CHRISTIAN SPIRITUALITY

CHRISTIAN SPIRITUALITY

LATER DEVELOPMENTS

PART I

FROM THE RENAISSANCE TO JANSENISM

By the REV. PIERRE POURRAT

Supérieur du Grand Séminaire de Lyon

Translated by W. H. MITCHELL, *M.A.*

VOLUME III

THE NEWMAN PRESS

WESTMINSTER, MARYLAND

1953

First published 1927
Reprinted 1953

NIHIL OBSTAT:

Fr. Innocentius Apap, O.P., S.Th.M.,
Censor Deputatus.

IMPRIMATUR:

Edm. Can. Surmont,
Vicarius Generalis.

Westmonasterii,
die 28ᵃ Julii, 1927.

Library of Congress Catalog Card Number: 53–5585

Printed in the United States of America

PREFACE

THIS volume begins with the Renaissance and ends with Jansenism, covering from the middle of the fifteenth to the middle of the seventeenth century. It takes in the great schools of spirituality of modern times : the Spanish, Italian, Salesian, and French Schools.

With the exception of the Salesian School, the others are divided between the great Catholic nations which filled the political stage of Europe during that period : Spain, Italy, and France.

Indeed, the principle of nationality asserted itself in a very remarkable way, especially from the time of the Renaissance. This tendency of each nation to converge upon the lines of its own genius and language and religion reacted upon every manifestation of its life, and therefore upon its spirituality. Hence we actually find in recent times a Spanish spirituality, an Italian spirituality, and a French spirituality, a spirituality which is fundamentally one and the same so far as it is Catholic, but differs in the way in which it is conceived and presented.

Therefore the schools of spirituality of the later period no longer appear simply as belonging to religious families, as in the Middle Ages, but as those of nations. In each school, no doubt, the various religious orders keep their peculiar characteristics ; but they owe much to the national bent and interests and to the special currents of doctrine distinctive of each country. Thus the spirituality of Spanish writers cannot be thoroughly understood without some knowledge of the truceless and merciless war waged by the Spanish Inquisition during the sixteenth century against Protestant heresy and false mysticism. The Inquisition reacted strongly upon Spanish spirituality by enlisting it on behalf of its own interests, and thus was realised the unity of the Spanish School.

In Italy unity was due to an analogous cause. Despite the diversity of the small States of the peninsula, we find in all of them during the sixteenth century the fear of an infiltration of Protestantism, along with a sincere desire for Church reform, on the lines laid down by the Council of Trent. The paganism of the Renaissance, too, had to be countered without rejecting whatever good there might be in humanism. Hence came that Italian spirituality which urges men on to

v

inward struggle, of which we have a grand example in *The Spiritual Combat*.

In France it was Cardinal de Bérulle's Oratory that gave unity to spirituality in the seventeenth century. All the great writers of that period were Berullians, and made what is called the French School. The counter-reformation in France was therefore Berullian.

Thus the history of the spirituality of the sixteenth and seventeenth centuries is clearly divided into four parts, which correspond to the four great schools: Spanish, Italian, Salesian, and French.

As everyone knows, the Renaissance and the Protestant Reformation have had an enormous influence upon the formation of the modern mind. A kind of humanism—a devout sort of humanism—is amalgamated in some spiritual books with Christian asceticism. But such fusion has not been wrought without difficulty, for if the Renaissance has its good side, we cannot forget that it revived the old paganism. Spiritual writers could not but react strongly against such paganism. It was indeed—at least I shall try to show it—the desire to keep the spiritual life free from the pagan spirit of the Renaissance that resulted in the development of methodical prayer. As the Christian found himself surrounded with nothing but enticements to evil, he had to fall back upon himself and encircle himself with the rampart of a method of prayer. He thus made a sort of inner sanctuary, closed to all unwholesome influences, and in it his supernatural convictions were guarded and fortified.

As for the frankly heterodox mysticism of Protestantism, there could be no doubt as to the attitude of Catholic writers towards it. Reaction against such false mysticism was one of the things which engrossed the strenuous attention of modern authors.

Therefore, at the risk of somewhat interrupting the plan of this volume, before beginning the study of the four great schools of spirituality, I have to speak of the Renaissance and the Reformation as well as of their influence on Christian asceticism.

Of late some very important critical studies of the great Spanish spiritual writers have been issued. The authors of the *Monumenta historica Societatis Jesu* have published the works of St Ignatius of Loyola and his first disciples according to the best manuscripts. The translation of the *Works* of St Teresa by the Carmelites of Paris is excellent. So, too, is the recent edition of the *Works* of St John of the Cross by P. Gérard, translated by H. Hoornaert. Other less important Spanish writers, whose influence has nevertheless been great, have also been carefully edited. As yet, however, we have no complete critical edition of Spanish spiritual writings of the sixteenth century, the great century, bubbling over with life.

The edition of the *Complete Works* of St Francis de Sales brought out by the Visitandines of Annecy is almost finished, and appears to be final.

M. Henri Bremond, of the Académie française, in his masterly work entitled l'*Histoire littéraire du sentiment religieux en France,* gives us a wonderful introduction to the French School.

There is no study of the Italian School as a whole. The works of the Italians in many cases have been imperfectly edited hitherto. Hence I shall be forgiven if, in this first inquiry, some important works have eluded my investigations.

Moreover, it has been my aim not to write a detailed history of spirituality, but to reveal its main outlines. Happy shall I be if, in this modest study, I have attained it !

TRANSLATOR'S NOTE

Though accepting full responsibility for the translation of this book as published, I have to thank Mr. S. P. Jacques for allowing me to use his translation of Chapter IX and onward, and to revise it so as to bring it into line with my own. I have also to thank Mr. A. G. McDougall for helping in the preparation of proofs for the press, during the course of which he made many suggestions which I was glad to adopt as improvements.

W. H. M.

CONTENTS

Contents

CHAPTER I

THE RENAISSANCE AND THE SYSTEMIZATION OF THE
SPIRITUAL LIFE—THE ORIGIN AND DEVELOPMENT OF
METHODICAL PRAYER—THE ORIGIN OF THE THREE
WAYS OF THE SPIRITUAL LIFE

TOWARDS the close of the Middle Ages, just at
the beginning of the fourteenth century, the
Hundred Years' War and the Great Schism
introduced anarchy into the churches and the
religious Orders. The war upset the social order,
especially in France. For the moment the Great Schism
actually broke up Catholic unity and thereby lessened ecclesiastical authority. Almost everywhere discipline was relaxed.
Such was the state of moral enfeeblement in which the
Renaissance found Christianity in the West.

It restored, as we know, the literature and art of antiquity;
it also revived the ancient paganism. For if there was, as
we shall see, a Christian and even a devout form of
humanism, there was also a pagan humanism, that of
Lorenzo Valla, of Poggio, of Leonardo Aretino, of Filelfo in
Italy, and of Rabelais in France. The fables of pagan
mythology were displayed in sculpture and painting. The
Epicurean notion of following nature revived the worship
of the flesh.[1] A thirst for enjoyment in its most various forms
became the ideal which the pagan humanists opposed to the
derided Christian spirit. Obscene writings popularized this
immoral teaching in Italy and France and Germany. Licentiousness of manners was its immediate consequence. Pro-
fligacy was observed, especially during the second half of
the fifteenth century, even in the papal court and, for some
years, on the very throne of St Peter.[2]

The tide of corruption threatened to submerge everything. The clergy and the monks—except the Mendicant
Orders—were not protected by a discipline sufficiently strict

[1] Rabelais says of the inhabitants of Thelema : " In their Rule there
was only this one clause : Do what you will " (*Gargantua*, Book IV,
chap. lvii).
[2] *Cf.* Ludwig Pastor, *Histoire des Papes depuis la fin du moyen âge;*
Furcy-Raynaud's translation, Vol. I, pp. 1-71; Vol. VII, chap. vii.
Jean Guiraud, *L'Église romaine et les origines de la Renaissance,*
Paris, 1904, chap. xi ; Imbard de la Tour, *Les origines de la Réforme,*
Vol. II, pp. 314 ff.; F. Mourret, *Histoire générale de l'Église,* Vol. V,
pp. 15, 274; Alfred Baudrillart, *L'Église catholique, la Renaissance, le
Protestantisme,* Paris, 1905, pp. 1 ff.

to afford them safety. They also possessed—and this was one of their great sources of weakness—an abundance of property which enabled them to procure the pleasures so much vaunted by the new Epicureans whose books were read on all sides. Besides this, there were the violent attacks made by the humanists upon the clergy and religious because they stood for the Christian ideal of renunciation.[1]

Surrounded with seducing influences, ridiculed by satirists and humanist pamphlets, poorly assisted by their superiors, how could the clergy and the monks withstand so rough a storm? Many held good; in what manner we shall see. Many, however, yielded to the onslaught and, borne along by the irresistible flood, abandoned all attempts as useless and gave up the struggle. In their discouragement they came to regard all resistance to passion as practically impossible. The surrounding decadence and their own laxity lulled their conscience in self-indulgence and in the dread of all endeavour. For them " such words as the conquest and mastery of self, as discipline, had hardly any meaning."[2]

Doubtless, in every age of the history of the Church, there is more or less evidence of failures amongst the clergy and the religious. The Middle Ages, as we know, had their full share of such troubles. But if, in the ages of faith, Christian morals were outraged by the lives of many, they still remained, for almost everyone and especially for the clergy, an undisputed ideal which men must endeavour to attain. The reprobate priest and the unfaithful religious, throughout that period, had each a deep feeling of his own

---

[1] J. Guiraud, *op. cit.,* pp. 304 ff. ; Imbart de la Tour, *Les origines de la Réforme,* Vol. II, pp. 199-212, 291-305.

[2] Denifle-Paquier, *Luther et le Luthéranisme,* Vol. I, p. 3, Paris, 1910. A contemporary work ascribed to Berthold of Chiemsee, entitled *Onus ecclesiae,* says : *Tota nostra inclinatio ad vanitatem tendit; quidquid mali unicuique in mentem venerit, hoc impune perpetrare audet,* cap. xl (Denifle, *id.,* p. 8); Erasmus of Rotterdam, about 1523, says the same in his *De contemptu mundi,* cap. xii : *Nunc plura monasteria mediis mundi visceribus admista sunt, nec aliter extra mundum sunt quam renes extra corpus animantis. In quibus adeo non viget disciplina religionis, ut nihil aliud sint quam scholae impietatis, in quibus ne liceat quidem esse puros et integros. Quibus titulus cultusque religionis nihil aliud praestet quam ut impunitius liceat quidquid libet;* Desiderii Erasmi Roterodami, *Opera omnia,* Lugd. Batav., 1704, tom. V, p. 1261. Cf. *Enchiridion militis christiani,* cap. vi, tom. V, p. 40. See, too, Louis de Blois (†1566), *Brevis regula tyronis spiritualis, Opera,* Antwerp, 1632, p. 355 : *Heu quam multi viri et feminae hodie se misere fallunt, qui monastico habitu suscepto, vota Religionis vovent, cum tamen parum aut nihil de perfectione vitae cogitent! Creaturis tenaciter adhaerent, et in eis delectationem inordinate quaerunt, externas consolationes avidissime appetunt, sese totos absque timore foras effundunt; mente vagi, moribus incompositi, sensibus incustoditi, verbis vani ac vani sunt; atque in sua negligentia suisque vitiis ad mortem usque perseverant.* See also Janssen, *l'Allemagne et la Réforme,* I, 575 ff.

unworthiness. They held to the faith, they recognized the value of their vows, they remained outwardly subject to the authority of the Church. The disgraceful contradiction between their beliefs and their lives filled them with dread when they thought of it. A fairly large number of them sometimes pulled themselves together and tried to break— were it only for a while—the bonds of iniquity. In short, the unchristian act was judged from a Christian point of view.[1]

In the age of the Renaissance it was not altogether thus. Men's minds were themselves perverted; public opinion in many countries became pagan. Evil was called good, and good evil. Erasmus in 1501 was able to write thus :

" Of the common run of Christians think this : that none were ever more corrupt, even among the pagans, in their notions of morals."[2]

The priest, the monk, and the faithful layman who wanted to do his duty could hardly discover anywhere outside his own interior life the means of protecting or of freeing himself from the evil influence of popular opinion. More than anything they wanted a thoroughly Christian mentality and unshakable convictions to set against the maxims of paganism. They wanted the mind of Christ and not the fancies of the crowd. The example and the words of Christ are the sole rule of right; to wander from them is inevitably to go astray. A man must be really convinced of this, whatever he may see or hear around him in the world or even in the Church and her rulers !

" Beware lest thou reason thus "—advises Erasmus with a touch of satire in his warning—" No one does any better than I ! This is how my forbears acted ! This learned philosopher and that eminent theologian think likewise ! So live our great men and kings ! So behave even the bishops and the popes ! Yet they are not the vulgar crowd !—Be not disturbed by these great names : I judge not vulgarity by its position, but by its want of moral worth."[3]

[1] See especially Gerson's *Dialogus super caelibatu sive castitate Ecclesiasticorum* (Lyons, 1443) in reply to those who demanded the suppression of the celibacy of the clergy because they thought it responsible for all the clerical disorders. The *Dialogue* is between Nature, which puts forward the current objections to celibacy, and Wisdom, which refutes them. Gerson writes thus in a spirit of resignation : *Hoc dicimus quod de duobus malis minus est incontinentes tolerare sacerdotes quam nullos habere (Opera, ed. Dupin, Antwerp, 1703, tom. II, 634). See, too, the Prologue of the *Lavacrum conscientiae*, published in Germany before 1500 by an unknown writer, and the *Reformatorium vitae morumque et honestatis clericorum*, Basileae, 1494, by Jacobus Philippi, brother of the Rector of the house of the Brethren of the Common Life at Zwolle.

[2] *Enchiridion militis christiani*, cap. viii, *Opera*, V, 40 : *De vulgo christianorum sic existimo, nullum unquam fuisse corruptius, ne apud ethnicos quidem, quantum ad opiniones de moribus attinet*.

[3] *ibid.*

Under the pressure of these grave difficulties the spiritual life was driven to adopt a stricter discipline than it had used in times gone by. Since, outside of it, neither ecclesiastical laws nor monastic rules nor public opinion could protect devotion, it had to make its citadel within the Christian soul. The spiritual life showed a tendency towards regulation even towards the close of the Middle Ages. The Renaissance drove it to shut itself up within definite borders, hard and fast barriers strong enough to bear rough blows without breaking down. Thus came about the methodization of the exercises, and especially of meditation, and the final graduation of the spiritual life. Everyone could then adapt, rather mechanically indeed, but appropriately the various religious exercises to the state and needs of his soul.

But for the better understanding of the goal of this evolution let us go back a little to take in at a glance its various stages. We shall see that the Middle Ages sketched in outline a method of prayer, and that it reached to the point of marking the steps of the threefold spiritual path : the purgative, the illuminative, and the unitive ways. Pardon me the somewhat technical character of this first chapter, which I shall abridge as much as possible.

I—MEDITATION AND THE GRADUATION OF THE SPIRITUAL LIFE BEFORE THE RENAISSANCE

A SPIRITUAL discipline has always been indispensable to the Christian life. Indeed, how is sin to be put off and to be kept at a distance, how can goodness be held fast and perfection aimed at unless we give ourselves up to a kind of moral gymnastics? St Paul advised Timothy to exercise himself (γύμναζε σεαυτόν) unto godliness, which is far more profitable than ardour in bodily exercise (σωματικὴ γυμνασία). The spiritual life demands a scheme of exercises more or less regulated from the beginning; in a word, a discipline. Ascetical authors always keep this Pauline idea in view.

In the third century, as we learn from Clement of Alexandria and Origen,[1] the Christians who mortified themselves by the practice of continence were called ascetics (ἀσκηταί), a word which implies a whole programme. *Askesis* is an ensemble of exercises. The continent were those who *exercised* themselves unto virtue by fasting and other austerities. A little later on Cassian regards fasting, vigils, reading, and denudation as " exercises " which mortify the body and enable the monk to attain to the topmost heights of charity.

---

[1] Clement of Alexandria, *Paedag.*, I, 8, etc. Origen, *In Jeremiam*, XIX, 7, ἀσκηταί = " those who exercised themselves in virtue."

Systemization 5

They are the "instruments" of perfection,[1] which must be
united with prayer and the practice of the virtues.

In the Middle Ages attention was directed to other exercises, which were called "spiritual exercises" or interior
exercises of the soul. These were reading, meditation,
prayer or contemplation, and examination of conscience. In
monasteries they took up the time left free from psalmody
and the other chief exercises of the Rule. They were also
a help to avoid idleness and their variety obviated boredom.[2]
It was especially timely to commend them to monks who
lived a hermit-life.[3]

These exercises soon gained greatly in importance, especially amongst the Carthusians;[4] so fitted were they to
promote the interior life of the religious. For "bodily exercises" such as fasting and vigils, in which the body plays
the chief part, have but one purpose—the facilitation of
"spiritual exercises."[5] In reality the true "exercise," the
only one that really counts, as St Bernard[6] says, is the
ascent of the soul towards perfection. Everything may be
brought down to that spiritual gymnastic training which lies
in climbing up the mystical ladder whereby we ascend
towards God. The rungs are *reading, meditation, prayer,* and
contemplation;[7] but meditation soon came to be regarded
as the primary one.[8]

[1] Cassian, *Coll.*, I, cap. vii, x.
[2] *Ep. ad fratres de monte Dei*, lib. I, cap. x, 23 : *Singulis horis
secundum communis instituti canonem sua distribue exercitia: cui
spiritualia, spiritualia; cui corporalia, corporalia: in quibus sic
exsolvat omne debitum spiritus Deo, corpus spiritui.* Aelred, English
twelfth-century Cistercian, *De vita eremitica,* XIV : *Quia mens nostra
. . . nunquam in eodem statu permanet, otiositas exercitiorum varie-
tate fuganda est, et quies nostra quadam operum vicissitudine fulci-
enda (P.L. XXXII, 1455).*
[3] In the twelfth century it is specially found in treatises intended
for Carthusians or for hermits and recluses. Guigues, a Carthusian
(† about 1190), recommends his monks to practise four exercises in
their cells : reading, meditation, prayer or contemplation, and manual
work. *De quadripartito exercitio cellae (P.L.* CLIII, 799-884).
[4] *Cf.* Dom A. Wilmart, O.S.B., *Les écrits spirituels des deux Guigues*
in the *Revue d'Ascétique et de Mystique* (Janv.-Avril, 1924). According
to Dom Wilmart, the Carthusians are those who wrote most of the
twelfth-century treatises which deal with meditation.
[5] *Ep. ad frat. de monte Dei,* lib. I, cap. xi, 32.
[6] *Sermo XXV de diversis,* 4; *In circumcisione, serm.* III, 11.
[7] *Scala Claustralium* or *Scala Paradisi,* cap. i : *Cum quadam die
. . . . de spiritualis hominis exercitio coepissem, quatuor spirituales
gradus animo cogitanti se subito obtulerunt: scilicet, lectio, meditatio,
oratio et contemplatio. Haec est Scala Claustralium, qua de terra in
coelum sublevantur (P.L.* CLXXXIV, 476). This treatise is ascribed
to Dom Guigues I, Prior of the Grand Chartreuse. It was translated
into French by Fuzet, *L'Échelle du ciel ou traité de l'oraison,* Lille-
Bruges, 1880.
[8] The *Scala Paradisi* and the *Ep. ad frat. de monte Dei* are the two
documents which speak most of meditation. At the beginning of them
will be found a method of prayer.

Meditation, in one form or another, has always been necessary for the sanctification of the soul. It helps us to discover the truth and to learn to love. Further, the Psalmist never tires of repeating that the law of the Lord " is his meditation all the day."[1] During his devout reflections " a fire flamed out "[2] within him. St Paul counselled Timothy to " meditate " upon his advice, to " be wholly in it "[3] that he might advance in goodness.

The first Christian ascetics, who slept with the Bible under their pillows, were lovers of meditation.[4] They regarded it as an efficacious means of overcoming the devil.[5] St Pachomius bade his monks to meditate on a few passages of Scripture or devout thoughts on their way from one monastery to another or while working or in the silence and solitude of their cells.[6] The Rule of St Benedict speaks of meditation which might be made by the monks after vigils when they ended before the time for Lauds.[7] St John Climacus[8] considered that prayer truly fervent which was united with meditation, especially with meditation on death.

The mystics of the Middle Ages threw into still higher relief the benefits of meditation. It is, according to them, an indispensable way of discovering the truth, scientific as well as religious truth. Without it no man can know himself nor examine the state of his conscience. Meditation preserves or delivers us from evil thoughts.[9] By it, too, we attain to a profounder knowledge of divine truths, a knowledge which is transformed into love. Looked at from all these various sides, it is that *consideration* in which St Bernard summed up all devotion.[10] Furthermore, it is the principal step to ascend if we would rise to mystical contemplation.[11]

This preponderating role of meditation is well described by the writer of the *Scala Paradisi*. Reading, he says,

---

[1] Ps. cxviii, 97, etc.   [2] Ps. xxxviii, 4.
[3] 1 Tim. iv, 15.
[4] St Athanasius, *De virginitate*, 12, 16; St Ambrose, *De virginibus*, III, 18, 20.
[5] *Vitae Patrum*, lib. VI, libell. I, 10.
[6] *Regula Pach.*, 2, 28, 36, 37, 59-60, 122 (*P.L.*, LXIII). Cassian advises constant meditation on the Scriptures. *Coll.*, XIV, cap. x.
[7] *Regula S Benedicti*, VIII.
[8] *Scala Paradisi*, gradus 28.
[9] Aelred, *De vita eremitica*, XXIX : *Nihil enim magis cogitationes excludit inutiles vel compescit lascivias quam meditatio verbi Dei, quod sic ad animum suum virgo debet assuescere, ut aliud volens, non possit aliud meditari. Cogitanti de Scripturis somnus obrepat. Evigilanti primum aliquid de Scripturis occurrat. Dormientis somnia memoria aliqua de Scripturis sententia condiat* (*P.L.*, XXXII, 1461).
[10] *De Consideratione*, lib. V, cap. xi. Cf. *De Imit. Christi*, lib. II, cap. v.
[11] *Scala Paradisi vel Claust.* cap. i ss.; Hugh of St Victor, *De modo dicendi et meditandi*.

presents the truth. It is meditation that cuts it up, masticates and ruminates it, and makes a kind of broth of it for the nourishment of the soul.[1] St Francis de Sales uses the same terms to define the word " meditate."[2] Meditation acquaints us with our own poverty, with our utter need of the truth, and with our impotence to follow it without the grace of God. Lastly, it fires us with the desire to pray for God's help.[3] Scarcely anywhere shall we hereafter find a better explanation of the influence of meditation upon prayer and of its indispensableness for the kindling of fervour in prayer.

Spiritual exercises—reading, meditation, prayer, and contemplation—are, therefore, bound together by a chain the main link in which is meditation :

" Reading apart from meditation is dry; meditation without reading is subject to error; prayer without meditation is lukewarm; meditation without prayer is barren; fervent prayer leads to contemplation; contemplation apart from prayer is either a very rare or a miraculous thing."[4]

I have read, says the writer of the *Scala* by way of explanation, this word of the Lord : *Blessed are the clean of heart, for they shall see God,* a word which stirs me to devout inquiry. Then comes meditation to delve into its meaning and scrutinize it syllable by syllable. It reminds me of what was said by the prophets of old in praise of purity. Then I reflect upon the happiness of seeing God face to face, the reward of the pure in heart. How I long to be one of them ! But neither reading nor meditation can make me clean of heart : only God can do that. So I ' take refuge in prayer,' and pray the Lord all the more ardently to make me pure, the more I desire to be made clean.[5]

Such fervent prayer wins even the grace of infused contemplation. *The eyes of the Lord are upon the just: and his ears unto their prayers ;*[6] but he does not wait until they

---

[1] *Quid enim prodest lectione continua tempus occupare, sanctorum gesta et scripta legendo transcurrere, nisi ea etiam masticando et ruminando succum eliciamus et transglutiendo usque ad cordis intima transmittamus? (Scala Paradisi,* cap. xi. *Cf.* cap. iii).

[2] " To meditate is the same as to masticate. . . . We must take the meat that nourishes the soul and masticate it—*i.e.,* meditate on it to swallow it and transform it into ourselves " (*Œuvres complètes,* Vôl. IX, 359, Annecy ed.).

[3] *Scala Paradisi,* cap. x-xii. Cf. *Ep. ad frat. de monte Dei,* lib. I, 31, 32.

[4] *Scala Par.,* cap. xii. Examination should be joined with meditation as its necessary complement. Any deviation between conduct and the way of perfection must be ascertained. *Ep. ad frat. de monte Dei,* lib. I, 22, 29; lib. II, 15.

[5] *Scala,* cap. iii-iv. Cf. *Ep. ad frat. de monte Dei,* lib. I, 42 : *Amorem ergo Dei, in homine ex gratia genitum, lactat lectio, meditatio pascit, oratio confortat et illuminat.*

[6] Ps. xxxiii, 16.

are over to answer them. Sometimes he " interrupts the flow of prayer " and suddenly breaks in upon the soul, inundating it with heavenly dew and filling it with joy.[1] At other times, however, he leaves the soul in aridity, a trial to be accepted with patience.[2]

The subject of meditation should be adapted, as far as possible, to the degree of everyone's spiritual life. Beginners will rather meditate upon episodes in Christ's life and try to find therein examples of virtue and helps to progress in the love of God. The easier passages of the Bible and from the works of the Fathers, as well as the lives of the saints, will be specially profitable to them. Having considered Christ as Man, they will succeed, as they advance in charity, in the apprehension and enjoyment of the divine perfections.[3]

The counsels given by the *Epistola ad fratres de monte Dei* to the Carthusians of the twelfth century were zealously followed in the next one. As we know, the pseudo-Bonaventure's *Meditations on the Life of Christ* was the standard work which provided subjects for prayer, but it was supplanted during the next century by the famous *Life of Christ* by Ludolph the Carthusian.

At the dawn of the later era, therefore, we find a theory of meditation. It is practised, and its benefits are proclaimed as well as its indispensableness for the religious who desires not to degenerate, and *a fortiori* for him who would increase in the love of God. David of Augsburg (†1272) affirms, indeed, that without the practice of meditation no religious can be worthy of his vocation.[4]

Are we to conclude that methodical meditation originated in the Middle Ages? No; if to *methodical meditation* is given the exact meaning which it bears to-day and as it is found in the works of Garcia Ximenes of Cisneros and of Ignatius of Loyola. To accomplish such a strict regularization of meditation, Christian life had to become more thoroughly systematized, and especially had the theory of the three ways of the spiritual life—the purgative, the illuminative, and the unitive ways—to become quite classical. Moreover, under the increasing pressure of outward circumstances upon the supernatural life of the soul, the need of systematizing the means of resistance with greater strictness had to make itself felt.

The Fathers of the Church graded the spiritual life quite empirically, if we may venture to say so. They distinguished

---

[1] *Scala,* cap. v-vi.   [2] *Ep. ad frat.,* lib. I, 46.   [3] *id.* 42-43.
[4] *De exterioris et interioris hominis compositione* (Quaracchi, 1899).

between the beginning, the progress, and the end of its
course. Obviously, the counsels and exhortations suited to
beginners would be useless to those who were more advanced
and to the perfect. Hence, their instructions are adapted
to the needs of their hearers. In summing up those who
had gone before him, Cassian explains that beginners are
led by fear, those on the way by the hope of reward, and
the perfect by charity alone.[1] Therefore, everyone is to be
dealt with according to the stage of spiritual life in which
he is found.

The twelfth century, which spoke so freely of the love of
God, liked to grade Christian life, as St Augustine did,
according to the degrees of that love. This did not hinder
it from usually keeping to the old arrangement of beginners,
the proficient, and the perfect.[2]

The spiritual exercises belonging to each degree of perfection were determined with care. Reading suited beginners, meditation the advancing, prayer and contemplation the perfect.[3] But we must not find in such principles
as these an exclusivism which was not in the mind of their
makers. The devotion of the Middle Ages was too spontaneous and too living to be shut up within hard and fast
barriers. Even the perfect were devoted to reading, and
whatever a man's spiritual state might be he could not
entirely dispense with the exercises of beginners.

Nevertheless, owing to the craving of the human mind
for synthesis, the systematization once begun never came to
a standstill. In the thirteenth century it was crowned by
the Platonic theory of contemplation of the Pseudo-Dionysius. According to the Areopagite, purification, illumination,
and consummation or perfection are the three stages of the
soul's ascent to mystical contemplation. Dionysian contemplation is above all an act of the mind; it demands an
intellectual as well as a moral preparation. The mind has
to be purified by stripping it of all sensible images and imperfect ideas which can be only an impediment to it when
anyone desires to see God. The mind must further be
enlightened by heavenly illumination to become capable of
discerning divine realities. When it has been thus perfected,

---

[1] *Coll.*, XI, cap. vii. St Thomas also likes to make use of the three
classes of *beginners*, the *proficient*, and the *perfect*, 2a, 2ae, Q. 24,
art. 9; Q. 183, art. 4.

[2] Cf. *Ep. ad fratres de monte Dei*, lib. I, cap. v : *Sicut stella a stella
distat in claritate, sic cella a cella in conversatione, scilicet incipi-
entium, proficientium et perfectorum*. *The Imitation of Christ* also has
this tripartite division. The *Scala Claustralium*, however, gives this
classification : *incipientes, proficientes, devoti* and *beati* (cap. x).

[3] See Hugh of St Victor, *De modo dicendi et meditandi*. The *Scala
Claustralium* restricts prayer to the *devoti* and contemplation to the
beati.

it will be finally united to God and thus contemplate him
directly.   No doubt the whole soul will be thereby purified,
illuminated,   and   perfected.   Mystical   contemplation   is
wrought by the love of God; but it is, nevertheless, in itself, of the intellectual order in this sense, that it is wrought
in the mind.

Especially during the first third of the thirteenth century
did Dionysian commentators favour the notion of applying
the threefold division of mystical contemplation to the normal
growth of Christian life.   But it is not easy to cast aside
the ideas of such an authority as Dionysius all at once.

The Victorine Thomas Gallus, Abbot of Vercellæ († about
1226),[1] the most famous " Master in Hierarchy " of the
period, who passed for the profoundest expert in Dionysian
thought, caught no more than a glimpse of the classical
theory.   He sums up all spiritual endeavour on the way
to sanctity in purification, illumination, and perfection; but
this endeavour seems to be of a too exclusively intellectual
kind.   According to Thomas Gallus, purification consists
in shaking off ignorance, illumination brings men to knowledge, and perfection gives them understanding and comprehension of that which is known.[2]   Here, we have not yet the
theory of the three spiritual ways.

That is the discovery of St Bonaventure.[3]   No doubt the
Seraphic Doctor took his inspiration from Thomas Gallus,
but went beyond him.[4]   It is the general and normal development of the Christian life that he means to explain and not
only the soul's ascent towards mystical contemplation.   In
the purgative way come conversion and purification from sin;
in the illuminative way the soul is enlightened as to God and
Christ and itself, and tries to imitate the Lord; in the unitive
way it is united to God by charity, and abandons itself to
the exercise of holy love.   St Bonaventure points out the
practices appropriate to each of these three ways.

Almost at the same time as St Bonaventure, the Carthusian
Hugh of Palma, who died towards the end of the thirteenth

---

[1] Besides his commentary on St Dionysius he left a *Commentarius
hierarchicus in Cantica Canticorum.*   Pez, *Thesaurus anecdotorum
novissimus,* tom. II.

[2] *Purgatio dicit recessum ab ignoto, illuminatio vero accessum ad
cognitum, perfectum vero ejusdem cogniti intellectum et comprehen-
sionem.*—*Extractio super quatuor libros magni Dionysii,* Puyol,
L'Auteur du Livre De Imitatione Christi, p. 189.

[3] Especially in the *De triplici via* or *De incendio amoris.*   Cf.
Christian Spirituality, Vol. II, pp. 177 ff.   P. Symphorien de Mons,
Etudes franciscaines, 1921, pp. 36 ff.   *Cf.* St Thomas, pars 3, Q. 27,
art. 3, and also Q. 184, art. 6, where we find purification and illumination in the Dionysian sense.

[4] *Cf.* Longpré, O.F.M., *La théologie mystique de saint Bonaventure*
in the *Archivum Franciscanum Historicum,* Ann. XIV, fasc. i-iii ff.

century, expounds an analogous doctrine[1] which must be noted on account of its great influence upon the creation of methodical prayer. Hugh of Palma depends rather upon Thomas Gallus than upon St Bonaventure. His aim is to lead the soul to divine wisdom and to mystical contemplation as understood by the Pseudo-Dionysius. His study is, therefore, above all mystical. But the principles which he sets forth will help to guide souls in the ordinary ways of perfection :

" Three ways," says he, " lead to God : the purgative way wherein the mind is disposed to learn true wisdom. The second is called illuminative, in which the mind by reflection is kindled unto love. The third is the unitive way, in which the mind is raised by God alone above all understanding, reason, and discernment."[2]

In the purgative way, as Hugh of Palma explains, the soul must be humble and conceive sorrow for its sins. By sin it has despised its Creator and tried to find its happiness outside of him. By prayer the sinner will obtain the cleansing graces that he needs for removing the rust of sin which hinders the influx of the divine light within him. The Christian will then enter into the illuminative way. By meditation upon the Lord's Prayer and by seeking for the mystical sense of Scripture he will rise up to the love of God. He will thus grow skilful in the discovery of the allegorical teachings of Holy Writ, an art so much appreciated afterwards by the makers of methods of prayer. Hugh of Palma calls this art *via illuminativa theorica*[3]—the theoretical illuminative way— the practical illuminative way being the actual experience of the love of God.

At the term of the unitive way comes wisdom, the most perfect knowledge of God which is to be found by the mind's unknowing—that is to say, without the help of imagination, reason, and understanding. This knowledge is a fruit of the divine love arising in the affective summit of the soul closely united with God.[4]

He who would traverse these spiritual ways must submit to discipline, give himself up to exercises, and use certain

[1] In his *Theologia mystica,* also called *De triplici via ad sapientiam et divinorum contemplationem* or else *Viae Sion lugent* from the opening words of the treatise. This was long ascribed to St Bonaventure and edited among his works; but in the 1755 Venice edition it is in Vol. XI. Cf. *Dict. de Théol. cath.,* art. Hugues de Palma.

[2] *Triplex est igitur via ista ad Deum, scilicet purgativa, qua mens ad discendam veram sapientiam disponitur. Secunda vero illuminativa dicitur, qua mens cogitando ad amoris inflammationem accenditur. Tertia unitiva, qua mens super omnem intellectum, rationem et intelligentiam a solo Deo sursum actu dirigitur* (*Mystica Theol.,* prologus, Venice Edition, XI, 345).

[3] *ibid.,* pp. 352-366.

[4] *ibid.,* pp. 366-375. This is an anti-intellectualist form of mysticism. Cf. *ibid.,* pp. 395-404. See also Gerson, *Opera,* tom. III, pp. 432 ff.

" devices," as Hugh of Palma calls them. Self-examination for sins committed—to be made discreetly so as not to disturb the soul with sinful recollections[1]—is obligatory at the beginning of the purgative way. Then meditation on death and the day of judgement, on the sorrowful passion of Christ, and on the goodness and bountifulness of God will fill the newly converted with lively contrition. Meditation will also stimulate prayer during the illuminative way, and thus increase in them the love of God. Its rôle continues until the threshold of contemplation, when the intellectual faculties are bound and become passive.

In proportion, as the degrees of the spiritual life get classified, meditation itself grows more methodical. We shall see how methodization was worked out at the end of the Middle Ages and at the beginning of the Renaissance, in the Low Countries and France, in Italy and Spain.

II—METHODICAL PRAYER IN THE LOW COUNTRIES, IN FRANCE, IN ITALY AND SPAIN, AT THE END OF THE MIDDLE AGES, AND AT THE BEGINNING OF THE RENAISSANCE

AT the end of the Middle Ages it was chiefly the Franciscan School[2] which inspired the founders of methodical prayer.

The works of St Bonaventure, especially the *De triplici via,* provided them with the theory of the three ways of the spiritual life in which the part played by meditation is of capital importance. David of Augsburg (†1272) was also one of their great favourites. His celebrated Directory,[3] in which he shows such competence in laying down the rules for the guidance of Franciscan novices, was in all hands from the middle of the fourteenth century. Outside the Franciscan School the most quoted writers are St Thomas Aquinas, Chancellor Gerson,[4] and the Carthusians, Hugh of Palma, Ludolph of Saxony, and Denys de Riken.

[1] Hugh of Palma, *Mystica theol.,* cap. i, particula ii.
[2] The Franciscan School was faithful to the doctrine of the three ways. The *Formula vitae christianae,* published in 1533 by Gaspar Hasgerus, Provincial of Germany, expounds it at great length.
[3] *De exterioris et interioris hominis compositione,* Quaracchi, 1899. Ubertino da Casale's *Arbor vitae* has also been sometimes quoted.
[4] Gerson never composed any method of prayer. In his treatise *On Meditation* he thus defines it : *Vehemens cordis applicatio ad aliquid investigandum et inveniendum fructuose.* He brings out clearly both its profitableness and its difficulties. He would prefer meditation to be affective rather than speculative. As to how it should be made, he refers everyone to his own spiritual director (*Opera omnia,* Antwerp, tom. III, 449-455). The treatises *De monte contemplationis* and *De mystica theologia* are those most quoted by writers on the theory of methodical prayer.

Methodical prayer sprang from the anxiety to reform the clergy and the religious Orders at the end of the Middle Ages and at the beginning of the Renaissance. The holy men who worked for this reformation were rightly concerned with giving intenser spiritual life to priests and monks by means of meditation. In their writings they constantly recur to the need of meditating, to the best hour for doing it, to the length of time to be spent upon it every day, and, lastly, to the subjects best adapted to meditation according to each person's stage in the spiritual life.

Thus was gradually formulated a method of prayer both precise and detailed. Towards the middle of the fifteenth century appeared the *Exercitatoria* or collections of exercises laid down for every day of the week.

In the Low Countries amongst the Brethren of the Common Life methodical prayer, properly so called,[1] seems to make its first appearance.

The Brothers of the Common Life and the Canons of Windesheim always held meditation in honour.[2] Gerard de Groot, their founder, recommended his followers to meditate on the passion of Christ, so that they might desire to imitate their crucified Lord.[3] He also proposed other subjects for meditation on a predetermined plan : first the teachings of the Gospel, then those of the Old Testament, lastly the teaching of the saints and the doctors.[4]

Florentius Radewijns[5] (†1400) closely follows St Bonaventure, and shows his disciples the importance of meditation in the three ways of the spiritual life. Gerard Zerbolt of Zutphen, too, proves how meditation may "reform" the three powers of the soul : the understanding, the memory, and the will upset by original sin. The place of these faculties in Ignatian meditation is well known. According to

[1] Hugh of St Victor's method of intuitive meditation could not be a method of prayer in the strict sense of the words. It is as much scientific as religious meditation. Severed from the philosophico-religious system to which it belongs, it very largely loses its significance.

[2] Here I shall follow P. Watrigant who has so well studied the history of methodical meditation in order to throw light upon the origin of the *Spiritual Exercises* of St Ignatius. *Histoire de la méditation méthodique* in the *Revue d'ascétique et de mystique,* Avril, 1922, Janvier, 1923, and *Collection de la Bibliothèque des Exercices de saint Ignace.*

[3] *Venerabilis Gerardi Magni Epistolae VII,* published by Mgr. de Ram, in the Report of the sessions of the Belgian Royal Historical Society, Brussels, 1860, p. 87.

[4] *De quatuor generibus meditabilium,* quoted by Mauburnus, *Rosetum exercitiorum spiritualium,* Bâle, 1504, CXLI.

[5] *Tractatulus de spiritualibus exercitiis seu Tractatulus de extirpatione vitiorum,* Freiburg im B., 1862. *Cf.* Symphorien de Mons, *Etudes franciscaines,* 1921, pp. 40 ff.

Gerard of Zutphen,[1] order is restored to the understanding by spiritual knowledge, to the memory by meditation, and to the will by the curbing of concupiscence. Gerard loves to dwell upon meditation. He points out what should be preferred in meditation in order to rise to the topmost heights of devotion. The subjects most strongly recommended are those which have to do with the last things and with the passion of Christ.

To facilitate such meditations as far as possible, in the Windesheim monasteries they made collections in which the mysteries of our Saviour's life, and particularly of his Passion, were arranged according to the days of the week.[2] They also divided the truths touching the last things. Every morning the religious had to meditate on a subject reminding them of God's blessings, or on some circumstance of the passion to kindle within them the love of God, and on another in the evening connected with the world to come, so that they might never lose the feeling of dread.[3] In those houses in which meditation was made only once a day, subjects of consolation alternated with such as inspired fear.[4]

Despite this wise distribution of subjects, meditation seemed to the religious of Windesheim a difficult thing. They were filled with distractions, and found it hard to reflect. They felt the need of a method, a kind of intellectual and moral discipline, which would compel their attention and keep their minds from wandering.

A friend of Thomas à Kempis, John Wessel Gransfort (†1489),[5] drew up a method for them, " a ladder for meditation "[6]—*scala meditatoria*—which was very popular. It appears to have been the first of all methods of prayer, for those that followed it are very like it. It consists of three

[1] Gerard of Zutphen, *De reformatione interiori seu virium naturae* and *De spiritualibus ascensionibus;* M. de la Bigne, *Maxima Bibliotheca Patrum,* Lugd., 1677, tom. XXVI, 237-289.

[2] *De spiritualibus ascensionibus,* cap. xlv, *de modo meditandi.*

[3] See the series of such meditations in the *Epistola de vita et passione Domini nostri Jesu Christi et aliis devotis exercitiis, secundum quae fratres et laici in Windesem se solent exercere,* in John Busch, *Chronicon Windeshemense,* Halle, 1886, pp. 226-244.

[4] *Consuetudines domus nostrae* of Thierry de Herxen (†1459), second Rector of Zwolle, in *Narratio de inchoatione Domus clericorum in Zwollis* (Amsterdam, 1908), p. 211. See, too, *Formula spiritualium exercitiorum seu meditationum pro novitiis in religione instruendis,* which contains several series of seven meditations (Watrigant, *Revue d'ascétique et de mystique,* 1922, pp. 145 ff.).

[5] A disciple of the Brethren of the Common Life at Zwolle, and afterwards professor of literature in the same house. He was a restless person who became a Nominalist. Luther, though doubtlessly mistaken, regarded him as a precursor of Protestantism.

[6] The work is entitled : *Tractatus de cohibendis cogitationibus et de modo constituendarum meditationum.* The *Scala* is found in chap. ix. *Aura purior, hoc est M. Wesselii Gransfortii Opera omnia,* Amstelodami, 1617, pp. 280 ff.

parts : preparatory steps (*gradus preparatorii*)—*i.e.*, driving
away thoughts unconnected with the subject of the meditation
and the retention of such as are best suited to it; ascending
steps (*gradus processorii*)—*i.e.*, for the orderly training of
the mind, the judgement, and the will; the final steps (*gradus
terminatorii*), which sum up the whole of the meditation by
entrusting to God the generous desires kindled in the course
of the whole exercise.   Each part includes a somewhat large
number of acts to be made,[1] and this renders the method complicated and even wearisome if carried out in all its details.

It was by such practices that the religious of the New
Devotion kept up the spirit of fervour and were able to carry
through the reformation of a large number of monasteries.
And it is easy to see how the practice of meditation was so
effective.   How could the religious, who daily meditated on
impressive and saving truths, and on the moving evidences
of Christ's love for men, remain hardened in sin?   Such a
state of mind is psychologically inconceivable.   A life of
laxity is only possible when the teachings of the faith are
forgotten.   When these are kept unceasingly in the fore-
front of consciousness by meditation, they soon exercise a
supreme, sway over a man's life.   Furthermore, if an
indifferent religious gives himself up freely to daily meditation, either he will reform his ways or else leave his monastery.   Whichever he does, the community to which he
belongs will soon become fervent, for before long it will consist entirely of religious who are faithful to their duties.

This is just what happened to the communities which
embraced the practices of the New Devotion.[2]   The secular
clergy, too, found in the Windesheim system of meditation
an effective means of reform.   The famous author of the
Reformatorium vitae morumque et honestatis clericorum[3]
recommends the clergy to meditate upon the same subjects
as those proposed to the Brethren of the house of Zwolle.

From the Low Countries the Windesheim reformation
spread to France.   John Mauburnus,[4] a religious of Mount

---

[1] The *gradus preparatorii* are two in number : *Excussio* (*repulsio
illorum quae minus cogitanda*), *Electio magis cogitandorum.*   The
gradus processorii are sixteen : *Commemoratio, Consideratio, Attentio,
Explanatio, Tractatio, Dijudicatio, Causatio, Ruminatio, Gustatio,
Querela, Optio, Confessio, Oratio, Mensio seu Commensuratio, Obse-
cratio, Fiducia.*   The *gradus terminatorii* are three : *Gratiarum actio,
Commendatio, Permissio* (*in Dei voluntate resignatio*).

[2] *Cf.* Busch, *Liber de reformatione monasteriorum,* Ed. Grube, Halle,
1886.

[3] This author is James Philippi, brother of Thierry de Herxen,
Rector of the house of Zwolle.

[4] John Mauburnus or Mombaer was born at Brussels.   He reformed
the Abbey of Saint-Séverin near Chateau-Landon (Seine-et-Marne),
and afterwards the Abbey of Livry.   He died in Paris in 1502.

St Agnes, who had known Thomas à Kempis, came thither with a few of his brethren. He reformed, in particular, the Abbey of the Canons Regular of Livry, near Paris.

Mauburnus urgently recommended meditation. He left a large collection of small treatises (*tituli*), a *Spiritual Rosary* (*Rosetum*), in which he puts forward exercises and meditations intended for the use of the religious for their own sanctification.[1] The nineteenth treatise is a Directory of Meditation (*Meditatorium*).[2] In it the writer reproduces the *Scala meditatoria* of John Wessel Gransfort, and comments thereon. But he introduces it with a fairly complete theory of meditation, the principles of which he borrows from Dionysius the Carthusian, from the author of the *De triplici via,* and, above all, from Gerson. After a preface pointing out the advantages, the prerogatives, and the necessity of meditation, he deals with the dispositions required in order to meditate, with appropriate subjects, with the devices to be used, and, in fine, with the method to be followed.

Mauburnus looks for this method in St Augustine, in St Bernard, in Hugh and Richard of St Victor, in Gerson, and in other writers prior to the fifteenth century: and since none of them had formulated one, it is not to be wondered at that he could not find it. He then puts forward with certain explanations the *Scala meditatoria* of John Wessels Gransfort.[3]

The reformation of several Benedictine abbeys was another fruit of methodical meditation.

It began in Italy, and its beginner was the Venerable Louis Barbo,[4] Abbot of St Justina of Padua, and afterwards Bishop of Treviso. The Benedictine monasteries, which received the reform after the fashion of St Justina's, combined with it to made the Congregation of St Justina of Padua. Among them, in 1503, stands out that of Monte Cassino.

---

[1] *Rosetum exercitiorum spiritualium et sacrarum meditationum,* published in 1494, then at Bâle in 1504, at Paris in 1610, at Milan in 1603, and at Douai in 1620. The first treatise is entitled *Eruditorium Exercitiorum* and is a kind of introduction. Then follows *Ordinarium vitae religiosae, Dietarium exercitiorum, Directorium solvendarum Horarum, Chiropsalterium,* or a means of fixing a man's attention during the chant; other treatises on Holy Communion and Feasts; *Examinatorium conscientiae, Destructorium vitiorum,* the *Profectorium virtutum* and the *Meditatorium,* or guide to meditation. Watrigant, *La genèse des Exercises de S Ignace* (*Études,* Vol. LXXIII, p. 203).

[2] Given in part by P. Watrigant, *Quelques promoteurs de la méditation au XVe siècle* (*Bibliothèque des Exercises de S Ignace,* n. 59, pp. 35-61).

[3] Mauburnus counsels meditation on the Mysteries of the Rosary, which was then becoming popular.

[4] He was first a commendatory of the Abbey of the Canons Regular of St George in Alga at Venice, of which St Laurence Justinian afterwards became Abbot General. He died in 1443.

Louis Barbo drew up a *Modus meditandi*,[1] which is rather a collection of meditations than a method of prayer in the strict sense. The Bishop of Treviso mentions three kinds of prayer: vocal prayer, which is the easiest and best adapted to beginners; meditation, which is the second degree of prayer; and contemplation, to which one rises by well made meditation. To help meditation, the seven days of the week[2] have fairly fully explained subjects divided between them. Brief hints as to how to meditate are thrown in.

Whatever be the merits of the *Modus meditandi*, it cannot compare with the *Ejercitatorio*, which was shortly to come from the pen of the Spanish Benedictine, Garcia Ximenes de Cisneros. It appears to have been by means of meditation that the reformation of many Spanish Benedictine monasteries was brought about towards the end of the Middle Ages and the beginning of the Renaissance; and it was meditation that reformed the Carmelite Order a little later on.

At the request of Pope Eugenius IV, Louis Barbo wrote to the Benedictine Congregation of Valladolid[3] to acquaint it with the Italian use of meditation. This Congregation was to be adorned in the sixteenth century by John of Castagniza,[4] the confidential adviser of Philip II, who honoured the Benedictine Order by his piety and knowledge. It was from the monastery of St-Benedict-of-Valladolid that Garcia Ximenes de Cisneros started in 1492 with twelve monks to rule the Abbey of Montserrat in the middle of Catalonia and to bring about its reformation.[5] He took away with him an extensive knowledge of methodical prayer and a strong conviction that with its help he would reform the monks of Montserrat. No doubt he had there come to know the principal works of St Bonaventure, the writers of the New Devo-

[1] First Ed., Venice, 1523, given by P. Watrigant in *Quelques promoteurs de la Méditation méthodique (Bibliothèque des Exercices,* no. 59, 1919). Other editions: Rome (1605), Salzburg (1634), Cologne (1644), Ratisbon (1856) following the *Exercitatorium* of Garcia de Cisneros.

[2] Meditation was to be devoted on Sunday to the love of God as Creator, on Monday to the fall and its consequences, on Tuesday to the birth of Christ, on Wednesday to the flight into Egypt, on Thursday to the persecutions of Christ, on Friday to the Passion, on Saturday to the descent into Hades, the Resurrection and the Ascension.

[3] Dom Besse, *La Congrégation espagnole de Valladolid (Revue bénédictine,* Vol. XIX.

[4] The chief works of John of Castagniza are: *Institutionum divinae pietatis libri quinque,* in which he sets forth some of the methods of the spiritual life; *De la perfeccion de la Vida Christiana.* This work is considered by some to give the original text of the *Spiritual Combat.* This controversy will be noticed farther on. John of Castagniza died at Salamanca in 1598.

[5] On Montserrat and its celebrated pilgrimage to the Blessed Virgin Mary, see Dom Besse, *Revue des questions historiques,* Vol. XVII (1897), pp. 22-31.

tion, and Gerson, who dealt with meditation.   He used them
in the compilation of his *Ejercitatorio*.[1]

III — THE FULL GROWTH OF METHODICAL PRAYER—GARCIA XIMENES DE CISNEROS

GARCIA XIMENES DE CISNEROS, and even St Ignatius of
Loyola, belong to the Spanish School, and stand forth, especially St Ignatius, among its most illustrious representatives.
I venture to set them apart from the other writers of this
school.   But they are so identified with the history of methodical
prayer that this study on the growth of that exercise would
be quite incomplete, and even altogether incomprehensible,
if we did not note at the outset the place they hold in it.

Garcia Ximenes de Cisneros[2] reformed the Abbey of
Montserrat by making all his monks follow his *Spiritual
Exercises*.[3]   Those who were held in the bonds of sin did
them to be converted and cleansed from their faults :

" The monk," says the holy Abbot, " who desires to bring
back from Jericho to Jerusalem his soul made in the likeness
of God (Gen. i, 26)—that is to say, to tear it away from
instability and disturbance to restore it to quietness and peace
—such a monk, I say, must imitate David's example, and

---

[1] Cf. *Revue bénédictine*, Vol. XVII, pp. 362-378. Watrigant, *Quelques promoteurs de la méditation méthodique*, pp. 69-76 (*Bibliothèque
des Exercices*, no. 59).

[2] Garcia de Cisneros, born at Toledo, related to the famous Cardinal
Ximenes, in 1475 entered the monastery of St-Benedict-the-Royal of
Valladolid at the age of twenty years. He was the first reformed Abbot
of Montserrat, where he died in 1510.   He left two Spanish works
printed in 1500 at Montserrat, where he had set up a printing press :
Ejercitatorio de la Vida espiritual and *Directorio de las Horas
canonicas*.   There have been numerous Spanish editions of the *Ejercitatorio*.   The last was in 1912, at Barcelona, by Dom Fausto Curiel, a
Benedictine of Montserrat.   Latin translations of the *Directorium
horarum canonicarum* and *Exercitatorium vitae spiritualis* have been
published as follows : At Paris in 1511, Venice in 1555, etc., and the
last at Ratisbon in 1856, *Exercitatorium spirituale cum Directorio
horarum canonicarum*.   French translations : *Exercices spirituels de
Dom Garcia de Cisneros* by Dom Anselme Thévard, Paris, 1655 ;
Exercices spirituels et Directoire des heures canoniales by Joseph
Rousseau, Paris, 1902.   The *Ejercitatorio* consists of four parts.   The
three first set forth meditations intended for the three ways ; the purgative, the illuminative, and the unitive ; the fourth has to do with contemplation.   The *Directorium horarum canonicarum* deals with spiritual
preparation for the recitation of the Office, with the manner of recitation, and with the means to be used to store up its fruits.

[3] A Montserrat MS. belonging to the time of Garcia de Cisneros
reads thus : *Exercitatorium vitae spiritualis, in quo opere pretium est
monachos esse apprime instructos et memoriter retinere universa illa
meditandi, orandi et contemplandi viae purgativae, illuminativae et
unitivae exercitia, et donec ea tam practice quam theoretice pleniter
noverit seu sciverit non permittatur in aliis libris legere vel studere*
(*Revue bénédictine*, tom. XVII, p. 369).

correct and purify his soul by spiritual exercises, setting it free from vice and sin and from all disorderly affections. Then only will it be able to receive heavenly graces and gifts."[1]

Even the fervent religious were not dispensed from doing the Exercises. They found in them an increase of zeal for all good. Novices were closely bound to them as the best means of training. To encourage the exercitant to enter resolutely upon the way of purification, Garcia shows him, in the first place, the necessity of turning his attention to set exercises, and then makes known to him the fruit to be gathered from them, the dispositions with which they should be begun, the way to arrange them, the place in which they are to be performed, which is the monastery chapel, and lastly, the hours of the day that are to be devoted to them, that is, immediately after Lauds or Compline, according to the subject of the meditation. Further, such subjects are fixed for every day of the three weeks normally assigned to the Exercises—the fourth part of the *Ejercitatorio* being specially intended for contemplatives.

The first week is given to the purgative way. The meditations will be in the morning, after Lauds: Monday, on sin; Tuesday, on death; Wednesday, on hell; Thursday, on the Judgement; Friday, on the Passion; Saturday, on the Blessed Virgin; Sunday, on heaven. Fear and contrition are the two chief feelings intended to be aroused within the exercitant during the first week.

Cisneros gives a detailed explanation of the method to be followed in these meditations. At the time laid down, the monk goes to the chapel, kneels down, makes the sign of the cross on forehead, lips, and breast, and recites the Antiphon: *Come, Holy Ghost, fill the hearts of thy faithful; and kindle in them the fire of thy love;* and thrice the verse: *O God, come unto my aid; O Lord, make haste to help me.* Then, he must practise recollection, and put himself in the presence of God, who is to be regarded during the first week as a strict Judge, angry with sin. Then come the three points of meditation. If he meditates on sin, he tries to conceive hatred of it by considering the sins of the fallen angels and of Adam, and of Sodom and Gomorrha, recalling the death of Jesus Christ and searching out his own sins. At the second point, he excites himself to repentance and sorrow for his shortcomings. At the third, he begs forgiveness with confidence, praying to God, to the Lord Jesus, and to the Blessed Virgin and the Saints. The prayer ends by thanking God for having granted him the blessing of contrition. He smites his breast three times, and says with the

---

[1] Chap. ii (Rousseau, p. 3).

publican : *O God, be merciful to me a sinner.* He then rises to recite a Psalm and a prayer, and retires in a state of recollection.

In the illuminative and unitive ways the method is the same, but the considerations made and the feelings aroused are different. Moreover, it is not always necessary to follow the method in every part. When devotion and love are stirred within, a man must abandon himself to them and take no further pains about applying the method. When the monk—and we must not forget that Garcia de Cisneros is writing for monks—has worked at his own purification for a certain period, even for a month if necessary, he passes on to the illuminative way, in which he becomes *illumined* and enlightened as to supernatural realities by the rays of the divine light. On entering into this stage, he will carefully examine his conscience for the purpose of confession. Cisneros gives a model of this examination, which is made in the evening after Compline during the time of the great silence. To arouse the love of God and contrition in the soul, this is followed by a week of meditations, always coming after Compline : Monday, on creation ; Tuesday, on elevation to the supernatural order ; Wednesday, on religious vocation ; Thursday, on justification ; Friday, on blessings personally experienced ; Saturday, on divine providence ; Sunday, on heaven. Meditation may also be made upon the life and examples of Christ and the Saints, and upon the Lord's Prayer.

In the unitive way, after the soul has been purified from its sins and illumined with heavenly light, it is lovingly united with its Creator, rejoicing in his excellence and desiring to please him alone. Deep recollection, contempt for this world's goods, and the constant thought of God's perfections are here indispensable. The divine perfections are the special subject of meditation during the third week. After the evening Office, on Monday God is considered as the principle of all things, on Tuesday as the beauty of the universe, on Wednesday as the glory of the world, on Thursday as sovereign charity, on Friday as a rule of every being, on Saturday as governing all things in profound calmness, on Sunday as supreme in liberality. Garcia de Cisneros, following Hugh of Palma, explains that in the unitive way the soul rises to God by love, and often without any intellectual act ; it feels and loves far more than it sees or understands. There are six degrees of unitive love according to the Saints'[1] way of looking at things : illumination and the kindling of the soul, sweetness, desire, satiety, and rapture. Some

[1] Richard of St Victor and St Bonaventure set forth a similar graduation of the love of God.

writers add two more : the sense of security and perfect
tranquillity.

The love which produces such effects is of the highest perfection; it is seraphic love. In order to attain to it, the
way of ordinary union must be surpassed, and contemplation
must be zealously embraced. Garcia de Cisneros therefore
adds a fourth part to his *Ejercitatorio* on contemplation. Its
beginning is in no way remarkable. Here we find a tran-
scription of Gerson's *De monte contemplationis*. What is
really noteworthy is the happy way in which the life and
passion of Christ are proposed for contemplation. According to Garcia de Cisneros there are three ways of contemplating our Saviour's life : we can either consider his holy
humanity, as St Bernard advised, and conceive an ardent
love of it, or consider Christ himself as God and man, or
else rise from his manhood to the knowledge and love of his
godhead. This last way of contemplation is the most perfect.
Each one must follow his inward attraction, conformably to
his degree of the spiritual life. Next, Garcia de Cisneros
proposes as subjects for meditation the principal episodes in
the life and Passion of Christ, but without dividing them up
into weeks. He allows contemplatives who are practised in
prayer a wide liberty in the choice of subjects for meditation.[1]

I have analyzed the *Ejercitatorio* at some length because
of its importance. Certainly the Abbot of Montserrat's book
had a great influence. It sets forth a definite and more
complete method of prayer than those hitherto found. He
who carries out the *Spiritual Exercises* with good will is
sure, we may say, to free himself from sin and to become
fervent. In a manner he fits himself into a spiritual gear
from which he only gets out when once converted.[2] The

---

[1] It is interesting to compare Garcia de Cisneros, in his teaching on
contemplation, with the English Benedictine, David Baker. Born in
England in 1575 and reared in Protestantism, Baker was converted to
Catholicism and went to Italy, where he became a Benedictine. He
was sent back to London, where he died in 1641. He explained Walter
Hilton's *Scale of Perfection* and wrote on contemplation. Dom S. de
Cressy abridged his teaching in a little treatise on contemplation,
entitled *Sancta Sophia,* recently republished in London.

[2] A few years later than Garcia de Cisneros, another eminent Benedictine, Louis de Blois (†1566), reformed the Abbey of Liessies with the
practice of meditation and other spiritual exercises. Like the Abbot
of Montserrat, he noticed that the exterior exercises of the cloister
only sanctify the monk in so far as they are vivified by spiritual union
with God : " Good, no doubt, and well-pleasing to God are such
exterior exercises," he says, " as the devout chanting of the divine
praises, the recitation of long vocal prayers, continued kneeling, the
giving of outward signs of devotion, fasting, watching, etc.; but
infinitely superior to them are spiritual exercises whereby man through
ardent desires, not by the senses and images but in a supernatural

religious were not the only ones to make use of it. Most of the numerous pilgrims who came to venerate the Blessed Virgin at Montserrat undertook to follow the *Exercises*. Among them, in 1522, is to be noted the famous soldier wounded at Pampeluna, Ignatius of Loyola.

Thus methodical prayer originated at the end of the fifteenth century. The Holy Spirit inspired the reformers of the religious life with this kind of exercise, which was destined to protect devotion just when society was ceasing to be Christian. And since the world, paganized by the Renaissance and upset by Protestantism, will doubtless take a long time to recover its full Christianity, methodical prayer will become more and more necessary. Moreover, it will be generalized and introduced into the lives of the ordinary laity, thanks to the work of St Ignatius of Loyola.[1]

---

manner, rises unto God to be united with him " (*Institution spirituelle*, chap. v, Benedictine translation, Paris, 1913, Vol. II, pp. 35-36). See the *Règle abrégée du novice*.

[1] *Cf.* E. Masure, *L'ascèse de saint Ignace et l'âme moderne* (*Mélanges Watrigant*, pp. 83-87, C.B.E., nos. 61-62). Early, indeed, was mental prayer introduced into the old religious Orders. We have seen it among the Benedictines. The Dominicans began to practise it in 1505, after the Chapter of Milan. The Chapter General of the Franciscans in 1594 also ordered it.

CHAPTER II

THE "SPIRITUAL EXERCISES" OF ST IGNATIUS—IGNATIAN SPIRITUALITY—FIRST JESUIT WRITERS IN THIS FIELD

A T the end of the evolution of methodical prayer we find a masterpiece: the *Spiritual Exercises* of St Ignatius of Loyola.[1] These are the crown of the systemization of the spiritual life which was slowly wrought age after age by the pressure of circumstances and difficulties and was completed at the time of the Renaissance. Like all the works which sum up a movement and are its final flowering, the *Exercises* owe much to the past. Whatever be his genius, whatever the stamp he impresses on the march of human thought, an author necessarily depends upon the time and environment in which he lives; and we know how far in the days of St Ignatius's conversion meditation had become methodized, prayer regulated, and the whole spiritual life organized and its various exercises so co-ordinated as to create a real system of moral reformation.

[1] The text is in the *Monumenta Historica Societatis Jesu*, Series II, Vol. I: *Exercitia spiritualia sancti Ignatii de Loyola et eorum Directoria,* Madrid, 1919. The *Monumenta* contain: 1. The original Castilian text— a copy of the Saint's manuscript corrected by himself and therefore called the *autograph.* 2. Five different Latin translations of the *Exercises:* That of Frusius made under the eyes of St Ignatius and published in Rome (1548) with Paul III's Brief—the Vulgate edition of the *Spiritual Exercises;* that of Father John Roothaan, published in Rome (1835); an old Latin translation, the *Versio prima,* made in Paris (about 1534) and ascribed by some to St Ignatius himself; a copy of the text of the *Exercises* left by Pierre Le Fèvre, the disciple and companion of the Saint in Paris, to the Carthusians of Cologne in 1544; and lastly, a Latin recension of the *Exercises* found in a manuscript collection made at Paris (1537) by John Helyar, a young Englishman.—Following the text of the *Exercises* in a Part II, the *Monumenta* publishes the principal *Directories* or collections of counsels intended for the director who gives the *Exercises* to his penitent. They are divided into three groups: 1. *Directories* written by St Ignatius— these are mainly notes; 2. *Old Directories* by John Polanco, Jacques Miron, Gilles Gonzales Davila, Fabio de Fabiis, etc.; 3. the two great *Directories* published by Claud Acquaviva in 1591 (*Monumenta,* chap. xxi, pp. 1075 ff.), and in 1599 (*id.,* chap. xxxix, 1179 ff.). In the two last *Directories,* the three ways—purgative, illuminative, and unitive— are described and adapted to the *Exercises.*—French translations by Pierre Jennesseaux from Roothaan's Latin text (Paris, 1857), and by Paul Debuchy from the Spanish autograph (Paris, undated).

I—SOURCES OF THE SPIRITUAL EXERCISES[1]

IT has been said that St Ignatius lived the *Exercises* before composing them. He has himself stated that " he did not make all the *Exercises* at one and the same time, but that he thought that the things which he observed within himself might be useful to others also, and therefore he wrote them down, [*e.g.,* what concerns] examination of conscience by the use of lines." Thus we shall find traces of his famous work in the story of his conversion.[2]

Ignatius was born in 1495, according to the Bollandists, at the castle of Loyola near the town of Azpeitia in Guipuzcoa, a Basque province bordering upon the French frontier. Until the age of twenty-six he gave himself up to the " vanities of the world, taking the greatest delight in the exercise of arms, being urged on, as he was, by a great and vain desire of worldly honour."[3]

On May 20, 1521, his right leg was crushed in the defence of the fortress of Pampeluna besieged by the French, in the war between Francis I and Charles V. After a short stay at Pampeluna he was borne to Loyola. And there it

[1] For historical records of the composition of the *Exercises* and the work of St Ignatius, see *Monumenta Historica Societatis Jesu*, Madrid, 1894 and after. It contains : the *Scripta de S. Ignatio*, 2 vols., 1904. In the first is the Spanish text of the autobiographical notes dictated by the Saint to Fr. Luis Gonzales de Camara in 1553-1555 (Latin translation in the *Acta Sanctorum*, July 31 ; French translation of the Spanish by Eugène Thibaut, entitled *Le récit du Pèlerin*, Louvain, 1922) ; *Epistolae P. P. Paschasii Broëti, Claudii Jaji* (disciples of St Ignatius), 1903 ; *Monumenta Xaveriana*, 1899-1913 ; *S. Francisci Xav. epistolae*, 1904-1918 ; *Monumenta Fabri* (Le Fèvre, St Ignatius' disciple), 1914 ; *J. Nadal, epistolae*, 1898-1905 ; *Polanco* (the Saint's secretary), *Chronicon Societatis Jesu*, 1894-1898 ; *S. Franciscus de Borgia*, 1894-1911.

Historians of St Ignatius : Ribadeneira, *Vida del bienaventurado Padre Ignatio de Loyola*, 1584 ; D. Bartoli, *Histoire de saint Ignace*, Paris, 1893 ; Henri Joly, *Saint Ignace de Loyola* (English Ed., Burns Oates and Washbourne).

Collection de la Bibliothèque des Exercices de saint Ignace, 1906 and after. A. Brou, *La spiritualité de saint Ignace*, Paris, 1914 ; *Les Exercices spirituels de saint Ignace de Loyola*, Paris, 1922 ; Watrigant, *La genèse des Exercices de saint Ignace* (*Études*, Vols. LXXI-LXXIII), Amiens, 1897 ; L. de Grandmaison, *Les Exercices spirituels de saint Ignace dans l'édition des Monumenta* (*Recherches de science religieuse*, September-December, 1920, pp. 391 ff.) ; Dom Besse, *L'Exercice de Garcia de Cisneros et les Exercices de saint Ignace* (*Revue des questions historiques*, Vol. LXI, pp. 22 ff.).

[2] Thibaut, *Le récit du Pèlerin*, no. 99, p. 102. In the Brief *Pastoralis officii* of July 31, 1548, approving the *Exercices*, Pope Paul III declares that Ignatius composed the *Spiritual Exercises* according to Holy Scripture and spiritual experience (*et vitae spiritualis experimentis*).

[3] Thibaut, *Le récit du Pèlerin*, no. 1, p. 11.

was, during his convalescence, that instead of the romances of chivalry, such as *Amadis de Gaul,* which could not be obtained, the *Life of Jesus Christ* by Ludolph the Carthusian and the *Flower of the Saints* by Jacobus de Voragine were put into his hands. These two books had been translated into Spanish.[1] St Ignatius gathered inspiration from them in composing his *Exercises.*

In fact, Ignatius was deeply impressed by such pious reading. From it he obtained the desire to do, himself also, great things for God. " St Dominic did thus," he would say, " and I, too, ought to do so; St Francis did that, and therefore I, too, will do it."[2] Just play of imagination at first rather than operative desire, for very soon his mind flew back to vain fancies, to the worldly reveries in which it habitually delighted. Long was his mind disturbed by this alternating flow of thought after thought, sometimes about God, sometimes of the vanities of this world. Later on, when he had gained experience in things spiritual, he saw in all this the action of different spirits; the spirit of God which drew him to the good, and the spirit of Satan desiring to keep him in the world.

However, his spiritual reading enlightened him fully as to the nothingness of creatures. He finally decided to serve God and planned, as soon as he was well, to make a pilgrimage to Jerusalem and to practise austerities. As his holy desires increased, his worldly fancies became less and less frequent and at last completely disappeared. His conversion was fortified by a vision of the Mother of God with the Holy Child, which left behind a deep disgust for his past life and an entire pacification of the senses which nothing could henceforth disturb. While waiting for his health to enable him to carry out his plans, Ignatius confirmed himself in his good resolutions by reading the lives of Jesus Christ and the Saints, from which he culled and copied many extracts.[3]

At the close of his life Ignatius declared to Fr. Gonzalès that the part of the *Exercises* which deals with elections was taken from " the diversity of mind and of idea which he had at Loyola when he was still suffering with his leg."[4] Great in meditation and profound in his knowledge of psychology, the writer of the *Exercises* was able to analyze the various spiritual states he experienced at the time of his conversion, and to deduce from his own religious experiences principles for the guidance of those who follow the same path. God and Satan contend for the soul who turns away from the world. Ignatius learnt the way in which each of them works : the thoughts inspired by God leave the

[1] *id., Le récit du Pélerin,* no. 2-5, pp. 12-14.   [2] *id.,* no. 7.
[3] *id.,* 8-12.   [4] *id.,* no. 99, p. 102.

soul in joy and peace; those that proceed from the devil please us at the outset, and are followed by uneasiness and discontent.

But all these conceptions were very confused when Ignatius recovered and left Loyola. " His soul was still blind," he says, having little beyond " a great desire to serve God."[1] He lacked spiritual knowledge. He was going to acquire it at Montserrat and at Manresa.

It was towards the middle of March, 1522, that Ignatius came to Montserrat, where rose not only the Benedictine abbey, but the church in which was the venerated image of our Lady. He made a general confession to the Benedictine Dom Chanones (†1569), who was his " director and first spiritual father."[2] Ignatius made but a short stay at Montserrat. On the vigil of the Annunciation he made a *watch in arms* all night before the Madonna. Next morning he went to Manresa, a neighbouring town. He returned from time to time to Montserrat to converse with Dom Chanones.[3]

According to the custom of his monastery Dom Chanones gave Ignatius the *Exercises* of Garcia de Cisneros and made him follow the meditations. We know that the Benedictines of Montserrat used the doctrine and method contained in this book in directing the pilgrims who came to practise their devotions in the sanctuary of our Lady. It would be astonishing, indeed, if any exception were made when Ignatius presented himself to Dom Chanones.

Moreover, Ribadeneira (†1611), one of the first companions of St Ignatius and his historian, recognizes as " very probable " the tradition handed down at Montserrat, to wit: that the " B. P. Ignatius at Montserrat came to know the *Exercitatorium* of Fr. Garcia de Cisneros and that he followed it in his prayer and meditation. Fr. John Chanones taught and instructed him in some of the things contained in the *Exercitatorium*."[4] Fr. Watrigant, who made a thorough study of the origin of the *Exercises* of St Ignatius, is " convinced that the saint had had the work of

[1] *Le récit du Pélerin,* no. 14.
[2] Ribadeneira, *Vida del B. P. Ignacio de Loyola,* Book IV, chap. iv.
[3] Antony de Yepez, *Cronica general de la orden de San Benito,* Valladolid, 1613, Vol. IV, p. 237 ; Bartoli, *Histoire de saint Ignace de Loyola,* Terrien's translation, Vol. I, p. 57.
[4] Ribadeneira's letter to Antony de Yepez, a Benedictine of Valladolid, on the Montserrat tradition in *Cronica general de la orden de San Benito,* by Yepez, Vol. IV, pp. 237, 238. Dom Besse gives a translation of the letter in the *Revue des questions historiques,* Vol. LXI (1897), pp. 35-38. The Montserrat tradition is also noted in Dom Thévard's translation of Cisneros, Paris, 1655.

de Cisneros in his hands."[1] Hence, we may infer without
rashness that Ignatius was acquainted with the *Ejercitatorio* of Garcia de Cisneros and even that "he used it for
his own spiritual life."[2]

To what extent was he helped by it in composing his
Spiritual Exercises?

It is hard to understand how the word plagiarism came
to be applied to this matter, as if St Ignatius had done no
more than appropriate the work of the Abbot of Montserrat.
Only partisanship or inadvertence can have given rise to
such an hypothesis, which the simple reading of the two
works is enough to demolish.[3] Hence, there is no point in
proving its fallacy. St Ignatius's work is conspicuously
original and, from that point of view, superior to that of
Garcia de Cisneros.

At the other extreme we find those who regard the influence of Cisneros upon St Ignatius as altogether or almost
nil; for, say they, there is not a single word for word
quotation from the *Ejercitatorio* in the *Exercises*. As for
similarities, they are confined to seven or eight passages,
and even these do not amount to the proof of any literary
dependence. Such is the point of view, indeed, of the
editors of the *Monumenta historica Societatis Jesu*.[4]

But the influence of a book does not depend solely upon
its borrowings or quotations. All admit—as does St Ignatius
himself—that *The Imitation of Christ* was made use of in
the composition of the *Exercises,* and nevertheless not a
single quotation from it is found in them.[5] Let us grant—
though this is far from sure[6]—that not a single passage
from the work of Cisneros can be found in any shape whatever in the *Exercises,* yet the latter may owe something to
the Abbot of Montserrat.

"What strikes one most at first sight," says Fr. Watrigant, "is the general design of the two writers: both of

[1] *La genèse des Exercices* (*Études,* LXXI, p. 529). Henri Joly,
S Ignace de Loyola, p. 46.

[2] Dom Besse, *loc. cit.,* p. 38.

[3] See also *Acta S. S.,* July 31; *Cf.* Dom Besse, *loc. cit.,* p. 45;
Watrigant, *La genèse des Exercices* (*Études,* LXXII, pp. 204-209).

[4] Series II, tom. I, *Exercitia spiritualia S Ignatii et eorum
Directoria,* Proleg., pp. 94-123. *Cf.* P. Codina, *Razon y Fé,* July,
August, September, 1917; *Los Ejercicios de san Ignacio y el Ejercitatorio de Cisneros.* See Fr. Watrigant's reservations with regard to the
too pronounced opinion of Fr. Codina, *Bibliothèque des Exercices,*
no. 59 (1919), pp. 65 ff.

[5] *Cf.* V. Mercier, *Concordance de l'Imitation de Jésus-Christ et des
Exercices,* Paris, 1885.

[6] See Dom Besse, *Revue des questions historiques,* pp. 40-44 and
Watrigant, *Genèse des Exercices* (*Études,* LXXII, p. 200), for re-
semblances between the two works.

them, in fact, wanted to provide a method to lead souls to
God by means of set *exercises.*" In both cases we find a
series of meditations to be made daily at fixed times on
subjects—several of which are the same—chosen beforehand in order to secure a definite and progressive spiritual
result : purification of soul and ascent in the Christian life.
Finally, in both cases, we find the systematization of the
spiritual life and of the exercises meant to develop it, especially of meditation.   But Ignatius could not have found this
notion of systematization anywhere else than in the *Ejercitatorio* of Garcia de Cisneros, just as Garcia had found it,
as Fr. Watrigant clearly proves,[1] in the works of writers
who had gone before him, particularly in those of the
religious of Windesheim.   Through Garcia de Cisneros, St
Ignatius took advantage of all the progress made during
fifteen centuries in the *methodization* of the exercises of
devotion.   It was from Cisneros that he gained the "idea
of a methodical course of spirituality following the classical
order of the three ways."   But he realized the idea on his
own account and in a conspicuously original manner.

The history of the composition of the *Exercises* confirms
this view.   The first draft of the *Exercises* was finished
in 1526, when Ignatius gave them at Alcala.   Next year,
at Salamanca, he had to submit "all his papers, which
were the *Exercises,*" to the knight bachelor Frias, who was
commissioned to examine them.   On February 2, 1528,
Ignatius arrived in Paris and immediately gave the *Exercises*
to many.[2]   Hence, the writing of the *Exercises* must be
dated between 1521, the year of his conversion, and 1526.
Subsequently the work "was modified in a few details and
completed in some points of secondary importance ";[3] its
essential parts were unaltered.

Now, in 1526, Ignatius had scarcely begun his university
course : he "had but the rudiments of learning."   How
could he have contrived the *Exercises* as they are had he
not then known the work of Garcia de Cisneros?[4]   Neither

[1] *Quelques promoteurs de la méditation méthodique au XVe siècle*
(C.B.E., no. 59).

[2] *Récit du Pèlerin,* nos. 57, 67, 73, 77.

[3] L. de Grandmaison, *Recherches de science religieuse* (1920), p. 394.
These conclusions, advanced by the editors of the *Monumenta (Exercitia,*
pp. 30-35), arise from the testimony of St Ignatius and his contemporaries.   Fr. Watrigant appears to set the drawing up of the
Exercises farther back : " St Ignatius did not finish, if one may say, the
draft of his *Exercises* before the period of his stay at Alcala ; and
probably the term should be put back a few years more " (*Études,*
LXXII, p. 211).

[4] " If the *Exercises,* as we now have them, had been written out in
full at Manresa itself, St Ignatius would very probably have been unable to consult any other master of spirituality than the Abbot of Montserrat." Watrigant, *La genèse des Exercices (Études, ibid.,* p. 210).

Ludolph the Carthusian's *Life of Christ,* nor Jacobus de Voragine's *Golden Legend,* nor even *The Imitation of Christ,* read in Castilian at Manresa,[1] could have really guided him. These works supplied him with certain ideas in the *Exercises,* but did not show him how to arrange them. The spiritual experiences of St Ignatius at the period of his conversion, however suggestive they may have been, could not have inspired him with the idea of an organic system of asceticism as definite and entire as that of the *Exercises.*

Was the knowledge of Ignatius supernatural, and must we seek a solution of the problem in enlightenment directly communicated to him by the Holy Ghost? Here is what Fr. Gonzalès has to tell us about it:

" One day he [Ignatius] was going out of devotion to a certain church, about a mile from Manresa, and I think it was St Paul's. The road runs by the river. Engaged in his devotions, he sat for awhile with his face towards the river flowing beneath him. As he was sitting there, the eyes of his mind began to open; it was not a vision, but he understood and knew many things, things of the spirit as well as those of faith and knowledge; and all that in so clear a light that they all appeared to him something altogether new. Nor is it possible to explain the particular points which he then understood, though they were many in number; but only that he received a great illumination of his understanding; so that when he recollects all the helps he has received from God, and all the things he has learnt during the whole of his life until the age of sixty-two, and gathers them together into one, it does not appear to him to come up to what he received in that one instance."[2]

Are we to infer from this that not only was Ignatius supernaturally enlightened as to the truths of the faith, and as to the spiritual life, but also that the detailed plan of the *Exercises* was revealed to him? Must we not rather say that the work of Garcia de Cisneros was the means used by Providence to disclose to him a method of asceticism—the outcome of a long development—perfectly adapted to the needs of his day?

Thanks to his divinely enlightened personal experience, enriched with reading, Ignatius was able to turn that method to account in a way amounting to genius.[3]

---

[1] We know that Ignatius used these three works in the composition of his *Exercises.* The Castilian translation of the *Imitation of Christ* was attributed in Spain to Gerson.

[2] Thibaut, *Le récit du Pèlerin,* no. 30, pp. 35, 36.

[3] I note here, by way of memorandum, the improbable opinion of unbelieving critics who like to think that St Ignatius derived his *Exercises* from the rules of Mussulman religious. *Cf.* Hermann Muller (a pseudonym), *Les origines de la Compagnie de Jésus,* Paris, 1898.

II—ANALYSIS AND EXPLANATION OF THE "EXERCISES"

LIKE Garcia de Cisneros, St Ignatius divided his *Exercises* into four weeks, but the subjects for meditation are differently distributed.

In both works, the aim of the First Week is spiritual purification. But whilst the Abbot of Montserrat's *Ejercitatorio* confines contemplation of the life and passion of Christ especially to the last week, the *Exercises* of St Ignatius assign the Second Week to meditation upon our Lord's Life up to and including Palm Sunday, the Third Week to the Passion, and the fourth to the Resurrection and Ascension. The theory of the three ways is latent rather than patent in the *Spiritual Exercises;*[1] it does not make their framework as in the *Ejercitatorio*.

The *Spiritual Exercises* open with twenty annotations, the result of St Ignatius' experience, and these make a kind of Introduction. The first gives a definite explanation of the *Exercises* and sets down their aim. The word " Exercise " designates " any way of examining one's conscience, meditating, contemplating, praying vocally and mentally, and other spiritual operations, as shall afterwards be told ; because as walking, going, and running are bodily exercises, in like manner all methods of preparing the soul to remove from herself all disorderly attachments, and, after their removal, to seek and find the divine will in the laying out of one's life to the salvation of one's soul, are called Spiritual Exercises." We must bear in mind that the first aim of the *Exercises* is to help the retreatant to purify his soul in order to discern his vocation and to follow it with generosity.

The other annotations contain general counsels meant for those who are giving or receiving the *Exercises;* for Ignatius always assumes that the exercitant is under the guidance of a director.

A certain amount of initiative is to be left to the retreatant in the meditation or contemplation of the subjects proposed. He should be filled with a greater sense of respect in those parts of the *Exercises* which induce prayer than in those which lead to simple reflection (II-III).

The *Exercises* last four weeks or about thirty days. But each week is not necessarily made up of seven or eight days. The week must be sometimes curtailed or prolonged, accord-

---

[1] *Cf.* the tenth annotation : " The enemy of human nature usually tempts a man more under the appearance of good when he is exercising himself in the illuminative life, corresponding to the Exercises of the Second Week, and not so much in the purgative life, corresponding to the Exercises of the First Week." Fr. Rickaby, *The Spiritual Exercises of St Ignatius*, p. 7.

ing to one's quicker or slower acquisition of the effect
sought. It is indispensable to the success of the exercises
to enter upon them with all one's heart. He who is giving
them must make sure that the retreatant is carrying them
out at the set times and as they ought to be done (IV-VI).

The director must treat the exercitant, who is tried with
interior desolation and temptations, with kindliness. He is
to give him instructions about spiritual desolation. He will
discover to him the wiles of the devil, explaining to him the
rules for the discernment of spirits in the First Week, and
even in the second, according to the dictates of prudence and
the needs of him who is making the exercises (VII-X).

It is well to follow the exercises of the First Week without
trying to find out those of the Second Week. A whole hour
or more should be given to each of the five exercises or
contemplations day after day. As a rule, the first exercise
will be made at midnight, the second directly after rising,
the third before or after Mass, the fourth at the time of
Vespers, the fifth before going to bed.[1] One must be on
one's guard against shortening the exercises, a temptation
chiefly arising during periods of inward desolation.

The director must prevent the exercitant from lightly
undertaking any promise or vow in the fervour of the
moment. He must not try to influence the retreatant in
the choice of any kind of life, but wait for God to show his
will. To let the Creator work more surely upon his soul,
the retreatant will endeavour to desire no work nor anything else except for the glory of God. And, to make sure
of the purity of his intention, he will faithfully discover his
thoughts to his director (XIV-XVII).

Lastly, the exercises must be adapted to the age, the
knowledge, the intellectual capacity, the health, the end in
view and to the occupations of each individual. The most
appropriate exercises are to be chosen according to circumstances. To those who have plenty of time at their disposal
and are sufficiently educated all the exercises should be
offered, and they should be advised to withdraw into solitude
apart from their relations and friends (XVIII-XX).[2]

St Ignatius opens the First Week with the *Preface* or
famous rule for the interpretation of the thoughts of others.
No doubt it was suggested to him by the attacks he had

[1] First Week, Observation, Jennesseaux, p. 78; Debuchy, p. 61.
[2] St Ignatius' Directory says: *Locus Exercitiis destinatus secretus
esto, nec cum aliquo verbo misceat exercitans, si exactam Exercitiorum
normam sequi velit.*—This Directory was first published in the
Recherches de science religieuse, May-September, 1916, pp. 248 ff., and
again brought out in the *Monumenta.* It has inspired most of the rest.

to meet in Spain, about 1527, when he was giving the
Exercises. When he appeared before the judges of the
Spanish Inquisition, they " put him a multitude of questions
not only on the *Exercises,* but also on theology." We know
how they imprisoned him at Alcala. As to the *Exercises,*
" they dwelt much on a single point which was at the beginning—viz., When a thought is a venial, and when it is a
mortal sin. And this they did because, though he was not
learned, he decided the question. And he made answer :
' Whether it is the truth or not, you must decide; and if it
is not the truth, condemn it.' And at last they, without
condemning anything, went away."[1]

Perhaps Ignatius met with prejudiced exercitants who
were much readier to blame his teaching than to be edified
by it. In Paris he must have had discussions with followers
of Erasmus and Luther whom he endeavoured to bring back
to the truth. These circumstances compelled him to formulate the Golden Rule which to-day would seem to us superfluous at the beginning of a retreat :

" In order that both he who gives and he who receives
the Spiritual Exercises may derive greater help and profit
from them, it must be presupposed that every good Christian
should be readier to excuse than to condemn a proposition
advanced by his neighbour; and if he cannot justify it,
let him inquire into the meaning of the author : if the latter
be in error, correct him lovingly; should that not suffice,
then let him employ every suitable means, so that his
neighbour, rightly understanding it, may be saved from
error."

Before beginning the first exercises with the retreatant,
Ignatius reminds him of the end in view : " To overcome
oneself and regulate one's life without being swayed by any
inordinate attachment."

The election or choice of a state of life according to the
divine purpose is the end to which everything in the *Exercises*
is subordinated, the central point towards which everything
converges : " The *Spiritual Exercises* keep in view above all
a concrete and clearly determined case : their aim is to put
a man—*i.e.,* one who is at liberty to choose his own career
and well equipped for the apostolate, in the position of being
able to discern clearly and to follow God's call."[2] At the
outset such a concrete case was that of Ignatius himself.
The *Exercises* made him an apostle as they made Francis
Xavier the most zealous of missionaries.

Wonderful as a method of winning recruits for the aposto-

[1] Thibaut, *Le récit du Pèlerin,* no. 68, p. 72. Note in Ignatius' replies
to the Inquisitors a certain amount of impatience with their cavillings.
[2] L. de Grandmaison, *Recherches de science religieuse,* September-
December, 1920, p. 400.

late, the *Exercises* are also a method for the restoration of the
spiritual life, and they are therefore adapted to many of the
faithful. Ignatius tells us that he used to give the *Exercises*
to those who came to see him in prison at Alcala.[1] Among
them many, no doubt, had already decided upon their vocation; for a man's election may not only determine the whole
course of his life, but it may simply aim at the reformation
of some important point in his spiritual life. This is the
election of amendment so much appreciated by Mgr. d'Hulst.[2]

From this point of view, however, the *Exercises* are less
easily explained. They are no longer to the same degree the
kind of drama in which we behold a "probable candidate for
missionary work" freeing himself from unruly passions with
energetic penances; contended for by God and Satan, trying
with the help of an enlightened counsellor to distinguish,
amidst conflicting inward attractions, those emanating from
the spirit of grace from those of the spirit of evil, and finally
determining to devote his life to the service of God and
strengthening himself in that determination by contemplating
the mysteries of the life of Christ.

To such a prospective missioner Ignatius proposes first of
all the principle which is to guide him in the discovery of his
way, the foundation upon which he will base the whole of his
spiritual building, the final goal of man.[3] Man was created
for God, to serve him and thereby to save his soul. Everything that is in the world was created to help man to secure
his salvation. Man's duty is to make use of it or to let it
alone in so far as it is profitable or unprofitable for that end.
The exercitant is consequently at once invited to take up an
attitude of indifference towards created things, and to desire
only whatever will best lead him to the fulfilment of his
destiny.

In his fundamental meditation Ignatius makes an allusion
to the notion which dominated his whole life: *Ad majorem
Dei gloriam.* Both in the *Exercises* and in his *Constitutions,*[4] and above all in his correspondence, he constantly
speaks of the service and the glory of God.[5] Habitual direction of thought and act towards the greater glory of God is
a well-known characteristic of the Ignatian spirituality.

---

[1] *Le récit du Pèlerin,* no. 60.
[2] Baudrillart, *Vie de Mgr. d'Hulst,* Vol. III, p. 555.
[3] *Cf.* Watrigant, *La méditation fondamentale avant saint Ignace*
(*C.B.E.,* no. 9).
[4] *Constitutiones Societatis Jesu latine et hispanice cum earum de-
clarationibus,* Matriti, 1892.
[5] "It is reckoned that in his *Constitutions* alone St Ignatius refers
259 times to the greater glory of God—*i.e.,* nearly once on every page"
(A. Brou, *La spiritualité de saint Ignace,* p. 10). *Cf.* F. Cavalier, *La
spiritualité des Exercices,* in the *Revue d'ascétique et de mystique,*
October, 1922, pp. 357 ff.

The exercitant under the guidance of Ignatius is regarded as knowing nothing of ascetic training. He needs instruction as to how to examine into his own thoughts, words, and deeds, to distinguish his serious sins from those which are venial, and to prepare for the general confession which is to precede his communion at the end of his First Week.[1] He is given models for self-examination. And he is to do five exercises or meditations every day in order to feel deep contrition for his sins. The first meditation will be on the fall of the angels, the fall of our first parents, and the fall of one cast into hell through one single mortal sin. The second will be on the retreatant's personal sins and on the divine attributes, principally on the mercy of God. Lastly, the fifth meditation will be on hell.

In the meditations for the First Week, St Ignatius gives his celebrated method of prayer according to the three powers of the soul : memory, understanding, and will.

Meditation is composed of a preparatory prayer asking God " to direct the intentions, actions, and operations of the exercitant," of two preludes, three or five points or parts of the subject of the meditation, and of a colloquy in which God is spoken with " as a friend talks with his friend or as a servant does with his master."

The first prelude is a composition, seeing the place. It consists in imagining the circumstances in which occurred the mystery in the life of Christ or of the Virgin Mary which it is desired to contemplate. When the meditation is on an abstract subject, we must make a representation of that which symbolizes it best. The second prelude is a prayer to God to beseech his grace in connection with the subject set before us. The two preludes thus vary according to the subject of the meditation.

The meditation rightly so called is divided into several points. In each of these Ignatius exercises the memory, the understanding, and the will,[2] the three faculties so much

[1] The Ignatian Directory advises that this confession should be made to someone other than the giver of the Exercises (*Direct.*, I, 5).

[2] This part of the Ignatian meditation varies and sometimes calls for the use of other faculties. According to these variations, as many as five methods of prayer are to be found in the *Exercises*.—The first is *Meditation according to the powers of the soul;* it is the best known and most used, the one above set forth.—The second is *Contemplation,* which is an ordinary meditation on some mystery of the life of Christ. After the preludes, we " contemplate "—*i.e.,* we consider, without exerting great effort, the persons, their utterances and acts.—The third is the *Application of the five senses* to the mystery on which we are meditating. We see the persons with the eyes of the imagination, we hear what they are saying, we inhale or relish the sweetness of the meditation, we touch with spiritual caresses the places in which the mystery occurred.—The fourth is entitled : *The second way of praying.* After

spoken of by the writers of the Middle Ages. This meditation is a kind of moral strategy. The powers of the soul are
like so many battalions held in reserve and launched one after
another at the right moment to the capture of the spiritual
objective by assault. Memory recalls facts and reasons,
understanding intervenes to make its inferences, and the will
evokes feeling and carries away the soul to the end desired.[1]

This method sets in relief the part played by man in the
work of his conversion and moral reformation; it stimulates
personal effort. No doubt it does not disregard God's part
since it both begins and ends with prayer for grace; nevertheless, it is mainly directed towards action. It explains
Ignatian spirituality, which is above all an excitant of energy.
The Christian who sets to work upon himself with meditation
and the particular examen is as duly conscious of his own
endeavour as if his spiritual training depended solely upon
himself. Ignatian meditation is " essentially active, practical, conquering virtues. In a certain sense it is Martha
rather than Mary, or rather it is an effective sort of contemplation for acquiring the possession of goodness. It is
active because it attains such virtues, not only by praying
for them, but by making the appropriate acts."[2] The retreatant is sanctified as much by acts of the will as by prayer.
The expression, " I will it, *id quod volo,"* recurs throughout
the *Exercises,* which are quite truly a school of will-power
and energy.

To meditation, which fires the soul to seek goodness,
Ignatius adds self-examination to verify its progress. Nothing
in the spiritual life must be left to whim or to chance. How
can self-knowledge be attained without self-examination?
And is not self-knowledge indispensable to the interior life?
Ignatius regards the particular examen as being as fundamental an exercise as meditation.

This particular examen, which is not found in Garcia de

---

the usual preparation we stop at each word of a prayer, such as the
Pater noster, as long as we find relish or good in doing so, and this
is done all through the prayer.—The fifth method, or *Third way of
praying,* consists in considering for the space of a single breathing
each of the words of some vocal prayer while we are saying it. *Cf.*
Fourth Week, the *Three ways of praying.* P. de Maumigny explains
these various methods in his *Pratique de l'oraison mentale,* 12th ed.,
Paris, 1916, I, pp. 320 ff.

[1] In the five first annotations which end the First Week, St Ignatius
adds a few counsels for securing the fruitfulness of the meditations:
before going to sleep at night, review the subject of the meditation;
think of it on awaking; after the meditation is over, note whether it
has been well or faultily made.

[2] Achille Gagliardi (†1607), *De plena cognitione Instituti Societatis
Jesu,* Bruges, 1882, pp. 98-99; A. Brou, *La Spiritualité de saint Ignace,*
pp. 29-30; Watrigant, *Des méthodes d'oraison dans notre vie aposto-
lique,* C.B.E., nos. 15-47 (1913).

Cisneros' *Ejercitatorio,* is far from being the same as the general examen prior to confession. Its purpose is to free a man from a besetting sin or from a dominant defect. This examen is made twice a day, after dinner and after supper. Every time a man's failures must be written down, and days and weeks are to be compared with one another to verify the progress attained. From the beginning the particular examen is prescribed for the retreatant; but it is to be continued even by the man who has advanced in the Christian life.[1]

The Second Week is "the most original and the most urgent part" of the *Exercises,* "which ends in the election of a state of life."[2]

The exercitant once purified from his faults by repentance, and having sufficiently mastered his unruly tendencies, is rightly disposed for hearing the divine call. And this call is an invitation to enrol in the army of Christ.

For St Ignatius regards the apostolate as an order of knighthood. When he betook himself to Montserrat after his conversion with his mind full of the romances of chivalry, he imagined Christ as a king summoning his subjects to a crusade.[3] How ardently did he desire to be one of these good knights!

Just when the exercitant has to decide to become one of Christ's knights Ignatius makes him meditate twice a day on "the call of a temporal king" to conquer "the whole world of unbelievers." If such a call "is calculated to strike our minds, how much more worthy of consideration is the sight of our Lord Jesus Christ, the eternal King with all the world before him, hearing him make his appeal to all and to each one in particular and saying : It is my will to subdue the whole world and all my enemies and thus to enter into my Father's glory. Let him who will come after me work with me, so that following me in toil he may follow me in glory."

But we must know Christ, the eternal King, and what he demands of his soldiers before we enrol in his service.

---

[1] To inspire the sinner with repentance and love so that he may be purified of his sins, such is the end of the First Week of the *Exercises.* To reach this point with greater certainty, Ignatius suggests further a few "devices"—*e.g.*, to keep strict watch over one's mind, to keep out the light by closing the doors and windows of one's room, to avoid laughing and talking, and, if needed, to undertake certain outward penances with prudence, such as limiting one's food and sleep, and chastising the body with the use of instruments of penance.

[2] L. de Grandmaison, pp. 401-402.

[3] Thibaut, *Récit du Pèlerin,* 17, pp. 23-24 : " He (Ignatius) went on his way towards Montserrat, thinking, as was his wont, of the great deeds he was to perform for the love of God. And, as his mind was full of the exploits of Amadis de Gaule and similar books, the thought of doing things of the same kind occurred to him."

To this end the exercitant must contemplate—for twelve days, if necessary—the mysteries of the childhood and of the public life of Christ. He will reflect long upon the Incarnation of the Word, the mystery of self-humiliation—on the Lord's Nativity, the mystery of denudation and poverty—on the Presentation in the Temple, and on the episode of Jesus left amidst the doctors, mysteries of detachment from creatures —on the hidden life of Christ at Nazareth, the mystery of obedience—on his public life, the mystery of the apostolate. In each contemplation, not only are the memory, the understanding, and the will exercised, but also the five senses— *i.e.,* the entire soul. Thus in the Lord's Nativity the exercitant is to imagine that he sees the chief characters concerned, that he hears their words, inhaling and relishing their grace and sweetness, touching and kissing their footprints. The exercitant will also feel that he is growing in the love of Christ, the Master of the Apostles, while he is learning the conditions of the apostolic life : abnegation, renunciation of honours and riches, and the practice of humility.

But what is more repugnant to a man who was lately flattered by the world than such a life of renunciation and poverty and humiliation? Ignatius knew it from experience. Day after day, when he was beginning to live a life of poverty and austerity, he was tormented by the thought of the difficulty of his enterprise : " How can you endure such a life as this all the seventy years you will have to live?" An inward voice kept on asking this question.[1]

Ignatius managed to triumph over these temptations to pusillanimity and bewilderment—the chief trial of the exercitant during the period of his election—by interspersing, in a disconcerting way at first, contemplations on the life of Christ, meditations intended to foil the ruses of Satan and the calculations of self-interest. The meditation on the Two Standards teaches us in a dramatic and quite military manner the opposite tactics of the two leaders or " captains " who are fighting one another for men : Jesus Christ and Lucifer. Lucifer draws men to himself by the love of riches, by vainglory, and pride, and he leads them to death. Jesus Christ, on the other hand, opposes riches with poverty, vainglory with opprobrium, pride with humility, and leads men to true life. Thus the exercitant is well taught in " the cheats of the bad leader " and in the requirements of Christ. All he has to do is to beseech our Lady to obtain from her Son the grace of being enrolled under his standard as an apostle, if he be pleased to do so.

And now we come to the revolts of selfishness.

The retreatant will overcome them by stirring himself to

---

[1] *Récit du Pélerin,* no. 20, p. 27.

generosity, and in the first place by the exercise of *the three classes of men*. A parable is set before him. Three classes of men there are who each of them possess "a sum of ten thousand ducats." All of them desire, for the sake of their salvation, to get rid of the attachment they feel for it. Those belonging to the first class would indeed like to be detached from it, but they do nothing to the purpose, a mere fancy; those of the second class are disposed towards detachment from it, but not to the point of stripping themselves of its possession, an unsatisfactory disposition; those of the third class are so far detached from it as to be stripped of it altogether if God required it of them; this is the right disposition, that of the exercitant who is about to make his election, and he will maintain it despite the natural repugnance he may feel for actual poverty.

Lastly, the exercise of *the three degrees of humility* will finish the victory over the future missioner's last resistance, his aversion to humiliations and obloquy. There is a degree of humility which is essential to salvation; it is that which subjects us to God's law when it is binding upon us under pain of mortal sin. In the second degree, which is more perfect, a man is in a state of complete indifference with regard to riches and poverty, honour and contempt, a long life or a short one, provided that God in all be glorified. For nothing in the world would he commit a venial sin. The third degree further requires us for the most perfect imitation of Jesus Christ to prefer, as he did, poverty to riches, contumely to honour. It is much to be desired that the retreatant should approach this degree of humility at the time of his election.[1]

The first condition for a good election is for the exercitant to consider only the end for which he was created : the glory of God and the salvation of his soul.[2] Then he will decide in favour of such and such a state of life, according to the leadings of grace.[3] For what he ought to choose is that for which God intends him.

God's will is manifested in various ways.[4] Sometimes a

---

[1] St Ignatius, *Directory*, III, 1 : *Det operam (qui dat Exercitia) ut in electionibus, quae fieri debent cum plena voluntatis resignatione et, si possibile est, cum approximatione ad tertium gradum humilitatis, ut exercitans magis propendeat, si aequale Dei servitium fore videretur, ad ea quae magis conformia sunt consiliis et exemplo Christi.*

[2] *Exercises*, Second Week, Prelude to the Election.

[3] The Election, as St Ignatius saw it, was that of a man who pledged himself irrevocably to the apostolate. But the *Exercises* have also in view the election of a man already irrevocably committed to a state of life determining to be more fervent in his vocation. Lastly, there is the variable election of such a thing as a benefice, which a man is free to accept or reject at will (*Exercises*, Second Week, Matter of Election).

[4] *Exercises*, Three Seasons favourable to the Election.

man is irresistibly drawn to a state of life, as were St Paul and St Matthew. Fairly often he receives flashes of illumination, and is disturbed in turns by consolations or desolation revealing God's purposes in regard to himself. At last he comes to have no particular feeling at all. Then he can make his election freely and quietly with the assistance of his natural faculties and reflection.[1] He prays and examines the pros and the cons, the advantages and the disadvantages of the various possible courses. He will ask himself how he would like to have made his present election had he been at the point of death, and in making his final decision he will be faithfully guided by this thought of his last end.

When the election has been made the man who has made it must be confirmed in his decision.

He will not be slow to experience, like Ignatius at Manresa,[2] great inward vicissitudes. Sometimes he will feel much joy in prayer, sometimes it will fill him only with disgust. The meditations of the Third Week on the Last Supper and on the Passion fasten more and more firmly to Christ the man who has just consecrated his life to him. His inward experiences of the spiritual life will increase. Prayer will grow more familiar, and he will learn discretion in things, especially in matters of mortification. Finally, during the Fourth Week in the contemplation of the mysteries of the risen Christ, he will become more and more closely united with God until he comes to the habitual divine union of the saints.

At the end of the *Exercises* come the rules for the discernment of spirits, required for the exercitant in the First[3] and

---

[1] St Ignatius proposes two exercises, or methods, to help reflection. In his *Directory*, III, 6, he thus defines them : *Ea autem quae deliberanda hic sunt: 1. consilia an praecepta; 2. si consilia, an in religione, an extra illam; 3. si in illa, in quali; 4. quando et quomodo; 5. si praecepta, in quo statu aut modo vivendi; et ita vadat discurrendo.*

[2] *Récit du Pèlerin*, no. 21.

[3] Fourteen rules for the First Week.—The evil spirit keeps the sinner in the pleasures of the senses, the good spirit fills him with remorse.—The devil tries to disturb the soul of the converted sinner, and God fills him with consolation and encouragement.—The third rule describes spiritual consolation and spiritual desolation.—Make no change in a resolution in a time of desolation, as the evil spirit advises; yet in the time of desolation it is good to pray and to meditate more and to do more penances.—Regard desolation as a trial permitted by God, to teach us to resist temptation with the help of grace.—Be patient in desolation.—Desolation may be a punishment for our lukewarmness and negligence. It is a trial. It is meant to teach us that good feelings come from God and not from ourselves.—During consolation let us think of desolation which will come, and take courage.—During desolation let us humble ourselves, because we can do so little without sensible grace.

Second[1] Weeks, then the rules for the distribution of alms, notes on scruples, and lastly, the famous rules for orthodoxy formulated by Ignatius at Paris for dealing with innovators, followers of Erasmus and Luther, whom he met there.

The *Spiritual Exercises* are not, strictly speaking, a complete manual of asceticism. They have a particular case in view : "they deal with a crisis . . . a missionary vocation studied, debated, and combated in a soul splendidly endowed." Ascetic teaching is largely used and explained, but only so far as is necessary. Hence "in the four famous Weeks we must not look for detailed lessons on normal, peaceable, everyday interior life."[2]

Nor must the work of St Ignatius be regarded as an initiation into the mystical ways. No doubt he raised himself to extraordinary spiritual states, and knew the graces of supernatural prayer; his autobiographical notes make this perfectly clear.[3] But it is no aim of his to lead the exercitant to that goal. His desire is to give God one more missioner. "It is God who has to decide whether his apostle is to be— in the technical sense of the word—a mystic. The author of the *Exercises* sets aside the thought of such possible calls."[4]

Perhaps, too, the false mysticism which swept over certain parts of Spain at the beginning of the sixteenth century put Ignatius on his guard against any exaggeration which might lead to illuminism, even by crooked ways. He was always very reserved as to the mystical states. While appreciating them as they deserved, he did not regard them as being in themselves signs of perfection. Besides, it is not in our own power to acquire them at will. So he insisted on ascetical exercises, the practice of the virtues, mortification, humility, and obedience.[5]

During consolation remember that we can do much with grace.—Firmness in temptation disarms the tempter, but weakness makes him terrible. —The tempter demands secrecy; he is powerless when we are open and sincere with our confessor.—Like a captain who would take a place by assault, the devil tries to find our weak point for his attacks.

[1] Eight rules for the Second Week.—The three first for ascertaining whether spiritual consolation comes from God or from the devil.—The other five reveal the ruses of the wicked angel, who sometimes changes himself into an angel of light.

[2] L. de Grandmaison, *loc. cit.*, p. 405; Watrigant, *La Genèse des Exercices* (*Études*, LXXI, p. 507).

[3] Cf. *Récit du Pèlerin*, chaps. iii, x.

[4] L. de Grandmaison, p. 406.

[5] See A. Brou, *La spiritualité de saint Ignace*, pp. 109 ff.

III—PRACTICE OF THE EXERCISES IN THE TIME OF ST IGNATIUS AND AFTERWARDS — IGNATIAN SPIRITUALITY : REACTION AGAINST THE PAGAN RENAISSANCE AND PROTESTANT QUIETISM; PROTECTION OF THE RELIGIOUS LIVING IN THE WORLD

As soon as Ignatius had finished the first edition of the *Exercises,* he made people go through them. He gave them at Alcala, as we know, in 1526, and through them many people " attained a knowledge of and a stronger relish for spiritual things."[1] In Paris during 1528 he had them made by three retreatants who " made remarkable changes in their lives," and " soon gave all that they had to the poor."[2] " By means of the *Exercises* " he won for God Pierre le Fèvre and Francis Xavier.[3] The precious manual in the hands of Ignatius was an effective means of gaining apostles for God and companions for himself. The spiritual exercises had already been made by those who took their vows with him at Montmartre on August 15, 1534 : Francis Xavier, Pierre Le Fèvre, Nicolas Bobadillo, James Laynez, Alfonso Salmeron, and Simon Rodriguez.

The *Exercises* are, above all, a spiritual method, and, like all methods, they must be constantly adapted to persons and circumstances and milieux. If, from the time of its composition till our own day, the booklet has continued to be an inestimable means of sanctification, that is because the sons of St Ignatius have always managed to adapt it to the needs of every age. Few suspect to-day that Ignatius intended the *Exercises* primarily to be a means of recruiting missionaries.

The oldest directories show how the first followers of Ignatius gave the *Exercises.*[4] The exercitant was isolated as far as possible in a solitary house. The director went to see him every day to give him advice. When the Society of Jesus had colleges and houses, it was able to receive the retreatants in them.

At the outset Ignatius and his first disciples made each person go into retreat by himself. But this limited the director's scope, for he could only attend to a small number of retreatants at the same time. Pierre Le Fèvre declared that he could not direct more than three persons at once.[5]

---

[1] *Le Récit du Pélerin,* no. 57, pp. 59-60.
[2] *id.,* no. 77, p. 79.
[3] *id.,* no. 82, p. 84.
[4] *Exercitia . . . et eorum directoria,* pp. 778 ff. *Cf.* A. Brou, *Les Exercices spirituels de saint Ignace de Loyola,* pp. 50 ff.
[5] *Monumenta Fabri,* 78.

From 1539, at Parma, Le Fèvre and Laynez inaugurated the idea of giving retreats in common.[1]

As we might expect, not all the retreatants used to reach the end of the Four Weeks. Most were satisfied with the First Week, and made a " retreat of conversion." Nevertheless, a certain number—especially those who felt a call to mission work—made the " election," and even went to the end of the *Exercises*.[2]

In his *Chronicle,* Polanco remarks the happy results everywhere following upon the *Exercises*. They led to the conversion of a large number of the clergy. Louis de Blois, as we know, used to send his religious and novices to the Jesuits of Louvain to be given the *Exercises,* and this contributed effectively to the reformation of the Abbey of Liessies.[3]

St Charles Borromeo used them for the reformation of his clergy.[4] In the seventeenth century St Vincent de Paul, in his famous retreats given to the candidates for ordination at Saint-Lazare, was inspired by the method of the *Exercises*.[5] And in modern times retreats, according to the Ignatian method, have become " a normal and ordinary function of the Christian life."[6] His Holiness Benedict XV, by an Apostolic Constitution of July 25, 1920, has proclaimed St Ignatius the patron of spiritual retreats.

In the era of its first appearance, Ignatian spirituality was one of the most effective means for the protection of Christian devotion against the paganism of the Renaissance and the fatalistic quietism of the Protestant Reformation.

According to Ribadeneira,[7] St Ignatius acted in conformity with this principle : " Let us work as if success depended on ourselves and not on God. Let us work with energy, but with this conviction in our hearts : that we are doing nothing, that God is doing everything." This great law of his own activity is also that of his spirituality.

[1] *Monumenta Fabri,* 33.
[2] *S Ignatii epistolae,* tom. I, p. 388; tom. II, p. 253; *Epistolae mixtae,* tom. I, p. 43.
[3] For information as to the history of the practice of the *Exercises,* see the *Mélanges Watrigant,* C.B.E., nos. 61-62, 1920.
[4] Mgr. Ratti (Pius XI), *Saint Charles Borromée et les Exercices de saint Ignace,* C.B.E., no. 32.
[5] *Saint Vincent de Paul et les retraites fermées,* C.B.E., no. 50; Watrigant, *Les Exercices spirituels à la naissance des Séminaires,* C.B.E., nos. 39-41.
[6] A. Brou, *Les Exercices spirituels de saint Ignace.* p. 105.
[7] *De ratione sancti Ignatii in gubernando,* 14 (*Scripta de sancto Ignatio,* p. 466. *Monumenta,* tom. I). It is the second of these *Sentences* attributed to St Ignatius : *Haec prima sit agendorum regula: sic Deo fide, quasi rerum successus omnis a te, nihil a Deo penderet, ita tamen iis operam omnem admove, quasi tu nihil, Deus omnia solus sit facturus.*

In the work of spiritual sanctification, there are two parts —God's and man's. Ignatius fixes his attention on the first to urge the importance of prayer for the securing of grace— God's part—and to call upon us to glorify God for all the good we do through him. He emphasizes still more, perhaps, man's part—radically eliminated by Luther, as we shall see—and impels us to action, indeed, as if success depended upon ourselves alone. His spirituality, if the anachronism may be allowed, is dynamically molinist; it is active and non-quietist, combative and not pacifist, methodical, and not just-as-you-will.

What Ignatius demands above all is personal effort, the active collaboration and the energetic work of the exercitant. He will not endure the retreatant's passivity, but makes him meditate, contemplate, and examine his conscience, and will not leave him to himself. He does not wait for God to work in the soul, for he is convinced that generous efforts on our part " often dispose us for the reception of greater inward illumination and heavenly consolation and divine inspiration."[1] The more a man does himself violence, the more he advances in goodness, says the writer of the *Imitation.* Ignatius, too, wishes a man to devote himself to the exercises, to act against himself and his own inclinations, and to change and conquer himself.[2] His is a spirituality of effort wonderfully adapted to counter the scandalous Lutheran quietism which denied man power to co-operate in his own salvation, and to stir men out of the *laisser-aller* in which some of the humanists took refuge under the pretext of resistance to man's passions being actually impossible.

It was also a combative spirituality. No doubt the spiritual combat is not an invention of St Ignatius, for it is of the very essence of Christianity : it is an indispensable condition of any serious spiritual life. No one has spoken of it more forcibly than St Paul. Since his day, perhaps, no one has understood it better than St Ignatius. His spirituality wears a military aspect. Christ is a captain who calls us to fight at his side. To answer his call is to join his army. His true soldiers " will not only offer themselves up wholly to the work, but also, when taking the offensive against their own sensuality and against their carnal and worldly affections, they will make offers still more precious."[3] Their

---

[1] *Exercises,* Third Week, fourth rule of " Temperance."

[2] " Discernment of spirits," sixth rule, etc : " The *Spiritual Exercises* combine the knowledge of self and the imitation of Christ into a school of energy. The representations, the feelings, and the virtues are so many tendencies to action. The whole of the interior life becomes a combat, the results of which have a social value." Etchegoyen, *L'amour divin, Essai sur les sources de sainte Thérèse,* p. 56, Bordeaux, 1923.

[3] *Exercises,* Second Week, The Kingdom of Christ, Debuchy, p. 73.

chief offensive weapon will be the particular examen which attacks some bad habit, sin, or failing, and especially their dominant passion. With God's help, victories will thus constantly be won. Christ's soldier conquers virtues as men carry fortified positions by storm. Others will get men to acquire virtues by the practice, which is also mortifying, of the love of God : Ignatius would have men show their love by fighting against their bad instincts.[1] He is not far from agreeing with the old monks that virtue must be preceded by the extirpation of the vices which are opposed to it.

Lastly, it was a disciplined spirituality, which was governed by precise methods leaving little room for the unforeseen. " St Ignatius assumes that a man knows where he is going and that he wants to get there, and that he is ready to take the best means and, therefore, to examine those which are offered and to weigh and to select them for well-known reasons."[2] The principal means is the meditation made daily at a fixed hour for a definite time on a subject chosen and prepared beforehand according to a method leading on step by step. Then follows the examen : the examen which superintends the way in which the prayer is made to eliminate hindrances and to keep the expedients that help;[3] the particular examen which records victories or failures day by day. It is, in a word, a strict supervision of every spiritual experience, indispensable to anyone who would defeat the wiles of the enemy within or from without. This may be called compulsion or spiritual tension. No doubt; but " unless thou do thyself violence," says the *Imitation,* " thou shalt not overcome vice."[4] The compulsion was most profitable for guarding the soul against the pagan seductions of the Renaissance ; furthermore, this compulsion and tension were compatible with a rightly understood freedom of will.

It is true that any maladroit or inexperienced person might apply these methods with too much severity and keep down the spirit from all upward soaring. We should then have " piety to order " with all its drawbacks.[5] But St Ignatius does not mean to straiten the action of grace nor to bind the soul to the point of keeping it from stirring and from going whither God would lead it. The object of his method is to prepare us for the action of the Holy Spirit; and it disappears as soon as his influence is felt, and we recover our freedom to follow the inspiration of God. The Ignatian

---

[1] *Exercises,* Second Week, The Kingdom of Christ, Debuchy, p. 73.
[2] A. Brou, *La spiritualité de St Ignace,* p. 82.
[3] *Exercises,* First Week, fifth Addition.
[4] Lib. I, cap. xxii : *Nisi tibi vim feceris, vitium non superabis.*
[5] Faber, *All for Jesus.*

method is not a set of drill-sergeant's commands. In the
Annotations and Additions incorporated with the *Exercises*
the director is advised not in any way to cramp God's action
upon the retreatant's soul.

The spirituality of the *Exercises* forms, too, men of
action and apostles while providing a discipline for the
interior life. It thoroughly forwarded the plans of Ignatius
as the founder of a new Order of religious devoted to mission
work amidst the world and driven to find their own safety
in a thoroughly sound spiritual training.

At the beginning of the sixteenth century many religious
congregations were inaugurated, especially in Italy, to take
charge of external works, such as the improvement of the
clergy, missions, the education of the young, and the care
of the sick. Later on, we shall study their spirit and their
teaching.

St Ignatius took part in the movement which urged men
on to the apostolate when he founded his Institute, the
principal aim of which was to be preaching and religious
instruction, especially the education of the young, and any
other charge which might be entrusted to it by the Holy
See. A fourth vow of absolute obedience to the Pope was
required of members of the Society.

In order that the new religious might have every oppor-
tunity of devoting themselves to their works, they were
" bound to say the divine Office according to the rite of the
Church, each one separately and privately, and not in
common and in the choir."[1] In this way a great change
was introduced into the old form of the monastic and
religious life. Ignatius made a real alteration in the centre
of gravity of the devotion of the religious. Until his day,
it revolved around the psalmody of the divine Office. Even
the Franciscans and the Dominicans, though they were pledged
to mission work, were bound to the choir Offices. The
Jesuit says his Office in private; this is the most important
of his religious exercises, but it is not the whole of his
devotion. Meditation and examination of conscience form
the framework of his spiritual life and make a rampart about
it and protect it efficaciously against the assaults of the
world amidst which it has to be preserved and to grow.

A means of protection, Ignatian spirituality is also an
inspirer of zeal. It develops the spirit of initiative and
conquering ardour. " The same offensive as it carries on
against the evil within us, it takes also against the evil

---

[1] Bull approving the Jesuits by Paul III, *Regimini militantis
Ecclesiae*, of September 27, 1540. *Cf.* Meschler, S.J., *La Compagnie
de Jésus, ses statuts et ses résultats*, Mazoyer's translation, Paris.

without us." Ignatius called his Society a "Company," taking the metaphor from military life. It is, indeed, a troop of soldiers of Christ, flung forward for the conquest of souls, that he wished to organize. And that each soldier might help on the common work effectively, his personal action was to be governed by a strict obedience to his leader.[1]

IV—THE FIRST JESUIT SPIRITUAL WRITERS

THE historians of the Society of Jesus relate the lives of the illustrious religious who were the offspring of the Ignatian spirituality. The compass of this work will not allow us to follow them. Let us be satisfied with mentioning those of the first disciples of Ignatius who have left us spiritual writings.

Blessed Pierre Le Fèvre,[2] who lived in Paris with Ignatius and Francis Xavier in the same room for students, has left behind him a sort of autobiography: *The Memorial.*

Born in Savoy, Le Fèvre has somewhat the same smiling character as Francis de Sales. A lover of purity and of the ideal, and with a great yearning for knowledge, he succeeded in triumphing over the temptations of youth which were not lacking in his case. God directed his steps in the way of perfection by trials of conscience, scruples and painful uncertainties as to his vocation. It was through Ignatius that he found peace and resolved, after making the *Exercises,* to become a missionary. He was one of the first apostolic workers to preserve South Germany from the inroads of Protestantism and there to keep alive the Catholic faith. He it was who attracted Peter Canisius to the Society of Jesus.

Le Fèvre was able to combine the active with the contemplative life: he shows in his charming *Memorial* how they react upon one another. He also had a very special devotion to the angels. He not only honoured the guardian angels of the faithful, but all the angels; those of cities and churches. He treated them as friends and thought that the angels were glad to have friends among men. St Francis

---

[1] St Ignatius' teaching on obedience is found in his celebrated letter to the Portugese Fathers in the *Thesaurus spiritualis Societatis Jesu,* and in the famous article of the *Constitutions: Quisque sibi persuadeat, quod qui sub obedientia vivunt, se ferri ac regi a divina providentia per superiores suos sinere debent perinde ac si cadaver essent, quod quoquoversus ferri et quacumque ratione tractari se sinit: vel similiter atque senis baculus qui ubicumque et quacumque in re velit eo uti, qui eum manu tenet, ei inservit.*

[2] He was born in Savoy at Villaret in 1506. As a child, he watched over his father's flocks. In 1525 he was sent to Paris, where he met Ignatius three years later. Le Fèvre's *Memorial* has been translated into French by Père Bouix, Paris, 1874.

de Sales admired this devotion of Pierre Le Fèvre for the Holy Angels, which is so reminiscent of that of St Bernard.

It was also a spiritual *Diarium*[1] that has been left us by St Francis Borgia. It includes several years of his life as General. It consists of simple notes in his own handwriting, often unintelligible to others. St Teresa had two conversations with Francis Borgia,[2] and calls him " a great contemplative." She consulted him as to the prayer of quietude and asked him how the active life and the contemplative life could be found united in it. Francis answered that " it was not at all impossible, and that it often happened so with himself."[3] Hence, in contemplation his soul was able never to lose sight of God amidst the overwhelming anxieties of the government of a religious Order. Without any painful striving he used to offer God every hour of the day for some definite intention. At one and the same time he fulfilled the office of Martha with that of Mary.

The same union of the active with the contemplative life is found in the case of St Peter Canisius[4] who, says Leo XIII, " is the second apostle of Germany after St Boniface." Canisius tells us of his spiritual life in two of his writings : his *Confessions,* in the class of those of St Augustine, and his *Spiritual Will.* His *Letters* also inform us about what was taking place in his soul. Ecstasies, raptures, and even visions rewarded him for his immense apostolic labours.

Of St Francis Xavier we have nothing but his *Letters.*[5] They are a lifelike expression of his fiery soul, which no fatigue could cast down, no suffering affright, when there were unbelievers to be converted. Xavier was favoured with mystical graces, and his ecstasies were many. He never ceased his prayers and never interrupted his most intimate

[1] Vol. V, pp. 729-887 of the M.H.S.J. Suau, *Saint François de Borgia,* Paris, 1910. Born in 1510, Francis Borgia was General of the Society of Jesus in 1565. He died in 1572. He defended Ignatius when he was first attacked, and had the *Exercises* approved by Paul III in 1548. He also composed a treatise called *The Christian's Works.*
[2] St Teresa, *Spiritual Relations,* relat. LIII.
[3] St Teresa, *Way of Perfection,* chap. xxxi. Cf. *Life,* chap. xxiv.
[4] Born in Guelderland at Nimeguen in 1521, he died at Freiburg in Switzerland. He founded many colleges in Germany, was a very popular preacher, and attended the imperial Diets. He was also sent to the Council of Trent, where he met his confrères, Laynez, Alfonso Salmeron, and Le Jay. His spiritual writings are : his *Conferences* and his *Will,* published with his *Letters* by Otto Braunsberger, *Beati Petri Canisii Epistulae et acta,* Freiburg, 1896 ff.; Vol. I, contains what is left of the *Confessions*—*i.e.,* the first book with a few other fragments, and the *Will.* Canisius published a German edition of the sermons and other works of the Dominican John Tauler, Cologne, 1543. Cf. Le Bachelet, *Dict. de Théol. cath.,* art. *Canisius.*
[5] Cros, *Saint François Xavier, sa vie et ses lettres,* 2 vols., Toulouse, 1900. A. Brou, *Saint François Xavier,* 2 vols., Paris, 1912.

intercourse with God, except for the labours of the mission-field.

Lastly, Pedro Ribadeneira,[1] the disciple and historian of St Ignatius, has edified generation after generation of Christians with his *Flowers of the Saints,* published in Spanish at Madrid in 1599, and soon translated into French. In this biographical work we must not expect to find the critical spirit to which we have grown accustomed since the time of the Bollandists. Certainly there may be found in it much unction and devotion, and a great desire for the sanctification of souls.

[1] Born at Toledo in 1527, he joined St Ignatius in 1540. He worked in succession in the Low Countries, in France, and in Spain. He died at Madrid in 1611. Besides *The Flowers of the Saints,* he wrote lives of St Ignatius, St Francis Borgia, and of Laynez and Salmeron.

CHAPTER III

CHRISTIAN HUMANISM AND DEVOUT HUMANISM—
THEIR SPIRITUALITY

AT the dawn of the Renaissance, while the monks were endeavouring within their cloisters to ward off the worldly spirit by means of mental prayer, Christian humanists were also working in their own fashion towards a restoration of the Christian life.

We note, in fact, a twofold tendency in the Renaissance : one, as we have seen, clearly pagan, which was consciously or unconsciously ruining all religion and morality by the study of antiquity; the other intending to remain true to Catholic faith and practice, and to bring literature and art into the service of Christian religion and piety. This second tendency is that of Christian humanism, a humanism which, according to many writers, was the forerunner of Protestantism. Besides its love for classical antiquity, it took an indulgent and optimistic view of human nature, which is the characteristic of what has been called devout humanism.

I—CHRISTIAN HUMANISM

THESE are the principal Christian humanists : in the Rhineland, Cardinal Nicholas de Cusa († 1464); in Italy, Pico della Mirandola[1] and Cardinal Sadolet († 1547); in England, Blessed Thomas More ;[2] in France, Lefèvre of Etaples ;[3] in Germany, Erasmus of Rotterdam.[4]

[1] The celebrated author of nine hundred theses submitted to Rome, thirteen of which were declared to be heretical. In 1489 he published his *Apologia* in self-defence. It is a manifesto of Christian humanism. He died at Florence in 1494, at the age of thirty-one. *Works*, Bologna, 1496, and Venice, 1498.

[2] Henri Bremond, *Le Bienheureux Thomas More,* Paris, 1904. (English trans., London, Burns Oates and Washbourne.)

[3] Lefèvre of Etaples, the greatest of French humanists, was born in 1455. He studied in Paris, and then in Italy and Germany. He retired to Saint-Germain-des-Près at Paris, and then to Meaux and Strasbourg. He died in 1536. He translated the whole of Aristotle with comments. He studied theology, which he wished to bring back to its sources, the Bible, and the Fathers. He also published the text of several parts of the Bible with a commentary. The two chief works in which his ideas on religion are to be found are : the Preface of the *Psalterium quintuplex,* in which the various texts of the Psalter are set in parallel ; and his *Commentaries* on the Epistles of St Paul, published in 1512. Luther justified himself by using the works of Lefèvre to support his two chief principles of private inspiration and justification by faith only. Lefèvre also wrote *Scholia* on Dionysius the Areopagite, Venice, 1556.

[4] Desiderius Erasmus was born at Rotterdam in 1464. When twelve years old he went to the celebrated school of the Brothers of the Common

They are usually regarded—at any rate, the two last—
as inspirers of Luther. Though they did not foresee this,
they certainly are so through their work of criticism and
through certain of their views. They reacted against the
formalism of the end of the Middle Ages in such a way as
to make the Christian religion appear a purely inward and
personal affair. They laughed at the abuse of Scholasticism
to the point of depreciating—doubtless unintentionally—the
dogmatic teaching of the Church. They criticized the
behaviour of the monks of their time in language that
appears to implicate the religious life itself. They recommended the reading of the Bible to all the faithful indiscriminately, as the Protestants were about to do. But their
manifest and dangerous exaggerations must not make us
fail to acknowledge the soundness of some of their work.
It is well to know it, because it has had a great influence
over the devotion of the Renaissance era, and it will help
us to understand Protestant mysticism.

It may be summarized in these three points : means for
keeping oneself from the corruption of the world; a return
to the inner life which is stifled by the use of formalist
practices; the direct study of the Word of God in Holy
Scripture for the purpose of edification, and not in order to
make subtle dissertations on idle questions.[1]

Life at Deventer. Being illegitimate, he could not enter the ranks of the
secular clergy. He joined the Augustinians in 1486, and took the
vows, despite his repugnance for the monastic life. Released from his
vows, he was ordained priest in 1492 by the Bishop of Cambrai. From
this time forward Erasmus began his cosmopolitan life. He travelled
in France, in England and in Italy, and was welcomed everywhere
on account of his world-renown in letters. Henry VIII of England,
Charles V, Francis I of France, and Popes Julius II and Leo X
endeavoured to keep him near them. In 1521 he settled at Bâle to
superintend the printing of his works. There he died in 1536.
Erasmus sums up in himself the tendencies of his period. Luther
tried, though in vain, to draw him into his own rebellion against the
Church. Erasmus contributed powerfully to the revival of learning by
his writings and by his editions of the works of ancient authors,
whether heathen or Christian. His edition of the New Testament
(Greek original and Latin translation) was very successful. His
religious opinions are to be found above all in his *Enchiridion militis
christiani*, a kind of humanist manual of the Christian life, published
in 1504; *Paraclesis, id est adhortatio ad christianae philosophiae
studium* (1516) and *Ratio seu methodus perveniendi ad veram
theologiam* (1518), which criticizes the theology of the School and
extols the new theology based upon Scripture and the Fathers of the
Church : *Colloquia familiaria* (1518), not a highly moral work. *The
Praise of Folly, Laus stultitiae* (1509), is a bitter and exaggerated
satire on monachism, and the licentiousness of the clergy and the
people. *Opera omnia*, Bâle, 1540; Leyden, 1703-1706, Ed. Clericus (Le
Clerc).

[1] *Cf.* Imbart de la Tour, *Les origines de la Réforme*, Vol. II.

Two works of Erasmus stand out in giving us an idea of this reaction of Christian humanism against the pagan corruption of the Renaissance : the *Enchiridion militis christiani*[1] and the *De contemptu mundi.*[2] They are written in such classical Latin as only the first Latinist of his day could write. They are also steeped in the spirit of humanism. St Ignatius Loyola, who read the *Enchiridion,* was bewildered by the tone in which it speaks, without any shades of the deference required, of theologians and devotional practices. But Erasmus, with his quite military manner of training the Christian, must have given him pleasure.

For Erasmus summons the Christian soldier to a real battle with the world. Is not the Christian life a perpetual combat? The enemies change : the devils " ever on the watch," the world " which attacks us right and left, on the front and from the rear," our passions " which are all the more dangerous from being within us and because we cannot get away from them." Therefore we must always be under arms : *Prima cura sit ne inermis sit animus.*[3]

The principal weapons recommended are : prayer, " which lifts up our hearts to heaven as to a citadel that our enemies cannot reach " ; and knowledge, which " furnishes our minds with wholesome thoughts." Knowledge of the Christian warfare is what Erasmus proposes to teach in his *Enchiridion.* At the outset he finds it in Holy Scripture, but as a good humanist he goes in search of it also in profane literature, in poets and philosophers, who have also formulated maxims which are helps to virtue.

Before all, we must come to know ourselves, since our fighting must be directed against ourselves. To possess a good knowledge of oneself, therefore, must be the primary condition of victory. Furthermore, the Christian has to study his body, his soul, his passions, and the opposition between the flesh and the spirit spoken of in Holy Scripture. Our humanist takes care to mention, by the way, the theories of the Stoics and the Peripatetics as to the passions.

Ignorance is the cause of the great inferiority of the Christian soldier. In order to get rid of it, Erasmus puts

[1] *Desiderii Erasmi roterodami Opera omnia,* tom. V, pp. 2-66, Lugduni Batav., 1704. The *Enchiridion* is addressed to Adolph, son of Philip of Burgundy. It was much read. Louis de Berquin translated it into French, 1529. There was a Spanish edition in 1528, and an English one in 1583.

[2] *ibid.,* pp. 1239-1262. The work of Erasmus has been very variously appreciated. Janssen (*L'Allemagne et la Réforme,* II, 6-22) is very severe in his judgement of Erasmus. *Cf.* F. Mourret, *Hist. gén. de l'Eglise, ibid.*

[3] *Enchiridion,* cap. ii.

forward twenty-two rules (*canones*), "general rules of true Christianity," which must lead to perfection, if they are followed.[1]

The Christian soldier will hold fast the purity of his faith. He will be ready to lose everything, even life itself, for Christ. He will die to the world and be convinced that the narrow way is more pleasant and more suitable than the broad way. The aim of his studies, his desires, and his efforts will be to reproduce Christ in himself. Thus, he will strive incessantly to turn aside from things visible to advance in things invisible. And above all—a practical piece of advice at the time of the Renaissance—he will hold himself aloof from the maxims and example of the common run of men to find in Christ alone the example of perfect devotion. "To depart from this example, even by a line's breadth, is to go astray." Besides, the more we advance in the love of Christ, the more we hate the world; the more we wonder at invisible realities, the more ugly we find what is passing away.

The other fifteen rules concern temptations and the way to resist them.

In addition to the struggle there must be meditation on the sufferings of the Saviour and on the hideousness of sin. God must be contrasted with Satan; by resisting we become servants of God, and by sinning the slaves of Satan.[2] We must also compare heaven with hell. We must remember the fragility of life and the sinner's risk of dying impenitent. Those who escape from licentiousness are so few! The *Enchiridion* ends with special counsels for overcoming sensualism, avarice, ambition, pride, and anger.

In the *De contemptu mundi,* Erasmus further insists on the dangers for the Christian in the world of the Renaissance. Is not the safest way to flee from them by retiring into solitude? "Nothing, indeed, is more miserable, nothing more vain, nothing more pernicious than the goods of this world." Real liberty and real peace are not for the worldly. And in the hour of death, must we not leave everything behind? Therefore let us renounce beforehand whatever we must inevitably give up some day!

Another humanist, Michel de Montaigne (†1592), was also able to enforce the same lesson from death in a moving way, but purely as a philosopher:

"To think upon death beforehand is to think upon freedom. He who hath learnt to die hath unlearnt to be an underling. Knowing how to die setteth us free from all subjection and

---

[1] *Enchiridion*, cap. viii.
[2] It is interesting to compare this passage from the *Enchiridion* with the meditation on the Two Standards of St Ignatius Loyola.

bondage. *There is no evil in life for him who hath well
learnt that the loss of life is no evil.*"[1]

We should become familiar with the thought of death,
and learn not to fear it:

" The goal of our career is death: it is the one thing
whereat we must aim. If it affright us, how can we go
forward, save in a fever? The remedy of the common folk
is not to think thereon. But what a brutish stupidity befalleth
them of such gross blindness? They must be made to
bridle the ass by the tail. . . . No wonder if they be often
taken in the snare. Our people are often afeared at the
mere name of death, and the more part do make the sign of
the cross thereat as at the name of the devil. . . .

" If (death) were an enemy man could avoid, I would
counsel him to use the arms of cowardice. But since he
cannot, and since it catcheth you when ye run away in
your poltroonery as well as if ye make an honest stand . . .
and since whatever be the temper of your cuirass, it cannot
cover you . . . learn ye with firmly planted foot to endure
death and give it battle. And to take therefrom its chief
advantage over us, let us choose a way quite contrary to
the common. Let us strip it of its outlandishness, let us
make it our practice and our habit to have in our heads
nothing so often as death. At every moment let us picture
it in our imaginations and in every form. At the stumbling
of a horse, at the fall of a tile, at the least pricking of a
pin, let us reflect of a sudden: What if this were death
itself? and therewith let us be hard and set our wills."[2]

This stoical attitude is grounded upon quite natural reasons
by " the good admonitions of our mother nature." Our
death is an essential part of corporal existence. It is " one
of the parts of the order of the Universe . . . a part of the
life of the world." Will Nature change " this fine con-
texture of things "[3] for us? No.

Erasmus is more of a Christian and less of a philosopher
when he speaks of death. He wrote a little book on the way
to prepare for it, the success of which in the sixteenth century was comparable with that of the *Imitation.*[4] To die
well, the most important thing is to purify the soul by the
reception of the last sacraments. Detachment from all that

---

[1] *Essais*, Book I, chap. xx, Ed. F. Strowski, Bordeaux, 1906, p. 107.
Montaigne was much appreciated by St François de Sales. See *Œuvres
de saint François de Sales,* Annecy, 1892; Vol. I, p. lxiii.

[2] *ibid.*, pp. 103-107.

[3] *ibid.*, p. 114.

[4] *De praeparatione ad mortem,* written in 1533, *Opera,* tom. V,
pp. 1293-1348. French translation, Lyons, 1538. This book of Erasmus
is often found bound up with and following *Internal Consolation (The
Imitation).* The humanism in this work of Erasmus had something
to do with its success.

is transitory is a condition, but not everything, for a good death. Nevertheless, the human motives of such detachment are so set in relief that we can understand the following judgement of Feugère with regard to the notions of Erasmus on death : " Here we already find the spirit of philosophy trying to dissipate the religious terrors as to the last hours of men. Erasmus, like Montaigne later on, is not far from envying the ancients for their peaceful death, which they reached without bitterness in a state of hazy somnolence."[1]

At the same time as he is preparing the Christian for the battle with the world, Erasmus trains him in the interior life.

Above all, he warns him beforehand against what he calls " the religion of the common people," which consists in the faithful observance of external practices without any effort to reform one's conduct and to become closely united with Christ :

" Thou art baptized," he says. " Think not that thou art indeed, therefore, a Christian, if thou hast disgust only for the world. Thou art a Christian in public, and in secret thou art more pagan than the pagans. And why? Because thou hast but the body of the sacrament and hast not its spirit. What is the good of bodily washing if the soul be defiled in will?"[2]

A life of purity, intimate and living union with Christ the Redeemer, these are the main part of Christianity. Instead of this, many are satisfied with a host of pharisaical observances which they join with a disorderly life, and that without remorse. Erasmus speaks of them in terms of implacable irony. Does veneration of the saints mean just making pilgrimages to their tombs, touching their relics, and at the same time despising the best of all that they have left behind for us : the example of a pure life? To imitate the faith of St Peter and the charity of St Paul is worth more than ten pilgrimages to Rome. What is the use of clothing oneself in the hour of death with the rough drugget of St Francis, if one has been not the least like St Francis during one's life? Furthermore, we are certain that the best way of honouring the Blessed Virgin is to imitate her humility.[3]

Yet Erasmus does not put forward any desire to do away with worship and outward observances. But he wishes them to be well understood : they are means for the cultivation of the inward life. They are necessary means, too; for religion

---

[1] *Erasme; Étude sur sa vie et ses ouvrages,* Paris, 1877, quoted by Janssen, *op. cit.,* II, p. 21.

[2] *Enchiridion,* cap. viii, *Opera,* tom. V, p. 31.

[3] *Enchiridion, ibid.* Montaigne also criticizes formalism : *Essais,* Book I, chap. lvi.

without external practices is not enough. Faith, however
perfect, without works worthy of it, far from being profitable does but complete one's damnation.[1]

Lefèvre of Etaples, in his reaction against formalism, shows
himself unable to keep within such just measure. He gives
such honour to justification by faith when he comments on
St Paul that he seems to throw good works overboard.[2]
Many perhaps wrongly regard him as the promoter of the
Lutheran theory of justification by faith only.[3]

This excessive reaction of the humanists against outward
practices, and what they called " the religion of the crowd,"
arises, like most of their other tendencies, from Platonist
idealism.

The Renaissance was a reaction from the Aristotelianism
of the School. Its Platonist[4] philosophy filled it with a
kind of aversion to whatever was material, and a marked predilection for a sort of religious symbolism bordering upon
dilettantism. Transcendent subjectivism—after the fashion
of Plotinus — which made the soul enter into direct communion with God, must have suggested to the humanists, as
we shall see, their doctrine of the symbolical and private
interpretation of Holy Scripture.

One of the great means of fostering the interior life, which
is forcibly urged by the Christian humanists, is, in fact, the
study of God's Word as contained in Holy Scripture, and not
as it is propounded by the decadent theologians of the Renaissance. These, according to the humanists, conceal the Word
of God beneath a heap of learnedly constructed syllogisms.
They go astray in a labyrinth of a host of subtle questions,
the solution of which is often impossible and, in any case,
quite useless for the Christian life.

To such argumentative and refined theology they oppose
a theology which is practical. To them religion is less a
fountain of knowledge than of life; it means union with

---

[1] *Enchiridion,* cap. viii, *Opera,* tom. V, p. 31.

[2] *Sancti Pauli epistolae XIV cum commentariis Jacobi Fabri
stapulensis,* 1515, tom. I, 16; VII, 3; VIII, 4.

[3] *Cf.* Lavisse et Rambaud, *Histoire générale,* Vol. IV, p. 479.

[4] Platonist idealism makes its first appearance in Italy with Gemistus
Plethon and Cardinal Bessarion (1472). But the great Platonist was
the Florentine Marsilio Ficino (†1499), the celebrated translator of Plato
into Latin (Venice, 1491), of Plotinus (Florence, 1492), and of Dionysius
the Areopagite (*Opera omnia,* Cologne, 1536, Paris, 1641, 2 vols.). He
undertook the work of a *Theologia platonica.* It was Giles of Viterbo
who compiled this Platonist Theology with a commentary on the
Sentences (*Recherches de Science religieuse,* July-October, 1923). In
Spain Miguel Servetus (†1563), in his famous book, *La Restauration
du Christianisme,* reproduces the pantheist doctrines of Plotinus.

God.[1] If the Lord has revealed religious truths, it is for our
guidance and not for the satisfaction of our curiosity. And,
in order to learn them, the heart and love are more helpful than reasoning and syllogisms. Theologians too often
forget this :

"For me," says Erasmus, "the true theologian is not he
who teaches with artificially made syllogisms, but by his
whole attitude and life, that we must despise riches, that the
Christian must not put his trust in the goods of this world,
but only in those which are from above. . . . For as to
how the angels communicate their thoughts to one another,
any writer who is even not a Christian can make dissertations thereon better than we. But to persuade us that we
ought to live a pure and angelic life, such is surely the work
of a Christian theologian."[2]

Yet theology thus understood ought to be scientific.

The humanists tried to recast theology on critical lines.
They wished to found it upon the Bible scientifically edited
and interpreted, as well as upon the undoubtedly authentic
teaching of the Fathers. Erasmus wanted "Christ preached
according to the fountain-heads." He wished men not to
let go the advantages which a classical training might supply
to theologians.[3]

To furnish Bible-readers with as accurate a text as possible of the original, the humanists made critical editions of
the sacred books.[4] But the Bible is not the book of the
learned only ; every Christian has the right to read it :

"Neither age nor sex, neither condition nor position, should
keep anyone from such reading. The sun does not more
belong to everybody than does the doctrine of Christ. . . .
I should like every woman to read the Gospel and the Epistles
of St Paul."[5]

In order not to go astray in the interpretation of the passages read, Erasmus advises men usually to follow the

---

[1] *Hic primus et unicus sit tibi scopus, hoc votum, hoc unum age,
ut muteris, ut rapiaris, ut affleris, ut transformeris in ea quae discis.*
Erasmus, *Ratio seu methodus perveniendi ad veram theologiam. Opera,*
tom. V, p. 77.

[2] *Paraclesis, id est adhortatio ad christianae philosophiae studium,*
tom. V, p. 140. *Hoc Philosophiae genus in affectibus situm verius
quam in syllogismis, vita est magis quam disputatio, afflatus potius
quam eruditio, transformatio magis quam ratio,* p. 144. *Cf.* Lefèvre of
Etaples, *Comment. in Epist. ad Rom.,* i, 15; xiii, 3.

[3] *Ratio . . . perveniendi ad veram theol., ibid.*

[4] "Begin by giving a few hours every day to searching the sacred
letters : first, in Greek, the New Testament and the Epistles of the
Apostles; and then, in Hebrew, the Old Testament." Rabelais, *Lettre
de Gargantua à son fils Pantagruel.* This letter is a little manifesto of
French humanism.

[5] *Paraclesis,* tom. V, p. 140. See Erasmus' Commentaries on the New
Testament, *Opera,* tom. VII.

Fathers and the commentators. He blamed Lefèvre of
Etaples for leaving out the traditional explanations in his
edition of the Psalms. Hence he does not demand an uncon-
ditional freedom of interpretation, for he knows that it is often
restricted, and principally by the dogmatic definitions of the
Church. But in questions which have not been finally settled
by ecclesiastical authority, Erasmus requires full and entire
liberty. Here the Christian is directly and exclusively taugh*
by God (θεοδίδακτος). As his guide he has the Holy Spirit,
who enlightens the pure in heart, and reveals to them the
teaching that they need.

"For," says Erasmus, "when we read the Holy Books,
God speaks to us more really and efficaciously than he did to
Moses in the burning bush, provided that we come to hold
converse with him with a clean heart. St Paul calls the
gift of the interpretation of Scripture prophecy and not
philosophy. And the Holy Spirit is certainly the origin of
prophecy.

"Thou must therefore prepare thy heart for this Spirit,
that thou too mayst deserve to be called by the prophetic
epithet (*i.e., taught of God*). Let thine eye of faith be as
simple as that of the dove, which can see naught but heavenly
truths. And let thy desire of instruction be immense ! . . .
When thou lightest upon any passage of special edification,
kiss it and worship it. . . . Thou wilt do thus with more
devotion when thou preparest thyself to receive the mysterious
teaching of the Holy Ghost. Whatever thou understandest,
receive it with delight; whatever is hidden from thee, that
worship with simple faith, and venerate it from afar. Away
with all impious curiosity !"[1]

Here we reach the central point of the mysticism of the
Christian humanists. The Christian who reads the Bible is
given a sort of personal inspiration to enable him to understand it. Here it is not only a case of such " inspirations "
or pious suggestions as grace arouses in us when we are
praying or making an edifying reading. It is God himself
who instructs the clean of heart, who is free from the bonds
of sin, so that he has no need to have recourse to ecclesiastical
teaching in those questions that have not been finally settled
by the Church. Piety is something altogether inward, absolutely spiritual.

This doctrine is partly the result of the humanist reaction
from the theology of the time and against the too external
and formalist religion of the crowd. It also depends, like
their philosophy, upon their tendency to seek for the rules
of the Christian life in immediate spiritual communications

[1] *Ratio . . . perveniendi*, tom. V, pp. 76-77. Cf. *Paraclesis, ibid.*,
pp. 143-144.

with God rather than in the direction of the theologians.
This is quite an old tendency which we have already met with
in many of the medieval mystics.   At the time of the Renaissance it was accentuated beyond measure.   The authority of
the ecclesiastical hierarchy was weakened by it, and the
notion of the Church somewhat impaired.   Lefèvre of Etaples,
the most mystical of the Christian humanists, in the Preface
of his *Psalter*[1] expresses himself in regard to this subject in
terms which suggest an idea of private inspiration.   His doctrinal audacities brought upon him the censures of the Sorbonne, despite the protection of Francis I, and Luther gave
his name as an authority.

The preference of the humanists for the spiritual and
allegorical sense of Scripture is also a consequence of their
mysticism.   What God teaches those who meditate on the
sacred text is to live holily.   But it is the spiritual sense that
chiefly contains this science of sanctity.   The literal sense
is the flesh of Scripture, the symbolical sense is its spirit.[2]

Erasmus ventures to say that often Scripture, when taken
literally, without any endeavour to discover its allegorical
meaning, is no more edifying than a poetical fable, and he
quotes by way of proof certain passages from the Old Testament.[3]   The mystical interpretation, on the other hand, is
always sanctifying.   Moreover, it is infinite in its variety
according to the needs of the reader.   It fills sinners with
fear, and the just with a greater love of virtue.   The same
Spirit suggests to everyone what he requires.   Furthermore,
Scripture is sterile, if the hidden meaning be not found
therein beneath the rind of the letter, for it is that which
must chiefly be examined and meditated on.[4]

This too exclusive inquiry into the allegorical meaning
made the humanists undervalue the primary importance of
the literal sense.   How did such conscientious editors of the
sacred text come to such a point as this?   Their reaction
from the religion of the crowd quite as much as their
mysticism carried them too far.   Erasmus, in his *Enchiridion*,[5]
brings a really ridiculous charge against the literal and

---

[1] *Psalterium quincuplex . . . cum commentariis a Jacobo Fabro,*
Parisiis, 1513, Praefatio.

[2] Erasmus, *Enchiridion,* cap. viii, 5: *Proinde ubique contempta
carne Scripturae, maxime Veteris Testamenti, spiritus mysticum rimari
conveniet. . . . Habet Evangelium carnem suam, habet et spiritum,*
tom. V, pp. 29-30.

[3] *Enchiridion,* cap. viii, 5: *At si citra allegoriam legeris, infantes
in utero colluctantes, vendito pulmento primogenita, benedictionem
patris dolo praereptam, Goliath funda David ictum, Samsoni derasum
capillum, non ita magni refert quam si poeticum legas figmentum.*

[4] *ibid.*   Hugh of Palma teaches that the gift of discovering the
allegorical sense of Scripture is granted to those who have entered
upon the illuminative way.

[5] Cap. viii, 5.

"carnal" sense of Scripture, which is adhered to by those
who materialize religion. Lefèvre of Etaples constantly
opposes "the literal-spiritual sense," which he favours, to the
"literal-vulgar sense," which he blackens. The first is what
we have to find out. It is that which the Holy Ghost has
concealed beneath the literal sense; it is revealed only to
those who are able to understand things divine in a non-
carnal way. To discover it, we have only to trust to the
help of divine inspiration.[1]

Christian humanism, as we know, was discredited by the
claim of Protestantism to regard it as a forerunner. If the
fruits were evil, then the tree cannot have been very good.
Thus the humanism of Erasmus and Lefèvre is judged rather
severely by most Catholic historians. It helped letters,
but was hurtful to religion.

This judgement would certainly have seemed unjust to any
devout person in the first half of the sixteenth century. At
that time the little devotional books by Erasmus and Lefèvre's
commentaries on the Psalms and on the Epistles of St Paul
were providing spiritual edification. Every educated Christian
carried in his pocket Erasmus' *The Christian Knight's Manual*
or his *Preparation for a Good Death*.[2] They were used for
meditations, and many found in them arms for waging victorious warfare against the paganism of the Renaissance.
The spiritual treasures of Scripture were brought within
the reach of the majority in the scriptural works of the
humanists. Real inward devotion was thus stirred up.
Many sincerely believed that the long expected reformation was
taking place. Lefèvre's followers, who formed what has been
called "the cenacle of Meaux," were quite convinced of it.[3]

What still further contributed to keeping up the illusion
was the startling rupture that broke out between the
humanists and Luther after 1520. The latter wanted people
to think that his work was the continuation and the full
flowering of that of Lefèvre and Erasmus. But after the
solemn condemnation of Luther by Leo X in 1520, one of
Lefèvre's disciples, Josse van Clichtove, published his *Anti-
Luther* in 1524. In 1525 Erasmus upheld free-will against
Luther, in a controversy that stirred up the whole of Europe.[4]

[1] Lefèvre. Prefaces to the *Psalterium* and to the *Commentarii initia-
torii in quattuor Evangelia*, Meldis, 1522.
[2] It was commonly said that Erasmus tried *cum elegantia litterarum
pietatis christianae sinceritatem copulare.*
[3] F. Mourret, *ibid.*, tome V, p. 400.
[4] *Cf.* André Meyer, *Étude critique sur les relations d'Erasme et de
Luther*, Paris, 1909. It must, however, be observed that several of the
humanists went over to the Protestant Reformation, and, among others,
Farel, who became an auxiliary of Calvin.

60 Christian Spirituality

Thomas More had already written his *Vindicatio Henrici VIII a calumniis Lutheri*[1] in 1523. Hence humanism tried to dissociate its cause from that of Protestantism.

Would it have been able to work this real reformation which was so much desired at the end of the Middle Ages? It is most unlikely.

True reformation means returning to the old discipline after it has been adapted to the new needs. The humanists well embodied the aspirations of their times, but they despised the customs of the ages which had gone before them. Their great weakness was in breaking clean away from the rules of the hated Middle Ages, in which they could find no good at all. This romanticism was of use to literature, but its help to the cause of religion was only indifferent. Bossuet, the preacher of tradition, speaks of it somewhat disdainfully :

" Indeed there is no one," says he, " who does not want to laugh as soon as he sees an Erasmus and a (Richard) Simon, on the strength of their superiority in letters and in languages, thrusting in to decide between St Jerome and St Augustine, and to award the prize as they please for the sound knowledge of sacred things. You would say that it all depends on the knowledge of Greek, and that to shake off one's illusions about St Thomas, it is enough to remark that he lived in a barbarous age; as if the apostles' style were highly polished, or as if the fine speaking of Latin made a man advance in the deeper knowledge of sacred things."[2]

Another obstacle to true reformation arose from a far too flattering idea of human nature and its so-called inherent goodness, which the humanists discovered in their study of classical antiquity. Their antipathy for Augustinian pessimism is easily understood. But between such pessimism and their optimism there is the mean of St Thomas Aquinas. If we must not depreciate the nature of fallen man we must not forget that it is in a state of revolt against divine law and that it must be held in check. The Christian humanist does indeed accept mortification, but only in moderation.[3] Erasmus considered the austerities of the saints blameworthy. They did not square with his ideal of the honest Christian who no doubt mortifies his passions, prays, and submits to external practices, but never goes beyond the limits of a nice moderation. Such is not the programme put forward by the saints who were the great reformers of their own times. The dilettante is never a real man of action. Erasmus taught

---

[1] H. Bremond, *Le Bienheureux Thomas More*, p. 95.
[2] *Défense de la Tradition et des saints Pères*, Book III, chap. xx.
[3] Erasmus, *Colloquia familiaria*, Pietas puerilis, *Opera*, tom. I, pp. 648-653. This conversation contains a sort of programme for a young man to follow if he wishes to train himself in the Christian life as understood by the humanists. *Cf.* Janssen, II, 19-20.

piety in his books, but hardly practised it himself. He " hardly ever said Mass . . . though he was a priest."[1] Indeed, he was accused of hearing it but rarely. Lefèvre of Etaples was more devout, but his work was spoilt by his individualism. Neither Erasmus nor Lefèvre were of the stuff of which real reformers are made.

II—DEVOUT HUMANISM

CHRISTIAN humanism is perhaps more closely related to the history of spirituality by its spirit, which continued, than by its still considerable influence upon Christian devotion at the beginning of the sixteenth century. The humanist spirit, inclined to think favourably of human nature and to avoid humiliating it, and not to condemn its inclinations but to moderate its impulses, this spirit survived in spirituality and became incarnate in what has been called "devout humanism," the humanism which we often meet with afresh in the spirituality of the sixteenth century.

" Devout humanism," says M. Henri Bremond, " applies to the needs of the interior life, and brings within the reach of all both the principles and the spirit of Christian humanism. . . .

" In theology, Christian humanism accepts the theology of the Church purely and simply. . . . Without neglecting any of the essential truths of Christianity, it prefers to bring into the light those that are the most comforting and cheering, in a word the most human, which it further regards as the most divine, and, if one may say so, as the most in accord with infinite goodness. Thus it does not look upon original sin, but on the Redemption, as the central doctrine. . . . Thus, too, it does not question the need of grace, but, far from measuring it out parsimoniously to some of the predestined, it sees it freely offered to all, more anxious to reach us than we can be to receive it. . . .

" The humanist does not regard man as contemptible. He is always and with all his heart on the side of our nature. Even if he sees it miserable and impotent, he makes excuses for it, he defends and restores it. With immovable confidence in the fundamental goodness of man, his whole philosophy depends upon these two words."[2]

---

[1] Janssen, *L'Allemagne et la Réforme,* Vols. VI-X.

[2] *Histoire littéraire du sentiment religieux en France,* Vol. I, *L'Humanisme dévot,* pp. 10, 11, 12, Paris 1916. In this volume M. Bremond studies " the vast movement " of devout humanism " from the time of the League to the majority of Louis XIV." The Jesuit Richeome (†1625), St Francis de Sales, the Jesuit Etienne Binet (†1639), Jean Pierre Camus, Bishop of Belley, the Capuchin Yves de Paris (†1679), are regarded in it as the principal representatives of such humanism. We shall meet with several of them again.

Devout humanism is, in fine, the humanism of Erasmus and Lefèvre, but wiser, more orthodox and more sincerely religious. It does not criticize as much, at any rate, the clergy and the monks. It is less disdainful of the Middle Ages, and yet hardly succeeds, apparently, in liking them. It grew side by side with the Reformation, and by its optimistic estimate of human nature was a permanent protest against Lutheran Manichæism. St Francis de Sales smiled upon such humanism, so that many rightly regard him as the greatest of the devout humanists.

The Bishop of Geneva showed, at all events, that he could avoid exaggerations. For devout humanism, as understood by some, is not altogether above reproach. Did it not humanize devotion too much? Did it not, of set purpose, shut its eyes to the imperfections of fallen man? Certain it is that, at the beginning of the seventeenth century, there was a reaction against it in France, which was afterwards pushed to extremes by the Jansenists.

CHAPTER IV

PROTESTANT MYSTICISM — THE REACTION WHICH IT
STIMULATED AGAINST SEVERAL MYSTICAL WRITERS
OF THE MIDDLE AGES

PROTESTANTISM is due, at least in part, to the spiritual crisis in the soul of a monk who broke his vows.[1]

Overcome by his passions, Luther asserted that they were irresistible. According to him, concupiscence, the effect of man's first fall, is absolutely invincible; it is useless to attempt to subjugate it. From this principle he deduced, with the vigorous dialectics which he possessed from his Aristotelian training, the whole of his theological system.

This moral crisis in one man's experience is not enough to account for the immensity of the religious revolution which it brought about. It was but the spark which set the huge fire ablaze, the drop of water which made the vessel overflow. If Luther carried away with him in his rebellion such a great number of the faithful and of monks and priests, it is because he preached to an audience thoroughly prepared to listen to him, for many of them were already, though unconsciously, practising the doctrines which he was bold enough to propound.

Humanism had accentuated to the highest degree the opposition between the allurement of the passions and Christian asceticism. It had stripped the veil from pagan humanity and elicited new aspirations, a thirst for enjoyment. On the other hand, it had somewhat discredited traditional asceticism by its contempt for the Middle Ages and its mordant sarcasms about the monks. The incongruity between the demands of nature, intensified by the Renaissance, and the moral restraints required by Christianity became more and more flagrant and vexatious to many people. It could not go on much longer. If only a false prophet were to arise and teach a new gospel, in which resistance to the passions was not required, his success was certain.

Such a false prophet was Luther. With a mind richly

---

[1] The causes of Protestantism are numerous and complex. I dwell upon one of them—Luther's moral crisis—because it has to do with asceticism. *Cf.* Denifle, *Luther und Luthertum* (French translation by J. Paquier, Paris, 1910-1913, 4 vols.).

endowed, but a sensualist by nature, Luther strongly felt the influence of the licentious humanism.[1] His doctrine was the reversal of the traditional Christian asceticism. To the *non concupisces* of the Decalogue he opposed his *pecca fortiter,*[2] and he found in an illusory mysticism means of salvation appropriate to his severe quietism.

I — THE MANICHÆAN QUIETISM OF LUTHER[3] AND CALVIN — THEIR CONCEPTION OF THE SPIRITUAL LIFE, OF DEVOTION TO CHRIST, AND OF THE RELATION OF THE SOUL WITH GOD

ACCORDING to the teaching of the Catholic Church, concupiscence is a consequence of original sin and not original sin itself. It constantly inclines us to evil in all its forms, but not invincibly. It may be dominated and mastered by the will with the help of grace. Its impulses do not make personal sins, unless they are elicited or accepted by the will which remains the master of its own acts.

Luther, on the contrary, taught that concupiscence is original sin itself. The spontaneous and totally involuntary impulses of concupiscence are actual sins and always grave sins. And since these impulses are inevitable, man is necessarily a sinner. But God does not impute the sin of concupiscence to those who call upon him and have faith in

---

[1] L. Pastor, *Histoire des Papes,* I, 31.

[2] *Esto peccator et pecca fortiter, sed fortius crede et gaude in Christo, qui victor est peccati, mortis et mundi. Peccandum est quam diu sic sumus; vita haec non est habitatio justitiae.*—Enders, *Dr. Martin Luther's Briefwechsel,* III, 208.

[3] Editions of Luther's *Works,* Jena, 1556, 4 vols.; Halle, 1743-1757, 24 vols.; Erlangen, 1826-1868, 67 vols.; Weimar, begun in 1883. De Wette edited Luther's *Correspondence,* in 6 vols., 1825-1856, and the publication was finished in 1884 by Enders. Ficker published the *Commentary on the Epistle to the Romans.* See Denifle, *Luther und Luthertum,* Paquier's French translation, Paris, 1910-1913; J. Janssen, *Geschichte des deutschen Volkes seit dem Ausgang des Mittelalters,* 8 vols., 1876-1894, translated by E. Paris, *L'Allemagne et la Réforme,* Paris, 1887-1907; Dollinger, *Die Reformation, ihre innere Entwicklung und ihre Wirkungen,* 3 vols., 1846-1848, translated by E. Perrot, *La Réforme, son développement intérieur et les résultats qu'elle a produits,* Paris, 1848-1849; H. Grisar, S.J., *Luther,* Freiburg im Breisgau, 1911 ff.; F. Mourret, *Histoire gén. de l'Eglise,* Vol. V, pp. 275 ff.; Georges Goyau, *L'Allemagne religieuse,* Vol. I; L. Christiani, *Luther et le Luthéranisme,* Paris, 1908.

On Calvin's doctrine: *L'Institution chrétienne; the Confession de foi de Genève* of 1537; the *Confession de foi des églises de France* of 1559. See the *Corpus Reformatorum . . . Joannis Calvini opera quæ supersunt omnia,* Brunswick, 1860-1900, tom. IX, XXII; *Dict. de théol. cath.,* art. *Calvinisme.*

On Melanchthon, see his works in the *Corpus Reformatorum.*

him and yearn for deliverance. Thus we are sinners, in fact, and nevertheless justified by faith.[1] By faith Christ's justice is imputed to us, for he has fulfilled the law in our stead.

Works are radically incapable of curing us of the evil of concupiscence, since we know from experience that whatever good we do, concupiscence still remains in us. Further, our passions are as untamable as Cerberus, as invincible as Antæus.[2] Free will is dead,[3] and man's will is irremediably subject to his passions.

Thus Adam's fall introduced an evil principle into man's nature, a predominant and compelling principle. Fallen man is doomed to evil. Luther thought that he found this doctrine in St Paul and in St Augustine.[4]

From this Manichæan conception of fallen humanity Luther deduced his false mysticism. Here are its main principles :

Since the passions cannot be mastered, it is useless to engage in striving against them :

"Who knows not," says Luther, " that this household and interior tyrant which abides in our members is no more under the power of our wills than the bad will of an external tyrant? And further, thou canst appease the latter by flattering speeches and bring him to thine own way of thinking;

---

[1] Luther, *Commentary on the Romans*, Ficker, II, 107-108 ; *Peccatum autem ipsa passio, fomes et concupiscentia, sive pronitas ad malum et difficultas ad bonum . . . opera peccati (peccata actualia) fructus sunt hujus peccati. Hoc malum, cum sit revera peccatum, quod Deus remittit per suam non imputationem ex misericordia omnibus, qui ipsum (peccatum) agnoscunt et confitentur [Deo] et odiunt et ab eo sanari petunt . . . Sic ergo in nobis sumus peccatores, et tamen reputante Deo justi per fidem. Cf.* Ficker, II, 117, 118. Luther wrote this *Commentary* in 1515-1516, at the time of his spiritual crisis and defection.

[2] *Commentary on the Romans,* Ficker, II, 145 : *Hic [fomes peccati] Cerberus, latrator incompescibilis et Anthaeus in terra demissus insuperabilis.* Sometimes, with some inconsistency, Luther advises us to strive against the evil tendencies of our nature. *Cf.* Grisar, *Luther,* I, 86 ff.

[3] *Liberum arbitrium est mortuum. Opera Lutheri,* Weimar, I, 360. See the treatise, *De servo arbitrio,* Weimar, XVIII. Despite his fundamental theory of the servile will, Luther contradicted himself and sometimes affirmed the possibility of resisting one's passions. Grisar, *ibid.* No doubt these contradictions arose from Luther's fear, which was the result of the great corruption of morals caused by his gospel. The same doctrine appears in Calvin's *Inst. christ.* Book II, chap. i ff.

[4] On Luther's misuse of certain passages of St Augustine, see Denifle-Paquier, *op. cit.,* II, pp. 398 ff. ; III, 29 ff. and 271 ff. Luther wrongly thought that Gerard of Zutphen, who wrote the *Tractatus de spiritualibus ascensionibus,* interpreted the consequences of original sin as he did (*Commentary on the Romans,* Ficker, II, 145). Gerard is strongly influenced by Augustinian pessimism, but falls far short of Luther's position.

whereas that tyrant within thee thou canst not tame by fair words nor by the most laborious efforts."[1]

Thus are man's evil instincts unloosed from all restraint. The Lutheran doctrine, like that of the medieval Beghards and, later on, of Molinos, ended, although by different paths, in the destruction of morality. An unbridled corruption of morals followed upon the preaching of the new gospel.[2] Luther was among the first to give an example of life which was the reverse of edifying.[3] The efforts he made afterwards, when contradicting himself, by advising men to resist their passions, proved vain.

Thus the principles of Luther led to a most radical kind of quietism.

In the work of salvation all human activity had to be got rid of. There was to be no inward act, such as the act of repentance of one's sins, in order to return to God. External acts, such as confession and the reception of the sacraments, were also useless. Faith was enough. Having faith, the sinner need do nothing but maintain a purely passive attitude, and Christ's justice will be imputed to him, and he will be justified.[4]

We need not pray. What is the use of praying since man's will is inevitably bound to evil? And so Luther, though sometimes acknowledging the profitableness of a certain sort of prayer, does not prescribe any prayer.[5] He even scoffed at having recourse to prayer in temptation.[6]

But what the reformer condemned with especial violence was the monastic profession. According to him, vows are bad. The vow of chastity was what exasperated him most. Is it not a resistance, and even a rebellion, against man's natural instincts, and therefore against divine order?[7]

Luther and Melanchthon, the better to discredit vows, particularly attacked "monastic baptism"—*i.e.*, the so-

---

[1] *Lutheri opera,* Weimar, VIII, 631; Denifle-Paquier, I, 173.

[2] About 1532 Luther wrote: " Scarce had we begun to preach our Gospel when a terrible rebellion broke out in the country, schisms and sects in the Church, and everywhere an utter downfall of honesty, morality, and good order. . . . Licentiousness and all forms of vice and filthiness, in every rank of life, are carried on much more to-day than they ever were under popery." *Opera,* Halle, V, 114; Döllinger, *Die Reformation,* Perrot's translation, I, 291. *Cf.* Denifle-Paquier, *op. cit.* II, 106 ff.

[3] From the time of his apostasy, Luther is remarkable for his obscene conversation and writings. Some passages of his *Works* are so scandalous and outrageous, from the point of view of morals, that the historians who quote them do not dare to translate them from Latin into living languages. *Cf.* Denifle-Paquier, *op. cit.,* I, 30, etc.

[4] *Commentary on the Romans,* Ficker, II, 219, 203; Denifle-Paquier, III, 262.

[5] *id.,* Ficker, II, 206.

[6] *Opera,* Weimar, VIII, 631. Denifle-Paquier, I, 184 ff.

[7] *De votis monasticis, Lutheri opera,* Ienæ, 1600, tom. II, p. 510b.

called equality claimed by certain Catholic writers, so far as efficacity is concerned, between the sacrament of Baptism and the Profession of the religious.[1] The writers of the Middle Ages, however, did not teach this equality.[2] Nevertheless, certain propositions might be found here and there, put forward by monks who were formalists, tending to lead people to believe that the profession of the religious worked a man's salvation, even if he did not live according to its requirements.[3] Luther takes unfair advantage of this to argue that the Middle Ages had corrupted the notion of the monastic life.

So, too, does Luther sometimes come across gibes in Catholic writers who had somewhat severely bantered the formalism of such religious—who were then rather too common—as did not take pains to live in keeping with the state of their vocation. He relies on this to affirm that these writers have decried the religious state and lowered the importance of the vows. Luther incessantly strives to connect his theories with the teaching of early writers to give them a traditional air.[4] And how he exaggerates for this purpose !

If man is incapable of all goodness and if he is in himself incurably sinful, his justification can only be external to himself and purely "nominalist."[5] He is just because Christ's justice covers him and hides his spiritual iniquities from God's sight. But his iniquities remain and are not destroyed.

The true interior life could not, therefore, exist within us. According to the Reformers, Christ was no longer the

[1] Article XXVII of the Confession of Augsburg.
[2] Denifle-Paquier, I, 353-354; II, 17 ff. The Fathers of the Church sometimes called the profession of a monk a *second Baptism: Vitae Patrum* (*P.L.*, LXIII, 994); St Jerome, *Epist.*, 39, 3 and 130, 7 (*id.*, XXII, 468, 1113); St Peter Damian, *Opusc.*, 16, 8 (*id.*, CXLV, 376); St Bernard, *Sermo XI de diversis*, 3; *De praecepto et dispens.*, cap. xvii (*id.*, CLXXXIII, 570; CLXXII, 889). The expression *Second Baptism* is grounded on the entire renunciation of the world implied in the monastic profession. This renews and completes the renunciation of the devil and the world which is promised at Baptism. Medieval theologians taught further, that religious profession might remit all penalties due to sin. St Thomas, 2a 2ae, Q. clxxxix, art. 3.
[3] Particularly did Matthew Grabon exaggerate the value of the religious state, as John Gerson blames him for doing (*Gersonii opera omnia*, I, 473 ff.).
[4] Thus, in article XXVII of the Confession of Augsburg, the testimony of Gerson is alleged, as if he had depreciated the religious state in his refutation of Matthew Grabon. Luther liked Gerson.
[5] On Luther and Occam, the head of the Nominalists (Weimar, VI, 195), see Denifle-Paquier, III, 191 ff.

life of our soul; he is not in us. His Spirit no longer
animates us. All our justice and all of our spiritual life
are outside of us. St Paul's saying, *Christ is my life,* has
no meaning in it. When the Protestant mystic practises
recollection and goes into the innermost depths of his soul,
there he finds no God, no virtue, nor any kind of good. This
depth of the soul, this inviolable sanctuary of Catholic mystics
in which they love to take refuge when the tempest of
temptation howls without, this deepest depth of the soul is
always in the Protestant's eyes filled with iniquity. How
then is he to enjoy the inward and sweet delights of a good
conscience? Never before had such a disheartening doctrine
been propounded !

And nevertheless, the Reformers were greedy for consolations. Like the mystics, they felt a great need of sanctification and of intimate union with Christ. They wanted to
feel that they were justified and beloved of God. Was not
this thirst for the certainty of his own justification the cause
of Luther's torment in the depths of his cloister at Witten-
berg?[1] The acquisition of such certainty became even one of
the chief aims of the revolution which he sought to effect in
the Catholic doctrine of justification.

For, according to Luther, it is by faith that man gets the
assurance of his justification. " It is certain beyond all
certainty that he is pleasing to God, that God is favourable
to him and forgives all the evil that he has done. . . . What,
indeed, were faith, if it were not such a conviction as this?"[2]
Thus Luther taught the identity of faith and justification.
He claimed to deduce this doctrine from his own mystical
experiences. He thought that he had an experimental knowledge of his union with Christ; he believed that he felt in
his own heart the faith that saves and that he was perfectly
sure that he pleased God.[3]

Calvin went still further and declared that we ought to be
certain of our eternal salvation, because sanctifying grace

---

[1] " Was it not . . . the profound accent, the penetrating charm of the
most kindly German mystics, which inspired Luther's pages when he
wrote of the love of God, describing the happiness of the soul united
with Jesus Christ with the ring of faith as a bride is united with her
bridegroom? (Jurgens, *Luther's Leben*, Vol. I, p. 577). This feeling
of man's decadence, of his need of sanctification, this conviction that
salvation comes not of works, but only of faith in Jesus Christ; this
appeal to the interior spirit and to the sole testimony of conscience;
had they not something strangely powerful and seductive, especially
for those who had serious grievances against the clergy, and were
tempted by a host of national prejudices to turn away from the Roman
Church? . . ." Baudrillart, *L'Église catholique, la Renaissance, le
Protestantisme*, pp. 128-129.

[2] Weimar, V, 395.

[3] On this certainty of justification according to Luther, see Denifle-
Paquier, III, 428 ff.

cannot be lost by those who are predestined. A rigid pre-
destinarianism, antecedent to creation and to the fall,
governs the whole of the Calvinistic system. Amongst mankind, some are destined to hell, the others to heaven. The
elect are assured of their own salvation; they can never lose
their justification : he who is once justified is justified for
ever. The important thing is to believe firmly that we are
justified by the imputation of the merits of Jesus Christ.[1]

The opposition between these fantastical views of the Reformers and true mysticism is plain.

The certainty of salvation was never sought with such
insistence by the medieval mystics.[2] They tell us, no doubt,
that at the time of their supernatural union with God, they
feel that the divine is within them beyond any possible
doubt. They would gladly permanently enjoy this sweet
certainty. But they know that such phenomena are transitory
and intermittent. More often are the mystics liable to experience interior desolation; and they sometimes believe that
they are abandoned by God. They are even assailed by an
agonizing fear that they are not saved. No spiritual state,
however perfect and extraordinary it be, carries with it the
certainty, in the strict sense of the word, of salvation. The
mystics, like ordinary mortals, can have no other permanent
and habitual mental condition than that of an entire and
pacifying trust in the mercy of God and in the merits of
Jesus Christ, and in the power and effectiveness of the
sacraments.[3]

This so-called certainty of salvation, which is the only
spiritual consolation of the Reformers, was also the sole
ground of their devotion to Christ.

What matters it to Luther that there are two natures in
Christ, and that all perfections are found together in him?
The thing that matters, in his eyes, is the fact that Christ
became his Saviour and Redeemer and is delivering him
from his sins.[4] Melanchthon, too, says that to know Christ
" means to know his blessings, and not, as [the Scholastics]
assert, to meditate on his natures and the possible modes

[1] Cf. *Institutio christiana,* Book III, chap. xxi-xxiv.
[2] Harnack, *Lehrbuch der Dogmengeschichte,* III, 759, appears to
believe that Luther, by his doctrine of the certainty of salvation,
corresponded with the tendencies of the medieval mystics. But he
adds that Luther " has surpassed mysticism." I quite believe it!
See, too, the same writer's *Das Mönchtum, seine Ideale, seine
Geschichte,* Giessen, 1901, in which similar notions are set forth with
regard to the medieval mystics.
[3] The doctrine of the Council of Trent, Session VI, chap. ix.
[4] Erlangen, tom. XXXV, 207; LVII, 208. M. L. Christiani quotes
many suggestive passages from Luther, Melanchthon, Calvin, etc., in
the review *Regnabit,* October-November, 1921; January-February, 1922.

of his Incarnation.''¹. Calvin assuaged his spiritual distress
by remembering that Christ's salvation was for the elect :

" It is quite certain," says he, " that when Christ prayed
for all the elect he asked for them what he had asked for
Peter, that their faith should not fail. Hence, we infer that
they are in no danger of falling mortally : seeing that the
Son of God, having demanded that they should stand firm,
was not refused his request. What did Christ wish to teach
us thereby but the assurance of eternal salvation, since he
has once for all made us his own ?''²

This Protestant religion is as far as possible from being
disinterested. It is egoistic and altogether *anthropocentric*.
The whole of the plan of redemption is brought down to
man's salvation. Do not ask this kind of mysticism for
acts of pure love. It is incapable of them. To pay to Jesus
the homage of praise and love, to which he is entitled by
his divine perfections, is far from its practice. It could not
lead to heroic virtues.

Protestant mysticism is still more defective when it has to
settle the relations of the soul with God. It does away with
all intermediaries and with all government. It is not for
Church authority to determine our faith nor to estimate
the worth of our religious experiences. The Holy Ghost
is the sole master and teacher of everyone, revealing to him
the meaning of Scripture and inspiring him as to what he
should believe and do. It is exclusively in private inspiration and in direct and immediate communication with God
that the soul finds the nourishment of its spiritual life.
Luther and the Reformers did not shrink from opposing
their assumed revelations to the infallible authority of the
Church.³

They used the names of the Christian humanists and of the
medieval mystics.⁴ These were accustomed to look for their

---

¹ *Loci communes rerum theologicarum,* Praefatio, Christiani, *ibid.,*
p. 444.
² *Institutio christiana,* Book III, chap. xxiv, 6.
³ Thus Protestant mysticism became illuminism. It showed all its
excesses in the sect of the German Anabaptists in the case of Thomas
Munzer, who started the Peasants' War in 1525.
⁴ Luther relies above all on the German mystics, on Meister Eckhart
and his disciples, and principally on Tauler. The work entitled
Theologia germanica also exercised a great influence over him. Pierre
d'Ailly and Gerson specially pleased Luther, who asserted that he
knew all d'Ailly's works by heart. See the list of German mystics
quoted by Luther in Denifle-Paquier, Vol. I, and in Goyau, *L'Allemagne religieuse.* Among these authors are many of little importance.
Luther also regarded Jerome Savonarola as a forerunner : " Christ
has canonized him," he said, " because he relied upon the meditation

leadings, their plans, and their rules of life in their direct
communications with God rather than in the hierarchical
guidance of the Church, and this appears to have exercised
a kind of fascination over Luther's mind. Taking certain
passages of their works in a literal sense, he inferred that
mysticism is above the laws of the Church :

" Here is a sentence," he says, " well known to the most
distinguished writers, and it has become proverbial in the
Church : ' Whenever a man is fulfilling the precepts of the
Church, if God raises him to a rapture of ecstasy or imparts
to him a special illumination, this man is bound to break off
the work which he has begun and to disobey the Church
It is better to obey God than man.' Writers tell us, indeed,
that when we are reciting the canonical Office, we ought to
turn our attention away from the words we are saying despite
the Church's prohibition, if our soul be touched by some
inward illumination or pious emotion."[1]

The writers of this " sentence "[2] were far from suspecting
the way in which Luther would misuse it. Despite the
extravagance of their utterances, they did not wish to make
a general rule of counsels concerning particular and exceptional cases. In the ordinary way, mystics, as well as the
common run of Christians, are subject to the laws of the
Church. But if a rapture seize them and deprive them of the
use of their senses, they are at the time incapable of obeying
anyone else than God.[3]

Many mystics of the Middle Ages insistently called for

---

of the Gospel of peace, and not upon vows or hoods, on the Mass, and
on the Rule " (César Cantu, *Histoire des Italiens,* Vol. VII, p. 255,
French translation, Paris, 1860.

[1] *Resolutiones disputationum de indulgentiarum virtute D. Martini
Lutheri ad Leonem decimum Pontif. Maximum*, Conclusio X, *Lutheri
opera*, Ienæ, 1612, tom. I, p. 73a.

[2] John Eck, Luther's famous adversary, attributes it to Tauler
(Joannis Eckii, *De Purgatorio contra Lutherum*, Parisiis, 1548, lib.
III, cap. xiii, p. 127). So does Louis de Blois, *Apologia pro D. Joanne
Thaulero adversus Joannem Eckium* (*Opera*, Antwerp, 1632, p. 345).
It is found, with a slight difference, in one of Tauler's *Sermons* (Frankfort ed.), *Third Sermon for the Fifth Sunday after Trinity*. Here is
the passage according to Sainte-Foi, II, 236-237 : " He who
observes closely his innermost self and all that occurs within him
either from within or from without; he who is ready to leave all with
joy for God and to become recollected in his own heart, that man soon
learns all that he ought to do or to leave undone. . . . If, then, a
monk or a nun, while singing or reading in choir, felt, by certain signs,
that God was calling him or her to inward recollection, and he or she
were unable to obey the call without stopping work, the work should
be stopped at once, and he or she should follow the inward attraction
and turn entirely to God." F. Vetter's critical edition of *Tauler's
Sermons* omits this one.

[3] *Cf.* Louis de Blois, *ibid.* To justify Tauler, Louis de Blois speaks
of St Francis of Assisi. He quotes Henry Harphius recounting certain
facts in the life of St Clare of Assisi.

Church reform. They sometimes ventured to communicate
to the highest dignitaries of the hierarchy orders believed
to come from heaven. Their audacities in behalf of reforms
were highly pleasing to Luther. He borrowed authority
from them to put forward his own proposals. But how
wrongly! For not a single Catholic mystic ever called for
a change in the faith or in the constitution of the Church,
as the Protestants did. It was the reformation of morals
that they keenly desired.[1] Ecclesiastical dogma did not in
any way check the upward soaring of their souls. It rather
verified them, for any private inspiration can only be valid
if it be in harmony therewith. And when the ecstatic mystic
came down from his Sinai and censured the conduct of the
heads of the Church, he bowed to their authority and never
disputed it. This Luther would not understand; and that
is how his mysticism differs essentially from that of the
Middle Ages. His true forerunners were those, like the
Albigenses, the Vaudois, and the Brethren of the Free Spirit,
John Wycliffe and Huss, who tried to ruin the Church on
the pretext of reforming it.

The Protestant Reformation gives a most important date
in the history of Catholic thought. The Council of Trent
defined all the points of Church doctrine disputed by the
Protestants. But these persisted in their rebellion. Thus
Catholic theology in modern times has been largely a work
of reaction. It had to combat heresy refusing to lay down
its arms. It constantly defines its doctrines in opposition
to Lutheran and Calvinistic errors. An analogous tendency
is manifested in the sphere of spirituality. The faithful have
to be put on their guard against Luther's quietism, and
against illuminism and private inspiration. In this direction,
the reaction, perhaps, went too far. It cast a kind of discredit on the mystics which lasted long.

II—REACTION AGAINST THE MEDIEVAL MYSTICS UPON WHOM LUTHER RELIED FOR HIS AUTHORITY

THE first to suffer discredit were the medieval mystics whom
Luther loved to quote. The praises ascribed by the heresiarch to a writer were—as we can easily understand—
singularly compromising. This is easily seen in the cases
of Tauler and, to some extent, of Gerson, to mention two
among others.

Tauler, as well as the author of *Theologia germanica,*
was the German writer most favoured by the head of the
Reformation :

[1] See Bossuet, *Histoire des Variations,* Book I, i.-v.

"I know that this Doctor (John Tauler)," he says, "is unknown in the schools of the theologians, and, therefore, perhaps contemptible. But for my own part, though he wrote nothing but German, I found in him more of solid and pure theology than has been found in all the scholastic doctors of all the universities, or than can be found in all their sentences."[1]

It is in his dissertations on Purgatory that Luther awards this extraordinary praise to Tauler. He thought he had found a confirmation of his doctrine in the accounts of visions of Purgatory or in the appearances of souls suffering in it, with which the famous preacher embellished his sermons.[2]

But what delighted him still more was the tendency which he thought he found in Tauler's writings to diminish the importance of works and of spiritual exercises, and to liberate the Christian's interior life, and especially the devotion of the religious, from all external rules.[3]

It is easy to understand the vexation of Luther's adversaries when he quoted against them in his controversies the authority of Catholic writers. Would it not be the quickest way, they thought, to fling overboard these troublesome people?

One of the first and of the most redoubtable of Luther's antagonists was John van Eck,[4] and he undertook " to put an end " to Tauler in his treatise *De Purgatorio contra Lutherum*. I quote a part of the passage which is a strange one. Though we must not take this violent accusation quite literally, it is an example of the passionate tone of the discussions of those times, of what has been called the *Rabies theologorum* of that period :

" Luther," he says, " in support of his opinion [on Purgatory] quotes Tauler, his dreamer of dreams (*somniatorem*

---

[1] *Hunc doctorem [Taulerum] scio quidem ignotum esse in scholis theologorum, ideoque forte contemptibilem. Sed ego plus in eo (licet totus Germanorum vernacula sit conscriptus) reperi theologiae solidae et sincerae quam in universis omnium universitatum scholasticis doctoribus repertum est, aut reperiri possit in suis sententiis. Resolutiones disputationum de indulgentiarum virtute* (Conclusio XV, *Opera*, Ienæ, tom. I, p. 76a).

[2] Luther deals with Purgatory with reference to indulgences in the *Resolutiones,* Conclusio VIII to XXIX. He gives Tauler as his authority, especially in Conclusio XV and XXIX. Luther also relies upon the opinion of Dionysius the Carthusian, according to which there are souls in Purgatory uncertain of their salvation (Conclusio XIX, p. 79b).

[3] In Tauler's *Sermons* may be found a few phrases, which may easily mislead us if they are taken out of their context. *Cf.* Vetter, pp. 56 ff., 68, 155, 181 ff. But Tauler never taught what Luther attributes to him.

[4] Born in 1486, was a professor and then Chancellor of the University of Ingolstadt. In 1519 he carried on a public controversy with Carlostadt and Luther. *Cf.* Janssen, *op. cit.,* I, 110-111; VII, 544-552.

suum). We shall refute him easily, because this writer has
indulged in the errors of the Waldensians and the Beghards[1]
enumerated in the Clementines (lib. V, tit. III, *De haereticis,*
c. 3). That he was infected by these condemned heresies
is plain, and further we shall prove it. As to Luther's
opinion of Tauler . . . whom he prefers to all the doctors
of all the universities, it shows such shameless arrogance,
such degrading presumption, and such blind jealousy that
it clearly proves one thing only : what a man this Luther
is, so humble, so patient, and so modest that he sets this
dreamer of dreams above all the lights of the Church and all
the most illustrious Fathers. Doubtless it was not enough
to be satisfied with putting them before others, but to make
his madness appear still more conspicuous, he declares that
in Tauler there is more sound theology than can be found,
and even—O climax of pride !—than could possibly be found,
in all the doctors of Scholasticism !''

Can Luther speak thus, continues John van Eck? Tauler
wrote but little. All his *Sermons* do not make as big a book
as the first one of the *Sentences* of Peter Lombard. Moreover, he is an unknown writer, and he is set above the
Pleiad of theologians who have illustrated the Church !

" After all, would to God that he were entirely in the shade
and that he had done no harm to the monasteries ! For (by
his mystical teaching) he destroys all rule and all religious
discipline and obedience itself, the pearl of price among the
virtues. Without obedience, what were monasteries but the
training schools of the devil?''

Had not Tauler said, in fact, that those religious " whom
God called to interior recollection " should follow their attraction and leave off the works prescribed by obedience? His
teaching, doubtless ill understood, had created disturbance
in some communities, but it above all filled Luther with
enthusiasm.[2]

This passionate harangue—need we say it?—oversteps

---

[1] This improbable accusation appears to have been made against
Tauler before Luther was born. *Cf.* J. van Eck, *De Purgatorio contra
Lutherum,* Parisiis, 1548, lib. III, pp. 125-128. Eck blames Tauler for
having approved of this Beghard error condemned by the Council of
Vienne in 1311 (Hefele-Leclercq, *Histoire des conciles,* Vol. VI, 682) :
" At the elevation of the Body of Christ, people should not rise nor
show any special veneration, for it would be an imperfection to come
down from the heights of contemplation to think of the sacrament of
the Eucharist.'' We cannot tell what gave rise to this charge. We
must note that there was then no critical edition of Tauler's *Works.*
Writings were attributed to him of which he was not the author. That,
too, may have occurred in the case of Luther himself.
[2] *De Purgatorio contra Lutherum,* lib. III, cap. xiii, pp. 125-128.
John van Eck also wrote a Commentary on Dionysius the Areopagite,
Commentarii in mysticam theologiam S. Dionysii Areop., Augsburg,
1519.

propriety. The fiery controversialist's excuse lies in his desire to defend the Church and to overthrow Luther's imposture. Besides, who calculates his blows in the thick of the battle? Tauler had the misfortune of winning Luther's appreciation. John van Eck, and others as well as he, hence inferred that he bordered upon heresy. It was part of the destiny of this great mystic to be the butt of contradiction, and all the more so because he was credited with writings which never came from his pen.

However exaggerated they were, Eck's attacks upon Tauler were not without effect. They so far discredited Tauler's books, says Louis de Blois, that they are no longer read.[1] The truth urgently needed to be re-established. The Abbot of Liessies undertook the work.

He personally esteemed Tauler greatly. He drew his inspiration from Tauler frequently in his own works. His famous *Institutio spiritualis* in many passages is a faithful echo of Tauler's teaching. In the first appendix of this treatise, Louis de Blois has gathered together the principal texts made use of for the purpose of documentary justification. Those from Tauler are the most numerous.[2] No one was more concerned for the good reputation of the Rhenish mystic than the Abbot of Liessies. He thus felt it necessary, when he sent the *Institutio spiritualis* to his friend Florentius du Mont in 1551, to add to it an *Apology for Tauler,* which he had written just when Eck published his *De Purgatorio*.[3]

Louis de Blois acknowledges the good faith of Eck, " the venerable theologian and invincible defender of the Catholic faith." His intention is excellent :

"Although he has condemned Tauler thoughtlessly and without examining him closely enough, we must not, therefore, think that he has acted wickedly. The consuming zeal against the heresiarch Luther, which carried him away, led him, as may be easily understood, to express a precipitate and unjust judgement about Tauler, a very holy man."[4]

---

[1] *Cum intellexissem plerosque a lectione librorum D. Ioannis Thauleri deterreri verbis Ioannis Eckii, operae pretium duxi paucis refellere ea quae in ipsum Thaulerum minus considerate scribit Eckius.—Ludovici Blosii Institutionis spiritualis appendix quarta sive Apologia pro D. Ioanne Thaulero adversus D. Ioannem Eckium,* cap. i, *Opera L. Blosii,* Antwerp, 1632, p. 344.

[2] Letter to Florentius du Mont, Preface of the *Apologia,* p. 344. See pp. 329-336 for this *Appendix prima desumpta ex libris D. Ioannis Thauleri aliorumque patrum.*

[3] Louis de Blois wrote the *Institutio* in the first instance for his own personal use some time before 1551, the year in which he sent it to Florentius (*Epistola ad Florentium,* at the beginning of the treatise, *Opera,* p. 287). Eck published his treatise *De Purgatorio* about 1530. It was between 1530 and 1550 that Louis de Blois wrote the *Apologia.* It makes the fourth appendix of the *Institutio.*

[4] *Apologia,* cap. vi, p. 352.

Except in intention, Eck's criticisms are altogether mistaken. Tauler, a most Catholic writer, is charged with heresy without proof. It is true that Luther praised him and claimed him in support of his authority. What is strange in all this? Did he not do the same with St Paul and with the great writers of the Church? To assert that Tauler wanted to withdraw the devout from the laws of the Church is a fearful calumny. Merely to read the *Sermons* is to be convinced of that. How can anyone discover the errors of the Beghards in his books, when one of his most famous *Sermons* is full of thunder against them?[1]

This *Apologia* did not altogether justify Tauler. Neither Laurentius Surius[2] nor Bellarmine succeeded in dissipating the prejudices against him which widely lingered on. The rapid growth of Protestantism was not calculated to help them. How, they thought, could anyone put confidence in a mystic who has expressed himself in such a way that heresy can rely on him for support? Thus Tauler continued to be a disputed writer. Bossuet held him to be " one of the soundest and most right of mystics."[3] The opinion of Suarez, on the other hand, was that, " as this writer does not speak with scholastic precision and subtlety, but in mystical language, we cannot build any strong foundation on his words when we would comply with his authority."[4]

Gerson met with much the same fate. However, his Gallicism did him as much injury as the favours of Luther.

The latter showed more appreciation for the theologian in him than for the mystic, and this he also did in the case of Pierre d'Ailly.[5] Gerson's spiritual doctrine is just the opposite of quietism. What could the head of the Reformation find in it in support of his teaching of the absolute passivity of man in the work of his own sanctification?

In the conference which he had in 1512, at the beginning of his apostasy, with Cardinal Cajetan, Luther relied upon the prestige of Gerson to maintain that " the authority of popes

[1] *Apologia,* cap. i-iv. To reply to Eck's accusations, Louis of Blois refers to Tauler's *Sermons* and to the *Institutions,* then regarded as authentic. We know that the *Institutions* are not by Tauler. The *Sermons* referred to Louis of Blois are : *The Second Sermon for the First Sunday in Lent* against the Beghards ; the *Sermon for the Eleventh Sunday after Trinity;* the two *Second Sermons for the Third and Fourth Sundays in Lent;* and the *First Sermon for the Third Sunday after Trinity* on the religious life ; the *First Sermon for the Eighteenth Sunday after Trinity.* They are not all in Vetter's edition.
[2] Preface to his translation of Tauler's *Works.*
[3] *Instruction sur les états d'oraison,* Book I, iii.
[4] *De virtute Religionis,* Tract. Quartus, lib. II, cap. xii, n. 17.
[5] The Occamist errors of Peter d'Ailly had already discredited him before the appearance of Luther's writings.

. . . is subject to the veto of councils."[1] He also alleged his testimony, as being favourable to himself, with regard to indulgences. [2]

But it was above all in controversies as to the monastic state that the Protestants made a misleading use of the writings of Gerson. One of their principal points is to put the state of the layman in the same rank as that of the religious, since monastic vows were null in strict right. Now it was in the very year 1418, at the Council of Constance, that the Chancellor of Paris must have got Matthew Grabon condemned for exalting the religious life beyond measure. According to him, the laity could not follow the evangelical counsels, nor make vows, nor practise poverty, chastity, and obedience without entering into one of the existing religious Orders which had been approved by the Church. Any work of perfection they sought to do while living in the world would be without merit, and even gravely unlawful. For man cannot do such works, which are only " of counsel," unless he is in a state of perfection—i.e., in a canonical religious Order ! [3]

Gerson rightly rose in indignation against such enormities. All, even the laity, can practise at least some of the evangelical counsels. It is not at all necessary to belong to a religious Order. In all conditions men can tend towards perfection.

" For the religious Orders, created by men," he adds, " are called improperly enough and by an abuse of language and somewhat pretentiously, states of perfection. Yes, indeed, because there are in them, as everyone knows, people far from perfect among the professed. . . . And this proves that the said expression is very badly chosen, that, according to those who have lately made use of it following holy doctors, it does not mean that the religious possess or have acquired perfection, like prelates, but only that they ought to acquire it. It is clear that perfection to be acquired is a very different thing from perfection that has been already acquired. Furthermore, religious profession would be better named if it were called the way and the means of perfection or the habit of tending thereto rather than the state of perfection. And verily, if the religious state leads and helps a certain number of people to practise the Christian religion in a more perfect manner, it turns aside and ruins many others

[1] Pallavicini, *Histoire du Concile de Trente,* Book I, chap. ix.

[2] *Resolutiones disput. de indulg.* Conclusio VIII. According to Luther, Gerson had condemned *indulgentias titulo multorum annorum donatas.* See Concl. XI and XXXVIII.

[3] See Matthew Grabon's erroneous propositions, *Gersonii opera,* 473. There are thirty-six, *quarum aliae sunt haereticae, aliae erroneae et aliae scandalosae ac piarum aurium offensivae,* p. 474.

who would have gained their salvation much better in the world. For, *an unfaithful and foolish promise displeaseth God* (Eccles. v, 3), a promise rashly made and not kept."[1]

Gerson's notion is certainly right. His way of putting it would have doubtless been very different in a treatise on the religious state which had nothing to do with polemics. Since Matthew Grabon extolled the religious life beyond measure, was it not necessary to bring it down enough to set it in its true place? To put a thing in its proper place is not to depreciate it. The Reformers, misunderstanding Gerson's mind, claimed this passage as an argument in their favour. Article XXVII of the famous Confession of Augsburg,[2] which is a bitter criticism of the religious state, ends thus :

" Lately Gerson has blamed the error of the monks as to the nature of perfection [which could not be practised outside the cloister] and he testifies that, in his time, it was a novelty to call the monastic life a state of perfection."

This abuse of Gerson's authority does not appear to have much impressed the Fathers of the Council of Trent.[3] Still, his memory suffered from it afterwards. His cultus, which was so popular at Lyons in the fifteenth and sixteenth centuries,[4] completely died out later on. Were not the Protestant controversies with which his name was so often mixed up at least partly responsible for it?

As for the *Theologia germanica* (*Theologia deutsch*) it was suspect from the day of its appearance. Written in the fourteenth century by an unknown hand, apparently of the school of Meister Eckhart, it was published by Luther in 1516, and republished by him in 1518 with a fuller text.[5] Revealing dubious tendencies, the *Theologia germanica* gave immense pleasure to the head of the Reformation.

" I declare," says he in his Preface to the second edition, " that I have not found any book, except the Bible and St Augustine, which has taught me more of the meaning of God, Christ, man, and everything."[6]

---

[1] *Opera*, I, 568.

[2] It is the work of Melanchthon, and was approved by Luther.

[3] They speak of him with respect, and attach much importance to his opinions. *Cf*. Pallavicini, *op. cit.*, Book VIII, chap. xix; XII, chap. xi; XVII, chap. xii, etc.

[4] Amongst others, see the account of the miracles wrought at Gerson's tomb, given by Etienne Verney, chaplain at St Paul of Lyons (*Opera* by Elie Dupin, tom. I, pp. clxxxviii ff.). See Canon Giraud's article, *Bulletin historique du diocèse de Lyon,* July-October, 1923.

[5] New editions and translations were numerous. Sebastian Castellion's French translation of 1558 was put on the Index in 1608. On the *Theologia germanica* see the *Étude sur la Théologie germanique*, by Maria Windstosser, Paris, 1911.

[6] Windstosser, p. 129. In spite of Protestantism, Germany and the Low Countries produced some Catholic spiritual writers : John of Staupitz, Augustinian, Luther's Provincial, *De amore Dei,* Frankfort,

This shows us how much he drew from this system of theology. It also shows us why Catholic orthodoxy felt such repulsion for it.

1524; John Tritheim, O.S.B., Abbot of Spannheim (†1516), *De triplici regione claustralium Opera,* Mainz, 1605. *Margarita evangelica* and *Templum animae,* by an unknown writer, published by Nicholas Eschius, priest (†1573), at Antwerp in 1539 and 1563. Francis Vervoort, *Chlamys sponsi sive de interna imitatione vitae et crucis Christi,* Antwerp, 1563; Adrian Adriaensens, S.J., *De divinis inspirationibus opusculum,* Coloniæ, 1601; Bernardine Rosignolo, S.J., *De disciplina christianae perfectionis pro triplici hominum statu,* Ingolstadt, 1600; Francis Amelry, Carmelite, *Dialogus de amante anima ad sponsi sui cognitionem perducta,* Coloniæ, 1605; Hugo Roth, S.J., *Via regia virtutis et vitae spiritualis,* Munich, 1689; John James Graft, *Speculum theologiae mysticae,* Strassburg, 1618.

CHAPTER V

THE SPANISH SCHOOL BEFORE ST TERESA

THE discredit that befell mysticism in consequence of Protestant heresy appears especially in Spain, above all in the first two thirds of the sixteenth century.

The sixteenth century marks the apogee of Spain. After the final expulsion of the Moors in 1492, Spain attained and kept the political supremacy of Europe during the reigns of Charles V and Philip II. She produced a Pleiad of theologians, several of whom gave lustre to the Council of Trent. In literature she had Cervantes; in mysticism, St Teresa and St John of the Cross.

The Catholic life of Spain, prosperous as it was, was nevertheless disturbed during the whole of the sixteenth century with the dread of Protestant heresy and by the false mysticism of the *Alumbrados* or *Illuminati*. The rigours of the Inquisition had to be let loose, and its labours were assisted by Philip II. His part, which in some ways may be thought marred by excesses, really resulted in maintaining orthodoxy in Spain.[1] But it so far hindered the growth of mystical theology that the history of Spanish spirituality during this period is partly bound up with that of the Inquisition.

It is well for the knowledge of this Spanish illuminism, against which the Inquisition had to fight so hard, to recall the philosophical tendencies and the religious doctrines of medieval Spain.

I—ARABIAN-SPANISH MYSTICISM IN THE MIDDLE AGES—THE FRANCISCAN RAYMOND LULL

THE Iberian peninsula, except a small portion in the northeast, was subject to the Moors for several centuries. Cordova, the Arabian capital until 1236, became a powerful intellectual centre under the Omayyad dynasty in the tenth century. There they studied Aristotle. Arabian writings from the East flooded it. The reaction of Eastern Islam in the eleventh century against the introduction of Greek phil-

---

[1] On the Inquisition, see F. Mourret, *Histoire générale de l'Eglise,* Vol. V, pp. 511 ff., which contains a bibliography. Alfred Baudrillart, *L'Eglise catholique, la Renaissance, le Protestantisme,* chap. vii, Paris, 1905, pp. 239 ff.

osophy into the religion of Spanish Mohammedanism but imperfectly checked this great scientific movement. Cordova
gave birth in 1126 to the most eminent Arabian philosopher
of Musulman Spain, Averroës (†1198), whose name and
teaching fill so large a space in the European theological
schools of the Middle Ages and of the Renaissance.

The Arabian-Spanish philosophical system is called Averroism, after the name of its last and most famous exponent.
It also constitutes a theology and even an ascetico-mystical
theology.

The end proposed to itself by this Arabian mysticism is
union with God by means of speculation or contemplation.

Aristotle had let it be understood that the life of the mind,
the life of thought, brings us into touch with God and makes
us participate in his felicity. The Arabian philosophers give
a definite shape to these mystical notions by their great theory
of the oneness of the intellect. The act of knowledge occurs,
according to them, by the co-operation of the passive or
subjective intellect with the active or objective intellect. The
first is a faculty of the soul; it is something individual. The
other is one and universal, something divine. The active
intellect alone is immortal and absolute, and in fine its
attributes are really proper to God alone.

In order to think, man must set his passive intellect, which
is his capacity for receiving the light, over against that sort
of divine sun, which is the active intellect. The sole *raison
d'être* of the passive intellect is to be united with the active
intellect to produce thought, " just as matter calls for form
to produce a material being." The union of the soul with
the active universal intellect may even become a kind of
identification. The soul is then like God. It attains its end,
its perfection.[1]

The Arabian-Spanish school was very taken up with this
union, the unique, real, and true fruit of our earthly life. The
great means of securing it is study, speculation. It is by
this that man becomes identified with the active intellect.

Thus reflection and meditation have a preponderant place
in Arabian mysticism.

But as a rule external means and ascetical exercises must
be added to them. The Arabian writer who has described
them most fully is Ghazali or Algazel (†1111). From the

---

[1] On this mysticism, see Avicenna (Ibn-Sina) in Roger Bacon, *Opus
majus,* ed. Jebb, London, 1733; Alfarabi (†950), in Munk, *Mélanges de
philosophie juive et arabe,* Paris, 1859, pp. 341 ff; Algazali or Algazel
(†1111), in Munk, *ibid.,* pp. 372 ff.; Carra de Vaux, *Gazali,* Paris, 1902;
Asin Palacios, *La Mystique d'Al-Gazzâli,* Beyrouth, 1914; Avempace
(Ibn-Babja, † about 1138), in Munk, pp. 388 ff; Averroës (†1198), in
E. Renan, *Averroès et l'Averroïsme,* 2nd ed., Paris, 1861, pp. 88 ff.
Not all of these Arabian philosophers lived in Spain, but their works
were widely read in that country.

philosopher that he was, Ghazali turned ascetic and lived as a hermit. While he taught philosophy at Baghdad and at Alexandria, he felt the vanity of the various philosophical systems of his day. For him philosophy is a deceptive science, which must be destroyed. In desperation he embraced mysticism.

His ascetico-mystical system appears to owe much to the Christian spirituality of the monks of the East.[1] Ghazali, born in Persia, was able to study it at leisure. Thus Musulman Spain through the Arabs came to know the spiritual teaching of the East in the same way as she received from them the works of Aristotle.

Ghazali makes his " devotee " go through the way of perfection in seven steps or stages. The first—as might be expected—is the step of knowledge, of rational speculation. The others are : repentance, victory over the hindrances scattered in our way—these are the world, bad examples, the devil, and concupiscence; the breaking of the shackles on our progress towards perfection; the use of the stimulants of hope and fear; purity of intention and the recollection of divine blessings in order to avoid hypocrisy and vanity; the seventh, and last, is the step of praise and thanksgiving to God. Ghazali intersperses his ascetic remarks with very practical and psychological counsels to help the " devotee " in his ascent toward the highest perfection. As we read him we often wonder to whom we are listening : Ghazali, the disciple of the Koran, or the Christian ascetics, to whom he owes his inspiration. But beneath this seemingly orthodox spirituality lurks a mysticism impregnated with pantheism. Besides, Arabian mysticism was not altogether protected from illuminism and the religious extravagances of oriental Islamism.

The brilliant works of the Arabian philosophers must have been in their way widely seductive to their readers. The Spanish mind had already been predisposed from the fourth century by Priscillianism towards the exaltation of a mystical sentimentalism. The Catalan Raymond Lull[2] (†1315), who well understood the dangers of the Arabian literature for the

[1] M. Asin Palacios sums it up in an analysis of the little book entitled *Minhadj*, by Ghazali, in the *Revue d'ascétique et de mystique*, July, 1923, pp. 275 ff., October, 1923, pp. 345 ff.
[2] *Acta Sanctorum*, June, tom. V, pp. 668 ff. Blessed Raymond Lull was born in 1232 at Palma in Majorca, which had been recently won from the Moors by James I of Aragon. He became a Franciscan, and died a martyr at Bougie (Algeria) in 1315. His chief mystical work is the mystical romance, *Blanquerna*, in which are found the *Art of Contemplation* and the *Book of the Lover and the Beloved*. Cf. Marius André, *Le bienheureux Raymond Lulle*, 2nd ed., Paris, 1900.

faithful, would have had the reading of it entirely prohibited.
Weak minds allowed themselves to be easily upset by the
many errors it contained. Thus, the fiery Franciscan undertook a spiritual crusade against Islam. He desired to destroy
it with the weapons of Catholic knowledge.

But error can only be destroyed by putting the truth in its
place. Efficiently to combat Arabian spirituality, Raymond
countered it with Christian spirituality. And to do this successfully he set forth the latter under the guise of a mystical
romance.

This style of literature was much liked by the Arabs. A
contemporary of Averroës, Ibn-Tufail, called Abubacer by
the scholastics, had written a philosophico-mystical romance.[1]
In it man's faculties are personified, and they attain to union
with God by their own ingenuity. This novel, written in
Catalan, achieved an immense success, and was translated
into several languages.

Raymond Lull tells us that he modelled himself on an
Arabian work when he wrote his mystical novel, *Blanquerna*,[2]
and thus he explains to us its apparently rather strange and
disconcerting aspect.   " A true romance of contemporary
manners . . . but a romance of religious manners and a
didactic romance, a novel with a purpose, in which the
mystical philosopher reveals his ideas as to the reformation
of the Christian world and the conversion of the infidels ; and
he gives a rule of life for five conditions of people : the
married, the religious, the prelates, apostolic lordship, and
the contemplative life."[3]

It is this fifth part that contains the *Art of Contemplation*
and the *Book of the Lover and the Beloved,* Lull's strictly
mystical works.

The Arabs are given to meditation. Then, as now, they
loved silent reflection. In this they found the great means
of becoming united with the universal active intellect. Raymond Lull well understood the Arab mind and thus explains
how the hero of *Blanquerna* became a hermit and contemplated the Christian virtues and the attributes of God. In
the *Art of Contemplation* he teaches us how to set in motion
the powers of the memory, the understanding, and the will,
and to apply them to the consideration of God and his virtues.[4]
These faculties of the soul intervene somewhat like the

---

[1] *Philosophus autodidactus,* Pocoke's ed., 1671.
[2] Critical ed., by Salvador Galmes, Palma, 1914. See E. Etchegoyen,
Mélanges d'Histoire et d'Archéologie de l'École de Rome, Vol.
XXXVIII, pp. 198-211 ; Probst, in the *Beiträge zur Geschichte der Phil.
des Mittelalters,* XIII, 2-3, Munster, 1914 ; J. Rosello, *Obras de Ramon
Lull,* Palmo, 5 vols. ; Marius, André, *L'Ami et l'Aimé,* Paris, 1921.
[3] Marius André, *L'Ami et l'Aimé,* p. xvii.
[4] We find an analogous procedure in the Ignatian method of meditation according to the three powers of the soul.

characters in a novel; each plays a given part and co-operates in the final result, which is union with God. Lull loved this kind of personification. In his great philosophical treatise, *The General Art,* does he not replace the metaphysical categories with personified abstractions?

The method of contemplation once given, he had to find the subject for contemplation. Lull remembered that the Arabs greatly relished short moral sentences of a somewhat enigmatical character, on which they concentrated their attention during the day. He, too, therefore puts forth a collection of three hundred and sixty-five sentences—one for each day of the year—on the love which joins the creature to Christ. This is the *Book of the Lover and the Beloved.* Each sentence, made of one or two phrases, conceals a hidden meaning, a symbol to be detected and a lesson sometimes profound.[1] The hymns of the Lover and the Beloved, as Lull himself tells us, are condensed parables which require an explanation and a commentary.

Raymond Lull's efforts to combat Arabian mysticism are the best proof of its powers of penetration. It spread through Europe with Averroism. We know that in the fourteenth century it gave its inspiration to the *Brothers and Sisters of the Free Spirit,* and to the heterodox Beghards. Gerson blamed the German mystics for not keeping sufficiently clear of it.[2]

But it was Spain that was chiefly threatened by this debased mysticism. Ferdinand the Catholic and Isabella of Castile in the fifteenth century finally destroyed the political power of the Moors in the peninsula. But they did not do away with their intellectual prestige to the same extent. The eminent Franciscan Cardinal Ximenes de Cisneros (†1517) tried to give a great splendour to Spanish Catholic thought in order to neutralize the fascination exercised by the Arabian learning. At Alcala in 1499 he founded a university which, with its elder sister of Salamanca,[3] was to make Spain, in the sixteenth and seventeenth centuries, the land of the most famous theologians. He also had published[4] in Cas-

---

[1] " The ways followed by the Lover in search of the Beloved are long and perilous, full of considerations, sighs and tears, and illumined with love " (Second Sentence). " The Lover was asked what was happiness, and answered : It is the unhappiness borne by love " (Sixty-fifth Sentence, E. Etchegoyen, *ibid.*).

[2] *Gersonii opera,* tom. III, pp. 1124-1125, Antwerp, 1706.

[3] The University of Salamanca was founded in 1259.

[4] He published in Castilian, amongst others, the *Contemptus mundi* (the *Imitatio Christi*) attributed to Gerson, the *Scala* of St John Climacus, the *Life of Christ* by Ludolph the Carthusian, the *Letters* of St Catherine of Siena, the *Stimulus amoris* of St Bonaventure, the *Moralia in Job* of St Gregory the Great, the *Letters* of St Jerome, the *Legenda* or *Flos sanctorum* of Jacobus de Voragine.

tilian and in Latin foreign works of spirituality, anticipating
any works which might be written in Spanish. His relation,
the Abbot of Montserrat, also endeavoured to procure such
works for his monks, and began to write himself. At the
end of the fifteenth century there was a great effort in Spain
to propagate Catholic spirituality. In spite of this, the old
pseudo-mystical leaven was not got rid of. Towards the
end of the Middle Ages it had acquired an increase of activity
from the immoral quietism of the Albigenses and the Beghards.[1] Hence the Spanish mind had a predisposition
towards false mysticism which led to the outbreak of the
heresy of the *Alumbrados*.

II—THE " ALUMBRADOS " OR " ILLUMINATI "[2]

It was particularly from the year 1509 that the sect of the
Alumbrados began to be talked of in Andalusia. It had
not then any definite or singular doctrine. Its adherents
were taught sentences, and were advised to take up practices
which led to quietism and stimulated excessive emotionalism.
The extravagance and the immortality of the old Islamic
superstitions were reproduced among these *Illuminati,* whose
excesses attracted the attention of the inquisitors. The
heads of the sect, who were sometimes renegade religious,
seduced and corrupted a great number of women. Before
the death of Cardinal Ximenes, a Franciscan of the province
of Castile was charged with accusations on this ground.
Toledo, Seville, and particularly Llerena in Estremadura,
experienced abominations of this kind. The *Alumbrados*
also had their thaumaturgists, impostors who deceived many
of the faithful. They were believed to be favoured with
ecstasies, visions, and stigmata.

The faithful ran extreme danger of perversion. The
Spanish temperament is inclined towards mysticism, and the
religious ignorance of the people was so great! Moreover,
the Inquisition pursued the *Alumbrados* unremittingly without being able to get rid of them. It published edicts against
them in 1568, 1574, and in 1623. This final edict summed up

---

[1] The Albigenses in the province of Leon, the Beghards in Catalonia
and in the kingdom of Valencia, had made their ravages.

[2] Menendez y Pelayo, *Historia de los Heterdoxos Españoles,*
Madrid, 1880, Vol. II ; Rinaldi, *Annales ecclesiastici,* ad ann. 1524 ;
Llorente-Pellier, *Histoire critique de l'Inquisition d'Espagne,* French
translation, Paris, 1818, Vol. II, pp. 3-4 ; Vol. III, pp. 102-126 ; Vol. IV,
pp. 123-127. Ribadeneira, *Vida del Padre Ignacio de Loyola,* Book I,
chap. 14, 16 ; Book II, 2, 6, 14, 29. Fermin Callero, *Vida de Melchior
Cano,* Madrid, 1871-1876 ; Louis du Pont, *Vie du P. Balthazar Alvarez,*
Couderc's translation, Paris, chap. xxxiii ; *Dict. d'Histoire et de
Géographie eccl.,* art. *Alumbrados,* Paris, 1913 ; R. Hoornaert, *Sainte
Térèse, écrivain,* Paris, 1922, pp. 66-67 ; 297-302.

the doctrines of the false mystics in thirty-five propositions,[1] and these enable us to form a fairly accurate notion of them.

There is no difficulty in discovering traces of Protestant teaching in them. From 1524 the Lutherans disseminated their books in Spain, and, despite the vigilance of the Inquisitors, they found a good many readers.[2] The leaders of the Reformation thought they could easily make use of the *Alumbrados* to spread their errors throughout the peninsula. In fact, the false mystics taught that "the intercession of the saints was a vain thing," and that the veneration of their images was useless. Their ideas of Purgatory and of the Eucharist were like those of the Protestants.

Their quietism reminds us of that of Meister Eckhart and his school. At the beginning of the sixteenth century the German mystics were known in Spain. Juan de Valdes, the theologian of the *Alumbrados,* drew inspiration from them in his *Hundred and Ten Divine Considerations;*[3] but he is far more indebted to pantheistic Neo-Platonist writers.

Like Plotinus, these false mystics thought that man's soul, having reached a certain degree of perfection, was then able, even in this life, to see the divine essence directly. This vision of God once obtained continues perpetually in us or is reproduced at will. In such pure contemplation the soul loses its personality, and is annihilated in the infinite essence. Its powers are reduced to nothing. The Christian in such a state of perfection can neither advance nor fall away; "grace so inundates his powers that it is impossible for him to go backwards or forwards." Further, "the perfect need not make any acts of virtue." Thus, works are useless, as well as all external acts of religion, such as attending Mass and hearing sermons. The inevitable consequence of such quietism was a corruption of morals. Michael Molinos, in the sixteenth century, revived all these doctrines and ended in the like immorality.

The error which is characteristic of the *Alumbrados,* and reveals traces of Arabian mysticism, has to do with mental prayer, the importance of which is exaggerated. "Mental prayer," said the sectarians, "is divinely commanded, and by fulfilling this command we discharge all our duties." It is by contemplation that the vision of the divine essence is attained, and even thereby does the soul become united with the universal active intelligence. All that hinders prayer

[1] It was Cardinal Andrew Pacheco who drew up this list of thirty-five propositions and had it read in all the churches of Seville.
[2] Hoornaert, *Sainte Térèse écrivain,* pp. 61-62; Lea, *A History of the Inquisition of Spain,* New York, 1906-1907.
[3] Hoornaert, p. 69.

must be ruthlessly set aside, even the consideration of Christ's humanity or obedience to one's superiors. For "the servants of God should not obey superiors in anything which might disturb contemplation." Here we recognize the famous counsel attributed to Tauler, about which Luther made such a stir. Thus it is "the Holy Ghost who rules the elect inwardly." The *Illuminati* can dispense with any other kind of direction : their thoughts and feelings come from God. Their transports and raptures during prayer prove that the Holy Ghost dwells and works within them.

The illuminism of the *Alumbrados* and their mystical sentimentalism were a perpetual danger to the ignorance and excessive sensibility of the Spanish people. In the first half of the sixteenth century spiritual writers did their best to guard them from it by their books, and after 1551 it was the Spanish Inquisition that intervened.

III—SPANISH SPIRITUAL WRITERS PRIOR TO THE INTERVENTION OF THE INQUISITION—THE FRANCISCANS : ALONSO OF MADRID, FRANCISCO OF OSSUNA, BERNARDINO OF LAREDO, AND ST PETER OF ALCANTARA

THE most signal service rendered to the cause of orthodoxy by the Spanish spiritual writers of this period was the putting into the hands of the faithful of good books in the vernacular.[1] Luis of Granada writes in the Prologue to his *Sinners' Guide:*

"Among the subjects for sorrow which we find in the heart of Christianity there is none more serious than the ignorance of Christians as to the laws and foundations of their religion. . . . Not only children, but even old men, scarcely know the first elements of this divine philosophy."

Disorder in morals and danger of heresy inevitably resulted from such religious ignorance. Was not the chief remedy the assiduous reading of books teaching how to make a good confession, a devout communion, and how to avoid sin, to practise virtue, and to pray to God with devotion? The *Sinners' Guide* and the *Treatise on Prayer,* by Luis of Granada, were the masterpieces of such works as these. At the beginning of the sixteenth century the great Cardinal Ximenes earnestly called for such books for popular use. At the time of his death, in 1517, he had succeeded in providing Spain with nothing but translations of foreign spiritual

---

[1] Luis de Leon (†591) says that it is the duty of those who can to write books of this kind in the language of the people (*The Names of Christ*, Book I, p. 40, French translation, Postel, Paris, 1862).

works. But St Teresa was born on March 28, 1515, at
Avila. The Cardinal's wishes were to be realized beyond his
desire.

It was the Order of St Francis which was the first to
answer to the yearnings of Ximenes. The Franciscan,
Alonso of Madrid, published *The Art of Serving God* (*El arte
de servir a Dios*[1]) at Seville in 1521. It is far more a book
of asceticism than of mysticism. Plainly the author wanted
to put his readers on their guard against the too sensible
manifestations of piety, which are so productive of illusions.[2]

The book is divided into three parts. The first contains
the general principles of perfection, and denounces the false
notions that may be formed of the spiritual life. The second
is practical. It teaches self-knowledge and how to practise
virtue, and to give oneself up to prayer. It is only in the
third that the reader is initiated into divine love. The writer
observes the restrictions demanded by the circumstances.
St Teresa read Alonso's treatise, and recommended it to her
religious for meditational prayer : " In this degree [of
prayer]," she said, " it is a good thing to make frequent acts
to stimulate one's generosity in the service of God, to kindle
one's love or to fortify one's virtues. This is the counsel of
a book entitled *The Art of Serving God,* an excellent work,
perfectly adapted to this degree, in which the understanding
is at work."[3]

Six years later, in 1527, there appeared at Toledo a
treatise on the prayer of recollection, Francisco of Ossuna's
Third Primer of Spirituality. It was a bold matter to
publish a treatise of mysticism in Spanish at this period,
especially since the writer, not satisfied with popularizing the

[1] In the *Nueva Biblioteca de autores españoles, Escritores mysticos
españoles,* Vol. I, pp. 588-634. It is a reproduction of the Alcala edition
of 1526. There is another edition by Jaime Sala. Valencia, 1903 ; a
reproduction of the 1570 edition. Then there is the *Meditations for
Holy Week*, by Alonso of Madrid. In 1523 and 1524 there appeared
at Toledo and Burgos the *Arte de bien confessar*, both anonymous.

[2] St Francis de Sales wrote to St Jane Chantal (April, 1606) about
this book. It " is good, but more embarrassed and difficult than you
need : *The Spiritual Combat* contains all that is in it, and is clearer and
more methodical."

[3] *Vie écrite par elle-même,* chap. xii, Ed. Polit, I, 158.

[4] Miguel Mir, Vol. I, pp. 319-587. This is the Burgos edition of
1544. Francis of Ossuna, an Andalusian Franciscan, wrote three
Primers. The first (of 1527) is the third in the complete edition ; then
the first appeared in 1528, and next the second in 1530. The complete
work *Abecedarios espirituales* was published at Seville in 1554. The
Abecedarios are thus called, because each of them contains as many
treatises as there are letters in the alphabet, each treatise beginning
with a letter. Francis of Ossuna also published *The Law of Love* in
1530, in which he sums up the three Abecedarios. *Cf.* P. Michel-Ange,
Revista de Archivos, 1912, I.

higher mysticism, seemed to rally some who were afraid
of it. If it was objected that these are dangerous matters
and that the devil may lurk beneath them, he replied he may
also hide behind the door of the Church, but that people did
not cease from entering thereby on that account.[1] The
prudent John of Avila declared that *The Third Primer* is not
suited to all the faithful, and that there are perhaps certain
objections to scattering it broadcast amongst the general
public.[2] It is a wonder that the author escaped the fulmina-
tions of the Inquisition, since it spared scarcely anyone a few
years later.

It is true that Francisco of Ossuna made some corrections
in those respects in which he might have been too daring.
He soon wrote the first and second *Abecedarios,* works of
ascetic theology. In the *First Primer* the pious Franciscan
speaks, as a true son of St Francis, of the passion and the
sorrows of Christ. The mysticism of the *Third Primer* was
thus enclosed in a doctrinal whole, the different parts of
which threw light upon each other.

But it was the mystical work of Francisco of Ossuna that
specially attracted the attention of posterity. It is this
which perhaps contributed most to the spiritual training of
St Teresa.[3]

In it is found a fairly complete synthesis of practical Franciscan mysticism, a sort of mystical therapy of the soul
which must be followed by it to attain to the prayer of
recollection.[4]

Francisco of Ossuna arranges his discipline according to
the psychology of the mystics of the Middle Ages. The
imagination and the external senses, the affections, the
memory, the spiritual senses, the will, and the understanding
successively undergo the mystical treatment which will make
them assist in attaining the desired recollection.

The imagination will be stripped of all created images, and
the senses must be cut off from outward impressions, for the
control of images is essential to recollection, and that of the
senses is equally necessary. Further, the soul's affections
must be turned from the carnal and increasingly directed
towards the spiritual. At the same time, the memory must
be filled with God and the thought of his benefits. This
mystical role of the memory was always considered most
important by spiritual writers :

"To think or remember that one is in the presence of

[1] Hoornaert, *op. cit.,* p. 329.
[2] *Epistolario espiritual,* ed. Ribadeneira, p. 321.
[3] Cf. *Vie,* chap. iv, *Œuvres de sainte Térèse,* Vol. I, pp. 70-71.
[4] The first five treatises of the *Tercer Abecedario* aim at detachment
from sin and things created. The sixth begins with recollection in the
strict sense of the word.

God, and to represent him as present before one are one and the same thing."[1]

This habitual remembrance of the presence of God increases the soul's relish for the divine. We possess a kind of "spiritual sensibility" which enables us to perceive the "touches" of heavenly consolations. Francisco of Ossuna, gifted with an Andalusian sensibility, gives much importance to this spiritual sense. He greatly prefers the "spiritual sense" to book-knowledge, for it imparts experience of the divine instead of a knowledge which is purely theoretical. Moreover, he cannot understand those who tell people not "to look for divine consolation and the enjoyment of things spiritual."[2]

Like St Francis of Assisi, the author of the *Third Primer* regards mystical joy as a necessary condition for interior recollection :

"In recollection," he says, "a man will advance the more, the more he keeps joy in his heart, which should be offered with joy when offered to God."[3]

Nothing is more fatal to devotion than a bad spirit of gloom. Holy enthusiasm in the service of God soon brings the will "to act for and through love only."[4]

"I have observed," says Francisco, "that in this way of recollection the down-hearted make but little progress, and that the joyous who consecrate their joy to God advance greatly."[5]

But joy and other feelings are but handmaids of the will which must finally rule the whole of man's interior life, for "all our spiritual progress depends upon the disposition and preparation of the will, and such good will is the measure of the graces bestowed upon us by the Lord."[6]

Lastly, the education of the understanding must also be made in the medieval fashion. The understanding must be kept in peace and silence; it has nothing to do with the prayer of recollection, in which by the silence of the understanding and the forgetting of images the soul withdraws into God and abandons itself to him in love.[7] "To practise recollection," says Francisco of Ossuna, "is in some sort to be transformed into the object of our recollection."[8]

---

[1] *Tercer Abecedario*, trat. XI, cap. iii ; Trad. Etchegoyen, *L'Amour Divin, Essai sur les sources de sainte Thérèse*, Bordeaux-Paris, 1923, p. 126. St Peter of Alcantara and Luis of Granada also speak of the "remembrance of God."

[2] *id.*, trat. XII, cap. iii.

[3] *id.*, trat. 3*, cap. v. Cf. *La loi d'amour*, XVII.

[4] Treatise XVI deals chiefly with such love. Treatises XVII, XIX and XX deal with outward mortifications.

[5] *Tercer Abecedario*, trat. XIII, cap. iv.

[6] *id.*, trat. XV, cap. vi. Etchegoyen, 152, 153.

[7] *id.*, trat. XXI.   [8] *id.*, trat. XIV, cap. vii.

Such recollection is the end of the fervent Christian's endeavours, and it has several degrees : (1) The recollection which gently quiets the powers of the soul; (2) that in which the intelligence is still working; (3) a more perfect kind in which the soul becomes enclosed within itself, as in a prison firmly locked, for the enjoyment of God; (4) ecstatic recollection.[1]

We can conjecture what St Teresa was to learn from the *Tercer Abecedario*. She was also much impressed by the style of this remarkable work, full of rich feeling and brilliant imagination. Francisco is a born writer. For the expression of mystical realities he found comparisons which were to become classical in Spain and to be immortalized by the authoress of the Carmelite reform.[2] Thanks to the mystics, the Spanish tongue begins to speak " the language of the angels."

The welcome given to the works of Alonso of Madrid and of Francisco of Ossuna encouraged the Franciscan Order to bring out other mystical publications. In 1535 there appeared at Seville the *Subida del monte Sion*[3] (*The Ascent of Mount Sion*), the work of an Andalusian Franciscan lay-brother, Bernardino of Laredo.[4]

The third part of *The Ascent of Mount Sion* is a real treatise on the prayer of quietude and of the prayer of union.[5] This it was that made the work of Bernardino famous, and calmed St Teresa when, about 1556, at forty-one years of age, she was raised to the prayer of quietude, and was " unable to meditate on the Passion," and felt that she was bereft of " the help of the understanding."[6]

It is just this twofold inability to meditate on the mysteries of the life of Christ and to reason discursively that characterizes the prayer of quietude, according to the *Subida del monte Sion*. In this mystical state the soul is united with God, and contemplates the divinity to the exclusion of all else :

" The perfection of love," says Bernardino, " does not con-

---

[1] *Tercer Abecedario,* trat. XXI.

[2] *Cf.* Hoornaert, *Sainte Térèse écrivain*, pp. 332 ff. F. of Ossuna already reveals traces of a preciosity of style which did injury to Spanish literature later on.

[3] There were many editions; the last at Alcala, in 1617, which also contains Bernardino's *Letters* and *Josephina,* an epitome of the praises of St Joseph.

[4] Born at Seville in 1482. He was doctor to John II of Portugal, became a Franciscan in 1510, and died at Seville in 1545.

[5] The first part teaches self-knowledge through discursive meditation, the second the knowledge and love of Christ by affective meditation; the third is strictly mystical.

[6] *Vie,* chap. xxiii.

sist in meditating upon the holy Humanity [of Christ], but in calm and perfected contemplation of the inaccessible Divinity."[1]

The absolute silence of the powers is the indispensable condition of such contemplation. "This sleep of the powers keeps the soul awake for the soaring of ardent love." Bernardino of Laredo tries to explain this powerlessness to reflect, this necessity of thinking of nothing (*No pensar nada*), of which all the mystics since the pseudo-Dionysius have said so much. Especially does he throw into relief the essentially gratuitous character of such quietude. No device of man can attain to such contemplation. Only the goodness of God can raise the soul thereto, and thus this kind of contemplation is clearly distinguished from that which is active and the result of mental work.[2]

The transition from active kinds of prayer, in which the understanding is still at work, to infused and passive contemplation, in which its working has entirely ceased, is particularly hard to make. St Teresa acknowledges that in her time there were "long discussions on the subject between several spiritual persons."[3] We must not try to encroach upon grace, she thought, nor to fetter the work of the mind, before God has introduced the soul into quietude. In support of her view, St Teresa alleges the authority of the most illustrious Spanish Franciscan mystic of the sixteenth century, St Peter of Alcantara,[4] the author of a *Treatise on Prayer and Meditation* (*Tratado de la Oracion y Meditation*).[5]

A man of prayer if ever there was one, St Peter of Alcantara had no fixed time for prayer. All times and places were proper for him to lose himself in contemplation. His spiritual concentration in God did not hinder him from giving himself up to other occupations and from keeping watch

---

[1] *Subida del monte Sion*, Part III, chap. ix.

[2] *id.*, Part III, xviii, xxv, xxvi.

[3] *Interior Castle*, Fourth Mansion, chap. iii, *Œuvres*, Vol. III.

[4] Born at Alcantara in Estramadura in 1499, when 16 he joined the Discalced Friars Minor. He became Provincial of the province of St Gabriel, and was the promoter of a most austere reform. The reformed convents founded by him formed the province of St Joseph. He died at Arenas, near Avila, in 1562. St Teresa praises him in justly famous words, *Life,* chaps. xxvii and xxxix. The saint left an account of St Teresa's prayer, *Œuvres de sainte Térèse*, Vol. I, pp. 444 ff. Cf. *L'illustre prédestiné* or the *Vie de saint Pierre d'Alcantara*, by F. Marchèse, French translation, Lyons, 1670; Paris, 1691.

[5] Published at Lisbon between 1556 and 1560, by Joannes Blavio, in a volume containing other little treatises by St Peter of Alcantara, and a treatise, by Savonarola, on the Three Vows. Recent ed. by P. Ubald d'Alençon, Paris, 1923. In the *Treatise* there are two parts, the first on prayer, the second on devotion.

over everything. Like Teresa, he was able to combine the contemplative with the active life.[1]

His *Treatise on Prayer and Meditation* is a summary of that of Luis of Granada.[2] To it he added his own experience of the spiritual ways. He aims at teaching the faithful such devotion as consists in doing good promptly and without repugnance, and this devotion is the fruit of prayer. Through Luis of Granada and St Peter of Alcantara, the Spanish School helps us to understand beforehand the teaching of St Francis de Sales' *Introduction to the Devout Life*.

The Christian who wishes to ensure his salvation must give himself up to meditation. This is hard. It demands effort. But let no one be discouraged. Meditation is the way to attain to contemplation in which there is no hardship. "When the ship has come into port navigation is over." Through the action of grace meditation is changed into contemplation, a transformation so deeply studied by St Teresa:

"When anyone," says St Peter of Alcantara,[3] "through the work of meditation has found repose and come to relish contemplation, he must then cease from that pious but toilsome endeavour. Satisfied with simply seeing and with the thought of God, as if he saw him present, he should restfully enjoy the feelings of love or of admiration or of joy, or any other such feeling as it may please God to give him. The reason for this advice and for such conduct is this : as the end of the soul's intercourse with God in prayer consists much more in love than in speculation of the understanding, when the will has already become seized and possessed by this affection, we should, as far as possible, avoid all discourse and all the speculations of the understanding in order that the soul may be wholly occupied with the enjoyment of the feeling of which we have just spoken."

The soul must then be enclosed within itself, where is the image of God, and there abide in attention, like a man listening to someone speaking to him from the top of a tower, or as if it held God within and was alone in the universe to converse with him.[4]

[1] Marchèse, Book IV, chap. x.
[2] This seems to be the upshot of the fairly lively controversy between the Franciscans and Dominicans on the priority of the *Treatise of Prayer and Meditation,* by Luis of Granada, over that by St Peter of Álcantara. See on Luis of Granada's side, P. Justo Cuervo, O.P., *Biographia de Fr. Luis de Granada,* Madrid, 1896; *Revista de Archivos,* Madrid, 1918 ff. On St Peter of Alcantara's side, see P. Michel-Ange, *Revista,* 1916 and 1917 ; *Estudios Franciscanos,* Barcelona, 1919-1921. Cf. *Études franciscaines,* Paris, 1923, pp. 198 ff. ; *Revue d'ascetique et de mystique* (1921), pp. 384-401 ; (1922), pp. 301-332.
[3] *Tratado de la Oracion y Meditación,* Part I, chap. xii, 8th notice ; R. Hoornaert, *op. cit.,* p. 380 ; Ubald d'Alençon, p. 145.
[4] The Order of St Francis had other spiritual writers in Spain in the sixteenth century. Among these was John of Bonilla, author of a

Let it not be supposed that during this period there are
nothing but works of mysticism. On the contrary, popular
books full of counsels for a devout Christian life are the
most numerous, if not the most famous.[1]

The illustrious Franciscan who was Court preacher to
Charles V, and also a fervent humanist, as well known
throughout Europe as Erasmus,[2] Antonio de Guevara insists
in his *Monte Calvaria,* published in 1528, on recalling the
principles of Christian morality. His *Oratorio de religiosos,*
of 1542, is a manual of the monastic and religious life noticed
by St Teresa.[3]

One of the most appreciated popularizers of spiritual teaching is the Canon Regular, Alonzo of Orozco. An eminent
preacher and John of Castile's confessor, he was also a
master of ascetical and mystical theology. He discovered
a wealth of symbolism in his description of the highest of
spiritual states while also inspiring simple Christians with
the love of true and sound devotion. Like Francisco of
Ossuna, Bernardino of Laredo, and especially St Teresa, he
had received from God the gift of describing the manifestations of mysticism.[4]

Tratado de la Paz de l'Alma, which appeared at Alcantara in 1580,
often republished, and once more at Paris, 1912. This *Treatise* of
fifteen chapters inspired certain parts of Scupoli's *Spiritual Combat.*
I shall speak of it again under Italian Spirituality. The teaching of
the *Treatise of the Soul's Peace* seems to be as much Italian as Spanish.
Several Italian and Spanish editions of the *Spiritual Combat* contain
this *Treatise* under the title, *Sentiero del paradiso.* On John of
Bonilla, see Wadding, *Annales ordinis Minorum,* Rome, Vol. IX, p. 335;
Scriptores ord. Minorum, Rome, 1650, p. 194. Note, too, Andrew of
Ortega, O.M., *Tratado del Camino del Espiritu,* Toledo, 1550; Gabriel
de Toro, O.M., *Teulugia mistica, union del alma con Dio,* Saragossa,
1548; Diego Murillo, *Escala spiritual,* Saragossa, 1598; John of the
Angels, *Los trionfos del amor de Dios,* Medina del Campo, 1590, republished with other mystical works at Madrid, 1912-1917 (*Nueva Bibl.
de Aut. Esp.,* Vols. XX, XXIV).

[1] In 1532 appeared the *Libro de doctrina cristiana* of Gutierre
Gonzalez; in 1534 the *Soliloquios de la Passion de N. S.,* the *Desper-
tador de peccatores,* the *Ejercitatorio de la Vida spiritual,* by Orozco
presumably; in 1535, at Valencia, an *Espejo de bien vivir.*—On
Poverty, Virginity, and Mortification, see the works of an anonymous
Franciscan: the *Mysterios de la devocion,* Burgos, 1537; the *Manual
para la eterna salvacion,* Saragossa, 1539; the *Vergel de Virginidad,*
Burgos, 1539.

[2] *Cf.* Montaigne, *Essais,* II, 2.

[3] He also published the *Menosprecio de Corte y Alabanza de Aldea,*
1539, a masterpiece of humanist morality.

[4] A collection (*Recopilacion*) of Alonzo of Orozco's works appeared
at Valladolid in 1555. It comprises six treatises of various dates:
Examination of Conscience for confession; *The Orchard of Prayer and
the Mountain of Contemplation,* Seville, 1544; *The Memorial of Holy
Love; the Rule of Christian Life; Spiritual Marriage; How to follow
the Gospel.* Alonzo of Orozco published other works afterwards.

IV — THE DOMINICANS: LUIS OF GRANADA,
MELCHIOR CANO, BARTHOLOMEW OF THE
MARTYRS—ST TERESA'S DOMINICAN CON-
FESSORS

THE science of prayer was taught in a still broader and more
personal way by the Dominican Luis of Granada, one of the
most influential authors of the Spanish School.

He was born at Granada in 1505.[1] In 1524 he joined the
Dominicans of Granada in their Convent of the Holy Cross.
He was much influenced by humanism. He became familiar
with the classics, and later liked to quote the ancient philosophers, even making collections of their moral maxims.
But he delighted especially in early Christian writers. He
drew much from the Fathers of the desert, as did also the
good-natured Alfonso Rodriguez, the writer of *The Practice of Christian Perfection.*

Returning to Granada in 1534, the famous Dominican
preached so successfully that the renown of his worth at last
reached the Court of Lisbon to which he was summoned.
There he became the director of Catherine, the Regent of
Portugal. He refused the archbishopric of Braga to keep
his time and strength for the instruction of the people by
preaching and writing. He died at Lisbon in 1588.

Teaching the people! Luis of Granada devoted his life to
it. In his zeal he was alarmed by the dangers which the
people's faith incurred through their ignorance of religion.
When people know not how to pray, nor how to confess,
nor how to communicate as they ought, they run great risk,
he thought, of being seduced by the artifices of heresy.

Luis of Granada was one of the best workers in the
spiritual crusade against the Protestants and the *Alumbrados.* Preaching was his chief weapon. He gave himself
up to it with an altogether apostolic zeal. His many sermons
for the Proper of the season and for the Feasts of the
Blessed Virgin and the saints, which St Charles Borromeo
loved to quote, form the largest part of his works.[2] But

Among others, the *Vitoria del mundo,* Alcala, 1570; *Epistolario
christiano,* Alcala, 1567; *The Story of the Queen of Sheba,* or how a
Christian should serve and worship Jesus, King of Kings, Salamanca,
1575.

[1] Luis Muoz, *Vida de Fr. Luis de Granada,* Madrid, 1788; Justo
Cuervo, O.P., *Biografia de Fr. Luis de Granada,* 1896.

[2] Complete edition of his *Works,* by Denis Sanchez, Madrid, 1679;
another edition, Madrid, 1787-1800. Recent critical edition, by Justo
Cuervo, *Obras de fray Luis de Granada,* Madrid, 1906 ff., 14
vols. have hitherto appeared. French translation, by Girard, Paris,
1667; by Simon Martin, Lyons, 1677; by Abbé Bareille, *Œuvres complètes de Louis de Grenade,* 22 vols., Paris, 1862-1868.

he believed that books in the vernacular should be added to preaching. The reading of good books is the principal remedy against religious ignorance, is it not? But all did not agree with him, and the learned Dominican had later on to endure very trying contradictions on this account.

Moreover, in 1554, at Salamanca, when he published his first book of spirituality, *Libro de la Oracion y Meditation,*[1] they were beginning to be uneasy in Spain about the diffusion of false mysticism. Luis of Granada, too, was careful to confine himself strictly to asceticism, and he avoids all questions connected with extraordinary states. Only two years later, as if the better to explain his mind, he brought out at Lisbon the sequel of his study on prayer, *The Sinners' Guide,* a work of pure asceticism. Despite these precautions, the two first books by Luis of Granada were put on the Index by the Spanish Inquisition in 1559. They had to be revised and republished in 1567.

Further on we shall revert to these occurrences.

Luis of Granada is one of the first spiritual writers, after St Ignatius of Loyola, to formulate a method of prayer intended for those living in the world.[2] His aim, like that of St Ignatius, is to lead all Christians, and not only monks and religious, to the practice of prayer. Hence, he was smitten with censure; his claim to teach everyone the practice without any exceptions was then in Spain considered dangerous and likely to promote illuminism.

Like everybody at that time, Luis of Granada grieved over the inconsistency of Christian conduct and belief:

" On all sides," he writes in the Prologue of his *Libro de la Oracion y Meditation,*[3] " we find a host of people who are irreproachable in faith, but disorderly in life. . . . Their faith is like money in a cash-box, or a sword in its sheath, or medicine on a chemist's shelf—that is to say, it is not used for the purpose for which it is intended. They readily

[1] Besides the *Sermons,* the chief works of Luis of Granada are the *Libro de la Oracion y Meditation,* Salamanca, 1559; the *Guida de Pecadores;* the *Memorial de la Vida Christiana;* the *Adiciones al Memorial; the Introduccion al Simbolo de la Fé;* a translation of *The Imitation of Christ,* and of *The Ladder of Paradise* of St John Climacus; the *Life of Bartholomew of the Martyrs,* Dominican, Archbishop of Braga, and the *Life of Blessed John of Avila.*

[2] Before him, however, several works, meant for all the faithful and dealing with prayer and contemplation, had been published in Spain. In 1541 Bernal Diaz de Lugo published the *Soliloquio* at Burgos; in 1542, an anonymous *Tratado de la Oracion.* In 1544 Alonzo of Orozco published a remarkable book, the *Vergel de la Oracion y monte de contemplacion;* in 1545 Martin of Azpilcueta published a *Tratado de la Oracion* at Coimbra. These are the principal treatises of this kind, meant to popularize the practice of prayer. None of them gives such a complete method of prayer as Luis of Granada's.

[3] Bareille's translation, Vol. XI, p. 5. *Cf.* Couissinier's translation, Paris, 1868, Vol. I, p. 3.

believe in what the Church believes, in the judgement, in the punishment in store for the wicked, and in the glory which will reward the just; but they believe quite unreflectingly, and never ask themselves what this judgement and these punishments and rewards may be."

There are, according to him, two great impediments to prayer. The chief one is inexperience; we know not what to think about or how to think about it. The other is a want of fervour and devotion which makes our meditation subject to distractions and aridities.

Luis of Granada wrote his book to remedy this evil. He first provides subjects for meditation and then sets forth a method. Afterwards he shows the difficulties involved in prayer and points out the means of overcoming them.[1]

Fourteen fully elaborated subjects for meditation are proposed at the outset for one week. Two meditations are provided for each day. In the morning the subject is to be the Saviour's Passion, and in the evening it is to be on the Last Things.[2] Here the influence of the *Ejercitatorio* of Garcia de Cisneros is plain.

Then comes the method of prayer to be followed by beginners and intended to guide their inexperience; but it is not required by others. It shows " novices the way . . . ; as soon as they have started on it, the Holy Spirit will teach them the rest."[3]

The method includes six parts: preparation, reading the subject, meditation, thanksgiving, offering, and petition.

Above all, there must be preparation of the heart. " To play the vielle we must begin by tuning it." Like St Ignatius, Luis of Granada counsels us to arrange for a review of the subject the night before, " like those who have to

---

[1] Luis of Granada drew upon the *Ejercitatorio* of Garcia de Cisneros and the *Spiritual Exercises* of St Ignatius and the *Tratado de la Oracion* (Alcala, 1551) of Antonio Porras. He is also much indebted to the Italian, Serafino da Fermo, Canon Regular of St Augustine, author of the *Treatises on the Spiritual Life,* which were translated into Castilian and published at Coimbra in 1551 and at Salamanca in 1552. We shall again meet with this writer when we come to the Italian School.

[2] *Libro de la Oracion y Meditacion,* Part I, chap. ii. In the morning : Monday, the Institution of the Eucharist; Tuesday, the Agony and Seizure of Jesus; Wednesday, Jesus at the Tribunal and the Scourging; Thursday, the *Ecce Homo* and the Bearing of the Cross; Friday, the Cross and the Seven Words; Saturday, the Lance, the Descent from the Cross, Mary's Sorrow, the Burial; Sunday, the Resurrection. In the evening : Monday, Knowledge of oneself and of one's Sins; Tuesday, the Miseries of this life; Wednesday, Death; Thursday, the Last Judgement; Friday, Hell; Saturday, Heaven; Sunday, God's blessings.

[3] *Libro,* Part I, chap. iii (Bareille, Vol. XI, p. 210). Luis of Granada sums up his *Libro* in the Sixth Treatise of the *Memorial of the Christian Life.*

knead dough next morning and must get it ready the
evening before.''¹ '' As soon as we are awake, let the
thought of our prayer be the first to fill the mind. In
the morning, when we have reached the place where we are
to pray, let us think of the incomparable majesty of him with
whom we are about to converse.''² Like Garcia de Cisneros,
Luis of Granada recommends us to put ourselves in the
presence of God at the beginning of the meditation. St
Francis de Sales made this a standard practice. As a preparation for prayer, it is also quite natural to be stirred to
repentance of our sins and to humble ourselves before God,
and to ask him to give us the grace to do these things well.
On all these matters Luis of Granada gives very useful advice.

The preparation is followed by reading the subject. This
must be done '' slowly and thoughtfully, trying to grasp
with the understanding the sense of the words and to relish
with the will the truths which they express.''³ Like St
Ignatius, Luis of Granada calls into play the understanding,
the will, and the memory, but he sets them going with a
less military swing. The reading must not be long, for its
aim is to stimulate reflections and especially prayer; and it
should cease as soon as its end is reached.

The meditation after the reading may be *imaginative* or
intellectual, according to whether it has to do with subjects
such as the facts of the Life or of the Passion of Christ,
which are easily imagined, or with realities such as the divine
perfections, which simply give rise to abstract considerations.
In the former case, it is a good thing to try to reconstruct
the scene in question, while avoiding exaggeration.

The thanksgiving is a natural consequence of the meditation. It is fitting to thank God for blessings which are most
closely connected with the subject of the meditation, and
also for all others which he has given us.

The duty of thanksgiving induces us to offer God, as a
proof of our gratitude, all that we have received from him.
This makes the Offering.⁴ To begin with, the Christian may
offer himself, along with all he has and is, to do the divine
will in all things. Next, in order to pay his debt of gratitude for the Lord's goodness, he may offer the merits and

---

¹ *Libro,* Part I, chap. iv (Bareille, p. 214).
² *Libro,* Part I, chap. iv, p. 211. Cf. *Memorial,* Treatise VI,
chap. iv.
³ *Libro,* Part I, chap. v, pp. 214-215.
⁴ Luis of Granada is silent as to this part of prayer in his *Libro.*
He added it, later on, in his compendium of it, and inserted it in
the Sixth Treatise of the *Memorial.* In his *Libro,* Luis only gives five
parts of prayer. The thanksgiving is immediately followed by the
petition. St Peter of Alcantara, in his *Treatise on Prayer,* sets forth
the six parts thus : Preparation, Reading, Meditation, Thanksgiving,
Offering, and Petition (Part II, chaps. v-xi).

works of Christ : they have become our own merits, and,
therefore, they are at our disposal.

" In return for so rich an offering, we can boldly turn to
the Lord and present our petitions to him." Our first request
will concern his glory ; may all the nations of the world know
and praise and adore him as their one and only God.   Then
we shall pray for the whole of the Church, and, lastly, for
ourselves and for our own particular needs.   We shall ask
for the necessary help against our passions and vices, and
for grace to keep our resolutions and to love God ever more
and more.   Luis of Granada constantly warns the Christian
against all selfish prayer.   Moreover, true prayer is not only
asking ; it also includes adoration, praise, and thanksgiving.

It is not enough to know how to pray in order to give
oneself up to prayer.   Want of devotion, as well as inexperience, may be an impediment.   In the sixth part of his
treatise, Luis of Granada has a profound study of devotion,
which is made use of by St Francis de Sales.   True devotion,
he says, is not " an affection of the heart poured out in
prayer," but " a quickness and readiness to do it well, and
to fulfil the commandments of God, and to do his service."[1]
It is important to know what is hurtful to him, and to be
able to baffle the wiles of the devil, the great enemy of the
devout.   We shall thus overcome the second impediment
which may give us a distaste for prayer, the loss of devotion
and spiritual fervour.[2]

Luis of Granada completes his ascetic teaching in his
famous *Sinners' Guide* (*Guia de Pecadores*).   It is a manual
of Christian virtues.[3]   It contains sound doctrine as to the
reasons for practising virtue, as to the spiritual and temporal
blessings to be looked for from a virtuous life, and as to the
excuses of those who choose evil.   It shows how to conquer
various failings, and man's duties to himself and to his neighbours and to God are clearly laid down.   It is a lofty teaching applying to all Christians, no doubt, but more especially
to those who aim at perfection, and it is set forth with width
of view and in fine humanistic style.

[1] *Libro,* Part II, chap. i (Bareille, pp. 250-251).

[2] In editions subsequent to 1566, Luis of Granada adds a third part
to his *Libro.*   Therein he deals with the profitableness and the necessity
of prayer, and with perseverance in it, and then with fasting and
almsgiving, " the wings which enable prayer to soar up to heaven."

[3] Similar works were written before that of Luis of Granada : In
1543, at Medina, the *Tesoro de virtudes,* by the Franciscan, Alonso de
la Isla ; in 1545, at Valladolid, the *Remedio de Pecadores,* by Juan
de Duenos ; and in the same year and in the same town the celebrated
Peter of Medina published the *Libro de la Verdad sobre la Conversion
del Pecador;* in 1550, at Valladolid, the *Victoria de si mismo,*
by Melchior Cano ; and in 1551 the *Danza de la Muerte,* by an anonymous Franciscan ; and in the same year the *Guia del Cielo,* by Pablo de
Leon.

The *Sinners' Guide* met with great success and made its author famous. The Inquisition put it on the Index, but that only checked its circulation for a time. In the seventeenth century the *Sinners' Guide* was in everyone's hands in France.[1] Of all the works by Luis of Granada, this is the one most readily recommended by St Francis de Sales.

In his spiritual teaching Luis of Granada always strove to be practical. He did not aim at being a theorist in spirituality, but a preacher of the Christian life. To set men free from sin and to lead them on to perfection was his sole ambition. He thought that a book which gave a compendium of ascetic teaching, " a complete and summary explanation of all that is needed for the heavenly life of the Christian,"[2] would fulfil the pious yearnings of his zeal. This book he wrote : it is his *Memorial of the Christian Life:*

" My design," he says in the Prologue, " is to form the perfect Christian, to lead him through the exercises of the Christian life from the beginning of his conversion up to the highest perfection. I take him in hand in the rough just as a workman takes a tree with its bark and its branches to turn it into a work of art worthy of unstinted praise."[3]

The circumstances in which Luis of Granada wrote did not allow him to linger over mysticism. He is, above all, an ascetic writer.[4] Nevertheless, in his *Libro de la Oracion* he gives the prayer of recollection and quietude as the desirable goal of many years of meditation :

" By abandoning all speculation and all reasoning, they (some Christians) establish their intelligence and their will in God, and they do all they can solely to enjoy the sovereign good. This state is the state of contemplation, which is the most perfect kind of prayer and the extreme goal of our endeavours. Contemplation does not strive to kindle love. With regard thereto, it is at the summit of its desire, and its one anxiety is fully to enjoy him whom it loves. . . . In contemplation there are at the same time both less effort and more enjoyment and profit. The work of meditation is

---

[1] French translation by Guillaume Girard, Paris, 1658. In the *Ecole des Femmes,* Molière makes Sganarelle say : " The *Sinners' Guide* is another good book; it does not take you long to learn how to live well from it."

[2] *Memorial,* Prologue.

[3] The *Memorial* comprises seven treatises : the Last Things ; Penance, Confession, and Satisfaction ; Holy Communion ; How to resist Sin and Temptation ; Prayer in general ; Prayer (*Oraison*) ; Love of God.

[4] At the beginning of the sixteenth century, when mystical works were more favourably regarded, a Dominican, Jerome of Alcozer, wrote a mystical work on the lines of that of Bernardino de Laredo, *Subida del Monte Sion,* Valentia, 1509.

excluded from it, and therewith a great deal of weariness of the flesh. The delight of deep recollection abides.''[1]

What a remarkable mystical writer Luis of Granada would have been had he lived in a less disturbed age! But he followed his zealous inspiration with much self-abnegation, and this bound him not to go beyond the region of asceticism. Moreover, he united with his intellectual gifts a gentle and conciliatory temperament ever ready to give way in the interest of peace.

Of a very different character was his illustrious colleague, Melchior Cano.[2] Zealous and irritable, incapable of enduring contradiction, impassioned in his views, Melchior Cano was often carried away beyond measure in his decisions and proceedings :

"I am greatly wanting in prudence and discretion," he humbly confesses. "Every day I catch myself tripping times innumerable in what I do and say, and I am no wiser one day than another. If I sometimes chance to get a good notion of what I ought to do at a particular juncture, it is generally not at the happy moment, but too late."[3]

He was one of the most ardent adversaries of the *Alumbrados*. But always intemperate, even in the best of his undertakings, he included true and sound mysticism in his reprobation of the false mystics. He saw illuminism in all directions ! Even ascetic books, if they were written in popular language, fell under suspicion ; and therefore he became the evil genius of the Grand Inquisitor Fernando de Valdes.

Though but a poor mystic, Melchior was a theologian of the first rank. Like his master, Francisco de Vitoria (†1546),[4] and even beyond his master, he was a reformer of theological studies. The humanists, as we know, had passionately attacked scholastic theology, which they found totally lacking in scientific spirit and written in a barbarous

---

[1] *Libro de la Oracion*, Part II, chap. v (Bareille, vol. xi, p. 398). Cf. *Guia de Pecadores*, Book I, chap. iv.

[2] Born at Tarancon in Spain in 1508. He was a professor of the University of Alcala (1542-1546), and then of Salamanca (1546-1552). In 1551 he was at the Council of Trent. In 1552 he was nominated to the bishopric of the Canaries, but did not take possession of the See. He died at Toledo in 1560. Fermin Caballero, *Vida del Illmo Fray Melchior Cano del Orden de Santo Domingo*, Madrid, 1871-1876.

[3] A kind of examination of conscience made by Melchior Cano in 1559 to convince himself that he ought not to accept the office of confessor of Philip II at the Court of Brussels. Caballero, *Vida*, p. 629. Translation by Mandonnet, *La victoire sur soi-même*, by Melchior Cano, Paris, 1823, pp. 21-22.

[4] Cf. Getino, O.P., *El Maestro Fr. Francisco de Vitoria y el renacimento filosofico teologico del siglo XVI*, Madrid, 1914.

style. It had to be rehabilitated in their eyes by giving it
a broader method, which would employ the newly restored
scriptural and patristic literature and enable it to make use
of noble language. This work was brilliantly begun by
Melchior Cano in his classic treatise *De locis theologicis*.[1]
The true theological method, alike positive and speculative,
was therein formulated and followed with a noteworthy
mastery according to the requirements of the humanists,
and in Latin of the highest elegance. Thus did the sacred
science recover the prestige which it had lost for over a
century. Henceforward, it could measure itself to advantage
with Protestant heresy.

Strange to tell, this fierce adversary of spiritual works in
the vulgar tongue left behind him a little ascetical treatise
in Spanish : *On the Conquest of Oneself*.[2] It is, however,
a publication with nothing dangerous in it. It is a treatise
against the seven capital sins, an adaptation of an Italian
book by the Dominican Battista da Crema.[3] It contains
nothing about the sensible or spiritual consolations of devotion. Except in the last chapter on the Crucifix, " the
universal remedy for all sins," which is fairly affective in
spirit, the book contains nothing but remarks on how to
discover our vices and counsels for overcoming them :

" The title of the book," writes Cano in the Prologue,
" is *On the Conquest of Oneself*—that is to say, of one's
own vices and passions; a conquest which is not so hard
as many people fancy. . . .

" Seeing how few books written in Spanish give such
teaching in a competent manner, I have decided to face the
fatigue of a few days' toil to write this treatise, the best part
of which I have taken from the Italian in which I found it
written by a man of great good sense and of great courage
in spiritual warfare. In it the reader will find the origin
and the cause of all our vices and the signs whereby they
may be recognized; he will find the remedies and medicines
most suited to each malady; he will find in what cases the
seven capital sins are mortal and in what cases they are
venial, and this, as I know, has not as yet been put in

---

[1] Published at Salamanca in 1563 after the author's death, and often
reissued. *Cf.* M. Jacquin, O.P., *Melchior Cano et la théologie moderne,*
in the *Revue des sciences philosophiques et théologiques,* 1920,
pp. 121-141.
[2] *De la vitoria de si mismo,* Valladolid, 1550. Often republished.
French translation by Maurice Legendre, Preface by P. Mandonnet,
Paris, 1923.
[3] John Baptist Carioni, generally known as Battista da Crema
(†1534), published *Le livre de la connaissance et victoire de soi-même,*
Milan, 1531. In 1538 Serafino da Fermo put an abridgement of this
book in his collection of *Traités de la vie spirituelle.* Battista da
Crema's Italian text was abridged by Melchior Cano. I shall refer to
Battista da Crema later on.

writing in the Spanish language. And this is as necessary
for penitents as well as for confessors as any other work
that could be written.''[1]

We shall come back to Melchior Cano again later on. His
work of antimystical reaction in Spain is of greater interest
to the history of spirituality than the little book *On the
Conquest of Oneself.*

The Venerable Bartholomew of the Martyrs (†1590) is
more celebrated for his action at the Council of Trent and
for his pastoral zeal in his diocese of Braga in Portugal
than for his spiritual writings. However, his *Compendium
vitae spiritualis*[2] contains a very good summary of spiritual
doctrine. It is a very practical book, which still further
extends the pastoral influence of the holy archbishop.

The Order of St Dominic had the signal honour of giving
St Teresa three confessors who directed her in the extra-
ordinary ways in which God used to lead her : Pedro Ibanez,
Dominico Bañez, and Garcia de Toledo.

Pedro Ibanez made his profession in the monastery of
Salamanca, and was teacher of theology in the convent of
Avila when St Teresa had recourse to his wisdom in 1560
and 1561. " He was at that time the most eminent theologian
in the town," she says, " and, in his Order, he had very
few superiors.''[3] Teresa, then in the monastery of the Incarnation at Avila, had framed her plan of reforming the
Carmelite Order and of founding the convent of St Joseph
of Avila. She talked of her plan to Pedro Ibanez.[4] A few
months later she made known to him all that was taking
place within her soul, to obtain his advice :

" I revealed to him," she says, " as clearly as I could,
all the visions I had had, my manner of prayer, and the great
graces which God was giving me, begging him to examine
everything seriously to see whether there was anything in
it contrary to Holy Scripture, so as to tell me what he
thought of it. He greatly reassured me.''[5]

Pedro Ibanez asked Teresa to give him a full account of
her life.[6] In 1563 or 1564 he wrote a report on the interior
ways of the saint, and after setting forth the traditional rules
for the discernment of spirits he concludes, " with all those
who have been consulted on the subject " that Teresa " was

[1] *La victoire sur soi-même,* Paris, 1923, pp. 36-37.
[2] Published at Lisbon, 1582, then at Venice, 1711, under the title
Compendium mysticae doctrinae, then at Rome, 1744. Le Maistre de
Sacy has published his *Life.*
[3] *Life,* chap. xxxii.　　　　　　*ibid.* and chap. xxxiii.
[5] *Life,* chap. xxxiii.
[6] St Teresa made then, in 1562, the first narrative of her life, which
was shorter than the one we have, and it has disappeared.

certainly led by the Spirit of God," and that the supernatural effects within her soul were "kept free from all illusion."[1]

Ibanez grew greatly in sanctity through his intimate relations with Teresa, and rapidly advanced in the extraordinary ways of the interior life. When he died at Trianos in 1565, the saint knew by revelation that, like St Peter of Alcantara and the Carmelite Diego-Matthias, he had gone to heaven without passing through purgatory.[2]

Celebrated in a very different way from Ibanez was his brother in religion, Dominico Bañez,[3] author of the theory of *physical predetermination*, at any rate as it was afterwards taught by the Dominicans, to reconcile man's free will with grace and the divine prescience. A man of superior mind, both gentle and firm in character, Bañez rendered St Teresa the most signal services. In 1562 he came to the Dominican convent of Avila, just when the monastery of the reformed Carmelites of St Joseph, but lately founded, was on the point of destruction. He saved Teresa's first foundation from ruin.[4] During the six years that he remained at Avila he was confessor to the saint and to her religious.[5] With his brother Dominican, Garcia de Toledo,[6] he asked Teresa to make a second edition of the *Book of her Life,* revised and completed. Then, in 1565, he ordered her to write *The Way of Perfection.* It was Bañez who revised the *Book of her Life;* at the order of the Inquisitors, he made an official examination of it at Valladolid in 1575.

We have the report which he made after this examination.[7] It was just the time when the false mysticism of the *Alumbrados* was at its height. Bañez begins by praising the book.

"In it I have found nothing," he says, "which, in my judgement, is erroneous. On the contrary, one finds in it much that is edifying and profitable to people of prayer.

---

[1] Ibanez's report is lost. Yepes quotes a few fragments from it in the Prologue of his *Life of St Teresa.* See *Œuvres complètes de sainte Térèse,* Ed. Polit, Vol. II, pp. 417-419.

[2] *Life of St Teresa by Herself,* chap. xxxviii.

[3] Born at Medina del Campo in 1528, Bañez entered the Dominican Order at the age of nineteen. He taught at Alcala, at Valladolid, and at Salamanca. He died at the convent of Medina del Campo in 1604. He wrote commentaries on the *Summa* of St Thomas.

[4] *Life of St Teresa by Herself,* chap. xxxvi.

[5] *Spiritual Relations of St Teresa,* n. liii.

[6] Garcia de Toledo advised Teresa to divide the *Book of her Life* into chapters. In her narrative she mostly addresses him. He examined the book with Bañez, but as her own confessor. Garcia de Toledo, belonging to the family of the Counts of Oropesa, went to the Indies in 1535 with the Viceroy Antonio de Mendoza and entered the Dominican Order. He had to do with St Teresa from 1562 to 1569. Provincial of Peru in 1577, he returned to Spain in 1569, and died in the convent at Talavera a few years later.

[7] *Œuvres complètes de sainte Térèse,* Vol. II, pp. 164-168.

Owing to her long experience, her prudence, and that humility which has made her have constant recourse to the enlightenment and knowledge of her confessors, she expresses herself on these matters of prayer with an accuracy which the best theologians do not always attain for want of experience."

Then come certain reservations demanded still more by the circumstances than by the prudence of the censor.

One point seems to claim his most careful consideration, " the revelations and visions which the book affords in great numbers." It is not in these that we must " place sanctity." They are, " on the other hand, a perilous reef for those who tend towards perfection, for Satan often changes himself into an angel of light and seduces such as are full of curiosity and devoid of humility : we have seen many examples of this in our own days." Bañez affirms that no one was more incredulous than himself as to the visions and revelations of Teresa, although he is inclined to think that they " might be the work of God, as in the case of some other saints." But he has better criteria for the appreciation of the sanctity of his penitent. He has subjected her to hard trials. He has " long put to the proof her sincerity, her obedience, her penance, her patience, her charity towards her persecutors, and her other virtues." She has always been admirable. Moreover, her undertaking to reform the Carmelite nuns is altogether in her favour. Bañez ends by declaring : " This book is not of such a kind as to be given to everybody, but only to men of knowledge, of experience, and of Christian wisdom."

V—BLESSED JOHN OF AVILA

SIMILAR reservations are to be found in the otherwise encouraging letter written by Blessed John of Avila[1] to St Teresa on the *Book of her Life*. We realize that at the time false mysticism was haunting everybody's mind. Teresa, too, was as alarmed as everyone else, and feared illusion ; she therefore took one step after another to get John of Avila's opinion about the special ways in which God was leading her.[2] She obtained it ; and it gave her his most reassuring approbation.[3]

[1] John of Avila, the apostle of Andalusia, did not belong to any religious congregation. He was born on January 6, 1500, at Almodovar del Campo. He studied at Salamanca and at Alcala. On the death of his parents, he distributed his goods amongst the poor, was ordained priest and devoted himself to preaching in Andalusia. He was beatified by Leo XIII on April 6, 1894. Among the *Works* of Luis of Granada, see the *Vida del venerabile maestro Juan d'Avila*. There is another *Life,* by Martin Ruis, Madrid, 1618.

[2] *Œuvres de sainte Térèse*, Vol. I, pp. 12-17.

[3] *id.*, Vol. II, pp. 159-163.

Nevertheless, several passages in his letter must have left Teresa in great anxiety.

"The book is not written," she read, "for the handling of many. . . . Certain things which may have been profitable to your own spiritual progress would not be so for those who might desire to seize upon them, for the particular ways whereby God leads some are not suited to others. . . . Inward voices have deceived many in our own times. Those from without are the least reliable. To perceive that the words are not the outcome of our own minds is easy; but to ascertain whether they come from the good or from the evil spirit, that is much harder. . . . Imaginary and corporal visions are the most dubious. They are not at all to be desired: they must be evaded as much as possible."

In his preaching, as in his books, John of Avila put the faithful on their guard against false mysticism as much as against Protestant heresy. To instruct the ignorant, to convert sinners, to exhort to the practice of perfection, to keep souls from sin, and to sanctify the clergy, such was the aim of his zeal. He restored to virtue a large number of those who had gone astray. He won Francis Borgia and John of God[1] to the religious life. Most of those who were eminent for sanctity in Spain during the sixteenth century had some relations with him. His authority was universally accepted and his guidance was much sought after. He wrote many letters addressed to all conditions of people, from dignitaries of the Church to the humblest of the faithful.[2] To all he gave the most appropriate advice proceeding from a heart burning with zeal for the sanctification of souls. His letters may be compared with those of St Francis de Sales.

John of Avila was raised to the highest of mystical states. To a rare degree he possessed the gift of the discernment of spirits. According to the testimony of St Peter of Alcantara, no one surpassed him in the knowledge of the spiritual ways.

His principal work, *Audi filia et vide*,[3] aims at leading the Christian through difficulties inherent in human nature or

[1] St John of God was born in 1495 at Montemajor-el-Novo in Portugal. His family was very poor. He was converted by one of John of Avila's sermons. He devoted himself to the service of the sick and founded a hostel at Granada. This was a model for all the rest. He instituted the *Order of Charity*, and died in 1550. Pope Pius V approved of the new Order, and gave its religious the Rule of St Augustine. *Acta SS.*, March 8. Cf. *Vie populaire de S Jean de Dieu*, by P. Ignace-Marie Magnin, Paris-Lille, 1887.

[2] Four books of *Spiritual Letters* are in the *Works* of John of Avila (French translation, 1588). His *Complete Works* were published at Madrid in 1618 by Martin Ruiz (French translation, Paris, 1673).

[3] *Esposicion del verso: Audi filia*, 1556, was first published without John of Avila's consent. He composed this mystical commentary for devout persons under his direction. He refrained from publishing it through fear of the Inquisition.

characteristic of the Spanish mentality at the time, and to help him to attain to the topmost heights of perfection. It is a mystical commentary on Psalm xliv, 11, 12 : " Hearken, O daughter, and see, and incline thy ear : forget thy people and thy father's house; and the King shall greatly desire thy beauty."

The Christian soul, the daughter of whom the Psalmist speaks, hears at first the various voices which must be despised : voices of the world, of the flesh, and of the devil. She must also close her ears to the words of heretics who, like the impious Luther, claim the right to reform the Church in order to restore her so-called primitive perfection.[1] Above all must she distrust the *Alumbrados,* the enemies of true devotion. They have tried to discover new ways of going to God, and shorter ways in their opinion. They imagine that it is enough to abandon themselves entirely to the Lord to be led by his Spirit. Hence they are so blind that they take their own notions for God's and do things against his commandments as if they were inspired by the Holy Ghost. John advises people not to desire revelations, visions, and other extraordinary things.[2]

Having put aside all hindrances to the Christian life, the soul must try to acquire self-knowledge. She will then devote herself to prayer and meditation, without which it is hard to acquire sanctity.[3] John of Avila's method of prayer resembles Luis of Granada's. Above all he would have us cleave to Jesus and contemplate him almost entirely in prayer. For when we consider ourselves, we find ourselves so imperfect that we are inclined to be discouraged. Let us then consider the highest of all beauty, which is Christ. Let us further take comfort because Jesus hearkens to us and looks upon us after we have listened to and regarded ourselves. By prayer the Christian soul thus enters into familiar communion with the Saviour. When she has renounced self-will and has been exercised in the practice of love, she will recover all her beauty, and the King will greatly desire her.[4]

---

[1] *Audi filia,* chaps. xxx-xlxx.   [2] *ibid.,* chaps. l-lv.

[3] *ibid.,* chaps. lxix-lxxxv.

[4] John of Ávila wrote several other little treatises or discourses : a discourse upon the need of having no will but God's ; two discourses on the priesthood and on the sanctity required for it ; a discourse on the love of God ; two collections of counsels for living a Christian life, both censured by the Inquisition. It is in the first of these collections that we find the passage upon the subject of a director which so much interested St Francis de Sales : " If God grants us the grace of meeting one [a good director] amongst a thousand. . . ." Cf. *The Devout Life,* Part I, chap. iv : " Choose one out of a thousand, says Avila ; and I say, one out of ten thousand. . . ."

VI—THE VIOLENT REACTION OF THE SPANISH INQUISITION AGAINST THE FALSE MYSTICISM OF THE "ALUMBRADOS"—THE ANTI-MYSTICAL REACTION

THIS wonderful blossoming of spiritual literature was cut short by the Inquisition.

Its task was a very hard one. Protestantism was endeavouring to enter into Spain. The *Alumbrados* held out a helping hand. Illuminism and false mysticism were filtering into the popular mind. At Cordova in 1544, Madeleine of the Cross, a Poor Clare, had a great reputation for sanctity.[1] Miracles were attributed to her. Her confessors ordered her to write her life and to give an account of the extraordinary graces with which she was favoured. But all of a sudden it turned out that it was all imposture, and that the miserable creature had sold her soul to the devil. Later on, a Dominican nun of Lisbon, Mary of the Incarnation, who simulated ecstasies and stigmata, took advantage of the honest confidence of Luis of Granada.

Reaction was certainly demanded to stop the evil. The Grand Inquisitor, Fernando de Valdes, Archbishop of Seville, began the work of purification by publishing the Index of Toledo in 1551.[2] It has the Protestants especially in view. The Index generally forbids the reading of any version " of the Bible in Castilian or any other vulgar tongue." All heterodox texts are prohibited, and Jewish and Lutheran Bibles or any others circulating in the kingdom.

This first blow was ineffective. Heresy and illuminism went on with their ravages. And then it was that, to put a stop to them more surely, it was decided to condemn any book that seemed in the least suspicious: book of Hours, treatise of spirituality, or manual of devotional practices.

Here Melchior Cano comes upon the scene.

About 1556 and 1557, in preaching at Valladolid against the Protestants and the *Alumbrados,* he also appeared to have the mystics in view. Moreover, according to him, in the circumstances of the time any devotional work in the language of the people was dangerous. Even simple explanations of the Catechism had their disadvantages.

In 1558 there appeared at Brussels the *Commentarios al Catecismo Cristiano* by Cardinal Carranza, Dominican and Archbishop of Toledo.[3] It was an excellent and entirely

[1] Menendez y Pelayo, *Heterodoxos Españoles,* II, p. 528.
[2] It is the Index of Louvain of 1546, republished at Toledo with a list of books forbidden by Fernando de Valdès.
[3] *Cf.* A. Tournon, *Histoires des hommes illustres de l'ordre de S Dominique,* Paris, 1743-1749, Vol. IV, Book XXIX.

practical work, a simple exposition of Christian doctrine in a form easy for all to understand. Was the Cardinal under suspicion? In any case the book was delated for trial to the Inquisition. Melchior Cano[1] was charged with the examination of it, and made a very unfavourable report. He found in it statements which were almost Lutheran! Especially were the explanations given in it much more suited, he said, to priests than to simple layfolk. Was it not the tendency of the *illuminati* and false mystics to reveal to everyone whatever is mysterious in Catholic doctrine? The book was condemned, and people were astounded to learn that the pious and learned Cardinal had been flung into the prisons of the Inquisition. Pope Pius IV could not obtain his discharge until after several years of insistence.

Decidedly, the Grand Inquisitor meant to strike dreadful blows in order to impress the people and to turn them away from error. If anyone went too far, so much the worse for him, provided that heresy and false mysticism were exterminated from Spain! They attacked even the wisest spiritual writers if they had written in Spanish.

Melchior Cano reproached his fellow Dominican, Luis of Granada, with desiring to lead all the faithful systematically to mystical prayer. Would it not fling them all into illuminism? He also thought that Granada's books were too full of sentimentality and of tendencies too much like those of the *Alumbrados*. Besides, all books that popularized mysticism were considered very dangerous and capable of promoting unhealthy illusions. Their reading must be forbidden.

Urged on by Melchior Cano, Fernando de Valdès issued the famous Index of 1559[2] at Valladolid. To the books already prohibited in 1551 was added a long list of works mostly written by authors of irreproachable orthodoxy. Besides Carranza's book, it included three works by Luis of Granada,[3] one by Francis Borgia,[4] one by John of Avila,[5] and the spiritual writings of Jorge de Montemayor. The reading of Eckhart, of the Institutions of Tauler, of the

---

[1] See *Vida*, by F. Caballero. Dominic de Soto (†1560), O.P., was charged with the examination of Carranza's book. He was a counsellor of the Grand Inquisitor. On this anti-mystical reaction, see Colunga, O.P., *Ciencia tomista*, May, July, November, 1914. A. Saudreau, *Le mouvement antimystique en Espagne au XVIe siècle* in the *Revue du Clergé français*, August 1, 1917, Vol. XCI, pp. 193 ff.

[2] *Catalogus librorum qui prohibentur mandato Illustrissimi et Reverendissimi D. D. Fernandi de Valdes, Hispalen. Archiepiscopi, Inquisitoris generalis Hispaniae*, Pinciæ, 1559. Reprint by Huntington, New York.

[3] *Libro de la Oracion y Meditacion; Guida de Pecadores; The Manual of divers Prayers and spiritual Exercises.* Luis appealed to the Council of Trent, which approved his *Libro*.

[4] *Obras del Cristiano.*   [5] *Aviso y reglas cristianas.*

Mystical Theology of Harphius, and of Dionysius the Carthusian's treatise on the Last Things was also forbidden.
The works of the " Mystics of the North " were considered
specially pernicious.[1]

This excessive reaction is explained by the end in view :
but it profoundly grieved the mystics. St Teresa wrote about
these condemnations.

" When the reading of a good many Spanish books was
prohibited, I was very sorry for it, since many of them gave
me pleasure, and henceforth I found myself deprived of them,
as they might only be read in Latin."[2]

A real panic spread among the writers of spiritual books.[3]
It was the rout of the mystics. Woe to him who dared to
write ! Luis de Leon, the famous Augustinian, having translated at the request of a nun the *Canticle of Canticles*, was
denounced to the Inquisition and imprisoned for five years.

By what miracle did the *Spiritual Exercises* of St Ignatius
of Loyola escape the Index of 1559? Opposition to the
Exercises was manifested, as we know, at Alcala and at
Salamanca, as soon as they began to be followed. Ignatius
finally left Spain in 1535, and his departure caused the attacks
to slacken, but about 1540, when his disciples returned,
prejudice against the *Exercises* revived and became more
violent than ever.

The papal approbation of the *Exercises* by Paul III in
1548 might have been expected to calm people's minds ; but
at that time the absolute power of the Inquisition was entirely
subject to Philip II, and the approbation and examinations of
Rome were but " feeble arguments " in Spain.[4] In any case,
they did not prevent the violent opposition of Melchior Cano.

As soon as the Jesuits returned to Salamanca, the terrible
Dominican, who was a professor there, started a campaign.
Both in his correspondence and in his still famous Memorandum[5] he unsparingly attacked Ignatius and his companions, those " latter-day seducers who delude the world."
The controversial amenities of the period swarm from his
pen ! According to him, the *Exercises* are " diabolical
artifices," and encourage illuminism ![6] Invective passed into

---

[1] These works had been translated into Spanish ; hence the reading
of them was forbidden.

[2] *Life,* chap. xxvi, *Œuvres,* Vol. I, p. 333.

[3] In 1565 there appeared a few rare works of ascetic theology ;
amongst others, De Montoya's *Obras de los que aman a Dios* at Lisbon.
Several treatises by Alonzo of Orozco were published from 1565 to 1570.

[4] *Monumenta historica Societatis Jesu, Epistolae mixtae,* Vol. III,
p. 666.

[5] Cf. *Crisis de la Compañia de Jesus,* Barcelona, 1900, pp. 152-159.

[6] In the sixteenth century the *Exercises* were considered conducive to
illuminism, and since then they have been said to bar the ways of
mysticism.

action : the Archbishop of Toledo, John Martinez Guijeño, appointed a commission to examine the *Exercises,* and it censured them as tainted with illuminism.[1]

These exaggerations issued in results contrary to those desired. Ignatius and his companions endured these unjust attacks without replying, and were content to countering them with the approbation of Rome. By degrees passions were allayed, and the *Exercises* escaped the Index of 1559.

These events naturally gave rise to a somewhat lively conflict between the theologians and the spiritual authors.

In 1562, when St Teresa consulted St Peter of Alcantara on her project—opposed by the theologians[2]—of founding monasteries in utter poverty, the famous Franciscan replied with energy :

" I assure you that I was very surprised to find you were referring to the judgement of theologians a question with which they have nothing to do. If matters of law or cases of conscience were at stake, it would be right to take the opinions of jurists or of theologians ; but when it is a question of perfection, we have only to consult those who practise it. Usually, indeed, conscience and pious dispositions are in harmony with the works that men do."[3]

Luis of Granada, in the new editions of his *Guia de Pecadores,* wrote prologues " in reply to certain persons, whose words are not lacking in gravity and who reject even good books in the vulgar tongue for the use of those who know not Latin."[4]

St Teresa, convinced " of the insufficiency of man's strength to quench the fire of heresy," recommended her religious in 1565 to pray for the defenders of the faith, in order, she acutely added, " that amongst so great a number of doctors and religious, many may be found possessed of . . . the qualities needed for the fulfilment of their mission, and that the Lord may give such dispositions to those who are as yet not fully endowed with them, seeing that one perfect man will do more than a large number of others who are not so."[5]

As long as she had put nothing into writing, the Inquisitors

---

[1] A. Astrain, *Historia de la Compañia de Jesus en la Asistencia de España,* Madrid, 1902, Vol. I, pp. 323-325, 367 ff. ; Polanco, *Chronicon Societatis Jesu,* Vol. III, pp. 503 ff. P. Brou gives a summary of the facts in *Les Exercices spirituels de saint Ignace de Loyola,* Paris, 1922, pp. 59 ff.

[2] *Life,* chap. xxxv.

[3] *Œuvres de sainte Térèse,* Vol. II, p. 420.

[4] Bareille, Vol. X, p. 15.

[5] *The Way of Perfection,* chap. iii. Cf. *Spiritual Relations,* Relation iii, *Œuvres,* II, p. 218.

did not alarm her;[1] yet she suffered indirectly from their exaggerated zeal. Fear of the Holy Office often led her confessors to subject her to hard trials, especially when she was beginning to receive extraordinary graces. To these trials the saint discreetly alludes, sometimes with severity, in the *Book of her Life* and the *Way of Perfection*.

" I have sustained considerable [harm]," she says in her *Life*,[2] " owing to the excessive fears to which some minds are liable.

" Among other things, this is what has happened to me. There was a meeting of a certain number of men of God, in whom I had much confidence, and that on just grounds. Yet I opened my mind to but one confessor, and only spoke to any others on his orders; but these conversed with one another about my spiritual interests, and as they were very devoted to me, they feared lest I might have illusions. . . . I believe there were five or six of them, all great servants of God. My confessor warned me that in their opinion the devil was the cause of what was taking place within me : according to them, I ought to receive Holy Communion less often and to seek distraction by shunning solitude. . . . These men were far more virtuous than I was, and, moreover, good theologians : how could I help believing them? I did my best to adopt their opinions. . . .

" A prey to desolation, I left the church [of the Jesuit College] and withdrew to an oratory. For some time I had been deprived of Holy Communion as well as of the solitude which was my whole joy. Further, I had no one to whom I could open my heart, since everyone was against me."

This attitude on the part of Teresa's confessors was not only inspired by the desire to " try her spirit." Mixed up in the conflict which stirred the peninsula, many may have been prejudiced by the surrounding hostility towards mysticism. They were " always distrustful."[3]

But St Teresa had to suffer still further from the Inquisition. In 1575 she was told that the *Book of her Life*, copies of which were being circulated against her will, had just been denounced to the Holy Office. She was alarmed about it, not on her own account, but for the sake of her foundations,

---

[1] Cf. *Life*, chap. xxxiii : " They came to tell me in much alarm that the times were evil, that some accusation might well be made against me, and that I might be delated to the Inquisitors. This idea seemed to me quite charming, and it made me burst out laughing. . . . So I answered that they need not worry : my soul would be in a very bad state if I had any reason to fear the Inquisition."

[2] *Life*, chap. xxv. Cf. *Life*, chap. xxviii; *Way of Perfection*, chap. v. The happenings in chap. xxv occurred at Avila, where Teresa was at the Monastery of the Incarnation.

[3] *Interior Castle*, Fifth Mansion, chap. i, *Œuvres*, VI, p. 133. Cf. *Foundations*, chap. viii.

which were fully prospering. " To incur the indignation of the Inquisitors was at the same time to incur the indignation of Philip II."[1] What was to become of the incipient reform? Happily the Dominican Bañez reported favourably on the book, and no condemnation occurred.

VII—TRIALS OF THE JESUIT BALTHAZAR ALVAREZ

THESE suspicions of mysticism were maintained by the persistence of false mysticism. Neither the Index of 1551, nor that of 1559, nor the *autos-da-fé* had been able to banish the *Alumbrados* from the peninsula. The cynicism and immorality of the sectaries, put on record once more in 1578 at Llerena, surpass all imagination. The Inquisition was acting rigorously. The superiors of religious communities were exercising keen watchfulness to keep their subjects from illuminism; and, as always in such circumstances, this watchfulness sometimes grew vexatious. It was particularly so in the case of Balthazar Alvarez.[2]

At the age of twenty-five, this Jesuit was charged with the direction of St Teresa just when she was entering upon the most extraordinary phase of her life. Though he was as prudent as the most sagacious of theologians, he could not refrain from criticisms.

First of all, he would not tolerate any imperfection in his penitent who was called to a high degree of sanctity. He asked her to give up " certain friendships which did not at all offend God,"[3] but which hindered her yearning for perfection. Having also remarked her too great eagerness in her enterprises, he desired to cure it.

" Once the saint, being very busy, wrote him a letter, while he was away from Avila, asking him for a speedy reply ' because she was tired out.' Father Balthazar, considering that it was more important to mortify her and to moderate

---

[1] For all this, see *Œuvres de sainte Térèse,* Vol. I, pp. 22 ff.

[2] Born in 1533 at Cervera in Spain, he entered among the Jesuits at the age of twenty-two. Ordained priest in 1558, next year he became the Minister of the College of Avila and was charged with the direction of St Teresa. He directed her for six years. In 1566 he became Novice-master and Rector of Medina del Campo, then Procurator of the Province of Castile at Rome in 1571, Rector of Salamanca in 1574, Rector of Villagarcia in 1577, Visitor of the Province of Aragon in 1579, Provincial of Toledo in 1580, the year of his death. Luis de la Puente, *Vida del V. F. Balthasar Alvarez,* Madrid, re-edited in 1880 by P. de la Torre (new ed., Madrid, 1921) with appendices; French translation by Bouix, Paris, 1873; Couderc, Paris, 1912. I quote the latter. See, too, Astrain, *Historia de la Compañia de Jesus en la Asistencia de España,* Vol. III, 189 ff.

[3] *Vie de sainte Térèse,* chap. xxiv.

such eagerness, answered the letter without delay, and wrote outside close to the address : ' *Not to be opened for a month.*' This she did, and it was no small mortification to her." [1]

He tried her still more—may we not say, to the point of hardship?—when nearly everyone was treating the saint as a visionary.

" Sometimes he told her purposely that everybody affirmed that what she experienced was an illusion of the devil, allowing her to understand that he shared their opinion. He kept her from Holy Communion for twenty days to see how she would endure it. He tried her with such mortifications that she was several times tempted to abandon him, so much did he distress and urge her ! But whenever she yielded to the temptation to leave him, she felt herself inwardly rebuked and urged not to do it." [2]

The trial was certainly pushed too far. Balthazar Alvarez wished to keep Teresa to discursive prayer by force. Distrustful of himself, he sought counsel on the subject : " His great humility," says Teresa with subtle delicacy, " was to me the source of many sufferings, for, although a man of much prayer as well as knowledge, he did not trust to himself in the matter, since the Lord used not to lead him by this way." [3]

The young confessor's humility did not, however, make him blind. He finally recognized very clearly the divine nature of Teresa's revelations and visions. These supernatural phenomena coincided with such an increase in the virtues of his penitent that they could not be of diabolical origin. Balthazar Alvarez, too, was himself treated as a visionary for believing in the visions of Teresa.

" He had to bear all kinds of troubles on my behalf," says St Teresa. " They told him, as I have learnt since, to beware of me, for if he gave the least credence to my words he would fall into the snare of the devil, and they mentioned what had happened to others. All this distressed me extremely. I feared a time might come when no one would be willing to hear my confessions and everyone would flee from me ; I did nothing but weep." [4]

Balthazar Alvarez was soon to experience, on his own account, similar contradictions.

---

[1] *Vie du P. Balthazar Alvarez,* p. 102, Couderc.
[2] *ibid.* Cf. *Vie de sainte Térèse,* chap. xxvi.
[3] *Vie de sainte Térèse,* chap. xxviii. Balthazar Alvarez was then at the College of St Giles of Avila, under the Rector Denis Vasquez, confessor and companion of St Francis Borgia, and a man of extreme severity.
[4] *ibid.* Later on, Balthazar Alvarez strongly encouraged the saint in founding monasteries. Cf. *Foundations,* chap. iii.

Sent to Medina del Campo in 1566 to exercise the functions of rector and novice-master, he was raised in the following year to the prayer of quiet and of union.[1] He then knew by experience the mystical state of which St Teresa had so often spoken to him.

At first he was not disturbed in any way. He was even reputed to have received from heaven much " enlightenment and understanding " on the question of prayer. He was also entrusted with a confidential mission.

In 1574 the Inquisition issued another edict against the *Alumbrados*. " On this occasion Father John Suarez, provincial of the province of Castile, wanting not even a shadow of such errors to be found among the Jesuits who practise mental prayer and are familiar with things spiritual, gave Father Balthazar . . . an order to compose a little treatise on the way to speak thereon in conformity with the truth and the spirit of the Church."[2]

The *Alumbrados,* as we know, exaggerated the need and the effects of mental prayer. "No one, apart from mental prayer," they claimed, "can be, or persevere, in a state of grace." On the other hand, " alone, such prayer is enough to make anyone perfect."[3] Moreover, these were not the only falsities of their teaching.

Balthazar Alvarez examines one after another their errors on prayer, on the soul's communications with God while on earth, on the sensible consolations of devotion, on confession and communion, on marriage, chastity, and the religious Orders. He criticizes them closely, and shows their entire opposition to the traditional teaching of the Church. His treatise is one of the best refutations of the false Spanish mysticism of the time.[4]

These events led anew to the over-excitement of men's minds. They spoke much of mental prayer and of methods of prayer. And, as often happens in such circumstances, the disciples of Balthazar Alvarez attributed compromising statements to their master :

" They spoke of prayer," says Luis de la Puente, " in terms far away from the thought of their master; they said or did things which led those who were well instructed and zealous to form no good opinion of the method that they

---

[1] *Vie du P. B. Alvarez,* chap. xxxiii, p. 314.

[2] *ibid.* The treatise of Balthazar Alvarez against the *Alumbrados* appears to be prior to the discussions about to be related. When the Inquisition published its edict against the false mystics, if the spirituality of B. Alvarez had been suspected, he would not have been asked for his treatise on prayer.

[3] *ibid.,* p. 316.

[4] A lengthy analysis of it is given in chap. xxxiii of the *Vie du P. B. Alvarez,* pp. 314-329. It is one of the most important documents for a knowledge of the teaching of the *Alumbrados*.

followed nor of the master to whom they attributed it, as if he were the one who used them as his mouthpiece. It was a still graver matter when they thought that certain ignorant or indiscreet persons appeared to despise the use of mental prayer by means of deductions, affections, demands and colloquies, as taught by the Blessed St Ignatius in his book of *Spiritual Exercises*. These, said they, are but perambulators, which are good enough for children till they have learnt to walk, and that is all; for when they can walk they are allowed to go as they please and without taking such trouble. The Holy Ghost will not be tied to rules and to methods of prayer; he 'bloweth where he will and as he will.' . . . Hence these imprudent persons, more presumptuous than experienced, wanted everyone to follow the road they took themselves, and turned them away from the path ordinarily used by the faithful."[1]

Balthazar Alvarez was then Rector of Salamanca. His followers' indiscretions ended in his kind of spirituality being disputed. Was not his exalted prayer mere illusion, "a work of Satan changed into an angel of light"?

"There were found even some who threatened to hand him over to the Inquisition, for they questioned whether he were not rather given to the error of the *Illuminati*. He was suspected of taking no account of methods of prayer by means of reasoning and meditation as used in the Society and approved by the saints, and of desiring to lead the religious by other singular and perilous paths."[2]

In fact, Balthazar Alvarez, being used to mystical prayer, in teaching his young religious, did not give what was regarded as a sufficiently important part to discursive meditation. He said clearly, indeed, that the mystical ways could not be followed by all as easily as the method of St Ignatius. "But," he added, "God can call everyone to them if he will."[3] And he ordinarily calls thereto all who have laboriously prepared themselves for them "by purity of heart, by mortification of their passions, and by long exercises of meditation."[4] Such preparation requires time. Those who "have to devote themselves to the salvation of their neighbours" will succeed still more surely in attaining such heavenly favours:

"That there are in the Society," added Alvarez, "wherein men are so desirous to please God, subjects who are raised to this degree [of prayer], this seems to me to be evident. But, to keep away those whom God our Lord has made to

---

[1] *Vie du P. B. Alvarez*, chap. xli, pp. 402-403.
[2] *id.*, chap. xl, pp. 394-395.
[3] *id.*, chap. xiii, p. 125.
[4] *id.*, chap. xiv, p. 135. *Cf.* chap. xiii, p. 125 : God calls "after a long use of meditation and reflection."

ascend thereto, especially if one has no experience of this manner, that appears to me not to be permitted in conscience and to involve a risk of injuring their souls and even their health. This is Ossuna's opinion in his *Abecedario:* 'We are not free from sin when we turn anyone aside from God's way.' Elsewhere we read : ' If a superior did this, God would shorten his life if he did not retract his decision.' To act thus by means of examination and trial is quite another thing, and the office of superiors enables them to do this.''[1]

The threat of Ossuna, as we shall see, did not intimidate the superiors of Balthazar Alvarez.

His provincial, John Suarez, asked him—Alvarez was still Rector of Salamanca—to "give an account of his prayer, and of what happened to him while he was engaged therein.''[2] Balthazar immediately composed a full account of what he had been asked for. Then, to the written objections of his provincial, he replied with a second memorandum :[3]

" Since our Lord has granted me this ' mercy,' " says Balthazar Alvarez, " my prayer consists in putting myself in his presence which I enjoy within, and also corporally, usually continuously, sometimes finding my joy with him. . . .

" At other times I am in prayer, reasoning according to the meanings given to the words of Holy Scripture and following inward teachings; sometimes I keep silence and relish a holy repose. This silent repose in the presence of God is a great treasure, because everything speaks to him, everything is open to his eyes, my heart, my desires, my aims, my trials, my feelings, my knowledge, and my capacity. . . .

" Usually there is no reasoning, but there is always petition : and whilst our Lord keeps my soul in a state of repose, it makes all sorts of acts of virtue, and consequently, of petition, not by an act which the theologians call ' marked,' but by an act ' exercised.' In fact, does this soul of mine, silent before God, trusting that, by appearing in his presence, its heart and all its heart's desires are manifested to him, cease from petitioning?''[4] . . .

Balthazar Alvarez calls his prayer " the prayer of silence," because the soul keeps in the presence of God without much speaking and even without speaking at all; it is in a state of " spiritual repose." The soul appears before God with its desires which " are to God what words are to man.''[5] In

---

[1] *Vie du P. B. Alvarez,* chap. xiii, pp. 125-126.
[2] *id.,* chap. xiii, p. 116.
[3] Luis de la Puente sums up these two accounts of Alvarez in chap. xiii and xiv of his *Life.*
[4] *Vie,* chap. xiii, pp. 119, 121, 124. Luis de la Puente also quotes extracts from this second memorial in chaps. xiv and xli.
[5] *id.,* xiii, p. 124.

fine, here we have the prayer of quiet and of union so much spoken of by St Teresa.

The intervention of the Provincial John Suarez does not appear to have been followed by sanctions. This was not the case with that of the Visitor Diego de Avellaneda in 1577.

As soon as he arrived in the province of Castile, Diego de Avellaneda asked Balthazar Alvarez, then Rector of Villagarcia, for a memorandum—the third—on his way of prayer.[1] The visitor, having taken knowledge of it, enjoined upon the rector to make no use " either in his own case or in the case of others of any manner of prayer differing from that of the *Exercises.*" It would not be enough for him to show " more esteem and affection for the method of prayer of the *Exercesis,*" but he should prefer it " to any other whatsoever, entirely following the method of prayer " of his Institute, " both in his own case and in the case of all whom he directed." The General of the Society, Everard Mercurian, approved of the conduct of the visitor.[2]

Measures were taken in consequence of these events. The religious of the Society were bound still more firmly to the method of prayer of the *Exercises,* which many of them appeared to disdain. They were also forbidden to read certain mystics, and especially Tauler and Harphius, without a special authorization.[3]

This severity proves that the Jesuit superiors were resolved to maintain their religious in asceticism and in the discursive prayer prescribed in the *Spiritual Exercises.* Did not prudence counsel thus? There were so many and such dangerous errors about prayer, and they were to be met with in Andalusia and even in Castile at every turn! Lastly, the Inquisition was on the watch, and woe to anyone whom it set upon! Later on, circumstances changed, and a General of the Jesuits, Claud Acquaviva, was able to put things right.[1]

The publication of works of mysticism was, in these circumstances, impossible.

In 1573 Ribera ventured to write a treatise *On Contemplation,* but he wrote it in Latin, and issued it at Cologne. We are astonished to find that the Augustinian Sebastian Foscari

---

[1] Luis de la Puente does not mention this memorandum. It may be found in Appendix xix of J. de la Torre's reissue of the *Vie de B. Alvarez* (1880).

[2] See Astrain, *Historia de la Compañia de Jesus en la Asistencia de España,* Vol. III, pp. 191 ff.; P. Dudon, *L'oraison du P. B. Alvarez* (*Revue d'Asc. et de Myst.,* 1921, pp. 36 ff.).

[3] *Cf.* Alphonsus Rodriguez, *Practice of Christian Perfection,* Part I, Treatise V, chap. iv.

was able to bring out at Madrid in the same year, a book on *Mistica Teologia.*[1]

In 1583 the Inquisition published another Index,[2] certainly less severe than that of 1559, but hardly likely to reassure writers. St Teresa died the year before in 1582. None of her immortal works were issued during her lifetime. The first to see the light, "the least compromising, the most moderate, the most purely ascetic in its tendency," was the *Way of Perfection,* published at Evora in 1583. It was only five years later that Luis de Leon issued the first edition of the saint's *Works.* This publication did not completely disarm all hostility to mysticism. But at any rate mysticism now wins once and for ever the right of citizenship in Spain.

VIII—THE AUGUSTINIANS: LUIS DE LEON AND THOMAS OF JESUS (D'ANDRADA)

LUIS DE LEON[3] is one of the greatest of Spanish writers and poets of the second half of the sixteenth century. His literary superiority is undisputed. Spanish owes a great deal to him. He wielded it with great suppleness, and contributed to its full development more than anyone else.[4]

He loved his mother tongue too much not to make use of it in preference to Latin, even in his theological works. To those who reproached him, he replied "that their national language had but small claims upon them, since that for its sake they detested what they would have approved of in another tongue. I confess," he added, "that I can hardly explain such revulsion, whereof our speech is certainly unworthy, nor their worship of Latin, which we know certainly to be no better than Spanish, although, truth to tell, we suspect not at all how rich is the latter. They find it strange, too, that in speaking the language of the people I put a

[1] At Saragossa, about 1570, appeared the *Union del alma,* by Enecon Aberca de Bolea.

[2] It was published by Cardinal Quiroga, then Grand Inquisitor. *Cf.* Fr. Reusch, *Die Indices librorum prohibitorum des XVI Jahrhunderts,* Tübingen, 1886, in the collection of the *Litterarisches Verein,* Stuttgart, Vol. clxxvi.

[3] Luis de Leon was born at Madrid (others say at Granada) in 1527. He studied at the University of Salamanca, joined the Augustinians of that town in 1544, and soon gained a great reputation owing to his learning. In 1588 he was elected Vicar General of the Augustinians, and then became Provincial of Castile. He died at Villa-de-Madrigal in 1591. *Cf.* Fray Vidal, *History of the Institute of the Augustinians of Salamanca,* Madrid, 1571. A good edition of the *Works* of Luis de Leon is that of Madrid, 1804-1816, 16 vols.: *Todas obras, reconocidas y cotejadas con varios manuscritos autenticos* por el P. M. Fr. Antolino Merino; Rivadeneyra, *Autores Españoles, Obras del maestro Luis de Leon,* Vol. XXXVII.

[4] *Bibliotheca Hispana nova,* Madrid, 1788.

certain amount of elegance into my discourses, seeking harmony of phrase, propriety of expression, and richly turned periods. They fancy that to use the common speech is to speak like the common people."[1]

It was not only his love of his mother tongue that led him to write in Spanish. Like Luis of Granada, he understood how necessary it was to write in the popular language to instruct the people in religious doctrine and to combat bad books. More than Luis of Granada he had to suffer for this innovation.

In 1561 he wrote in Spanish a short explanation of the *Canticle of Canticles* for a nun. Denounced to the Inquisitors, he was cast into the dungeons of the Inquisition, and remained there five years. It was during his captivity that he had the idea of composing his masterpiece : *Los nombres de Cristo* (*The Names of Christ*).

After the fashion of the *Octavius* of Minucius Felix, Luis de Leon makes three Augustinians discourse upon the various names of Christ taken from the Scriptures. This pious colloquy sets forth a deep spiritual christology, which is a forerunner of that which was to be taught by the French School a few years afterwards.

" The name . . ." says Luis de Leon, " is a word which is put in place of the thing or person whereof we speak, and it is taken for that thing or person."[2] To explain the various names of Christ is therefore to speak of what he is, of his greatness, his virtues, his offices, and of our duty towards him. In a word, it means to base our piety on devotion to the Saviour.

Why does Holy Scripture give several names to Jesus?

" The reason," says Luis de Leon, " lies in his infinite greatness, in the treasure of his perfections, as well as in the diversity of his offices and of the goods that flow from him to us. The soul cannot embrace all this with a single glance, nor can it be expressed with a single word. Thus, as he who pours water into a vase with a long and narrow neck fills it drop by drop and not all at once, so the Holy Spirit, knowing how narrow and limited is our understanding, does not put before us all this immense greatness at the same time, but he offers it to us, so to speak, in fragments, revealing to us one part of it under the veil of a

---

[1] *Los nombres de Cristo,* Book III, see Rivadeneyra, *Autores Españoles,* Vol. XXXVII. The other chief works of Luis de Leon are : *In Cantica canticorum explanatio,* Salamanca, 1580; *In psalmum XXVI comment.,* Salamanca, 1580, in which he complains of his captivity; *La perfecta Casada* (*The Perfect Wife*), 1583. After his death in 1618, the *Explanation of the Psalm " Miserere "* was published at Madrid.

[2] Postel's French translation of *The Names of Christ,* p. 50 (Paris, 1862).

Name, another part under that of a different Name, and so forth throughout. Hence the number of the names given to the Saviour in Holy Scripture."[1]

Amongst these names the writer selects a few which seem to him of greater importance and more inclusive, and then explains them.[2]

The wealth of doctrine and charm of style secured an extraordinary success for the *Nombres de Cristo*. This cele-brated work found its way into all the literary collections of the peninsula, and was included in all libraries of devotional reading. It gave its author a henceforth undisputed authority, so that, when the Carmelites thought of publishing the first edition of the *Works* of St Teresa, they begged the famous Augustinian to take charge of it. "By his knowledge and the authority of his name no less than by his admiration for St Teresa, Luis de Leon seemed eminently fitted to carry out this delicate and important business with happy results."[3]

Of less literary value than his Spanish brother, the Portu-gese, Thomas d'Andrada, better known as Thomas of Jesus,[4] edified many by his meditations on the *Sufferings of our Lord Jesus Christ*.

He wrote them during his long and hard captivity among the Moors in Africa, whither he had accompanied the luck-less Portugese army in 1578. Thomas of Jesus was interned in a narrow cell, and, being unable to care for the imprisoned soldiers, wrote in order to encourage and comfort them. His work was thought out "in his actual experience of the cross." And with what realism does he describe the Saviour's suffer-ings! Thomas of Jesus appears to have suffered them him-self, such is the unction with which he speaks. And what outbursts of love does he utter, sanctified as he is by the

---

[1] Postel's French translation of *The Names of Christ,* p. 65.

[2] These are : Jesus Christ the Offshoot or Fruit—the Face of God—the Way—the Shepherd—the Mountain of God—the Father of the world to come—the Prince of Peace—the Spouse—the Son of God—the Well-beloved—the Lamb of God—and above all, the Name of Jesus.

[3] *Introduction aux Œuvres de sainte Térèse,* Polit, Paris, 1907, p. xxxii.

[4] Thomas d'Andrada was born at Coimbra in Portugal about 1530. At the age of fifteen he joined the Augustinians of Lisbon. He tried, though not quite successfully, to reform the Portuguese Augustinians. In 1578 he accompanied King Sebastian in the tragic African expedi-tion, in which he underwent a long and hard captivity among the Moors, and he died in prison in 1582. The work of Thomas of Jesus, *The Sufferings of our Lord Jesus Christ,* appeared first of all in Portuguese. It was very soon translated into Spanish, Italian, and Latin under various titles. One of the first French translations was entitled *The Works of Jesus,* a tasteless allusion to *The Works of Hercules,* by Collucio Salutati. Fr. Alleaume, S.J., published a French translation at Toulouse in 1820.

torments of his imprisonment endured in close union with the sufferings of Christ !

The work of Thomas of Jesus—and this has not been sufficiently noticed—is not only a collection of aspirations founded on the various sufferings of our Saviour, it is also a little treatise of true devotion. In the *Spiritual Counsels* preceding the meditations, the pious Augustinian reminds the many who then forgot that perfection does not consist in extraordinary graces :

" Too often it happens," he says, " that those who aspire to Christian perfection are mistaken as to the way in which they understand things spiritual. When they read of the actions of the saints and consider their austerities, fervours, ecstasies, and other extraordinary graces wrought by the Holy Spirit in such strong souls, they are drawn towards the marvellous in them without reflecting on the foundation of the noble structure and the way by which sanctity has been attained. . . .

" Now (the spiritual life) consists of two things, mortification and the love of God. Mortification, if it does not lead to the love of God, is to be suspected. He who would draw near to God must not separate these two things which are at once the foundation and the summit of perfection."[1]

The reader is very naturally led to conclude that meditation on the sufferings of the God-man is eminently calculated to perfect the faithful.

Thomas of Jesus explains how the meditation must be made. His method is like that of Luis of Granada, and he adds some counsels as to the examination of conscience. Then come fifty meditations on the sufferings of Jesus, which form the greater part of the work.[2]

Thomas of Jesus, like the writer of the *Imitation,* regards " all the life of Christ as a cross and a martyrdom." Jesus suffered most of all in his Passion : he also suffered in all the circumstances of his life. Thus Thomas of Jesus runs through all the mysteries of the earthly life of Christ from his conception in the virginal womb of Mary till his last breath upon the cross, and he reflects in each of them upon the suffering which it contained. It is the suffering Christ who is set before us by the writer. Luis de Leon shows us Christ in his beauty and splendour and divine glory. He stirs us to admiration and draws us powerfully to the Spouse of our souls. Thomas of Jesus makes us contemplate Christ in pity as the Man of Sorrows on our behalf. He fills our hearts with compassion, he sets our tears flowing, and,

---

[1] *Avis spirituels,* chàp. i, Vol. I, pp. 9, 12, Alleaume's translation.
[2] Each meditation is followed by a colloquy with our Lord on the particular suffering of that meditation.

despite our natural repugnance for suffering, we come to desire to suffer with Christ and for Christ.

Luis de Leon and Thomas of Jesus have left us fine examples of the way in which many regarded devotion to Christ in Spain in the sixteenth century.

CHAPTER VI

THE SPANISH CARMELITE SCHOOL—SAINT TERESA

THE Carmelite Order,[1] in the sixteenth century, gave Spain St Teresa and St John of the Cross. Thus it shed upon the Spanish School such a brilliance as will never be surpassed, perhaps not even equalled, by any other school of spirituality. In St Teresa we may study the saint, the reformer, the foundress, and the mystic.[2] Here we shall deal only with the mystic.

I—CHARACTERISTICS OF TERESIAN MYSTICISM

St Teresa is a mystical writer of the first rank.[3] More than anyone else did she teach the Spanish tongue to speak " the language of the angels." She " is the writer most

[1] The Carmelites were a flourishing Order in the twelfth century. Berthold, a Calabrian crusader, was living as a hermit on Mount Carmel with ten companions, about 1156. Their Rule was probably that of St Augustine. About 1209, St Albert, Patriarch of Jerusalem, drew up the Carmelite Rule. The Order had several convents in the Holy Land, as many as the incursions of the Saracens permitted. In the thirteenth century the Carmelites came to Europe. The first Prior General was St Simon Stock. The Rule of St Albert was modified by Pope Innocent IV in 1247 in order to change the eremitic into the cœnobitic life. In 1431 this Rule was mitigated by Pope Eugene IV, and the latter Rule was carried out, so far as he could get it observed, by Bl. John Soreth. It was while he was General that the first convent of Carmelite nuns was founded under the Rule of the brethren. Towards the end of the fifteenth century there were houses of Carmelite nuns in France, Italy, and Spain. It was into one of the last, the Convent of the Incarnation at Avila, that St Teresa entered, in 1535, at twenty years of age. She reformed this house, and devoted it to the contemplative life, to poverty, and to strict enclosure. She also set up a reformation among the men Carmelites. See *Dict. de Théol. cath.*, art. *Carmes, Acta Sanctorum,* St Cyril, March 6; St Berthold, March 29; St Albert, April 1. André de Sainte-Marie, *L'Ordre du Mont-Carmel,* Bruges, 1910; Cosme de Villers, *Bibliotheca Carmelitana.*

[2] Chief biographies of St Teresa: Diego de Yepes, *Vida, virtudes y milagros de la Bienaventurada Teresa de Jesus,* Madrid, 1587; Francisco de Ribera, S.J., *La vida de la Madre Teresa de Jesus,* Salamanca, 1590; Julian de Avila, *Vida de Santa Teresa de Jesus,* 1881; Henri Joly, *Sainte Térèse,* Paris, 1902; *Acta Sanctorum,* October, Vol. VII.

[3] St Teresa's Works: Chief edition, *Los libros de la Madre Teresa de Jesus,* by Luis de Leon, Salamanca, 1588; *Escritos de Santa Teresa,* Collection of *Autores Españoles,* Rivadeneyra, 1861, Vols. LIV and LV;

gifted with personality produced by the Spanish genius and
perhaps by the Latin genius. In her . . . [there are]
brilliant faculties, exquisite sensibility, surprising philosophical intuitions, a steadiness of gaze which enables her
to plumb the depths of man's soul, to discover its hidden
springs and to analyse its most secret workings, and, lastly,
a rare good sense allied with a frankness and good grace
which enchant and captivate us."[1]

She has to the point of excellence the very rare gift of
making a fine analysis of her own spiritual psychology, and
of describing its various states with astonishing sureness
and luminous precision. We may find in others the same
extraordinary graces; but no one able to express them with
the same talent :

"To receive one of God's favours is a first grace," she
said; "to know wherein it consists, is a second; lastly, it
is a third grace to be able to give an account of it and to
explain it."[2]

We shall have a fuller notion of her intellectual temperament and literary genius if we remember that she fed from
childhood upon the reading of the romances of chivalry.[3]
Like St Ignatius of Loyola and all the Spanish nobility of
the time, she was passionately fond of such books :

Phototypical editions of the *Vida* and the *Fundaciones*, by La Fluente
and Selfa, Madrid, 1873, 1880; of the *Castillo*, by Lluch, Seville, 1882;
of the *Camino* and the *Modo de visitar,* by Herrero Bayona, Valladolid,
1883. Silverio de Santa Teresa, O.C.D., *Obras de Santa Teresa de
Jesus*, Burgos, 1915-1919 (without the *Letters*).

French translations are many. Among them may be mentioned
the following : De Bretigny, Paris, 1601; D'Andilly, Paris, 1670;
Bouix, S.J., Paris, 1852-1861, in 6 vols., since then improved;
Œuvres complètes de sainte Térèse de Jésus, by the Carmelites of Paris,
6 vols., Paris, 1907-1910, from which I shall quote. There is no
critical edition of St Teresa's *Letters.* There is a new translation of
them by Fr. Gregory of St Joseph, Pustet, 2nd ed., 1906, 3 vols.

[1] *Œuvres de sainte Térèse,* Vol. I, p. xxiii.
[2] *Vie,* chap. xvii, *Œuvres,* I, p. 213. St Teresa improved in the
art of explaining her mystical states : "Then (1558) I had not, as now
(1565), the light needed for giving good explanations" (*Vie,* chap. xxx,
Œuvres, I, 384).
[3] The chief ones were *Amadis de Gaule,* in twenty-four Books. The
first four were published at Seville in 1496. *Amadis* was followed by
a whole series : *Amadis of Greece,* in 1532; *Florisel of Niquea, the son
of Amadis of Greece,* etc.; French translation of *Amadis de Gaule,* by
Hugues Vagany, Paris, 1918. In 1511 appeared the *Palmarin de Oliva.*
This was followed by a series the most famous of which was the
Palmarin de Inglaterra, written in 1547. Then *Don Belianis de Grecia,*
etc. Preachers and moralists made war upon these books, which
certainly exalted chivalrous ideals, but by their amorous adventures
"turned the heads of young women." *Cf.* Malon de Chaide, *The
Conversion of the Magdalen,* Prologue (*Autores Españoles,* Rivadeneyra, Vol. XXVII); Luis de Leon, *Nombres de Cristo,* Introduction
(*ibid.,* Vol. XXXVII).

"I thought there was no harm," she humbly tells us in her *Life*,[1] "in spending many hours of the day in so frivolous an occupation, even hiding from my father, and I became so absorbed in it that I could never be happy without a fresh book."

According to her biographer, Ribera, she even wrote along with her brother Rodriguez a chivalrous and sentimental romance, which was received with appreciation by her friends. Later on she saw that this taste for romances injured her soul.[2]

If she renounced—and how generously, God knows—such frivolities, her imagination, like that of St Ignatius of Loyola, kept the impression of pictures of chivalry which refined her sensibility. For her, too, Christ is a king, a conqueror who calls his vassals to the holy war and desires to lead them to victory over themselves. In the depths of the poor monasteries of Segovia and of Avila, she recalls the splendid castles of the great men of Spain and the magical descriptions of the old romances. All round, the moats are full of water, swarming with serpents and venomous creatures. The many-mansioned castle rises in its majesty, and it stands for the devout soul. The heavenly Spouse is in the central room, and there awaits his bride; and she will pass through all the mansions to reach him and to unite with him in a mystical marriage which is indissoluble.[3]

A chivalrous imagination in the noblest sense of the word, "a delicate and finely emotional sensitiveness," "a keen intelligence, both positive and practical,"[4] these natural gifts of Teresa are extraordinary; they explain the incomparable charm of her writings.

But whence comes the deep and sound mystical teaching which they contain?

Her old biographers were fond of saying that she received from divine Wisdom the beautiful teaching which she gives us. There is nothing bookish in the mysticism of St Teresa. Like St Bernard before her and many others, she "imparts to us what it had been granted her to enjoy and know." She gives us of her own inmost spiritual experiences; she has received supernatural light to discern them, and to translate them into human speech. It is not from spiritual writers that she has learned: she has read but very few of them; she never quotes them. She often complains of the bad

---

[1] Chap. ii, *Œuvres*, I, p. 51.   [2] *ibid.*, p. 50.
[3] *Œuvres,* Vol. VI, pp. 6, 41, etc.
[4] R. Hoornaert, *Sainte Térèse, écrivain*, p. x.

memory which prevents her from remembering what she
has read or what has been explained to her :

" If only God had given me a little ability and memory !"
she says with a sigh. " Then I could turn to some advantage what I have read or heard. But I am as lacking as
possible in all that. If, then, I say anything useful, it is
because God willed it to be thus, to bring some good out
of it."[1]

According to her own testimony, Teresa owes only to
God the doctrine she teaches us.[2]

This view of most Teresians is beginning to be modified
in consequence of a closer study of the literary sources from
which the saint drew.[3] Never mind ! " Far from taking
anything away from Teresa's personality," these studies
" will only accentuate it."[4]

They teach us that Teresa tried to get instruction in the
supernatural ways by the human means within reach. Help
thyself and God will help thee ! " One of the essential
tendencies of her mind is an insatiable and fruitful curiosity.
She knows how to question her confessors as well as how to
answer them; she is fond of talking to theologians " who
are learned and talented "; she listens to sermons and
homilies with eager attention, but, above all, does she read
and re-read, underline, and make notes on the solid Castilian
treatises which bring the traditional doctrine within her
reach.[5] When she afterwards writes down her experiences
of the interior life, she makes use of what she has learnt.

---

[1] *Vie,* chap. x, *Œuvres,* I, 140. In the Prologue of the *Interior
Castle* (*Œuvres,* VI, 38), Teresa complains, too, of her bad memory.
Doubtless, it is this defective memory that explains some appearances
of contradiction to be found in her writings.

[2] See this opinion of the majority of Teresians in the general Introduction to *Œuvres,* Vol. I, p. xxiii.

[3] On the sources of St Teresa, see Morel-Fatio, *Les lectures de sainte
Térèse,* in the *Bulletin hispanique,* Vol. X, January-March, 1908,
pp. 17-67; R. Hoornaert, *Sainte Térèse, écrivain,* Paris-Lille-Bruges,
1922; Gaston Etchegoyen, *L'amour divin, Essai sur les sources de
sainte Térèse,* Bordeaux-Paris.

[4] Hoornaert, p. ix. M. Etchegoyen rather exaggerates in writing
thus : " St Teresa had a genius for assimilation and synthesis rather
than for invention," p. 29.

[5] Etchegoyen, p. 30. Copies of the Castilian books used by Teresa
have been preserved. They are annotated in her own handwriting.
They are : The *Letters* of St Jerome (*Vie,* chaps. iii, xi ; *Castle,* VI,
chap. ix); the *Morals* on the book of Job, by St Gregory the Great (*Vie,*
chap. v); (*Way of Perfection,* chap. xii); *The Carthusians* (*los
Cartujanos*). This was the name of the Spanish translation of the *Vita
Christi,* by Ludolph, the Carthusian (*Vie,* chap. xxxviii; *Castle,* VII,
chap. iv). *The Imitation of Jesus Christ* or *Contemptus mundi* (*Way
of Perfection,* chap. xxxviii; *Castle,* V, chap. ii). The *Confessions* of
St Augustine (*Vie,* chap. ix). St Teresa also read the principal works
of Luis of Granada (St Teresa's Letter to Luis of Granada, December
28, 1573). We know that she read the writings of Alonso of Madrid,

Her reading helped her to take cognizance of her own spiritual states and to unravel them :

" Scarcely had I begun to read the *Confessions* of St Augustine," she says, " than I seemed to have discovered myself."

It was at the time when she finally gave up her " frivolous and dissipated life " to yield herself entirely into the hands of God.

" When I had reached his (Augustine's) conversion," she adds, " the voice which he heard in the garden, the Lord, I believe, made it ring in my ears, so keenly was my heart touched. Long I remained bathed in tears, overwhelmed with grief and regret."[1]

Later on she took this work of St Augustine as the model for her own biography for which her confessors asked.

It was the Franciscan Francisco of Ossuna who revealed to her the prayer of recollection. His book, the *Tercer Abecedario,* gave her much pleasure, she says, and she resolved to follow the way which it opened out to her with the greatest possible fidelity.[2] But the most signal service was rendered to her by Bernardino of Laredo's mystical book, the *Ascent of Mount Sion.* Teresa had just been habitually favoured with the prayer of quiet, and often with that of union. She could not succeed in explaining this kind of prayer to herself, and dreaded illusion. What tormented her still more was that she did not know how to tell what she experienced :

" I consulted books," she says, " to see whether they would help me to give an explanation of my prayer. In a work entitled *The Ascent of Mount Sion,* in the place where the union of the soul with God is spoken of, I met with all the marks of that which I experienced with regard to an inability to reflect. And it was just this inability that I specially remarked in this kind of prayer. I noted the passages in question with a line."[3]

Teresa also found in the books that she studied the images, metaphors, and allegories taken from the Bible or nature or social and family life, which are usually employed to express the love of God and to describe its mystical effects in the soul. From this point of view she owes much to the Spanish spiritual writers who preceded her. They also revealed to her the traditional and classic terminology used in speaking

of Francisco of Ossuna, of Bernardino of Laredo, and of St Peter of Alcantara. In her *Constitutions,* St Teresa also recommends to her prioresses the *Lives of the Saints* (*Flos Sanctorum*) and finally the *Oratory of the Religious,* by Antonio de Guevara.

[1] *Vie,* chap. ix, *Œuvres,* I, p. 131.
[2] *id.,* chap. iv, *Œuvres,* I, pp. 70-71.
[3] *id.,* chap. xxiii, *Œuvres,* I, p. 297.

of supernatural occurrences and of the different degrees of prayer, but she wrote in a style so fresh, so full of personality and genius, that everything appears to proceed from herself.

One of the most striking singularities of Teresian mysticism is its lack of theory. Teresa recounts her own experience, describing what takes place within her soul. She does not try to give a philosophical explanation of mystical union. She never launches out into metaphysics, but always confines herself to psychology. Teresa tells her own story, and does it in a captivating way.

Her writings are, in fact, her own mystical autobiography. Her *Life,* the *Interior Castle,* and even the *Way of Perfection* are the story of her own seraphic soul. The different degrees of prayer which she describes in them are the stages which she has herself passed through to reach the heights of divine love.

The mysticism of Teresa, full of genius as it is, is therefore not pure and simple mysticism. Let me explain. St Teresa describes her own experiences, the ways by which God has led her. Let us not therefore conclude that all mystics necessarily pass by the same way thereto. Teresa herself expressly says the contrary. Very often she reminds us that she is explaining her own experience, the way in which God has led her, but the paths that run towards perfection are infinitely various.[1] If she divides her ascent towards the highest kind of prayer into seven stages, if she reckons seven mansions in the castle of the soul, it does not follow that in the case of everyone and of all the saints there must necessarily be seven degrees of the spiritual life. To think so would be to run the risk of bringing false notions into mystical theology.

Since St Teresa's writings are an autobiography, the best way to understand them is to apprehend their teaching in act, in the very life of the saint. If we constantly check Teresa's teaching with the story of her life, we shall be enabled to follow its unfolding with safety. But it is sometimes a difficult matter. St Teresa does not always reckon with chronology; she is often in confusion as to the dates of occurrences. She wrote during the last twenty years of her life, from 1562 to 1582,[2] and her memory is now and then at

---

[1] See *Œuvres,* Vol. I, p. xxx.
[2] The *Life* was drawn up in 1562, then revised and completed at St Joseph of Avila's from 1562 to 1565. The *Way of Perfection* was first drawn up in 1562 at the same monastery, and then for the second time, probably at Toledo, during the foundations in 1569 and 1570. The *Constitutions,* intended for the nuns only, were composed at Avila about 1563. The *Exclamations*, or impassioned ejaculations of divine

fault. Here, too, as elsewhere, history is but an imperfect approximation to living reality.

II—ST TERESA'S TEACHING[1]—HER SPIRITUAL BIOGRAPHY—MEDITATION

A—THE SPIRITUAL BIOGRAPHY OF ST TERESA

IT is in the *Interior Castle* that St Teresa has best described her religious experiences.

Her biographer, Yepes, in his deposition for her canonization, thus relates how the book was written :

" On the vigil of the feast of the Most Holy Trinity (1577), while she was asking herself what the fundamental idea of this treatise should be, God, who orders all things with wisdom, answered her prayers and provided her with the plan of her work. He showed her a splendid globe of crystal in the form of a castle with seven mansions in it. In the seventh, in the very centre of it, was the King of glory, shining in brilliant splendour which lighted up and embellished all the mansions as far as the enclosure. The nearer they were to the centre, the more they participated in the light. The illumination did not extend beyond the enclosure : outside it there was nothing but darkness and uncleanness, frogs, vipers, and other venomous creatures."[2]

This castle represents the Christian soul. The entrance-gate is prayer which, by means of recollection, withdraws the soul into itself. As long as it lives outside of itself, in dissipation, more or less the slave of the senses, it stays in the enclosure outside of the castle, along with the reptiles and other venomous creatures, exposed to their bites which may

---

love, appear to have been written in several monasteries from 1566 to 1569. The *Thoughts on the Canticle of Canticles* no doubt date from 1574, when the saint was at Segovia. The *Book of the Foundations* was begun at Salamanca in 1573, continued at Toledo in 1576, and finished at Burgos in 1582. The *Record of the Visitation of the Monasteries* goes back to 1576, at Toledo. The *Interior Castle*, or *Mansions of the Soul,* was composed in 1577, first at Toledo and then at Segovia and Avila, on the advice of Fr. Jerome Gratian, Carmelite, who was then Apostolic Commissary of the Carmelite reform. The *Interior Castle* was to replace the *Life,* the manuscript of which had been kept by the Inquisitors. The *Counsels* and the *Spiritual Relations* belong to various periods. Cf. *Œuvres,* Vol. I, pp. xxi-xxii.

[1] See Poulain, S.J., *Les Grâces d'Oraison,* Ed. 10, Paris ; Saudreau, *Les degrés de la vie spirituelle,* Paris, 1905 ; *La Vie d'union à Dieu d'après les grands maîtres de la spiritualité,* Paris, 1900 ; *La Vie spirituelle,* October, 1922 ; A. Tanqueray, *Précis de théologie ascétique et mystique,* pp. 889 ff.

[2] *Œuvres complètes de sainte Térèse,* VI, 6.

be mortal. When it begins to give itself to prayer, it enters
into the first mansions of the castle.[1] If it perseveres, it will
pass through these first mansions—the first three symbolize
the ordinary kinds of prayer—and it will traverse the four
others—the mystical mansions—until it reaches the central
chamber to unite with its divine Spouse in spiritual marriage.

Such is the mystical biography of St Teresa. In her youth,
until she was sixteen, she loved worldly frivolities; she dwelt
outside the castle with the reptiles in danger of offending
God. She was converted; then entered the Carmelite Convent
of the Incarnation of Avila at the age of twenty-one and a
half. She then dwelt in the first mansions of the castle until
she was twenty-three, during which period she experienced
times of fervour as well as of slackness. She even abandoned
prayer for some time. Lastly, she succeeded in breaking
through the impediments which kept her from soaring God-
ward, and finally entered into the mystical mansions.

It is in the first chapters of her *Life* that St Teresa relates
the period of her youth spent in the enclosure outside the
castle. They remind us of the *Confessions* of St Augustine.
It is with the same humility and with the same grief[2] that
she reveals, as far as obedience allows, what she calls the
" great sins " of her " sad life."[3]

Brought up piously by her parents, when she was about
the age of sixteen, Teresa allowed the spirit of the world to
enter into her soul. Her passionate fondness for novels, the
want of supervision, especially after her mother's death, the
frequent visits of rather flighty cousins, and her own natural
friendliness with which God had " prodigally endowed her,"
exposed her extremely to " lose herself altogether." She
was reassured by the thought that this intercourse with the
world might " happily end in a marriage."[4]

Her father grew uneasy at this state of mind, and thought
it well to isolate Teresa and to have her taken to the
Augustinian Convent of *Santa Maria de Gracia,* in which she
became a boarder. There God opened her eyes to the dangers
she had been through; she began to think seriously, and,
becoming ill, she saw " the nothingness of the world." At
the age of twenty-one and a half she joined the Carmelite
Convent of the Incarnation of Avila without obtaining her
father's consent, with a courage which clearly shows the
temper of her soul.

---

[1] *Castle,* First Mansion, chap. i.   [3] *Life,* chap. ix.
[2] *Life,* Prologue. St Teresa's biographers assure us that she never
knew a single mortal sin. Her writings give a contrary impression,
but saints are apt to exaggerate their faults. *Œuvres,* Vol. I, p. 7.
[4] *Life,* chap. ii, *Œuvres,* I, pp. 56-57.

"When I left my father's house," she says, "I felt such an excess of grief that I think that the hour of my death cannot hold in store for me anything more cruel. I felt as if my bones were breaking asunder. As the feeling of the love of God was not strong enough to counterbalance that which I had for my father and my kin, I was forced to do myself incredible violence, and had not God come to my aid all my reflections would not have sufficed to make me go through with it. But at this moment he gave me the courage to overcome myself, and I carried my enterprise out to the end."[1]

In the convent Teresa was sheltered from great dangers. She again knew, as we shall see, times of slackness and lukewarmness; but she ran no risk of sinning gravely.

All her life long she had such a keen and sorrowful feeling for the days of her youth, during which grave sin constantly lay in wait for her. In her latter years, when she was writing the *Interior Castle,* her mind was almost haunted with the notion of the soul in a state of mortal sin. She saw it "totally impotent, like a man closely bound and garrotted, with a band over his eyes keeping him from seeing, unable to walk or to hear, and finally engulfed in the depths of darkness." For such a soul she felt an unspeakable pity and an insatiable desire to deliver it from so fearful a state. To set it free, "there was no suffering that appeared to her to be anything but light."[2]

It is also to this period of her life that belongs the celebrated vision of hell which she had about 1560.[3]

"One day, while engaged in prayer, I found myself in a moment, I know not how, borne entirely away into hell. I understood that God desired to show me the place prepared for me by devils, and deserved by my sins. . . .

"The entrance seemed to me much like one of the longest and narrowest of alleys, or rather like a low, dark, and cramped oven. The ground appeared to be like miry water, extremely filthy, with a pestilential smell, and full of poisonous creatures. At the end was a hollow made in a wall, a sort of closed recess, in which I saw myself confined and very pinched for room. . . .

"In my soul I felt a fire, the nature of which I cannot explain, and at the same time I was the victim of intolerable bodily sufferings. During my life I have experienced some which were very sharp, and, according to the doctors, some

[1] *id.,* chap. iv, *Œuvres,* I, p. 66.
[2] *Spiritual Relations,* XXI, *Œuvres,* II, pp. 1-4; *Castle,* First Mansion, chap. ii; Seventh Mansion, chap. i.
[3] *Life,* chap. xxxii, *Œuvres,* II, pp. 1-4. She was then raised to the mystical kinds of prayer. Her description of hell reminds us of the *oubliettes* in the fortified castles of the time. In visions, God makes use of images which are already in the imagination of the saints.

of the most cruel that can be endured on earth, for all my nerves contracted when I became a cripple, not to speak of other torments of various kinds, some of which, as I have said, were instigated by the devil. Well, all that is as nothing compared with what I experienced there, and, as I understood, these tortures would be endless and uninterrupted. I repeat it, all that was as nothing compared with the spiritual agony. It is an anguish, an oppression, a pain so poignant, united with such bitter and desperate desolation, that I give up any attempt to describe them. To say that your soul is being torn out of you at every moment is but little, for then it is another who is taking your life, while here it is the soul that is rending itself. No, I cannot tell how to depict this interior fire, this despair added to such cruel torments and such atrocious pains! I could not see who was inflicting them on me, and yet I felt that I was burning and being hacked into a thousand pieces. . . .

" In this pestilential place, from which the least hope of relief is for ever banished, there is not any way of sitting or of lying down. There is no room in the sort of hole made in the wall, for in it the very sides are horrible to see and appear to crush you with their weight. One is stifled in every way. There is no light, and nought but deep darkness, and yet, inexplicable as it is, in this absence of light you can perceive everything which can offend your sight."

Teresa declares that her " dread was unutterable." Six years later when she described her vision, about 1565, her terror was still so lively that her blood froze in her veins.

"The way of fear is not that which befits my soul," she adds. We know, indeed, that God led her especially by love. However, fear acted strongly upon her at the time of her conversion. " I told myself with alarm that death would have found me on the road to hell." It was also rather fear than love that drove her to the cloister.[1]

In the work of the purification of her soul, Teresa experienced, like everyone else, the salutary fear of the judgement of God. Must one not generally pass by this way to reach the way of love?

Before joining the Carmelites of the Incarnation of Avila, Teresa had already made her way by prayer into the First Mansion of the Castle of the soul. " My experience of this First Mansion," she says, " will enable me to speak of it from full knowledge."[2] She will tell us how, for more than eighteen years, she used to pray with difficulty, and how she gave it up and took to it again. Before being finally admitted into the mystical mansions of the castle she dwelt long in the first rooms.

[1] *Life,* chap. iii.   [2] *Castle,* First Mansion, chap. ii.

B—First Degree of Prayer or Ordinary Prayer—Meditation.[1]

St Teresa's celebrated comparison for expressing the effects of prayer and for marking its different degrees is well known.

" He who begins to pray," she says, " must imagine that he is undertaking to turn an altogether uncultivated piece of ground covered with weeds into a pleasure garden for our Lord. It is our divine Master himself who uproots the bad weeds and plants the good flowers, and we think that all is done when we have resolved to give ourselves to prayer, and that we are already busy in it. Our task, as good gardeners, is to work with God's help in cultivating and watering the plants to keep them from dying and to make them yield fragrant flowers for the enjoyment of our good Master. Then he will often come into our garden for refreshment and take pleasure in seeing virtues bloom therein.

" Now let us see how we can water it, so as to know well what we have to do, what the work will cost us if the gain is to exceed the trouble, and lastly, how long our toil must go on.

" It seems to me that there are four ways of watering a garden. First of all, we may laboriously draw the water from a well. We may also make use of a noria and buckets set in motion by a winch. . . . We may also bring the water from a river or stream : the watering is then more thorough, the earth drinks in the water more deeply and it is not necessary to water it so frequently, and the gardener is far from having the same amount of fatigue. Lastly, there is plenty of rain, and this is incomparably the best way, the Lord thus doing the watering himself, without any toil on our part.

" And now I intend to apply to my subject these four ways of distributing the water needed by a garden for its maintenance, and without which it would die. Thus, I think, I shall be able to give some idea of the four degrees of prayer to which the Lord, in his mercy, has sometimes raised my soul."[2]

[1] *Life,* chap. xi-xiii ; *Castle,* First, Second, and Third Mansions ; *Way of Perfection,* chaps. xvi-xxviii. The comparison of the soul to a garden is found in Spanish mystics prior to St Teresa ; in particular, in the *Tercer Abecedario* (IV, 3) of Francisco of Ossuna. St Teresa says, indeed : " Here is a comparison which I think I have read or heard somewhere " (*Œuvres,* I, p. 117).

[2] *Life,* chap. xi, *Œuvres,* I, pp. 147-148. The first degree of prayer is meditation ; the three others are kinds of mystical prayer. St Teresa wrote this about 1565. In 1577, when she wrote the *Interior Castle,* she had attained the summits of mysticism. In it she reckons that there are four kinds of mystical prayer, one more than in the *Life.* Cf. R. Hoornaert, *Le progrès de la pensée de sainte Térèse entre la " Vie " et*

The first degree of prayer, that of the "beginners," is meditation. It is marked with effort. Those who begin to pray "draw water from the well" by hand labour, "and hard toil it is." In mystical prayer of various kinds there is much less effort and sometimes none at all.

St Teresa knew eighteen years of this toil of meditation, and describes it in detail.[1] The beginner must first of all gather together his "senses which have been accustomed to get scattered abroad."[2] "We meet with those who are so used to live amidst things external that there is no way of disentangling them from them : they appear to be powerless to withdraw into themselves." Yet they must become recollected for prayer. Later on, if they persevere, recollection will come without effort.[3]

"To draw water from the well . . . is to work with the understanding," for this first degree of prayer is meditation and consideration. Reflection may be difficult. Sometimes we experience nothing but "dryness, boredom, and repugnance." Distractions supervene, and there is no consolation. Prayer must not be given up whatever be the obstacles we encounter. "He (the gardener) must look to the satisfaction of his master, and not to his own. . . . Let us do what we can." God will repay us "for the arduous toil of lowering the bucket so often to draw it up empty."[4]

Teresa knows these troubles from her own experience. She has endured them year after year, so as to think herself fortunate when she has succeeded "in getting but a single drop of water from the blessed well."[5] God has not given her "the talent of discursive understanding," nor that "of employing her imagination profitably." She dared not pray without a book, which she used as a "buckler," to ward off the "assaults of intrusive thoughts." If she had no book immediately her mind went all astray."[6]

Reflections and the exercise of the understanding are excellent things in prayer; acts of love, silent prayer, and union with Jesus are better still.

"It is a good thing," says Teresa, "to reason discursively

---

le " Château," in the *Revue des sciences philosophiques et théologiques*, January, 1924, pp. 20 ff.

[1] *Life*, chap. iv.   [2] *id.*, chap. xi.

[3] *Castle*, First Mansion, chap. i; *Way of Perfection*, chap. xxviii.

[4] *Life*, chap. xi, *Œuvres*, I, p. 150. Cf. *Castle*, Second Mansion.

[5] *id.*, chap. xi, p. 151. Cf. *Relation* LIII, *Œuvres*, II, p. 277 : "She (Teresa) thus spent nearly twenty-eight years amidst great aridities." *Life*, chap. viii (I, p. 122) : "Very often—and it went on for years—I was more filled with wishing for the end of the time I had decided to give to prayer, more eager for the striking of the clock, than for pious considerations."

[6] *id.*, chap. iv, *Œuvres*, I, p. 74.

for some time, to fathom the sorrows endured by our Lord
. . . and his purpose in embracing them, to think of the greatness of him who suffered and of the love wherewith his
sufferings were accompanied. But we must not tire ourselves
out unremittingly in exhausting our subject; we must also
keep close to our Lord in the silence of our understanding.
We must try to permeate our mind with the idea that he is
looking at us; we are in his company, we are speaking to
him, we shall make our requests to him; we shall fling
ourselves down at his feet, we shall find joy in him, and
recognize how unworthy we are to dwell in his presence.
If we can reach this point, even at the beginning of our
prayer, we shall greatly profit thereby, for this way of prayer
is one of the most useful; at least it has been so with my
own soul.[1] . . . Mental prayer is nothing but an intimate
friendship, a frequent converse, heart to heart, with him
whom we know to be our lover."[2]

Here Teresa is describing what has since been called
affective prayer,[3] in which prayer and loving impulse exceed
the part played by reasoning. St Teresa recommends two
forms of it: *the simple look of affection* and *interior recollection* (active recollection), for the soul has sometimes to
strive hard to withdraw within itself. St Teresa thus describes this kind of recollection in the *Way of Perfection*.

" In seeking (for God) the soul needs not to take wings,
it has only to go into solitude, to look within and not to
depart from such an excellent guest. Let it speak to him
as it would speak to a father. As to a father, too, let it
address its demands to him, tell him of its troubles, and beg
him to remedy them. . . .

" This way of praying, though vocal, causes the mind to
become much more rapidly recollected. It is a kind of prayer
which possesses many advantages. It is called the prayer
of recollection, because the soul therein gathers together all
its powers and withdraws within itself with its God. By this
way more than by any other its divine Master will teach it
and give it the way of quiet. Hidden in itself, it can think
of the Passion, represent to itself the Son of God, and offer
him to the Father without having to weary the mind by
going to look for him at Calvary or in the Garden or at the
Column.

[1] *Life,* chap. xiii, *Œuvres,* I, p. 178. Chap. iv : " I did all I could
to consider continuously Jesus Christ, our Master, present within me :
that was my way of prayer. If I meditated on the mystery, I represented it to myself within, but I specially applied myself to reading
good books." *Œuvres,* I, 72. *Cf.* chap. ix.

[2] *id.,* chap. viii, *Œuvres,* I, p. 120.

[3] Also called *Acquired Contemplation.* See *Conclusions of the
Teresian Congress* of 1922, Theme IV, 7; *Mensajero de Santa Teresa,*
March 15, 1923; *Études Carmelitaines,* January-July, 1924.

"Those who can thus enclose themselves in the little heaven of the soul where its Creator dwells as much as on earth, who practise control of their sight and praying in a place where nothing can distract their outward senses, must believe that they are in an excellent way and that they will succeed in quenching their thirst at the fountain. And they will really make much progress in a short time."[1]

Such was Teresa's prayer during her noviciate and the first years of her religious profession : meditation with the help of a book, struggling against distractions, and affective recollection of a more or less laborious nature. She was "converted" by such prayer. And with what eloquence does she recommend it to all who would truly serve God and attain salvation![2]

Sufferings, too, helped Teresa to advance in sanctity. During the winter of 1537-1538, the saint had a terrible illness. She had an alarming nervous crisis. She felt at intervals that "sharp teeth were biting deep into her heart. They thought at last that it must be madness." She was tortured from head to foot. "Doctors declare," she says, "that nerve pains are intolerable, and as my nerves were all contracted, I suffered a cruel martyrdom." She became crippled; her "contracted limbs were gathered into a ball." And it was in this state that, after two years absence, she was sent back to the convent of Avila. Her paralysis lasted three years.

These sufferings courageously endured united her soul closely with God. Teresa was raised "rapidly and transitorily" to the prayer of quiet and even to that of union.[3] This state of prayer lasted but a short time, hardly for an Ave Maria, but it wrought great results in her soul. It taught Teresa "what loving God means." She felt a deep contempt for the world. Evil-speaking she held in horror. She carefully avoided the occasions of sin. Spiritual reading became her delight, and occasions for speaking of God were most pleasing to her.[4]

Teresa obtained her cure through the intercession of St Joseph. In her gratitude she exalted the holy patriarch's power of intercession in justly celebrated pages which did much to enhance his cultus amongst the faithful. "I want," she says, "to lead everyone to devotion to this glorious saint, so greatly have I experienced his influence with God. . . .

---

[1] *Way of Perfection,* chap. xxviii, *Œuvres,* V, pp. 203-204.
[2] St Teresa treats of this quasi-indispensability of prayer in her *Life,* chaps. viii, xix; *Way of Perfection,* chaps. xx-xxiii; *Interior Castle,* Second Mansion.
[3] *Life,* chap. iv, x.   [4] *id.,* chap. vi, *Œuvres,* I, p. 89.

So far I cannot remember having asked him for anything without his having given it me."[1]

The soul of Teresa, visibly called to the enjoyment of intimacy with God, ought apparently to have risen henceforth unchecked to the highest peaks of mysticism. Unfortunately, whatever be the degree of a soul's spiritual life, deterioration and even downright falls are yet possible.

The monastery of Avila, according to the custom of the times, was not then strictly enclosed. The nuns might receive and even pay visits. Teresa was cured, and, in the intoxication of recovered health, resumed her external relationships. Soon, the consequence was a frivolous and relaxed manner of life. She gave up prayer. "Having regard to my aberrations," she says, "I began to fear to return to prayer." She was afraid of entering into such intimate communion with God in the state of tepidity in which she found herself.[2] She resumed prayer only after her father's death in 1544 on the advice of the Dominican Vincent Baron; she was twenty-nine. Then followed a kind of struggle between her and God.

"On the one hand," she says, "God called me; on the other, I followed the world. I found much joy in the things of God, and the things of this world held me captive. I wanted, apparently, to unite these two contraries, so opposed to one another: on the one hand the spiritual life and its consolations, on the other the diversions and the pleasures of the senses."[3]

But in this combat God was to be the winner. He would have Teresa for himself, he intended to give her exceptional favours.

Teresa attributes her final conversion to mental prayer, the immense gains of which she extols in lyrical[4] language. But this long period of relaxation and lukewarmness, following upon years of spiritual progress, filled her with deep humility. The uncertainty of this life with regard to perseverance filled her with a kind of alarm. Later on, she told her sisters to cling to a salutary fear and always to be on the watch.

"Do not trust to the enclosure nor to the austerity of your life," she said, thinking of herself, "and do not rely upon your constant occupation with the things of God, nor upon your continual exercises of prayer, nor upon your separation from the things of this world, nor upon the horror you may seem to have of them. All that is good; but, as I have said, it is not enough to take away from us every reason for fear. Therefore, repeat this text and call it often to mind: *Beatus vir qui timet Dominum.*"[5]

---

[1] *Life,* chap. vi, *Œuvres,* I, pp. 92-93. [2] *id.,* chaps. vii, xix.
[3] *id.,* chap. vii, *Œuvres,* I, p. 111. [4] *id.,* chap. viii.
[5] *Interior Castle,* Third Mansion, chap. i, *Œuvres,* VI, p. 79.

III—KINDS OF MYSTICAL PRAYER ACCORDING TO ST TERESA

ABOUT the age of forty-three, Teresa entered into the mystical mansions of the castle of the soul. During her great illness, she had formerly been introduced into them in a transitory fashion, and then she had returned for some time to the First Mansion. Henceforward she was to receive super-natural favours uninterruptedly.

She distinguishes them thus from what she had experienced in the First Mansion :

"Before this I had felt, somehow continuously, a tender-ness of devotion, which is, I believe, the result of our effort. It is a feeling of consolation which is neither entirely sensible nor entirely spiritual. It is clear that we receive all from God. In this, however, we can, I think, help ourselves much, either by considering our lowness and ingratitude . . . or by rejoicing in the works of the Lord. . . . If thereto is added a little love, the soul expands, the heart is touched, and tears flow."[1]

These loving impulses are a reward for our goodwill. When we draw water with manual labour from the spiritual well our soul is sweetly watered therewith.

But in the other degrees of prayer, the soul "touches the supernatural. In fact, whatever be its effort, it cannot obtain of itself that with which we now have to do."[2]

A—IS EVERYONE CALLED TO THE MYSTICAL KINDS OF PRAYER? —THE SPECIAL NEED OF DIRECTION FOR MYSTICS

Does God call all souls of goodwill to the mystical kinds of prayer?

To this question St Teresa seems to make a hesitating reply. In her *Life* we find nothing definite about it.

When she teaches her religious abouf prayer in the *Way*

[1] *Life,* chap. x, *Œuvres,* I, p. 135. *Castle,* Fourth Mansion, chap. i : "We may, apparently, call consolations the feelings of happiness obtained by means of meditation and prayers addressed to our Lord. These consolations . . . therefore arise from the laudable act which we fulfil, they are in some sort the effect of our work." *Œuvres,* VI, p. 98. See chap. ii, pp. 107 ff.

[2] *Life,* chap. xiv, *Œuvres,* I, p. 179. Cf. *Castle,* Fourth Mansion, chap. ii : "To understand this well, let us imagine that we are look-ing at two springs filling two basins with water. . . . These two basins are filling in different ways : one receives its water from a distance through long pipes and by artificial means; the other is built close to the spring and fills noiselessly. . . . The water laid on by a pipe represents the consolations acquired by meditation. We bring them, indeed, by our reflections on created things and by a troublesome effort of the understanding. . . . In the other basin, the water issues from the same spring, which is God." *Œuvres,* VI, pp. 108-109.

of Perfection, she declares that the gift of contemplation is not intended for all.

" How, if we are humble," she says, " can we ever per-suade ourselves that we are virtuous enough to be among the contemplatives? That God can make us such is certain ; he can do so in his goodness and mercy. But if people will follow my advice they will always take their seats in the lowest place, according to the counsel and example of our Lord. Then we must be prepared in case it be God's good pleasure to lead us by the way of contemplation. If he does not do so let us have recourse to humility. Let us think our-selves happy to serve the servants of God. . . .

" It is not without good cause that I speak thus : for—I repeat it and it is most important to understand this—God does not lead souls by the same road. Whoever thinks that he is walking by the lowest way is perhaps the highest in the eyes of the Lord. Thus, because in this monastery all give themselves up to prayer, it does not follow that all must be contemplatives. It is impossible, and not to know this truth might cast into desolation those who are not at all so. Contemplation is a gift of God. Since it is not necessary for salvation and God does not demand it, none of you should imagine that he will require it of her. A soul will not fail to be very perfect provided that she fulfils what we have said. She may even have much greater merit, because she will work the more at her own cost. The Lord is leading her as a strong soul, and holds in reserve for her to be given all together all the consolations that she has not enjoyed in this world. Therefore, let her not be discouraged. Let her not give up prayer, and go on doing what the others are doing. . . .

" Let the master of the house have his way. He is wise and powerful and knows what befits you, and also what befits himself. If you do what you can and prepare yourself for contemplation by the perfect life we have shown you, and then find this gift denied you—and yet I am inclined to be-lieve that you will receive it if your detachment and humility are real—be sure that our Lord is keeping this joy for you to add to all those that await you in heaven."[1]

A little further on, in chapter xix, St Teresa appears to contradict herself. After comparing contemplation with a fountain of living water, she adds :

" Think that the Lord invites everyone. He is the very Truth, therefore the thing is beyond doubt. If the feast were not general, he would not call us all, or when calling us he would not say : I will give you to drink. He would

---

[1] *Way of Perfection,* chap. xvii, *Œuvres,* V, pp. 132-133, 136. *Cf.* chap. xviii.

say : Come all of you, you will lose nothing by it; and I will give to drink unto whom I think good. But he says without restriction : Come all of you; and thus I hold it sure that all those who do not stop on the way will receive this living water."[1]

The saint is conscious of this apparent contradiction, for she writes at the beginning of chapter xx :

" There is apparently a contradiction between what I have just said in the preceding chapter and what I said farther back when, wishing to console those who do not attain to contemplation, I showed that there are different ways of going to God, as there are different mansions in heaven. And, nevertheless, I maintain what I have said."[2]

If we now open the *Book of the Mansions*—i.e., *The Interior Castle*—we again find the saint advising her sisters not to seek for the mystical kinds of prayer. " The *Book of the Mansions* is the last and most finished of St Teresa's works, and it represents the experience of her whole life, and, therefore, we rightly look to it for the last word she has to say about the interior ways and the mystical states."[3] Now this is what she has to say of the spiritual tastes or the supernatural prayer of quiet :

" You want to acquire this kind of prayer directly, my daughters, and for good reasons, for, once more, the soul cannot comprehend the graces which are then received from God and the love with which he comes to it. There can be nothing more legitimate than to desire to know how to obtain such a favour. Therefore I will tell you what I have learnt about it. Let us put aside the case in which the Lord is pleased to grant it merely because he thinks well to do so. He knows the reason, and we have nothing to do with it.

" First, do what was counselled to the dwellers in the former mansions, and then—humility, humility ! It is thereby that the Lord yields to all our desires. And would you know whether you possess this virtue ? First of all see whether you think yourselves unworthy of these graces and divine tastes, and whether you are convinced that they will never be granted you in this life. You will say to me : But how are we to obtain them if we do nothing towards it ? I reply that the best way is the one I have just pointed out—that is to say, to do nothing to get them."

And St Teresa gives several reasons for this.

" The first is, that to obtain these graces, nothing is more necessary than to love God disinterestedly. The second is, that there is a slight want of humility in thinking we can obtain so great a good by such poor services as ours. The third is, that the true disposition for us who, after all, have offended our Lord, is not to aspire to receive consolations, but to desire to suffer and to make ourselves like him. The fourth is, that his Majesty has not bound himself to give us these spiritual tastes as he has bound himself to give us beatitude if we keep his commandments. We can be saved without them, and he knows best what befits us and who are those who love him in reality. There is one thing certain, and I have no doubt about it, that there are people—and I know some of them—who walk in the way of love as we ought to walk in it, that is to say, with the sole desire of serving Jesus crucified, and who not only do not ask him for spiritual tastes and do not desire to have them, but even implore him not to give them any in this life. This is mere truth.

" The fifth reason is, that it means tormenting ourselves in sheer waste. As this water is not brought through pipes like the former water, if the spring will not give it we shall tire ourselves out in vain. I mean that we shall multiply our meditations to no purpose and strain our hearts and shed our tears, it will be all useless. That is not at all the way in which this water comes. God gives it to whom he will, and he often does it at the moment when the soul is thinking of it least. We are his, my sisters : let him do what he will with us ; let him lead us by the path that pleases him."[1]

After this it is surprising to find Teresa saying at the beginning of the Fifth Mansion :

" All of us who wear the holy habit of Mount Carmel are called to prayer and contemplation : there is the place of our first institution, we belong to the race of the holy Fathers of Mount Carmel who, in such deep solitude and in such entire contempt of the world, sought for the treasure, the precious pearl of which we are speaking. And nevertheless, I declare to you that very few among us prepare themselves to see the Saviour reveal it to them."[2]

Lastly, a few pages further on, St Teresa appears to say that we may reach the prayer of union by two ways. One of these ways is mystical and supernatural, and it is only followed by the few who are called to extraordinary states. The other is not mystical, but is accessible to all who renounce " their own wills to cleave to God's."[3]

---

[1] *Castle,* Fourth Mansion, chap. ii, *Œuvres,* VI, pp. 111-113.
[2] *ibid.,* Fifth Mansion, chap. i, *Œuvres,* VI, p. 128.
[3] *ibid.,* chap. iii, *Œuvres,* VI, pp. 150-151 : " According to all that I have said, this [Fifth] Mansion has still, I think, a certain amount of darkness. But since it is so good for us to enter it, it will be well not to take away the hope of it from those whom the Lord does not gratify with such supernatural favours. Real union, indeed, may be quite well obtained with our Lord's help, if we try to **acquire** it by renouncing our own will to cleave to the will of God."

St Teresa's thought remains indefinite. From it we can apparently draw no really sure conclusion.

Before reaching the mystical states great sufferings must be undergone. Teresa knew them by experience. She describes them at considerable length in the *Interior Castle.* She points them out merely for her nuns in the *Way of Perfection,* encouraging those who may experience them.

"I tell you, my daughters, whom God does not lead by the path of contemplation, that those who walk by that way have to bear a cross no lighter than yours. This is what I have seen and known. You would, indeed, be surprised if you knew the crosses which God makes them bear. I am well acquainted with what concerns them both. Well, I see quite clearly that the sufferings God sends to contemplatives are intolerable. They are so great that did he not sustain them with the heavenly tastes, they could not hold fast. And that is easy to understand: God leads by the way of suffering those whom he specially loves, and the more he loves them, the greater are their sufferings."[1]

Certain of these sufferings sometimes arise—as Teresa knew by her own experience—from the confessor's lack of experience. Those whom God leads by extraordinary ways need directors who have knowledge personally, if possible, of the mystical states, or have at any rate studied them in books. The contemplative cannot do without direction. If his confessor is an ignorant man he will make very regrettable mistakes and subject his penitents to painful anguish.[2]

B—The Different Kinds of Mystical Prayer

In the writings of St Teresa we find two different classes of mystical prayer.

According to her *Life,* written from 1563 to 1565, the extraordinary kinds of prayer are: the *prayer of recollection,* the *prayer of quiet,* the *prayer of the sleep of the powers,* the *prayer of union and ecstasy.* *Spiritual Relation* LIV gives a similar classification.

In 1577, in the *Interior Castle,* St Teresa says nothing of the *prayer of the sleep of the powers,* but she adds the *spiritual marriage,* the highest degree of mystical prayer, of which she was ignorant when she wrote the *Life.* The saint's final idea of the classification of mystical prayer is therefore this: *prayer of recollection, prayer of quiet, prayer of union* with or without ecstasy, and the *spiritual marriage.* This

---

[1] *Way of Perfection,* chap. xviii, *Œuvres,* V, pp. 138-139.
[2] *ibid.,* chaps. iv-v. Cf. *Castle,* Fifth Mansion, chap. i, *Œuvres,* VI, p. 153.

classification is considered by theologians as more exact than the first. It denotes a real advance in Teresa's thought.[1] I shall follow it giving all the variations of the *Life,* the *Way of Perfection,* and of *Relation* LIV.

1. *Prayer of Recollection*[2]

We note that Teresa feels her way to some extent with regard to this kind of prayer.

In the *Life* she makes it a supernatural prayer, which is indistinguishable from the prayer of quiet : " Here," she says, " the soul begins to enter into recollection : it touches the supernatural." By its own efforts it cannot reach this second degree of prayer, which " corresponds with the second way instituted by the Master of the garden for obtaining water. By means of a wheel and buckets the gardener gets a larger quantity of it with less fatigue, and he is no longer forced to give himself up to unceasing labour. To apply this second mode of watering to the prayer called that of quiet, such is the aim I have now in view.[3]

The *Way of Perfection,*[4] on the other hand, clearly distinguishes the prayer of recollection from the prayer of quiet, but it is no longer a supernatural prayer; it is the prayer of active recollection described higher up.

Lastly, in the *Interior Castle* and in *Relation* LIV St Teresa separates the prayer of recollection from that of quiet and considers it as a supernatural prayer.[5] Such, on this point in mysticism, is the final mind of the saint. Moreover, Teresa declares, when she comes to the description of the Fourth Mansion of the *Interior Castle,* that she had " a little more light on these favours granted to certain souls " than when she wrote the *Life.*[6]

The recollection in question cannot be obtained " by the

---

[1] *Cf.* R. Hoornaert, *Le progrès de la pensée de sainte Térèse entre la " Vie " et le " Château "* (*Revue des sciences phil. et théol.,* January, 1924).

[2] *Life,* chaps. xiv-xv; *Castle,* Fourth Mansion, chap. iii; *Spiritual Relation,* I, LIV.

[3] *Life, ibid., Œuvres,* I, p. 179.   [4] Chaps. xxviii-xxix.

[5] *Castle,* Fourth Mansion, chap. iii : " I shall deal with a kind of prayer which almost always precedes this [of quiet]. . . . It is a recollection which seems to me to be also supernatural. . . . I spoke in the first place [on coming to the Fourth Mansion] of the prayer of the divine tastes, or of quiet, then I passed on to the prayer of recollection. I ought to have treated of the latter prayer first." *Œuvres,* VI, p. 114.

[6] *Castle,* Fourth Mansion, chap. i, *Œuvres,* VI, p. 97. In *Relation* LIV, St Teresa says this : " From this recollection sometimes springs a quiet, a delicious interior peace. The soul seems to want nothing more; speaking—I mean praying—vocally and meditation become a burden; it wants only to love." *Œuvres,* II, pp. 295-296. This *Relation* belongs to 1576, a year before the *Interior Castle.*

work of the understanding, trying to think of God within oneself, nor by that of the imagination representing him to oneself within. . . . We are not concerned with the manner of working which is in everyone's power, always, of course, with God's help." Here all is different. "Sometimes, even before we have begun to think of God," the senses and the powers of the soul "are already found to be within the castle." It is God himself who produces such recollection without any effort on our part. "The monarch who dwells within the royal residence of the castle" makes his voice heard as a very low "whistling" by the senses and the powers which wander round the walls. Immediately they "re-enter the castle" and the soul feels, without incurring the least fatigue, "a sweet impression of recollection."[1]

"The powers withdraw within themselves the better to relish the pleasure which they enjoy; they are not, however, suspended or put to sleep." In the prayer of recollection "the will alone is occupied, and, without knowing how it is made captive, it allows itself to become God's prisoner." The understanding, the memory, and the imagination desire to act and to help the will. In reality, they hinder it, but it "must pay no attention to them" and "remain in the enjoyment of its repose." If it tried to fetter them, it would lose its own recollection.[2]

Contrariwise to what is said by several spiritual writers, St Teresa thinks that, in the prayer of recollection, we cannot "fetter the action of the mind without doing more harm than good."[3] It is in the most perfect kinds of prayer that the powers of the soul are bound. But to explain this diversity of opinion, it must be remarked that all mystics do not distinguish, as St Teresa does, the prayer of recollection from that of quiet. The passage of the *Treatise of Prayer and Meditation* (ch. xii, Counsel 8) of St Peter of Alcantara, to which the saint refers, has to do with the state of a "man . . . who has reached repose and the taste for contemplation"[4]—that is, the prayer of quiet.

---

[1] *Castle*, Fourth Mansion, chap. iii, *Œuvres*, VI, p. 116.
[2] *Life*, chap. xiv, *Œuvres*, I, p. 180. St Teresa has but little appreciation for "the work of the understanding" in prayer. For her "the progress of the soul does not consist in much thinking, but in much loving." Then she flings out this sally : "I only want to make it well understood that the soul is not the mind, and that the will is not at all ruled by the latter, which, indeed, would be a very unhappy thing for the will." *Foundations*, chap. v, *Œuvres*, III, pp. 97-98.
[3] *Castle*, Fourth Mansion, chap. iii, *Œuvres*, VI, p. 117. Cf. *Relation* LIV, *Œuvres*, II, p. 295.
[4] *Castle, ibid.*, p. 118.

2. *The Prayer of Quiet or of the Divine Tastes*[1]

Here the powers of the soul, without being properly bound, are as if they were laid half asleep :

"In the prayer of the divine tastes, in which the water gushes from the spring itself without being brought through pipes, the understanding stops, or rather finds that it is stopped, because it sees that it does not itself know what it wants. Then it inclines first to one side and then to the other, as if it were numbed and incapable of concentrating upon anything."[2]

Distractions are harder than in the prayer of simple recollection. However, the will has a little trouble to bear " this agitation of the understanding," but its repose is not disturbed thereby. It is, indeed, in the will, because it " is fixed upon its God," that the quiet dwells.[3]

God begins to make his presence felt in the soul; he captures it and makes it happy :

" Here, indeed, the soul is immersed in peace, or rather, the Lord immerses it therein by his presence, as he did in the case of the just Simeon. Then all the powers are at rest and the soul comprehends in a very different way from that of the external senses, that it is close to God and that it is very near becoming one with him by union. . . .[4] Then there are spiritual blessings which are unutterable, and even the soul itself cannot understand what it is actually receiving."[5]

In this kind of prayer the soul enjoys perfect repose and relishes a most sweet pleasure. It is quite " happy with its God." The will " is so exquisitely busy without knowing how " that all the endeavours of the understanding and the memory " cannot deprive it of its content and happiness."[6]

[1] *Life,* chap. xiv-xv; *Way of Perfection,* chap. xxxi; *Castle,* Fourth Mansion, chap. ii : " What I call the divine tastes and have elsewhere named the prayer of quiet." *Œuvres,* VI, p. 108. *Cf.* chap. iii.

[2] *Castle,* Fourth Mansion, chap. iii, *Œuvres,* VI, p. 121. *Relation* LIV.

[3] *Castle, ibid.; Life,* chap. xv : " The understanding and the memory wander in vain, the will remains united with God, the quiet and repose persist." *Œuvres,* I, p. 189.

[4] *Way of Perfection,* chap. xxxi, *Œuvres,* V, pp. 222-223. In the *Castle,* Fourth Mansion, chap. i, Teresa appears to modify this explanation : " In my opinion, the powers here are not united to God, but only, as it were, inebriated, and they ask in astonishment what it can really be. . . . It is by the effects and ensuing works that we can tell the real graces of prayer."

[5] *Castle,* Fourth Mansion, chap. ii, *Œuvres,* VI, p. 110.

[6] *Life,* chap. xv, *Œuvres,* I, p. 189. See chap. xxii : " I thought [in the prayer of quiet] that I felt the presence of God, which was true, and I tried to keep recollected close to him. If only God shows himself at all favourable, this is a most agreeable state of prayer, which fills one with delight." *Œuvres,* I, p. 274.

St Teresa thus describes the effects of such prayer when persevered in :

" There appear very plainly in the soul a dilatation and enlargement. Imagine a spring without an outlet, and with a basin so made as to increase in size as the water becomes more abundant. Well, thus it is with this sort of prayer. God—not to speak of many other wonders then wrought in the soul—prepares it and makes it fit to contain all that he desires to fill it with. This sweetness and interior enlargement may be known from the following effect : the soul no longer finds itself bound as before in the service of God, but its action is much more extended. The fear of hell ceases to disturb it. Whilst the dread of offending God increases in it, servile fear disappears. . . . Formerly it was afraid of crosses, but now it fears them less because its faith is more living. . . . Knowing his [God's] greatness better, it has a lower opinion of itself. As it has experienced the delights that come from him, the pleasures of the world are but dung in its sight. . . . Lastly, it grows in all the virtues, making continual progress, if indeed it draw not back and do nothing to offend God."[1]

In the *Way of Perfection,*[2] St Teresa notifies another favour, which is " very difficult to grasp if one has not had a great deal of experience," granted by God " when the quiet is deep and prolonged." It is the favour of combining the active life with the contemplative, of fulfilling the Office of Martha and that of Mary at the same time :

" [Those who possess it] perceive very well that they are not altogether in what they are doing : they are lacking in the main thing—that is to say, in the will, which, as it appears to me, is then united with its God. As for the other powers, God leaves them free to busy themselves with what belongs to his service. For this, indeed, they are much more fit than they usually are. But if they have to do with worldly matters, they seem to be dull and, sometimes even, as if they were stupefied. . . . Then we serve the Lord in all sorts of ways at the same time : the will is at its own business—I mean at contemplation—without knowing how it is performing it, and the two other powers are doing the work of Martha."[3]

When St Teresa was raised to this state, she did not know

---

[1] *Castle,* Fourth Mansion, chap. iii, *Œuvres,* VI, pp. 121-122.

[2] Chap. xxxi. St Teresa does not speak of this result of the prayer of quiet in the *Interior Castle.* In *Relation* LIV, she attributes it to the prayer of the sleep of the powers. *Œuvres,* II, p. 296. So, too, in the *Life,* chap. xvii, *Œuvres,* I, pp. 211-212. In the Seventh Mansion of the *Castle,* the soul in the state of the spiritual marriage experiences a similar effect, but it is more perfect.

[3] *Way of Perfection,* chap. xxxi, *Œuvres,* V, pp. 224-226. Cf. *Relation* LIV, *Œuvres,* II, p. 296.

how to explain it. She consulted Francis Borgia, who " replied that there was nothing at all impossible in it, and that the same thing happened to himself."

According to the *Life*[1] and *Relation* LIV, between the prayer of quiet and the prayer of union is found an intermediate degree of prayer, called the *prayer of the sleep of the powers*. St Francis de Sales[2] and St Teresa's commentators think that this *sleep of the powers* does not differ from the *prayer of quiet*.

This is how St Teresa describes it in her *Life:*

" Let us now speak of the third kind of water that waters our garden. It is running water, coming from a river or fountain. We must still, it is true, take the trouble to bring it, but the watering is much less tiring. Here the Lord so far helps the gardener as to take his place in some sort, doing almost all the work himself.

" This prayer is a sleep of the powers, wherein these, without being entirely suspended, do not understand how they work. Consolation, sweetness, enjoyment are incomparably greater than in the preceding state. The soul is so plunged in the water of grace that it can go neither forward nor backward nor see how to do so; it aspires only to enjoy such felicity. It is as if someone were holding a candle that had been blessed in his hand and expecting death at any moment, but a death ardently desired. In the act of dying, the soul is inundated with unutterable delight. In my opinion, this is to die almost entirely to the things of this world and already to enjoy God. . . . The soul itself no longer knows what it ought to do. Must it speak or be silent, laugh or weep? It does not know. It is in a glorious delirium, a heavenly madness, that we learn true wisdom."[3]

In this kind of prayer, there is not as yet the full union of all the powers with God, but " this union surpasses that of the preceding state."[4] The faculties of the soul can still act, but only " to attend to God." Even if we tried hard, we could not succeed in drawing them away from him; then thousands of words of praise ascend to God, but without any order, unless the Lord himself order them : at any rate, the understanding is powerless to arrange them." In this state St Teresa exhaled her love in " verses full of utterance . . .

---

[1] Chaps. xvi-xvii.
[2] *Treatise of the Love of God,* VI, chap. viii.
[3] *Life,* chap. xvi. *Œuvres,* I, pp. 201-202.
[4] *ibid.,* chap. xvi, *Relation* LIV : " From this prayer (of quiet) usually proceeds what is called the sleep of the powers. These are then neither absorbed nor so suspended as to call this a state of rapture : nor is it altogether union." *Œuvres,* II, p. 296.

under the sway of this holy and heavenly madness."[1] She complained of the torments of exile and wanted to die. She gave herself up entirely to the good pleasure of God.

St Teresa had been enjoying these spiritual favours for five or six years when she gave an account of them in her *Life*. She acknowledges that she did not altogether understand them at first:

" Until now," she says, " I had no skill in them, and I was incapable of giving an account of them. Moreover, I had decided, when I reached this point, to say but very little or even almost nothing about them. I well understood that in this state there was not an entire union of the powers, and, nevertheless, it was clear to me that this union surpassed that of the preceding state [of quiet]. But I confess that I could not discern and thoroughly grasp in what the difference consisted."[2]

God enabled her to take full knowledge of this state of prayer one day after Holy Communion. At the same time he taught her how she should find expressions to explain it, and how the soul should behave in it.[3]

" This state seems, at first," she says, " to be the same as the prayer of quiet, and nevertheless there is a difference between them. In the prayer of quiet, the soul tries to avoid any movement of whatever kind; it enjoys the holy idleness of Mary. In the state of which I am speaking, it can also play the part of Martha. . . . This mode of prayer seems to be a very evident union of the whole soul with God. Only God wishes, apparently, to enable the powers to understand and to enjoy the greatness of his work in them. . . . What cannot be doubted is, that the virtues gain much more vigour from this state of prayer than from the preceding one, which is that of quiet. The soul becomes quite changed."[4]

Ten or twelve years later, when she wrote the *Interior Castle,* St Teresa makes no further mention of the prayer of the sleep of the powers. She passes directly from the prayer of quiet to the prayer of union.

3. *The Prayer of Union:*[5] *its Nature and Object*

This is " the fourth kind of water," that " which falls from heaven to flood and drench our garden," without any effort on the part of the gardener. " This rain from heaven often falls just when it is least expected by the gardener."[6]

---

[1] *Life,* chap. xvi, pp. 202-203.
[2] *ibid.,* chap. xvi, *Œuvres,* I, p. 202.   [3] *ibid.*
[4] *ibid.,* chap. xvii, pp. 210-211.
[5] *ibid.,* chaps. xviii-xix; *Castle,* Fifth Mansion, chaps. i-iv; *Relation* LIV.
[6] *ibid.,* chap. xviii, *Œuvres,* I, p. 223.

Its suddenness is, indeed, one of the notes of this grace of union :

" While I was keeping in spirit near Jesus Christ . . ." says St Teresa, " or else while I was reading, I was suddenly seized with a lively sense of the presence of God. I could then have no manner of doubt of his presence within me nor that I was myself entirely lost in him."[1]

Here God makes his presence felt in the mystic's soul beyond all doubt, so complete is the union :

" In the beginning," says St Teresa, " I was so ignorant as not to know that God is in all beings. Now, on the one hand, the most intimate presence of which I am speaking appeared to me to be incredible, and on the other, I could not help believing that God was there, for I had what seemed a clear view of his real presence. . . .[2] God then establishes himself in such a manner in the innermost part of this soul that when she comes to herself she cannot doubt but that she had been in God and God in her. This truth is so thoroughly impressed upon her spirit that if years were to elapse without this grace being renewed she could neither forget nor doubt but that she had been in God. And that is quite apart from the results effected. . . . This certitude is the capital point."[3]

It is not " by means of a vision " nor by reasoning that the soul acquires the knowledge of God's presence in it, " but by its abiding conviction which God alone can give."[4]

During the union, there is a " simultaneous suspension of the powers." Distractions are impossible in this state of prayer ; they might still supervene in the former ones. The " little lizards "—that is to say, the " little thoughts arising from the imagination " or otherwise—may come into the Fourth Mansion of the Castle. But " however agile they may be, these lizards cannot get into the Fifth Mansion with which we are dealing, because there is neither imagination nor memory nor understanding to be an obstacle to the good we enjoy there."[5]

" Here we feel nothing at all, we only enjoy without knowing what we are enjoying. We see that we are enjoying a good which includes all goods, but we do not understand wherein this good consists. All the senses are so absorbed in this joy that none of them is free to engage in anything else either within or without. . . .[6] Here we are asleep—and deeply asleep—to the things of this world and of ourselves ; and, therefore, during the short period of union, we

---

[1] *Life,* chap. x, *Œuvres,* I, p. 134.
[2] *ibid.,* chap. xviii, pp. 226-227.
[3] *Castle,* Fifth Mansion, chap. i, *Œuvres,* VI, p. 134.
[4] *ibid.*   [5] *ibid.,* p. 131.
[6] *Life,* chap. xviii, *Œuvres,* I, p. 218. St Teresa also says : " Here all the powers are bound and totally suspended," p. 216.

are, as it were, without feeling : even if we would, we cannot think. Then there is no need of any contrivance to suspend the activity of the mind. . . . Lastly, we are absolutely dead to the world in order to live the more unto God. And this is a delightful death : a death, because the soul is withdrawn from all the operations that it can perform while united to the body; and delightful, because if the soul appears really to be separated from the body, it is in order to live the better unto God."[1]

St Teresa has just told us that this union is short. In her *Life,* she remarks that " the time of the suspension of the powers is always very brief," at most but " half an hour." Even when such state of prayer lasts as long as that, it " does not injure one's health."[2]

This state of union " leaves the soul filled with an extreme tenderness of love. . . . It feels that it is full of courage, and if it were then torn asunder for God's sake, it would greatly rejoice. Then arise promises and heroic resolutions and burning desires, a horror of the world, and a clear perception of its vanity." The soul discerns plainly its unworthiness " in all its fulness; just as, in a room full of sunshine, not a single thread of a spider's web escapes our sight."[3]

In the *Interior Castle* Teresa compares the soul in the state of union with " a most lovely little white butterfly " coming from a silk-worm, escaping from its cocoon. It has quite other aspirations than it had as a worm; it flies instead of crawling; and nowhere does it find its true repose. It is the same case with the soul in the prayer of union; it has an intense desire to get away from this world. It " cannot recognize itself any longer. . . . Now, indeed, it looks for great crosses, and the desire to bear them is irresistible. It is athirst for penance, it yearns for solitude, it wants God to be known by all men, and, hence, it is deeply grieved when it sees them offend him."[4] The suffering felt by St Teresa when she saw souls perishing gave her some idea of the sufferings of Christ. In fact, the grace of union is not given for the soul's own sake. Our neighbour should profit by it. Further, one of the fruits of such prayer is an increase of fraternal charity, an advance in our zeal for the salvation of mankind.[5]

In the prayer of union we contemplate eternal realities. What, exactly, is the object of such contemplation : the

[1] *Castle,* Fifth Mansion, chap. i, *Œuvres,* VI, p. 129.
[2] *Life,* chap. xviii, *Œuvres,* I, pp. 224-225.
[3] *ibid.,* chap. xix, *Œuvres,* I, pp. 228-229.
[4] *Castle,* Fifth Mansion, chap. ii, *Œuvres,* VI, pp. 142-143.
[5] *ibid.,* chap. iii.

divinity alone, or the humanity of Christ? St Teresa tries to give us an answer.

She knows that most mystical writers think that in high contemplation the soul is applied to God to the exclusion of all else, and even of the humanity of Christ:

"These writers," she says, "strongly exhort (those who have attained to contemplation) to set aside all corporal representations to concentrate upon the divinity alone, for, say they, even the humanity of Christ becomes an obstacle and an impediment to perfect contemplation. . . . (This last) is an entirely spiritual thing, and any corporal thing may encumber it and bar its way. Consider yourself surrounded by God on all sides, see yourself immersed in him: that is what they tell us to aim at."[1]

Teresa does not hesitate to declare that this teaching is "mistaken."[2] She cannot understand how the humanity of Christ can be a hindrance to contemplation. Her own experience proves, on the contrary, that it is "the gate whereby we must enter, if we would have the sovereign Majesty discover high secrets to us."[3] She acknowledges, however, that:

"[When] it pleases God to suspend all the powers [of the soul], as we have seen that he does in the various kinds of prayer above dealt with, it is plain that, in spite of ourselves, the presence of the holy humanity escapes our notice. That it is so then, well and good. . . . But that we ourselves should try of set purpose, instead of forming the habit of having this most holy humanity ever before us—and would to God that it always were so!—to do exactly the opposite: that, once more, is just what I disapprove of."[4]

Despite these modifications, the mind of St Teresa, on an important point of mystical theology, is in disaccord with the majority of contemplatives. St Teresa is very individual. Despite her great docility towards her directors, she does not fear from time to time to set her own experience against the views of the theologians, making the subtle remark that, in mysticism above all, "God leads souls by many ways and by many different paths."[5]

The prayer of union paves the way towards the spiritual marriage, a kind of "interview" of very brief duration between the soul and its Lord:

"The soul sees in a merely mysterious way who he is whom she is about to take as her Spouse. The knowledge which she thus acquires in a short space of time she could

---

[1] *Life,* chap. xxii, *Œuvres,* I, pp. 272-273. See, too, *Castle,* Sixth Mansion, chap. vii.

[2] *Life, ibid.,* p. 274.   [3] *ibid.,* p. 278.
[4] *ibid.,* p. 279.   [5] *ibid.,* p. 273.

not obtain in a thousand years by means of the senses and the powers. The Spouse, being what he is, by this single sight of himself makes her worthier of his hand, as we say. The soul is then so lost in love that she does all that she can that nothing may hinder the divine espousals."[1]

For the devil makes desperate efforts to prevent the soul from attaining to the heavenly marriage. Teresa points out the way to defeat his wiles and to be strictly faithful to the divine call.

But before being admitted to the spiritual marriage, the soul must be further purified. God makes her pass through the painful way of mystical purification and by that of rapture and ecstasy. This is the subject of the Sixth Mansion of the *Interior Castle,* which must be reached before attaining to the mystical marriage of the Seventh Mansion.

Before going any further, let us note the wonderful effects in the way of zeal wrought in St Teresa by the mystical union. Not in vain did God accord her such extraordinary prayer and the favours which accompanied it. She had a very important mission to fulfil : the Carmelite reform. The period of her life in which she was raised to this degree of prayer, and to the most extraordinary of her other states, was exactly coincident with that of her numerous foundations.[2]

4. *The usual Preparations for the Spiritual Marriage: Passive Purifications*[3]*— Raptures — Ecstasy — Visions and Revelations*[4]

" O God !" says St Teresa, " what inward and outward pains do we not endure before entering into the Seventh Mansion ! Of a truth, when I think of it, it seems to me

---

[1] *Castle,* Fifth Mansion, chap. iv, *Œuvres,* VI, p. 161.

[2] In 1562 she founded the monastery of the Carmelites of St Joseph of Avila, where she spent five years (1562-1567), " the sweetest of her life," she says. During the next four years (1567-1571) she founded nine monasteries, seven for nuns : Medina del Campo, Malagon, Valladolid, Toledo, Pastrana, Salamanca, and Alba; and two for men : Duruelo and Pastrana. Her three years' priorate at the Convent of the Incarnation of Avila (1571-1574), which she was charged to reform, stopped the foundations for a time; the only exception was that of Segovia. On regaining her freedom, she resumes her travels and works. In less than a year (February, 1575-January, 1576), she gives three new convents of nuns to the Reform : Beas, Seville, and Caravoca. Then persecution was let loose upon her work and brought it within a hair's breadth of destruction. All foundations were suspended until 1580. On the other hand, the last three years of her life (1580-1582) were to see the erection of five new monasteries : Villanueva de la Jara, Palencia, Soria, Granada, and Burgos. *Œuvres,* III, p. 17. How can it be said that St Teresa was a sick woman, and that what was extraordinary in her inner life belongs to pathology?

[3] *Life,* chaps. xxx-xxxi ; *Castle,* Sixth Mansion, chaps. i-ii.

[4] *Life,* chaps. xx, xxiv-xxix, xxxii, xxxvii-xl ; *Castle,* Sixth Mansion, chaps. iii-xi ; *Foundations,* chaps. vi, viii ; *Relation* LIV.

that if we knew of them beforehand, our natural weakness would find it very hard to resolve to face them, whatever gain might be otherwise promised us."[1]

These troubles—to begin with the least of them—are the ill-natured comments, the criticisms, and the calumnies of the people with whom we are connected. According to them, we are wandering astray and cheated with illusions, we are, like a host of others, the playthings of Satan, we bring virtue into disrepute and deceive our confessors. "There will be endless scoffing and all sorts of things said against us."[2]

The Lord also usually sends very serious illnesses. "This torment far exceeds the foregoing one, especially if the pains we suffer are sharp."[3] When she was writing the *Interior Castle*, St Teresa declared that since she received the grace of union—that is to say, during forty years—she had not passed a single day without suffering.[4]

Amongst her interior troubles must be placed those she had to endure when she happened to meet with an ignorant or inexperienced confessor to whom everything seemed suspicious and who condemned all spiritual favours, "putting everything down to the devil or to melancholia."[5] No one ever experienced this sort of suffering more than Teresa.

This attitude on the part of the confessor gives rise to another torment. The soul thus rebuffed imagines that owing to its sins God allows it, in fact, to deceive itself:

"My mind became so darkened," relates St Teresa, "that I fell into innumerable doubts and perplexities. I said to myself that I had understood nothing of what was taking place within me, perhaps it was all mere reverie, and it ought to be enough for me to be misled myself without misleading honest people. I felt that I was so detestable that I believed that by my sins I was the cause of all the evils and heresies which have appeared in our days."[6]

When the confessor happens to reassure his poor afflicted penitent, "the torment subsides only to return." Furthermore, she succeeds in persuading herself that she is really deceiving her confessor.[7] God alone can quell such tempests. He sometimes does so, but only for a short time. For he permits other inward and more painful afflictions, especially the belief that he has abandoned us.

[1] *Castle,* Sixth Mansion, chap. i, *Œuvres,* VI, p. 168.
[2] *ibid.,* p. 169. St Teresa alludes specially to the criticisms, gibes, affronts, and persecutions of which she became the butt from 1562, the year of the foundation of the first monastery of bare-footed Carmelites at Avila. *Cf.* H. Joly, *Sainte Térèse,* pp. 121 ff.
[3] *Castle, ibid.,* p. 171.
[4] *ibid.,* p. 172. Cf. *Life,* chap. xxx, *Œuvres,* I, p. 387.
[5] *Castle, ibid.,* pp. 172, 173.
[6] *Life,* chap. xxx, *Œuvres,* I, p. 387; *Castle, ibid.,* vi, pp. 173-174.
[7] *Castle, ibid.*

This torment is inexpressible : " The anguish and affliction of spirit are such that one knows not what name to give them," says St Teresa. As to all that is good, there is no light; we see only the evil we have done. God altogether hides himself and we feel as if we had never loved him. The devil tries to make us doubt the divine goodness : "The soul regards God as putting everything to fire and sword; it pictures his justice, and, while keeping faith in his mercy—which the devil cannot go so far as to take away— it draws no consolation from it." In this state, mental prayer is hard, for " the powers are incapable of it." Even vocal prayer gives no consolation :

" Yes, of a truth," says St Teresa, " it appears to me that the devils are playing ball with my soul, and that my soul cannot escape them. It is impossible to tell what the soul then suffers. . . . In my opinion, it is a sort of foretaste of hell; and the comparison is quite accurate, as God showed me in a vision. The soul, indeed, burns inwardly; but it knows not by whom and in what manner the fire is kindled; it knows not how to fly from it or to put it out."[1]

By these sufferings, compared by St Teresa to those of purgatory,[2] God purifies the soul and makes it acknowledge his sovereignty. He thoroughly humiliates it and thus prepares it for the reception of great spiritual favours.

The period of purification once begun, the heavenly Spouse sends forth his call to the spiritual marriage.

This is first heard in " impulses springing from the very depths of the soul, so delicate and subtle " that it is hard to give any true idea of them :

" Often when one is not in the least thinking of it, and one's mind is not occupied with God, his Majesty suddenly awakens the soul : it is like a shooting star or a clap of thunder. . . . The soul clearly understands that God has called her. He makes her feel his presence, and yet does not reveal himself in such a way as to let her enjoy it."[3]

God calls the soul in yet another way :

" He speaks to her. . . . His words are of many kinds : some seem to come from without, others from the innermost depths of the soul, others from the higher part. Lastly, others seem so external that they are perceived by the ears; one seems to hear an articulate voice."[4]

[1] *Life,* chap. xxx, *Œuvres,* I, pp. 388, 389. *Cf.* chap. xx, Vol. I, pp. 247-248. *Castle,* Sixth Mansion, chap. i. St Teresa also experienced outward temptations of the devil. *Life,* chap. xxxi.

[2] *Castle,* Sixth Mansion, chap. xi.

[3] *Castle,* Sixth Mansion, chap. ii, *Œuvres,* VI, pp. 179-180.

[4] *Castle,* chap. iii, *Œuvres,* p. 185. Cf. *Life,* chaps. xxv, xxvi. In her first rapture, St Teresa heard our Lord utter these words :

But here illusion is easy, and Teresa explains at length the signs by which one may distinguish a divine source from what is diabolical or merely pathological.[1]

When the divine call has been heard, the soul is led to the spiritual marriage by means of *raptures*. They are like the "betrothal," they free the soul from the senses and make her capable of close union with God. It was about the year 1562 that the great raptures began which prepared St Teresa for the spiritual marriage with which she was favoured ten years later.

"Rapture, elevation, flight of the spirit, transport, these are all the same, and the different names express but one thing, which is also called ecstasy."[2] St Teresa describes them with her usual precision.

She first notes the effects produced in the body of the ecstatic:

"At the moment when the rapture begins," she says, "one ceases breathing and, if one keeps one's other senses for a very short time, one loses the power of speech immediately. At other times, one loses the use of all one's senses suddenly; the hands and the whole of the body are frozen to such a point that the soul seems to have withdrawn. Sometimes we have to ask ourselves if we are still breathing. This is but for a little while, at least so far as it is a fixed state, for when the great suspension begins to decrease, the body seems to become somewhat reanimated. But if it recovers a little life, it is only to die afresh and to leave the soul more alive. Nevertheless, such a high degree of ecstasy is but of brief duration."[3]

Rapture is sometimes accompanied with the raising of the body from the ground. It is the phenomenon of levitation that mystics are so afraid of. It is the spirit that is carried away first of all:

I wish thee to converse no longer with men but with angels. These words were spoken in the innermost part of the soul. *Life,* chap. xxiv, *Œuvres,* I, p. 309.

[1] *Castle,* Sixth Mansion, chap. iii.
[2] *Life,* chap. xx, *Œuvres,* I, p. 241.
[3] *Castle,* Sixth Mansion, chap. iv, *Œuvres,* VI, p. 207. *Life,* chap. xx, *Œuvres,* I, pp. 242 ff : " During such raptures, the soul appears no longer to animate the body. We very plainly perceive the natural heat departing and the body getting colder and colder, but in an unspeakably sweet and pleasant manner. . . . The body is often as if dead and utterly impotent : it stays just as it happens to be overtaken, with the hands open or closed. Consciousness is but rarely lost. Yet I have sometimes lost it altogether. . . . Generally the eyes are closed involuntarily ; and, if they happen to remain open, I repeat that we do not distinguish or apprehend anything." Cf. *Relation* LIV, *Foundations,* chap. vi.

" Sometimes," says Teresa, " the soul feels that she is transported with such a sudden motion, and the spirit seems carried away with such velocity that one experiences, especially at first, a real alarm. This is why I told those whom God intends to receive such graces that they need great courage. Do you think, indeed, that anyone in full possession of her faculties feels but little disturbed when she is aware of her soul being thus raised—and her body, too, as we read of in the case of some people—without knowing whither she is going or who is carrying her away or what it all means? For just when the sudden motion occurs, we have no certainty as yet that it proceeds from God. But is it not possible to resist? No. . . . With the same ease with which a giant carries off a straw, so does our divine Giant in his power carry away the spirit."[1]

St Teresa often tried to resist. She did it with all her might, especially when she was seized with ecstasy in public. Once, when she was about to communicate, she felt herself rising from the ground. She seized the grille with both hands to cling on to it. She sometimes succeeded in somewhat neutralizing the force which was carrying her away, " but at the cost of an extraordinary lassitude." At other times, " all resistance was impossible."[2] She also tried to lie down on the ground when she perceived that an ecstasy was coming on; her nuns surrounded her to keep her where she was. Lastly, she besought our Lord to grant her no such favours. The raptures continued, but they were only rarely accompanied with the raising of her body.[3]

These external phenomena, however extraordinary, are of much less importance than the graces imparted to the soul in moments of rapture. The soul is rapt in ecstasy by an interior grace : it is " suddenly struck by a divine word remembered or heard." The spark of love is powerfully rekindled in it until it is thoroughly afire. At the same time our Lord unites with the soul " in a manner known only to both of them." And further, the soul is afterwards unable to give any real account of it.[4]

[1] *Castle*, Sixth Mansion, chap. v, *Œuvres*, VI, pp. 210-211. A little farther on in the same chapter, we read : " I return to this rapid carrying away of the spirit. Such is its impetuosity that the spirit appears really to be parting from the body. . . . For some moments the (person in ecstasy) cannot tell whether her soul is in the body or out of it. She believes that she is transported . . . into some other region." Cf. *Life*, chap. xx.

[2] *Life*, chap. xx, *Œuvres*, I, p. 243 : " When I wanted to resist, I felt as if there were amazing forces under my feet and that they were carrying me away. . . . There is a terrible struggle, and it is of very little use when God means to act." *Œuvres*, I, p. 245.

[3] *Life, ibid.*

[4] *Castle*, Sixth Mansion, chap. iv, *Œuvres*, VI, pp. 199-200. *Ibid.*, chap. v : " As swiftly as the bullet leaves the arquebus when it is fired,

In rapture, although " the powers (of the soul) are so absorbed as to be dead, and the senses also," the soul has never been " so awake to the things of God " or " so enlightened and conscious of his majesty." St Teresa makes no attempt to explain how that may be; but, according to her, unless the soul, when raised to such states as these, sometimes heard such " secrets," the divine character of its raptures would be open to doubt. God usually reveals supernatural truths to the ecstatic by intellectual or imaginative visions of which more will be heard later on.[1]

When the soul is thus "beyond itself" it rapidly acquires a threefold knowledge : that of God's greatness revealed in such wonderful effects, that of its own nothingness and lowness despite which the Lord comes to it, and that of the vanity of the things of this world. The soul becomes supremely detached from all creatures. " In an hour, and even less, it gains such a wonderful liberty that it does not know itself." It is no longer fettered by any created thing.[2]

Moreover, divine love grows at a bound during ecstasy. When the soul has entirely come to itself, it feels an incredibly ardent desire to serve God in every way. It " wants to have a thousand lives to devote them all to God, it would have everything in the world changed into tongues to bless him with; its thirst for penance is insatiable. . . . It sees clearly that the torments of martyrs were easy for them to endure, because such help from our Lord makes everything easy."[3] The soul itself suffers " a martyrdom both delightful and cruel," which it can neither describe nor explain. It is like a painful ecstasy arising from the loss of the vision of God.

In short, " before experiencing ecstasy the soul is convinced that it is careful not to offend God, and that it is serving him to the utmost of its powers. But no sooner has it received this grace than the sun of justice shines upon it and makes it open its eyes."[4] It sees how imperfect it is; but the graces of rapture very soon transform it.

Amidst these both " painful and delightful " effects of rapture, our Lord imparts to the soul from time to time " certain jubilations and a kind of strange prayer, the nature of which is inexplicable." There are " loving transports of incredible vehemence " :

" In my view," says St Teresa, " there is a very close

within the soul arises an impulse, which I call a soaring. . . . It transports one so evidently that illusion is impossible " (pp. 215-216).
[1] *Castle*, Sixth Mansion, chap. iv, *Œuvres*, VI, pp. 200-201. Cf. *Life*, chap. xx.
[2] *Castle*, *ibid*., chap. v, *Œuvres*, VI, pp. 216-217. *Life*, chaps. xx-xxi.
[3] *Castle*, Sixth Mansion, chap. iv, *Œuvres*, VI, p. 208.
[4] *Life*, xx, *Œuvres*, I, 261.

union between the powers [of the soul] and God; only they retain, along with the senses, the freedom to enjoy their happiness. But what do they enjoy, and how do they enjoy it? This they know not. This is like Arabic, and yet it is pure truth. The soul experiences such excessive joy that it would not be alone in feeling it, but would proclaim it everywhere, to be helped to thank our Lord for it, since to that is it borne by an irresistible impulse. Oh! if it were in our power, what festivals should we celebrate, what demonstrations of joy, to impart our happiness to all the world! . . .

"Such were the transports that befell St Francis, I think, when he was met by robbers while he was shouting aloud in the open country, and told them that he was the herald of the Great King. And how many other saints fled into the desert to be able, as he did, to proclaim the praise of God!

"I knew one such—to judge by his life, I may put him among them—who acted in the same way. This was the friar Peter of Alcantara. At the present time those who have heard him still believe that he was mad. O happy madness, my sisters, would to God that we were all touched with it!"[1]

It was in one of these transports of love that St Teresa, about the year 1560, received the signal grace known as *Transverberation*:

"I saw an angel near me," she says, "on my left, and in bodily form. . . . He was not tall, but short and very beautiful; his fiery face seemed to show that he belonged to the highest hierarchy, that of the spirits all on fire with love. These are, I think, those called cherubim [seraphim]. . . .

"I saw in the angel's hands a long golden dart, the iron point of which was tipped with a little fire. Sometimes he seemed to me to be thrusting this dart through my heart, and to plunge it deep within me. When he withdrew it, I was left all on fire with the most ardent love of God. So intense was my pain that it made me utter the feeble plaints of which I have spoken. But at the same time the sweetness caused by this unspeakable pain is so excessive that one would take care not to ask for it to end. . . .

"During all these transports I seemed to be beside myself. I wanted neither to hear nor to speak, but to give myself up entirely to my torment, which for me was a bliss beyond all created joy."[2]

In an extraordinary state of prayer God sometimes com-

---

[1] *Castle,* Sixth Mansion, chap. vi, *Œuvres,* VI, pp. 224-225. Cf. *Life,* chap. xxix.

[2] *Life,* chap. xxix, *Œuvres,* I, pp. 378-379. This vision of the transverberating angel was granted to St Teresa "several times," p. 378.

municates with the soul by *visions*. These are of three kinds : *intellectual, imaginative,* and *corporal.*

She declares in her *Relation* to Father Rodriguez Alvarez, S.J., appointed by the Inquisitors in 1576 to examine her spirit, that she "never saw anything with the eyes of the body nor heard anything with her bodily ears except twice only. And then she never grasped anything that was said to her nor knew who was speaking to her."[1]

Christ once appeared to St Teresa in an *intellectual vision.* He was neither perceived by her bodily eyes, nor by those of the soul, but by a sort of mental intuition :

"Being engaged in prayer," she says, "on a feast-day of the glorious St Peter,[2] I saw near me—or rather I felt, for I saw nothing with the eyes of the body nor with those of the soul—it appeared to me, I say, that I saw Jesus Christ close to me. At the same time I understood that it was he whom I believed that I heard speaking to me. . . . It appeared to me that Jesus Christ kept constantly by my side ; however, as the vision presented no image, I could not see what form he had, but that he was always at my right hand, that I felt clearly. He was the witness of all my acts, and if I kept the least recollected or undistracted, I could not be unaware of his presence close to me."[3]

Such an intellectual vision is not to be confounded with the feeling of the presence of God experienced by those "who are favoured with the prayer of union or of quiet."[4] By the effects wrought by God within them, they understand that he is there. In the former case all occurs quite otherwise. Christ kept close to St Teresa without her seeing him. She understood so clearly that it was he "that all doubt was impossible."[5] She knew quite well that it was he, Christ himself, who usually spoke to her. The vision sometimes lasted a long time.[6]

St Teresa first of all was frightened. She was afraid of being the victim of a diabolical illusion. She "went away quite cast down to find her confessor," who did nothing to reassure her, for he could not understand how his penitent could know that Christ was near her, since she never saw him.[7] She was not fully enlightened until later on by St

---

[1] *Relation* LIII, *Œuvres,* II, p. 290. Cf. *Life,* chap. xxviii, *ibid.,* I, p. 354.

[2] Probably on June 29, 1557.

[3] *Life,* chap. xxvii, *Œuvres,* I, pp. 336-337. Cf. *Castle,* Sixth Mansion, chap. viii, *ibid.,* VI, p. 241. *Relation* LIII, Vol. II, pp. 293-294.

[4] *Life,* chap. xxvii, *ibid.,* VI, p. 338.

[5] *Castle, ibid.,* VI, p. 241.

[6] *Life,* chap. xxvii. St Teresa says that she had this vision for some time "in some sort continually" and that she did not leave her state of prayer. *Life,* xxviii, *Œuvres,* III, p. 352.

[7] *Castle, ibid.* Cf. *Relation* LIII.

Peter of Alcantara and " other great theologians." Intellectual vision is of " the highest kind " ; it is " that in which the devil has the least admittance." Towards the close of her life, when Teresa remembered what the ignorance of her directors had then inflicted upon her, she recommended her nuns, when in doubt, to consult great theologians who were "advanced in spirituality." You should prefer, she would say, " a man eminent in doctrine," even if lacking in piety, to " a man devoted to prayer," but of little learning.[1]

Amidst her fears Teresa was reassured by the conviction that Christ was near her, and especially by the graces that accompanied the vision. When our Lord said *Fear not, it is I*, she could not cast a doubt upon the authenticity of these words :

" Such excellent company filled her with courage and joy; she found it a powerful aid in thinking of God continually, and in keeping herself very carefully away from all that might displease him, whose look seemed to her to be always fastened upon her. If she wanted to speak to our Lord either during her prayer or at other times, she always found him so near that he could not but hear her. As for his words, she did not hear them according to her inclination, but unexpectedly and when necessary."[2]

St Teresa was further favoured with intellectual visions of another kind, in which God imparted to her wonderful enlightenment as to supernatural realities.

One of them told her " how all things are seen in God, and how he contains them all within himself." The malice of sin was disclosed to her, for she saw " that it is in God, yes, in God himself, that we commit the most monstrous sins." And this truth filled her with fear.[3]

Another vision showed her God as the supreme truth, " the truth which cannot lie." She understood why humility is so excellent a virtue. " It is because God is the supreme truth, and humility is nothing else than walking in truth. . . . We have nothing good of ourselves . . . misery and nothingness are our lot." Not to know that is to walk in lies. To be convinced of it is to walk in truth.[4]

A soul in the state of grace was also shown her in a " very extraordinary" intellectual vision. She saw that " the Holy Trinity was with this soul, and a companionship so divine communicated to it a sovereignty over the whole world."[5]

---

[1] *Castle, ibid.*, pp. 246-247. Cf. *Life*, chap. xiii, *Œuvres*, I, pp. 175-176.
[2] *Castle*, Sixth Mansion, chap. viii, *Œuvres*, VI, p. 242. Cf. *Life*, chap. xl.
[3] *Castle, ibid.*, chap. x, p. 262. Cf. *Life*, chap. xi, *Œuvres*, II, p. 147.
[4] *Castle, ibid.*, pp. 264-265. Cf. *Life*, chap. xl, *Œuvres*, II, pp. 141-144.
[5] *Relation* XXI, *Œuvres*, II, p. 242.

Finally, in the last years of her life Teresa had an intellectual vision of the Blessed Trinity, as she will explain to us later on in dealing with the Seventh Mansion of the *Interior Castle*.

Towards the end of 1557, a few months after her first intellectual vision, Teresa saw *in imagination* our Lord's humanity.[1]

His holy humanity was shown to her gradually, as if to prepare her little by little to bear its glory. First of all the Saviour showed her only his hands. Their beauty was so marvellous, she says, that it is impossible to depict it. Soon afterwards Teresa also saw the holy face of the Saviour, and was altogether ravished by it. Lastly, one day on the feast of the Conversion of St Paul she saw the Saviour's humanity in its entirety, " as it is represented after the resurrection, in extraordinary beauty and majesty."[2] She cannot express the beauty of the vision :

" Had I spent year after year," she says, " trying to picture to myself anything so beautiful, I should have neither the power nor the talent to succeed in doing it, so far do its singular whiteness and brightness surpass all that can be imagined here below. It is a brightness that dazzles not, a whiteness full of sweetness, an infused splendour that charms one's sight delightfully without wearying it. As for the clear light which enables one to perceive such wholly divine beauty, it is an entirely different light from that of this world. The shining of the sun seems indeed to be so dull compared with this brightness, which is presented to our inward gaze, that afterwards we want never to open our eyes again."[3]

Teresa often had this vision during two years and a half, probably the years 1558, 1559, and 1560. Her womanly curiosity sometimes fastened upon certain details of the vision :

" While our Lord was speaking to me," she says, " and I was contemplating his wonderful beauty, I noted the sweetness and sometimes the severity with which his most beautiful and divine mouth uttered his words. I had an extreme desire to know the colour of his eyes and the dimensions of his height, so as to be able to speak of them ; but I never merited to take knowledge of them : any attempt for that purpose is quite useless."[4]

[1] An imaginative vision, in which the imagination receives supernaturally and passively an image which God desires to present to the soul. Such is the vision of hell related on p. 199.
[2] *Life,* chap. xxviii, *Œuvres,* I, p. 353.
[3] *Life,* chap. xxviii, *Œuvres,* I, pp. 355-356. Cf. *Castle,* Sixth Mansion, chap ix.
[4] *Life,* chap. xxix, *Œuvres,* I, p. 369.

Our Lord then showed her that her curiosity was indiscreet by withdrawing the vision.

Teresa tries to explain how she saw Jesus. It was not with the eyes of the body; the vision was altogether inward:

"On some occasions," she says, "what I saw seemed to me to be an image, but on many others, it was not so; it seemed to me to be Jesus Christ himself. That depended upon the clearness with which he condescended to show himself to me. Sometimes it was in a rather uncertain manner, and then I thought I saw an image, but an image that has nothing in common with the representations of this world, however perfect they may be. . . . If it is an image, it is a living image. It is not a dead man; it is the living Christ, and he lets it be clearly known that he is God and man, not as he was in the tomb, but as he left it in rising again. . . . Sometimes he appears in such majesty that no one could doubt but that it is the Saviour himself."[1]

Just because the vision occurs in the imagination, it runs the risk of producing many illusions. The devil and the imagination itself may bring them about. Hence came the difficulties of the confessors when Teresa resorted to them in order to discern the origin of such visions. One day one of them told her "that they plainly came from the devil." Since the vision forced itself on her and could not be driven off, she must make the sign of the cross whenever it appeared, and treat it with a gesture of contempt. We can easily surmise Teresa's anguish, convinced as she was that the vision came from God and yet bound as she was to obey her confessor.[2] He had, indeed, gone too far.

Ten years later Blessed John of Avila, after an examination of Teresa's *Life,* condemned such direction: "Imaginative and corporal visions," he wrote, "are the most dubious. They are not at all to be desired: we must escape them as far as we can, but without using gestures of contempt, unless the intervention of the evil spirit is demonstrated. What was done in this respect really horrified me, and I was grieved by it."[3]

Finally, Teresa had many *revelations.* God spoke to her with interior words which revealed the future or made hidden things known to her:

[1] *Life,* chap. xxviii, *Œuvres,* I, p. 358. These visions forced themselves upon Teresa. She could neither have them at will nor dismiss them when they occurred.
[2] *Life,* chap. xxix, *Œuvres,* I, pp. 371-372.
[3] John of Avila's letter to St Teresa, *Œuvres,* II, pp. 160-161. Cf. *Foundations,* chap. viii, *Œuvres,* III, p. 136. St Teresa also saw the Holy Spirit in the form of a dove; she contemplated Jesus Christ in the Father's bosom; she had a vision of Purgatory, which many souls were leaving (*Life,* chap. xxxviii). She saw the throne of God, and the glory of Mary in her Assumption (*Life,* chap. xxxix).

" These words," she says, " are perfectly distinct, but they
are not usually heard by the ears of the body. Yet they are
much more clearly perceived than if they were audible, and
they cannot be resisted; it is impossible not to perceive
them. When we have to do with human speech, if we
do not want to hear it we can stop our ears or fix our attention upon something else, so as not to understand what is
said to us. In the case of words spoken to the soul by
God, everything is vain; despite ourselves, we are obliged
to hearken, and our mind must attend to what God is
saying to it. . . .   He shows that he is our real
Master.''[1]

Teresa heard the Saviour so often that he became to her
a living book teaching her all truth :

" Once," she says, " for an hour and more our Lord stood
close to me and revealed marvellous things to me.''[2]

Like St Paul, in her raptures she was given to contemplate the things of heaven, and she was powerless to express
them :

" One evening . . . I was seized," she tells us, " with a
rapture of irresistible power. I seemed to be transported
into heaven, and the first persons I saw there were my father
and mother. In the space of an *Ave Maria* I saw wonderful
things. . . .

" Since then I have happened—and still sometimes happen
—to get the knowledge of yet higher secrets. But the soul
has neither the means nor the possibility of seeing anything
beyond what is shown it. . . .   Such were these marvels
that the least of them was enough to strike my soul with
admiration, and to help it to make great progress in forgetting and despising the things of earth. I should like to
give some idea of what was least lofty in the knowledge then
imparted to me, but it is in vain to try to do so, and I see
that it is impossible.''[3]

Many events were foretold to her when in prayer, sometimes two years beforehand. She always saw them fulfilled. In particular, she had several revelations as to the
Carmelite reform. Three years before anyone ever spoke of
it, she knew she was to found the first monastery of Discalced Carmelites at Avila.[4]

Although St Teresa was certain that these revelations
came from God, she had them supervised by her confessor,
especially when they concerned things to be done : " To act

---

[1] *Life,* chap. xxv, *Œuvres,* I, pp. 311-312. The *Spiritual Relations*
specially abound in our Lord's instructions, encouragements, and
reprimands addressed to St Teresa.
[2] *Life,* chap. xxxviii, *Œuvres,* II, p. 103.
[3] *Life,* chap. xxxviii, *ibid.,* pp. 101-102.
[4] *Relations* III and LIII, *Œuvres,* II, pp. 220-277.

otherwise, and to be led in such circumstances by one's own feelings, is, in my opinion, a very dangerous thing."[1]

When St Teresa's mystical training was finished, God granted her the signal favour of spiritual marriage. In the middle of November, 1572, "in the Octave of St Martin," the Saviour appeared to her and said: *From to-day thou shalt be my spouse: hitherto thou hast not merited it. . . ."*[2] Teresa tells us in what this supernatural favour consisted so far as she was concerned : it lasted till her death.

5. *The Spiritual Marriage*[3]

The celebration of the spiritual marriage takes place in the innermost Mansion, the "centre of the soul," of which mystics have so much to say.

"This mysterious union takes place in the innermost centre of the soul, which is, I think," says St Teresa, "the dwelling-place of God himself, and into which, according to me, he enters without going through any doorway. If I say that no door is needed, it is because, in the other graces which I have described, the senses and the powers are in some sense used as intermediaries. . . . What takes place in the union of the spiritual marriage is very different. The Lord appears in the centre of the soul without any imaginative vision, but by means of an intellectual vision still more refined than those of which I have spoken, and in the same way as he appeared to the apostles without passing through doors when he said to them : *Pax vobis.* . . . At this moment the Lord condescends to show the soul the beatitude of heaven in a way the sublimity of which surpasses that of all other visions and of all the spiritual tastes."[4]

In raptures and in the prayer of union "the soul did not feel itself called to enter into its own centre with the power that invites it thereto in this Mansion : it was attracted only in its higher part."[5]

The feeling of the union of the centre of the soul with God is permanent in the spiritual marriage. This is what differentiates this degree of prayer from all the rest in which the union is conscious only from time to time. The other graces of prayer are like "spiritual betrothals" in which the favour of union is not at all permanent. "In the spiritual marriage," says Teresa, "it is quite otherwise : the soul

---

[1] *Castle,* Sixth Mansion, chap. iii, *Œuvres,* VI, p. 193.
[2] *Relation* XXV, *Œuvres,* II, p. 246.
[3] *Castle,* Seventh Mansion.
[4] *Castle, ibid.,* chap. ii, *Œuvres,* VI, pp. 285-286.
[5] *ibid.,* chap. i, p. 279. In her *Life,* chap. xl, Teresa relates that she saw her soul in the fashion of a clear mirror. In the centre of it was our Lord, *Œuvres,* II, p. 144.

abides always with God, in the centre of which I have spoken." God is so closely united with the soul that he makes it one spirit with himself.

"All that we can say of it," observes St Teresa, "is that the soul, or rather its spirit, becomes, so far as we can judge, entirely one with God. . . . Perhaps this is what St Paul meant when he said : *He who is joined to the Lord is one spirit* (1 Cor. vi, 17), and desired to speak of this sublime marriage, which assumes that the Lord has already drawn close to the soul by union."[1]

St Teresa carefully avoids, both in her words and in her comparisons, anything like pantheism, when she is speaking of this very close union. It is wonderful to hear her describe this lofty and little-known mystical experience with such ease and justness and clarity.

This permanent union of the soul with God is also much more conscious than the passing union of the states of prayer prior to the spiritual marriage.

"Hitherto," says St Teresa, "when the Lord united my soul with himself, he made it blind and dumb, as St Paul was at the time of his conversion. He thus deprived it of the means of knowing what was the favour that it enjoyed and how it enjoyed it. The immense delight felt by the soul when thus flooded came from the fact that it saw that it was close to its God; but at the very moment when it found itself united with him, it had no kind of knowledge at all, for its powers were altogether lost.

"Here it is quite otherwise. It pleases our God, in his goodness, to take away the scales from the eyes of the soul, so that it may understand, but in an extraordinary way, something of the favour with which he gratifies it."[2]

According to St Teresa, in the mystical marriage the soul enjoys an intellectual vision of the Blessed Trinity :[3]

"Once [the soul] has entered into this Mansion, the three Persons of the Most Holy Trinity, in an intellectual vision, discover themselves to it by a certain representation of the truth, and in the midst of a kindling fire, which, like a resplendent cloud, comes right into its spirit. The three divine Persons are shown to be distinct, and by a wonderful notion which is imparted to it, the soul knows with an absolute certainty that all the three are of one substance, one power, one knowledge, and one God. Just as we believe by

---

[1] *Castle,* Seventh Mansion, chap. ii, *Œuvres,* VI, pp. 286-287. St Teresa calls " the centre of the soul " or " the spirit of the soul " what other mystics call the " bottom of the soul " or " the apex of the soul." It is the most spiritual part of the soul, wherein God unites with it.

[2] *Castle,* Seventh Mansion, chap. i, *Œuvres,* VI, 279.

[3] *Castle,* Seventh Mansion, chap. i; *Spiritual Relations,* XIV, XV, XXII, XLI, XLII, XLIII, LIV, LXVI.

faith, so does the soul, as we may say, perceive by sight.
And yet we see nothing either with the eyes of the body or
of the soul, because here is no imaginative vision. Then
all three divine Persons communicate themselves to the soul,
speak to it and reveal to it the meaning of the passage of
the Gospel in which our Lord says that he will come with
the Father and the Holy Ghost to dwell in the soul who
loves him and keeps his commandments."[1]

Have we here to do with a vision, properly so called, of
the Blessed Trinity? Certain expressions used by Teresa
would lead us to think so. Moreover, she takes care to
distinguish this " vision " of the divine Persons from the
simple, yet very perfect, knowledge which she had before
of the mystery of the Trinity of which she speaks in her
Life:[2]

" One day, while I was reciting the Psalm (Creed)
Quicumque vult, I was given to understand how there was
one God in three Persons, and that so clearly that I was
filled with wonder and joy. . . . Now, when I think of the
most Holy Trinity or hear it spoken of, I seem to understand how this mystery is possible, and it gives me great
consolation."

But in the spiritual marriage, on many occasions Teresa
speaks not of simple knowledge, but of " seeing " the
presence of God within her. " The sight of this divine
presence," she says, " is not always so complete." It is
intermittent, " otherwise it would not be possible to do anything else, or even to live among men."[3] What Teresa says
is not easily explained if we have to do merely with an
infused divine light, and not with a vision properly so called.

But this " sight " of God does not hinder Teresa from
action because it is not constant. Her soul is continuously
in close union with God, and at the same time she gives
herself up to external occupations :

" You will perhaps think," she says to her nuns, " that
this soul is as it were beside herself and in such a transport
that she cannot do anything at all. It is just the contrary :
she finds it much easier than before to take part in all that
has to do with the service of God."[4]

While in this state there were two operations going on in

[1] *Castle,* Seventh Mansion, chap. i, *Œuvres,* VI, pp. 279-280. St
Teresa's vision of the Blessed Trinity was not permanent, but the
feeling that the divine Persons were in her did not leave her (p. 281).
[2] Chap. xxxix, *Œuvres,* II, pp. 139-140.
[3] *Castle,* Seventh Mansion, i, *Œuvres,* VI, p. 284. Cf. *Relation* XIV,
Œuvres, II, p. 236. *Relation* XLII, p. 265 : " One day when I was
enjoying the presence of the three divine Persons, whom I bear in
my soul, the light in which I saw them within me was so clear that I
could not doubt that the living and true God was really there."
[4] *Castle, ibid.*

Teresa. "Her soul appeared to her to be in some fashion divided": one part enjoyed the presence of God, and the other was "grappling with a great number of trials and occupations":[1]

"This may seem to you to be an extravagance," she said to her daughters, "and nevertheless it really happens to be so. Clearly, the soul is one. However, what I have just said is not mere imagination; it is a very ordinary state. This is why I said above that certain interior effects make it certain that in some respects there is a very real difference between the soul and the spirit. Although in reality they make but one, we sometimes perceive a division between them, and it is so fine that one of them works in one way and the other in another, according to the different taste which the Lord is pleased to give them. I think, too, that the soul differs from the powers, that it is not one and the same thing as these."[2]

Mysticism, indeed, opens out many, and some unsuspected, vistas to the Christian philosopher!

The spiritual marriage is destined to give rise to much work for the glory of God and for the salvation of our neighbour.[3] Whoever is favoured with it overflows with activity in the service of our divine Master.

Teresa was the Prioress of the Convent of the Incarnation of Avila in 1572, when she was raised to this high spiritual state. She had begun her foundations: she was yet to bring into being nine new monasteries. What ardour did she display! "This mistress of mystical knowledge, accustomed to the regions of contemplation and ecstasy . . . deals with affairs, she begs, negotiates, organizes, and with what skill, practical good sense, perseverance, and success! Everywhere she makes friends, and what devoted ones!" When she travels alone or with one or two companions she makes long journeys on mules or donkeys, but more often in lumbering conveyances, in which it is baking in summer and freezing in winter. And how picturesque are these travels! How tragic or merely diverting are the happenings! You should read the *Foundations* with its lively account of them adorned with unexpected episodes. The description of the inns of those days, where the Carmelites had to take refreshment or pass the night, is most enlivening. Amidst the incidents, the perils, the privations, the fatigues, the holy mother and her daughters are inviolably faithful to the minutest prescriptions of the monastic life. And when, after hearing Mass and communicating, they set

---

[1] *Castle, ibid.*, p. 282.
[2] *Castle, ibid.*, p. 283.
[3] *Castle, ibid.*, chap. iv, *Œuvres*, VI, p. 308.

forth on their way, the hours of prayer and silence are strictly observed, thanks to a little bell which they had brought for the purpose.[1]

If one part of St Teresa's soul was in heaven, united to God, the other was surely on earth, and played a wonderful part thereon, with a keen sense of its realities.

In the last chapters of the *Interior Castle* Teresa makes known the new life of the soul after the spiritual marriage.[2]

It is totally forgetful of itself; it is "entirely devoted to procuring the glory of God." It has "an immense desire of suffering." If it is the victim of persecution, it feels the keenest joy within. It no longer wishes to die to enter into the joy of our Lord, but desires to "live many a year amidst sharp trials" to procure God's glory and the salvation of souls.[3]

Such were, indeed, the feelings of Teresa during the persecution of the Carmelites from 1575 to 1579, a persecution stirred up by the Mitigated Carmelites, which very nearly ruined the work of the reform:

"This grieved me incomparably more," she said, "than my personal sufferings, which, truth to tell, gave me rather a real joy. I looked on myself as the cause of all the torment, and it seemed to me that if I were cast into the sea, like Jonas, the tempest would be stilled."[4]

Calm was restored, thanks to the intervention of Philip II.

The wonderful delights experienced by the soul in the spiritual marriage nevertheless suffer passing eclipse at times. Teresa thought that in the Seventh Mansion of the Castle "one hardly ever met with dryness or with the interior troubles that occur at certain moments in all the rest."[5] Nevertheless, when she founded the monastery of Segovia in 1574, two years after she had been raised to the mystical marriage, she experienced "interior pains" from which she "suffered through dryness and a profound spiritual

---

[1] *Œuvres*, III, pp. 6 ff., Introduction to the *Foundations*.

[2] Teresa also describes this new life in several of her *Relations*, particularly in the LXVIth: "My soul enjoys an ineffable peace," she says. She also alludes to the spiritual marriage in some of her *Letters*. In detail they do not always agree with the last chapters of the *Castle*. Thus, in chapter iii of the Seventh Mansion, Teresa declares that in the spiritual marriage "the soul has no more raptures . . . transports and flights of the spirit." But in her letter of January 17, 1577, to her brother, Laurence, she complains of having repeated irresistible raptures. Cf. *Œuvres*, VI, pp. 30-31.

[3] Cf. *Relation* LXVI, *Œuvres*, II, 323.

[4] *Foundations,* chap. xxviii, *Œuvres*, IV, p. 97.

[5] *Castle*, Seventh Mansion, chap. iii, *Œuvres*, VI, p. 299. *Cf.* p. 296: "They (these souls) have no dryness nor interior pains."

darkness."[1] She also taught that the soul, "when it has become one with the mighty God by this sovereign union of spirit with spirit," participates in his might.[2] And yet, when she was busy with her last foundations from 1574 to 1580, she often notes her impotence and moral dejection, and even her pusillanimity.[3]

However perfect be the state of the soul which has reached the Seventh Mansion, it is not exempt from all wretchedness, nor is it there more sure of its salvation nor "protected from all relapse."[4]

In spite of that, there is nothing higher on earth than "the effects wrought by God in the soul when he unites it to himself by the kiss asked for by the Spouse. In my view," says Teresa, "this is when the favour she implored is granted to her. This is when the wounded dove stanches her thirst with the living waters. This is when she is filled with delights in the tabernacle of God. This is when the dove sent forth by Noe to see if the storm is over finds her olive-branch to show that she has found dry land amidst the deluge and the tempests of this world. O Jesus, would that I knew enough passages of Scripture, for they would surely describe this peace of the soul for us!"[5]

IV—ST TERESA'S ASCETIC TEACHING—THE RELIGIOUS VIRTUES OF THE CARMELITE NUN

IT would be a great mistake to think that St Teresa wrote of nothing but mysticism. She generally wrote for her nuns, and she knew that they were not all raised to mystical states. Her quick sense of realities warned her that to desire to urge them on to mysticism off-hand or indiscriminately would mean falling into that very illuminism which was so much combated in Spain. She recommends them to follow the ordinary spiritual ways until it please God, if he think right, to make them take another path.

According to St Teresa, perfection is not to be found in extraordinary states, but in the full and entire conformity of man's will with God's :

"Sovereign perfection," she says, "does not consist in

[1] *Foundations*, chap. xxi, *Œuvres*, III, p. 279. In her letter of January 17, 1577, to her brother, Laurence, she notifies an intense aridity, which lasted a whole week.

[2] *Castle, ibid.*, chap. iv, p. 310.

[3] *Foundations*, chaps. xxv, xxviii, xxix, *Œuvres*, IV, pp. 50, 103, 130 ff.

[4] *Castle, ibid.*, chap. ii, p. 290.

[5] *Castle, ibid.*, chap. iii, *Œuvres*, VI, p. 301.

interior consolations, nor in sublime raptures, nor in visions, nor in the spirit of prophecy. It consists in making our will conform with God's, so that, as soon as we know that he wills a thing, we set our whole will to it; so that we finally accept with the same joy the sweet and the bitter, as soon as we know the good pleasure of his Majesty. . . . Such is the power of perfect love that it makes us forget to please self in order to please him who loves us."[1]

"To make our will one with God's will," such is "real union" far to be preferred to mystical states:

"Such is the union that I desire for myself," says Teresa, "and such is that which I would see all of you possess rather than the delightful transports, no doubt deservedly called "union," if they are preceded by that of which I have just spoken. But if, after the suspension is over, we have little obedience and much self-will, then in my opinion our union will have been with our own self-love and not with the will of God."[2]

What is "the readiest and the most effective way of attaining this happy state"? Prayer? No. Teresa answers without hesitation: Obedience. Father Gratian, the censor of her works, appears to be quite surprised at this. And yet, how right the saint was! For our own will to be subject to God's, it must renounce itself by obedience which subjects it to our reason and our reason to God.[3] Thus do we offer God "a pure will which he can unite with his own." And so we beg him "to send from heaven the fire of his love to consume this sacrifice and to strip it of all that may be displeasing unto him. We, indeed, have done all that lies in our power: at the cost of innumerable efforts we have laid the victim upon the altar, and, as far as we are able to prevent it, it no longer has anything to do with this world."[4]

Such obedience must appear especially in the use of spiritual direction:

[1] *Foundations,* chap. v, *Œuvres,* III, pp. 103-104. Cf. *Castle,* Second Mansion: "The sole ambition of one who begins the way of prayer . . . should be to work courageously to bring his will into conformity with the will of God . . . therein consists the whole of the highest perfection to be attained in the spiritual way. . . ." *Œuvres,* VI, p. 74. *Cf.* p. 92: "Perfection does not consist in tastes, but in love and in works wrought according to justice and truth."
[2] *Foundations, ibid.,* p. 106. Note that St Teresa wrote this in 1573, when she had been raised to the state of the mystical marriage. Cf. *Way of Perfection,* chap. v: "The first stone of the [spiritual] building is a good conscience, the careful avoidance of all sins, even venial, and aiming at what is most perfect." *Œuvres,* V, p. 65. See *Foundations,* chap. xxxii, pp. 233 ff.
[3] *Foundations, ibid.,* iii, pp. 104-105.
[4] *ibid.,* 105-106.

"Even those alien to the religious life," says St Teresa, "will find it most helpful to follow, as many do, the advice of a guide in order to do nothing of their own self-will; for that is ordinarily the cause of their ruin."[1]

And in order to renounce their own self-will the more surely, they ought not to look for a director "who is, as the saying goes, one of their own kidney."

But it is, above all, when we make progress in the ways of prayer that "we must submit to the leading of a guide."[2] Teresa constantly repeats it. She obeyed her confessors even when convinced that they were mistaken. Hence she is all the readier in demanding that directors should be as experienced as possible in the spiritual ways, and, in any case, that they should have a wide knowledge of theology and enough independence of mind not to be influenced by the disparagers of mystical states.[3]

Openness with one's director is essential.[4] He must be told of our temptations, imperfections, and repugnances in order to give counsel and suggest means of overcoming them.

Those in the way of prayer "usually have much affection for their spiritual guide, when they see that he is holy and feel that he understands them." St Teresa advises such people "not to worry whether they have or have not affection towards him." In her opinion, "such affection may conduce to our making great progress, if the confessor is holy and spiritual and tries to help the soul forward." But if the confessor has not these qualities, "it might be dangerous, and if he knew of one's affection for him, much harm might follow." The safest way, then, is to have a talk with another confessor and to act upon his advice.[5]

Christ has given us the Eucharist to help us to submit our wills fully to the will of God. "In fact, he abides with us [in the Blessed Sacrament] only in order to help us and to encourage us to do the divine will which we have asked to

[1] *Castle,* Third Mansion, chap. ii, *Œuvres,* VI, pp. 93-94.
[2] *Life,* chap. xiii, *Œuvres,* I, p. 165. *Cf.* I, pp. 175, 176, 240, 291, 321, 331; II, pp. 146, 147. Teresa demands the greatest freedom for direction. *Way of Perfection,* chap. v, *Œuvres,* V, pp. 64 ff; chap. xviii, p. 143. By following a capable confessor, "more progress is made in one year than would otherwise be made in a great many."
[3] See especially: *Way of Perfection,* chap. v; *Life, Œuvres,* I, 78, 79, 91, 173, 256, 366; II, 44-45, 146, 289. *Interior Castle, Œuvres,* VI, p. 94, 102, 133, 246, 247.
[4] *Counsel:* "Try to speak of the things of your soul with a spiritual and learned confessor. Be open with him and follow his counsel in everything." *Œuvres,* V, 481. See p. 476.
[5] *Way of Perfection,* chap. iv, *Œuvres,* V, pp. 60-63 (various readings from the Escurial MS.).

be done within us,"[1] in the *fiat voluntas tua* of the Lord's
Prayer.

St Teresa liked to remind her nuns how invaluable for the
sanctification of the soul are the moments that follow upon
Holy Communion :

"Then, after you have just received our Lord," she said,
"and have his very Person present within you, close the
eyes of your body and open those of the soul and look into
your heart. . . . We know that, as long as our natural
heat has not consumed the accidents of the bread, the good
Jesus is in us. . . . How should we doubt that, being in
our house, he will grant us what we ask of him? His
Majesty is not wont to pay poorly for his sojourn at the
inn of our soul, when he receives a good welcome therein."[2]

It is for the confessor to regulate the frequency of our
communions. On this point Teresa gave her nuns very
definite counsels :

"Those who approach our Lord so frequently," she
observes, "must be so convinced of their unworthiness as
not to do it of themselves. An order under obedience must
come to make good our deficiencies for approaching so
august a Master, and, indeed, in how many things are we
lacking !"[3]

If we make good use of our communions and other means
of sanctification, we shall make rapid strides in the practice
of virtue.

Christian virtues, these again, and not extraordinary kinds
of prayer, make sanctity.

"More to be praised," says Teresa, "are those marked
with humility, mortification, and obedience than the nuns
led by God in altogether supernatural ways of prayer, even
were they adorned moreover with the same virtues."[4]

Spiritual consolations of contemplatives, "though good,
are not always perfect, and there is always more security in
humility, mortification, detachment, and the other virtues.
So fear nothing," Teresa told her daughters, "and say to
yourselves that you will not fail to reach perfection as well
as the great contemplatives."[5]

[1] *Way of Perfection*, chap. xxxiv, *Œuvres*, V, 247.
[2] *ibid.*, pp. 252, 254.
[3] *Foundations*, chap. vi, *Œuvres*, III, p. 123.
[4] *ibid.*, chap. viii, p. 141. *Cf.* Etchegoyen, *op. cit.*, pp. 111 ff.
[5] *Way of Perfection*, chap. xvii, *Œuvres*, V, p. 135. See chap. xviii,
p. 142 : We must not consider whether we have " more spiritual tastes
in prayer, more raptures, visions, and other favours of that kind which
God sometimes gives to souls. To know the value of such goods we
must wait for the next life. . . . But there is a current coinage, a safe

A good treatise on the virtues of Christians and religious
might be extracted from the works of St Teresa.

We know her definition of humility, which " is nothing else
than walking in the truth." The spiritual building is founded
" entirely " upon it. " The nearer we come to God the more
must this virtue increase; and, if it be otherwise, all is
lost." [1] Humility is intimately connected with self-knowledge, in which we must train ourselves, especially in the
First Mansion of the Castle, "before starting off on our
flight towards the others, for it is the way that leads to
them." [2] When we know what we are worth we do not
want to be proud of it, and if we would, we could not.

Do you want, St Teresa asked her nuns, " to know your
degree of progress " in the spiritual life? " Let each one
consider whether she esteems herself as the most contemptible
of all, and if she translates her conviction into practice." [3]

Again it is humility that protects mystics from the wiles
of the devil, and helps them to turn to advantage the supernatural graces granted to them :

" If there is humility," says Teresa, " a vision proceeding
from the devil can do no harm; but if humility be wanting,
a vision from God will do no good. Indeed, when a soul
receives a grace meant to increase humility, and glories in it
instead, acknowledging her unworthiness of it, she is like
the spider which changes whatever it eats into poison,
instead of imitating the bee, which turns everything into
honey. [4] . . . Humility is like the bee." [5]

Besides, humility is not pusillanimity. Teresa very often
condemns " false humility," which, on pretence of unworthiness, would refuse divine favours or check any desire for
them. [6]

St Clare of Assisi would have liked to enclose her monasteries in the high walls of humility and poverty. Teresa,
with her great love of humility, also regarded poverty as
one of the strongest ramparts, one of the stoutest supports
of the Carmelite reform :

" Everywhere let us have poverty," she said to her
daughters, " in our house, in our clothes, in our words, and

---

return, a perpetual revenue. . . . I mean to refer to deep humility,
complete mortification, perfect obedience to the least wish of our
superior. . . ."
   [1] *Life,* chap. xii, *Œuvres,* I, p. 159. Cf. *Castle.* Sixth Mansion,
chap. x.
   [2] *Castle,* First Mansion, chap. ii, *Œuvres,* VI, 56
   [3] *Way of Perfection,* chap. xviii, *Œuvres,* V, p. 142.
   [4] *Foundations,* chap. viii, *Œuvres,* III, 137.
   [5] *Castle, Œuvres,* VI, p. 55.
   [6] *Way of Perfection,* V, 203, 204, 283, 284; *Life,* I, 97, 105, 120, 136,
etc.; *Castle,* First Mansion, chap. ii, VI, p. 57.

much more in our thoughts. As long as you do thus, be not afraid : with God's help, religious perfection will not decay in such a convent."[1]

"Our arms are holy poverty," she is fond of repeating. She wants her religious who have renounced the possession of incomes also to renounce " all anxieties as to maintenance, otherwise all were lost." It is the heavenly Spouse who will provide for their needs :

"The less the convent has of necessaries, the more calm am I," she affirmed, "and our Lord knows well that I am more troubled when we have what is considerably more than we need than when we run short of something."[2]

This passionate lover of poverty sings the praises of her beloved virtue in the fashion of St Francis of Assisi. She wanted to be " not poor in spirit," as her profession required, " but mad in spirit." She loved " holy poverty " madly, as the story of her foundations proves. She sees an epitome of the other virtues in poverty :

" Poverty in spirit is a good that includes in itself all the other goods of this world. Yes, I repeat it, you become the master of all the goods of this world by despising them. . . . True poverty . . . bears a dignity which impresses everyone. It has not to please anyone but God; but because it needs no one, it is sure to have many friends.[3] . . . There is always more of the interior spirit and even more inward cheerfulness when there is a lack of corporal comforts than when you find yourself liberally and comfortably housed."[4]

Poverty is not the only virtue in which the Carmelite should excel. In exhorting her religious to the observance of the Rule, Teresa insists upon " detachment from everything created." She requires renunciation of one's family, of oneself, one's comfort, and even of one's health. The austerities of the Rule, which are great among the reformed Carmelites, are to be welcomed with joy.[5]

The Carmelites live in community. Hence, they specially need mutual love to bear with one another. When we live side by side, jars are frequent. Little occurrences in the community are apt to take exaggerated importance in a woman's mind. Teresa gives very wise counsels on the subject. Fraternal charity is the great remedy for the difficulties arising from the common life. " Indeed, there is nothing vexatious that is not easily borne by those who love one another, and a thing must be very hard indeed if it is to provoke indignation."[6]

[1] *Way of Perfection,* chap. ii, V, p. 42.
[2] *Way of Perfection, ibid.,* pp. 38-39.
[3] *ibid.,* pp. 40-41. *Cf.* chap. xxxviii, pp. 280-282.
[4] *Foundations,* chap xiv, *Œuvres,* III, p. 188. *Cf.* pp. 208-209.
[5] *Way of Perfection,* chaps. viii-xii.
[6] *ibid.,* chap. iv, V, p. 55. Cf. *Castle,* First Mansion, chap. ii.

Let them, then, keep the commandment to love one another. "But, either from excess or from defect, we do not succeed in practising it to perfection." From excess, when we let ourselves drift into particular friendships which are "an evil" in any religious, and "a pest" in a superior.[1] From defect, when we do not endure the imperfections of others.

Let us have "real affection," "spiritual love." Those who possess it "take all the troubles to themselves and want others to have all the good they do."

"How precious and worthy of the name," cried Teresa, "is the love of a sister who is able to serve all the rest because she sacrifices her own interests for them."[2]

This forgetfulness of self will sometimes be carried a very long way by the Carmelite nun:

"You ought also to try," advises St Teresa, "to be gay with your sisters when they need recreation. I say the same of the usual time of recreation, when it makes no appeal to you. When we bear ourselves in it with prudence, all becomes perfect love."[3]

In communities the very smallest detail may become a stimulus to fraternal charity. Yet superiors should be on the watch to get rid of novices who might make mutual forbearance too difficult, especially such as are lacking in right judgement. This defect, says St Teresa, is particularly intolerable in small communities.[4]

It is also necessary never to accept subjects who are given to melancholy, the neurasthenia of those days. If a nun suffered from this complaint, she was to be withdrawn from solitude and contemplation and to be trained in the active life and in mastering the will.[5]

Love of one's neighbour is essential to holiness; the more it is practised, the more perfect we become. But finally it all comes back to the love of God, which is the synthesis of all the virtues.

Teresa uses quite seraphic language in speaking of it. Love of God is won by deciding to "follow in the way of prayer him who hath so much loved us." Unfortunately we do not rise rapidly to the perfection of this love. We cannot enter "into the enjoyment of a good so precious without paying a high price for it." This price is the full giving up of self:

[1] *Way, ibid.*, p. 57. *Cf.* chap. vi.
[2] *Way of Perfection,* chap. vii, *Œuvres,* V, p. 83.
[3] *ibid.*, p. 82. *Cf.* chap. xli, pp. 299-300.
[4] *Way of Perfection,* chap. xiv, pp. 116 ff.
[5] *Foundations,* chap. vii, *Œuvres,* pp. 126-134. In this chapter St Teresa describes *melancholy* and points out the moral treatment it requires.

"But we are so miserly, so little eager to give ourselves entirely up to God, that we never succeed in putting ourselves into the desired dispositions. . . . We think we have given all; but in reality we offer God the revenue or the fruit, while keeping the right of possession for ourselves."[1]

We embrace poverty and then engage "with eagerness" in getting superfluities for ourselves. We have renounced human honour, yet we are irritated "at the least thing that touches it." Thus, it is because our giving up is not whole-hearted, that we do not receive all at once the treasure of divine love."[2]

True love is active. Teresa insists upon this mark of the love of God. The more we love God, the more do we desire his glory, and the more do we pray and act for the realization of our desire:

"To love," she says, "is not to have many spiritual tastes, it is to resolve firmly to please God in everything, it is to make every effort not to offend him, it is to pray constantly for the increase of the honour and glory of his Son, and for the exaltation of the Catholic Church."[3]

Teresa thinks that "souls kindled with love and burning to show God that they are not out for gain" are not stimulated to serve him by the prospect of future reward. "They think only of satisfying love, whose property it is to act always and to act in every way."[4]

Towards the end of her life, when she had attained to the loftiest heights of mystical love, Teresa very distinctly developed from contemplation towards action. Did she consider the office of Martha more in harmony with real love than that of Mary? In fact, she united them both in herself:

"The soul asks to do great things in the service of God and of her neighbour; for this prize she joyfully renounces the delights and sweetnesses [of contemplation]. What she asks for, indeed, belongs to the active rather than to the contemplative life, and if she gets it, she apparently must lose by obtaining it. Nevertheless, in this new state, Mary and Martha almost always go together, because, in such activity and in the midst of what seems to be external, the inward is at work."[5]

To prefer the sweetnesses of retreat to the deeds of charity is to let oneself be drawn into "a very subtle kind of self-love, which creeps in in such a fashion imperceptibly that we seek rather our own satisfaction than God's. It is evident, in fact, that when we have begun to taste how sweet the

[1] *Life*, chap. xi, *Œuvres*, I, pp. 143-145.   [2] *ibid.*
[3] *Castle*, Fourth Mansion, chap. i, *Œuvres*, VI, p. 101.
[4] *ibid.*, Sixth Mansion, chap. xi, p. 260. Cf. *Foundations*, chap. v, *Œuvres*, III, p. 98.
[5] *Thoughts on the Canticle of Canticles*, chap. vii, *Œuvres*, V, p. 460.

Lord is, we take more pleasure in keeping the body in repose and the mind in a state of spiritual joy than in giving ourselves up to activity."[1]

Teresa is expressing only her own personal experience. How many journeys, how many fatigues and annoyances of all sorts did she undertake during the last twenty years of her life! She could well say:

" Oh! the charity of those who truly love our divine Lord and know the inclination of his heart! Rest becomes impossible for them, if they think they can contribute ever so little to the good of a single soul and to its progress in the love of God, or even comfort it in its troubles, or deliver it from a danger. What a burden to them then is their own repose!"[2]

Love is an active and mighty fire; those in whom it burns cannot but act.[3] They take an interest in all that is good:

" Those who really love God love all that is good, help on all that is good, praise all that is good, unite with the good, support and defend the good, and love only what is true and worthy of love."[4]

In solitude, some may say, there " are fewer occasions for offending God, and purity is more easily kept." But, replies Teresa, when " obedience or charity bids us run the risk of occasions," love comes out far more clearly than it does in " the recesses of solitude. . . . Believe me, we make much greater gain and that beyond comparison, even if we commit more faults and suffer some slight losses."[5]

How greatly are we impressed by the sight of this Carmelite, inebriated with the love of God, burning to be in heaven with her divine Spouse, and yet, like St Martin, willing to remain on earth amidst the cares and the sufferings of the life of action in order to make men know and love and serve God! These various feelings she expresses in passionate and poetical phrases in " her tender and fiery aspirations " entitled her *Exclamations:*

" O my life, my life! How can you go on apart from your own Life? In such solitude, what are you about? what can you do? . . .[6] O my Joy; sovereign Master of all beings! O my God! . . . How long must I wait for thy presence? . . . How long and bitter is this life that is no life! . . . How long, O Lord, how long? O death! O death! How can we fear thee, since thou givest us life? . . .[7] O my Jesus, how great is the love thou hast for men! The

---

[1] *Foundations,* chap. v, *Œuvres,* III, p. 99.
[2] *Foundations, ibid.*   [3] *Way of Perfection,* chap. xix.
[4] *ibid.,* chap. xl, *Œuvres,* V, p. 289.
[5] *Foundations,* chap. v, *Œuvres,* III, p. 107.
[6] *Exclamation* I, *Œuvres,* V, p. 321.
[7] *Exclamation* VI, pp. 332-333.

highest service we can give thee is to leave thee for the love of them and to do them the most good we can. Then it is that we possess thee most fully. The will, indeed, is less inebriated with the joy of thee, but the soul rejoices in pleasing thee. . . .[1] The soul heaps up devices to find friends for its love, and gladly leaves the happiness that floods it in the hope of helping others to try to find it."[2]

When we can do nothing, we ought to pray. When Teresa heard of the calamities that devastated France and of the ravages of Lutheranism there, she would have "given a thousand lives to save but one of these souls which were being lost in such large numbers in that country." She asked her nuns to "pray for the defenders of the Church, and for the preachers and theologians who were upholding her cause."[3] She exhorted them thus to use all their powers for the salvation of souls. Carmelites must help with their prayers the clergy who are carrying out such a difficult work. It is their vocation.[4]

The daughters of St Teresa have always been most faithful to these counsels of their holy Mother.

[1] *Exclamation* II, p. 324. [2] *ibid.*, pp. 323-324.
[3] *Way of Perfection,* chap. i, *Œuvres,* V, pp. 33-34.
[4] *ibid.,* chap. iii.

CHAPTER VII

THE SPANISH CARMELITE SCHOOL — THE QUARREL
BETWEEN THE MITIGATED AND THE REFORMED
CARMELITES : JEROME GRATIAN AND ST JOHN OF
THE CROSS—THE SPIRITUAL TEACHING OF ST JOHN
OF THE CROSS

DESPITE the excellence and soundness of their teaching, the writings of St Teresa met with opponents in Spain. People asked whether it was not dangerous to publish visions and revelations at a time when false mysticism was making such inroads? Did they want to foster illuminism? Others thought it very indiscreet and even unseemly to give the public the intimate writings of a woman, which were intended for her confessors only.[1] In 1589, the year after the appearance of the first edition of the saint's *Works*, Luis de Leon had to reply to their adversaries.

But soon Teresa's readers took upon themselves the defence of her writings. The juridical depositions for her canonization contain numerous and very genuine testimonies of their enthusiastic admiration. Why should anyone find fault with the publication of such edifying books? Was it not plain that God had chosen Teresa to teach and to touch souls?

Moreover, the attention of the religious public of Spain was somewhat distracted from these controversies by the quarrel between the Mitigated and the Reformed Carmelites; the former wishing to keep to an observance which had nothing austere in it, the latter accepting the Reform of St Teresa and St John of the Cross.

St Teresa went through the beginning of this quarrel and even through the most critical period of it. No sooner had she founded the first convents of the Discalced Carmelites than the Mitigated party, fearing, it is said, that if the reform were allowed to develop, they would be obliged to reform themselves, impeded the progress of the new observance.

The principal upholders of the reform were Father Jerome Gratian[2] and St John of the Cross.

[1] *Œuvres,* General Introduction, I, pp. xxxvii-xxxviii.
[2] On him and his critics, see Father de Saint-Joseph, *Le P. Jérôme Gratien et ses juges,* Rome, 1904. See, too, Cosme de Villiers, *Bibliotheca Carmelitana,* 1752, Vol. I, pp. 645 ff.; P. André de Sainte-Marie, *L'Ordre du Mont-Carmel,* Bruges, 1910.

Jerome Gratian, who "belonged to a noble family of Valladolid, remarkable for elevation of mind, distinction of manners, and rare intellectual culture," was Commissary Apostolic and the first Provincial of the Carmelite Reform. St Teresa held him in particular esteem. She assisted him with her counsels in directing the Discalced Carmelites. She bore him an affection which was "both filial and maternal." She treated him with the solicitude and care of a dearly beloved son, and she obeyed him in everything in the sphere of conscience "as a father given her by the hand of our Lord himself to direct her until the end of her life."

Deeply learned in the science of mysticism, Father Gratian revised several of St Teresa's manuscripts, adding valuable marginal notes which confirm and explain what she has written.[1] He was keenly interested in the works of the Carmelite reformer. It is he who ordered her to finish the story of the *Foundations,* though she was tempted to give it up.[2] It is he, too, who asked her to write the *Interior Castle* to take the place of her *Life,* the manuscript of which was in the hands of the Inquisitors with little hope of being recovered at the time. Teresa's vivacity of spirit and facility with the pen filled him with admiration. "She wrote her works," he says, "without any erasures and very rapidly."[3] In his *Dilucidario del verdadero spiritu de la Madre Teresa de Jesus,* he has given priceless testimony to St Teresa and to her real mind, a witness which shows how deeply he entered into her spirit.[4]

Despite his high merit and talents, and perhaps on account of them, he did not succeed in satisfying all the religious of the reform. One party—that of the *fervent*—reproached him for his lack of firmness in the application of the Rule and for dragging the Discalced Carmelites, a mainly contemplative Order, too far into the external work of ministering to souls. Thus, to the persecutions of the Mitigated Carmelites were added the vexations of those who pursued the same ideal as his own !

As long as St Teresa was alive, these reproaches did not do too much harm to Father Gratian, but after her death, passions broke loose. He was not re-elected Provincial at the Chapter of Lisbon in 1585. Such was his disgrace that after having been "declared rebellious to his superiors and

---

[1] On these *Notes marginales du P. Gratien,* see *Año Teresiano,* Vols. VI, dia 23 de junio, and VII, dia 7 de julio.

[2] Cf. *Foundations,* chap. xxvii.

[3] *Dilucidario del verdadero spiritu,* I Parte, cap. v. Fr. Gratian also published, with a dedicatory letter, the Latin translation of *The Life,* etc. (1610), by Fathers John of St Jerome and John of Jesus Mary.

[4] This is the *Dilucidario,* etc. (Brussels, 1608), so often quoted by the editors of St Teresa's works.

unfaithful to his vows," he was driven out of the Order in 1592. He was exiled, and died at Brussels in 1614 in a convent of the Mitigated brethren.

The Carmelite reform brought no less suffering upon St John of the Cross.[1] But his trials came chiefly from the Mitigated Carmelites, the implacable adversaries of the new observance.

In these afflictions, as in those of St Teresa and of Jerome Gratian, may be seen the ransom paid for the Carmelite Reform. They are also a luminous expression of the mystical spirit of John of the Cross :

" O truth unheeded !" he writes in his *Spiritual Canticle,*[2] " when shall we make people understand that the depth of the wisdom and of the infinite riches of God is beyond the reach of those who reject suffering and do not desire it and find no spiritual consolation therein ? When will they be convinced that, if they really would aspire to divine wisdom, they must begin by sounding the depths of the sufferings of the cross ?"

Since " Suffering is the best means of advancing farthest in the delectable and profound wisdom of God," John of the Cross loves suffering passionately. If it does not come to him of itself, he will go to fetch it.

In 1567, three years after his profession in the Carmelite Convent of Medina, having brought his studies in theology at Salamanca to a brilliant finish, he felt he was called to a stricter Order than the one he had entered. More and more privations and renunciations ! Such was his device. He was thinking of the Carthusians, when he decided, in his first

[1] Juan de Yepes was born in 1542 at Hontiveras, near Avila. At the age of twelve or thirteen he lost his father, and, to earn his living, had to become a sick attendant in the hospital of Medina del Campo. While looking after the sick he managed to follow the classes of the Jesuit College of that town. At the age of twenty-one he joined the Convent of the Carmelites of Medina, and made his profession there in 1564 as John of St Matthias, and then he was sent to Salamanca to study theology. In the month of August, 1567, he had his first interview with St Teresa, during which he decided to undertake the reform of the Carmelites under her direction. At Duruelo he founded the first house of the Discalced Carmelites. The success of the reform brought persecution upon him. The Mitigated brethren imprisoned him at Toledo in a narrow cell from December 4, 1577, to August 15, 1578. Miraculously delivered from captivity, he spent a few months at the Convent of Calvary in Andalusia, then became Rector of Baeza, and founded several convents of the Discalced. He died at the Convent of Ubeda on December 14, 1591. He was canonized by Benedict XIII on December 27, 1726. *Cf.* Demimuid, *Saint Jean de la Croix,* 3rd ed., Paris, 1916; Fr. Jérôme de Saint-Joseph, *Vie de saint Jean de la Croix,* in the *Œuvres* edited by the Carmelites of Paris, Vol. I.

[2] Part IV, Strophe xxxvi, H. Hoornaert's translation, Vol. IV, p. 218, Paris-Bruxelles, 2nd ed., 1923.

interview with St Teresa, to undertake the reform of the Carmelite religious. Next year, September 30, 1568, he set up the first Convent of the Discalced Carmelites in a poor hovel at Duruelo. What was its state of poverty? There is no difficulty in surmising it. John of the Cross was thus living through his dark nights of the senses before expounding his theory of them in his books.[1]

To these voluntary sufferings were added others from without. The success of the reform was quicker than could have been expected. People began to exalt the Discalced and to turn away from the Mitigated Carmelites. These displayed irritation and began to persecute John of the Cross.

First of all he was compelled to move frequently and unjustifiably by his superiors, who were of the Mitigated party. Finally, in 1571, to put a stop to his work of reform, they sent him to Avila as confessor to the Carmelite Convent of the Incarnation, "the main fortress of the Mitigated Carmelites." St Teresa was appointed Prioress of the Convent to hinder her, too, from carrying on the Carmelite reform.

Desiring to ruin the reform in every way, even by violence, the Mitigated Carmelites, on the night between the third and fourth of December, 1577, got John of the Cross carried off by force of arms from his house at Avila. He was dragged to the Convent of the Mitigated Carmelites in that town, and was there flogged to the blood. He was then taken to Toledo and interned in the Carmelite Convent.[2] All this was done with the greatest secrecy.

His prison was a dark recess, a real dungeon cell without ventilation. His daily food was a morsel of bread and a sardine. Rough handling was not spared him.[3] And it was in this cell that John of the Cross composed his first work, the *Spiritual Canticle*,[4] the expression of a soul purified with suffering and inebriated with love.

This poem of mystical love consists of forty strophes of five verses each. It takes its inspiration from the *Canticle of Canticles*; it is a dialogue between the soul and her divine

---

[1] At Duruelo the saint changed his name from John of St Matthias to John of the Cross to show his love for suffering.

[2] St Teresa said of the vexations of John of the Cross and of Jerome Gratian: "Poor Fathers! I would rather see them in the hands of the Moors."

[3] It was then that St Teresa wrote to Philip II of Spain to complain of the Mitigated Carmelites (Bouix, Vol. II, p. 301). The quarrel died down when Pope Gregory XIII, in his Brief of June 27, 1580, decided that the convents of the reform should become an autonomous province with a Provincial of the Reform. But it did not altogether cease until the two observances were separated—each having its own Superior General—decreed on December 20, 1593, by Clement VIII. Neither St Teresa nor St John of the Cross saw the end of the dispute.

[4] In 1584 he added the *Explanations* to it in prose. The finished work is thus the last composed by St John of the Cross.

Spouse. In the first part—which he calls the purgative way or the way of novices in the mystical state—the Bride seeks her Beloved and asks creatures to tell her where he is. The second part—that of proficients in the illuminative way—gives the answer of the Spouse who has just become spiritually betrothed to the soul. In the third—the unitive way—the mystical marriage is celebrated. Finally, in the last strophes the Bride sings of the joy given her by her intuition of the happiness of heaven.[1]

St John of the Cross wrote this *Canticle* "through need of expansion" amidst his unheard-of tribulations. His heroic endurance of his trials won him extraordinary graces. He was quickly raised to the most perfect stage of union with God, and poured forth his joy in lyrical poetry. He turned the *Canticle* into a kind of treatise of speculative mysticism by adding thereto his *Explanations* towards the close of his life.

His studies at Salamanca had indeed prepared him for mystical speculation. He had a deep knowledge of scholastic theology, and was steeped in the works of the Areopagite. There is every reason to suppose that he had also read the Flemish and German mystics.[2] Not long after his escape from imprisonment in Toledo, about the end of 1578, he was appointed Prior of the monastery of Calvary. There it was that he began to write *The Ascent of Mount Carmel* and *The Dark Night*.[3] He finished them in 1583 at Grenada, where he filled the office of Prior. At Granada he also wrote *The Living Flame of Love* in 1584.[4] In these three famous treatises the saint sets forth the theory of the mystical states which he had himself experienced.

St John of the Cross, despite the exceptional merits of his works, will certainly never have as many readers as St Teresa. This is to be regretted. But would that he had

---

[1] See the text of the *Canticle* in H. Hoornaert, Vol. IV, pp. 5-16.

[2] Cf. *Collationes brugenses*, tom. XVII, pp. 233, 499.

[3] *Études carmelitaines*, 15 juillet, 1913.

[4] St John of the Cross also wrote *Maxims* and *Spiritual Counsels*. All his works were written in Spanish. The first appeared in 1618 at Alcala; it contained *The Ascent of Mount Carmel, The Dark Night*, and *The Living Flame of Love*. It was republished at Barcelona in 1619. Another edition appeared at Seville in 1703 and included also *The Spiritual Canticle*. A critical edition was undertaken in 1754 by Fr. Andrew of the Incarnation, but was not published. The work was resumed by Fr. Gerard of St John of the Cross, who published (in 1912 and subsequently) the critical edition of the saint's *Works* at Toledo. In 1880 the Carmelites of Paris made a complete translation of the 1703 edition, and this has gone through many editions. Fr. Gerard's edition has been translated by H. Hoornaert, Paris-Bruxelles, 2nd ed., 1922-1923; and this is the edition I shall quote.

written with more simplicity! Instead of a concrete
mysticism, clothed in the charm of style, John of the Cross
delights in a sometimes rather subtle psychology; he expounds his doctrine, which is often fairly abstruse, under
complicated symbols, in conformity with the Spanish " man-
nerism " of his times.[1] He was, however, a poet, and he
could have revealed to us with dazzling brilliancy and clarity
that divine " poetry of religion,"[2] which is known as
mysticism. Did he not sing in lyrical strains of the joys of
a soul united with God?

But had he done so, he would have thought himself lacking in Christian renunciation, which he pushed to its utmost
limits in practice. He knew by experience what God requires
in the way of mortifications from a soul called to mystical
union. Before tasting " these intense delights, this joy of
soul and mind " resulting from such union, the purgatory of
purification had to be passed through. Before the flame of love
is seen in all its brightness, we must traverse the dark night
of the senses and of the spirit. Why should we be astonished
if there is no light in that dark night, and that he who is
leading us through the darkness makes us feel it?

" Since we have to make known the Dark Night, the
only way that leads to God," he writes in the Prologue of
The Ascent of Mount Carmel, " the reader will not be
astonished if he sometimes meets with what looks like darkness. This will be his feeling, I think, as he begins to read.
As he goes on, he will better understand what has gone
before; one page will throw light upon another. If he undertakes a second reading, I believe that it will give him further
light, and that the doctrine will come out more completely.
If, however, the second reading does not give full satisfaction, let the reader be good enough to blame my scanty
knowledge and defects of style; for indisputably the matter
is good in itself and strictly necessary."[3]

It is not only through his own bent that this passionate
lover of the cross describes the state of purification in which
God places holy souls. If he clings to this forbidding subject rather than to " the moral questions of an attractive
spirituality enjoyed by souls who seek God by the way of
consolations,"[4] it is because he knows how good it is for
them :

" Certain confessors and spiritual fathers," he says, " for
want of experience in these ways, far from coming to the

[1] This may be noted especially in his last two works, *The Living
Flame of Love* and *The Spiritual Canticle.*
[2] Demimuid, *op. cit.,* 126.
[3] H. Hoornaert, *Œuvres spirituelles de S Jean de la Croix,* Vol. I,
p. 5.
[4] *ibid.,* p. 6.

rescue of souls, load them with obstacles and do them
harm. . . . For the soul there is no more disquieting and
painful state than that of not being able to see clearly within
itself, and of finding no one who can understand it. Led
by God over the heights of dark contemplation and aridity,
it thinks that it is going astray, and amidst the darkness
and the sufferings and the anguish and the temptations,
the director will tell it as did Job's comforters: this is melancholy[1] and infirmity; perhaps you are keeping back some
hidden wickedness, whence comes the abandonment in which
God is leaving you. The confessor concludes that the soul
must be or must have been very guilty, since it is burdened
with such troubles. Others will say that this must be a
relapse, since the soul finds neither relish nor comfort in the
things of God as it used to do."[2]

These ill-advised counsellors impute to the soul, thus distressed, troubles for which it is not responsible, such as really
come from God and prepare the way for extraordinary graces.
"They are like the builders of Babel, who, because they
could not understand one another, did not bring useful things
but supplied others, so that the work came to a standstill."[3]

All the mystics mention these purifications usually allotted
by God to souls who are called to the highest kinds of prayer.
None have analyzed them as thoroughly as St John of the
Cross, and this it is that gives such great interest to his
writings: it is also the chief characteristic of his mysticism.
He describes these purifications, these mystical *nights,* in
two celebrated treatises: *The Ascent of Mount Carmel* and
The Dark Night. The first deals with *active* purifications—
i.e., the mortifications which the soul must practise *spon-
taneously* to do its utmost to prepare itself for close union
with God. The second, *The Dark Night,* tells of the passive
purifications which the soul must undergo. Here, it is God
himself who alone acts and strips the soul of all interior
impediments to the highest contemplation.

The soul who has passed through these dark nights and
has "reached the shining summit" of the mystic mount, after
climbing up "its rough and steep slopes,"[4] possesses God in

[1] The neurasthenia which St Teresa mentions.
[2] Hoornaert, *ibid.,* pp. 3-4. St John of the Cross has fifteen spiritual
maxims on "the spiritual teacher" and on direction. "To direct
souls," he says, "is not the business of the first man you meet, for to
judge soundly or to be mistaken in so grave a matter is a thing of the
highest importance." H. Hoornaert, Vol. II, p. 153.
[3] *ibid.,* p. 3.
[4] St John of the Cross himself sketched the design intended for the
frontispiece of his works. It represents a mountain. On the summit
is shown perfect union with God. At the foot of the mystic mountain
three roads are revealed to the soul. Only one of them leads to the
summit, the road of the complete renunciation of everything. This is

the union of perfect love. This is the subject of two other works of St John of the Cross : *The Spiritual Canticle* and *The Living Flame of Love*.

I—THE SPIRITUAL TEACHING OF ST JOHN OF THE CROSS[1]—ACTIVE PURIFICATIONS WHICH PREPARE THE WAY FOR ACTIVE CONTEMPLATION

ACTIVE purifications, as we have seen, are those which the soul, with the help of grace, can realize in itself, and does, in fact, realize by its own initiative, as contrasted with those which are wrought by God himself. In the latter, the soul is passive in God's hands.[2]

It is the whole of the soul that has to be purified : in the first place, its *senses;* then, its *spirit—i.e.,* its *mind, memory, and will.* Like the mystics of the Middle Ages, like St Ignatius of Loyola and St Teresa, St John of the Cross bases his spiritual psychology on this division of the faculties of the soul.

He calls these various purifications "dark nights." Let us not be too alarmed by such mannerisms of style. Purification strips the senses and the faculties of the soul from that which attracted them. It deprives them of material, just as darkness in the night does away with light and thus deprives the eyes of all that they see. Thus purified, the senses and the faculties of the soul are in the darkness of the void, just as the eyes are without light.[3] To enter into heaven, the soul usually must be purified in purgatory. And the soul

---

the central road. Of the two others, the one is that in which souls attached to the goods of this world go astray; the other is that wherein souls take pleasure in the enjoyment of spiritual goods.

[1] In the translation of the *Works* of St John of the Cross, by Fr. Cyprian of the Nativity (1641), will be found an Introduction and explanations of this teaching by Fathers Jerome of St Joseph, Nicholas of Jesus, and James of Jesus. In the Toledo edition of Fr. Gerard (1914, Vol. III) are also to be found the explanations of Father Diego de Jesus, O.C.D. (1570-1621), and the *Don que tuvo S Juan de la Cruz para quiar las almas a Dios,* by Fr. Joseph of Jesus Mary, C.D. (†1626), the author of a *Subida del alma a Dios,* Madrid, 1656, and other books enumerated in the edition of St John of the Cross by Fr. Gerard (Vol. I, p. lix). *Cf.* R. P. Wenceslas of the Holy Sacrament, *Fisionomia de un Doctor,* Salamanca, 1913; Ludovic de Besse, *Eclaircissements sur les Œuvres mystiques de S Jean de la Croix,* 1895; P. Berthier, *Lettres sur S Jean de la Croix* to the Marquis de Créqui; R. Garrigou-Lagrange, *Perfection chrétienne et contemplation selon S Thomas d'Aquin et S Jean de la Croix,* 1923; Mgr. Landrieux, *Sur les pas de S Jean de la Croix,* Paris, 1924; A. Tanqueray, *op. cit.,* pp. 890 ff.

[2] *Ascent of Mount Carmel,* Book I, chap. xiii, Hoornaert, Vol. I, p. 47.

[3] *Ascent of Mount Carmel,* Book I, chaps. ii, iii.

called to the heights of contemplation must also pass through
the mystical purgatory of purifications; and this purgatory
is as dark as night.

A — THE NIGHT OF THE SENSES OR THE ACTIVE PURIFICA-
TION OF THE SENSES

The first night, *that of the senses,* corresponds with what
ascetic authors call the purgative way.[1] St John of the
Cross powerfully demonstrates the necessity of mortifying
to the utmost " our unruly appetites " or passions. He
describes at length their " harmful effects " and the damage
they inflict upon us. All our voluntary appetites, he says,
" even the least which have to do with simple imperfections,
must be entirely eliminated " if " we would attain to entire
union " with God.[2] Then he shows what must be done to
enter into the night of the senses.

First, the soul must habitually desire to imitate Christ in
everything. His sole satisfaction in this world was to do
his Father's will. Next, all that appeals to the senses and
does not tend " purely to the honour and glory of God,"
must be renounced " through the love of Christ."[3] If the
senses are thus mortified, the passions will also be mortified:

" For instance," says St John of the Cross, " if the things
that are spoken of please you, even if they have nothing to
do with the service of God, abstain from enjoying them and
do not listen to them. If the pleasure of the eyes inclines you
towards things that do not raise your mind to God, abstain
from the enjoyment of them and turn your eyes away from
them; and mortify yourself, too, if you want to say or do
something to please yourself. In all your senses without
exception, do away with the power of attraction, when you
can do it without drawing anyone's attention; but if you
cannot do that, it will suffice to renounce the satisfaction
which you cannot interrupt. Thereby your mortified senses
will be freed from attraction and, as it were, left in
darkness."[4]

Let us not forget that here we have to do with rules of
perfection, with renunciation and satisfaction in things permissible. It is by the way of absolute abnegation that the
saint would lead us to union with God.

To make still more sure the death of the passions, he
proposes the following most crucifying practices:

[1] *Ascent of Mount Carmel,* Book I, chaps. iv-xv. St John of the
Cross always assumes that souls who have actively entered into the
dark night are already completely detached from sin. He demands an
absolute detachment even from simple imperfections of the least voluntary kind.
 [2] *ibid.,* Book I, chap. xi, p. 39.
 [3] *ibid.,* chap. xiii, Vol. I, p. 48.   [4] *ibid.*

" Seek preferably : Not the easiest, but the hardest. Not the most to your taste, but the most insipid. Not what pleases you, but what does not attract you. Not what comforts you, but what grieves you. Not what relieves you, but what demands hard toil. Not more, but less. Not the highest and the most precious, but the lowest and the most despised. Not to desire things, but to be indifferent to them. Not what is best in anything, but what is worst."[1]

St John of the Cross further reveals his mind with regard to the mortification of man's threefold concupiscence :

" In the first place, strive to despise yourself and desire to be despised by your neighbour, this is salutary for the concupiscence of the flesh. In the second place, try to lessen yourself by what you say and to get your neighbour to lessen you, this is salutary for the concupiscence of the eyes. Thirdly, endeavour to have a sense of humiliation with regard to yourself and to get others to have the same opinion of you, this is salutary for destroying the pride of life."[2]

To attain to such renunciation of the things of sense, the soul is helped by the love of God. " By putting her relish and power " in this love, she finds the necessary vigour and confidence for easily abandoning any other affection.[3] To the fire of the passions she opposes the still more burning flame of the love of her heavenly Spouse. Moreover, she tastes in such complete renunciation a great joy, the joy of deliverance. " Since the sin of the fall, the soul is really the captive of our mortal body, subject to the passions and natural appetites." When she has passed through the night of the senses, she enters " into possession of true liberty." John of the Cross sings of this deliverance in lyrical accents.[4]

B—THE NIGHT OF THE SPIRIT OR THE ACTIVE PURIFICATION OF THE SPIRIT

However, the soul has not yet attained union with God. The night of the senses is succeeded by the *Night of the spirit.* Or rather, as St John of the Cross explains,[5] it is the second part of the night that now begins and this is darker than the first. The night of the senses is like the twilight which follows the setting of the sun, wherein we can hardly see anything. The night of the spirit, especially that of the understanding, corresponds with midnight; it is utter darkness. For, in the night of the senses, the intelligence was still active and took cognisance of things; but now it totally ceases from its natural operations. The soul is thus

[1] *Ascent of Mount Carmel*, pp. 48-49.
[2] *ibid.*, p. 49.
[3] *ibid.*, chap. xiv, p. 52.   [4] *ibid.*, chap. xv, p. 53.
[5] *ibid.*, Book II, Introduction and chap. i.

in total darkness. The third part of the night, the night of
the memory and the will, is already near the break of day.
It is in some sort the dawn before the divine sunrise in which,
during contemplation, the soul "loses herself in an ecstasy
of heavenly light."

What St John of the Cross calls *spirit*—let us bear it in
mind—comprises the understanding, the memory, and the
will. The understanding enters into the dark night by faith,
the memory by hope, and the will by love.[1]

The understanding must be stripped of all its natural
cognitions and thoughts if it desires to attain to the contemplation of God; this is a kind of axiom with spiritual writers.
Let us call to mind the teaching of the Areopagite. To see
God in contemplation, we must first have nudity of the intelligence. St John of the Cross, too, speaks of this "nudity
of the understanding." He had read the Dionysian writings;
he had no doubt also read the German and Flemish mystics.
Sometimes he seems to reproduce their expressions. According to him, the night of the spirit is "nudity and the void,"
wherein it must be left so far as its operations are concerned.
If we would come to the possession of God, we must "enter
into this extreme nudity and void of the spirit."[2] For the
thoughts and "the knowledge acquired and kept as its own
by the understanding are rather hindrances than means"
towards union with God. They are limited and imperfect:
but God is infinite and perfect:

"In this life," he explains, "for the understanding to
attain to union with God, so far as that is possible, it must
use the proper means towards union, means having a close
likeness to the end. Note well that amongst all creatures,
whether superior or inferior, none affords this close likeness
or possesses the required resemblance to the divine Being.
According to the theologians, all of them, indeed, have
a certain relation to God and are marked with a divine imprint, more accentuated in some than in others, according to
their degree of excellence; but between them and God there
is no affinity, no essential likeness. In reality, the distance
between the divine and created beings is infinite; hence it
is impossible for the understanding to enter truly into God
by means of creatures, whether heavenly or earthly, since all
proportion and likeness between them is lacking."[3]

Therefore the understanding will of itself renounce its
human activity and forms and representations provided by the

---

[1] *Ascent of Mount Carmel*, Book II, chap. v, Vol. I, p. 73.
[2] *ibid.*, chap. vi, pp. 76-77.
[3] *id.*, Book II, chap. vii, Vol. I, p. 83.

corporal senses and taken from things visible. It will put
out its natural light and thus be in darkness.

This extinction does not destroy the understanding; but on
the contrary it makes its illumination by faith all the easier.
The more the understanding is mortified, the more does faith
increase in it, the more, too, does it become capable of union
with God. For there is no close means of union with God
apart from faith. " Faith is so intimately connected with
God that believing by faith and seeing in the beatific vision
have the same object."[1] When the soul has concentrated the
action of her powers, her inclinations and spiritual appetites
in pure faith, she can unite " with her Beloved by the union
of simplicity, of purity of love, and of likeness."[2] But faith
is obscure, this is one of its characteristics. Its light is
supernatural; it eclipses all human brightness of the understanding. The latter believes the truths revealed without
understanding them. Hence it remains, humanly speaking,
in a dark night. It is the *dark night* of the understanding.

To put the understanding into this night and to immerge
it in faith only, it must—going from the more outward to
the more inward—be stripped of the perceptions of the
external senses, then of those of the internal senses, especially
of the imagination, and lastly of those that are purely mental
or of ideas.[3]

According to what was said of the *Night of the senses,* he
who would unite with God must have already purified his
outward corporal senses by depriving them of all perceptions
that do not lead to God. But the understanding may have
previously received perceptions and knowledge through the
corporal senses. It must be stripped of them so that none of
its former perceptions and no sensible images remain. It
will thus be in the night so far as the outward corporal
perceptions are concerned.

St John of the Cross goes still further. He demands that
contemplatives shall renounce supernatural phenomena, such
as visions, revelations, and interior words which sometimes
affect the external senses. The more the soul " makes of
such phenomena," he says, " the more does it turn away
from the true road and from the security of faith."[4] Evidently
he is here reacting—and how energetically—against illuminism and the pseudo-mystical sense-illusions of the
Alumbrados. Let us listen to him:

[1] *Ascent of Mount Carmel,* Vol. I, p. 87.
[2] *ibid.,* p. 57.
[3] See the whole of Book II of the *Ascent of Mount Carmel,* chaps.
i-xxx, Vol. I, pp. 56-207.
[4] *id.,* Book II, chap. x, Vol. I, p. 92.

" It may happen, and often does happen, that spiritual persons are supernaturally affected by representations and things that affect the senses. Their eyes are struck by figures, by persons of another world, by visions of saints, of good or bad angels, by lights and extraordinary brightnesses; the ear hears certain strange words, uttered by persons in visible shape or said apart from any apparition; the sense of smell perceives sweet perfumes, the source of which is undisclosed. The sense of taste may likewise be affected by a most charming savour, and the sense of touch by deep delights. These are sometimes so strong as to rejoice both marrow and bones till they dilate and are steeped in pleasure. Of this nature is what is called spiritual unction, which is imparted to the members of pure souls. . . . We must take account of this: though all these phenomena may come from God and affect the bodily senses, they must never be the subjects of satisfaction or acceptance; I will go farther, they must be fled, and that absolutely, without trying to find out whether their source is good or evil. From the very fact that these communications are mainly external and physical, it may always be presumed that their origin is not divine."[1]

St John of the Cross declares without ambiguity that such sensible manifestations " are a source of hindrances and hurts to the soul," and that by not shutting our eyes to them " we depart from the means to union with God," which is faith.[2]

He is just as severe in dealing with supernatural imaginative visions, perceived by the internal senses, which are " imagination and fancy."

" I declare, then," he says, " that all perceptions and visions of the imagination, every shape and sensible species presented as a figure, image or particular cognition, whether regarded as false and coming from the devil, or as true and coming from God, ought not to preoccupy or nourish the understanding. The soul cannot desire their communication or retain them when they come, so that she may keep herself free, denuded, pure and simple, as is required for union with God."[3]

The reason of this is plain. Besides that imaginative visions are subject to the risk of diabolical illusion, all these " forms, from the fact that they are perceived, are confined to the modes and manners of limitation," whereas the divine wisdom knows " no limit of form, species, or image." The

[1] *Ascent of Mount Carmel,* Book II, chap. x, Vol. I, p. 91.
[2] *ibid.* St John of the Cross makes an exception, however, in the " very rare " cases in which a director might judge otherwise (p. 98).
[3] *ibid.,* chap. xiv, pp. 120-121. St John of the Cross distinguishes between " imagination " and " fancy," *ibid.,* chap. xi.

soul can only unite with it on condition of not being " enclosed in " a particular form.[1]

As much must be said, *a fortiori,* of the images shaped in our minds by the normal and natural play of imagination. " All these images and perceptions must be cast out of the soul, for she must become dark, in this sense, to attain to divine union."[2] However, since meditation, which is a discursive exercise, belongs to the sphere of the imagination, beginners will make use of this faculty. It will also be used sometimes during the period of first arriving at contemplation. But as soon as contemplation has become habitual, imagination must finally go into the night.[3]

Lastly, we come to the very innermost of the soul, wherein purely spiritual perceptions take place. Here again St John of the Cross demands entire denudation. No idea, however spiritual, can enable us to contemplate God, for it is necessarily imperfect and limited. The mind must be put " in the Night of faith."

But there are purely spiritual perceptions of the supernatural order, to wit : intellectual visions, revelations, interior words, and spiritual feelings. Moreover, such phenomena, when divine, produce happy results in the soul. Nevertheless, St John of the Cross will not have us seek for nor desire them. He goes much farther. He counsels us to forget the forms and the impressions left by intellectual visions. We must go to God in the negation of everything.[4] We must also forget revelations and interior words. " It is better always to go to God by unknowing."[5] The saint incessantly advises the soul to keep to herself " prudently all these communications, if she would reach, pure and free from illusion, by the night of faith, unto union with God."[6]

As we see, St John of the Cross would have the soul renounce all that is below mystical union properly so called ; she is to renounce visions and other like phenomena which might create illusion. Thus does the saint react against illuminism.

St John of the Cross has just given us a description of the *Dark Night* of the understanding. We have now to learn

---

[1] Although St John of the Cross is unfavourable to visions and other imaginative perceptions, he does not deny that the saints had some that were real. He attempts to characterize them, and he affirms that even those which come from God may give rise to errors. See *ibid.,* Book II, chaps. xv-xx.

[2] *Ascent of Mount Carmel, ibid.,* chap. xi, p. 99.

[3] *ibid.,* Book II, chaps. xi-xiii.

[4] *ibid.,* Book II, chap. xxii, pp. 179-189.

[5] *ibid.,* chap. xxiv, p. 190. [6] *ibid.,* chap. xxv, p. 194.

of the *Night* of the memory and of the will.[1] We must remember that the whole soul has to pass through the purgatory of purification.

It is faith that has stripped the understanding and made it enter into the night. It is hope that will create " in memory the void of all possession," and it is charity that will produce " the void in the will, the stripping away of every affection for and joy in what is not God."[2] For—and John of the Cross constantly repeats this with the Areopagite— " just as the soul must know God rather by what is not than by what is, so must it go towards him rather by denial than by admission ; it must reject the least of the perceptions, whether natural or supernatural, which it might conceive of him."[3]

The memory must therefore get rid of all impressions and memories which come to it through the five bodily senses, " so that no trace of them is left therein, and that it may remain as void and clear as possible, as if nothing had come through it, in its forgetfulness and freedom from everything."[4] Thus will the soul be delivered from the evil memories left by the world, distractions will be fewer, and the temptations of the devil less readily arise. Peace and tranquillity of mind will be more secure.

If memory retains supernatural memories of visions, revelations, and interior words, even though of divine origin, they, too, must be got rid of. St John of the Cross regards them as " an obstacle to divine union in pure and perfect hope."[5] For he considers that it is hope that " empties and darkens the memory," and of this he gives the following somewhat subtle explanation :

" To hope for a thing is not to possess it, and the less we possess it the greater is our capacity and readiness for expecting what we hope for, and the more perfect is our hope. On this principle, it is in proportion to the divestment of the memory, setting aside the forms and memories which are not God, that it will immerse itself the more in God, and will prepare a greater void for the hope that God will fill it completely.

" To live in pure and perfect hope in God we must therefore not stop short at cognitions, forms, and distinct images —as we have explained. Whenever they occur we must immediately turn our soul, free from all that, to God in an impulse of tender love."[6]

---

[1] This is the subject of Book III of the *Ascent of Mount Carmel,* Vol. II, p. 1-110.
[2] Book II, chap. v, Vol. I, p. 73.
[3] Book III, chap. i, Vol. II, p. 4.   [4] *Ascent, ibid.,* p. 5.
[5] Book III, chap. vi, Vol. II, p. 19.
[6] Book III, chap. xiv, Vol. II, pp. 33-34.

Memories must only be recalled so far as the fulfilment of our duties requires. Then the Spirit of God will tell us what we ought to know.[1]

It is by charity that the will is purified in the *Dark Night* of the spirit. This virtue " makes a void in all the things of the will, since it binds us to love God above all things, and that is only realised by renouncing everything so as to refer everything to God."[2]

To throw such renunciation into full relief, St John of the Cross explains in four short treatises how the will should mortify the four passions characteristic of it : joy, hope, grief, and fear. Of these four treatises only one has survived, and that is unfinished. It teaches us how the will is purified of the enjoyment of supernatural and spiritual goods.[3] The counsels given by the saint for attaining to the entire renunciation of the will present no peculiarity.

However, we note in the last chapters of the *Treatise on the Will,* his astonishing insistence upon renouncing the " enjoyment " of supernatural favours which are inferior to the mystical union that God sometimes grants.[4] His first editors were alarmed at it, and they found it necessary to explain and justify his line of thought. The reasons for such detachment given by St John of the Cross do not, indeed, appear to suffice. The favours received may certainly, as he says, contribute to the soul's *amour-propre* and lead it to forget God for the sole sake of sensible consolations. But such dangers as these are met with in every age. Spiritual writers have warned the faithful against them, yet have not required them to renounce the enjoyment of such favours when God willed to grant them. When St Teresa spoke of " the joys and consolations afforded by meditation," she said, " they are to be highly esteemed, provided that humility makes it plainly understood that we are none the better for them."[5] Hence we may consider that when St John of the Cross pushed renunciation to the point of rigorism, he wanted to react against the false mysticism of the *Alumbrados,* who

[1] St John of the Cross explains (Book III, chap. i) how those whose memory is thus stripped may still act and fulfil their duties. God makes it up to them and " reminds them of what they have to remember."

[2] Book II, chap. v, Vol. I, p. 74.

[3] Book III, chaps. xv-xliv. St John of the Cross here refutes Protestant theories counter to the worship of images.

[4] Yet St John of the Cross does not demand the renunciation of enjoyment arising from mystical union through contemplation of the divine Essence. He describes this joy in *The Living Flame of Love* and in *The Spiritual Canticle.*

[5] St Teresa, *Castle,* Fourth Mansion, chap. i, *Œuvres,* VI, p. 100. *Cf.* pp. 91-93. *Way of Perfection,* chap. xxviii.

thought that spiritual joys were the sum and substance of piety.

He requires of the contemplative under his guidance every kind of mortification and detachment; nothing must be left that is not God. Well did he deserve the name of the doctor of *Nada* (*Nothing*), as they liked to call him in Spain.[1]

C—" Spiritual " or Active " Contemplation "

When the soul's purification is finished and when it has passed through the Night of the Senses and of the Spirit, it will be able to contemplate God.

This contemplation, which is prepared for by active purifications, is not as yet infused or passive contemplation, for the latter will be preceded by passive purifications. It is called *active* contemplation, because anyone led by ordinary grace can attain thereto by using the ordinary means.[2] St John of the Cross calls it " spiritual contemplation," because " the spiritual senses alone are in action therein."

This is how he explains " this matter " which, he says, was " rarely dealt with " in his time.

Between discursive prayer—*i.e.*, meditation in which imagination and " the sensitive powers " are in action—and infused or mystical contemplation, there is an intermediate kind. This is " spiritual " contemplation. It consists " in gently imposing silence at the opportune moment on the understanding, and in keeping quiet in faith while fastening our spiritual gaze affectionately upon God, rejoicing in the contemplation of him, and realizing that God, too, is looking on us and helping us in our contemplation.[3] It is " contemplation or the simple regard with the spiritual powers."[4] Later on it is called the prayer of simplicity or of simple regard.

In it imagination, memory, and understanding are at rest : " the soul is glad to find itself alone with God, fixing its attention lovingly upon him without any particular consideration, with inward peace, quiet, and repose, without any acts or exercises of a really discursive kind of the powers—the understanding, the memory, and the will—through the association of ideas. It is contented with knowing and with a general and loving attention . . . without any particular perception of anything else."[5]

The repose of the powers of the soul is facilitated by the

[1] *Nada=nothing,* constantly occurs in his Maxims.
[2] *Cf.* H. Hoornaert, Introduction to *Œuvres,* I, pp. xii ff.; III, pp. xix ff.
[3] *Ascent,* Vol. III, p. xxi.
[4] *Ascent,* Book II, chap. xii, Vol. I, p. 109.
[5] *Ascent, ibid.,* chap. xi, p. 104.

purification to which they have been subjected. This general
and loving knowledge of God is the result of faith; it is a
" spiritual light striking the eyes of the soul which are the
understanding."[1] With the help of this light, the soul looks
at and contemplates God. This look and this contemplation
are obscure like faith itself. They are not vision, as is sometimes the case in mystical union; for here we have nothing
extraordinary or supernatural so far as it is a state of prayer.

When the soul is quite pure and stripped of cognitions
and particular notions that may affect the understanding or
the senses, this light is in itself particularly clear, pure,
simple, and perfect.[2] The light of faith entirely permeates
the soul.

" Imagine the sun shining on a window-pane," says St
John of the Cross; " if the glass is darkened with spots or
dirty straws, the rays will not succeed in shining through it
and in completely transfusing it with light, which is what
would take place if the pane was clean and free from all grime.
It would not be the fault of the sunshine, but of the window-
pane. If it were quite clean and clear the light would transform it; it would shine with the same brightness as the rays
of the sun which transfused it."[3]

In this kind of contemplation the soul is in action. It not
only uses effort for preparation for it, but also to put itself
into such a state and to keep therein as long as was intended.
This exercise is not in the same case as mystical contemplation, which depends upon God alone.

When must discursive prayer be given up for contemplation? St John of the Cross considers that the time is
determined by the difficulty found in fixing one's imagination
and senses upon some particular subject, by the disappearance
of all relish for reflections, and especially by a persistent desire
for " the repose of contemplative knowledge."[4] However,
" it is profitable, when we first enjoy a general knowledge of
contemplation, sometimes to resume discursive meditation
and the use of the natural faculties."[5] Discursive meditation

---

[1] *Ascent of Mount Carmel,* chap. xii, p. 110.   [2] *ibid.,* p. 109.
[3] *Ascent,* Book II, chap. iv, Vol. I, pp. 70-71. *Cf.* chap. xii.
[4] These three signs of readiness to give up discursive meditation are
classic in spiritual writers. Here is the statement of St John of the
Cross : " *First sign:* Meditation becomes impracticable, the imagination is inert, the relish for this exercise vanishes, and the enjoyment
of the thing imagined has changed to aridity. . . . *Second sign:*
This appears in an entire lack of the desire to fasten either the imagination or the senses on any particular subject, either inward or outward. . . . *Third sign:* This is the most decisive one : the soul takes
pleasure in finding itself alone with God, fastening its attention upon
him without any particular consideration. . . ." *Ascent,* Book II,
chap. xi, Vol. I, pp. 103-104.
[5] *ibid.,* chap. xiii, p. 115.

is the way to prepare for active contemplation ; it purifies the powers of the soul, and therefore it is not a good thing to leave it altogether until contemplation has become habitual.

II—PASSIVE PURIFICATIONS WHICH PREPARE THE WAY FOR MYSTICAL UNION TRULY SO CALLED, FOR INFUSED CONTEMPLATION

" After having begun the ascent of Mount Carmel, in following the Narrow Way of the five renunciations (the senses, the imagination, the understanding, the memory, and the will), by active contemplation the soul attains to enter into the mystical life, and is henceforth led by God himself in the passive ways. The new progress of the soul henceforth depends upon the vocation given it by God's special leadings and upon its correspondence with the graces imparted to it."[1]

The end of such graces is to purify the soul passively and thoroughly. Human nature is sinful. Even when purified from its faults their root remains. Simple purification from voluntary manifestations of sin suffices for active contemplation. The very roots of sin must be extirpated for infused contemplation, which unites the soul to God in a supereminent way.

The soul which is destined for mystical union will therefore enter into a special Dark Night, wherein, through great suffering, it will undergo an " essential " purification. Such is the subject of the work which St John of the Cross calls *The Dark Night,* a night not to be confounded with that of *The Ascent of Mount Carmel.* Here we find the most original part of the mysticism of our saint, and in it he describes the passive purifications of the senses and of the spirit very fully.

A—The Passive Purification of the Senses or Passive Night of the Senses

The purification or passive night of the senses " eliminates the principal imperfections which have withstood (in *The Ascent of Mount Carmel*) personal endeavour and ordinary grace."[2] These imperfections are our innate inclinations to cling to sensible consolations in spiritual work.

[1] H. Hoornaert, *Œuvres spirituelles de S Jean de la Croix*, Vol. III, Preface, p. xxx. St John of the Cross writes at the beginning of the First Book of *The Dark Night:* " The soul has just come out of the *Narrow Way* by the purification due to its own activity. It is united to God, while retaining certain imperfections, and if God call it to a higher spiritual life, he will subject it to a twofold passive purification (of the senses and of the spirit)." Vol. III, p. 3.

[2] *Dark Night.* Vol. III, p. 3.

" Many people think," says St John of the Cross, " that spirituality consists in being faithful to practices [that yield consolations]. . . . Nevertheless, in a really spiritual sense, what they do is very feeble and imperfect. The motive of such practices and exercises is consolation, the attraction which charms them. Since their hearts have not been trained by arduous struggles in the practice of virtue, even in spiritual works they commit faults and incur numerous imperfections."[1]

St John of the Cross sets forth " these numerous imperfections in order and in their relations to the seven capital sins."[2] God banishes them by " purifying aridity" into which he plunges the soul, which suddenly loses all its pleasure and satisfaction in religious exercises: it finds nothing but aridity.

But here we must be on our guard against illusion. These aridities are not always solely intended to purify the sensitive appetite; they may also be the result of " sin, imperfection, lack of energy, lukewarmness, and even of an unruly humour and bodily indisposition."[3] How can we tell whether they are really purifying or that they do not arise from some fault?

St John of the Cross gives us three signs. First, the soul which is undergoing passive purification no longer finds any taste for or consolation in creatures rather than in or for things divine; the dark night of the sensitive appetite is complete. Next, it retains " usually in the thought of God an uneasiness and a painful anxiety." It fears that it is not doing enough for the Lord and that it is losing ground. Lastly, discursive meditation becomes more and more difficult. People in this state suffer keenly. They think they are on the wrong road and that God is abandoning them. They need enlightened and comforting direction; and if they find it they will make great spiritual progress.[4]

B—PASSIVE PURIFICATION OF THE SPIRIT OR PASSIVE NIGHT OF THE SPIRIT

The passive night of the senses precedes and prepares the way for the passive night of the spirit. This " is exceptional in its full manifestation; and its frightful torments are compensated for by marvellous graces."[5] Taken by itself it prepares the soul for the highest union with God. " It is but

[1] *Dark Night,* Book I, § 1, *Œuvres,* Vol. III, p. 7. I take no notice of the division of the treatise into strophes.
[2] *ibid.,* p. 8. Thus there is spiritual pride, spiritual avarice, spiritual anger, spiritual greediness, spiritual envy and idleness. Book I, ii-viii, Vol. III, pp. 8-27.
[3] *ibid.,* Book I, x, p. 29.
[4] *ibid.,* Book I, xi ff., pp. 34-53.
[5] *ibid.,* Book II, i, Vol. III, p. 54.

rarely experienced, and little has been written or taught about it.''

According to St John of the Cross, '' the soul which is called by God to the highest perfection does not enter into the night of the spirit as soon as it has passed out '' of that of the senses. '' An indefinite period, which may last for years,'' '' usually '' comes between the two nights. During this interval, God prepares and comforts the soul with raptures, ecstasies, or revelations, before introducing it into the fearful night of the spirit.[1]

As soon as the soul is about to enter into it, purification begins.

Even after the passive night of the senses, there remain habitual imperfections which '' resemble roots left in the spirit where the purification of the senses has been unable to reach.'' When we have cut down a tree we have not torn out its roots. Still harder work remains to be done. Further, besides such habitual imperfections, even in those who enter into the passive night of the spirit, there are a few actual imperfections arising from their lack of an entirely pure intention.[2] Their old man has not yet altogether disappeared.

[In order to annihilate it] '' God deprives these proficients [in the mystical ways] of their powers, affections, and senses, both spiritual and sensible, both inward and outward, leaving the understanding in darkness, the will in aridity, the memory with no recollections, and the spiritual affections overwhelmed with grief, bitterness, and anguish. They have neither feeling nor relish for the spiritual goods which formerly attracted them, and God uses this deprivation as a requisite of the spirit to make room for the spiritual form which is loving union. Our Lord works all this in the soul by a pure and obscure sort of contemplation.[3] . . .

'' This dark night is a divine influence in the soul which purifies it of its ignorance and its habitual imperfections. Contemplatives call it infused contemplation and mystical theology, wherein God teaches the soul secretly and in the perfection of love, without any intervention of its own and without its knowing wherein this infused contemplation consists.''[4]

This contemplation puts the understanding in the dark, the '' divine darkness '' of which the Areopagite has so much to say. It also brings about sufferings and torments in every part of the soul, and afflictions and tortures in the will. In fact, infused contemplation '' darkens the spirit '' by its too great light. '' The more we want to look at the sun the weaker grows our sight, and our enfeebled eyes are filled

<hr>

[1] *Dark Night,* pp. 55-56.   [2] *ibid.,* pp. 57-58.
[3] *ibid.,* Book II, iii, Vol. III, p. 60.
[4] *ibid.,* p. 62.

with darkness." Thus is it with contemplation before the soul is entirely purified. The divine light cast into the soul by God is in excess of its capacity, and is therefore dark so far as it is concerned. This explains why the enlightening brightness of divine wisdom produces "profound darkness in the mind."[1] It is because of its impurity that the spiritual vision cannot endure such brightness; the soul is keenly conscious of it, and therefore suffers much.

The other sufferings are still more excruciating. One of them is " inexplicable," says St John of the Cross. It is the impression of being invaded by the divine that destroys all the remnants of the old man. It is God who thus transforms the soul into himself. The soul is absorbed " in a deep and absolute darkness so as to feel melted and annihilated in a cruel death of the spirit."

" It feels," says the saint, " as if it were being swallowed alive by some beast, and digested in its dark belly with the anguish experienced by Jonas in the hollow recesses of the great sea-monster. And it has to pass through this dark death to attain to its expected resurrection."[2]

At the same time it feels—and this is another great suffering—" a profound emptiness, a cruel dearth of the three kinds of goods capable of comforting it—i.e., temporal, natural, and spiritual blessings." Just as fire eats away the rust from iron, thus does God thoroughly purify the internal and external powers of their inclination towards such goods ; and as such attractions are deeply rooted in the substance of the soul, it is subjected to the " torment of an inward dis-assimilation which is added " to the distressful impression of absolute emptiness.

" To do away with the rust of the [imperfect] affections in the centre of the soul, it must somehow destroy and annihilate itself, since its passions and imperfections have become a part of its nature. . . . The soul must pass, like gold, through the crucible.

" By these trials does God humiliate the soul profoundly to prepare it for the great exaltation in store for it. . . . The contemplation of its inward unworthiness sometimes reaches a point so keen that the soul sees hell open to swallow it up for ever. Of such souls it may be said that they literally go down alive into hell [purgatory] ; they are purified on earth in the same way as down there. . . . Hence it is that a soul thus treated on earth either escapes the place of expiation in the other world or stays in it scarcely at all ; and an hour of such suffering in this life is far more efficacious than many hours of purification after death."[3]

---

[1] *Dark Night, ibid.*, p. 63. [2] *ibid.*, pp. 65-66.
[3] *ibid.*, pp. 67-69. On the mystical purgatory, see pp. 93-96.

In this state of anguish and affliction the soul believes that it is abandoned for ever by God whom it formerly served with happiness. Temptations to despair assail it violently, though it is convinced that it loves God and that it would give a thousand lives for his sake.

" As the soul finds itself very miserable, it cannot be persuaded that God can love it now or ever. In it there is nothing except that which fills it with horror, a hopeless horror of God and of all things. Hence it suffers from seeing within itself nothing but reasons justifying its being forsaken by him whom it passionately loves and desires."[1]

Prayer becomes very difficult, for the soul " can no longer, as formerly, rise to God either in mind or heart." If it does happen to pray, " it is with such aridity as to think that God neither hearkens to it nor takes any notice of it."[2]

This very detailed description of the mystical purgatory is plainly taken from the experience of St John of the Cross. If God wills certain souls to pass through such sufferings it is because he intends to load them with favours. This hope sustains them in their cruel trial. St John of the Cross thus explains the favours which are the happy results of this passive night.

" If it [the night] darkens the spirit," he says, " it is to enlighten it about everything; if it humiliates it and makes it miserable, it is to exalt it and set it free; if it impoverishes it and strips it of all natural possessions and affections, it is to enable it to relish divinely the sweetness of all the blessings of heaven and earth."[3]

The soul is wholly transformed into heavenly fire by infused contemplation, just as—according to a comparison of Hugh of St Victor repeated by St John of the Cross—wood is transformed into fire by burning.[4] In this dark night of sorrowful contemplation the spiritual fire of love begins to inflame the soul. It is the awakening of divine love. While the understanding remains in total darkness the soul is " very sharply wounded " by that love. All its powers and appetites being altogether severed from their natural objects, they are exclusively concentrated in this inflaming of love."

" It is possible," says St John of the Cross, " to form some notion of this inflaming of love in the spirit, in the centre in which God makes all the powers, the faculties and appetites of the soul, both spiritual and sensitive, converge in a mighty harmony of powers and virtues, having no other object than his love alone. Thus it is that the soul comes to fulfil really

[1] *Dark Night,* Book II, Vol. III, p. 76.
[2] *ibid.,* p. 76. [3] *ibid.,* p. 80. [4] *ibid.,* pp. 85-89.

the first of the Ten Commandments, which excludes all that remains of man's self-love : *Diliges Dominum Deum tuum ex toto corde tuo et ex tota anima tua et ex tota fortitudine tua: Thou shalt love the Lord thy God with thy whole heart, and with thy whole soul, and with thy whole strength* (Deut. vi, 5)."[1]

Those who have undergone these passive purifications really love God with an unmixed love. Whatever they do or think in the different situations in which they are, they " only love in various ways." This is the life of love in its truest sense, the life of those who have reached the top of Mount Carmel.[2]

C—PASSIVE OR INFUSED CONTEMPLATION

I have dealt with the passive purifications at some length, because they are the most novel part of the teaching of St John of the Cross. Mystical union will not need such space.

It is specially treated in *The Living Flame of Love* and in *The Spiritual Canticle*. Yet these two works are entirely independent of *The Ascent of Mount Carmel* and *The Dark Night*. Their teaching is not presented as the climax of the purifications of the senses and of the spirit. The work of the saint, which included the normal sequel of these purifications and described " the wonderful effects of the spiritual enlightenment and of the union of love with God," is lost. Hence we are obliged to substitute for it *The Living Flame* and *The Spiritual Canticle*,[3] the subject of which is analogous.

These two works are hymns divided into strophes. They are full of lyrical feeling. They should be read : they cannot be analyzed any more than the divine love which is their theme.

The union of love takes place in the *centre of the soul*.[4] Thus does St John of the Cross name the higher part of the soul, " the seat of the theological virtues." Other mystics call it *the bottom of the soul, the summit of the soul, the*

---

[1] *Dark Night,* Book II, Vol. III, pp. 90-91.

[2] At the end of *The Dark Night*, St John of the Cross notes further effects of the passive purification of the spirit in his explanation of the end of the first strophe and of the second strophe of Book II. His style is particularly obscure and mannered. Vol. III, pp. 102-141. These effects are included in those previously described.

[3] Part III of *The Canticle* deals with the unitive way and the spiritual marriage, Vol. IV, pp. 139 ff. Part I treats of the dispositions which are indispensable for the marriage, Part II of " the spiritual betrothal."

[4] St John of the Cross also uses other analogous expressions : the *substance of the soul*, the *higher part of the spirit*, the *innermost part of the spirit*, the *heart of the soul*. Vol. III, pp. 148 ff.

highest part of the spirit, the highest point (or *apex*) *of the reason.* There take place assent to revealed truths and the union of man's spirit with God.

This centre of the soul is inaccessible to the senses and to the devil. After the passive purifications, the soul is completely freed from the senses. Furthermore, in these passive states " the soul does nothing of itself "; it has " to do nothing but receive what comes from God. In the centre of the soul he alone can set it in motion and operate without the intervention of the senses."[1] Here we must call to mind the German theories of *the bottom of the soul,* remarking well that St John of the Cross was able to avoid any disconcerting expression.

Divine love is unifying and transforming. The more it increases in the soul the more perfectly does it unite it with God and transform it into him. A moment comes—but never fully in this life—when the soul is transformed into God in its innermost centre :

" If it [the soul] attains to the highest [degree of love], divine love will have wounded it in its deepest centre, and this will mean the transformation of the soul, the illumination of its whole being according to the power and the desire of which it is capable, and to such a point that it will appear as God. It is then like a crystal of extreme purity and transparency in sunlight. The more bright the sun's rays, the more does the crystal concentrate them in itself, and the more does it shine; and if the light received by it is superabundant, the crystal itself will be confounded with it; the rays will no longer be perceived, for the crystal will absorb their brightness as far as it can and will appear to have become light itself."[2]

The soul will then see the sweetest relations established between the divine Persons and itself. Its understanding will be " divinely enlightened by the wisdom of the Son . . . its will will delight in the Holy Spirit . . . and the Father will engulf it [the soul] mightily and profoundly in the abyss of his love."[3]

In *The Spiritual Canticle,* a real mystical epithalamium, John of the Cross defines the object of the revelations made to the soul enlightened by divine Wisdom :

" In the higher life of the spiritual marriage," he says, " the Spouse readily and frequently discovers to the soul his faithful companion, his marvellous secrets, for a sincere and perfect heart has no secrets for the beloved. What he specially delights in revealing to her are the sweet mysteries of his Incarnation, and the dispensation of the Redemption

---

[1] *Living Flame,* first strophe, Vol. III, p. 152.
[2] *ibid.,* p. 154.   [3] *ibid.,* p. 155.

of mankind; and as this work is amongst the most astounding of those of God, nothing can be compared with the happiness of the soul who enters into them."[1]

As for the delight of the will in the Holy Spirit, St John of the Cross celebrates it in *The Living Flame of Love*. This wholly spiritual delectation is now free from danger: it specially belongs to mystical union. The soul feels the Spirit of her heavenly Spouse within her. He is not only the fire which consumes her, but also the fire which bursts into flame. Through the action of the Holy Spirit the soul acts, and is transformed into the fire of love. Her acts are bursts of flame, burnings of love breaking out from the divine fire. It is the Holy Spirit who stimulates these acts of love and makes the flame burst forth. "Every time that the flame breaks forth, producing a divinely sweet and powerful love in the soul, she thinks that she is entering into eternal life because she is in the state of acting in God."[2]

These divine flames tenderly wound the soul and burn her in a delightful manner, inflicting wounds of love upon her. Wounds, burns, and sores are sources of joy to the soul.[3] They appear to her to be the forerunners of death. It seems as if each of them must break the thread of her earthly existence to unite her to her heavenly Spouse in glory. But every time she is disappointed:

"O flame of the Holy Spirit, who piercest the substance of my soul so tenderly and intimately, who burnest her with thy glorious heat, how kind art thou to show thy desire to give me life eternal! . . . Break, then, the fine thread of my life and let it not last till old age and years cut it in twain according to natural law, so that I may love thee thenceforth in the fulness and satiety my soul longs for, measureless and unending!"[4]

And St John of the Cross sings on in all the tones of mysticism of the loving languors of the soul burning with the desire to be united with her Well-beloved, yet kept on earth perforce.

[1] *The Spiritual Canticle,* Part III, strophe xxii, Vol. IV, p. 144.
[2] *The Living Flame,* strophe i, Vol. III, pp. 148-149.
[3] *id.,* strophe ii. St John of the Cross also calls the flame of love a " delicate touch."
[4] *id.,* strophe i, Vol. III, pp. 170-171. The mystical marriage made St Teresa desire to remain upon earth to work for the glory of God and for the salvation of souls. In St John of the Cross the longing for heaven is more apparent in it, and this is in conformity with his strong leaning towards the contemplative life.

CHAPTER VIII

THE SPANISH SCHOOL AFTER ST TERESA AND ST JOHN OF THE CROSS — THE CARMELITES — THE JESUITS— MARY D'AGREDA

THE works of St John of the Cross no more escaped criticism than did those of St Teresa.[1] They were first published in 1618, twenty-eight years after their writer's death. The prejudice against mysticism had not ceased, far from it. The ascetic school continued its opposition to mystical books, and sometimes with violence. Further, the persistence of illuminism in Spain seemed to justify this attitude.

It will be remembered how severely the Spanish Inquisition in 1559 had proscribed mystical works published in Spanish. Many thought such strictness opportune, even in the beginning of the seventeenth century, and they were very displeased because St John of the Cross had written in Spanish not only simple devotional books but real treatises of mystical theology. Ought theology to speak any other language than Latin? In fact, the new departure made by St John of the Cross seemed all the more daring in that the matters of spirituality which he explained were higher and more delicate and, therefore, more subject to erroneous interpretations by the common people.

One of these questions raised particularly lively controversies. St John of the Cross was one of the first, not to discover—for the discovery was made before his day—but to bring out well into the light active or " spiritual " contemplation, as he calls it.[2] This mode of contemplation, which is intermediate between discursive prayer and infused contemplation, does not require extraordinary grace. Everyone may aspire to it, and those who take pains reach it. It is totally different from passive or " infused " contemplation, which depends entirely upon divine action. John of the Cross thereby thought to reassure the partisans of pure asceticism. If there be a kind of contemplation open to all, which does not belong to the domain of mysticism properly

[1] See R. P. Wenceslas of the Blessed Sacrament, O.C.D., *Fisionomia de un Doctor,* especially Vol. II, and his Introductions to the *Works* of St John of the Cross.
[2] *Cf.* H. Hoornaert, *Œuvres spirituelles de S Jean de la Croix,* Vol. III, pp. xix ff.

so called, must not people be led thereto? And can it not be done with no risk of illuminism? St John of the Cross explains carefully, as we know, the signs whereby the moment is recognized for passing from meditation to such contemplation.

This theory seemed to be novel. In reality, only the explanations of John of the Cross were new, particularly his explanation of the psychological phenomenon of aridity, occurring at the time of transition from discursive meditation to active contemplation. But this novelty is a happy discovery, a "precious contribution" to spiritual theology.

John of the Cross has been blamed for the rigour of his mysticism. He constantly speaks of *emptiness, annihilation,* and of the *death* of the senses and powers of the soul. He demands that the soul shall be stripped of every perception, image, and idea. We must renounce even spiritual favours granted by God. Is not this asking for more than the preparation for supernatural states requires? Besides, how can any mysticism, if it be based on the radical suppression of the use of our natural faculties, be reconciled with the needs of active daily life?

It must be admitted that the mysticism of St John of the Cross is perhaps not much to the taste of men of action. They are free to prefer that of St Teresa or of St Francis de Sales; but if we except his renunciation of spiritual favours—which needs to be rightly understood—the doctrine and the terminology of St John of the Cross are to be found in the great theorists of mysticism from the time of Dionysius the Areopagite. In their writings we meet with terms which, at first sight, seem exaggerated, and are not to be taken in an absolute sense. And besides, who can say how far self-abnegation should be carried by one whom God himself is purifying before uniting him with himself?

Despite the good grounds for such explanations, the writings of St John of the Cross were denounced to the Inquisition. Learned theologians, like Suarez, had to undertake their defence.[1] However, criticism diminished by degrees in proportion to the growth of the famous mystic's reputation for sanctity. And since his canonization the Church has put this passage in his office : " To explain the mysterious operations of God in souls, equalling St Teresa, in the judgement of the Apostolic See, St John of the Cross was divinely taught, and has written books of mystical theology full of heavenly wisdom."

[1] P. Wenceslas, Vol. II, chap. vi.

I—THE CARMELITE SCHOOL IN THE
SEVENTEENTH CENTURY

THE views of St John of the Cross upon active contemplation
were accepted in Spain by the religious Orders : they effected
a real reconciliation between pure asceticism and mysticism.
There is a kind of contemplation open to all, the result of
our efforts with the help of grace. Properly mystical contemplation, which is infused and the fruit of a special
grace, is a passive state which does not depend upon ourselves.[1]

The Carmelite School kept to this doctrine and propa-
gated it.

John of Jesus Mary,[2] the contemporary of St Teresa,
afterwards General of the Carmelites, recorded it in his
Disciplina claustralis, the spiritual directory of the novices
of the Order. Therein he treats at length of discursive
prayer, and sets forth a method resembling that of Luis of
Grenada and St Peter of Alcantara. It has the same principles : preparation for prayer, reading, meditation, affections
of the will—*i.e.,* thanksgiving, offering, and petition.[3] As to
contemplation, he distinguishes it into three kinds :

" The first," he says, " is natural, and it belongs to the
spirit clinging to God as the creator of nature and to the
truths contained in this order : this is the contemplation of
philosophers. . . .

" The second is supernatural, and, by a higher light than
nature's, it discovers some mystery of grace, and, by a
simple and loving look issuing from previous meditations,
fastens thereon and feeds and rests thereon. This is the
contemplation of Christians who are practised in prayer, and
it is that, too, of certain of the Church's prophets. To this

---

[1] *Contemplatio fidelium quae fidem praesupponit dividitur in duas
species, scilicet in acquisitam et infusam. . . . Acquisitam eam nun-
cupamus, quam industria et exercitatione propria, non tamen sine
divina operatione et gratia acquirimus; infusam vero, quae ex sola
gratia sive inspiratione divina promanat et Deus in nobis sine nobis
operatur.* Antonii a Spiritu Sancto (†1667) *Directorium mysticum,*
tract. III, disput. i, sect. 6, Parisiis, 1904, p. 238. Antony of the Holy
Spirit reproduces Philip of the Holy Trinity, *Summa theologiae
mysticae,* pars II, tract. I, art. ii, Paris, 1874, tom. II, p. 45.

[2] Born in 1564 in the diocese of Osma in Spain : died in 1615. With
John of St Jerome he wrote the book, *Vita et mores, spiritus, zelus et
doctrina servae Dei Theresiae de Jesu,* published by Fr. Gratian in
1610. Bossuet (*Mystici in tuto,* pars I, cap. xv) quotes with praise a
chapter on contemplation from the *Disciplina claustralis* of John of
Jesus Mary.

[3] *La discipline claustrale,* Part IV, chaps. i-vii, Paris, 1669, pp.
171-190.

kind of contemplation may be referred the knowledge of the truths of the natural order, which has been acquired by supernatural enlightenment.

" The third is divine, coming from the gift of wisdom with the help of a supereminent light, which regards nothing but God and the divine perfections. . . ."[1]

Thomas of Jesus, whose doctrinal authority is undisputed among the Carmelites, founds his spiritual teaching on the distinction between infused and acquired contemplation.[2] The latter, he declares, is equally suited to beginners and to those who are most advanced. He gives the requisite directions for all to practise it. A like doctrine is found in the works of the French Carmelite, the celebrated Philip of the Holy Trinity,[3] and in those of the Portuguese Antony of the Holy Spirit.[4]

The Carmelites have kept their tradition intact. It is always taught to their novices;[5] and recently, on the third centenary of the canonization of St Teresa, the Discalced Carmelites held a Congress at Madrid, where the existence of acquired or active contemplation was affirmed, and also its distinction from infused or passive contemplation. By

[1] *La discipline claustrale,* Part V, chap. i, pp. 207-208.

[2] The Venerable Thomas of Jesus was born in Andalusia about 1564. Provincial of Castile, then Definitor General of the Order, he died in Rome in 1627, reputed for sanctity. His mind as to infused contemplation is seen in his *De contemplatione divina libri sex,* published in 1620. He treats of acquired contemplation in the *Via brevis et plana orationis mentalis,* published in 1610, and in an unpublished work issued in 1922 at Milan by Fr. Eugene of St Joseph, entitled *De contemplatione acquisita,* in which are treated the nature, effects, and properties of acquired contemplation. My knowledge of this work was obtained from a French adaptation, by Fr. Berthold Ignace de Ste Anne, entitled, *La meilleure part ou la vie contemplative.* The *Works* of Thomas of Jesus were issued at Cologne in 1685.

[3] Born in 1603 in the diocese of Vaison (Vaucluse), he lived at Lyons. Then he was a missionary in the Levant. Returning to Lyons, he was raised to all the offices of his Order in succession, and finally elected as General of the Carmelites at Rome in 1665. He died at Naples in 1671. He wrote a great many books : *Summa philosophiae,* Lyons, 1648; *Summa Theologiae,* Lyons, 1653; *Summa Theologiae mysticae,* Lyons, 1656; a *Chronologia* from the creation of the world and a curious *Itinerarium orientale,* 1649, etc.

[4] Antony of the Holy Spirit was born at Monte Morovelho in Portugal. He was a professor at Lisbon and a famous preacher. He became Bishop of Angola in Africa, and died about 1677. His *Directorium mysticum* appeared at Lyons in 1677, then at Venice in 1697, and often afterwards. Republished at Paris in 1904. The plan of the work is that of the three ways. The author treats of the active and the passive purifications, of active and of passive enlightenment, of active and of passive or infused contemplation. He merely abridges the *Summa* of Philip of the Holy Trinity.

[5] *Cf.* Theodore of St Joseph, O.C.D., *Essai sur l'oraison selon l'école carmélitaine,* Bruges, 1923. He explains the *Disciplina claustralis* of John of Jesus Mary.

proclaiming this doctrine the Congress intends to continue faithful to the real mind of the foundress of the Carmelite Reform.[1]

II—THE SPANISH JESUITS AT THE BEGINNING OF THE SEVENTEENTH CENTURY: ALPHONSO RODRIGUEZ, LUIS DE LA PUENTE, ST ALPHONSUS RODRIGUEZ, ALVAREZ DE PAZ

AT the beginning of the seventeenth century we may still remark among the Spanish Jesuits some distrust of mysticism, and this is accounted for by the occurrences of the end of the century before.[2]

We recall the unfortunate infatuation of the followers of Balthazar Alvarez for mystical prayer, which necessitated the intervention of their superiors and resulted in penalties.

It was just at this period, in 1577, that Alphonso Rodriguez[3] was novice-master at Montilla, in Andalusia, and had to make the regular spiritual exhortations weekly in all the society's houses. According to the official directions, he had to put his brethren on their guard against methods of prayer differing from those of the *Spiritual Exercises.* His treatise on the *Practice of Christian Perfection* is an epitome of his exhortations.   Now, what he teaches on

---

[1] *Resolutions of the Madrid Congress,* First Section, The Spiritual Life, Themes IV-VI, in the *Mensajero de S Teresa,* Madrid, March 15, 1923. See *Études Carmélitaines,* January-July, 1924, pp. 89-91. Among Spanish Carmelite writers of this period, note: another Thomas of Jesus, author of a *Summary of the Degrees of Prayer* in Spanish, 1609; the French translation (Paris, 1612) also contains a *Traité de l'oraison mentale;* Michel de la Fuente, *Libro de las tres vidas del hombre, corporal, racional y espiritual,* Toledo, 1623; Cecilia del Nacimento (1570-1646), *Tratado de la transformación del alma en Dios* (1632-1633), and *Tratado de la unión del alma con Dios* (in the *Obras* of St John of the Cross, Toledo, 1914, Vol. III); Maria de Aquila y Canali, *Vie intérieure et spirituelle,* Madrid, 1634; Joseph of the Holy Spirit (†1739), *Cursus theologiae mystico-scolasticae,* Seville, 1720-1739; Antony of the Annunciation, professor at the College of Alcala de Henares, *Disceptatio mystica de oratione et contemplatione,* which is the Carmelite Manual of mysticism since 1686.   On the Carmelite tradition, see *Études Carmélitaines,* January-July, 1922, pp. 13-17.
[2] But see Antony Martinez (Garcia del Valle, S.J.), *Camino a la unión y comunión con Dios, recogitado de diversos autores de la compañia de Jesus,* Alcala, 1630.
[3] Alphonso Rodriguez was born in 1526 at Valladolid.   At the age of twenty he joined the Jesuits, then still governed by St Ignatius.   On leaving the noviciate, he taught moral theology, and twelve or thirteen years later he became novice-master of Montilla in Andalusia, and had to deliver weekly exhortations in the Jesuit houses.   In 1593 he was sent to Cordova for the same purpose.   In 1606 he was novice-master at Seville.   There he wrote his famous treatise, *The Practice of Christian Perfection,* issued in Spanish at Seville in 1614.

mystical kinds of prayer is right, but its tone betrays some anxiety and even fears:

" There are two kinds of mental prayer," he says, " one simple, common, and easy; the other very exceptional and very sublime, and it is received rather than made. . . ."

" Perfect [mystical] prayer is a special grace from God, and he grants it to whom he will; sometimes as a reward for services rendered to him and for mortifications endured for the love of him, and sometimes gratuitously, without regard to the past, as the pure outcome of his liberality; for, as he himself says, he is free to do good to whom he will (Matt. xx, 15). . . .

" This divine call to the soul to enter into the Lord's sanctuary, converse with her heavenly Spouse, and to be inebriated with his love, is an altogether special grace, a signal privilege granted only by God to whom he will. It is not the Bride who herself enters into the retreat of her Spouse, but it is he who takes her by the hand and leads her into it."[1]

To desire such a favour and to claim to attain to it when not called thereto is a " presumptuous " attempt, " making him who dares it run the risk of losing, as a penalty for his pride, the grace of ordinary prayer and of finding himself stripped of everything because he has set his desires too high.[2]

" If we had perfect humility we should be satisfied with praying like most of our brethren; we should even regard it as a special grace of God that he willed to lead us by the common way rather than by some other higher and harder road in which we might perhaps go astray and get lost."[3]

Moreover, mystical prayer " is a gift so much above man's understanding that we can neither teach it nor comprehend it." Only those who are privileged to enjoy it can speak of it; " nor can even those thoroughly know the nature of it, nor tell what it is, nor how it is made."[4]

---

[1] Part I, Treatise V, *On Prayer,* chap. iv, Crouzet's translation, Paris, 1895, Vol. I, pp. 346 ff. *Cf.* Treatise VIII, chap. xxx, Vol. II, pp. 204 ff.
[2] *ibid.,* Vol. I, p. 350.
[3] *ibid.,* chap. xx, p. 430. Father Everard Mercurian, General of the Jesuits, writes thus to his Spanish subjects: " There are many who hear of an exercise of divine love which is still higher than ordinary prayer and of certain anagogic acts and some strange silence of the faculties of the soul, and wish, rather from want of discernment than in obedience to a real desire for spiritual progress, to rise prematurely to the practice of the life of union as to the highest peak of perfection, from the top of which the human passions are more easily subdued; but since they have not gained enough strength, they lose much time in vain endeavours and make so little progress that after many years they are as much carried away by their vices and as selfish and opiniated in their minds and wills, as much the slaves of their material well-being, as if they had never had any intercourse with God. . . ." Quoted by Rodriguez, *ibid.,* chap. vi, p. 359.
[4] *ibid.,* chap. iv, pp. 347, 349.

"Further," continues Rodriguez, "quite rightly the reading of certain authors has been condemned, who have fancied that, by means of certain rules, a man could be made a contemplative, and have tried to teach what no one could learn and to reduce to a human science what is altogether above art and nature. In a book written by Gerson against Ruysbroeck, he rebukes the latter severely for such a rash pretension as this. . . . Moreover, what mean these analogies, these transformations of the soul, this silence of all the faculties, this annihilation, this immediate union, and all the subtle and obscure terminology of Tauler? Can one make anything out of all that? As for myself, I frankly acknowledge my ignorance about it."[1]

If Rodriguez does not understand the obscure theories of the German mystics, he nevertheless knows "perfect prayer." He describes it along with discursive meditation in his treatise on prayer, not to urge his readers thereto but to give them a notion of it. What he recommends with warmth and conviction is "ordinary mental prayer."

He does not, however, make the whole of prayer consist in meditation and considerations. These are but means to attain to acts and "affective motions of the will."

"The masters of the spiritual life," he says, "counsel the avoidance of too lengthy meditations, especially when they are taken up with subtle and fine-spun reflections, because they paralyze the affective motions of the will which ought nevertheless to be the goal and end of prayer.[2] . . . This sort of affective outgush of the will is the highest degree of prayer. Then do we no longer try to stir ourselves up to the love of God with the stimulus of meditation; the heart is filled with the love which it so ardently yearned for, and it delights and rests therein as being at the consummation of its desires and endeavours."[3]

The soul has thus attained to "active" contemplation, which was then well known in Spain, and is the result of the efforts of spiritual meditation:

"In prayer," adds Rodriguez, "meditation and other functions of the mind are all directed towards contemplation; they must be used as steps to ascend to this summit of prayer."[4]

This attitude of Rodriguez towards mysticism explains the character of his work. It is a treatise of pure asceticism, and, from that point of view, remarkable.[5] Not only is his

[1] Chap. iv, p. 349. See H. Bremond, *Histoire littéraire du sentiment religieux,* Vol. V, Appendix, for interesting evidences of Rodriguez's mind on mysticism.
[2] Chap. xiii, p. 385.　　　　[3] Chap. xii, p. 382.
[4] Chap. xii, p. 382. *Cf.* Part II, Treatise VII, chap. iii.
[5] The book is divided into three parts, and each part into treatises. The First Part comprises these treatises: Of the Esteem of Perfection

teaching very sound and very definite, but it is set forth
with warmth and unction. He charms his reader with his
familiar and amiable simplicity. A large number of quotations, taken from the Fathers—no matter whether the texts
be genuine or not—or from the lives of the saints, support
his principles of spirituality; and we feel that the very subtle
psychological remarks interspersed with his doctrinal teaching show the writer's great experience in the direction of
souls.

Rodriguez wrote his book especially for "the members of
the Society." But, as he tells us in his Preface, he has used
a method which makes it "a good book . . . for all religious
in general," and also "for all who aspire to the perfection
of the Christian life." The *Practice of Christian Perfection*
has really been a classical handbook of spirituality in
universal use for many centuries: few works have had such
a deep and wide influence.

Luis de la Puente,[1] the contemporary and compatriot of
Alphonso Rodriguez, does not partake of his distrust of
mysticism. The historian of Balthazar and of Dona Marina

—Of the Perfection of Ordinary Actions—Of Uprightness and Purity
of Intention — Of Union and Fraternal Charity — Of Prayer — Of
Examination of Conscience—Of the Presence of God—Of Conformity
with the Will of God.

The Second Part contains the treatises: Of Mortification—Of Modesty
and Silence—Of Temptations—Of Inordinate Love of One's Parents—
Of Humility—Of Sadness and Joy—Of Meditation—Of the Passion—
Of Holy Communion and of Mass.

The Third Part deals with the religious life: Of the Aim of the
Society of Jesus—Of Vows and Religious Profession—Of the Vow of
Poverty—Of the Vow of Chastity—Of the Vow of Obedience—Of the
Observance of Rules—Of Confidence in One's Superiors and Spiritual
Fathers—Of Fraternal Correction.

[1] Born at Valladolid in 1554, he joined the Society of Jesus in 1575.
He was too weak in health to take up active employments. He gave
himself up to direction and to writing spiritual books. His works
are: *Meditaciones de los mysterios de la nuestra santa je*, Valladolid,
1605. In these *Meditations* the art of meditating is taught according
to the method of St Ignatius. *Guida espiritual de la oración, meditación y contemplación*, Valladolid, 1609. This *Spiritual Guide* teaches
one how to meditate and to attain to contemplation. *De la Perfección
cristiana:* a *Treatise of Christian Perfection in every State,* Valladolid,
1612-1616; *Vida del Balthazar Alvarez,* Madrid, 1612; *Expositio moralis
et mystica in Canticum canticorum,* Monocerote, 1622, Paris, 1646;
Directorio espiritual, Madrid, 1625; *Vida maravillosa de la venerabile
virgen Marina de Escobar.* This *Life* of Doña Maria de Escobar was
finished by Fr. Cachupin and published at Madrid, 1665. Marina
de Escobar (†1633) founded the Order of Recollection of St Bridget.
She was born at Valladolid in 1554. She often had visions of St
Gertrude, St Bridget, and St Matilda. She also had revelations as to
heavenly things. Luis de la Puente was her confessor for thirty years.
Marina de Escobar was well versed in mysticism. There are two

de Escobar, two true mystics, he made a close study of supernatural states and described them. Moreover, a letter of Claud Acquaviva, General of the Jesuits after Everard Mercurian, had expressed the official mind of the Society as to mysticism, and this mind was favourable.

Luis de la Puente sums up his spiritual teaching in his *Life* of Balthazar Alvarez, a work of his closing years, which benefits by the experience of a lifetime.[1] Its central part is concerned with prayer. Moreover, it was just the way in which this exercise was understood and practised that was then being discussed in Spain.

Like Rodriguez, he declares that the way of mystical prayer can only be embarked upon through a special call of God. He expresses himself in the same words:

"Intimate and familiar converse with God our Lord," he says, "and the gift of calm and perfect contemplation . . . are so sublime a good that Father Balthazar, as he himself says in his account of it, could only be raised thereto by a special call of God. He calls thereto whom he will; it has no place nor year nor fixed time, for all depends upon his most holy will who findeth "his delight in conversing with the children of men." But with some he converses more familiarly than with others; and this is through a special and gracious privilege which we call "vocation." It is an inspiration, an impulse, or a great affection impressed on the soul, which urges it on to this high way of prayer, and at the same time communicates to it the aptitudes and means to follow that mode. For all are not called thereto, all are not adapted to it, and they should not rashly set themselves to aspire to it."[2]

If it is rash to aspire to extraordinary states of prayer when not called thereto, it would also be most regrettable not to answer the divine call when there is one:

"For two things may do great harm: to dare to aspire, without being called thereto, to ascend higher than one can; to resist the divine call when we have ascertained that it is God's will to lead anyone by that way. We must appeal to the judgement of some prudent and experienced spiritual Master, whose special mission it is to examine the different

posthumous works by Luis de la Puente: *How to help towards a Good Death*, 1670, and the *Memorial*, 1671. His *Life* was written by Fr. Cachupin and published at Salamanca in 1652.

[1] Luis de la Puente is above all an ascetic writer; but he deals with mysticism in the *Vida del Balthazar Alvarez*, in the *Expositio in Cantica canticorum*, and in the *Guida espiritual*, Treatise III. Compare him with Diego Monteiro, S.J., in the *Arte de orar*, Coimbra, 1630.

[2] *Vie du P. Balthazar Alvarez*, chap. xv, Couderc's translation, p. 139. *Cf.* chap. ii, p. 12: "There are two modes of mental prayer: one ordinary and practised in general by the just, the other extraordinary, the lot of the few." See, too, chap. xiii.

ways in which God guides his servants' steps so as not to lead them astray therefrom, but, on the contrary, to direct and to encourage them therein, so that they may walk in them with prudence and with profit."[1]

This vocation is manifested sooner or later, according to God's good-will :

"Sometimes . . . our Lord, by a privilege and special gift, raises up some of them, even from infancy or from the first days of their conversion, to such a sublime state of prayer and sometimes to extraordinary favours; yet, in general, he calls thereto only those who have devoted themselves to ordinary prayer in meditation and reflection on the divine mysteries. And to such meditation everyone is called and more or less interiorly drawn according to his capacity."[2]

We cannot "claim to tie God down as to the time of his visits and mercies." Balthazar Alvarez was kept for sixteen years to ordinary prayer :

" Also," continues Luis de la Puente, " look with suspicion upon the claim to lay down as a general law that, if we follow such and such a method for so many years and so many months, we shall obtain this or that divine favour, or else such and such a degree of virtue."[3]

It is according to these principles that Luis de la Puente wrote his books, especially those which deal with prayer.

First of all he teaches how the prayer of meditation is to be made according to the method of St Ignatius, which he uses invariably.

" The book of the *Spiritual Exercises* . . ." he says, "contains all that is needed for perfect mental prayer, to which all can aspire if they co-operate diligently and keenly with the motion inspired by God and his grace, which ever prevents and stimulates us to act along with it."[4]

Whoever uses Luis de la Puente's *Meditations* learns theoretically as well as practically " the art of meditation and prayer." The great Christian truths and the events of our Saviour's life are the successive subjects of his devout reflections. Well-ordered themes of prayer, full of doctrine, unction, and piety are set before him.

While keeping his readers in the ways of asceticism, Luis de la Puente never forgets that perhaps many of them may be

[1] *Vie,* chap. xlii, p. 422. Luis de la Puente adds : " Everyone should be helped and encouraged in his own way, for directors are only God's co-operators and coadjutors in the conduct of souls. God himself is the guide and master in chief, and the others have but to follow him, as has been said. And, unless our Lord intervene by some special grace, those general rules are to be observed which he left to his Church."

[2] *ibid.,* chap. xv, pp. 139-140.

[3] *ibid.,* chap. xlii, p. 421.

[4] *ibid.,* p. 423.

called to mount higher. Further, he himself explains his method :

"Let us remember the preparations to be made," he says, "the subjects and the mysteries we have to meditate on, the sentiments we must conceive, the conversations and colloquies we have to hold with God, the manner in which all this is to be applied to the faculties of the soul; the fruits and gains to which we should aspire; the reflections and examens to be made with regard to all these operations, in order to purify and improve such fruits. Afterwards we learn how to attain to contemplation and to the perfect love of God, to enjoy peacefully and interiorly all that we have perceived in our meditations. All this I have explained at length and in detail in the two books of *Meditations* and in *The Spiritual Guide*."[1]

With regard to the mystical union, Luis de la Puente tries less to determine its degrees than to explain the different names then given it. St Teresa's terminology had not then become classical. The divergencies of nomenclature among the old writers on mysticism engendered much confusion.

"This mode of prayer," he says, "is called very particularly prayer of the presence of God, because through him, the intellect is enlightened with divine light, and, for no other reasons, considers God as so present near it and in it that it seems to feel[2] with whom it is speaking and in whose presence it stands. It is like that which St Paul says of Moses, that he dealt with the invisible God as if he saw God. Hence, and as it were naturally, come respect, admiration, inclination of the will—that is to say, pleasure and the joy of being in his presence. . . .

"Hence it is that this mode of prayer is also called prayer of repose, or of interior recollection. It puts an end, indeed, to the great number and variety and tumult of our imaginings and reasonings. The higher powers of the soul, the memory, the understanding, and the will are gathered up and fixed in God and in the contemplation of his mysteries; their acts are wrought in a perfect peace and repose. This is what is most exactly called contemplation. . . . Contemplation . . . by a simple look regards the sovereign truth, admires its greatness, and delights in it.

"It is also called the prayer of silence. Therein, indeed, the soul is silent, listens with close attention to what her Master says to her heart, to what he teaches her, and discloses to her of himself and his mysteries. But we must not think, as do some who are ignorant, that if the soul is

---

[1] *Vie,* chap. xlii, p. 423.

[2] Alvarez de Paz (tom. III, lib. V, pars III, cap. iv) says, too, that in the prayer of quiet and of union God makes his presence felt by the soul.

silent and stops to wait in silence, she ceases altogether
from acts of her inferior powers; for that is impossible,
except in sleep, and it would be very difficult and even dangerous, because it would rather result in idleness and loss
of time and run the risk of having the imagination encroached
upon by a host of chimeras, or the mind disturbed by the
devil through bad or improper thoughts. . . .

"Sometimes there are imaginative representations impressed upon the soul by our Lord; at others there is a purely
intellectual and most high enlightenment. . . . Then is the
divine Being known in a manner so lofty as to be united
with it so intimately and divinely that God alone can raise
one to such a height by his special grace and favour; and
despite the greatness of that which one then knows, that
which one does not know appears to be an infinite abyss."[1]

In this kind of prayer there are sometimes extraordinary
effects. When the interior illumination and the ardent affections of love and union are particularly strong, "the soul is
disconnected with the outward senses and the corporal movements are interrupted, and there is *suspension* or *ecstasy*."[2]
If this happens suddenly and very powerfully there is *rapture*. When the divine working is more gentle within, it is
called *flight of the spirit*. In this case, fairly frequently the
body is raised from the ground, and follows the motion of
the spirit which mounts to the contemplation of heavenly
things. For, as Luis de la Puente insists, "the spirit is
neither idle nor asleep. It ceases not to see, to understand,
to hear something, to admire, to rejoice, and to love."

The works of Luis de la Puente did away with the prejudices against mysticism. The occurences which gave such
trouble to Balthazar Alvarez were, moreover, already at a
distance and somewhat forgotten. A contemporary Brother
Coadjutor of the Society of Jesus, St Alphonsus Rodriguez,
himself raised to states of extraordinary prayer, was putting
a final touch to the dissipation of old prejudices.

St Alphonsus Rodriguez[3] wrote his spiritual autobiography
in memoranda for which he was asked as to what was taking

[1] *Vie de Balthazar Alvarez,* chap. xiv, pp. 128-130. Similar explanations are to be found in Part III of the *Spiritual Guide.*
[2] *ibid.,* p. 131-132.
[3] Born at Segovia in 1531. He was first of all in business. He lost
his wife and his two children and experienced reverses of fortune. He
entered the Society of Jesus as Brother Coadjutor in 1571. After his
noviciate at Valencia he was sent to Majorca, where he dwelt until
his death in 1617. He wrote twenty-one memoranda on his mystical
states and therewith composed his *Life,* which was translated into
French by Fr. de Bénazé, Paris, 1890. The opuscula written by
Rodriguez were published at Barcelona as *Obras espirituales del
Beato Alonzo Rodriguez.* Several were translated into French:

place in his soul. He went through the different degrees of the states of prayer which were known to Balthazar Alvarez. He seems to have distinguished them according to the intensity of the feeling of the presence of God in his soul :

"The soul," he says, "knows without any discourse (because it has passed beyond this degree [of discursive prayer]) how God is within it, since God gives it the grace of communicating himself to it in this way. This feeling of the presence of God is not obtained by way of the imagination; but it is in it as a certainty received from on high; it is a spiritual and experimental certainty that God is in the soul and in every place. This presence of God is called an intellectual presence. It usually lasts a long time. The more we advance in the service of God the more is this presence felt and continuous, since God communicates himself daily more and more to the soul, if it dispose itself thereto by a generous mortification of itself."[1]

In his frequent ecstasies this feeling of the presence of God became a sort of vision of God :

"This person," he says, speaking of himself, "put himself into the presence of God by saying to him lovingly in heart and word : ' Lord, make me know thee.' And immediately he was raised above all created things. . . . His knowledge of God, which was immediate and without reasoning, and consequently his love of God and his intimate familiarity with him reached such a point that it seemed to him, so to speak, that God willed to discover himself to him as if to the blessed."[2]

Very high teaching about this knowledge of God and of oneself is to be found in the treatise he wrote *On the Union and Transformation of the Soul in Jesus Christ*. The more we know God, the more we love him. On the contrary, we hate ourselves the more the more we know of ourselves, and the more do we keenly desire " blessed sufferings."

The love of sufferings perpetually inspires the spirituality of Rodriguez and is also the explanation of his life. To make him suffer was to lay him under an obligation :

"Let us hold as our best friend and benefactor," he said, " him who persecutes us most, and let us behave ourselves towards him as towards a benefactor, thanking God for not forgetting us and for regarding us with tender love, since

L'explication des demandes du Pater, Desclée, Lille, 1894; *De l'Union et de la transformation de l'âme en Jésus-Christ,* a booklet followed by other treatises on the Holy Spirit, the Blessed Virgin, the Angels, the Celebration of Mass, and the *Jeux de Dieu avec l'âme,* Desclée, Lille, 1899. These are to be found in Vol. II of the *Obras del Beato Alonzo Rodriguez.*
[1] *Vie,* de Bénazé's translation, no. 40.
[2] *Vie,* n. 12. St Alphonsus Rodriguez experienced the trials reserved for mystics, *Vie,* no. 18.

he gives us the grace of suffering with patience for the love of himself and of thus winning a magnificent and glorious crown."[1]

Moreover, it is God's will to try those whom he loves. He "plays," to use Rodriguez' own word, "with those who are devoted to him." We might be tempted to say, did it not imply a shade of want of respect, that he teases them. Rodriguez knows how to tell us in a naïve and charming way of God's dealings with the devout soul:

"God bears himself," he says, "towards such a soul as a tender mother towards her poor little child whom she loves more than her own life. Such a mother holds her son in her arms and plays with him; she gives him little pats on the cheek, and the child makes faces and begins to cry. His mother is happy, and soon kisses him tenderly and gives him her breast, and quiets him with her caresses. She is so pleased to play with him that she often starts the loving game over again; the child begins to cry out and weep anew, which makes his good mother laugh with pleasure; and all this behaviour arises from the mother's tender love for the fruit of her womb."[2]

God indulges in a similar game with the soul, and he goes on with it until the soul has given itself up to him without reserve.

There is no prejudice against mysticism to be found in the works of Alvarez de Paz.[3] In these there is nothing but peace: we move in the serene region of theological principles.

He made the first complete synthesis of ascetical and mystical theology, much more the work of the theologian than of the psychologist. Alvarez de Paz is not inclined to observe with patience the mystical experiences of those around him. Rather rarely does he describe his own or anything he had remarked in those whom he directed. His is largely the science of books. He knows fairly fully the

[1] De l'Union et de la transformation de l'âme en Jésus-Christ, Lille, 1899, p. 110.
[2] ibid., pp. 212-213.
[3] He was born at Toledo in 1560, and entered the Society of Jesus in 1578. He studied at Alcala. He was sent to Peru, where he was successively Rector of the Colleges of Quito, Cuzco, and Lima. He taught philosophy and theology in the latter town. He died at Potosi in 1620. The first volume of his works, De vita spirituali ejusque perfectione, is divided into five books, Lyons, 1608 and 1611; Mayence, 1614. The second, De exterminatione mali et promotione boni, contains five treatises also, Lyons, 1613, 1623; Mayence, 1614. The third, De inquisitione pacis sive studio orationis, Lyons, 1617, 1619, 1623; Mayence, 1619; Cologne, 1620. This, too, has five books. Œuvres published at Paris, Vivès, 1875-1876.

ascetical and mystical teaching of the Fathers of the Church
and of the medieval doctors. The writings of contemporaries
he almost ignores. He never read St Teresa, but, on the
other hand, nothing of the teaching of the early schools is
overlooked by him. He knew how to sum up the spirituality
that preceded later days.

He wrote in Latin a treatise of ascetical and mystical
theology. It is not surprising to find therein a methodical
mind sometimes rather fastidiously dividing up the matter of
its studies. But piety and unction tempered any dryness
there might be in philosophical speculations. For Alvarez
de Paz not only desires to impart spiritual teaching, but also
to make men love and practise it. It is related that when he
lectured or preached, he became so fired in speaking of
things spiritual that he used to faint away. He was as much
an orator as he was a theologian. We feel this in his
writings, which are rather prolix and tire the hurried reader.
If we indeed wish to follow and listen to him, we are soon
gripped by his eloquence, and feel a desire to become holier.

Alvarez de Paz takes his disciple—who is a religious—at
the beginning of the spiritual life and leads him on to perfect
contemplation, if he be called thereto.

First of all, he exhorts him to have a high esteem for the
religious life. He next explains the nature of the spiritual
life—which is sanctifying grace—and lays down its degrees.
It may be cultivated in those who are engaged in the life of
action as well as in those whom Providence has called to a
contemplative or mixed life. If the spiritual life grows
normally, it will attain to perfection. Alvarez de Paz defines
such perfection—which consists in the union of the soul with
God by ever-increasing charity—and he shows its excellence
and proves how desirable it is.[1]

When perfection is known and desired, we must tend
towards it by fleeing from evil and by doing what is right.
This is the subject of the Second Part of the work of Alvarez
de Paz.[2] The teaching of spiritual writers on the avoidance
of sin, the destruction of vicious habits, resistance of temptation, and the mortification of the passions are explained at
length. Then we find a treatise on the Christian and religious
virtues and on the way to acquire them. Humility, poverty,
chastity, and obedience are given the chief place amongst

[1] The five books of tom. I (Lyons edition of 1611) are thus entitled :
*De incitamentis religiosorum ad vitam spiritualem consectandam; De
vita spirituali et ejus partibus (de quindecim gradibus; de vita activa,
contemplativa et mixta); De natura perfectionis; De mirabili dignitate
perfectionis; De excitando desiderio perfectionis.*
[2] The titles of the five books of tom. II (Lyons, 1612): *De fuga
peccatorum, extinctione vitiorum et victoria tentationum; De mortifica-
tione virium animae et abnegatione; De adeptione virtutum; De
humilitate; De paupertate, castitate et obedientia.*

these. This part of the work of Alvarez has been translated
and published by itself.[1]

The great means of perfecting the spiritual life is prayer,
vocal and mental. Alvarez de Paz, according to the Spanish
tradition of the period, enters into this subject in detail.[2] He
has set down certain particularities of mental prayer which
must be made known.[3]

After his own method he sets forth the patristic teaching
as to the nature and necessity of mental prayer, as to the
preparation it demands, and the means required for practising it well and to good advantage. Preachers delight in
his pages, which overflow with pious considerations.[4]

Alvarez de Paz distinguishes between four kinds of mental
prayer: *discursive prayer* or *meditation*—which he calls " intellective "—then *affective prayer,* next the *beginning of contemplation,* and lastly, *perfect contemplation.* This point of
view was adopted by spiritual writers who came after him.
The first three kinds of prayer are accessible to all; the fourth,
which is properly mystical, is assigned to those who are
called thereto.

So far no one had clearly defined the nature of affective
prayer, which follows immediately after meditation and precedes " the beginning of contemplation "—*i.e.,* the " active "
contemplation of later writers. Alvarez de Paz gave this
kind of prayer the name which suited it—affective prayer
(*oratio adfectiva*)—and this name has clung to it:

" Since mental prayer," he says, " consists in raising the
mind and will to God, it follows, according to spiritual
writers, that there are two kinds of prayer: intellective,
which takes its name from the intelligence; and affective,
which is so named because it is made by the affections of the
will."[5]

[1] Under different titles: *Exercice journalier des vertus,* Douai, 1625;
and *Traité des vertus,* Brouillon, Paris, 1838.

[2] The whole contents of tom. III, in five books (Lyons, 1617): *De
oratione tum vocali tum mentali; De his quae praecedunt, comitantur
et sequuntur orationem mentalem; De materia orationis mentalis; De
affectibus orationis mentalis; De perfecta contemplatione et de dis-
cretione spirituum.*

[3] At the beginning of tom. III (lib. I, pars I and II) Alvarez shows
the need and explains the effects of prayer in general. He then shows
how to pray well vocally by reciting the Hours. The rest of the volume
deals with mental prayer.

[4] Lib. I.-II. With regard to discursive meditation, Alvarez de Paz
(lib. I, pars III) recalls all the medieval theories (*cogitatio, meditatio,
contemplatio*). In Book III, he sets forth the subjects of prayer (*materia
orationis mentalis*). The subjects for beginners are sin and the last
things, those of the proficients are the mysteries of our Lord's life, and
those of the perfect are the attributes of God. The subjects of the proficients may be had in French, *Méditation sur la vie de Notre-Seigneur,*
Le Muller, Besançon, 1847, 1848; Tournai, 1860.

[5] Lib. I, pars III, cap. vi, tom. III, col. 205, Lyons, 1617.

But he explains that intellective prayer is not made up solely of speculative considerations : it would then be simply a study. If we reflect, it is to attain to prayer and to doing what is good. In the same way, affective prayer does not entirely exclude reflections. Both kinds of prayer are characterized by what predominates in them.

Alvarez de Paz sets out at length the theory of the affective states and shows how to use them in the pursuit of the good. Affection is the movement of the soul turning towards what pleases it or away from what displeases it. It starts from the will when originating from an idea, and from the sensibility when resulting from a sensation. Its end is good or evil.[1]

The aim of prayer is to give rise to strong affective impulses which make us hate vice and love virtue. The role of the intellect is to stimulate them by means of the idea. In affective prayer, ideas are few, but pious desires and emotions fill the soul. The will and the feelings are thus strongly borne towards God and goodness. Energetic resolutions then carry out what is felt.[2] Affective prayer also obtains divine help more effectively, for it is nothing but pure prayer.

" Even if you were to make no petition," says Alvarez, " if you are in the presence of God and desire the good, groaning because you have gone away from it, you will be answered just as if you had made a petition. And even if you have expressed no desire, yet if your heart is ready to act and is prepared to do the right, putting its trust not in itself but in God, such readiness will be counted as a prayer, and the grace needed for action will be granted you."[3]

Alvarez de Paz has a preference for affective devotion, and herein follows the tradition of St Teresa and the Spanish School.

Whoever has followed out the ways of discursive meditation and affective prayer with devout fervour will merit being raised to contemplation.[4] But here it is important to observe that there is a degree of contemplation, " the beginning of contemplation (*inchoata contemplatio*), which we must endeavour to attain, and another, " perfect contemplation " (*perfecta contemplatio*), which may be desired and even asked for, but which it would be indiscreet to pursue, for only a special grace can bring us thereto :

" If it be a question," says Alvarez de Paz, " of the beginning of contemplation (*de inchoata contemplatione*), in which

---

[1] Tom. III, lib. IV, Proemium, col. 934.

[2] Tom. III, col. 937 ff.

[3] Col. 943. Alvarez de Paz shows how beginners, proficients, and the perfect practise affective prayer, lib. IV, part. I-III, tom. III, col. 950-1220.

[4] Tom. III, lib. V, col. 1221.

anyone leaves all reasoning and keeps himself in the presence
of our Lord Christ or of the Blessed Trinity, with his heart
burning with love, to me it seems certain that a soul purified
from its vices, freed from bad and unruly affections, and
adorned with virtues, can, and ought, after having practised
meditation, to try to attain it. . . .

" If we now speak of perfect contemplation (*de perfecta contemplatione*), let us remember that it is of two kinds. There
are, first of all, the extraordinary gifts of contemplation
bestowed by God on some holy souls, such as ecstasies,
raptures, corporal or imaginative apparitions, and other
things of the sort. It is neither permitted to desire such gifts
nor still less to try to bring them about. It would be an act
of ridiculous pride. . . . The other kind of perfect contemplation consists in a simple knowledge of God, without any
mental consideration, effected by the gift of Wisdom raising
the soul, suspending the powers, throwing it into a state of
admiration, giving it joy, and enkindling it with the fire of
ardent love. Souls called to perfection, if very mortified,
and if they have cultivated virtue and are devoted to prayer,
must prepare for this contemplation by greater purity and
by the means of which I have spoken. May they also desire
it keenly and ask it humbly of God? Why not? It is the
most efficacious way of winning perfection. . . . However,
though it be expedient and right for the perfect who are
stripped of their vices and possess all the virtues to ask it of
God in all humility, yet no one should seek to attain it or try
to abide in it; for that does not depend on man's efforts, but
on God's liberality."[1]

Thus, according to Alvarez de Paz, there are two kinds
of contemplation, one accessible to all indiscriminately, for
which all should prepare. It depends upon us alone to attain
to it with the help of ordinary grace. This is " the beginning of contemplation," later called " active " or " acquired "
contemplation. Alvarez de Paz does but echo the Spanish
School, which threw this sort of contemplation into relief and
defined its nature. The other is perfect contemplation, the
" infused " contemplation of the moderns.

His terminology is less precise when he is enumerating
the degrees of perfect contemplation. He reckons fifteen of
them ![2] Here, indeed, he does but compile and heap together,

---

[1] *Nemo debet ad eam conari, aut quasi in ea se ponere, quia non est
id in potestate humana, sed venit ex benignitate divina.* Lib. V,
pars II, cap. xiii, col. 1381-1382. Alvarez de Paz speaks at length of
the preparations for contemplation. He draws much from Gerson,
col. 1231-1324. So, too, when he treats of the nature of contemplation,
col. 1323.

[2] These are : intuition of the truth, interior recollection, spiritual
silence, quiet, union, hearing God's voice, spiritual sleep, ecstasy,
rapture, corporal visions, imaginative visions, intellectual visions,

without sufficient discernment, the teaching he found in the old spiritual writers. The gradation of the contemplative states which he gives does not correspond with the reality, nor was it followed afterwards. Often he takes some secondary circumstance of a mystical state for a specifically different degree of contemplation. On the other hand, he passes over in silence the mystical marriage, which is regarded as the highest degree of mystical union. Alvarez de Paz considers that the highest degree of perfect contemplation is the intuitive vision of God.

For very short moments, is it possible for man to enjoy such ineffable vision while on earth? There is much controversy about it among spiritual writers. All agree that Moses, St Paul, and the Blessed Virgin Mary enjoyed this privilege; several think that it has been accorded to other holy persons, and in particular to St Benedict and St Ignatius of Loyola. There are some, indeed—St Bonaventure, Harphius, and Ruysbroeck are among them—who believe that those who are raised to a very high degree of sanctity see God intuitively from time to time with the swiftness of a flash of lightning. Alvarez de Paz is not among these. He reckons that—excepting Moses, St Paul, the Blessed Virgin Mary, and perhaps two or three other saints—no one on earth intuitively perceives the divine Essence.[1]

III—THE THREE CONCEPTIONS OF MYSTICAL CONTEMPLATION: "QUIETIST" CONTEMPLATION, "ANTI-INTELLECTUALIST" CONTEMPLATION, AND "INTELLECTUALIST" CONTEMPLATION—FRANCIS SUAREZ[2]

WHEN Spanish theologians were synthesizing spirituality at the beginning of the seventeenth century, various problems,

divine darkness, the clear manifestation of God, the intuitive vision of God. Luis de la Puente used several of these terms to designate mystical union or contemplation.

[1] Lib. V, pars III, cap. xv, col. 1463 ff. In chap. xvi Alvarez de Paz speaks of the most keen spiritual sweetness which accompanies contemplation. Then he finishes his work with a treatise on the discernment of spirits (pars IV). We must also note, among the Spanish Jesuits, Pedro Sanchez, who wrote the *Libro del regno de Dios* for the Fathers of the Society, Madrid, 1594. French translation by G. Levite, O.P., Paris, 1608-1609. Alonzo d'Andrada wrote *Meditations for every Day in the Year,* and translated the ascetical works of Bellarmine into Spanish.

[2] Francis Suarez, like Alvarez de Paz, summed up and discussed the opinions of his forerunners and contemporaries. He is rather theologian of dogma and morals than of spirituality. Nevertheless his treatise *De Oratione,* especially Book II, dealing with prayer and contemplation, is a treatise of spirituality. His treatise *De statu perfectionis* contains

only suspected hitherto, stood clearly forth.   One of the most interesting of them concerns the very essence of contemplation, the nature of mystical union.   Can contemplation arise without any knowledge of the mind and without any act of the will?

The different solutions put forward showed the diverse conceptions of mysticism formed by the early or modern writers.

In the opinion of many spiritual writers, the soul is entirely passive in mystical contemplation.   It is so absorbed in the object of contemplation that neither its understanding nor its will are in a state of activity.   " This kind of prayer," says Suarez, " is called the prayer of silence, the spiritual sleep."[1] The soul says nothing, it does not act; it waits for God to speak to it.   This sort of contemplation may be termed " quietist," giving the word its etymological meaning.

This notion of contemplation comes from the Areopagite, who counsels the mystic, if he wishes to be united with God, always to become disentangled not only from the senses, but from every operation of the mind, and to raise himself by *unknowing* to the divine darkness.   The German mystics, and particularly Tauler, accept this view.   No doubt the soul prepares for contemplation by its own efforts, but when it has reached it, it must cease to act and remain passive under the action of God : *Potius divina patiens quam agens.*

On metaphysical grounds scholastic theologians reject this teaching : " No mode of mental prayer can be imagined," says Suarez, " in which the understanding and the will would be absolutely passive."[2]   If we do not think of God in any way, how can we know that we are praying to him?   And if the will be not attached to him, how can we say that it loves him?   To that the reply is that the mystics discover higher spiritual regions unexplored by metaphysicians.   They call them the " bottom " or " summit of the soul " or otherwise, and there it is that they believe that intimate union with God takes place in the silence of all the faculties.

However, most spiritual writers reject such radical notions. According to them, the soul is but partially passive.   The

the classic notion of perfection (lib. I, cap. iii-iv).   Therein he studies the religious state and the vows of the religious life.   Francis Suarez, the Jesuit theologian, was born at Granada in 1548.   He taught theology with great success at Alcala, Salamanca, and Coimbra in Portugal.   He died at Lisbon in 1617.   His works were published at Lyons, 1630, at Venice, 1740, and at Paris in 1859 (Vivès).

[1] Suarez, *De Oratione*, lib. II, cap. xii, 1.
[2] *ibid.*, 2.   Cf. Melchior de Villanueva (†1606), *Libro de la oracion mental,* Toledo, 1608.

mind does not act in contemplation, but the will is active and makes acts of love. When the mystic is raised to the highest states, he loves God without any actually accompanying knowledge of him. The soul behaves as if it were solely affective and without understanding. Everyone knows that the more perfect mental prayer becomes, the more is it simplified and the rarer are its reasonings. A time may come when the mind altogether ceases to act; only the will continues to do so by expressing its love for God. Such is "anti-intellectualist" contemplation. What are we to think of it?

"It is a question long and sharply disputed, not only by the spiritual writers, but also by the doctors of the school," says Alvarez de Paz.[1] He considers that at the beginning of mystical prayer there is a knowledge of God, but that afterwards nothing but love remains. The soul is united to God by the will only. Alvarez de Paz, as we know, favours affective devotion. He dissertates at length on affective prayer. It is not surprising that he believes in the possibility of a purely affective contemplation in which the understanding takes no part. A good many medieval spiritual writers set forth, as we have seen, an anti-intellectual kind of mysticism. Nicolas of Cusa, and the writer of the *Docta Ignorantia,* Hugh of Palma, are the most famous among them.[2] They thought that no knowledge was necessary for mystical union, either before or whilst it was taking place: *Sine cognitione praevia aut concomitante.*

But according to most of the scholastic theologians, contemplation is always intellectual: "It is probable," states Suarez, "that it is impossible for the affective part of the soul to act without the previous knowledge required for its action."[3] Thus, the will is unable to make an act of love for God if the intellect has no actual knowledge of him whom it loves. It can only tend towards its object when this is previously known. This celebrated theologian proves this thesis at length and leaves not one of the anti-intellectualist objections unanswered. His conclusion—which is regarded as classical among the scholastics—is that, even in the highest mystical states, the intellect is never altogether passive. The outward senses alone, in ecstasy, may be totally suspended.

However, on other points, Suarez diverges from the generally received views. Thus, he considers that the intuitive vision of God may occur in the soul without being accompanied by ecstasy.[4] Christ, in fact, enjoyed such vision, and nevertheless he acted as other men do. Hence we may

[1] Tom. III, lib. IV, pars III, col. 1123 ff.
[2] St Bonaventure and Gerson are strongly in favour of purely affective mysticism.
[3] *De oratione,* lib. II, cap. xiii, 7.   [4] *ibid.,* cap. xvi.

infer that ecstasy is rather a sign of the weakness of man's organism, than a condition of the highest spiritual union with God. It is a "crisis of growth." When anyone is raised to the most perfect states, it ceases to occur. Such, too, was indeed the idea of St Teresa : " When the soul has once reached this place (the Seventh Mansion of the Castle), it has no more raptures, or, if it has, which very rarely happens, they are not uplifting and flights of the spirit such as I have spoken of."[1]

The problems raised about the subject of prayer have always aroused the passionate interest of the spiritual writers of Spain. In the seventeenth century treatises on prayer swarmed in that country.[2]

IV—THE VENERABLE MARY OF AGREDA[3]

MARY OF AGREDA originated a new kind of mystical writings. This is partly the reason of her name becoming the butt of such lively contradictions.

[1] *Interior Castle,* Seventh Mansion, chap. iii, *Œuvres,* VI, p. 300.

[2] Here are the principal Spanish treatises on prayer belonging to the seventeenth century : *Arte de bien vivir y guia de los caminos del cielo,* 1608, by the Benedictine, Antonio de Alvarado, who reproduces in his treatise a *Tratado del conocimiento oscuro de Dios,* attributed to St John of the Cross (*Obras de San Juan de la Cruz,* tom. III) ; *De la oración mental, y via unitiva,* Valencia, 1611, by Antonio Pascal, O.M. ; *De oratione et contemplatione,* Lisbon, 1611, in Portuguese, Alphonso de Medina, O.M. ; *Exercicios espirituales de las excelencias, provecho, y necesidad de la oración mental,* Burgos, 1615, by the Carthusian, Antonio de Molina ; the *Obras* of Blessed John Baptist of the Conception, Trinitarian (†1613), Rome, 1830 ; *Navegación segura para el cielo,* Valencia, 1611, by Jerome de Segorbe, Capuchin ; *Vuelo del espiritu y escala de perfección,* Seville, 1612, *El solitario contemplativo y guia espiritual,* Lisbon, 1616, by George of St Joseph, of the Order of Mercy ; *De la vida espiritual, y perfección christiana,* Valencia, 1612, by Antonio Sobrino, O.M. ; *Mística Theulugia y doctrina de la perfección Evangelica,* by the Minim, John Breton, Madrid, 1614 ; *Luz de las maravillas que Dios ha obradas per visiones y hablas corporales, imaginarias, y intelectuales,* by the Benedictine, Leander de Granada, Manriquez, Valladolid, 1617 ; *Desengaño de religiosos y de almas que tratan de virtud,* by Mary de la Antigua, religious of Mercy (†1617), Seville, 1678 ; *Mystica theologia et exercitium Fidei divinae et orationis mentalis,* by the Minim Ferdinand Caldera, Madrid, 1623, French and Italian translations ; Philip de Luz, Augustinian, *Tratado da vida contemplativa,* Lisbon, 1627 ; Jerome Planes, *Examen de revelaciones verdaderas y falsas, y de los raptos,* Valencia, 1634 ; Gabriel Lopez Navarro, Minim, *Theulugia mistica, union y junta perfecta del Alma con Dios por medio de la contemplación,* Madrid, 1641 ; Augustine of St Alphonsus, Augustinian, *Theulugia mistica: scientia y sabiduria de Dios, mysteriosa, obscura, y levantada para muchos,* Alcala, 1644 ; Paul de Vasconellos, of the Order of our Lord Jesus Christ, *Arte spiritual que ensina o que he necessario para a meditaçao e contemplaçao,* Lisbon, 1649.

[3] Born at Agreda in Spain in 1602, she entered the monastery of the Immaculate Conception of the Order of St Francis in the same

This famous Franciscan nun was the first, apparently, to have the idea of completing the Gospel story with her own special revelations. Anne Catherine Emmerich, at the beginning of the nineteenth century, resumed the same kind of enterprise with greater success.

In fact, Mary of Agreda claimed to write a detailed history of the Blessed Virgin Mary. We know how sparing of information are the Gospels about the earthly life of the Mother of God. Could not the mystics who had revelations fill up this gap? Mary of Agreda believed she was called to fulfil this task. Her famous *Mystical City of God* is presented as "a divine story and a life of the Virgin Mother of God." She relates minutely, and as revealed by angels, all the occurrences that preceded Mary's birth, then those of her life until her death. The story is interspersed with edifying mystical considerations.

Apparently there are no errors of doctrine in the work of Mary of Agreda, but what historical improbabilities! Often imaginative fancies are taken—in perfect good faith—for authentic revelations. And what is more, Mary of Agreda seems to be well up in such apocryphal writings as *The Infancy of Jesus* and *The Nativity of the Blessed Virgin Mary*. Her work was bound to incur criticism.

This was not slow in forthcoming. The book appeared in Spanish at Madrid in 1670, five years after the death of Mary of Agreda. Its novelty and also its author's reputation for sanctity won an extraordinary vogue for it. But very ardent controversies arose, so that Pope Innocent III in 1681 forbade the reading of the *Mystical City*. However, advice deferring the execution of his decree on the pressure brought to bear on him by Charles III of Spain.

The French translation of Mary of Agreda's book, published at Marseilles in 1695, revived the discussions, and next year they became more impassioned than ever. On September 17, 1698, the Sorbonne condemned *The Mystical City of God* as containing rash assertions and apocryphal revelations "of such a nature as to expose the Catholic religion to the

town. She was Abbess of this monastery until her death in 1665. She enjoyed a great reputation for sanctity. Her cause for canonization was introduced in 1673, but was not successful. Mary of Agreda was a correspondent of Philip IV of Spain. This king's letters were published at Madrid in 1890 : *Cartas de la ven. madre sor Maria de Agreda y del señor Rey Felipe IV*. The most celebrated mystical work of Mary of Agreda is a history of the Blessed Virgin Mary, founded on her revelations : *La mistica ciudad de Dios . . ., historia divina y vida de la virgen madre de Dios . . .*, written from 1655 to 1660 and published at Madrid in 1670 after the writer's death. Mary of Agreda left other ascetical and mystical writings which were never published. The bibliography of Mary of Agreda will be found in the *Dict. de theol. cath.*, art. Agreda (Marie d').

contempt of the ungodly and of heretics." Bossuet[1] pronounced a very harsh judgement on the book. Eusebius Acort, the learned Canon Regular of Pollingen, is no less formidable than the Bishop of Meaux in his attacks on the work of Mary of Agreda.[2]

These sharp discussions did harm to the memory of the celebrated nun. They put a stop to the cause of her canonization.

---

[1] Remark on *The Mystical City of God.*
[2] *De revelationibus, visionibus, et apparitionibus privatis regulae tutae*, Augsburg, 1744; *Controversia de revelationibus Agredianis . . .*, Augsburg, 1749.

CHAPTER IX

THE ITALIAN SCHOOL IN THE SIXTEENTH CENTURY—ITS
GENERAL CHARACTERISTICS — THE CHIEF ITALIAN
SPIRITUAL WRITERS[1]

SPANISH spirituality, which was of a practical nature at the beginning of the sixteenth century, became theoretical and scientific with and after St John of the Cross. Italian spirituality was always directed towards the practical and was less speculative. As was the case in France in the sixteenth century, it is spirituality in action, in the religious communities and in the lives of the saints, rather than spirituality in theory or in books. It was, moreover, spirituality as opposed to the paganism of the Renaissance and to Protestant heresy.

Those responsible for the Renaissance in Italy, or many among them, were frankly pagan. The lively Italian imagination had been dazzled and fascinated by the new birth of antiquity. Hence, the great decline in morality, against which the spiritual writers reacted. This spirit of reaction against the almost universal laxity is shown in their teaching. Italian asceticism was definitely arrayed in spiritual combat against self, for when self is vanquished and vice subdued the corruption around is little to be feared. This movement of energetic spirituality and inward conflict seems to have begun first among the Theatines and the Barnabites. John-Baptist Carioni, the Dominican, often known as Baptist da Crema, from the place of his birth, who acted as director to St Cajetan of Thiena, founder of the Theatines, and of St Antony Mary Zaccaria, one of the originators of the Barnabites, brought all his spirituality to bear on the knowledge of and victory over self.[2] It was from his circle of disciples that there was to come later on that famous book *The Spiritual Combat,* in which we are urged to continual warfare against ourselves.

Heresy was even more to be feared than worldly-mindedness : "As regards heretics and their dangerous opinions,"

[1] *Cf.* G. Tiraboschi, *Storia della Letteratura italiana,* Florence, 1805-1813; Tachi-Venturi, *Storia della Compagnia di Gesù in Italia, La vita religiosa in Italia durante la prima età della Compagnia di Gesù,* Rome, 1910, Vol. I.
[2] *Concerning the Knowledge of and Victory over Self,* Milan, 1532, is the title of one of his chief works on spirituality.

St Angela Merici (✝1540) counselled her daughters the Ursulines, " as soon as you hear of a preacher or anyone else that
he is suspected of sharing in these errors and allowing these
novelties, contrary to the teaching and practice of the Church
or to the principles which you have received from us, immediately keep your daughters [pupils] away."[1]

The universal advice given to those who desire to preserve
intact their faith was not to dispute with error, but to fly
from it. " If the enemy suggest to you some false and
captious reasoning, be on your guard against arguing with
him," advises the author of the *Spiritual Combat*.[2] Protestantism made fewer ravages in Italy than elsewhere. Its
coldness, lacking all æsthetic form, with nothing to appeal
to the senses, bewildered the expansive Italian temperament,
which yearns for outward demonstration. The Inquisition,
nevertheless, must have dealt vigorously with it from time to
time. The discreet and individual work of the spiritual-
minded was doubtless a still more efficacious means of pre-
servation.

Italian spirituality furthermore was one of the best agencies
of the Catholic counter-reformation. It was in the sixteenth
century in Italy, as in Spain, that there arose those magnificent institutions for the renewal of Christian life. The
Theatines of St Cajetan, the Oblates of St Charles Borromeo,
and the Oratorians of St Philip Neri (✝1595) laboured to
uplift the secular clergy. The Fathers of Christian Doctrine
of Cæsar de Bus (✝1607), the Fathers of the Pious Schools
of St Joseph Calasanza (✝1648), the Ursulines of St Angela
Merici, and others, undertook to instruct and bring up young
boys and girls. The mysticism of these holy persons impelled
them to action; like all true mysticism it was creative. After
reforming self others must be reformed. " He has conquered
himself, he has overcome the world and the flesh " was said
of St Charles Borromeo. His life " is so exemplary that
through example he does more good in the Court of Rome
than all the decrees of the Council of Trent."[3] Living his
asceticism he knew how to find the means of bringing others
to live it also.

" In the Catholic Church, as everywhere else, reforms are
first of all the work of certain individuals who earnestly desire
them, and end by imposing them on public opinion and on the
regular agencies of the hierarchy. This is what happened in

---

[1] *Souvenirs ou avis de Sainte Angèle,* 7ᵉ souvenir, *Sainte Angèle
Merici et l'ordre des Ursulines,* Paris, 1922, Vol. I, p. 417. " Know,"
she says again, " that you will have to defend your little flock against
wolves and thieves, two kinds of plagues which I point out to you :
I mean worldly-mindedness and heretics." *Ibid.*

[2] Chap. lxiii.

[3] De Hubner, *Sixte-Quint,* French translation, Vol. I, p. 64, Paris,
1870.

the sixteenth century."[1] It is thus that Catholic mystics
have acted in every age.

Italian mysticism, moreover, effected reform in another way
which carries us back to the heart of the Middle Ages, to the
time of St Bridget and St Catherine of Siena. In the sixteenth century, as much as in the centuries preceding it, the
reform of the Church was spoken of by all. St Angela Merici
recommended her religious to pray and to make others pray
" that God forsake not his Church, but reform it himself in
accordance with his good will and in the way he knows to
be best for us and most able to promote his glory."[2] St
Magdalen dei Pazzi (†1607) was not content only to pray.
In her Carmel at Florence she dictated letters during her
ecstasy, addressed to the Cardinals of the Roman Curia, to
the bishops, and even to Pope Sixtus V, begging them on
behalf of God to labour for the renewal of the Church. In
1586 she wrote to the " Most illustrious cardinals present at
the Apostolic See " :

" The humble servant of the Lamb that was slain and of
the Word incarnate, Christ crucified, compelled by the sweet
truth and unity of the most Holy Trinity, and especially by
her loving Spouse—I say : compelled, and let them be pleased
to note what I say : compelled—to reveal to them something
that is not less pleasing to God than profitable to creatures,
to wit, his wish to reform the Church his Spouse, through you
his ministers and the chief members of this same Church."[3]

And in fiery accents she goes on to unfold the urgent
reasons for undertaking this work of Catholic restoration
without delay.

Another mystic belonging to the Dominican convent of
Prato near Florence, St Catherine de Ricci (†1590), who also
was fired with the desire for the reform of the Church, wrote
urgent letters to warn the cardinals, to reprimand when needful
the bishops, and to encourage those who laboured for the
glory of God.[4]

This display of reforming activity, this inward combat,
resolute and austere against self, is usually found hidden
beneath attractive externals. Italy of the sixteenth century

---

[1] A. Baudrillart, *L'Église catholique, la Renaissance et le Protestantisme,* p. 225.

[2] *Sainte Angèle Merici, ibid.,* p. 417.

[3] *Lettres de sainte Marie-Madeleine de Pazzi,* French translation by
M. Vaussard, *Revue d'ascétique et de mystique,* April, 1924, p. 160.
These *Letters* were never sent to those for whom they were destined.
The saint's superiors were opposed to it. They were published in 1893
at Florence in the saint's *Complete Works.*

[4] Cesare Guasti, *Letters* of St Catherine de Ricci, Prato, 1861,
Florence, 1890.

possesses a lovable spirituality which gives the impression
of moderation and balance. " The warlike soul of Spain
vibrates in St Ignatius and St Teresa."[1] Its most wonderful
outbursts and its most ardent affective impulses almost always
show forth the austerity which maintains them.

This austerity exists—who can doubt it?—in Italian
spirituality, but more often than not it is delicately veiled.
St Francis de Sales carefully noted this characteristic of
mystical Italy and his piety was impressed with it.

Doubtless it is in Italy that the Renaissance exercised the
greatest influence on spirituality. The Christian humanists
of the peninsula dreamed of a religion " wholly of art and
charity, of beauty and of love."[2] The optimistic calm and
joyous rhythm of Raphael belong much more to their spirit
than does the pessimism of Michael Angelo. Cardinal
Sadolet, secretary to Leo X and Bishop of Carpentras, is a
perfect type of this humanism. " His Christianity enlarges
the heart because in it are summed up goodness and charity;
he has no bitterness or sadness, he becomes all things to all
men in order to win all things and all men."[3] It may be
thought, however, that this Christianity is too forgetful of
mortification. The Italian mystics, as we have already seen,
eschew this forgetfulness. But for the greater part they
found delight in the beautiful and consoling aspects of
Christian life, in whatever dilates the heart and attracts souls.
St Philip Neri, " the loving saint *par excellence* " had hymns,
canticles, and Palestrina's motets at the gatherings of his
first disciples in Rome. He ever had on his lips these gentle
words : " My children, be joyful. . . . The spirit of joy wins
Christian perfection more easily than does the spirit of sadness."[4] There must be no melancholy, even among thorns,
says in turn St Catherine de Ricci. And again St Magdalen
de Pazzi declared that " God does not want a sad heart. He
wants it to be free and joyous."[5] God is a Father even
more than a Judge.

A religion of art and beauty, Christianity is above all a
religion of love. Italian humanism repeats this often enough
and in a manner gives proof of it. It says : " Christianity

[1] A. Baudrillart, p. 218.
[2] De Maulde la Clavière, *Saint Gaëtan*, Paris, 1905, p. 17.
[3] *id.*, p. 69.
[4] Cardinal Capecelatro, *Life of St Philip Neri*, Bézin's French translation, Vol. I, p. 512, Paris, 1889.
[5] *Œuvres de sainte Marie-Madeleine de Pazzi*, French translation
by Bruniaux, Paris, 1873, Vol. I, p. 512. *Cf.* pp. 176-177, where the
saint speaks of the happy consequences of original sin. *Heureuse
faute!* There is the same optimism in the spirituality of Blessed
Bellarmine. *Cf.* Monier-Vinard, *Le Bienheureux Cardinal Bellarmin et
St François de Sales* (*Revue d'ascétique et de mystique*, July, 1923,
pp. 225 ff).

is less an ultimate knowledge of things than the bond between men and God and between themselves, a bond of love and grace . . . the role of religion is to produce tenderness, to make men gentle and by means of this to give them real personal energy and other social virtues, goodness, unity—in a word, happiness."[1] In the Middle Ages the mystics of Italy, St Francis of Assisi and St Bonaventure among others, well knew how to act on the feelings in order to raise man to God, though in quite another way.

With the thought of these mystical tendencies of the Middle Ages the humanists mingled the teachings of Plato. We know that the Platonic theories were held in high honour in Italy of the Renaissance. Many looked upon them as an introduction to mysticism.[2] " The idea that the visible world was created by the God of love, that it is the reproduction of a design, pre-existing in him, and that it will ever receive from its creator its life and movement,"[3] that the human soul is able to expand, to become indefinitely enlarged, thanks to divine love, this idea was drawn as much from the writings of Plato as from the teachings of ecclesiastical writers. Moreover, the humanists delighted to discourse on love. Bembo, secretary to Leo X, who wrote only too well of human love, maintains that " love is one, and from particular love we pass to love that is ideal, and from the ideal to love that is divine."[4] A more accurate conception of the genesis of divine love will be found in the *Dialogues* attributed to St Catherine of Genoa, in the *Works* of St Mary Magdalen dei Pazzi and in the ascetic treatises of Blessed Robert Bellarmine.

In spite of everything the humanists rendered the doctrine of divine love familiar. It is to be found, more or less, mingled, in all the religious writings of the Italy of the sixteenth century. It took so great a hold on the public mind that in 1516, at Rome, they started the secret society, which very soon became famous, of the *Oratorio del divino Amore*. Its members busied themselves with the beauty of religion and with the needed reforms of the Church, and took up the work of charity towards the unfortunate. The *Divino Amore* very soon " increased in Italy by means of numerous branches like a kind of freemasonry."[5] Its chief

[1] De Maulde la Clavière, p. 167.
[2] Stephen Conventius, a religious of the Congregation of St Saviour, wrote a book of this kind : *De ascensu mentis in Deum ex platonica et peripatetica doctrina libri sex*, Venice, 1563. See also *Philosophia platonica,* by the Franciscan, Peter Calauna, Palermo, 1599.
[3] J. Burckhardt, *La civilisation en Italie au temps de la Renaissance,* French translation, Schmidt, Vol. II, pp. 346-347.
[4] In his *Dialogues on Love (Gli Asolani)*, John Francis Pico de la Mirandola also produced a treatise, *De Amore divino,* dedicated to Leo X.
[5] De Maulde la Clavière, *St Gaëtan,* p. 32.

founder was Ettore Vernazza, a disciple of St Catherine of
Genoa, the great founder in the sixteenth century of Italian
hospitals.[1] Sadolet and St Cajetan were the first to join it.
This association was not unconnected with the magnificent
outburst of charitable works of every kind which were so
admirable in Italy of the Renaissance.

I—JOHN BAPTIST CARIONI, DOMINICAN (BATTISTA DA CREMA), AND SERAFINO DA FERMO, CANON REGULAR, LEADERS OF THE CANONS REGULAR—THE FOUNDERS OF THE CONGREGATIONS OF THE ITALIAN CLERKS REGULAR

JEROME SAVONAROLA (†1498) in his sermons and in his
writings strove vigorously in Florence against the pagan
morals of the Renaissance. Some years later his less famous
confrère, John Baptist Carioni,[2] the Dominican, was to become one of the originators of the Catholic reaction in Italian
spirituality.

Baptist da Crema, as he was commonly known, was a fine
worker in the reform of morals, both as a preacher and as a
director of souls.[3] To extend his influence he wrote several
spiritual treatises, in which he dealt especially with the need
of reaction against the general corruption, and also with
men's prevalent vices, both inward and outward, and with
the remedies against them. Like all reformers, he insists on
personal effort. He " marches at the head of this movement
in spirituality which was to go on increasing in the course
of the sixteenth and seventeenth centuries, in which so much
stress is laid on voluntary effort and the expansion of outward
activity. Baptist da Crema is a teacher of spiritual energy

[1] F. Von Hügel, *The Mystical Elements of Religion as Studied in
Saint Catherine of Genoa and her Friends,* London, 1908, Vol. I,
p. 140; Tacchi Venturi, *Storia della Compagnia di Gesù in Italia,*
Rome, 1910, Vol. I, p. 497; L. Pastor, *Histoire des Papes,* French
translation, Vol. VIII, 2nd edition, p. 345.

[2] Born at Crema near Milan, he died at Guastalla, in the duchy of
Parma, in 1534. He joined the Dominicans of the Province of Lom-
bardy. He was a gifted preacher and a good director of souls. *Cf.*
G. Salvadori, *San Gaetano da Thiene et la Riforma cattolica italiana,*
French translation with historical notes added, by Maulde la Clavière;
Premoli, Barnabite, *Fra Battista da Crema secondo documenti inediti,*
Roma, 1910; by the same author, *San Gaetano Thiene e Fra Battista
da Crema (Revista di Scienze storiche, Pavia,* VII, 1910, *fasc.* VII-
VIII); and also *Storia dei Barnabiti nel Cinquecento,* Roma, 1913,
pp. 4-6, 13-15, 30-32, 108-113, 198-200.

[3] *Via di aperta verità,* Venice, 1523, often republished; *Della cogni-
tione et vittoria di se stesso,* Milan, 1531, republished several times;
Specchio interiore, Milan, 1532; *Filosofia divina,* Venice, 1545. Cf.
Storia dei Barnabiti, pp. 108 ff., 510.

for the work of reform of self and of Christian society. From this point of view, as well as several others, he takes a prominent place with the initiators of the prevailing spirit and spirituality of the Clerks Regular."[1]

Was this spirituality, quite " Molinist " in anticipation and inspired by the writings of Cassian, the cause of certain difficulties which Baptist da Crema had with his Order? Semi-pelagian tendencies were constantly thought to be found in his writings, nor did he treat the question of pure disinterested love with accuracy. Lively discussions arose, and, after the death of Baptist da Crema in 1552, ecclesiastical authority, which was as specially rigid at this period in Italy as it was in Spain, placed his writings on the Index.[2]

The disgrace was posthumous. When he was alive, in spite of difficulties which his superiors, Baptist da Crema exercised a real influence on several choice souls. St Cajetan, founder of the Theatines, and St Antony Mary Zaccaria, the chief founder of the Barnabites, were directed by him at a moment when they were seeking their way. The Countess of Guastalla, Louisa di Torelli, who instituted the congregation of the Angelicals or Guastallines, in order to help the Barnabites in their apostolate among women, had also been led towards the religious life by the zealous Dominican.

One of the great admirers of Baptist da Crema was Serafino Aceto da Portis, Canon of the Lateran, more often known as Serafino da Fermo. Serafino published a collection of tracts at Milan in 1538,[3] more or less inspired by the Dominican de Crema, which were translated into Castilian in 1551. Luis of Granada had read them when he published his famous Book of Prayer and Meditation in 1554. Serafino da Fermo became the defender of Baptist da Crema. He wrote an apology for his teaching,[4] which, however, did not prevent it from being condemned. Desirous as he was for the reform of the Church, the pious canon greatly encouraged

---

[1] P. Mandonnet, O.P., Preface to the Victoire sur soi-même de Melchior Cano, Paris, 1923, p. 11.

[2] They are no longer on the Index since 1900. With reference to this incident which troubled the Order of Barnabites, see Premoli, Storia dei Barnabiti, cap. vii, pp. 108-112; cap. xii, p. 197-200. Melchior Cano thought Baptist da Crema as dangerous as Tauler and Harphius.

[3] Operette spirituali. These tracts are : Of the Conversion of the sinner; Of the Victory over Self (translated into Spanish by Melchior Cano); Of Discretion; Of the Mirror of the Soul; Of One Hundred Questions and Answers respecting Prayer. Serafino da Fermo died in 1539. Before him another Canon Regular, Peter of Lucca, had published the Regule della vita spirituale e secreta theologia, Bologna, 1507. The Spanish translation by Luis of Granada (Seville, 1548) may possibly be known.

[4] Published in the 1541 edition of the Operette spirituali. Fr. Premoli has reproduced it in Il Rosario Memorie Dominicane, 1918, pp. 29-34, 71-76, 107-113.

the founders of the Barnabites and seconded their projects.
Together with Baptist da Crema, though in a lesser degree,
he gave an impetus to the first Clerks Regular.

The illustrious penitents of Baptist da Crema, St Cajetan,
St Antony Mary Zaccaria, and the Countess Louisa de Torelli,
noted that in order to establish a Christian society the instru-
mentality of the clergy was needed. A pure, fervent clergy,
living the life of religious, but mingled more than they with
society; instructing, preaching, hearing confessions, directing schools; this it was that rightly seemed to them to be
the best means of Christian reform. A double end would
thus be obtained: the people would be evangelized and the
secular clergy reformed by example. For the latter could not
be reformed in a body. Councils had issued laws, and with
threats had exhorted the clergy to amend.[1] The results
thus obtained were very small. It was hoped that, by
addressing themselves individually to priests, by preaching
and by example, something better might be achieved.

Such were the ideas which inspired the founders of the
Italian congregations of Clerks Regular. When St Ignatius
came to Rome in 1357 he brought with him similar ideas.
They wrought a new transformation in monasticism; to the
older conception of monk and friar there was added that of
the Clerk Regular.

This transformation began with the three religious Orders
of Theatines, Somaschi, and Barnabites. These three Orders
were born about the same time, at three different points in
Italy.[2] At Rome in 1525, St Cajetan[3] started the Theatines;
at Milan in 1530, St Antony Mary Zaccaria[4] and two other
priests founded the Clerks Regular of St Paul or Barnabites;

[1] Especially the fifth Council of the Lateran (1512-1517) under Leo X,
the regulations of which had little practical result.
[2] Cardinal Capecelatro, *Life of St Philip Neri*, French translation,
Bézin, Vol. II, p. 12, Paris, 1889.
[3] St Cajetan was born at Vicenza in 1480, of an illustrious family.
He was first of all a Roman prelate. Then, with John Peter Caraffa,
the future Pope Paul IV, Boniface Colli, and Paul de Ghisleri he
founded an order of Clerks Regular in Rome called Theatines, because
Caraffa, the first Superior, retained the title of Archbishop of Tiene
(Chieti). St Cajetan died at Naples in 1547. The principal document of
the history of St Cajetan is his *Life*, by the Theatine, Antony Caracciolo,
published at Cologne in 1612. See De Maulde la Clavière, *St Gaëtan*,
Paris, 1905, in which a complete bibliography will be found. There
are *Letters* of St Cajetan, published by the Abbé de Barral in 1785,
Paris, reproduced in De Maulde, pp. 182-201. The Italian text is in
G. Salvadori, pp. 48 ff.
[4] Born at Cremona, in the Milan district, he studied at Padua. After
becoming a priest he showed his zeal by labouring, with much fruit, at
the reform of the morals of the faithful. At Milan he founded the
Barnabites, with the assistance of Bartholomew Ferrari and James
Morigia. Their chief object was the preaching of missions and the

finally, in 1531, at Venice, St Jerome Emilian[1] formed the Somaschi. After these several holy persons, in this marvellous sixteenth century, established similar congregations in Italy to respond to the various needs of the time.

The Italian religious congregations of this period are divided into two classes. The one was principally concerned with the reform of the clergy and with the moral improvement of the people by means of missions and other zealous works; these were the Theatines, the Barnabites, the Oratorians of St Philip Neri, the Oblates of St Charles Borromeo, and the Minor Clerks Regular (clerici regulares minores) of St Francis Caracciolo and John Adorno. The other was occupied with the education of youth or with the care of the sick in the hospitals. Among these may be cited: the Somaschi of St Jerome Emilian, the Fathers of Christian Doctrine of Cæsar de Bus, the Piarists or Fathers of Pious Schools of St Joseph Calasanza, the Ursulines of St Angela Merici of Brescia, the Fathers of a Good Death of St Camillus de Lellis, the Clerks of the Mother of God of Blessed John Leonardi.[2]

The founders of these congregations, with very few exceptions, have left no spiritual writings.[3] They were animated

---

management of schools. St. Charles Borromeo greatly loved them. St Antony Zaccaria died at Cremona in 1539. A collection of *Detti notabili* of St Antony Zaccaria was published at Venice in 1583. French translations with the titles *Œuvres spirituelles,* Paris, 1600, and *Les hautes maximes de la vie spirituelle,* Lyons, 1625. Latin translation *Axiomata sacra . . .,* Rome, 1671. *Cf.* Premoli, *Storia dei Barnabiti nel Cinquecento,* Rome, 1913; *Le Lettre et lo spirito religioso di S Anton. M. Zaccaria,* Rome, 1909.

[1] Born at Venice in 1481, he was converted after a wild youth. Being greatly touched at the sight of the numerous orphans after the war, he gathered them together in Venice. At Somasco, near Bergamo, he founded his congregation, devoted to the education of orphans and to the instruction of youth. Jerome died in 1537. His *Life* has been written by Fr. Augustine Turtura (*Acta Sanctorum,* February 8).

[2] It is desirable to mention the reform of the Franciscan Order brought about in 1525 by Matthew de Baschi, who made his religious wear a beard and a pointed hood (*capuche*), whence the name *Capuchins.* The Rule of St Francis was literally restored and followed. In 1619 the Capuchins formed a distinct branch of the Franciscan Order. One of the first saints of the new Capuchin foundation was the lay brother, St Felix of Cantalice (†1587), the friend of St Philip Neri. *Cf.* Capecelatro, *Life of St Philip,* Vol. II, pp. 318 ff. St Francis of Paula, born at Paula in Calabria in 1416, founded the Order of Minims. It was he who assisted Louis XI, King of France, at his death. See his *Life,* by Fr. Hilarion Coste.

[3] Although he did not compose writings on spirituality properly so-called—the *Recordi al popolo,* published during the plague of Milan, is not so—St Charles Borromeo has left very important documents on the reform of the clergy and faithful in his diocese of Milan. They are to be found in the *Acta Ecclesiae Mediolanensis,* Mgr. Ratti's (Pius XI) edition, Milan, 1890 ff., and in the *Documenti circa la Vita et le geste di San Carlo Borromeo,* published by A. Sola, Milan, 1857-

by the spirit of the first Clerks Regular, especially that of
the Theatines and of the Barnabites.   St Cajetan of Tiene,
more largely than others, engendered this spirit.   A lively
zeal for poverty, great inward mortification in order to attain
to a joyous calm of soul, an intense and disinterested love
of God and one's neighbour, such was the pervading spirit
of this magnificent movement towards Catholic reform by its
first beginners in Italy in the sixteenth century.   It is the
teaching of that admirable book, the *Spiritual Combat,* which
produced the asceticism of the Italian Clerks Regular.

II—THE " SPIRITUAL COMBAT "

THE authorship of the *Spiritual Combat* is not definitely established.

This book was sometimes published under the name of the
Spanish Benedictine, John of Castagniza.[1]   Several writers
of the Society of Jesus have attributed it to the Jesuit
Achille Gagliardi.[2]   There are doubtless traces in the work
of Spanish asceticism and Ignatian spirituality.[3]   But the
imprint of the Italian School is so evident that it is impossible
to place the author of the famous work elsewhere than among
the Clerks Regular, especially among the Theatines.   We
know that in the opinion of the greater number of critics[4]
this author was the Theatine Laurence Scupoli.

1861. See also the various biographies of St Charles. St Philip Neri
was accustomed to give those whom he directed spiritual *Maxims* or
Sentences. They were brought together after his death. The collection
was published at Turin under the title *Ricordi e Dette di san
Filippo Neri.* The *Sentences* are arranged according to the number
of days in the year, one sentence for each day. The Abbé A. Bayle
gave a translation in his *Vie de saint Philippe de Néri,* Paris, 1859,
pp. 398 ff. Cardinal Capecelatro has inserted in his *Vie de saint
Philippe* certain *Letters* of the saint (Vol. I, pp. 540 ff. of the French
translation of Fr. H. Bézin). The members of the Oratory of St Philip
Neri take no vows. In this they are distinguished from other Clerks
Regular. In the same way the Oblates of St Charles are a society of
secular priests to which was given charge of ordinands and the direction of the Seminary at Milan.

  [1] Especially by the printer Berthier, at Paris in 1675, in a volume
which also contains the *Treatise on the Peace of the Soul* or *The Path
of Paradise* of John of Bonilla, the Spanish Franciscan, and the
Meditations on the Sorrows of our Saviour Jesus Christ, by Blessed
Battista Varani, Italian Franciscan, written about 1490.

  [2] Sommervogel, *Bibl. des Ecrivains de la Compagnie de Jésus,*
Vol. III, 1095.

  [3] Franciscan influence has also rightly been noted. Ubald d'Alençon,
Études franciscaines, Vol. XXVII (1912), pp. 72 ff.

  [4] *Cf.* Vezzosi, *Scrittori teatini,* Vol. II, pp. 276 ff. Discussion on
this subject will also be found in the various editions of the *Spiritual
Combat,* especially in those of Alexis de Buc, Paris, 1696, and of
A. Riche, Paris, 1860. Scupoli was born at Otranto, in the kingdom
of Naples, in 1530; he died at Naples in 1610.

It may be asked with regard to the *Spiritual Combat* as with the *Imitation,* if it is not rather the collective work of a religious family than that of one single writer. The *Combatimento Spirituale* was not produced in the first instance as we have it. The first edition, which appeared in 1589 at Venice, had only twenty-eight chapters. Subsequent editions then appeared with thirty-three, thirty-seven, forty, and finally sixty chapters. Certain parts of it seem to point to a compilation rather than to a single author. The chapters often lack logical sequence. And, above all, the style of the later editions is very different from that of the earlier. Much of the naïve grace and impressiveness is lost.

At the beginning of the *Spiritual Combat* is found the idea of Christian perfection. The spiritual life " does not consist in external practices."

" It consists in nothing else but the knowledge of the goodness and the greatness of God, and of our nothingness and inclination to evil; in the love of him and the hatred of ourselves, in subjection, not to him alone, but to all his creatures for love of him, in entire renunciation of all will of our own and absolute resignation to all his divine pleasure; furthermore, in willing and doing all this purely for the glory of God and solely to please him, and because he so wills and merits thus to be loved and served."[1]

Christian perfection is wholly internal. It results from the combined effect of the virtues which cause us to die to ourselves in order to be fully subjected to God through love. Here we find the inward mortification which the school of the Clerks Regular pushed so far.

Note also in the *Spiritual Combat* the clear insistence on the need of pure love in those who wish to attain to perfection. According thereto we cannot tend towards the perfect Christian life unless we serve God *solely* for his glory and " with a view to pleasing him." Our own interest ought never to count, and we must as far as possible exclude it. There are motives for being virtuous which are good in themselves, such as that of escaping hell and reaching heaven. Perfection demands that we act unto the sole glory of God.[2]

[1] Chap. i (French translation, Tournai, Desclée, 1894). French translations are numerous.

[2] Chap. i. *Cf.* chap. x : " The most insignificant action, done with a view to please God alone, and for his sole glory, is (if we may so speak) of infinitely greater value than many others of the greatest dignity and importance done without this motive. Hence a single penny given to a poor man with the sole desire to please God is more acceptable to him than the entire renunciation of all earthly goods for any other end, even for the attainment of the bliss of heaven; an end in itself not only good, but supremely to be desired."

St Francis de Sales is very careful not to define so precisely the nature of divine love required for perfection. He feared, not without reason, to discourage beginners in the Christian life. We also know that St Bernard declared the impossibility of that state of pure love in which man unceasingly forgets himself in order to please God alone.

" The summit of perfection " is attained by the fight against self, by this combat so much spoken of by the Clerks Regular. In reading the *Combatimento* we seem to be assisting at a course on spiritual strategy. We there learn how to struggle victoriously against " all the evil affections " of the heart, however slight they seem to us.

Four arms, without which victory is impossible, are recommended to us : *Distrust of ourselves,* for reduced to our own strength we can do nothing ; *trust in God* with whom we can do all things ; *the good use of the faculties of soul and body ;* finally, the *exercise of prayer.*

It is above all in reference to the good use of our faculties that the spirituality of the *Spiritual Combat* is made most manifest. These faculties are the intelligence or understanding, the will and the outward or bodily senses.

The intelligence ought to be on its guard against two enemies by which it is unceasingly attacked : ignorance and curiosity (vii-ix).

But it is in the exercise of the will that the struggle is necessary because of the opposition which exists between the " reasonable and higher will " and the " other which has its seat in the senses, known by the name of the lower and sensual will, and more commonly under the names of appetite, sense, or passion." " For a true will, the assent of the superior will " is needed. Hence ensues a combat without truce between the two wills, or between the passions and the reasonable will (xii).

It is not expedient to attack all the passions at once ; there is an order to be followed in the struggle. The " passion which besets us " and " tyrannizes over " our heart should be attacked first of all (xvii). And the struggle should be undertaken thus (xiii).

First of all direct resistance to the insurgent passion :

" First, whenever thou art assailed and buffeted by the impulses of sense, oppose a valiant resistance to them, so that the higher will may not consent " (xiii).

This first victory gained, in order to repress the passion " with greater vigour and force," it is good to provoke a second struggle. In this way the habit of crushing it more completely is acquired, and hatred and horror of it is produced. But these tactics must never be used in the combat against carnal passion, which can only be overcome by flight " with the greatest care from every occasion and every person presenting the least danger " to us (xix).

Whilst resisting the passions and provoking renewed combats we must cultivate acts of those virtues that are opposed to them.

Finally we must keep watch over the senses.

" The sensitive appetite is, so to speak, the captain of our corrupt nature. . . . It makes use of the outward senses, like so many soldiers and natural instruments, in order to seize what it desires " and misuse it. We must then know how to govern the senses if we desire not to be overcome in the battle against self.

Before all, " take good heed not to let thy senses stray freely where they will; nor to use them when pleasure alone, and not utility, necessity, nor any good end, is the motive " (xxi).

But as the senses cannot be wholly withdrawn from the outer world, let us direct them towards God and employ them in the contemplation of heavenly realities. The beauties of creation are able, if we so desire, to uplift us towards the Creator. The author of the *Spiritual Combat* here gives some examples of the spiritual aspirations which the sight of things created may suggest to the devout.[1] There, as well as in other parts of his work, he shows himself much more a theologian and philosopher than poet. Then he writes a very beautiful chapter on the manner of passing from the consideration of the outer world " to the meditation of the life and passion of the Word incarnate " (xxii), wherein we note the Ignatian method of prayer by the application of the five senses.

The voice of Ignatius, too, constantly echoes through the clash of arms in the *Spiritual Combat,* ordering the tactics and planning the battle. The author of the *Combatimento* only adapts and then passes on the commands of his chief. The exhortation, " the order of the day," given in the morning before the beginning of the daily battle, is little else than a paraphrase of the meditation on the Two Standards of the *Spiritual Exercises.*

" On awaking in the morning the first thing to be observed by thine inward sight is the listed field in which thou art enclosed, the law of the combat being that he who fights not must there lie dead for ever. . . . On the right hand, behold thy victorious Captain Jesus Christ, the Virgin Mary and her beloved spouse St Joseph, and an innumerable host of angels and saints . . . on the left hand, the demon, with all his armies, ready to excite this passion and to persuade thee to

---

[1] *Cf.* Augustine Capece, Theatine, *Il monte di Dio,* 1645.

yield to it " (xvi). . . . " Then think you hear the voice of
your guardian angel" strengthening your courage.

So the fight begins and proceeds in accordance with the
rules already given. If in the struggle we feel wounded and
on the point of being overcome and vanquished, we must
never allow ourselves to yield to discouragement or give up
the fight (xiv, xxvi). We should then pray more earnestly.
But it is essential, if victory is to be gained, to retain a
"good morale." So also does the *Combatimento* urge the
soldier of Christ, amidst the struggle, to keep tranquillity of
soul and peace of heart and to avoid with all possible
care anything that might disturb them (xxv).[1]

"If distrust of self, trust in God, and the right use of
our faculties be so needful in this spiritual conflict, needful
above all is prayer (the fourth weapon above mentioned) "
(xliv).

The last part of the *Spiritual Combat* maps out a plan for
the Christian's life of prayer. The three practices specially
commended are : prayer or meditation, communion, and examination of conscience. The influence of the Spanish
School is plainly seen, but the Italian writer simplifies the
exercises.

He recommends two forms of prayer : short prayers—*i.e.,*
ejaculatory prayers—which should be used often, above all
in the midst of the battle ; and the longer form of prayer
combined with meditation.

The first is "a raising of the soul to God, in which we
ask him for those things which we desire." We may ask
for them verbally by using mental words, or tacitly by showing our needs to God without speech, or finally by "a simple
look of the soul towards God," which is a tacit reminder of
the grace already asked for (xlv).

To the already mentioned longer form of prayer lasting
"half an hour, an hour, or longer," must be "added meditation on the life and Passion of Jesus Christ" (xlvi-xlvii,
li-lii).[2] Our Saviour's Passion, according to the *Spiritual
Combat,* is the great subject for meditation :

"Jesus crucified—there is the book which I give thee to
read, that from it thou mayest copy the true picture of

---

[1] The *Spiritual Combat* describes at length the wiles of the devil
(xxvii, xxxii, xlii-xliii). *Cf.* the Rules of St Ignatius on the
Discernment of Spirits. Chapters xxxiii-xli contain advice in detail
as to the way to acquire and make progress in virtue : it is a kind of
small treatise on Christian virtues.

[2] The method is simple without any preamble as is found in the
Ignatian method ; but with considerations on the subject of the meditation, accompanied by acts of love.

every virtue. For it is the real *book of life,* which not only instructs the understanding by words, but enkindles the will by its living example " (lii).

It is in this book that patterns of every virtue and the most urgent motives for practising them must be sought.

It will be noticed that the *Combatimento* draws the attention of the devout to the inward and " mental " sufferings of Christ (li). Meditation on the thought of what Jesus suffered in his soul was very much in favour in Italy in the sixteenth century. About 1490 the Franciscan nun, Blessed Battista Varani, whom we shall meet again later, wrote a book on the sorrows of Christ's soul during the Passion (*Dolori mentali di Cristo*).[1] Her work was known to Lorenzo Scupoli. St Mary Magdalen of Pazzi also was moved to pity " by the sorrow and compassion which divided the heart " of Jesus, " at the sight of so great a number " for whom his precious Blood " must be shed in vain." She also referred " to the distress of love and compassion (of his divine heart) for all the just, for all the pains " which the elect would have to suffer " till the end of the world."[2]

It is also good to meditate on the Blessed Virgin Mary, for whom the author of the *Spiritual Combat* has a very trustful devotion (xlviii-xlix). He desires us to have daily recourse to her. We should also take as our " chief advocate and protector, St Joseph, Mary's spouse." Also, " in our prayers, we may make use of the help and protection of the angels and saints " (l).[3]

This devotion to the angels is characteristic of Italian spirituality. Pierre Lefèvre, that disciple of St Ignatius who wrought his apostolic ministry for some time in Italy, greatly loved the holy angels. In a letter—of doubtful authenticity, but which well reflects the devout thought of the time—St Cajetan explains at length to a nun the nature and being of the angels and their activities.[4] St Mary Magdalen of Pazzi describes the love of the angels for men. " It is," she says, " an intense love which has its source in

---

[1] See the *Études franciscaines,* Vol. XVII, 1907, p. 687, on Bl. Varani. The *Dolori mentali di Cristo* (Latin version *Acta Sanct.,* May, Vol. VII, pp. 488 ff.) contains meditations on the Saviour's inward sufferings as to : the sins of the damned, the sins of the elect, the sorrows of Mary, the love of Mary Magdalen, his well-beloved disciples, the loss of Judas, the ingratitude of the Jews and others. The *Combatimento* of Rome, 1615, contains also the *Sentiero del Paradiso* and the *Dolori mentali di Cristo.* The author of the *Spiritual Combat* must have been inspired by the *Dolori mentali.* Cf. *Études franciscaines,* Vol. XXVII, 1912, p. 76.

[2] *Œuvres,* Part I, chap. xiv, Bruniaux, Vol. I, pp. 164-165.

[3] The *Spiritual Combat* often speaks of the guardian angel and his role in the struggle waged by the Christian against sin (xvi).

[4] De Maulde la Clavière, *Saint Gaëtan,* pp. 198-201; Salvadori, p. 103.

the heart of the Word, because they see in the Word the
dignity of creatures and the love he has for them.[1] . . ."

Holy Communion is the most effective means of overcoming our adversaries. With our other weapons "we
struggle against our enemies through the virtue of Jesus
Christ; with this we battle with them in company with
Jesus Christ, and it is Jesus Christ who fights with us
against them" (liii). Moreover, it is through the Eucharist
that our hearts are inflamed with the fire of divine love
(lv). It is thus needful to communicate, whenever we have
permission, as frequently as possible, and to make good
preparation (liv-lv).

This permission at that time was not granted so easily
as it is to-day. So, instead of the wholly desirable daily communion, the *Combatimento* recommends communion by desire,
which is possible not merely every day, but every hour (lvi).
This is the exercise known as *spiritual communion*. It arose
at a time when communions were not frequent and was
intended to do duty for daily communion. This exercise
loses its importance as the custom of approaching the holy
table daily becomes more and more general among those of
the faithful desirous of tending towards a perfect Christian
life.[2]

Such are the main points of the spirituality of the *Combatimento*.[3]

Although the work is not a complete treatise on asceticism,
it is surprising not to find in it a chapter devoted to spiritual
direction. This direction is very often assumed. The
author of the *Combat* recommends talks with the "spiritual
father" (xix). We also know that the first founders of the
Clerks Regular, St Cajetan and St Antony Zaccaria, were
directed by Baptist da Crema.[4] The direction given to his
penitents by St Philip Neri has become famous.[5] None the

[1] *Œuvres,* Part IV, chap. xxvii, Vol. II, p. 342.
[2] Spiritual communion will always be preserved as a means of unceasingly producing virtue and the spirit of the Saviour within us.
It is a kind of prayer.
[3] The last chapters—added afterwards—do not follow logically. They
contain two parts of Luis of Granada's method of prayer: thanksgiving and the oblation of oneself to God (lvii-lviii), which fit in with
nothing else; a chapter on dryness (lix), and another on examination
of conscience (lx), which ought to be placed after those which treat of
prayer. Finally the treatise ends with six chapters (lxi-lxvi) on the
struggles of the soul at the hour of death.
[4] St Jerome Emilian had as director a canon of the Lateran (*Acta
Sanct.,* February, 8, p. 229). Treatises on direction were written in
Italy, especially that of the Friar Minor Conventual, Trebatio Macrotti
della Penna, *Discorsi spirituali per direzione delle anime,* Turin, 1590.
[5] St Philip had as penitents, among others, St Camillus de Lellis,
Blessed John Leonardi, and Cardinal Frederick Borromeo, cousin of
St Charles.

less, direction does not appear as yet to have had all the importance in Italian spirituality which it was to possess later on. It is St Francis de Sales who rendered it really popular.

III—THE MYSTICS: ST MARY MAGDALEN DEI PAZZI OF THE CARMELITE ORDER, ST CATHERINE DE RICCI AND BLESSED OSANNA DE ANDREASSI OF THE ORDER OF ST DOMINIC, BLESSED BATTISTA VARANI, POOR CLARE — FRANCISCAN SPECULATIVE MYSTICISM

THE wholly Italian spirituality of St Mary Magdalen dei Pazzi[1] has the reforming spirit. Her writings embody the tendencies of the Italian Catholic reformers of the sixteenth century.

Born at Florence, April 2, 1566, of one of the most famous families of Tuscany, she employed all the influence of her position to demand the reform of the Church. As Carmelite, she laboured by exhortation and by her writings to bring the religious of both sexes to a more regular and more fervent life. As mystic, she felt authorized by her visions and revelations to bring home the lesson to the clergy and to urge them to a better life. Her mission in many ways resembles that of St Catherine of Siena. In her ecstasies she obtained teaching from the Sienese Virgin concerning the virtues of religious life.[2]

Her vocation, above all, was to pray and to do penance

---

[1] Catherine de Geri dei Pazzi was born at Florence in 1566. Her father was Governor of the town of Cortona. She was brought up in the monastery of the Sisters of Charity of St John the Less. She entered the Carmelites of St Mary of the Angels at Florence, where she made her profession, May 27, 1584, and took the name of Mary Magdalen. She was novice-mistress from 1598 to 1604, then she became sub-prioress. She died at Florence, May 27, 1607. *Life of St Mary Magdalen de Pazzi,* by Vincenzo Puccini, confessor to the Monastery of St Mary of the Angels, Venice, 1675, *Acta Sanct.,* May 25.—The *Opere di Santa Maria Maddalena de Pazzi carmelita di S Maria di Firenze* were collected and published by Lorenzo Brancaccio, Carmelite of the strict observance, Florence, 1609. Another edition with the saint's *Letters,* Florence, 1893. An abridged French translation by the Carthusian, D. Anselm Bruniaux, 2 vols., Paris, 1873. The *Works* of the saint are divided into five parts. The first contains contemplations on the mysteries of faith and of the life of Christ, the second deals with religious life and virtues, the third comprises uplifting thoughts on passages from Holy Writ, the fourth lofty contemplations on the divine perfections, the fifth contains *Exclamations* similar to those of St Teresa.

[2] *Œuvres,* Part II, chap. x-xii; Bruniaux, Vol. I, pp. 408 ff.

in order to obtain the reform " of all states of the Church " :
religious, priests, the faithful, and even heretics and pagans :

" I desire to offer thee, O my God," she exclaims, " all
creatures state by state, and I shall begin with the virgins,
thy brides who are so dear to thee. . . . Thou hast chosen
all religious women, but they are not all acceptable because
they fail to perform all those duties for which thou hast
chosen them. . . . I implore thee, O my God, to make them
know their obligations, and I offer thee on their behalf the
Blood thou didst shed in the Garden of agony. . . .

" And what must I say of thy priests, O Word? thou
makest me to see a multitude of them who . . . trample
under foot their honour by making themselves the slaves of
vile and despicable creatures. Those eyes which see thee
descend in the Eucharist from the bosom of thine Eternal
Father, allow themselves to gaze on abominable sights and
the wretches dare approach the altar in this dreadful state.
. . . O Word! I shall leave thee not until thou dost grant
me the conversion of some among them. . . . Tell me,
I beseech thee, what I must do to obtain it; whatsoever it
be I shall do it with all my heart. . . .

" I offer thee, O Word, for all the members of Holy
Church of which thou art the head, the numberless drops of
Blood that thou didst shed from all thy members in thy
cruel scourging. . . . O Word divine! I shall only be content when I see myself wholly consumed with the desire to
bring back to thee these souls astray. . . .

" Would that I had the strength to gather all [the un-
faithful], to lead them into the bosom of thy Church. I
should pray her to purge them from their unfaithfulness
through the beneficent breath of her mouth, to give them
new life. . . . But alas! I can only deplore my impotence
and my ingratitude, which is its cause. . . .

" I now offer thee, O Word, those incarnate devils—for
thus I think they may be called because of their malice—I
mean all heretics and all sects, such as they are known to
thee, and I offer thee for these the Blood thou didst shed
when thou wast stripped of thy garments on Calvary,
because these wretches make every effort to tear thy robe
by their poisonous deeds and words. . . ."[1]

It is in flashes of fire and with impassioned accents that
she pours forth her prayer to God for the salvation of sinners
for the expiation of whose sins she is ready " to sacrifice her
own life " :

" O my God! How can this wickedness be plucked out
from the hearts of men? Oh, that I were found worthy to

---

[1] *Œuvres,* Part V, 2nd *Exclamation,* Vol. II, pp. 377 ff. *Cf.* Part
IV, chap. xxi, pp. 291 ff.

give my life for the salvation of souls and to destroy this evil, how happy should I be! How great a torment it is to live and to die every moment; to see that one is only able to be of use to creatures by giving one's life and yet to be unable to do it. O charity, thou art a file which little by little wears away both body and soul. . . ."[1]

In all that she wrote St Mary Magdalen had in view unceasingly this reform " of all states of the Church." She lived only to bring it about.

The *Works* of the great Carmelite nun contain not only exclamations and prayers; deep theological teaching on such subjects as creation, the fall, the atonement, and the divinizing of man through Christ the Redeemer are also to be found there. As in the *Dialogue* of St Catherine of Siena, the influence of Thomist theology is to be seen.[2] Dogmatic considerations on the divine Unity, the Trinity of Persons, the Incarnation, and the work of the Holy Ghost in souls are frequent; very often, too, as in the writings of the Sienese Virgin, the teaching is expounded in the form of a dialogue with the heavenly Father, or the Word, or the Blessed Virgin. Finally—and this completes the resemblance between the two saints—it is during ecstasy that St Mary Magdalen expounds her teaching, and with such rapidity that it was necessary to give her six secretaries, who wrote for hours, and even for whole days, under her dictation.[3] She had also read the *Meditations on the Life of Christ* of the pseudo-Bonaventure and the *Life of Christ* by Ludolph the Carthusian. We find once more, in her chapters consecrated to the Passion, the famous scene of the farewell between Jesus and Mary before the last departure for Jerusalem.[4] But the colloquies of Jesus with Mary are not so pathetic as in the work of the holy Franciscan. They contain above all theological considerations on the love of Christ for men and the benefits which his death ought to procure them.

---

[1] *Œuvres,* Vol. II, pp. 295-296.

[2] She distinguishes between the two appetites, concupiscible and irascible (Vol. I, pp. 7-8); and gives a kind of treatise on the theological and cardinal virtues (pp. 10 ff.), and a psychological explanation of the Holy Trinity (pp. 58 ff.), " God is most pure act," p. 92, etc.

[3] The six secretaries thus divided their duties: the first wrote, as No. 1, the first portion of the saint's discourse; the second followed as No. 2, and so on; after this the first became No. 7, the second No. 8, etc., and they continued to write in this way until the end. After the ecstasy one of them transcribed the whole, following the numerical order, and by order of the Mother Prioress, the saint heard it read through, approved what was correct, and altered anything inaccurate. *Life of St Magdalen,* by Father Virgilio Cepari, one of her confessors. Bruniaux, *Œuvres,* Vol. I, pp. xiv-xv. It is difficult for a work composed in this way not to suffer certain accidental alterations.

[4] *Œuvres,* Part I, chap. xii, Vol. I, pp. 136 ff.

St Mary Magdalen yields at times to the desire to supplement, through her revelations, the silence of the evangelists on certain circumstances of the life of the Saviour. She greatly wished in particular "to know what the most holy soul of Jesus did during its separation from his body" until the moment of the resurrection. In a long dialogue with the Eternal Father, she obtained this knowledge. During one of her ecstasies she also witnessed the visit made by Jesus to the "blessed souls in Limbo."[1]

The famous Carmelite had a poetic soul. She felt strongly the charm of the beauties of nature. Her style is coloured with the marvellous tints of Tuscan scenery, which again adds to the interest possessed by her *Works*. Further, her influence increased more and more. After her death she continued through her writings to insure that Catholic reform for which she had so greatly prayed and suffered.[2]

The *Letters* which St Catherine de Ricci[3] wrote in order to procure the reform of the Church—unlike those of St Mary Magdalen dei Pazzi—reached those to whom they were addressed. Among these were cardinals, bishops, superiors of religious Orders, and princes. They were impressed by the prudence and sanctity of their illustrious correspondent.

In these heavenly raptures in the Dominican convent of Prato in Tuscany, St Catherine, with groanings, recommended the whole Church to her divine Spouse:

"Oh! how many are the Judases in the Church," she says to him. "Oh! Oh! Oh! Here I must be silent. Renew, renew, O Lord, thy Church. . . ."

She gave courage to those who were inflamed with the desire to renew the Church: "I pray the divine Majesty," she wrote to St Philip Neri, "to restore you and to main-

---

[1] *Œuvres*, Part I, chap. xxi-xxv, pp. 199 ff. We would note that, according to St Mary Magdalen, the visit to Limbo only took place after the resurrection (chap. xxv).

[2] Note here three Italian Carmelites: Amanzo di Santa Rosa, *Opere spirituali*, Naples, 1615-1619; Dominic of Jesus and Mary, General of the Carmelites, *Sententiario spirituale,* 1620, French translation, Paris, 1623; Eliseus Vasallo, *Il cristiano invitato al Paradiso* (the three ways), Naples, 1643.

[3] Alexandrina de Ricci was born in Florence in 1522. In 1535 she entered the Dominican Convent of St Vincent of Prato, near Florence. She took the name of Catherine. She was Prioress of her convent for a long time and died in 1590. Her *Letters* were published by Cesare Guasti, at Prato, in 1861, with an excellent introduction; re-edited at Florence, in 1890, by Gherardi. Her *Life* was written in Italian by Serafino Razzi, Lucca, 1594, and in France by Fr. Hyacinth Bayonne, Paris, 1873. The Dominican Order was also made famous in Italy by the foundress of the Monastery of the Cross of Florence, Dominica dal Paradiso (1473-1553), whose life was written in Italian by Ignatius del Nente, O.P., Venice, 1624.

tain you in good health because Holy Church has too great need of you."[1] Between these two generous souls a tender and wholly celestial friendship was established which was shown by a correspondence, unfortunately almost totally lost.[2]

St Catherine's mysticism was directed wholly towards the reform of the Church and is characterized by its holy gladness. In this she resembles St Philip, "who was the most beautiful type of Christian gladness that the Church has ever had." The historians of the saint relate that "God changed and transformed her heart in a most happy ecstasy, rendering it like that of the most Blessed Virgin. Then it was that Catherine felt herself flooded with an infinite and unspeakable gladness, and became conscious of being quite other than she was before."[3] In her ecstasies she also experienced the sufferings endured by Christ in his Passion. The greater number of the mystical phenomena which we admire in St Catherine of Siena were reproduced in this other daughter of St Dominic in the convent of Prato.

The same change of heart and the same mystical graces were granted to another famous Dominican nun, Blessed Osanna de Andreassi,[4] likewise for a social mission. God inspired her to become a tertiary of St Dominic, but yet to remain in the world "for the salvation and consolation of many."[5] She consecrated her life to prayer and penance for the conversion of sinners. Like another Geneviève, she rallied the courage of the inhabitants of Mantua[4] during the French invasions of Italy.

The Italian women mystics appear to be of much the same type as that of St Catherine of Siena, whose life was everywhere read with eagerness.[6] We find renewed the mystical ring, the symbol of the spiritual espousals with Christ; the invisible and painful stigmata; the frequent and prolonged ecstasies during which the visions and revelations occurred.[7]

---

[1] Cesare Guasti, *Letter LVIII.*

[2] *Cf.* Capecelatro, *Life of St Philip Neri,* Vol. II, pp. 372 ff.

[3] *ibid.,* p. 377. *Cf.* Serafino Razzi, *Vita Cat.,* lib. II, 6.

[4] Born at Mantua in 1449 she became a tertiary of St Dominic though remaining in the world. She died at Mantua in 1505. *Libello della vita sua propria e de doni spirituali da Dio a lei collati,* Mantua, 1507, reproduced in Latin in the *Acta Sanctorum,* June 18, following the *Lives* of Silvester Ferrara, O.P., and Jerome of Mantua, Olivetan.

[5] *Acta Sanctorum,* June 18 (Vol. IV, p. 563, Paris, 1867).

[6] St Mary Magdalen dei Pazzi and Blessed Osanna saw St Catherine of Siena in their ecstasies (*Acta S.S.,* June 18, p. 574).

[7] For Blessed Osanna see *Acta Sanctorum, ibid.,* and for St Mary Magdalen de Pazzi, *Acta Sanctorum,* May, Vol. VI, pp. 219 ff. *Œuvres,* Bruniaux, Vol. I, p. 80. See also the *Life* of Blessed Veronica de Binasco, Augustinian of the fifteenth century (*Acta Sanctorum,* January 13), and Matthew Silvaggi de Catania, O.M., *De nuptiis animae cum Christo,* Venice, 1542.

Occasionally the ecstatics give some mystical teaching during their raptures. The change or transforming of the heart through divine love is a phenomenon often found in Italy. We meet with it in St Cajetan, and, above all, in St Philip Neri.

Blessed Battista Varani, Poor Clare, Princess of Camerino in Umbria, also had her heart wholly inflamed with pure love.[1] Like St Mary Magdalen dei Pazzi, she found the source of this love in the heart of Jesus suffering for us.[2] She often meditated on the sorrows of the divine heart endured during the Passion. Her meditations have come down to us in the small work *Dolori mentali di Cristo,* which so largely contributed in the sixteenth and seventeenth centuries to inspire the faithful with devotion to Christ in his expiation of our sins.

Blessed Battista Varani was very specially drawn by the sorrows of the soul of Christ at the sight of sin. She herself thought so often of her own sins, and the many committed in such numbers at the time of the Renaissance. She was, in this connection, beset by a horrible temptation to blasphemy; to wit, that God was the author of evil. This temptation obsessed her to such a degree that she thought she was consenting to it and constantly committing acts of blasphemy. She was in despair and believed herself to be damned. This trial lasted for three years.[3] St Mary Magdalen dei Pazzi also passed through a similar trial during which, to use her own expression, she was " in the den of lions."[4]

The Seraphic Order also produced works of speculative mysticism. The Italian Franciscans who wrote them, according to the taste for Platonism in vogue at the time, delighted to comment on Dionysius the Areopagite. They desired to explain the union of the mystical soul with " the supereminent light," the light divine. Their explanations were occasionally disputed, and caused the intervention of ecclesiastical authority.[5]

[1] Born in 1458, at Camerino, Camilla Varani, after her " conversion," entered the Convent of the Poor Clares of that town. She died about 1526. She wrote her *Life* for her director, then a small work, the *Interior Sorrows of Christ,* and some *Spiritual Letters*. The Latin translation of all her writings is in the *Acta Sanctorum,* May 31. Her name in religion became Battista. Her *Life* was written by the Comtesse de Rambuteau, Paris, 1906.

[2] She often speaks of the heart of Jesus, which she invokes (*Acta Sanctorum,* May, Vol. VII, pp. 476, 478, 495, Paris, 1866).

[3] *Acta Sanctorum,* May 31, p. 484.

[4] *Acta S.S.,* May, Vol. VI, pp. 194 ff., Paris, 1866.

[5] Here are the names of several of the Franciscan writers of treatises on mysticism commenting on Dionysius the Areopagite : Antony de

IV—BLESSED ROBERT BELLARMINE[1]—
CLAUD ACQUAVIVA

LIKE St Mary Magdalen dei Pazzi and St Catherine de Ricci, Blessed Robert Bellarmine made heard "the groanings of a dove"—that is to say, of the Church, which weeps over sin, the sins of clergy and laity and the laxity of religious.

The spiritual writers of the Renaissance all lament the disorders of which they were the saddened witnesses. The spectacle of these disorders is a source of the pious tears shed by those faithful who were inflamed with the desire for the reform of the Church. This gift of tears of the Italian School is well known. St Cajetan[2] and St Philip Neri possessed it to a high degree :

"Pious tears flow from two principal sources," says Cardinal Bellarmine, "evil and good, sadness and joy. They are bitter or sweet according to whether they be tears of sorrow or tears of love."[3]

Monelia, *Sursum corda, Directorium inflammandae mentis in abissum divini luminis. Ejusdem expositio super librum de mystica theologia,* Bologna, 1522; Jerome Acceti, O.M., *De triplici theologia symbolica, scholastica et mystica,* Cremona, 1582; Angelo del Pas of Perpignan, O.M., *Breve trattato del conoscere et amar Iddio,* Rome, 1596; Ignatius of Bergamo, Franciscan, *Theologica mistica,* Bergamo, 1599. Occasionally the commentators of Dionysius the Areopagite were not fortunate. The *De unione animae cum supereminenti lumine,* Perugia, 1538, of Bartholomew de Castello, O.M., was placed on the Index, March 8, 1584. *Il paradiso de Contemplativi,* Venice, 1622, of Saluzzo, is appraised. See his *Opere,* Venice, 1639.

[1] Robert Bellarmine was born October 4, 1542, at Montepulciano in the ancient Duchy of Tuscany. In 1560 he entered the Jesuits in Rome, where he studied philosophy at the Roman College. He made his theological studies at Padua. Then he became Professor at the University of Louvain (1569-1576), and afterwards at the Roman College (1576-1592), where he wrote his famous *Controversies.* Created Cardinal in 1599, he was made Archbishop of Capua, 1592-1604. He laboured for the reform of his diocese. On his return to Rome he wrote in defence of the rights of the Church and of the Pope. He died there September 18, 1621. The ascetic treatises of Bellarmine were written towards the end of his life, from 1614. They are here given in chronological order : *The Ascent of the Mind towards God by the Ladder of Creatures; The Eternal Happiness of the Saints* (a pious treatise on heaven); the *Groaning of the Dove,* that is to say, of the Church, on the sins of the clergy and layfolk, on the laxity of the religious, etc; *The Seven Words of our Lord on the Cross; The Art of Holy Dying.* Cf. *Opera omnia Roberti Bellarmini,* published by J. Fèvre, Paris (Vivès), 1874, Vol. VIII, pp. 239-620; Raitz v. Frentz, *Les Œuvres ascétiques du Bx. Bellarmin,* in the *Revue d'ascétique et de mystique,* July, 1923, pp. 243 ff., January, 1925, pp. 60 ff.

[2] *Acta S.S.,* VII, August, p. 263.

[3] *De gemitu columbae sive de bono lacrymarum,* lib. I, cap. i, Vol. VIII, p. 415. After the Cardinal's death, certain religious, thinking that they were aimed at, protested. Thence sprang a war of pamphlets. *Cf.* J. Thermes, *Le B. Bellarmin,* Paris, 1923, p. 176.

For divine love makes us shed tears, but tears of joy. The pious Cardinal treats at length the cause of these sweet tears and their beneficial effects on the spiritual life.

He wrote his ascetic treatises towards the end of his life, using the method propounded in his famous *Controversies.* He defines, he divides, he cites abundant texts from Scripture and from ecclesiastical writers. The affective note is rare, and this is to be regretted. It is, however, to be found in the *Ascent of the Mind towards God,* which is the most beautiful of Bellarmine's spiritual works, wherein his optimistic piety, overflowing with divine love, is best made manifest.

It will be recalled that the author of the *Spiritual Combat* recommends the pious soul to be raised from the consideration of created beings to God who has given them motion, life, and beauty. The Italian School delights in this method of prayer. Bellarmine teaches us to look at creation as an immense ladder—a staircase, as St Francis de Sales translates it—wherewith to mount towards God. Fifteen steps, each represented by a group of creatures, must be climbed. The first is man himself, who in himself is a small universe (*mundus minor*). Then the great universe (*major mundus*)[1] and all the elements which compose it : the earth, water, air and fire, the sun, moon, and stars. Then the spiritual world, the reasoning soul, and the angels. Finally, God, his essence, his omnipotence, his wisdom, his providence, his mercy, and his justice, which the immensity, the order, and the power of nature make manifest. A magniloquent panorama of all the ways which lead to God. We can understand Bellarmine's predilection for this treatise : " My other works," he said, " I have re-read only from necessity, but this one I have read three or four times, and I have resolved to read it again frequently."[2]

In the last years of his life he meditated more often on heaven. The collection of his meditations, made in writing, form a booklet *On the Eternal Happiness of the Saints,* a work of theology as much as of piety. Bellarmine answers most of the questions that can be put regarding the blessed and the happiness which they enjoy. Finally, in order to prepare himself immediately for death, he wrote, in 1620, his last work on the *Art of Holy Dying,* which recalls the well-known work by Gerson on the same subject.

The work of a theologian even more than a mystic, the ascetic treatises of Bellarmine were nevertheless much appreciated. " They delighted St Francis de Sales." And for us they are one of the best sources of Italian spirituality.

[1] *De ascensione mentis in Deum per scalas rerum creatarum,* gradus secundus, *Œuvres,* Vol. VIII, p. 246.
[2] J. Thermes, p. 174.

The contemporary of Bellarmine, Claud Acquaviva,[1] General of the Society of Jesus, brought peace to the controversy relative to the predominance of asceticism over mysticism, which, as we have seen, troubled the Spanish Jesuits. Greatly versed in spiritual theology, the author of several ascetic works, gifted with great prudence, he recommended his religious to follow the methods of prayer of the *Spiritual Exercises,* but not to trouble those among them whom God might raise to the mystical state.[2]

[1] He was born in 1543, in the kingdom of Naples. In 1581 he became General of the Jesuits. He died in 1615. His ascetic works are : Certain *Letters* on various subjects of spirituality, some *Meditations* on Psalms xliv and xciii, an *Oratio de Passione Domini.* His best known work, *Industria ad curandos animos,* has been translated into French under the title *Manuel des supérieurs,* Paris, 1776.

[2] We would also mention : Antony Cordeses, S.J., *Itineraria della perfettione christiana,* Florence, 1607, Latin translation, Messina, 1626; Virgilio Cepari, S.J., *Exercitio della presenza di Dio,* Milan, 1627; Thomas Massucci, S.J., *De caelesti conversatione per internam orationem et exercitia spiritus,* Rome, 1622; J. B. Rossi, S.J., *Opuscula spiritualia,* Rome, 1642; James Callesi, S.J., *Vita del Servo di Dio Padre Giulio Mancinelli* (1537-1618), Rome, 1668.

CHAPTER X

THE ITALIAN SCHOOL: ITS TEACHING

THOSE who laboured in the sixteenth century for the restoration of the Church in Italy very rightly had in view the bringing about of this restoration through the clergy. They strove first of all to give them a high ideal of their dignity and mission. They then urged them, as they did the laity, to inward combat against self, sustained by an optimistic piety and an ardent love of God and one's neighbour.

This programme of moral reform sums up all Italian spirituality.

I—THE CLERGY—THEIR DIGNITY AND MISSION

We know how earnestly the reform of the clergy in the sixteenth century was desired. The disciplinary decrees of the Council of Trent are the best proof of this. Nearly everywhere God raised up apostles vowed to effect the sanctification of the priesthood. In Spain, Blessed John of Avila had formed the design of renewing the clergy through his preaching. He has left us two discourses on the excellence of the priesthood and the sanctity required of it; a feeble echo of the eloquent exhortations which he addressed to the clergy of his time.

In Italy, especially among the Franciscans, we find cogent teaching as to the excellence of the sacerdotal dignity. We may recall the earnest respect of St Francis of Assisi for priests on account of the character bestowed on them and his insistent recommendations to the religious of his Order on the subject.

St Bernardine of Siena, the great Franciscan preacher of Renaissance Italy, knew also how to inspire the faithful with a great " veneration " for the divers orders of the ecclesiastical hierarchy. The clergy are entitled to very great respect, above all, the priests, on account of the divine powers which raise them above all created beings. In an eloquent sermon —perhaps more eloquent than strictly theological—St Bernardine shows that the powers of the priest are greater than those of the devil, the angels, the archangels, and even the Virgin Mary, however astonishing this may appear:

"O Virgin full of love and blessing," he exclaims with touching emotion, "forgive me for placing above thee the power of the priest. I do not, however, say anything against thee, when I speak the truth which thy Son declared himself to be. He himself placed the priesthood above thee in the temple where thou didst present him, as has already been explained."[1]

These thoughts were later on to be very often made use of as a theme of exhortations on the priesthood.

"I presume to hold in my hands," wrote St Cajetan to Laura Mignani, a nun, "and to offer as a propitiatory victim to his Father, even him from whom the day-star receives its light and who gives being to the whole universe. Ah! what a miracle of charity is this that God has separated me from the rest of the faithful, to raise me to the rank of his minister!"

This divine election, as he well understands, calls for great sanctity. How can such a ministry be worthily fulfilled without eminent virtues?

"But alas!" he continues, "how does this choice, so little merited, render me deserving of compassion! I must choose between these two things: either to cease to offer the holy Victim in consideration of my unworthiness; in a word, to pass my days in deep humility, or else to fulfil my ministry before the Lord in a humble spirit, as a sacred trust, as a faithful dispenser of the abundant treasure of his graces."[2]

The sense of his misery did not turn St Cajetan from the daily celebration of the holy Sacrifice. He prepared himself therefor with care, and occasionally by several hours of meditation. His eucharistic zeal caused him to exhort those priests who celebrated Mass badly or rarely[3] to follow a better way.

St Philip Neri also counselled those priests whom he directed to celebrate holy Mass every day, when no legitimate reason prevented them. He himself celebrated every morning, and with what devotion! "Whilst each priest makes

---

[1] *Sermo* XX; *Quanta veneratione honorari debent ecclesiastici gradus*, art. II, cap. vii : *Quanto quoque superat [sacerdotis potestas] potestatem Virginis gloriosae et omnium creatorum. Virgo amorosa et benedicta, excusa me apud te, quia non alloquor contra te, cum veritatem, quam dixit se esse Filius tuus, fatear coram te, et sacerdotium, sicut supra dictum est, in templo ipse praetulit supra te. In quatuor excedit sacerdotis potestas Virginis potestatem. Primo in brevitate, secundo in majoritate, tertia in immortalitate, quarto in replicabilitate. Sancti Bernardini Senensis, O.M. Opera omnia*, Lyons, 1650, Vol. I, p. 99, Joachim de la Haye, ed.

[2] *Lettres de St Gaëtan*, de Maulde la Clavière, pp. 182-183; Salvadori, *San Gaetano*, pp. 49-50. Similar thoughts on the sanctity of the priesthood are found in the writings of St Laurence Justinian, Bellarmine, and other holy persons of the time.

[3] *Acta Sanctorum*, August 7, p. 267, Paris, 1867.

great efforts for the mind to be recollected in God before celebrating, Philip was obliged to make great efforts to distract his mind from God. Without this he would have lacked the necessary attention to the outward acts of the holy Sacrifice, and, instead of saying Mass, he would have passed long hours absorbed in God."[1] In spite of these precautions, he was often rapt in ecstasy while he celebrated.

Christ is the true model whom the priest should strive to imitate. St Cajetan bewailed the fact that " neither inwardly nor outwardly " did he resemble Jesus Christ. He asked the Reverend Mother Laura Mignani " to obtain for him to be very conformable to the divine Master."[2] This resemblance to Christ the High Priest, so much preached by the reformers of the clergy, St Philip Neri strove to reach : " From the first day, when he was clothed with the sacred ministry, he always had his eye on Christ the High Priest, and he became one with him in such a way that his work was in substance the work of Christ, wrought by means of him. In the sacerdotal life of Philip, he was like the branch united to the vine, and that vine was Jesus Christ."[3]

" Alas ! to-day there is no one like Christ," said St Cajetan sadly.[4] How ardently must he and the holy priests of his time have preached sacerdotal virtue ! so well did they understand how needful it was !

When a clerk has been convinced of the dignity of his state and of the obligation which binds him to avoid, in his own life, the faults which he is charged to correct in others, a programme of perfection must be set before him. This programme must not be too severe, so that it may be within the compass of all. It was the secular clergy that needed reform, by being shown the true sacerdotal life by example. The Clerks Regular would not have been able fittingly to undertake this reform were they submitted to an austere monastic rule, good for the cloister but unsuitable to priests exercising their ministry outside.

The founders of the Clerks Regular understood this well. They themselves, nevertheless, practised austerities. St Cajetan, the first Barnabites,[5] St Charles Borromeo, to cite

---

[1] Card. Capecelatro, *Vie de saint Philippe de Néri*, translated by Bézin, Vol. I, p. 251. The writer adds : " The thing appeared most strange, and I should hardly have believed it if I had not seen it so often affirmed in the process of canonization of Philip by witnesses most worthy of trust."
[2] De Maulde, p. 194; Salvadori, p. 70.
[3] Capecelatro, Vol. I, p. 250.
[4] De Maulde; Salvadori, *ibid*.
[5] Premoli, *Storia dei Barn.*, p. 473.

only these, made themselves remarkable by their heroic penance. But what they urged on their disciples was spiritual mortification, inward self-denial.[1]

Thus the absolute poverty of the mendicant Orders was not imposed on them. They were required to have the spirit of poverty, which renounces what is superfluous, which learns, if needful, to be content with little, and, above all, to avoid covetousness, a vice that was fairly frequent among the clergy of the Renaissance. With regard to this poverty of mind and heart, they knew, as did St Charles Borromeo, when he became Cardinal, how to give the example of a return to evangelical simplicity. St Francis de Sales later on desired his Visitation Nuns " to have their feet well shod, but the heart discalced and naked of all earthly affection; to have the head well covered and the mind well uncovered by perfect simplicity and the stripping of self-will."[2] The influence of St Philip Neri, who proposed to himself " to inspire and to promote, throughout the whole Church, poverty of heart and mind," is here seen.[3] And St Mary Magdalen dei Pazzi, who reflects the spiritual teaching of her time so faithfully, said, in connection with the spirit of ownership among religious :

" The salvation of a religious who has everything in abundance may be looked upon as certain, provided that this abundance comes to him from his superiors, and that he does not desire something more. On the contrary, there is no hope of salvation for the one who, though ill-nourished and ill-clothed, cries for possession by desire, and who strives to stifle remorse of conscience by this outward appearance of poverty. If he do not promptly strip himself of all he possesses in affection, he hopes for heaven in vain; it is not for him."[4]

The clergy ought to be unselfish, pure, filled with the spirit of religion; qualities which were often lacking in them at that time. Bellarmine relates that on one occasion he received hospitality at the palace of a rich prelate, who belonged to the nobility. Everything was luxurious, apart-

---

[1] This spirituality is beautifully expressed in the treatises *Of Inward Self-denial, Of Christian Perfection,* Cremona, 1585, by a nun of Milan whose name is unknown. These treatises were published at Cologne in 1642, under the name of Achille Gagliardi, Jesuit.

[2] *Œuvres de Saint François de Sales,* Lyon-Annecy, Vol. XIV, p. 232.

[3] Capecelatro, Vol. I, p. 100. The importance of spiritual mortification is one of the characteristics of St Philip Neri's spirituality, Vol. I, chap. xi.

[4] *Œuvres,* French translation, Bruniaux, Vol. I, p. 394. St Cajetan did not at once attain to the true definition of poverty for the Clerks Regular. He himself practised absolute outward poverty (*Acta Sanctorum,* August 7, p. 261). It was the same with the Barnabites, Premoli, p. 75.

ments, plates and dishes, the table. Early next morning the
cardinal betook himself to the church attached to the palace
in order to celebrate there the holy mysteries. But how great
was his surprise to find it completely bare and repulsively
dirty. He dared not say Mass there.[1] We can imagine the
sadness of the pious cardinal, who, like St Charles, "could
find nothing beautiful enough or rich enough for the house
of God." St Cajetan, St Philip Neri, and all the founders
of the Clerks Regular, loved the beauties of worship and
devoted themselves to the artistic decoration of their
churches.[2] In this way were the faithful edified, God
glorified, and ministers at the altar inspired with the spirit
of religion.[3]

II—THE WAR AGAINST SELF

THE condition needed for the production of this inward
spirituality is the struggle against self. The means recommended to both clergy and faithful was that of the *Spiritual
Combat* and of the *Spiritual Exercises* of St Ignatius, for the
Italian School is stamped with the impress of Ignatian
spirituality.[4] To die to self is to become virtuous. It is
also to glorify God.

"I am well aware," said St Cajetan, "that the greatest
glory of God consists in perfect submission and in generous
dying to self."[5]

---

[1] *De gemitu columbae*, lib. II, cap. v, *Œuvres*, Vol. VIII, pp. 435-
436.

[2] As regards the Barnabites, see Premoli, *Storia*, pp. 188, 327 ff.

[3] The famous picture of the true clerk, made, in 1562, by the Council
of Trent (Sess. XXII, *De reformatione*, cap. i), well corresponds with
the ideal of the Clerks Regular at this epoch : *Nihil est quod alios
magis ad pietatem et Dei cultum assidue instruat, quam eorum vita et
exemplum qui se divino ministerio dedicaverunt: cum enim a rebus
saeculi in altiorem sublati locum conspiciuntur, in eos tanquam in
speculum, reliqui oculos conjiciunt, ex iisque sumunt quod imitentur.
Quapropter sic decet omnino clericos in sortem Domini vocatos, vitam
moresque suos omnes componere, ut habitu, gestu, incessu, sermone
aliisque omnibus rebus nil nisi grave, moderatum ac religione plenum
prae se ferant, levia etiam delicta, quae in ipsis maxima essent,
effugiant, ut eorum actiones cunctis offerant venerationem.*

[4] The Theatines and Barnabites began before the coming of St
Ignatius into Italy (1537). The Jesuits were first of all called Theatines,
because of their resemblance to the religious of St Cajetan. St Teresa
sometimes gives them this name (*Letters*, Vol. I, pp. 7, 154, 437, etc.,
ed. Gregory of St Joseph). The *Spiritual Exercises* were not slow in
becoming famous in Italy. St Charles had drawn up a practical commentary on them. The people said of the Bishop of Milan : "The
Jesuits, added to his natural gifts, have caused him to adopt the life
he leads" (De Hurner, *Sixte-Quint*, Vol. I, p. 65). In her ecstasies,
St Mary Magdalen dei Pazzi heard St Ignatius, who gave her instructions respecting humility (*Œuvres*, II, chap. xiv). *Cf.* Tacchi Venturi,
Storia della Compagnia di Gesù in Italia, Rome, 1910.

[5] De Maulde, p. 51.

We are struck by the prominent place given to the struggle against self-love in Italian spirituality. An exaggerated love of self is quite rightly considered as the meeting-place of all the passions. Our will, according to the *Spiritual Combat,* is "infected and ruined by self-love."[1] In the *Dialogues of St Catherine of Genoa,* the worst role is played by self-love. St Mary Magdalen dei Pazzi sees in this the most mortal enemy of divine charity. These are in direct conflict at every moment.[2]

To draw the greater attention of the faithful to this inward battle, spiritual writers dramatized it. The *Dialogues of St Catherine of Genoa* help us to assist at the struggle waged by the mind and soul against the body and self-love, which are finally overcome. St Mary Magdalen dei Pazzi is filled with admiration for the charity which arms for the battle against self-love, "clothed in an armour which so perfectly protects all its members that the blows appear to it like puffs of wind and the wounds like the bite of an insect."[3] She was greatly stirred by a combat between humility and vainglory.

"I see," she said, "vainglory filled with boasting, and humility on the contrary calm and peaceful. . . . I desire to pause here in order to witness the battle; I feel that they are about to slay one another. Vainglory is well armed, but humility is no less so, and its arms are better sharpened. Vainglory tries to give its blows on the head; humility strikes from beneath. She will certainly have the advantage. She has already given her enemy a blow which has laid him at her feet. Beware, thou brave humility, vainglory is not yet dead. I desire to see the end of this battle, for I do not yet find perfect humility within me."[4]

Tranquillity of soul and inward peace were strongly urged on the fighters. Trouble and care produce discouragement. Moreover God brings about great things in a soul that is at peace.

"Keep therefore," says the author of the *Spiritual Combat,* "a sentinel always on the watch, who, as soon as he discerns the approach of anything likely to disquiet or disturb thee, may give thee a signal to take up thy weapons of defence. . . . So may the untoward accident do us much good, if we keep our souls in peace and tranquillity; otherwise all our exercises will produce little or no fruit."[5]

St Philip Neri also counselled holy joy and gaiety to those whom he directed. St Magdalen of Pazzi, too, desired her religious to be joyful and contented.[6] The enjoyment of this

---

[1] Chap. xliv.   [2] *Œuvres,* I, p. 421; II, p. 297.
[3] *ibid.,* Part II, chap. xii, Bruniaux, I, p. 421.
[4] *ibid.,* chap. x, p. 408.   [5] *Spiritual Combat,* chap. xxv.
[6] *Œuvres,* Part II, chap. vii, Vol. I, p. 387.

tranquillity of soul was the dream of the Christian humanists of Italy. The brief of Pope Clement VII, June 24, 1524, instituting the Order of Theatines, declares that the first founders are brought together with the desire to serve God " with most perfect tranquillity of soul."[1] Blessed Robert Bellarmine, in his autobiography, stated that it was on reflecting " very seriously one day on the means of arriving at true peace of soul " that he resolved to enter the Society of Jesus.[2]

Tendencies such as these account for the success which the *Treatise on the Peace of the Soul,* by the Spanish Franciscan, John of Bonilla, obtained in Italy in the sixteenth and seventeenth centuries. This inward peace was truly the *Path to Paradise (Sentiero del Paradiso).*[3]

III—OPTIMISTIC PIETY OF THE ITALIAN SCHOOL

IT is optimistic not only in insisting on the beauties of religion and on the consoling aspects of Christian mysteries, but also in its kindly feeling and sympathy for human nature. Strict as are the Italian writers in order to assure success in the fight against self,[4] they are equally indulgent in regard to other spiritual exercises.

Thus they counsel frequent communion, under conditions which, owing to the almost total neglect of the sacraments throughout Europe, were difficult at this period. St Cajetan was among the first to urge the faithful to the daily reception of the Eucharist. He was inspired above all by their need of it to counter the paganism of the Renaissance.[5] St Philip Neri, as all know, had made the frequenting of the sacraments of penance and the Eucharist one of the great

[1] This brief was drawn up by Cardinal Sadolet. F. Mourret, *Hist. gen. de l'Eglise,* Vol. V, p. 535.

[2] Joseph Thermes, *Le Bx Robert Bellarmin,* Paris, 1923, p. 11.

[3] This *Treatise on the Peace of the Soul* must have inspired the author of the *Spiritual Combat (Études franciscaines,* Vol. XXVII, 1912, pp. 76 ff.). It is added to several editions of the *Spiritual Combat.* Italian, as well as French, editions call it the *Path to Paradise.* The Trinitarian, St Michael of the Saints (1591-1635), also published a *Breve tratato de la tranquillitad dell' almo* (published with other small works at Rome, 1915). In Italy, Ignatius del Nente, O.P., published an analogous treatise, *Della tranquillita dell'animo nel lume della natura, della fede, della Sapienza, e del divino Amore,* Florence, 1642.

[4] For example St Philip Neri, who was kindness itself, in order to conquer the self-love of his famous disciple, the great Baronius (†1607), the immortal author of the *Ecclesiastical Annals,* obliged him to act as cook to the Community of the Oratory for some time, and inflicted other humiliations on him. Capecelatro, Vol. II, p. 125.

[5] *Acta Sanct.,* August 27, p. 67. In the sixteenth century the Theatines were the first to react against the desertion of the holy table.

means of propagating devotion in the city of Rome. Before him in 1540, Blessed Pierre Le Fèvre, one of the first companions of St Ignatius, exhorted to weekly confession and communion at Parma.[1] St Magdalen dei Pazzi advised frequent communion even for those whose dispositions left a little to be desired.

For if in the ordinary way, she said, we find God " inclined towards us, as we are towards him, yet very often his mercy closes his eyes to our lack of preparation, his goodness prevails over our neglect, and he gives us consolation, even when our imperfect dispositions render us unworthy to receive that plenitude of grace which this heavenly nourishment brings."[2]

The sympathy of Italian spirituality for poor human nature is also shown by simplicity of method in prayer.

The temperament of the Renaissance Italians was ill-disposed to what was intricate or restrictive : it needed air and space. Any hindrance of its movements was unbearable. Doubtless the spiritual combat requires force : it is impossible to overcome without doing violence to self. Yet in exercises of piety the soul should move at its ease so as to approach God without being compelled by a kind of pious, and possibly hampering, etiquette. As a matter of fact, we do not find that so much importance was attached to mechanical methods of prayer and examination of conscience in Italy as in Spain, the Low Countries, or in France.[3] The methods counselled in the *Spiritual Combat*[4] are as simple as possible, and yet we may assume that they came from Spain through John of Castagniza or through St Ignatius. There is no doubt that St Philip Neri, who was so exacting as to spiritual mortification, insisted much more on Christian gladness—one of the chief notes of his asceticism[5]—than on the explanation of divers methods of mental prayer. Nevertheless, like all the

[1] Cf. *Recherches de Science religieuse*, March-April, 1910, p. 174. St Jerome Emilian, after his conversion, communicated every week. *Acta S.S.*, February 8, p. 229.

[2] *Œuvres*, Part I, chap. ix, Vol. I, p. 102.

[3] There are, however, exceptions owing to the influence of the *Spiritual Exercises* of St Ignatius. Thus St Charles Borromeo followed the Ignatian methods of prayer and had them followed by those around him. But it is a fact that the Italian writings on methodical prayer are incomparably fewer than the Spanish. In the sixteenth century the most noteworthy are those of Serafino da Fermo and the *Specchio di orazione*, Parma, 1537 (French translation, Paris, 1601), of Bernadino of Balbano, O.M. An anonymous Franciscan work, *Trattato della meditatione e stati della santa contemplatione*, Rome, 1654. *Pratica dell'Oratione mentale*, Venice, 1592, of Bellintani Matthia, Capuchin.

[4] Chap. xlvi-xlviii, lx.

[5] Cardinal Capecelatro characterizes thus the ascetic school of St Philip : *the charitable, mortified, gladsome, and simple school. Life*, Vol. I, p. 518.

saints, and notably St Charles Borromeo,[1] he was insistent on advocating prayer.

He knew how to teach it and had a method, but one that was very simple. As regards his religious, " he gave preference to prayer in common rather than to psalmody in common, because his wish was to unite his priests and layfolk together in prayer."[2]

" In order to learn to pray," he said, " an excellent means is to realize that we are unworthy of it. True preparation for prayer consists in the practice of mortification. To wish to give ourselves to prayer without mortifying ourselves is to be like a bird which desires to fly before it has feathers."

To one of his penitents who begged him to teach him how to pray he answered : " Be humble and obedient and then the Holy Spirit will teach thee how to pray."[3]

In prayer he counselled the faithful to follow the impulse of the Holy Spirit. If a book were used, the reading of it should cease as soon as some pious emotion was felt within. In a state of dryness and aridity we should behave as beggars before the good God. Above all, we should not cease to pray.

" Prayer," he said, " is in the supernatural order what speech is in the natural. A man who does not pray is like an animal who does not speak. There is nothing that the devil fears more than prayer, and what he seeks for most is to destroy this spirit of prayer in souls."[4]

St Philip Neri " made himself the master of a mild, sweet, tender, compassionate asceticism. Throughout his life hardly two or three instances of moderate severity are to be met with ; and, on the contrary, an infinite sweetness of charity towards one's neighbour is seen at every step. . . ." " I do not desire confessors," he said, " to make the path of virtue too hard, above all for recent converts. I do not wish them to be galled by harsh reproaches. Dismayed by fear and by the difficulties of the new way, they might turn back. . . . Let us act otherwise : by compassion, gentleness, and love let us strive to win them for Jesus Christ ; let us sympathize with their weakness as much as we are able, so that our whole effort may be to inflame them with the love of God, who alone works great things." Thus did St Philip and his school speak.[5]

[1] St Charles, we know, decreed that at Milan the ordinands at their examinations should be specially asked if they used mental prayer and the subjects of their meditations.
[2] Capecelatro, Vol. II, p. 203.   [3] *id.*, p. 521.
[4] Bayle, p. 247. St Philip Neri trained men in the world to prayer, as did St Francis de Sales.
[5] Capecelatro, I, pp. 483, 485. Leopold Ranke, the historian, characterizes St Philip Neri in the same way : " He was good, of playful humour, strict as regards things essential, indulgent in those which were only accessory ; he never commanded, but restricted himself to

Such also, speaking generally, was the Italian School.[1]

" You must be kind and friendly towards your daughters," St Angela Merici counselled the Ursulines, " that they may be humble, kindly, models of charity and patience in every word and act " . . . and the Mothers in charge of the sisters : " I recommend you most insistently to seek ever to draw and rule the sisters by love, with a soft and gentle hand, without pride and harshness. In every circumstance be kind to them."[2]

IV—DIVINE LOVE IN THE ITALIAN SCHOOL

THE teaching of divine love holds a large place in the spiritual writings of Italy in the sixteenth century, which knew the *Oratorio del divino Amore*.

Divine love wrought marvels in the soul of St Cajetan, one of the founders of this society. " To speak to him of divine love floods him with joy and throws him into ecstasy. His delights are made manifest by abundance of tears. He loved, then he wept. . . . This ' holy madness ' transformed him; it produced in him, even physically, an incredible power of resistance. . . . ' When one loves God,' he exclaims, ' all is easy !' And he marches on mad with love . . . the flame which fires him expands his breast and distresses him. But it seemed impossible not to love him, because of his lofty flights and his fire, which wonderfully fed the energy of his soul. His word was on fire. . . . He burnt with love."[3] In his *Letters* to Laura Mignani, he frequently asks his pious correspondent to pray to God that his soul might become " a flaming brasier." This passage in the *Dialogues* attributed to St Catherine of Genoa, he interprets thus : " He who could well express what is felt by a heart burning with the love of

---

giving counsel, beseeching, so to speak, those who were expecting to receive his orders; he did not teach but conversed, possessing as he did the needful discernment to distinguish the special bent of each mind. His Oratory increased through the visits paid him, and by the attachment of some younger men who regarded themselves as his pupils and desired to live with him; the most famous among these was the Church annalist, Cæsar Baronius." *Histoire de la Papauté pendant les XVIe et XVIIe siècles,* French translation, Haiber, Paris, 1838, Vol. II, pp. 337-338. One of the Maxims of St Philip was : " Do you wish to be obeyed? Then command little." Bayle, p. 191.

[1] A somewhat more severe tone, however, is to be noted in St Charles Borromeo.

[2] *Ste Angèle Merici et l'Ordre des Ursulines,* Paris, 1922, I, pp. 413-421.

[3] De Maulde, pp. 35-36, which sums up the text of the *Acta Sanctorum,* August 7, pp. 263 ff.

Its Teaching 265

God would make all other hearts melt or break, even though
they were harder than the diamond and more stubborn than
the devil."[1]

In the catacombs of St Sebastian, where he often went to
pray, St Philip Neri, on the day of Pentecost 1544, was so
violently overwhelmed by the fire of divine love that " his
heart leapt . . . needed to dilate and to have more room "
and miraculously bent two of his ribs.[2] This is the famous
mystical phenomenon of the wonderful dilation of his heart.

St Aloysius Gonzaga (†1591) was also one of the most
pure victims of divine love. After his death he appeared to
St Magdalen dei Pazzi and to other mystics in order to
exhort them to let themselves be consumed by the flames of
divine charity.[3]

St Magdalen dei Pazzi herself was rapt in God whenever
the word *love* was mentioned in her presence.[4]

But still more interesting than these wonders is the teaching of the Italian mystics of this period on the love of God.
It is to be found chiefly in the *Dialogues* attributed to St
Catherine of Genoa. These *Dialogues* must have been written
by Battista Vernazza, daughter of Ettore Vernazza, the
disciple of St Catherine of Genoa, who was one of the
founders of the *Oratorio del divino Amore.* Composed about
1548, they reflect the great Genoese mystic's thoughts on
divine love.[5]

They are a kind of mystical history of the converted soul
which is freed from passion and becomes purified in the flames
of divine love, attaining the closest and most extraordinary
union with God.[6] Several holy persons belonging to six-
teenth-century Italy, such as St Jerome Emilian and St
Camillus de Lellis, are here to be recognized.

All the marvels of grace described in the *Dialogues* are the
effects of pure love, the pure love so much enlarged on by
St Catherine of Genoa, Baptist da Crema, and many others
at this time ; but later on it brought Fénelon and Bossuet into
conflict.

[1] *Dialogues,* Part II, chap. iv, de Bussière's translation, Paris, 1914,
p. 284.
[2] Capecelatro, Vol. I, pp. 185 ff.
[3] *Acta Sanct.,* May 25.
[4] *Œuvres,* Bruniaux, Vol. I, p. xiii.
[5] Ettore Vernazza and Cattaneo Marabotto, the confessor of St
Catherine, edited, about 1530, the *Life* of the saint and her *Treatise on
Purgatory,* in her own words. About 1548, Battista Vernazza composed
the *Dialogues* which were added to the *Life* and the *Treatise on
Purgatory* in 1551. At this period the *Works* of St Catherine of Genoa
were determined. F. von Hügel, *The Mystical Element,* Vol. I.
[6] The dialogues take place between the Soul, the Body, Self-love,
the Spirit, the Natural Man or Humanity and Christ. Usually the
subject of the dialogues is Pure Love.

Pure love is, first of all, that disinterested love with which we are loved by God.

"Know," says the Lord to the soul in the *Dialogues,* "that I am God, unchangeable, and that I loved man before creating him with an infinite and pure and simple love, without any cause : I cannot but love what I have created and destined, each in its degree, to contribute to my glory.[1] . . . My love is pure, simple, and free, and I cannot but love with such love as this."[2]

This pure love is next that purifying love which destroys evil passions and even the smallest imperfections in the converted soul.

"A ray of love was shed in his heart, and this ray was so ardent and penetrating, and pierced him inwardly through so completely, that it took away all loves, appetites, delights, and belongings that he ever had or could have in this world. His soul remained thus deprived of all things . . . it held human nature of no more account than if it had never had part therein ; it esteemed neither the flesh nor the world nor the evil spirit."[3]

The fire of pure love next consumes our imperfections, however small they be. It makes the soul pass through "a purgatory" which purifies the least stains and submits it to a "long martyrdom." "The grindstone of divine love" crushes all that is not itself.[4]

Pure love, again, makes men renounce all consolation, no matter what, either corporal or spiritual. The "spiritual tastes" are as dangerous as the "corporal tastes," if not more so. In the *Dialogues,* the Spirit says to Humanity :

"As for me, I aspire only to pure and naked love which cannot be attached to anything which flatters the taste or the spiritual or corporal senses ; and I declare to thee that I fear much more attachment to the spiritual sense than the corporal. The reason of this is that the spiritual entangles man under the appearance of good, without his being able— unless with the greatest difficulty—to be made to understand that it is quite other than good ; and thus the creature delights in that which proceeds from God. But I say to thee in truth, that he who desires God alone ought of

---

[1] *Dialogues,* Part III, chap. i, Vicomte de Bussière's translation, Paris, 1914, p. 306.

[2] *id.,* Part II, chap. v, p. 285. The same thought is found in the *Spiritual Combat,* chap. lv.

[3] *Dialogues,* Part I, chap. xii, pp. 246-247. See also in the *Œuvres* (Part II, chap. xiii) of St Magdalen dei Pazzi the combat between Divine Love and Sensual Love.

[4] *id.,* pp. 250, 278, 284, 294, 298, 302, 324, 328, etc.

necessity to avoid these things, for they are as poison to Pure Love."[1]

St Philip Neri, who counselled a holy gladness to those whom he directed, would have found such renunciation exaggerated. The *Dialogues,* it is true, expound an extremely high programme of perfection, accessible to a few only. It is, moreover, as we know, the programme of the *Spiritual Combat* and of the greater part of the Italian writers.

" I wish thee, O blessed soul," said Blessed Battista Varani,[2] " to follow my counsels. Thou shouldst serve God not as a slave through fear of temporal punishment or of eternal pain, not as a sinner for a reward, but as a child who renders God love for love, blood for blood, death for death. Such is the short way to sanctity, the hidden but sure way, unseen of men but known and admirable in the eyes of God, to whom all is naked and open."

The *Dialogues* consider that even true friendship is contrary to pure love.

" Nor again do I desire thee," says the Spirit to Humanity, " to contract friendship with anyone nor to retain a special affection for thy parents. I require thee to love each one, poor and rich, friends and neighbours, but without preferences, without human love or attachment. I desire thee not to distinguish one from the other and not to bind thyself to anyone, however religious and spiritual."[3] To act thus is to practise very great renunciation; but pure love, properly understood, certainly does not demand it. Let us note these exaggerations in passing.

The *Dialogues* explain the mystical effects of pure love more correctly.

When it has stripped the soul of all evil passion and all imperfection, love dispossesses it again of itself and of its natural operations.

" After this creature had been stripped of the world, of the flesh, of goods, of exercises, of affections, and of all things —God alone excepted—the Lord desired yet to strip it of itself *unto the division of the soul and spirit* (Heb. iv, 12). This separation is accompanied by very great and most subtle suffering, difficult to express and to understand by one who lacks the knowledge of it by personal experience enlightened by divine light. God poured into her heart a new love so im-

---

[1] *Dialogues,* Part I, chap. xv, p. 253. *Cf.* pp. 251, 258. The *Dialogues* recognize, however, that the soul filled with charity " no longer feels anything but love and jubilation, and thinks itself in paradise " (pp. 283 ff.).

[2] *Acta Sanct.,* May 31, p. 495.

[3] *Dialogues,* Part I, chap. xviii, p. 261.

petuous as to draw unto himself her soul with all its powers,
as though they were removed from her natural being."[1]

Then the powers of the soul are bound : the understanding,
the memory, and the will are submerged " in this sea of divine
love " and drawn " out of the conditions in which the soul
was created."[2]

" Stripped in this way it [the spirit] is naked in God, and
is retained there as long as it pleaseth the Lord, who leaves
it only what is needful for the life of the body."[3]

This " nakedness of the spirit," of which mystics speak so
much, is an effect of love, that " Pure Love which must be
absolutely bare " and admit of nothing else than itself.[4]
When love reaches such purity in the soul the latter is
ineffably united to God.

The sources of this pure love are the Saviour's wounds,
from which, as from " five fountains," flow " drops of burning blood and of fiery love for men."[5] These wounds are
channels which pour forth in us the sweet and precious cordial of love. The true source is the Heart of the Incarnate
Word. Let us hearken to St Magdalen dei Pazzi :

" What is the name of the vessel which contains this sweet
cordial [of love]? It is called the Heart of the Word. Small
though it be, it nevertheless contains it in spite of its abundance, and it yearns to pour it into a still smaller vessel, which
is the heart of the creature. . . . Oh! how right it is that
the Heart of the Word Incarnate was chosen to be the source
of this precious cordial ! From what mountain has there ever
been seen to flow so abundant a source? What fountain
has clearer waters than this most pure love? These waters
are so abundant that they water both heaven and earth."[6]

The conditions for receiving this divine cordial which flows
from the heart of Jesus and for living on it are summed up
by the saint in what she calls " the alphabet of love."[7]

---

[1] *Dialogues,* Part II, chap. i, pp. 273-274.
[2] *ibid.,* p. 275. *Cf.* p. 335.
[3] *id.,* p. 274. *Cf.* pp. 334-335, 337-340.
[4] *id.,* Part I, chap. xiv, p. 251. *Cf.* John of Fano, Capuchin, *Arte della unione con Dio,* Brescia, 1548, and the commentary by Dionysius of Montefalco, Capuchin, *L'Arte d'unirsi a Dio del R. P. F. Giovanni di Fano* . . ., Rome, 1622.
[5] *Dialogues,* Part I, chap. xii, p. 247. *Cf.* St Magdalen dei Pazzi, *Works,* Part III, chap. vii.
[6] *Œuvres,* Part III, chap. xxii, Vol. II, pp. 300-301. Like St Bonaventure, St Magdalen entered into the Heart of Jesus through the doors of his five sacred wounds (*Œuvres,* Part III, chap. vii). She is, as was Battista Varani, an important witness to the ancient tradition of devotion to the Sacred Heart of Jesus.
[7] *Œuvres,* Part IV, chap. i, Vol. II, pp. 132-133 : " A=abounding love. B=good. C=blind (*cieco*). D=Desirous. E=exalted. F=fervent. G=generous. H=humble. I=integral (integrity in). L=luminous.

This alphabet must be known in order to possess the love of God.

Among these conditions one of the chief is devotion to our neighbour. Has not divine love God and our neighbour as its object? Moreover the members of the society of the *Amore divino* were strongly urged to relieve some of the wretchedness of the time. These miseries were immense on account of the wars and political troubles which disturbed Italy. We may well call to mind the horrors resulting from the sack of Rome in 1527, when on all sides were seen the sick without care, orphans abandoned, and youth left in ignorance and depraved morals. It was with a view to assisting so many unfortunates that there were founded the hospitals, orphanages, schools, and many other charitable institutions at that time.

The *Oratorio del divino Amore* recruited within it the servants of the sick.[1] Ettore Vernazza, its founder, was also the initiator of this great movement of charity, which caused hospitals to be raised in divers parts of Italy, and provided them with kindly and devoted nurses. Indeed, we may ask whether we truly love God if we refrain from succouring the sick when we can.

"Thou wilt do all that I shall urge on thee," says the Spirit to Human nature in the *Dialogues;*[2] "thus thou wilt cleanse the sick and, if asked to do this even when speaking to God, thou wilt leave everything and promptly go to whoever asks thy help and wherever thou art led. Nor wilt thou consider either who it is that calls thee or the work thou hast to do."

The care of the sick occasionally calls for very great renunciation.

"There were to be found at that time beings full of all kinds of filth, covered with vermin, and whose stench was all

---

M = mortified. N = negative. O = easeful—that is, not occupied with self but with God. P = pitiful (sympathetic). Q = plaintive (*queritante*) as a bride unable to bear the absence of her husband. R = red with the Blood of the Word. S = safe and silly; wise in choice and foolish in ecstasy. T = threefold—*i.e.*, love of God, one's neighbour, and oneself. V = vehement. Z = zealous. RU = ruminant, that is thinking only of the well-beloved. The whole of this alphabet should be known by him who desires to possess love."

[1] Almost all the holy persons of Italy in the sixteenth century, from St Cajetan to St Camillus de Lellis, served in the hospitals. St Philip Neri nursed the sick in the hospitals of Rome (Capecelatro, I, chap. iv). "An ardent charity in the service of the sick," he said, "is a short way to attain perfect virtue." Bayle, p. 405.

[2] *Dialogues de St Catherine de Gênes,* Part I, chap. xviii, p. 260.

but unbearable : some of the sick gave utterance to terrible words of despair because of the dreadful misery and affliction in which they were. Thus, entering such places seemed like going into tombs, which horrifies everyone.''[1]

In order to overcome this natural repugnance, divine love may suggest putting the vermin and filth of the sick into one's mouth, as several saints did.[2]

Charity towards the suffering was to carry impartiality to the finest point. To shun the gratitude of the sick is a condition of true love. The *Dialogues,* which seem to analyse the souls of the great servants of the poor sick at that time, remark that '' sometimes . . . sick folk are to be met with who, besides their filth and their stench, were always crying out, complaining of those who served them and insulting them.''[3] Nature suffers from this, but true charity does not let itself be repelled by anything. In this connection let us call to mind the charming lesson which Bernadino da Feltre († 1494), that great friend of the poor and unfortunate, gave one day to the sick and to the nurses of a hospital :

'' In the book of the sick,'' he said, '' should be written : *Patience, patience, patience,* and in that of those who help them : *Charity, charity, charity.* But each should rest content with reading his own book and not look at the contents of the other, for in the midst of the thousand little incidents brought about by human weakness, if one ask of the other : where is your charity? he endangers his patience, and if the other replies : where is your patience, he endangers his charity. Let us not be like the schoolboy who, instead of learning his lesson in his own book, curiously peeps into his neighbour's ; this boy will not be able to answer his master's question, and will be punished.''[4]

Divine love often prompted generous persons to live in the hospitals to render service and to consecrate their lives to the relief of the sick. The *Dialogues* thus explain this form of heroic charity :

'' In proportion as it [humanity] had lost the habit of self-love, it had acquired the possession of pure and simple love, which had made it more and more humble, by entering and dwelling therein. Thus this soul, burning with love, was consumed in the divine fire, and as the fire constantly

---

[1] *Dialogues,* p. 262.
[2] *ibid.,* p. 265. In the *Dialogues,* divine love prompts human nature to eat the vermin of the sick in order to conquer its repugnance.
[3] *Dialogues,* art. I, chap. xix, p. 262.
[4] E. Flornoy, *Le Bienheureux Bernadin de Feltre,* Paris, 1897, p. 70. Blessed Bernardino da Feltre, Friar Minor and famous preached, was the organizer and defender of the pawnshops in Italy in the fifteenth century. He thus fought successfully against usury. *Cf.* Ludovic de Besse, *Le Bienheureux Bernadin de Feltre et son Œuvre,* 2 vols., Paris, 1902.

increased, it was consumed more and more. This is why it performed its [hospital] service with great speed and never rested, in order to get relief from the fire that beset it daily more and more."[1]

Is it not a love such as this which impelled St Camillus de Lellis and many others to care for the sick with as much delight as they would have tended Christ himself?[2] It was divine love again which suggested to St Jerome Emiliani the thought of founding an institute of Clerks Regular to take up the education of orphans. What unseen, incessant, and untiring devotion is needed to instruct these abandoned children and train them in habits of Christian virtue![3] It is a work of love, and without love cannot succeed.

In this connection St Angela Merici said to her Sisters :

"You will be affable and kindly towards your daughters. You will have no other motive regarding them than the love of God and zeal for souls, whether you warn them, give them counsel, exhort them to piety, or strive to make them avoid evil. . . . It is charity which leads all to honour God and to help souls; it is that which will teach you discretion and discernment. From charity alone is learnt how to be sometimes indulgent, at others severe, according to circumstances.[4]. . ."

[1] *Dialogues,* Part I, chap. xxi, p. 268.

[2] St Camillus de Lellis (†1614) contemplated Jesus so perfectly in the poor that he asked them for grace and forgiveness of his sins, behaving himself in their presence with the same respect as though really in the presence of God.

[3] See the *Life* of St Jerome Emilian, by Augustine Turtura, lib. III, cap. vii, in the *Acta Sanct.*, February 8.

[4] *Souvenirs et avis,* 2e Avis, *Sainte Angèle Merici et l'Ordre des Ursulines,* Paris, 1922, Vol. I, p. 413. In her *Testament,* St Angela required of the Mothers who were to rule the Ursulines after her, that "their sole motive in the government of the Company must be the love of God and zeal for the salvation of souls," p. 420.

CHAPTER XI

SAINT FRANCIS DE SALES—DIRECTOR OF THOSE IN
THE WORLD—FOUNDER OF AN ORDER—MYSTIC

ST FRANCIS DE SALES forms a school of spirituality by himself alone. He is its beginning, its development, its sum-total.[1]

In the ordinary way the founder of a school conceives some new idea, suggests its principles : then the disciples draw consequences from it and formulate the teaching with exactitude. This is a work which becomes developed in a religious family or in a nation. Thus it was with St Benedict, St Francis of Assisi, Bérulle. The disciples of St Francis de Sales are legion. None of them seem to have added anything of importance to the thought of the master.[2] All they have done is to repeat; they think themselves happy if they are able to imitate and reproduce.

Few writers are so subjective. In this way he may be compared to St Augustine, to St Bernard, to St Thomas Aquinas, or to St Teresa.

Not that he was self-centred or over didactic. He studied the writers who came before him and was affected by their influence. He owed much to the Spanish School, to John of Avila, to Luis of Granada, and above all to St Teresa. The Italian School, several representatives of which had become known to him in his studies, deeply influenced him. Was not the *Combatimento spirituale* his bedside book for more than sixteen years?[3] But he made their teaching so thoroughly his own; presented it in a light so peculiar to

---

[1] See the first three *Lives* of St Francis de Sales, by Father de la Rivière, John de Saint-François, and Charles-Auguste de Sales. More recent *Lives* are by Hamon (revised by Gonthier and Letourneau) and A. de Margerie. Books on St Francis de Sales are innumerable, and I shall only mention those of which I make use.

[2] St Chantal is an admirable witness to the life, the spirit, and the teachings of St Francis de Sales. It does not appear that she has added anything of her own either to the Salesian spirit or to Salesian spirituality. The same must be said of Pierre Camus, Bishop of Belley, the author of *L'Esprit du bienheureux François de Sales* (1639-1641). Some critics doubt whether it always reflects the " true " spirit of the Bishop of Geneva. *Cf*. De Baudry, *Le véritable esprit du Saint François de Sales*, Lyons-Paris, 1846. According to this writer, the work by Camus " does not always show with accuracy the spirit and teaching of the saintly Bishop of Geneva," a somewhat severe judgement. *Cf*. Henri Bremond, *Hist. du sent. relig.*, I, pp. 149 ff., 273 ff.

[3] *Œuvres de Saint François de Sales,* complete edition, Annecy, Vol. I, chap. xliii, pp. 189 ff. This edition is always quoted.

himself, with infinite shades; he adapted it so thoroughly to the thousand needs of human nature, dealing with every sort of temperament you will, that we might think that it was all his own work. For it is not exactly his teaching which makes St Francis de Sales original. What he said had been stated or perceived before him; yet never had it been said as he could say it. That which characterizes a spiritual writer is less what he teaches—which must of necessity be traditional doctrine —than the way he teaches it, the spirit which animates him. Now in St Francis de Sales this way is very special; in fact, unique. " The flower-girl Glycera " was clever enough to make " a great number of nosegays " with the same flowers. St Francis de Sales was also able to present " the lessons of devotion," in a new way :

" I am indeed unable," he writes in the Preface to the *Introduction to the Devout Life,* " nor do I wish, nor ought I in this *Introduction* to write what has formerly been made known on this subject by our predecessors; they are the same flowers, dear reader, which I offer thee, but the nosegay which I make of them will be different from theirs because of the variety of its arrangement."[1]

It is then, above all, the knowledge of the temperament of the Bishop of Geneva, of the nature of his soul, of the charm of his spirit, which the characteristics of his spirituality reveal.

I—THE SALESIAN SOUL—SALESIAN SPIRITUALITY

GOODNESS, gentleness, tenderness—but not exclusively indeed—form the groundwork of St Francis de Sales' nature. Though gentle and peaceful, he could be firm in directing, and was able to rule, knowing what he wanted and how to obtain it. But he must have made an effort in order to become so. St Charles Borromeo was naturally a man of authority, impatient of opposition. St Francis de Sales was by temperament inclined to conciliation, to compliance, disposed to yield, given to looking on men with kindliness, indulgent to their faults, skilful in discovering their better side, compassionate with them in their wretchedness. In order to remain at all times thus kindly to all, he struggled all his life against a keen temptation to impatience to which intercourse with men exposes even the most gentle. He overcame it so completely that his intimate friends reproached him with being too easy-going.

His kindness sprang from a sensitive heart, easily moved to pity :

[1] *Œuvres,* Vol. III, pp. 5-6.

" Have we not a human heart and a sensitive nature?" he wrote to the Baroness de Chantal, who grieved for the death of her youngest daughter. " Why not weep a little over our dead, since the Spirit of God not only permits but invites it?"[1]

He himself wept over the death of his sister Jeanne de Sales: " Alas ! my daughter," he wrote to Mme de Chantal, " I am but a man and nothing more. My heart is saddened more than I could ever have thought; but the truth is that my mother's and your distress have both greatly contributed towards it, for I feared for your heart and that of my mother. But for the rest, praise be to Jesus ! I shall ever be on the side of divine Providence, which does all things well and orders all for the best."[2]

In giving an account of the last moments of his mother to the Baroness de Chantal, he said :

" I had the courage to give her the last blessing, to close her eyes and mouth, and to give her the last kiss of peace at the moment she passed away; after which my heart swelled, and I wept over this good mother more than I have done since I was ordained; but it was without spiritual bitterness, thanks be to God."[3]

But this exquisite sensitiveness was always moderated by a very perfect piety. He loved to tenderness, but this love was always supernatural. Let us not think of St Francis de Sales as simply a sentimentalist ! This is how he himself speaks of his heart in a letter to St Chantal :

" I believe that there are no souls in the world who cherish feelings more cordial, tender, and, saying it in all good faith, more loving than mine : for it has pleased God so to fashion my heart. But, nevertheless, I love souls that are independent, strong, and not effeminate ; for this great tenderness confuses the heart, disquiets and distracts it from loving prayer to God, and preve/.s entire resignation and the total extinction of self-love. Hŏw does it come about that I feel such things, I, who am the most tender-hearted man in the world, as you, most dear mother, know? In truth, however, I do feel them; but it is a marvel how I make all this fit together, for it is in my mind to love nothing at all but God and all souls for God."[4]

To these gifts of heart there were added remarkable social qualities. St Francis de Sales, in a home full of affection, received the upbringing fitted for a nobleman, which rendered yet more perfect the happy disposition of his nature. A man of the world like few others, he was exceedingly fascinating. The charm of his society was of special service in the work of directing souls. He knew how to be attractive, and was so without effort, quite naturally. Nor did his noble manners

---

[1] *Œuvres,* XIV, p. 264.   [2] *id.,* XII, p. 330.
[3] *id.,* XIV, p. 262.   [4] *id.,* Vol. XX, p. 216.

ruffle in the least any of those who came in touch with
him :

"The manner and speech of this blessed one," said St
Chantal, "were full of majesty and dignity, yet always the
most humble, the most gentle, the most simple that I have
ever met . . . he spoke in a low voice, gravely, sedately,
and wisely."[1] St Francis de Sales carried this attractiveness everywhere : in his person, in his dealings with others,
in his piety, and in his direction. He is identified with
lovable devotion :

"I in no way desire," he wrote to one of his penitents,[2]
"a fantastic, meddlesome, melancholy, vexatious, gloomy
devotion; but one that is mild, gentle, agreeable, peaceful—
in a word, one that is a wholly sincere piety which first loves
God and then men."

Italian spirituality gave zest to this natural inclination to
put that which is beautiful, touching, captivating in
Christian virtue in high relief. It taught our saint how the
devout soul may be inwardly mortified—and that to the
highest degree—without allowing this deep-rooted austerity
to appear outwardly; and this teaching he himself gives, in a
masterly manner, in each page of the *Introduction to the
Devout Life* and in his letters of direction. He thus knew
how to "humanize" virtue "in its environment,"[3] to make
it beloved by the world, and to place it within reach of all.

Humanism achieved what education had begun. The
natural gifts of St Francis de Sales were refined by the
Humaniores litterae which the Jesuits taught him in their
college of Clermont and in Paris, and afterwards at Padua.
Humanism, even that of Maldonatus and Possevin,[4] could
not alone produce the Salesian spirit. So perfect was its
affinity therewith, however, that at least it led to its complete development. It also contributed to the formation of
that inimitable style, "richly adorned, well finished, at times
euphuistic, as proper to the period, always courtly,"[5] which
caused devotion to be so much beloved.

Finally, let us not forget the great influence which the
Savoy landscape had on St Francis de Sales' imagination.
He himself declared that he discovered one of the sources of
his inspiration in that delightful country. One day, "on the

[1] *Œuvres de sainte Chantal,* II, pp. 221, 222.
[2] Mme. de Limojon, *Œuvres,* Vol. XIII, p. 59.
[3] F. Vincent, *Saint François de Sales, directeur d'âmes,* Paris, 1923,
p. 18.
[4] The Jesuits Maldonatus and Possevin taught first at Paris, at the
College of Clermont, and afterwards at Padua.
[5] F. Vincent, p. 19. With reference to this pictorial or intimate style,
which "touches the heart deeply," see Mgr. Lavallée, *Le réalisme de
St François de Sales,* in *La Documentation catholique,* March 10, 1923,
pp. 579 ff.

little plateau of St Germain," he marvelled at beautiful nature, above all at the azure sheet of the lake of Annecy which, surrounded by high and picturesque mountains, spread out at his feet.

" O God," he exclaimed, " how we desire never to leave this place ! Here is just the retreat for the right service of God and his Church with our pen." And, addressing the Prior of the Abbey of Talloires who was with him : " Do you know, Father Prior, that thoughts would pour down here as thick and fast as the winter snows."[1]

From the castle of Allinges, during the Chablais mission, he very often contemplated that emerald sea, Lake Leman. He loved nature and flowers and living creatures. He had in his heart something of St Francis of Assisi's love for animals. Hence, he liked to find rustic comparisons.[2] But he had no time to study the properties of plants or the habits of beasts for himself. He obtained them from the old naturalists and from the bestiaries of the Middle Ages. His flora and fauna are very largely book lore. Having become obsolete they have, therefore, slightly marred his style.

To this human side of the Salesian spirit must be added sanctity, sanctity of high degree. Grace does not destroy nature, it perfects it. St Francis de Sales is a startling proof of this. His natural gifts of goodness and gentleness received from divine love their final perfection. An heroic mortification, though hidden beneath an outward charm, set aside without pity any obstacle that might hinder, ever so little, the predominance of divine charity in his soul that was made for love. The gifts of grace are combined with those of nature to make St Francis de Sales one of the most perfect and most attractive of all the saints.

Salesian spirituality could not be other than optimistic; it is its dominant, though not its only, note.[3] For optimism, when not held within proper bounds, leads to error.

[1] De la Rivière, *Vie de l'Illustrissime et Reverendissime François de Sales*, Book III, chap. xviii (*Œuvres*, I, p. xxxv).
[2] His idea of the world is very like that of Hugh of St Victor. In his *Lettre sur la prédication* addressed to the Archbishop of Bourges, October 5, 1604, we read : " The world made by the Word of God everywhere reflects this Word; every part sings the praises of the Workman. It is a book which contains the Word of God, but in a language which all do not understand. Those who understand it by meditation do most well to use it, as did St Antony, who had no other library. And St Paul says : *Invisibilia Dei per ea quae facta sunt intellecta conspiciuntur;* and David : *Caeli enarrant gloriam Dei.* This book is good for similitudes, comparisons *a minori ad majus,* and for a thousand other things " (XII, p. 307).
[3] *Cf.* Henri Bremond, *Histoire du sentiment religieux,* I, pp. 104-127. F. Vincent, pp. 25-98.

St Francis de Sales wishes us to fear God, but lovingly.[1]
Yet it is love far more often than fear that flows from his
pen. His spirituality, like that of St Augustine, is summed
up in love. It views the Christian life from its inward principle, which is that of charity. All is reduced to this charity
and is explained by it. God is, above everything, a good
and merciful Father, who loves man beyond anything we can
conceive. If he deals with sin, no doubt it is to punish it,
but this again is because it frustrates his loving designs
towards man.

In the same way Salesian spirituality considers human
nature not so much in its original fall as in its restoration
through Christ. It does not display the wounds of fallen
man, but rather shows them dressed and healed by the
Redeemer. Restored humanity appears to it, to some extent,
returned to its state of innocence. It is not a contami-
nated thing which cannot be touched without our becoming
soiled. It is, in spite of its wretchedness, an image of divine
perfection. St Francis de Sales has nothing of the pessimism
of St Augustine.

Nevertheless he was Augustinian from other points of
view:[2] first of all, in his spirituality of love, as we have
just said; and then, like St Augustine, he sets in relief the
work of grace in our sanctification. Not that he restricts
the power of the will, as Camus,[3] Bishop of Belley, would
seem to have us believe. He does not dream of this:

"What is as wonderful as it is true," he said in his
Treatise on the Love of God, "is that when our will follows
its attraction and gives consent to the divine impulse,
it follows it just as freely as, when it resists it, it freely
resists, although the consenting to grace depends much more
on grace than on the will, whereas resistance to grace
depends wholly on the will; so loving is the hand of God in
the handling of our heart, so adroitly also does it communicate its strength to us without taking away our liberty."[4]

Salesian thought is perfectly precise and safeguards our
free will. But, nevertheless, it takes delight in describing
divine love and heavenly allurements, which urge on the will
towards the way of sanctity. On this point it is more Augustinian and Thomist than Ignatian.

[1] "Let us have no fear but of God, and let that too be a loving
fear" (Vol. XIII, 300).

[2] He had a particular affection for the Bishop of Hippo. He spoke
of him as "the great St Augustine."

[3] *Esprit de S. Fr. de S.,* Part III, section 2. *Cf.* De Baudry, *op.
cit.,* Vol. IV, pp. 109 ff.

[4] *Treatise on the Love of God,* Book II, chap. xii, *Œuvres,* IV, 127.
We would note that the famous letter of St Francis de Sales to Lessius
only speaks of predestination *post praevisa merita,* a more humane
doctrine to which the young Francis de Sales came round after his
temptation to despair. Lessius will be dealt with in the next volume.

Salesian spirituality, like that of St Bernard, is very affective. It ever intermingles pious upliftings and ejaculations with doctrinal thought. The loving soul of the Bishop of Geneva cannot be retained by pure speculation; heavenly charity bears it quickly away to God. It has even been said that the *Treatise on the Love of God* was as much a collection of prayers and meditations as a work of mystical theology.

St Francis de Sales is before all things a man of action. He wrote only when the interests of his ministry demanded it. "I write only by chance and in emergency," he says in his Preface to the *Treatise on the Love of God*. Providential events, indeed, led him to take up his pen. It may be said of him that he lived his books before composing them, like the monastic lawgivers who themselves followed and made others follow their rules long before prescribing them.

The *Introduction to the Devout Life* is an "enlightening revelation" of the religious experiences of its author and of those whom he directed. St Francis de Sales shows himself therein to be a most zealous and experienced director of souls. When he wrote it, between the Lent of 1607 and the summer of 1608, his ministry had brought him, above all, in touch with people in the world:

"My intention is to instruct those persons in the world who very often, under colour of an alleged impossibility, are not willing even to think of undertaking the devout life, because they are of opinion that, just as no beast dare taste the herb called *palma Christi,* so no one ought to aspire to the palm of Christian piety whilst living in the midst of the press of worldly occupations."

Yet he himself was persuaded that "a vigorous and constant soul can live in the world without receiving any worldly taint, can find springs of sweet piety in the midst of the briny waters of the world, and can fly among the flames of earthly concupiscences without burning the wings of the holy desires of the devout life."[1]

This "vigorous and constant soul" was Mme de Charmoisy. Ever since he knew her, about 1607, the Bishop of Geneva had progressively given her "teachings meant to lead her to the Promised Land of true devotion." These are the *Advice,* the *Exercises,* the *Spiritual Memoirs* spoken of by the saint in his *Letters.*[2] These, with necessary additions and the "grouping" proper to a work, form the *Introduction,* the first edition of which appeared in 1609.

[1] *Devout Life,* Preface, *Œuvres,* III [English translation, Allan Ross (B.O.W.)].
[2] Preface by Dom Mackay, III, xiii-xv.

Next year St Francis de Sales founded the Order of the Visitation. He became director to the nuns. He gave spiritual conferences to the first Visitandines in order to instruct them in true perfection.[1] After having taught people in the world how to practise devotion he now had to explain the duties of the religious life. The teaching of his *Spiritual Conferences* is necessarily more elevated than that of the *Introduction.* The holy founder does not limit himself to the principles of asceticism; at times he rises to the most lofty teaching.[2]

Nevertheless, in the midst of all his preoccupations, St Francis de Sales nourished the thought of writing a treatise on the love of God. This project was even in his mind before bringing out the *Devout Life.* Divine love wholly dominated his life. His direction had no other end than to make this love permeate souls and grow in them. He wrote, on February 5, 1610, to Mme de Chantal:

"I am about to put my hand to the book on *The Love of God,* and I shall endeavour to write it as much on my heart as on the paper."[3]

At first he had no intention of writing a treatise on mystical theology. But in instructing and directing the first Visitandines and especially Mother de Chantal, he soon witnessed the extraordinary work of the Holy Spirit in them. He had to adapt his spiritual teaching to the needs of these souls, thus raised to the mystical state.[4] This led him to modify his first idea:

"I proposed to write on holy love," he says in the Preface to the *Treatise on the Love of God,* "for some time, but this project was in no way comparable to what this occasion has led me to produce."[5]

The Daughters of the Visitation, and especially their foundress, thus in their way collaborated in the composition of the book. They also urged their blessed Father to hasten it. And he devoted every moment he was able to "tear from the pressure" of his other duties. The work appeared in 1616.

[1] Cf. *Œuvres,* VI, pp. 8-9: "Our holy Founder," writes St Chantal, "often visits us, hears our confessions every fortnight, and gives us little spiritual conferences, in order to instruct us in true perfection."

[2] *Treatise on the Love of God,* Preface: "And as their purity and piety of mind [the Visitandines] has often given me great consolation, so also have I endeavoured to repay this to them frequently by the distribution of the holy word . . . it was often necessary to deal with the most delicate feelings of piety, passing beyond what I had said to Philothea." *Œuvres,* IV, p. 20.

[3] *Œuvres,* XIV, p. 247.

[4] *Treatise on the Love of God,* Preface: "And a great deal of what I now communicate to you I owe to this blessed assembly," wrote St Francis de Sales. *Œuvres,* IV, 20.

[5] *Œuvres,* IV, 21.

If it be possible to condense such great spiritual riches into phrases which are ever insufficient, and to confine so overflowing a spiritual life within limits that are of necessity too narrow, we would distinguish three stages in the historical development of Salesian spirituality : (1) the direction of people in the world; (2) the founding of the Visitandines; and (3) the elaboration of the mysticism of divine love. The *Introduction to the Devout Life,* the *True Spiritual Conferences,* and the *Treatise on the Love of God* mark these several stages.[1]

II—DIRECTION OF PEOPLE IN THE WORLD—THE "INTRODUCTION TO THE DEVOUT LIFE"[2]

IF we would understand the spirituality of the *Introduction* we must constantly recall to ourselves the end proposed by its author.

In the sixteenth century many spiritual directors believed that perfection was impossible outside the cloister. If those in the world wished to aspire to it, they required them to live, as nearly as was possible, the contemplative life. Hence, that prejudice, "the so-called impossibility," against which the Bishop of Geneva protested with such energy, of being able to unite the devout life with the "business of the world." Spiritual writers, instead of reacting against this prejudice, scarcely ever wrote for any but those much withdrawn from temporal affairs, or else they taught "a kind of devotion which led to such entire withdrawal." St Francis de Sales' intention, on the contrary, was "to instruct those who live in towns, in households, and at Court, whose circumstances oblige them to lead *outwardly* an ordinary life."[3]

He teaches them that devotion is, above all, inward, "it is the perfection of charity." It is acquired by the spirit of prayer, even more than by the multiplicity of exercises. Pious exercises, however, are needful. They are recommended almost as much as to the religious, but they must always be subordinated to the entire and joyful fulfilment of the duties of one's calling.

---

[1] The *Letters* must be added, which are a necessary complement to these three works.

[2] The first edition was finished in August, 1608, and appeared in 1609 (*Editio princeps*). The final edition was dated 1619. It is this latter which Dom Mackay gives in Vol. III of the *Works of St Francis de Sales,* Annecy, 1893. The first edition is added in an Appendix to this same volume.

[3] *Devout Life,* Preface. *Cf.* Part I, chap. iii : "It is an error, nay, rather a heresy, to wish to banish the devout life from the army, from the workshop, from the courts of princes, from the households of married folk" (Allan Ross). I quote from the edition of 1619, according to Dom Mackay's rendering.

For "the practice of devotion must be accommodated to the strength, to the affairs, and to the duties of each individually. . . . Devotion when it is true never spoils anything, but rather perfects all things, and when it becomes inconsistent with the lawful vocation of anyone it is certainly false."[1]

That mortification which is necessary for becoming truly devout must also be almost exclusively inward.[2] It must consist in that kind of death to self which destroys all affection for sin, however slight. The virtues which we ought chiefly to practise should be those pertaining to intercourse with others, in order best to fulfil the obligations imposed on us in our dealings with the world, and also to render devotion beloved. Besides, ought not he who is devout to be a thorough man, possessing as much as possible all natural qualities as well as Christian virtues? In this way the most solid virtue will become reconciled with the life of intercourse and with the affairs of those in the world. It was thus that St Francis de Sales' Philothea was to act.

We may assume that the Italian School, which so accentuated inward piety, aided the author of the *Devout Life* in forming this most clear and practical idea of devotion.

A—Definition of Devotion—Direction—The Purification of the Soul

If in fact we compare the idea of Christian perfection given by the *Spiritual Combat* with the "description of true devotion" at the beginning of the *Devout Life,* we are struck by their resemblance.

According to the Italian author perfection consists in the love of God. "Outward works are but the means of acquiring sanctity; but it cannot be said that they constitute Christian perfection."[3] St Francis de Sales completes this idea with Luis of Granada's conception of devotion. According to the famous Spanish Dominican, who, moreover, was inspired by St Thomas Aquinas, devotion is nothing else than "the readiness and ardour with which we tend to do good, to observe the commandments, and to serve God in all things."[4] The Bishop of Geneva gives exact expression to these thoughts, adapts them to his end, and reclothes them with the grace of his style :

[1] *Devout Life,* Part I, chap. iii.

[2] Cf. *id.,* Part III, chap. xxiii : "For my part, Philothea, I have never been able to approve of the method of those who, to reform a man, begin with the exterior. . . . On the contrary, it seems to me that we must begin with the interior."

[3] *Spiritual Combat,* chap. i.

[4] Luis of Granada, *Treatise on Prayer and Meditation,* Part II, chap. i.

"True and living devotion, Philothea, presupposes the love of God; nay, rather it is no other thing than a true love of God; yet not any kind of love; for, in so far as divine love beautifies our souls and makes us pleasing to his divine Majesty, it is called grace; in so far as it gives us strength to do good, it is called charity; but when it reaches such a degree of perfection that it makes us not only do good, but do so carefully, frequently, and readily, then it is called devotion. Ostriches never fly; fowls fly, but heavily, low down and seldom; but eagles, doves, and swallows fly often, swiftly, and on high. In like manner sinners fly not to God . . . good persons who have not reached devotion, fly towards God by their good deeds, but rarely, slowly, and heavily; devout persons fly towards God frequently, readily, and on high."[1]

This active charity is not limited to the mere observance of God's commandments, but "it urges us on to do promptly and lovingly as many good works as we can, even though they be in no way commanded, but only counselled or inspired."

St Francis de Sales does not content himself with giving "an air of novelty" to that teaching which his "predecessors" gave regarding devotion. He is often most individual, and is not afraid, when he thinks good, to accentuate certain principles of traditional asceticism. His teaching on direction is, in this connection, particularly noteworthy.[2]

Before the *Introduction to the Devout Life,* the universal need for direction had not been so definitely stated.[3] Nor was there anywhere to be found so complete a teaching regarding it.

In every age, as we know, spiritual direction has been recommended. It was always practised in monasteries. We have heard how John of Avila and St Teresa counselled it to

---

[1] *Devout Life,* Part I, chap. i. St Francis de Sales multiplies comparisons in order to describe devotion : " Charity and devotion are no more different from one another than is the flame from the fire . . . devotion adds nothing to the fire of charity, except the flame which renders charity prompt, active, and diligent " (chap. i). " If charity be a milk, devotion is a cream; if it be a plant, devotion is its flower; if it be a precious ointment, devotion is the odour of it " (chap. ii).

[2] Respecting Salesian direction, see Part IV of that fine book by F. Vincent : *St François de Sales, directeur d'âmes,* pp. 397-547.

[3] The Baroness de Chantal said after she had met St Francis de Sales : " Although I was brought up by virtuous people, and I never had other than becoming conversations with them, nevertheless I have never heard a director or spiritual master speak in a manner in any way approaching his." Mère de Chaugy, *Sainte Jeanne de Chantal, sa vie et ses Œuvres,* Paris, 1893, p. 38.

those who wished to advance without hindrance in the spiritual way. St Ignatius of Loyola places those in retreat under the strict control of the one who is giving the *Exercises*. And his disciples have extended, even beyond the period devoted to the pious exercises, their role of counsellors to the faithful. St Philip Neri, in Italy, directed a great number of priests and layfolk, and his direction was much appreciated. But nobody so far seems to have spoken out so strongly as to " the necessity of a guide in order to enter into, and to make progress in, devotion," a necessity for all, and one which appears to admit of no exception : " It is," says St Francis de Sales, " the admonition of admonitions."[1]

Do we see, in this strictness, a wish to react against the theories of individual inspiration, Protestant and Christian humanist?[2] Perhaps. But St Francis was not in the habit of going further than what was in his mind, even when reacting. His teaching on the universal necessity for direction is the result of reflection and experience :

" One thing is very certain," he said to his nuns of the Visitation; " it is that all are not led by the same road [in the spiritual life]; but again it is not for each one of us to know by which road God calls us. This belongs to Superiors, who have the light of God for this. It must not be said of them that they do not know us well, for we ought to think that obedience and submission are always the true marks of good inspiration."[3]

No one, in fact, is a good judge in his own case. We nearly always deceive ourselves, whether it be with regard to the sickness of our bodies or of our souls. And this in spite of the knowledge which we may possess :

" Why, then," said our saint, " should we be masters of ourselves in that which concerns the spirit, since we are not so in that which has to do with the body? Do we not know that doctors, when they are ill, send for other doctors to decide as to the remedies they need? In the same way that advocates do not plead their own cause, so also is reason likely to be led astray by self-love."[4]

Moreover, direction ought not to hamper the action of the Holy Spirit in the one directed, but to facilitate it and be

[1] *Devout Life*, Part I, chap. iv.
[2] The saint seems to allude to these theories in the *Twelfth Spiritual Conference:* " There are souls," he says, " who, from what they say, desire only to be led by the spirit of God, and it seems to such that everything that they imagine comes from the inspiration and movement of the Holy Spirit, who takes them by the hand and guides them in all that they wish to do, like children; in this they are greatly deceived." Vol. VI, 214.
[3] *Spiritual Colloquy*, XII, Vol. VI, p. 215.
[4] *Sermon for the Feast of our Lady of the Snow*, Vol. IX, p. 95.

regulated thereby. It guides the soul, adapts itself to its temperament, without checking it.[1] St Francis de Sales knew wonderfully well how to use this method. But in no part of his writings does he put forward a theory of direction in general. He addresses himself to his penitents and instructs them in their duties as penitents. It is not his purpose to give instruction to directors.

The attitude towards her director which he suggests to Philothea is at the same time traditional and yet new.

The spiritual guide was looked upon by the ancients as, above all, the representative of God. St John Climacus, in this connection, relates the beautiful words of a monk who was ever ready to obey. When he was asked the secret of his obedience he answered: "I see Jesus Christ in the person of my superior; and so I do not look upon the order given me as coming from man, but as coming from God."[2] In the same way St Francis de Sales, with a slightly more human touch, declares:

"When you have found him [your guide] do not look on him as a mere man nor trust in him as such nor in his human knowledge, but in God who will favour you and speak to you by means of this man, putting into his heart and into his mouth whatever shall be requisite for your happiness, so that you ought to listen to him as to an angel who comes down from heaven to conduct you thither."[3]

Regarded thus, the director inspires a wholly supernatural respect and confidence. But the opening of the heart of the penitent is not necessarily made easy by it. In order to render this more easy St Francis de Sales counsels our looking on the director also as a "faithful friend." Between himself and his penitents there should exist a strong and tender "friendship . . . wholly spiritual, sacred, holy, and divine." Let us note this accumulation of epithets; because, if this friendship become too humanized, most regrettable consequences might result from it for both director and directed. It is wonderful to see how St Francis de Sales, whose direction is affective, who had "the gift of making himself beloved"[4] maintained, without ever failing, his heart and that of his Philothea in the sure sphere of an affection purely for God. He knew how to give infinite shades to this mingling of respect and affection, which enables the penitent to deal with his director without discomfort and yet "with an open heart, in full sincerity and faithfulness."

"Have the greatest confidence in him," he advises,

---

[1] M. François Vincent has clearly shown that the direction of St Francis de Sales possesses all these qualities. *Op. cit.,* chaps. vii-viii.

[2] *The Spiritual Ladder,* IVth Degree, obedience.

[3] *Devout Life,* Part I, chap. iv.

[4] *Cf.* F. Vincent, pp. 481-515.

" mingled with a holy reverence, yet so that the reverence
diminish not your confidence nor your confidence hinder in
any way your reverence; confide in him with the respect of a
daughter for her father, and respect him with the confidence
of a son in his mother."[1]

Thus understood, direction calls for very high qualifica-
tions in the director. " He must be full of charity, of knowledge, and of prudence; if one of these three qualities be
wanting in him, there is danger." St Francis de Sales
even goes so far as to say, " there are fewer than can be
imagined that are fitted for this office." A severe indict-
ment, though perhaps true, of the clergy of those days, or
maybe, it shows an extraordinarily high conception of the role
of director. It is by prayer, above all, that Philothea will
obtain this rare guide. If she pray " with great earnestness "
God will hear her, " even though he should have to send
an angel from Heaven, as he did to the young Tobias."[2]

In order to reach perfection, " the first purgation which
must be made is that of sin," the second is that of " affections, which are connected with sin."

The exercises which St Francis de Sales recommends in
order to become purified from mortal sin by meditation on
the last ends and a general confession, are borrowed from
St Ignatius. The " solemn protestation, to engrave on the
soul the resolution to serve God and to conclude the acts
of penance," also seems to be an adaptation from the election
of St Ignatius.

The " second purgation," that of affection for sin,
occupies a very important place in the Introduction to the
Devout Life. Without this complete renunciation of all
attachment to sin, there can, in fact, be no true conversion
nor impulse towards perfection. Nay, more, Philothea was
called to live in the world, in the midst of dangerous occasions. She must needs then detest with " a powerful and
vigorous contrition " not only sin but also " all affection
for it and all that springs from or leads to it."[3] Like
" the pirastes which fly in the flames without burning their
wings," she also will be able to " fly among the flames of
earthly concupiscences without burning the wings of the
holy desires of the devout life."

This is why this " purgation " of the soul can never be
pushed too far. It must be extended to " all affection " for
deliberate venial sin, and even to all attachment to dangerous
things which are not evil in themselves but which expose us
to the danger of offending God, such as " games, balls,

[1] Devout Life, Part I, chap. iv.   [2] ibid.
[3] ibid., Part I, chap. viii.

feasts, pageants, and plays." Philothea should never be
attached to them. If occasionally obliged to mingle in them,
it should be but rarely and of necessity, never from love or
inclination.[1] Finally, true devotion should never tolerate
" defects and shortcomings " which spring from our character
and temperament. These are not sins, properly so called,
for usually the will has no part in them. Nevertheless, we
must labour to correct them in ourselves, " in order to become
better,"[2] and to render devotion pleasing.

The soul thus mortified inwardly will be in a manner
insensible to the unhealthy incitements of the world. St
Francis de Sales wrote to the Baroness de Chantal with
regard to Mme de Charmoisy, who was forced to spend
some time in court :

" The good Mme de Charmoisy does much; you will find
her well advanced in affections and in the effects of true
devotion. But, O God, there she is with one foot on the
threshold of the door of the court. I hope God will hold
her through it all by the hand; at least, he gives her good
resolutions."[3]

Is not this a living commentary on the first part of the
Introduction? Mme de Charmoisy is so dead to the world
inwardly that she will not suffer from its attacks.

B—EXERCISES OF PIETY

It is divine love which brings about and completes the
" purgation of the soul." And love is developed within us,
becomes prompt and active, by means of exercises of piety.

St Francis de Sales puts forward these exercises in the
second part of his *Introduction:* mental prayer daily for one
hour, prayers morning and night, examination of conscience,
spiritual reading, the practice of inward recollection or
" spiritual retreat," ejaculatory prayers, weekly confession
and frequent communion. These are the exercises which the
Clerks Regular of the sixteenth century usually practised.[4]
The *Spiritual Combat* recommends almost all of them.
Mental prayer in common became substituted more and more
among the religious of this period for the choir office.

The great novelty, it might even be said boldness, of St
Francis de Sales was to impose these exercises on devout
persons living in the world, and to unite thus the contemplative with the active life. No one before him had dared

---

[1] *Devout Life,* chap. xxiii.   [2] *ibid.,* Part I, chap. xxiv.
[3] Letter to the Baroness de Chantal, 1609, Vol. XIV, p. 131.
[4] These are so much the exercises of the religious life that, later
on, several religious congregations took the *Introduction* as their
spiritual directory.

to do this definitely. Almost all thought it impossible. After the publication of the *Devout Life,* the Bishop of Montpellier, Fenouillet, reproached its author with forcing Philothea "too far in advance" in the interior ways.[1] But experience showed that it is possible, without too great difficulty, to place people in the world in an environment of monastic piety. It is true that Philothea is a great lady, mistress of her time, and generally free to arrange her manner of life. It was possible for her to give herself to the prescribed exercises almost at any given moment, rather like a nun in her cloister. We should have liked to see St Francis de Sales drawing up the life of prayer for a working man or for a mother of a family whose whole time is absorbed by material occupations.[2]

Philothea's rule was, nevertheless, extremely flexible. Her exercises are not to be prejudicial to the duties of her state.[3] Mme Acarie, to whom St Francis de Sales acted as director for some time, did not hesitate to shorten her practices of devotion when necessary, in order not to annoy her husband. So also with Philothea. But she should always be able, even when her worldly affairs absorbed her, to practise interior recollection and make "aspirations" and "ejaculatory prayers":

"Remember, then, Philothea, always to make many withdrawals into the solitude of your heart, whilst you are outwardly in the midst of intercourse and business; and this mental solitude cannot be hindered by the multitude of those who are about you, for they are not about your heart, but only about your body, so that your heart may remain all alone in the presence of God alone."[4]

Like St Catherine of Siena, who had "a little inward oratory in her mind," in order to pray, Philothea should

---

[1] *Œuvres,* Vol. III, p. xl. St Francis de Sales refutes these objections in Part V of the *Devout Life,* chap. xvii. In 1604 he already recommended the same exercises to Mme de Chantal (XII, p. 352).

[2] It would seem that in the thought of St Francis de Sales, members of every profession ought to adapt themselves to the exercises of piety notified above. "You must . . . pass from prayer to all sorts of actions which your vocation or profession justly and lawfully requires of you, though they seem very far removed from the affections which you have received in prayer. I mean that the advocate must learn to pass from prayer to pleading; the merchant to business; the married woman to the duties of her state and to the cares of her household. . . ." *Devout Life,* Part II, chap. viii.

[3] Often in his *Letters* St Francis de Sales insists on the pre-eminence of the duties of one's state. *Œuvres,* XII, p. 270; XV, p. 88, etc. In his famous *Letter* to St Chantal, October 14, 1604, he wrote: "If you greatly love obedience and submission, I desire you, if just or charitable occasion for leaving your exercises arise, to take it as a sort of case of obedience, and to make up for your omission with love." XII, p. 359.

[4] *Devout Life,* Part II, chap. xii.

often withdraw herself within her heart and bring forth there-from acts of "tender love" for her divine Spouse.

The "spiritual retreat" and ejaculatory prayers are only to take the place of the other exercises when it is not pos-sible to do better. Ordinarily, they form but a part of the spiritual programme for the day; they are in order to main-tain the soul in recollection and the spirit of prayer.

In this spiritual programme mental prayer holds a very important place.

Before the time of St Francis de Sales this exercise was very little employed by people in the world. During retreats and on other occasions dealing specially with the salvation of the soul, meditation was used, but it was not always methodical prayer :

"But perhaps you do not know, Philothea, how to make mental prayer; for it is a thing which unhappily few persons in this age of ours know how to practise."[1]

The *Introduction to the Devout Life* popularized this exercise. From this time on, the practice of devotion was not complete without mental prayer. There remained but to adapt it to the position or degree of culture of each one, but it was necessary for all. It creates within us solid supernatural convictions which enlighten us as to the good to be done. It also produces affective states which encourage us to the realization of this good :

"Inasmuch as prayer places our understanding in the clearness of the divine light, and exposes our will to the warmth of heavenly love, there is nothing which so purges our understanding of its ignorance and our will of its depraved inclinations; it is the water of benediction, which, when our souls are watered therewith, makes the plants of our good desires revive and flourish. . . ."[2]

St Francis de Sales, inspired by the Italian School, which had no love for complicated exercises, suggests a "simple and brief method" of prayer.[3] For "many are greatly deceived, thinking that so many things, so many methods, are needful" in order to meditate properly.[4] The method of the *Spiritual Combat* is simple, but not sufficiently concise. That of St Ignatius is too complex, and the same may be said of Luis of Granada. The Bishop of Geneva drew up one which comprises the essential elements of the methods both of St Ignatius and of Luis of Granada, but is better adapted to the inexperience of people in the world.

[1] *Devout Life,* Part II, chap. ii.   [2] *ibid.,* chap. i.
[3] *ibid.,* Part II, chap. ii.
[4] *Sermon for the Feast of the Purification* (1620), Vol. IX, p. 259.

It is composed of four parts : preparation, considerations, affections and resolutions, and the spiritual bouquet.[1]

The preparation has three parts : the act of placing oneself in the presence of God, the invocation, and the subject proposed.

Like Luis of Granada and the greater number of the framers of methods of prayer, St Francis de Sales wishes us first of all to put ourselves " in the presence of God." This is done either by an act of faith in the " omnipresence of God " in the universe or in our hearts by grace, or else by picturing to ourselves the Saviour looking down on us from on high or near us as a friend. This part of the Salesian method is noteworthy. Writers on the subject of mental prayer after him never fail to make use of it. The invocation and the subject proposed are borrowed from St Ignatius. They consist in asking of God the grace to meditate well and in proposing the subject by the " composition of place." The outward aspect of the mystery on which we desire to meditate is recalled through the imagination. St Francis de Sales brings the imagination under discipline. He is of opinion that this faculty, by producing distractions, may easily become a hindrance.[2] It is with the understanding and will or with the heart that prayer should, above all, be performed.

For the end in view in prayer is to influence " the will or the affective part of our soul." The action " of the understanding which we call meditation, which is nothing else than one or several considerations," tends to " rouse our affections towards God and divine things." If now and then, " immediately after the preparation, the affection is stirred up to God : then, Philothea, you must give it the rein, without trying to follow the method."[3] The end of prayer is attained, provided that we convert " these general affections . . . into special and particular resolutions " for our spiritual amendment.

The conclusion of Salesian prayer contains, in abridged form, the three last parts of the prayer of Luis of Granada : the *act of thanksgiving* to God for favours received in the meditation ; the *offering,* " by which we offer to God his own goodness and mercy, the death, the blood, the virtues of his Son (these are the very words of Granada) and in conjunction with these our own affections and resolutions "; the " *supplication* by which we ask of God " to grant us and those whom we love " the graces and virtues of his Son."

The spiritual bouquet or " nosegay of devotion "[4] is peculiar to St Francis de Sales. It is equivalent to the re-

---

[1] *Devout Life,* Part II, chaps. ii-vii.
[2] F. Vincent, pp. 316 ff.
[3] *Devout Life,* Part II, chaps. vi-viii.   [4] *ibid.,* chap. vii.

commendation in ancient writers to recall, during the day, some thought from the morning's meditation.

It will be seen how careful the author of the *Introduction* is to preserve, whilst simplifying them, the traditional elements of exercises of piety. We shall be even more struck by this in comparing his method of examination of conscience with that of St Ignatius. There is no question of making this examination in writing, or of drawing up weekly statistics of shortcomings. There is the consideration, based on serious self-reflection, as to how " each hour of the day " has been spent. Then, thanksgiving to God for any good that we have been able to do, or begging forgiveness for evil committed. Finally a recommendation of ourselves to divine Providence before taking the rest which he " wills us to need."[1]

St Francis de Sales advises Philothea to communicate every Sunday. He thus sanctions a custom which was apparently tending to become general in Italy. There the devout were admitted easily enough to weekly communion. Thus it was with St Aloysius Gonzaga, St Jerome Æmiliani, after his conversion, and many others. Blessed Pierre Le Fèvre wished the fervent to communicate every week.[2] The Bishop of Geneva definitely established the rule of Sunday communion for devout persons. He showed it to be lawful from the text of Gennadius—attributed at the time to St Augustine—which permits communion " every Sunday, provided that the mind be without any affection for sin." This is the case with Philothea, and those aiming at perfection and free from all attachment to evil.[3]

C—The Exercise of Virtue—Temptations— Union with Christ

The final edition of the *Introduction,* in the part " concerned with the exercise of virtue," differs notably from the *editio princeps.* In the latter St Francis de Sales puts in the first place the " three great virtues," obedience, chastity, and poverty, which are the " three arms of the Cross . . . the three great means wherewith to acquire perfect devotion." They are also the ends of the three vows of the religious life. When they are thus " vowed," they place man in " the state of perfection," but " they do not place him in perfection except in so far as they are observed."[4]

---

[1] *Devout Life,* Part II, chap. xi. Cf. *Letter* to Mme Travernay, September 29, 1612, Vol. XV, p. 269.
[2] St Philip Neri also recommended frequent communion, without defining it.
[3] For daily communion, St Francis furthermore demands " our conquest of most of our evil inclinations." *Devout Life,* Part II, chap. xx.
[4] *Œuvres,* Vol. III, Appendix, pp. 90-91.

The order followed in the *editio princeps* was that of the greater number of religious writings. As they were meant for religious, they treat first of all of the virtues of their state. St Francis de Sales conformed to the received custom, even though he wrote for people in the world. Although he possessed so new and personal a manner of viewing the practice of the Christian life, he had no desire for innovation.

On reflection, however, he came to the conclusion that the old plan of the virtues, " as far as the order of their exercise is concerned," was less suitable for those " amidst the pressure of temporal affairs." The question which Philothea must solve without delay is how to " unite an exalted piety with every social requirement." She must try first of all to perfect herself in the social virtues : patience in putting up with others, humility, gentleness with her neighbours and herself, calmness in business. Afterwards, " the three great virtues." Then, what are called the natural virtues : friendships, conversations, suitable dress, " counsels about speech," games, " permissible though dangerous pastimes," such as balls.[1] St Francis de Sales looks at these natural virtues in a very Christian way. But he desires the devout person to be a thoroughly " honest man." He means to improve the whole man.[2] The truly devout, then, must have all natural qualities, as much as possible, even to " the just and reasonable mind."[3] He will thus make devotion loved :

" You should not only be devout and love devotion," wrote our saint to Lady-President Brulart, May 3, 1604, " but you ought to render it lovable to everyone. Now you will render it lovable if you make it useful and agreeable. The sick will love your devotion if they are charitably consoled by it ; your family, if thereby you are admittedly more careful of their good, more gentle in emergencies, more kindly in reprimand, and so on; your husband, if he sees that in the measure in which your devotion grows, you are more cordial towards him and sweeter in the affection you have for him; your relations and friends, if they notice in you more frankness, help, and compliance in meeting their wishes when not contrary to the will of God. In short, you must, as far as possible, render your devotion more attractive."[4]

In the final edition of the *Introduction*, the counsels as to the exercise of virtue form Part III, at the beginning of which there are two chapters on the choice " we ought to make in the exercise of virtues." Here are the principles that guided the saint's own choice, and they explain the changes in the last editions of his work :

[1] St Francis de Sales also adds the famous " Counsels for the married." Part III, chaps. xxxvii-xxxix.
[2] F. Vincent, pp. 217-290.
[3] *Devout Life*, Part III, chap. xxxvi.   [4] Vol. XXII, p. 270.

" Among the virtues, we should prefer that which is most conformable to our duty and not that which is most conformable to our inclination. . . . Among the virtues which do not concern our particular duty, we should prefer the most excellent and not the most evident."[1]

Among these St Francis de Sales places in relief those which he calls the " little virtues," the conquest of which our Lord has proposed to our care and travail, such as patience, meekness, mortification of heart, humility, obedience, poverty, chastity, consideration for others, bearing with their imperfections, diligence and holy fervour."[2]

" Little virtues," not so in themselves, but in opposition to the extraordinary states to which mystics are raised, which do not depend on ourselves :

" Let us walk along the low valleys of the humble and little virtues," wrote our saint to Baroness de Chantal in September, 1605, " there shall we find roses among the thorns, charity which breaks forth amidst sorrows, both within and without; lilies of purity, violets of mortification, and what not. Above all do I love these three little virtues : gentleness of heart, poverty of spirit, and simplicity of life. . . . No, we have not yet arms wide enough to reach the Cedars of Lebanon, let us be content with the hyssop of the valley."[3]

As to the method to be followed in order to make progress in virtue, St Francis de Sales counsels attachment to the virtue that is opposed to our ruling passion. Thus shall we overcome our enemy, and " not fail to make progress in all the other virtues," for we cannot do our poor best to perfect one virtue without the concurrence of all the rest.

This method rests on one of the fundamental principles of Salesian spirituality, which is wholly that of love. Love is not only that which constitutes perfection, it is also the means of acquiring it. We become perfect, less by fighting a vice directly than by loving the contrary virtue strongly.

" All must be done by love and nothing by force," wrote St Francis de Sales to Baroness de Chantal; " we must love obedience more than we fear disobedience."[4]

Indeed, love is more stimulating than fear. Besides :

" Charity never enters into the heart without bringing with her the whole retinue of the other virtues, exercising them and setting them to work, as a captain does his soldiers."[5]

It is wonderful to see how the Bishop of Geneva can rejuvenate the subject of temptation, which is old as the

[1] *Devout Life,* Part III, chap. i.   [2] *ibid.,* chap. ii.
[3] *Œuvres,* Vol. XIII, p. 92.   [4] *id.,* Vol. XII, p. 359.
[5] *Devout Life,* Part III, chap. i.

world.[1] The counsels he gives in order to repel evil suggestions, to preserve peace of soul amidst moral tempests, have
their living commentary in the letters of direction, above all, in
those addressed to Baroness de Chantal, who was obsessed
by temptations and devoured by scruples, during the first
years that he directed her.

Finally, the Fifth and last Part of the *Introduction* contains "exercises and counsels for renewing the soul and con-
firming it in devotion." This is the annual retreat which
Philothea should make, "being withdrawn rather more than
usual into a solitude that is both spiritual and real." Her
"protestation to serve God," made at the beginning of her
conversion, should serve as a theme for her reflections and
examination of conscience. Then she must examine the
state of her soul "towards God," herself, and her neighbour. Subjects for appropriate prayers are also drawn up
for the days of the retreat.

If the exercises of the *Introduction to the Devout Life* be
well performed, Philothea will become more and more
identified with Christ. It is in this happy state of hope that
St Francis de Sales leaves her :

"You must," he tells her at the end of his book, "often
repeat with your heart and lips these burning words of
St Paul, St Augustine, St Catherine of Genoa, and others :
No, I am no longer my own; whether I live or die, I belong
to my Saviour; I have nothing left of myself or of mine :
My 'self' is Jesus; to be 'mine' is to be his."[2]

Bérulle a few years later said : "I desire that there be
no more I in myself; I desire to be able to say with St
Paul : *I live; now not I, but Christ liveth in me* (Gal. ii, 20)."[3]

In one page of the *Introduction,* not enough emphasized,
St Francis de Sales shows this life of union with Christ to be
the first and most precious fruit of meditation :

"For by beholding him [the Saviour] often in meditation
your whole soul will be filled with him; you will learn his
demeanour, and you will form your actions after the model
of his. He is the *light of the world,* and therefore it is in
him, by him, and for him that we must be enlightened and
illuminated. . . . Children, by listening to their mothers,
and prattling with them, learn to speak their language, so
we, by keeping close to the Saviour in meditation, and

[1] It is Part IV of the final edition of the *Devout Life.* In the first
edition temptations are dealt with in Part II, together with the virtues
and exercises of piety.
[2] *Devout Life,* Part V, chap. xvi. This passage is to be found in the
first edition of 1609 (*Œuvres,* Vol. III, p. 181).
[3] *Grandeurs de Jésus, Discours* II, xii (Migne, p. 181).

observing his words, his actions, and his affections, shall learn, with the help of his grace, to speak, to act, and to will like him. We must stop there, Philothea, and believe me, we cannot go to God the Father but by this door."[1]

This already anticipates Berullian spirituality.[2]

III—ST FRANCIS DE SALES THE FOUNDER OF A CONGREGATION—HIS RELATIONS WITH ST JANE DE CHANTAL[3]

It was on March 5, 1604, in the Sainte-Chapelle at Dijon, where he was preaching the Lent, that St Francis de Sales saw Baroness de Chantal, the future foundress of the Visitation of St Mary, for the first time.

Although they had never met they knew each other. Before leaving for Dijon, the Bishop of Geneva had a vision in which he learnt that he was to found an Order of religious women. She who was to be the first Superior was shown him, and he recognized her among his listeners. The Baroness on her side recognized the bishop, of whom she had caught sight in a vision some time before, in the famous preacher. It was at a time when she was praying very earnestly to God to enable her to find a good director. During the vision she heard a voice saying to her : " There is the man, beloved of both God and men, in whose hands you ought to place your conscience."[4]

She did not dare to place herself under the guidance of the saint immediately. She had as director a religious, who imposed on her a vow, tyrannical and invalid, of speaking to no other person on matters of conscience. Nevertheless she could not fail to recognize the call from God to follow another guide; hence, she was tortured by scruples when she

[1] *Devout Life*, Part II, chap. i. The same passage is to be found in the first edition (Appendix, p. 67).

[2] St Francis de Sales thus did honour to the Heart of Jesus : " The other day when in prayer," he wrote to St Chantal in 1608, " contemplating the opened side of our Lord and seeing his heart, it was brought home to me that our hearts were all around him, doing homage to him as the sovereign King of hearts. So may it ever be with our heart. Amen." Vol. XIV, p. 14.

[3] *Cf.* H. Bremond, *op. cit.*, II, pp. 537 ff.

[4] Mère de Chaugy, *Sainte Jeanne-Françoise de Chantal,* Part I, chap. x, p. 40, Paris, 1893. Born at Dijon, January 23, 1572, St Chantal founded the Visitation in 1610. She died in 1641. Her *Life* was written by Mère de Chaugy, secretary to the saint and fourth Superior of the Monastery at Annecy, in 1642. The *Works* and the *Letters* of St Chantal were published in eight volumes in Paris (Plon Nourrit). The first volume contains the *Life* of St Chantal, by Mère de Chaugy. The *Divers Works* of the saint form the second and third volumes, which are Vols. I and II of the *Œuvres de Ste Chantal.* Her *Letters* are contained in the other five volumes.

had recourse to the ministry of St Francis de Sales. The latter, from motives of delicacy, did not wish, first of all, to withdraw her from her director. It was not until August 25, six months after the first interview at Dijon, at St Claude, where he met her, that he finally agreed to be her guide.[1]

God united these two souls with a wholly sacred affection, destined as they were to accomplish a great work. From June 24, 1604, before becoming her spiritual guide, St Francis de Sales speaks of this affection, which is "all of God," to the Baroness de Chantal, with whom he will work in the interests of her soul.

"What does it matter to you to know whether or no you are able to retain me as your spiritual director, provided that you know how my soul stands towards you and that I know how yours stands to mine? I know that you have entire and perfect confidence in my affection; of that I have no doubt whatever, and derive consolation therefrom. Know also, I beg you, and believe it wholly, that I have a lively and extraordinary desire to serve your spirit to the utmost of my power. I cannot explain to you either the quality or the greatness of this affection I have for your spiritual service; but I would clearly say that I think it comes only from God and on that account I cherish it dearly and see it grow and notably increase day by day. . . . Value then my affection, employed in all that God has given me for the service of your spirit. Thus am I wholly yours and so think no more in what form or to what degree I am so. God has given me to you; hold me then as yours in him and call me what you will, it matters not."[2]

This holy and truly enveloping affection could not but increase the great confidence which Mme de Chantal had in St Francis de Sales; and when he spoke of "this charity and true Christian friendship" the "bond" of which is "indissoluble and never relaxes,"[3] he must have had premonitions of his future relations with the pious Baroness.

Yet he did not let her conjecture anything, at first, of the project he had of making use of her some day to found a new Order of nuns. In the month of May, 1605, he made her a first overture in obscure terms: "Some years ago," he told her, "God communicated something to me regarding a manner of life, but I do not wish to tell you of it for a year."[4]

At this period the Baroness was too necessary at home. The education of her children kept her in the world for several years.

[1] With regard to this drama of St Chantal's conscience, see Mère de Chaugy, Part I, chaps. xii-xv, and the *Letters* of St Francis de Sales to St Chantal from June 14 and June 24, 1604 (XII, pp. 277, 282).
[2] Vol. XII, pp. 284-285.   [3] *ibid.*, p. 285.
[4] Mère de Chaugy, chap. xvii, p. 71.

St Francis de Sales directed her with great care. First of all he drew up a rule for her consisting of the exercises of piety which were to be recommended in the *Introduction to the Devout Life*.[1] The direction of St Chantal, almost as much as that of Mme de Charmoisy, guided St Francis de Sales in the production of his masterpiece. One of the chapters of the Baroness' rule was concerned with visiting the sick and poor.

But the important thing was to form the interior spirit. Ardent and impulsive, the Baroness de Chantal had need to be put on her guard " against the impetuosities and abrupt sallies of a character in which there was naturally more of masculine energy and generosity than of gentleness."[2] She would have to watch over herself in order to make her devotion lovable. She allowed her uplifted soul to be easily tormented by hastiness, anxiety, and scruples. Great temptations, especially against the faith, were to try her and to throw her into much inward pain and sorrow.

St Francis de Sales taught her, before all, the spirit of liberty, of gentleness, and of love, which places the exercise of charity before exercises of piety:

" The effects of this liberty," he wrote, " are a great sweetness of spirit, a great tenderness and sympathy with all that is not sin or a danger of sin; it is that temper which is gently pliable to the action of all virtue and charity. For example, a soul which is attached to exercises of piety, if interrupted, will be seen to come out from it with annoyance, hastiness, and astonishment. A soul possessing true liberty will go out with an even expression and kindly heart to the place of the intruder who has caused the disturbance, for to such a one it is all the same whether God be served in meditation or in helping a neighbour; either is the will of God, but the helping of one's neighbour is necessary at that moment."[3]

The pious Baroness followed these counsels so well that her servants said:

" The first director of Madame only made her pray three times a day, and we were all put out; but Monseigneur of Geneva makes her pray all day long and that troubles no one."[4]

St Francis de Sales apparently found it more difficult to calm the eagerness of this generous and anxious soul, ever fearful that she was neither doing enough nor well enough.

---

[1] *Letter* of October 14, 1604. This should be compared with the Rule of Baroness de Chantal described by Mère de Chaugy, Part I, chaps. xvii-xviii.

[2] A. de Margerie, *S. François de Sales,* Paris, 1908, p. 187.

[3] *Letter* of October 14, 1604 (XII, p. 363-364).

[4] Mère de Chaugy, Part I, chap. xvii, p. 73.

" There is something in me," she wrote to her director, " which has never felt satisfied, but I cannot tell what it is."[1] She would have liked to have reached perfection all at once.

The lack of proportion between her desires and what she was able to accomplish threw her into great dejection. The sense of her impotence was to her a kind of torment. The remnants of self-love were not lacking in this state, as St Francis de Sales delicately hinted to his dear daughter. In order to soar towards perfection we must first wait till we have wings :

" Do not distress yourself," he wrote, " you will see that you will thus be all the better for it, and your wings all the stronger. This anxiety, then, is a defect in you and a vague kind of dissatisfaction; thus it is a lack of resignation. You are indeed resigned, but it is with a *but;* for you want to have this or that, and you strive in order to obtain it. A simple desire is not contrary to resignation; but a panting heart, the flapping of wings, an agitated will, a throng of yearnings, these are certainly a lack of resignation . . . since as yet you have not your wings to fly and your own impotence bars your efforts, do not strive at all, do not be anxious to fly, have patience until you have *wings* to fly *like a dove.* I am infinitely afraid that you have too much ardour for the prize, that you are too eager and heap up your desires a little too fast."[2]

This insatiable eagerness, this excessive discontent with self, belonged to St Chantal's temperament.[3] It was her cross. The devil made use of it to tempt her against the faith. Other inward trials also tortured her for several years. In these doubtless are to be seen those passive purifications through which souls that are called to extraordinary states must pass. Her saintly director wrote for her consolation wonderful letters, which have also comforted and will comfort

[1] In the *Letter* of St Francis de Sales of November 21, 1604 (XII, p. 384).

[2] Same *Letter* (XII, pp. 384-385).

[3] She herself admits it in her account, in 1637, of her first mystical prayers " of a simple sight and sense of the divine presence." " This grace of prayer has continued with me," she says, " even though on account of my unfaithfulness I have greatly offended against it; letting fears of my being of no use in this state enter into my mind, and desiring to do something on my part, I spoilt everything. . . . If I think of strengthening my soul by thoughts and by discourses, by resignation and acts, I expose myself to new temptations and pain, and can only do so with great violence which leaves me dry. So that it is needful for me to return promptly to that simple surrender, for God seems to make me see from this that he desires a total cessation of the efforts of my mind and of its working in this. And the activity of my mind is so great that I always need to be comforted and encouraged to do so. Alas! My blessed father has told me this so often!" *Œuvres de St Chantal,* IV, pp. 735 ff.

those who pass through the same inward trials.[1] He does not, however, appear to have thought that the Baroness was as yet in the mystical ways. He brought her on to accept these trials with a holy indifference, like Jesus in the garden of Olives :

" What does it matter to us whether it be by the desert or by the fields that we pass, provided that God be with us and that we go to Paradise? . . . Think of the great abandonment which our Master suffered in the garden of Olives. See how this dear Son, having begged his good Father for consolation, which he willed not to grant him, thought no more of it, was no longer anxious for it, and sought it no further, but, as though he had never claimed it, bravely and courageously carried out the work of our redemption. . . . For the honour of God acquiesce wholly in his will and do not believe that you can serve him otherwise; for he is never well served if not served as he wills."[2]

St Chantal must not only be resigned but full of joy in carrying her cross. " You would not offend God for anything in the world; surely this is enough to live joyously," he wrote on June 24, 1604.[3] And on August 28, 1605, when her temptations were at their height : " Live joyously and be generous; God whom we love and to whom we are vowed, desires us to be thus."[4] These kindly and strong exhortations to inward detachment led the Baroness de Chantal to acts of heroic virtue. Not only did she consent to see M. Anlezy the unintentional murderer of her husband, but she had the courage to hold his newly born son at the baptismal font. She visited the sick, dressed their most loathsome wounds, and even kissed them.[5] Her desire to quit the world increased more and more. Thus she prepared herself to make the supreme sacrifice, to leave all her own, in order to go to Annecy and found the Order of the Visitation.[6]

A—The Salesian Conception of the Religious Life —The Visitation

When the Baroness de Chantal reached Annecy on April 4, 1610, St Francis de Sales had a definite idea of the new institute he wished to establish. He had already explained it clearly enough to his famous penitent in 1607, when she was at Annecy.[7] His enterprise was a novelty.

[1] See above all the *Letters* written at the end of the year 1604 and during the years 1605, 1606, and 1607 (Vols. XII and XIII). *Cf.* Mère de Chaugy, Part I, chap. xvi.
[2] *Letter* of February 18, 1605 (XIII, pp. 5-6).
[3] Vol. XII, p. 288. [4] Vol. XIII, p. 89.
[5] Mère de Chaugy, Part I, chaps. xviii-xix, pp. 77-88.
[6] Mère de Chaugy has related the famous scene (chap. xxviii) of St Chantal's farewell to her family. It took place March 29, 1610.
[7] Mère de Chaugy, Part I, chap. xxi, p. 96.

The future Congregation was to unite the active and the contemplative life, the vocation of Martha with that of Mary. The sisters were to be half-enclosed. Entrance to their monastery would be forbidden to strangers quite as strictly as in other Orders of women. But the sisters could go out at certain hours of the day in order to visit and tend the sick.[1] The neglect of the sick poor, the tending of whom as yet no congregation, properly so-called, had undertaken, had moved the compassionate heart of the Bishop of Geneva. He remembered with what charity the Italian *Oratory of Divine Love* was working for the suffering members of Jesus Christ. He himself had exhorted his penitents—and Mme de Chantal in particular—to visit the poor and the sick with pious tenderness.

The sisters were to practise corporal mortification in moderation; first of all, because of the fatigues entailed by the service of the sick, and also in order that the new institute might receive persons in delicate health, called to the religious life but incapable of standing the austerities of the Poor Clares or Carmelites.[2] These austerities had been hitherto regarded as essential elements of the religious life. St Francis de Sales—and this was to be his other innovation—replaced them by interior mortification pushed to its furthest limit.[3] " A generally feasible mortification of the mind, the heart, and the will was here to compensate for such mitigation; defects would be reformed and virtues acquired more by the attractiveness of love than by the rigour of penance; here they would be devoted more to interior recollection than to a multiplicity of prayers, to renunciation than to poverty, to charity than to solitude, to obedience than to hard observances."[4]

This conception of religious life was already spreading in Italy among the congregations of men. It fully corresponded to the temperament of the Bishop of Geneva and to his manner of directing souls. Moreover, when the immovable

[1] De Chaugy, Part II, chap. v, pp. 158-159. The visiting of the sick, although not strictly speaking a secondary work of the Visitandines, was yet not the chief end of the Congregation, which, according to the idea of its founder, was primarily a contemplative Order, very different from the Congregation of the Sisters of Charity, founded later on by St Vincent de Paul.

[2] St Francis de Sales established his Congregation " so that no great harshness might turn away the feeble and infirm from joining the ranks to apply themselves to the perfection of divine love." Constitutions of the Visitation : *Of the end for which this Congregation was instituted*. See *Discourse* XIII, *Of the Spirit of the Rules,* Vol. VI, p. 229.

[3] " The fervour of charity and strength of very intimate devotion makes up for all that [an austere austerity]." Addition to the first Constitution.

[4] A. de Margerie, *St F. de Sales,* p. 202.

opposition of the Archbishop of Lyons, Mgr. de Marquement, had obliged the Visitandines to keep strictly enclosed and to give up visiting the sick, the Salesian idea of religious life none the less remained. The sisters continued to live behind their grating without corporal austerities, but rigorously applied to the practices of interior mortification in order to attain " the perfection of divine love."

The Salesian conception of the religious life, as also of the Christian life in general, rests on the principle of the self-sacrificing power of divine love. The end is death to self, complete inward mortification; the means is love, not austerities, " the fervour of charity and the power of a very intimate devotion."[1] Love undertakes to immolate the soul, provided that the latter yields thereto. It is thus the end and the means of the religious life. St Francis de Sales declares at the beginning of the *Constitutions* that in his institute it is proposed to " apply oneself to the perfection of divine love."

Let us hold fast to this idea. It will help us to understand the counsels given by the holy Founder to his religious in his wonderful *Spiritual Discourses*.

The *Constitutions* do not bind under pain of mortal sin.[2] God is only offended when they are violated, if it be done from contempt or is a cause of scandal. After recalling the theological principle, the Saint immediately soars to the heights:

" The Daughters of the Congregation, through the sweet violence of love, should observe their Rules with the same exactness, by God's help, as if they were obliged thereto under pain of eternal damnation."[3]

This readiness to act in all things through love, this " devotion," the sisters should make " particular profession to nourish in their hearts." It should be intimate " so that . . . nothing be done from custom, but by choice and application of the will " ; it should be strong " to bear temptation " ;

[1] An addition to the first Constitution, Vol. VI, p. xxx. Cf. *Discourse* I, *Obligation of the Constitutions:* " The daughters of the Congregation have very few outward rules, few austerities, few ceremonies, few offices : let them willingly and lovingly adapt their hearts thereto, making the outward spring from the inward and nourishing the inward with the outward." Vol. VI, p. 13.
[2] A violation of the *Constitutions* must not be confused with that of the vows; this, when grave, is a matter of mortal sin. *Discourse* I, Vol. VI, p. 12.
[3] *Discourse* I, Vol. VI, p. 12. Cf. *Discourse* XIII, *Of the Spirit of the Rules:* " We cannot love the commandment if we love not him who gave it. . . . Some are attached to the law by chains of iron, others by chains of gold . . . the religious and those who care for their perfection are attached thereto by chains of gold : that is to say, by love." Vol. VI, p. 239.

lastly, generous " so as not to be astonished at difficulties,
but, on the contrary, thereby to increase its courage."[1]

B—The Virtues of the Religious Life

St Francis de Sales considers the great virtues of the
religious life, poverty, obedience, and chastity, less in themselves than in the consequences which love deduces from
them. He strives towards those higher virtues which are the
full expansion of them : self-renunciation or poverty of spirit;
modesty, which is the flower of chastity; the giving up of our
own judgement, which is the highest obedience.[2]

Detachment means that we deprive ourselves of "three
kinds of goods : outward, corporal, spiritual or cordial." Outward goods are " houses, possessions, relations, friends, and
such like " that are left " outside religion." We must deprive ourselves of these in reality and in affection. Nevertheless, for our relations and friends, we must ask our Lord for
the " affection which he desires us to have for them." For
" everyone should be loved in his degree, and it is charity
which gives order in affection." We must also renounce
corporal goods, by being " equally content in sickness or in
health " in the higher part of the soul. " Cordial goods are
the consolations and comforts which are found in the spiritual
life." We must " place them in the hands of our Lord to
dispose of them as he pleases, and we must serve him as well
without them as with them. . . . All our deprivations and
renunciations of the above things should be performed,
not from contempt of them, but from abnegation, from the
sole and pure love of God. . . . Every sister must leave her
own will outside the door [of the monastery] in order to have
only that of God."[3]

Modesty properly so-called, " is the maintenance of a
decorous exterior."[4] It is opposed to looseness either of
gesture or look," or to " affected looks." This virtue " is
powerful to restrain us." It obliges us unceasingly to a
demeanour which has nothing in it contrary to the delicacy
of chastity :

" It subjects us not only for a time, but always and in
every place, as much when alone as when with others, at

[1] *Discourse* I, Vol. VI, pp. 13, 14.
[2] Nevertheless, on account of its importance for communities, St
Francis de Sales devotes two discourses to the virtue of obedience.
Discourses X and XI.
[3] *Discourse* VIII, *Of Renunciation,* Vol. VI, pp. 122-123.
[4] St Francis also calls three other virtues modesty : " Inward propriety of our understanding and of our will "; the absence of " boorish-
ness " and " gossip " in our conversation; " modesty and seemliness
in attire " as opposed to " squalidness and to superfluity." *Discourse* IX, Vol. VI, pp. 131-132.

every time, even while asleep, because the angels are always present with us, and God himself in whose eyes we bear ourselves with modesty."[1]

St Francis de Sales desires his sisters to practise loving obedience. Such obedience is " blind," it is obedience of the understanding. It " is practised when, being commanded, we accept and approve the commandment, not only with the will, but also with our understanding, approving and esteeming the thing commanded and judging it better than any other thing that might have been commanded on that occasion." Again it is prompt and persevering. The religious, like our Saviour, ought to obey all her life indefatigably.[2] So perfect an obedience necessitates the renunciation of our own judgement, which is the summit of renunciation. The saintly founder admits that it is a rare thing. And, nevertheless, this " love of our own judgement . . . is infinitely contrary to perfection."[3]

Salesian abnegation, already pushed so far, also includes the most subtle manifestations of self-love which some might mistake for virtues—that is to say, the claim to attain perfection " at once," the restless desire for correction of faults, and the vexation at not succeeding as quickly as desired.[4] We are reminded of the excessive eagerness of the Baroness de Chantal in this regard. This spiritual lack of mortification, this " tenderness " of mind, troubles the peace of souls and may trouble still more the peace of communities.

Humility must also be one of the favourite virtues of the Visitandines :

" I wish for you," says the Saint, " above all other perfection that of humility, which is not only charitable but sweet and pliable; for charity is an ascending humility and humility a descending charity. I love you better with more humility and less of the other perfections than with more of the other perfections and less humility."[5]

The special spirit of the Visitation is a " spirit of profound humility towards God and a great kindliness towards one's neighbour."[6] Further, the Saint invites his sisters to practise the love of abjection, that perfection of humility which keeps the soul in peace in little annoyances, in the daily clashing of

[1] *Discourse* IX, Vol. VI, pp. 132-133.
[2] *Discourses* X, XI, *Of Obedience.*
[3] *Discourse* XIV, *Of Our Own Judgement,* Vol. VI, p. 245. See pp. 170, 199.
[4] *Discourse* XXIII, *Of Firmness,* Vol. VI, pp. 48, 49. *Cf.* pp. 257, 331. " It is not possible for you to be so mistress of your soul that you hold it in your hand so absolutely at the beginning. . . . We must put up with others, but first with ourselves, and have patience to be imperfect." Letter to Mme de la Flachère, April 8, 1608, Vol. XIV, p. 2.
[5] *Discourse* VIII, *Of Renunciation,* Vol. VI, p. 130.
[6] *Discourse* XIII, *Of the Spirit of the Rules,* Vol. VI, p. 229.

characters, which the common life entails. We have need of
"the love of our abjection . . . at every moment, however
advanced we may be in perfection."[1]

According to St Francis de Sales, humility depends upon
divine charity; he moreover defines the virtues as the work of
divine love. It is this love which corrects our defects for us
and makes us advance in virtue. It ends by simplifying the
operations of the soul, and brings it to forget itself wholly
in order to be taken up only with God. Simplicity, a virtue
so beloved of our Saint and so insisted on in his counsels to
his religious, is thus reached :

"It is, then, an act of simple charity which makes us only
regard and have no other end in all our actions than the sole
desire of pleasing God . . . this is simplicity, a virtue which
is inseparable from charity so far as it looks straight to God,
without ever being able to suffer any admixture of self-
interest, otherwise it would no longer be simplicity."[2]

Simplicity banishes from the soul the restless search for
"exercises and means" of loving God. "We should not try
to double our desires or our exercises, but our perfection in
performing them."[3] When we have this simplicity we leave
to God "all the care of ourselves," not only "in things
temporal," but also "in things spiritual and in the advancement of our souls in perfection."[4] The soul only thinks of its
Beloved, it only seeks to please him in the accomplishment
of duty every moment. "Let us do quite simply all that is
commanded either by the Rules or the Constitutions, or else
by our Superiors, and then remain in peace respecting all the
rest, as near to God as we are able,"[5] such is the law of this
loving simplicity. It will maintain us "in continual even-
ness, in both adverse and prosperous things, in desolation as
well as in consolation, and finally amidst dryness as well
as amidst delicacies."[6] We shall no longer have any other
desire than that of loving God.[7]

St Francis de Sales desires his religious to have great
tranquillity of soul, "the principal means" of personal sanctification. To insure this inward peace is indeed one of the
ends of Salesian spirituality, as it was also of the asceticism

[1] *Discourse* XVI, *Of Aversions*, Vol. VI, p. 298. *Cf.* p. 71. The
counsels given to the Visitandines greatly resemble those which St
Francis de Sales gave to the Baroness de Chantal in 1608 and 1609 :
"The virtues of a widow are humility, contempt of the world and of
self, simplicity. Her exercises are love and her own abjection. . . .
We must exercise ourselves in the little virtues, without which the
great are often false and deceptive." Vol. XIV, pp. 109-110.
[2] *Discourse* XII, *Of Simplicity,* Vol. VI, p. 203.
[3] *Discourse* VII, *Of the Three Spiritual Laws, ibid.,* p. 114.
[4] *Discourse* VII, *ibid.,* p. 105.
[5] *ibid.,* p. 448, Appendix, *Of the Discourse of Our Own Judgement.*
[6] *ibid.,* p. 117, *Of the Three Spiritual Laws.*
[7] Cf. *Discourse* XXI, *Of asking Nothing,* Vol. VI, pp. 383-389.

of the devout humanists of Italy. This individual tranquillity maintains, through holy contagion, the peace of communities.

In order that the Sisters should ever preserve this peace among themselves, the holy Founder desired that their relations should conform to the rules of good company. This would not be mere worldly politeness which is wholly outward, but the exercise of those Christian virtues inspired by most pure charity : humility, sweetness, mutual forbearance, cordial simplicity. These virtues must be practised unceasingly. St Francis, in this matter, enters into the smallest details.

He counsels even obedience to equals and inferiors. In this disposition to obey all are comprised, according to him, the social virtues :

" Obedience consists in two points," he says. " The first is to obey superiors; the second to obey equals and inferiors. But this second belongs to humility, sweetness, and charity, rather than to obedience; for he that is humble thinks that all others surpass him and are much better than he, so that he considers them as superiors and thinks that he ought to obey them."[1]

This spirit of universal submission inspires gentleness towards others and strength to put up with their defects. It checks wounding words. It favours " cordial love "[2] between the Sisters, love which must not be sentimentalism. And in time of relaxation it gives " a holy liberty and freedom to converse on subjects which help the spirit of joy and recreation."[3] To be joyous in all simplicity in order to amuse the others is an act of charity.

IV—THE MYSTICISM OF ST FRANCIS DE SALES

A—St Francis de Sales and Mysticism before the " Treatise on the Love of God "

At first St Francis de Sales appears not to have been very favourable towards mysticism. His Ignatian training made him give preference to the sure ways of asceticism. He also feared illusions. His relations with the Protestants and the history of the first reformers had unveiled to him the ravages of a false mysticism.

Baroness de Chantal was very quickly raised to passive prayer; " her heart," says Mère de Chaugy, " was wedded

---

[1] *Discourse* X, *Of Obedience*, Vol. VI, p. 157.
[2] *Discourse* IV, *Of Cordiality*, Vol. VI, p. 54.
[3] *Discourse* XII, *Of Simplicity*, Vol. VI, p. 209.

early to the beautiful Rachel of contemplation."[1] Even
before she was under the guidance of St Francis de Sales,
she had been raised, from time to time, and without knowing
it, to the prayer of simplicity.[2] She hastened to obtain instruction in this kind of prayer. Towards the end of 1605
she had conversations on this subject with the Carmelites of
Dijon, especially with Mother Mary of the Trinity. She felt
herself habitually prompted to this "most spiritual mode
of prayer, separated from things sensible"[3] in which the
imagination and the understanding have no part. But on
this matter she conferred with the Bishop of Geneva, not
wishing to do anything without his consent. He brought
her back rather firmly to common prayer :

"To make no use in prayer either of the imagination or of
the understanding is not possible," he replied to her in 1606.
"This good Mother [Mary of the Trinity] says that we need
not make use of the imagination in order to represent to ourselves the sacred humanity of the Saviour. No, perhaps not
for those who are already far advanced on the mountain of
perfection; but for us others, who are as yet still in the
valleys, although desirous of ascending, I think that it is
expedient for us to make use of everything, and of the
imagination too. . . . This is the great highway, my dear
daughter, from which we must not yet part until the daylight
be a little clearer and we are well able to discern the foot-
paths. Let us remain, my dear daughter, a little longer here
in the low valleys, let us kiss the Saviour's feet a little more ;
he will call us, when he pleases, to his sacred mouth."[4]

To maintain his penitent in profound humility was also
one of his aims.

Some months later, the Saint wrote to him again that she
was still counselled not to "make use of the imagination or
of the understanding" in her prayers. He answered her,
June 8, 1606, that he did not approve of the complete abandonment of these two "powers" of the mind in meditation.[5]

Moreover, it is not only Baroness de Chantal, but also his
other penitents whom he retained in "the low valleys" of
ordinary prayer : it was a principle in his direction. He
wrote, in 1607, to the Lady-President Brulart :

"I would approve of your still holding on to the lesser
course, preparing your mind by the lesson and the disposi-

[1] *Sainte Jeanne de Chantal,* Part III, chap. xxiv, p. 498.
[2] St Chantal speaks of her beginnings in this prayer. See *Œuvres,* I,
p. 21 ; II, p. 337 ; IV, pp. 735 ff.
[3] Mère de Chaugy, p. 498.
[4] *Œuvres de Saint François de Sales,* Vol. XIII, p. 162.
[5] *ibid.,* pp. 183-184. M. Gallemand, the priest who aided M. de
Bérulle in introducing the Carmelites into France, united with Mother
Mary of the Trinity in exhorting St Chantal to make the passive
prayer of simplicity.

tion of the points, without any use of the imagination other than that required to help the mind. Now, then, I am well aware that when we happily meet and find God it is good to linger to look upon him and remain with him; but, my dear daughter, to think thus to meet him unexpectedly every day, without preparation, I do not believe that this is yet good for us who are novices and need rather to consider the virtues of the crucifix, one after another and in detail, than to admire them all together."[1]

Towards 1608, he again wrote to Baroness de Chantal to exercise herself in the " little virtues," in the " virtues of a widow " :

" For, as regards ecstasies, insensibilities, and these deific unions, elevations, transformations, and similar virtues, and when we think it a distraction to serve God in his humanity and its members, and take no pleasure except in the contemplation of the divine Essence, these must be left for the rare and lofty souls who are worthy of them. We do not deserve such rank in the service of God; we must first serve him in the low offices before being called to his cabinet."[2]

In the *Introduction to the Devout Life,* which he wrote about this time, he says the same things in still more emphatic terms.[3]

Nevertheless, Baroness de Chantal might well be of the number of " these rare souls " raised to the mystical state. The prudent director, towards the end of 1609, left more freedom to his penitent. He noted the extraordinary work of God in her. He does not wish to hinder her and writes :

[1] Vol. XIII, p. 162.
[2] Vol. XIV, p. 109.
[3] " There are certain things which are thought by many to be virtues, but which are by no means such, and of these I must say a word : I mean ecstasies or raptures, states of insensibility and impassibility, deific unions, transports, transformations, and other such perfections of which certain books treat, which promise to raise the soul to a purely intellectual contemplation, to an essential application of the Spirit, and to a super-eminent life. Note well, Philothea, that these perfections are not virtues. They are rather rewards which God gives for virtue. . . . But for all that we should not aspire to such graces, since they are in no way necessary to the true service and love of God. . . . Let us willingly leave the lofty heights to the souls who have been raised so high : we merit not so exalted a rank in the service of God; we shall be only too happy to serve him in his kitchen and in his pantry; to be his lackeys, porters, and chambermaids; it is for him, afterwards, if it seem good to him, to advance us to his privy council " (*Devout Life,* Part III, chap. ii). This passage is in the final edition of 1619, which appeared three years after the publication of the *Treatise on Love of God.* The last idea of the Saint was then, towards the end of his life, as always, that the extraordinary graces are not intended for all.

" Remain thus [in the arms of the Bridegroom], dear daughter, and like another little St John, whilst the others eat many meats at the table of the Saviour, repose and lean, with simple confidence, your head, your soul, your mind on the loving breast of your dear Saviour; for it is better to sleep on this sacred pillow than to keep awake in any other posture."[1]

But this sleep on the breast of the Saviour is only a passing state. In the ordinary way Mme de Chantal must keep to the common rules of meditation.

In 1610, she again submitted to St Francis de Sales the counsels which Mère Louise de Jésus, Prioress of the Carmelites of Dijon, had given her, not to prepare her prayers, but to abandon herself herein to the divine action. The Saint finds this " rather hard "; he does not understand and wanted full knowledge of the " foundations " of this method :

" As regards these precepts of prayer," he replied on March 11, 1610, " which you have received from the good Mother Prioress, I shall say nothing for the present; only I beg you to learn as much as you can the foundation of all this, for, to speak frankly to you, although two or three times last summer, having put myself in the presence of God without preparation or intention, I found myself full of joy in the presence of his Majesty, with a single and very simple and continual affection of love, almost imperceptible yet very sweet, still I never dared to leave the high road to make this my ordinary way. I only know that I love the way of the holy and simple forerunners. I do not say that when preparation has been made and in prayer one is drawn to this kind of prayer, it is not necessary to follow it; but to take it as a method not in any way to prepare, that to me is rather hard, as again it is to leave the presence of God, at once, without thanksgiving, without offering, without definite prayer. All that may usefully be done, but that it should be the rule seems to me, I must confess, rather repugnant. Nevertheless . . . I do not claim to know so much that I should not be glad, I would say extremely glad, to alter my opinion and follow that of those who should very reasonably know more than I."[2]

In 1610, three years after having begun his *Treatise on the*

---

[1] Vol. XIV, p. 214. Mère de Chaugy gives a different version (p. 499) : " Whilst the others eat many meats . . . *through divers considerations and pious meditations.* . . ."

[2] Vol. XIV, 266. Later St Chantal said of the prayer of the Visitandines : " I have recognized that the almost universal attraction for the daughters of the Visitation is that of a very simple presence of God, through an entire abandonment of themselves to divine Providence." *Œuvres de Sainte Chantal*, II, p. 337. " The great method of prayer is that there is none at all . . . prayer should be made by grace and not by artifice." *Ibid.*, p. 260.

Love of God,[1] the very year of the foundation of the Visitation, St Francis de Sales admitted the need he had to be instructed in the knowledge of mystical prayers. This knowledge he was fully to acquire by directing his religious, who were thus, unconsciously, his collaborators in the composition of the mystical part of the famous treatise.[2] He, too, began, without intending it, he says, to learn of the mystical states by experience. Henceforth, he grew to know them more and more. " As his pen wrote of the marvellous transports of divine love, he himself happily experienced it."[3]

" My dear daughter," he declared in 1615 to St Chantal, " thank God for the leisure he has given me these two days for a little extraordinary prayer; for truly his goodness has shed so many lights into my mind, and into my poor heart so great an ardour to write in our dear book of holy love, that I know not where I shall find words to express what I have conceived."[4]

Too often, alas, his many occupations obliged him to set aside the pen, just when his soul overflowed with mystical impulses and he had the greatest ease in expressing them. He was " very grieved " at this and confided his sorrow to his " very dear Mother " de Chantal :

" This blessed one," she said at the process of beatification, " wrote an admirable treatise in twelve books on this subject [the Love of God], in which I perceive that he naïvely depicted himself."[5]

It was indeed in a sort of ecstasy, the heart overflowing with love, that our Saint composed his treatise. He admitted later on to St Vincent de Paul that when re-reading it, after finishing it in 1616, he wept abundant tears.[6] What happy tears and how contagious ! How many readers have in their turn wept over these pages, " all perfumed with most intimate devotion !" It is because their writer filled them with the fire of his soul and with the beatings of his heart, revealing a living love, love in action far more than in theory.

Nevertheless, neither his own mystical experiences nor those of the first Visitandines were the only sources from which he drew. He studied, as he states in the Preface to his treatise, the principal writers, both ancient and modern,

[1] It was begun in 1607. Cf. *Letter* to Baroness de Chantal, February 11, 1607 (Vol. XIII, p. 265).
[2] M. Henri Bremond has very well demonstrated this influence of the Visitandines on the *Treatise of the Love of God*. *Histoire du sentiment religieux,* Vol. II, pp. 564 ff.
[3] Dom Mackey, Vol. IV, p. xiii.
[4] *Œuvres,* Vol. IV, p. xiv.
[5] *Déposition,* art. XXVI, *Œuvres de Sainte Chantal,* Vol. II, published separately as *The Soul of St Francis de Sales revealed by St J. F. de Chantal,* Annecy, 1922, p. 51.
[6] De la Rivière, *Vie,* Book IV, chap. xliv.

who have written on divine love. Among the modern, the Spanish writers, and especially St Teresa, held a prominent place.[1]

"I say nothing," he humbly said, "that I have not learnt from others; but it would be impossible for me to remember from whom I have received each thing in particular."[2]

B—THE TEACHING OF THE "TREATISE ON THE LOVE OF GOD"[3]

St Francis de Sales tells us that he wanted "to represent . . . the history of the birth, progress, decline, operations, properties, advantages, and excellencies of divine love."[4] He admits that in his treatise may be found "excrescences" and apparently useless digressions. In his description of the genesis of divine love he goes far back. He explains teaching which apparently would have been better placed in a work of dogmatic theology:

"The first four Books," he says, "and certain chapters in others, might doubtless be omitted at the will of those who only seek the simple practice of holy love, but all that would still be very useful to them if they regard it with devotion."[5]

It is "all that follows from what belongs to the treatise of heavenly love." To cut out a part was to risk the charge

[1] Four Spanish or Portuguese writers, without counting St Teresa, have been mentioned: Luis of Granada; Stella Diego (1524-1598) a Portuguese, *De amore ·Dei meditationes,* Salamanca, 1578; Fonseca Christophe (1540-1616), *Del Amor di Dios,* Barcelona, 1591; John of Jesus Mary (1564-1615), *Ars amandi Deum.* Also three French writers: Louis Richeome, S.J., of Provence (1544-1625), *La Peinture spirituelle ou l'art d'admirer, aimer et louer Dieu en toutes ses Œuvres,* Lyons, 1621; J. P. Camus, Bishop of Belley, *Parénétique de l'amour de Dieu,* Paris, 1608; Laurens de Paris, Capuchin (†1640), *Le Palais de l'amour divin entre Jésus et l'Ame chrestienne,* 1614. One Italian, Cardinal Bellarmine, *De ascensione mentis in Deum per scalas rerum creatarum.* Still other writers inspired St Francis de Sales, especially St Catherine of Genoa.

[2] *Œuvres,* Vol. IV, pp. 10-11.

[3] The *Treatise on the Love of God* has twelve books. The first deals with the will of man and his affections, the description of love in general; the second, with the heavenly origin of divine love; the third, with the progress and perfection of love; the fourth, with the decline and ruin of charity; the fifth, with the love of happiness and goodness; the sixth, with mystical prayer; the seventh, with raptures and death through love; the eighth, with the love of conformity to the will of God; the ninth, with the love of submission to the good pleasure of God; the tenth, with the commandment to love God above all things; the eleventh, with the pre-eminence of love over all other virtues; the twelfth, with some advice on progress in holy love.

[4] Preface, Vol. IV, p. 8.

[5] Vol. IV, *ibid.,* p. 9. The digressions are also explained by the fact that the writer wrote "amidst many distractions" by fits and starts. *Ibid.,* p. 8.

of being incomplete, which no one would dream of making against the Bishop of Geneva.

The work begins with a small treatise on the will and the passions, according to the teaching of St Thomas Aquinas.

The will is supreme over all the powers of the soul; but it " governs them differently," for it has not an absolute sway over each of them. The " sensual " appetite, in particular, is a " rebellious, seditious, restless subject."

In this connection St Francis de Sales explains his conception—a fundamental point in his spirituality—of the " two parts " of the reasonable soul :

" In our soul," he says, " since it is reasonable, we clearly note two degrees of perfection, which the great St Augustine, and after him all the doctors, have called two parts of the soul, the lower and the higher : of which that is said to be lower which debates and draws its consequences from what it learns and experiences through the senses; and that is said to be higher which debates and draws its consequences according to intellectual knowledge, which is not founded on the experience of the senses, but on the discernment and judgement of the spirit; and this higher part is generally called the spirit or mental part of the soul, as the lower is usually called sense or feeling and human reason."[1]

Our Saint very often makes use of this doctrine to console his penitents amidst their temptations. It may happen, in the violent assaults of the devil, that all the lower part of the soul is in his power :

" See, my daughter, my soul," he wrote to the Baroness de Chantal in February 18, 1605; "this is a sign that all is taken; that the enemy has won everything in our fortress, save the impregnable keep, which is unconquerable and can only be lost through ourselves. In the end it is this free will, which, all naked in God's sight, resides in the highest and most spiritual part of the soul, depending only on its God and on ourselves; and when all the other faculties of the soul are lost and subject to the enemy, it alone remains mistress of itself in order not to give any consent.[2]

In the *Treatise on the Love of God*, analysis is pushed further, for it is necessary to determine, as soon as possible, what part of the soul is the seat of the mystical state :

" In the higher part of the reason [in mysticism this only is concerned] there are two degrees; in one of which occur

[1] *Love of God*, Book I, chap. xi, Vol. IV, p. 63.
[2] Vol. XIII, p. 10. Cf. *Devout Life*, Part IV, chap. iii : " We have two parts of our soul, the one the lower and the other the higher . . . it often happens that the lower part takes pleasure in the temptation without the consent—nay, against the will—of the higher."

debates on questions of faith and supernatural light, and in the other the simple acquiescences of faith, hope, and charity."[1]

St Francis de Sales has in view here the apex of the soul of which mystics so often speak :

" [It is] a certain eminence and supreme point of the reason and spiritual faculty which is not led by the light of argument or reasoning, but by a simple view of the understanding and a simple feeling of the will, by which the mind acquiesces and submits to the truth and the will of God."[2]

Our Saint, following many other writers, compares this " extremity and summit of our soul, this highest apex of our spirit " to the sanctuary of Solomon's temple :

" In the sanctuary," he says, " there were no windows to give light ; in this degree of the mind there is no enlightenment from discourse. In the sanctuary all light entered through the door ; in this degree nothing enters into the mind except by faith, which produces, like rays, the sight and the sense of the beauty and goodness of the good pleasure of God. None entered the sanctuary but the High Priest ; in this apex of the soul discourse has no access, but only the great, universal and sovereign feeling that the divine will must be supremely loved, approved, and embraced. . . . The High Priest, entering into the sanctuary, darkened still more the light which entered by the door ; and all that comes into view in the highest apex of the soul, is in a certain way darkened and veiled by the renunciations and resignations performed thereby, willing less to look upon and see the beauty of the truth and the truth of the beauty presented to it than to embrace and adore it : so that the soul would desire almost to close its eyes, as soon as it begins to see the worthiness of the will of God, so that, no longer being busy with considering it, it may accept it more potently and perfectly by absolute compliance uniting itself and submitting infinitely thereto."[3]

In the mystical states the role of the mind is quite curtailed. The Bishop of Geneva in this adheres to tradition. The " apex of the mind " does not reason, but all passes within it " by a simple sight and a simple feeling of the divine will," by " the simple acquiescences of faith, hope, and charity."[4]

St Chantal had well noted these mystical facts in St Francis, who seems to describe them from experience :

" As regards myself," she says in her deposition at the process of beatification, " I clearly recognize that this gift of faith which our blessed father had received, was accompanied

[1] *Love of God,* Book I, chap. xii, Vol. IV, p. 69.
[2] *ibid.,* p. 67. [3] *ibid.,* p. 68.
[4] *ibid.,* p. 69.

by great clearness, certainty, relish, and an extraordinary sweetness; that, with simple sight, he saw the truths of faith; and I know that he subjected his understanding to these truths with an absolute peace of mind and will. He called the place in which these clear visions took place the sanctuary of God, where nothing enters but the soul alone with its God.''[1]

If St Francis de Sales thus analyzes the soul and its faculties, it is the better to demonstrate how love rules it. For all the affections and passions of the soul spring '' from love as their root and source.'' Love, whatever it is, also governs the will, yet without doing violence thereto.''

Our Saint first of all gives a description of '' love in general.'' He shows how it is produced and developed. He gives a history of it. This history is summed up in five motions of the will.

Love is born from the '' very close concord '' between '' the will and the good.'' This affinity of the will with the good is such that '' as soon as it perceives it, it turns towards it in order to take pleasure in it.'' Delight in the good perceived is the second motion of the will. The third is the effort of the will to be united with the thing loved. The fourth is the search for the means to realize this union. Finally, at the end of these movements union is achieved.

'' Love comprises all this together, like a beautiful tree, the root of which is the concord of the will with the good, its foot is the delight, its stem is the motion; the seekings, the pursuits, and other efforts are its branches; but the union and enjoyment are its fruit.''[2]

Divine love has a similar history, but it is wholly supernatural.

The true good for man is God. St Francis de Sales teaches that, even from the natural point of view, there exists between God and man a concord '' which is not without its usefulness.'' It is doubtless not able to produce divine love, supernatural charity. But God '' makes use of it as a handle in order to take hold of us more gently and draw us to himself.''[3]

---

[1] *Deposition,* Article xxiv, *Œuvres de St Chantal,* Vol. II. *L'âme de Saint François de Sales,* pp. 43-44.

[2] *Love of God,* Book I, chap. vii, p. 41.

[3] Book I, chap. xviii. *Cf.* chaps. xv-xvii. Bossuet thought, quite wrongly, that in these chapters St Francis de Sales teaches that natural love of God may, of itself, become a supernatural love. Cf. *Œuvres de St François de Sales,* IV, p. lxxii. '' Sacred love is a miraculous child [like Isaac, Jacob, and Joseph] since the human will cannot conceive it if the Holy Spirit do not spread it in our hearts.'' Book I, chap. vi, Vol. IV, p. 39.

Divine love springs from the consideration of the divine
perfections and the eternal charity of God for man. How
can we help loving God who is so perfect? His supernatural
Providence operates upon us in so touching a manner, above
all by " a most abundant redemption," and by " the diversity
of graces which he distributes to men."[1] Is it possible for
us not to love a God who is so good to us? Like St Bernard,
the Bishop of Geneva most lovingly expounds the motives
which urge us to love God. He then shows how faith, hope,
and penance combine together to make charity spring up in
the soul.[2]

Love is the last thing to arise in us. It should be preceded specially by faith and hope. But once it has entered
the soul everything must be subject to it, even the understanding and the will. "If it be not master, it ceases to
exist and perishes." It " must always be king or nothing ";
but it reigns by gentleness:

" Holy love makes its abode in the highest and most uplifted region of the mind . . . so that from so exalted a
place it may be heard and obeyed by its people—that is to
say, by all the faculties and affections of the soul which it
governs with a sweetness without equal; for love has no
convicts or slaves, but reduces all things to its obedience by
so charming a power, that, though nothing is so strong as
love, nothing also is so lovable as its strength."[3]

Having explained the origin of divine love, it might be expected that St Francis de Sales would at once speak of its
exercise. He prefers, however, first to study love's progress
and perfection.[4]

We can always make progress in it during this life. The
most beautiful model of such progress is given us by the
Virgin Mary. The Bishop of Geneva contemplates it with
admiration:

" Of this heavenly Queen," he says, " I declare with all
my heart this loving but most true thought; that at least at
the end of her mortal life her charity surpassed that of the
Seraphim. . . . And going beyond this, I think, too, that
as the charity of this Mother of love surpasses that of all the
saints of heaven in perfection, so also did she exercise it more
excellently, I say, even in this mortal life. She never sinned
venially, as the Church declares; she had, then, no vicissitude

[1] This is the subject of the Second Book of the *Treatise on the Love of God*.
[2] Book II, chaps. xiv-xxi.
[3] Book I, chap. vi, Vol. IV, p. 39.
[4] This is the subject of the Third Book. St Francis de Sales
incidentally speaks (chaps. iv-v) of the final perseverance of divine
love, or of a good death.

or delay in the progress of her love, but mounted from love
to love, advancing perpetually. She never felt any opposition from the sensual appetite; and hence, her love, like a
true Solomon, reigned peacefully within her soul and acted as
freely as it wished. The virginity of her heart and of her
body was more worthy and more honourable than that of the
angels; and this is why her mind, not being divided or parted,
as St Paul says, was *wholly occupied in thinking of divine
things, how to please her God.* And finally, maternal love,
the most pressing, most active, and most ardent of all, an
indefatigable and insatiable love, what must it not have been
in the heart of such a mother for such a son?"[1]

The end of divine love is the union of the blessed with God,
a union which is brought about in heaven by the beatific
vision; and in dealing therewith St Francis de Sales wrote
beautiful passages about the Blessed Trinity, the end of such
vision.[2]

"Our love towards God," says our Saint, "is exercised
in two chief ways: the one affective, and the other effective
or, as St Bernard says, active." The first is the love of
willingness and of goodwill, the other is the love of obedience.

The whole of the Fifth Book is consecrated to the love
of willingness and of goodwill.

"Love is none other," as we know, "than the motion and
flow of heart which is directed towards the good by means of
our delight therein." [When we think of the infinite perfections of God] "it is impossible for our will not to be
touched with delight in this good. . . . We delight in the
divine pleasure infinitely more than in our own."[3]

This pleasure which our heart feels when it considers the
divine goodness is again made manifest by the sympathy
which it feels at the sight of the sorrows of the Word
incarnate. Love is compassionate towards the sufferings of
the one who is loved. This explains the extraordinary attraction of the saints and of the devout towards meditation on
the Passion of Christ.

Goodwill in love is exercised "by way of desire." It
incites the soul to wish for good things for God, as though
he lacked them: an imaginary and conditional desire—for
God lacks nothing—but it has the value of an act of
love.

"This desire," says St Francis de Sales, ". . . by imagining
impossible things, may sometimes be usefully practised

---

[1] Book III, chap. viii, pp. 191-192.
[2] *ibid.,* chaps. xi-xiv. In the Fourth Book of the *Treatise on Divine
Love,* St Francis de Sales points out how divine love may be lost.
[3] Book V, chap. i, Vol. IV, pp. 255-256.

amidst strong emotions and during extraordinary fervour; it is moreover said of the great St Augustine that he often practised the same, in his excess of love exclaiming thus: 'Lo, Lord! I am Augustine and thou art God; yet if that were which neither is nor could be, if I were God and thou wert Augustine, I would desire to change with thee and become Augustine that thou mightest be God.' "[1]

If the love of goodwill is able to give nothing to God who is infinitely perfect, it " at least desires that his name be blessed, exalted, praised, honoured, and adored more and more." It sings " the benediction of its dear Beloved."[2] In its ardour for the glory of God, it calls upon all creatures, in union with the angels and saints and with the Virgin Mary, to sing the divine praises. It is happy to make its own Christ's praise of God, which is of infinite value.[3]

It is chiefly by prayer that the love of compliance and of goodwill is exercised. St Francis de Sales speaks of this exercise in the Sixth Book of his treatise, and he considers it exclusively from the point of view of love.

He calls prayer " mystical theology," because it has God as its object, but " God in the measure in which he is supremely to be loved." It tends less to the knowledge of God than to the love of God, by which it is distinguished from speculative theology. " It is called mystical because the converse therein is entirely secret, and nothing is said in it between God and the soul except from heart to heart, by communications incommunicable to any other than to those who make them."[4]

In this sense simple meditation belongs to mystical theology. Moreover it is the " mother of love,"[5] and its daughter is contemplation.

The Bishop of Geneva describes contemplation in differentiating it from meditation. " Contemplation is nothing other than a loving, simple, and permanent attention of the mind to divine things." This is the traditional definition, with a suggestion of meaning that accentuates the part played by love. Contemplation " is practised with pleasure," because " it presupposes that we have found God and his holy love and that we rejoice and delight therein."[6]

Divine love it is which also produces passive recollection and the prayer of quiet.[7] St Francis de Sales explains these

---

[1] Book V, chap. vi, Vol. IV, pp. 276-277.
[2] *ibid.*, chap. viii, pp. 282, 284. [3] *ibid.*, chaps. viii-xii.
[4] Book VI, chap. i, Vol. IV, pp. 303-304.
[5] *ibid.*, chap. iii, p. 313. The title of chapter ii is as follows: " Of meditation, the first degree of prayer or mystical theology."
[6] *ibid.*, chap. vi, p. 323. [7] *ibid.*, chaps. vii-ix.

by drawing from St Teresa. He very skilfully unravels the
divers degrees of " holy quiet." The mystical experiences of
St Chantal and the first Visitandines must have specially
guided him in this.[1]

Before reaching ecstatic union the Bishop of Geneva notes
several mystical phenomena brought about by love : " The
flowing or liquefaction of the soul in God," the " wound of
love," the " loving languor of the heart wounded by delight." [2]

Mystical union of the soul with God is brought about by
love. It has different degrees. The highest is that of rapture
or ecstasy in which the union suspends the faculties of the
soul, totally or partly, according to its intensity.[3]

The supreme effect of affective love is to unite the soul
with its God by slaying the body.

The pages of the *Treatise on the Love of God* which explain this effect are specially moving. St Francis de Sales
must have wept with love when he wrote the account taken
from the *Sermons* of St Bernardine of Siena,[4] of the nobleman
who traversed all the regions of Palestine sanctified by the
presence of Christ in the body, and died with love on the
Mount of Olives uttering this prayer : " O Jesus, my sweet
Jesus, I know not now where to seek thee or follow thee on
earth. Ah, Jesus ! Jesus my love, grant this heart then to
follow thee and take flight to thee above !"[5]

Several of the saints died of love ; the Bishop of Geneva
enumerates them with joy.[6] But above all does the death of
the Blessed Virgin enrapture him. This " glorious Virgin
died of a supremely sweet and tranquil love."

" The phœnix is said, when very old, to gather on the
mountain heights a quantity of aromatic wood, upon which,
as on a bed of honour, it prepares to end its days, for when
the midday sun sends forth his hottest beams, this quiet,
peerless bird, in order to add to the strength of the sun, beats
its wings unceasingly upon its funeral pile until it sets it on
fire, and burns with it, and is thus consumed, dying amidst
the sweet-smelling flames. In the same way, Theotimus,
the Virgin Mary, having gathered up in her mind, by most
lively and continual memory, all the most lovable mysteries
of the life and death of her Son, and ever receiving directly

---

[1] Book VI, chaps. x-xi. We may compare these chapters with the
Œuvres of St Chantal, Vol. II, pp. 260, 337, etc.
[2] *ibid.,* chaps. xii-xv.
[3] Book VII, chaps. iii-viii. St Francis de Sales is again inspired
by St Teresa.
[4] First Sermon on the Ascension.
[5] Book VII, chap. vii, Vol. V, pp. 45-47.
[6] *ibid.,* chaps. ix-xi. Among the holy persons cited is found the
name of Jean Gerson, Chancellor of the University of Paris (chap. ix).

therefrom those most ardent inspirations which her Son, the *Sun of Justice,* has cast upon the world at the highest midday of his charity; besides making also on her part a perpetual act of contemplation, the sacred fire of divine love finally wholly consumed her as a holocaust of sweetness, so that she died of it, her soul being wholly rapt and transported into the arms of the love of her Son.   O death, in love giving life; O love, in life giving death !"[1]

Affective love, if it be true, becomes effective love, that is love in conformity with the divine will.   This conformity springs from the loving heart's delight in God.

" By dint of delight in God, we become conformable with God, and our will is transformed into that of his divine Majesty by its delight therein.   Love, says St Chrysostom, " either discovers or draws the likeness."[2]

The love of goodwill also gives us this holy conformity in another way.

" For goodwill desires all honour for God, all the glory, and all the recognition that is possible to be rendered him, as a certain outward good which befits his goodness."[3]

Now, the best " outward good " which we are able to give to God is the obedience which he wills or permits.

God's will may be his " will signified " or his " will of good pleasure."   He who loves fully submits himself to both of them.

St Francis de Sales explains at length, in the Eighth Book of his treatise, how his will is signified by the Ten Commandments, by the evangelical counsels, and by the inspirations of grace.

" Christian doctrine," he says, " clearly proposes to us the truths which God wills us to believe, the goods for which he wills us to hope, the punishments which he wills us to fear, that which he wills us to love, the Commandments he wills us to observe, and the counsels which he desires us to follow; and all this is called the signified will of God, because he has signified and made it manifest that he wills and intends that all this should be believed, hoped for, feared, loved, and practised."[4]

Contempt of the counsels " is a great sin."   Each one should love and practise what he can.   But the faithful are not obliged to practise them all.

We should also make our will conform to that of God by following his inspirations; these also belong to his signified will.   Such " inspiration is a heavenly ray which sheds into

---

[1] Book VII, chap. xiii, Vol. V, pp. 51-52.
[2] Book VIII, chap. i, Vol. V, p. 60.   [3] *ibid.*, p. 63.
[4] *ibid.*, chap. iii, p. 65.

our hearts a warm light by which he [God] shows us the good and incites us to the pursuit of it."[1]

God thus inspires us in a thousand ways, either in order to make us practise virtue with extraordinary perfection or know our vocation or persevere in the way in which we are. He who loves truly unites his will with that of God in all such inspirations.

The love of God is still better shown by submission to the divine good pleasure, as made known by events.

" Nothing, except sin, is done but by the will of God which is called absolute, or the will of good pleasure, which no one can prevent, and it is known to us only by its effects, the occurrence of which shows us that God has willed them and determined them."[2]

To such belong spiritual tribulations, trials, and afflictions. We should unite our will to the divine good pleasure by resignation and by indifference. Indifference in all things, " things of the service of God . . . in what concerns our advancement in virtue," and even in a certain way, " in the permission of sins."[3]

The will should love God with a wholly pure and dis-interested love. Like a musician that has become deaf— this is St Francis de Sales'[4] comparison—who plays the lute in the court of an indifferent prince. This musician does not enjoy the sweetness of the airs he makes heard, since he has lost his hearing. He has not the satisfaction of pleasing his prince, for the latter goes away and leaves him to play all alone, from obedience. In the same way the soul ought to sing the canticle of love, not to please itself, but solely to please God. And often even, without knowing if its song be pleasing to its Lord, it must continue to sing " amidst the spiritual anguish," which renders its love extremely pure and clear. It will be deprived of all pleasure which might attach it to God. Thus love " joins us and unites us to God directly, will to will, heart to heart, without any medium of contentment or of expectation."[5] Nowhere, so much as here, is felt the influence of St Catherine of Genoa on St Francis de Sales. Pure love is crucifying.

The will is thus dead to self. It lives " purely in the will of God," in the most perfect indifference. It is " a most lovable passing away."

St Francis de Sales again explains this doctrine by another

---

[1] Book VIII, chap. x, Vol. V, p. 89.

[2] Book IX, chap. i, p. 109. All this Ninth Book is devoted to this will of good pleasure.

[3] *ibid.*, chaps. iv-viii.　　　　　　[4] *ibid.*, chaps. ix and xi.

[5] *ibid.*, chap. xii, pp. 147-148. This disinterestedness and in-difference of soul never make it cease to hope for its salvation. Quietists have wrongly cited this Book IX of the *Treatise on the Love of God* in favour of their erroneous teaching.

comparison more enlightening than any discourse. The passage is constantly quoted.

" The daughter of an excellent doctor and surgeon was in a state of constant fever, and knew that her father loved her tenderly. She said to one of her friends : ' I am in great pain, but, nevertheless, I do not think of remedies, for I do not know what could help my cure ; I might want one thing, yet really need another. Do I not gain, then, by leaving the care of all this to my father who knows, and can and will do everything required for my health? I should do wrong to think about it, for he will think enough for me ; I should do wrong to want anything, for he will want enough of everything that is good for me. I shall only wait for him to will what he thinks needful, and interest myself in watching him when he is near me, thus giving him proof of my filial love and letting him know of my perfect trust.' And with these words she fell asleep, whilst her father, judging it expedient to bleed her, made the necessary arrangements ; and coming to her as she awoke, after inquiring how she felt after her sleep, he asked if she were willing to be bled in order to get well. ' Father,' she replied, ' I am yours ; I do not know what to wish for in order to be cured, it is for you to wish to do for me all you think good ; for me, indeed, it is enough to love you and honour you with all my heart, which I do.' With this her arm was bound and her father himself cut the vein with a lance ; but while he was cutting it and the blood spurted out, not once did his loving daughter look at her wounded arm nor at the blood flowing from her vein, but remaining thus, with eyes fixed on her father's face, she said nothing except occasionally and quite softly this : ' My father loves me well, and I am altogether his ' ; and when all was over, she did not thank him, but only repeated the same words of affection and filial trustfulness."[1]

What a touching and expressive symbol of the total indifference, of the full and entire abandonment of the soul filially submissive to God. St Francis de Sales had reached this supreme degree of conformity to the divine will when he said towards the end of his life :

" I wish for few things : and what I desire I desire but little ; I have scarcely any desires, but were I to be born once more I should have none at all. If God were to come to me [to grant me a sense of his presence], I also should go to him ; if he willed not to come to me, I should keep still and not go to him [I mean I should not seek to have this sense of his presence, but be content with the simple apprehension of faith].

" So I say that we must neither ask nor refuse anything,

[1] Book IX, chap. xv, Vol. V, pp. 156-157.

but leave ourselves in the hands of divine Providence without gratifying ourselves with any desire, save willing what God wills of us."[1]

Here the treatise might have ended. But the writer is captivated by his subject; he cannot leave it. At the risk of once more breaking the logical connection of the parts of his work, he explains, in the tenth book, the great commandment to love God above all things and one's neighbour as oneself (Matthew xxii, 37-39). In connection with the love of one's neighbour St Francis de Sales speaks highly of zeal, and also of the qualities of goodness and prudence which are needed.[2] Then he shows " the precious influence of sacred love " on all the other virtues.[3] He ends his magnificent work with some advice for the making of spiritual progress in holy love.[4]

The *Treatise on the Love of God* was received with enthusiasm, above all in France, where, at the beginning of the seventeenth century, arose a splendid movement of Christian reform. But it seems to be the fate of great works to be disputed. Posterity judges them from points of view unknown to their authors. This change of perspective often prevents them from being justly appreciated.

St Francis de Sales dwells at great length—as we have seen—on perfect conformity to the will of God and on holy indifference in all things. He rightly sees in this the highest exercise of divine love, the complete stripping of the soul in order to be united to God. And then there arose, a few years later, quietism. Its supporters claim that true charity, pure

---

[1] *True Spiritual Conferences,* Dialogue XXI. *Of asking nothing,* Vol. VI, pp. 383-384. See the variants in the notes, *ibid.* St Chantal says this in her *Deposition* at the process of beatification of St Francis de Sales, art. xxvi : " The ordinary confessor of the Blessed One told me, and I am also sure that it is so, that our Blessed Father did nothing in order to avoid hell or to gain Paradise ; but he did all his actions purely and simply for the sole honour of God, whom he feared because he loved him, and loved him because he merited it, and for the love of [God] himself. Moreover, he said that his heart had ' as its sovereign law the greatest glory and love of God.' "—We can understand how these kinds of expressions must have disturbed the opponents of quietism in the height of the controversy. They are, however, understood when placed in the historical circumstances which belong to them. It is so true that St Chantal does not intend to say that the Bishop of Geneva suppressed the virtue of hope, that in the preceding article (xxv) she speaks of the manner in which he practised this virtue.

[2] Book X, chaps. xii-xvi.

[3] This is the subject of Book XI. The writer there shows " how charity comprises in itself the gifts of the Holy Spirit." Chaps. xv-xviii.

[4] Book XII, and the last.

love, exclude hope, induce the soul to become disinterested even in its eternal salvation. What is most astounding, they imagine that they find such teaching in the Salesian *Treatise on the Love of God*.[1] Bossuet, their opponent, had no difficulty in justifying St Francis de Sales, not, however, without subjecting him to certain criticisms.[2] Hence, the great work suffered some slight discredit; a discredit, it is true, that was but momentary, but one that did not wholly disappear until Pius IX proclaimed St Francis de Sales a Doctor of the Church.[3]

The *Treatise on the Love of God*, then, in spite of the controversies which arose in connection therewith, remains one of the most beautiful masterpieces of Christian spirituality.

[1] *Cf.* Dom Mackey, Translator's *Introduction to the Treatise on the Love of God*, pp. vi-xxiii.

[2] *Instruction sur les états d'oraison*, Books VIII-IX. The criticisms are chiefly in the *Préface sur l'Instruction pastorale* de M. de Cambrai, section 11, no. cxxiv ff.

[3] The decree was promulgated July 7, 1877, and confirmed November 16 of the same year.

CHAPTER XII

THE FRENCH SCHOOL BEFORE BÉRULLE — CARDINAL
RICHELIEU — PIERRE DE BÉRULLE — THE TREATISE
ON THE GREATNESS OF JESUS — GENERAL CHAR-
ACTERISTICS OF BERULLIAN SPIRITUALITY

ST FRANCIS DE SALES had considerable influence
in France at the beginning of the seventeenth
century. First of all through his works and afterwards through intercourse.

In 1602, charged with some diplomatic mission,
he made a stay in Paris. There he met the Doctors of the
Sorbonne, Asseline and André Duval, the masters of Bérulle,
the Carthusian Beaucousin, and Bérulle himself. He must
have had conversations with Mme Acarie, "a new Teresa,"
with Marie de Beauvillier, the future reformer of the Abbey
of Montmartre, and with others.[1] Not, indeed, ephemeral
conversations, for later on he exchanged letters with his
Paris friends. His advice was appreciated and his direction
sought and followed.

After his death his influence still increased. He had, too,
some faithful interpreters : St Chantal, first of all, who
" shaped herself according to his pattern; she drew life from
him and from his thought : people came to her as a living
relic of Francis de Sales."[2] Then " two Salesian masters,"
the Jesuit Étienne Binet,[3] and the Bishop of Belley, Jean-
Pierre Camus.[4] Finally, the great number of those who go

[1] *Cf.* H. Bremond, *Hist. du sent. relig.*, p. 92 ff. Respecting Mme
Acarie (Blessed Mary of the Incarnation), see André Duval, *La vie
admirable de Mme Acarie,* 1621.

[2] Bremond, *ibid.*, p. 129.

[3] See *ibid.*, chap. iv. Étienne Binet was born at Dijon in 1569. He
very soon became acquainted with St Francis de Sales, perhaps in
Paris or at the College of Clermont. Becoming a Jesuit in 1590, he
was obliged to go into exile in Italy until 1603. He was an eminent
director. His relations with St Chantal were frequent, but not always
peaceful. He died in Paris in 1639. His chief works : *Les attraits
tout puissants de l'amour de Jésus-Christ,* Paris, 1631 ; *Le grand chef-
d'œuvre de Dieu et les souveraines perfections de la Sainte Vierge,*
Lyons, 1649 ; *Essai des merveilles de la nature . . .,* Paris, 1639.

[4] Jean-Pierre Camus was born in Paris, November 3, 1584. Made
Bishop of Belley at twenty-five he was consecrated by St Francis de
Sales at the Cathedral of Belley, August 30, 1609. He died in Paris,
April 25, 1652. His best known work is *L'Esprit du bienheureux
François de Sales,* published in 1639, 1640, 1641, in six 8o volumes. He
wrote several works on spirituality, especially devout stories, in the

more easily to God by the way of love than by that of fear. The Salesian spirit is always likely to charm the greater number.

The French School, however, was not Salesian. Circumstances directed it much more towards St Paul and St Augustine than to the Bishop of Geneva. Nevertheless, its founders were affective. They knew how to transform theological speculations into prayer, as Asseline was requested to do in a famous letter from St Francis de Sales.[1]

The French School was prepared, towards the end of the sixteenth century, by a group of holy men whose religious influence was deep : " There is matter," wrote M. Bremond, " for a very fine book on the interior life of French Catholicism during this time of upheaval."[2] But this interior life was revealed much more by works than by books. The religious wars and the divisions caused by them hindered literary composition. It was a period of action and not of writing.

Under the peaceful reign of Henry IV writing revived. Some interesting spiritual writers may be then noted, especially among the Jesuits,[3] Carmelites,[4] and Capuchins. Many

---

taste of the time. *Cf.* Henri Bremond, *Hist. du sent. relig. en France,* Vol. I, pp. 149-173, 273 ff.; Boulas, *Un ami de S Fr. de Sales, Camus, évêque de Belley,* Lons-le-Saunier, 1878, in which a complete list of the works of Camus will be found; De Baudry, *Le véritable esprit de S Fr. de Sales,* Lyons, Paris, 1846.

[1] Letter to Dom Eustache de Saint-Paul Asseline (Cistercian), November 15, 1611, respecting the project of a *Summa* of Theology : " I approve of your stating the arguments for your opinions in this [affective] style wherever it could suitably be done. . . . The opinions might be drawn up in affective style. . . ." Vol. XV, pp. 119-120.

[2] *Hist. du sent relig.,* II, p. 7.

[3] Louis Richeome, Fr. Coton, and Etienne Binet. Richeome was born at Digne in 1544. His books were both controversial and ascetic. *Œuvres,* Paris, 1628. The ascetic works are in Vol. II. The chief of these is *La Peinture spirituelle ou l'art d'admirer, aimer et louer Dieu en toutes ses œuvres,* Lyons, 1611. Fr. Coton, confessor to Henry IV and controversialist, was born at Néronde in le Forez, in 1564, and died in Paris in 1626. His book *L'intérieure occupation d'une âme dévote* comprises letters of direction a little like St Francis de Sales' *Introduction.* Fr. Binet has already been mentioned.

[4] Jean de Saint Samson, lay brother, was the St John of the Cross of the Carmelite reform in France. Born at Sens in 1571, blind from the age of three, at thirty-five he entered the Carmelite Convent of Dôle. Very soon raised to the mystical state, he delivered discourses to his brethren on the spiritual life and dictated treatises. His works were published in the seventeenth century in two folios, by Fr. Donatien de Saint Nicolas : *Les œuvres spirituelles et mystiques du divin contemplatif et mystique Jean de Saint-Samson.* His teaching is obscure, like that of the German mystics. *Cf.* Sernin-Marie de Saint-André, O.C.D., *Vie du Ven. P. Jean de Saint-Samson,* Paris, 1881. The

of them were formidable antagonists of the Protestants. All of them spread the Christian spirit around them and were centres of the interior life. M. Bremond has devoted some charming and well-known pages to them.[1]

The Capuchins, quite newly settled in France, took an active part in this religious restoration. Two of them, above all, deserve notice on account of the extent of their influence : Bennet Canfield and Fr. Joseph Tremblay, "the grey cardinal."

William Fitch, the future Bennet Canfield,[2] was born at Canfield, Essex, in England. He came while still young to France. He entered the Capuchins in 1586. His chief work is his *Règle de perfection réduite au seul point de la volonté divine.* To become fully and heroically abandoned to the divine will, such, *par excellence,* is the means of reaching perfection. This book had a great success when it appeared a few years after the death of its author. But it had not only admirers : many found its teaching subtle and rather dubious.[3]

Joseph, the Clerk of Tremblay,[4] is the author of an *Introduction à la vie spirituelle par une facile méthode d'oraison.*[5] It is an adaptation of the Ignatian method to the seraphic spirit. The *Spiritual Exercises* were used in almost all the religious Orders. It was therefore opportune to introduce them among the daughters of St Francis de Sales, though with all needful modifications. The *Exercises* tended in France, as they did in Spain and Italy, to become more and more important.

---

mysticism of Marguerite Acarie, Carmelite, daughter of Mme Acarie, has been explained by Fr. J. M. de Vernon : *Conduite chrétienne et religieuse selon les sentiments de la V. M. Marguerite,* Paris, 1691 (2nd ed.).

[1] *Hist. du sent. relig.,* Vols. I and II. It was also at this time that "the great Abbesses" brought about the reform of the abbeys of Paris. Marie de Beauvillier reformed the Abbey of Montmartre, Marguerite d'Arbouze that of Val de Grâce. All thus prepared for the great century.

[2] *Cf.* J. Bruosse, *La vie du R. P. Ange de Joyeuse . . . ensemble la vie des R.R. F.F. Benoit Anglais . . .,* Paris, 1621.

[3] Above all in Part III. This was specially the opinion of St Francis de Sales, *Œuvres,* IV, p. ix. The accusation of quietism seems to be exaggerated.

[4] Born in Paris, in 1577, he received a humanist education, and travelled in Italy and in England. Entering the Capuchin Order in 1599, about 1613 he became *l'Éminence grise* attached to Richelieu. He died in 1638. *Cf.* Dedouvres, *Études franciscaines,* April-June, 1921 and ff.

[5] Published about 1616, reissued at Mans in 1897, under the title *Méthode d'oraison du P. Joseph Tremblay,* by P. Apollinaire de Valence.

I—CARDINAL RICHELIEU'S "TREATISE ON CHRISTIAN PERFECTION"

WE cannot well separate Fr. Joseph from Cardinal Richelieu, particularly from Richelieu the spiritual writer, rather than Richelieu the Minister of State. Does this mean that Fr. Joseph collaborated with the famous cardinal in the *Treatise on Christian Perfection?* It is very likely.

Richelieu, in spite of his overwhelming cares and crushing responsibilities, interested himself particularly in spiritual writings, primarily for his own personal sanctification. Fr. Cloyseault, historian of the beginnings of the French Oratory, tells us that the great cardinal thought so highly of Bour-going's *Meditations,* " that he generally read one of them on the days when he said holy Mass, and that more often than not he took them with him in his carriage so that he could read them when he was alone."[1] He also devoted his pious attention to many other spiritual books. He desired, too, to write some himself. Those that had been written, in spite of their merits, did not appear to him to be sufficiently practical. Let us hear what he says in the introduction to his treatise :

" I candidly grant the virtue and merit of all those who have written on the subject of which I treat ; but the greater number of their works seem so lengthy or so difficult that many minds are only able, with great trouble, to find what they seek in them ; charity, to which nothing is impossible, makes me undertake to describe a road, as easy as it is short, towards attaining Christian perfection."

Such a declaration, after the publication of the *Introduction to the Devout Life,* is surprising. But we must remember that many found Philothea, too, " wrapped up " in devotion. She could not be suggested as a model for many ! Richelieu, in a small treatise of forty-six chapters, traces " a road as easy " as it is " short." Everyone may pass along it and reach perfection without too great difficulty.

The treatise was begun in 1636, during the siege of Corbie. But a Minister of State is not master of his time ! The work did not appear until after the author's death. The Duchesse d'Aiguillon, the cardinal's niece, published it in 1646.[2]

There is no trace of Berullian spirituality to be found in

[1] Quoted by Fr. Ingold in the Preface to the 33rd edition of Bour-going's *Méditations*, Paris, 1906, Vol. I, p. xiii.

[2] In the dedication to the Blessed Virgin there is an allusion to a vow made by Louis, February 10, 1638, just when Richelieu was writing his book. Migne has reproduced the *Treatise on Christian Perfection* at the end of his *Dictionnaire d'ascéticisme,* Vol. II, pp. 1017-1190. This is the edition I shall quote. Richelieu (1585-1642) also composed the *Instruction du Chrestien,* Paris, 1626, a catechetical work, and also some works of controversy with the Protestants.

it. But the influence of the *Introduction to the Devout Life* is seen, above all, in the chapters in which it is shown that " in every condition of life it is possible to arrive at Christian perfection," and that true devotion requires, beyond everything, entire solicitude for the duties of our station.[1]

As for the rest, the work progresses very differently from that of St Francis de Sales. The whole doctrine of perfection is reduced to the theory of the three ways of the spiritual life. Perfection is reached in the unitive way :

" The third degree of the spiritual life is the unitive life, which is no other than the care which the Christian, cleansed from sin by the purgative life, enlightened and inflamed by the illuminative life, takes to become united to God through perfect charity. This gives him so great a conformity of will with God that without in any way considering himself, he no longer desires anything that is not willed by God, and desires it only from the consideration that God wills it."[2]

Here again we have pure love in the notion of Christian perfection.[3]

" The practice of mental prayer " is " the principal part of the illuminative life " ; for " mental prayer is an operation of our soul in which, by the penetration of a truth of faith, our will is incited to will and to ask God for Christian perfection, or to make some notable advancement therein."[4]

Moreover, with regard to the second degree of the spiritual life, the writer gives us a fairly complete treatise on prayer, which reproduces the traditional teaching on the subject. Of these we confine ourselves merely to the then famous scholastic theories " concerning divers kinds of mental prayer." These matters we are told are abstruse. " Great obscurity is found in what contemplatives write on this subject,"[5] says Richelieu. He strives therefore to be very clear. Nevertheless, to follow him we must be acquainted with the Thomist system of knowledge.

We may, he explains, conceive of " two kinds of prayer. . . . The first is called ordinary prayer or meditation. The second extraordinary prayer or contemplation."

" Meditation is performed by means of images or of species which we receive by the outward senses, which perceive objects represented to them. . . . In this way the consideration of a stone or anything of the kind will bring man to

---

[1] Chaps. xli-xliv. We also find there the influence of Luis of Granada and of St Teresa.

[2] Chap. vi, Migne, p. 1039. In the first five chapters the writer develops the motives which ought to lead man to assure his salvation. In the chapters on the purgative way we would note the pointing out, as against the Protestants, of the divine institution of confession and the invitation to frequent communion. Chaps. ix-xxii.

[3] *Cf.* Chap. xl.   [4] Chap. xxvi, Migne, p. 1109.

[5] Chap. xxxi, Migne, p. 1129.

God; as it is impossible to think that this stone of which he has the image or sensible species in the imagination is a creature, without recognizing that God is its Creator and Master."[1]

This meditation may be performed by the reason alone—and we then arrive at the simple knowledge of the existence of God—or by reason enlightened by the light of faith. By this second and more perfect means, the Christian knows "many things which cannot come from the senses." He knows not only "that God is, but what he is; so that we are able to conceive with evidence the perfections of his being as they are."[2]

Extraordinary prayer or contemplation "is that in which man sees and knows God without any use of the imagination and without discourse." The mind has no need to make any effort nor has it any labour to perform.[3] It is God who enlightens the soul supernaturally, and this in three principal ways.

"One by the infusion of intelligible species, which are not drawn from the senses, but formed by God expressly in the mind of man." These species, not being produced through the senses or coming from creatures, are much better fitted to enable us to know God:

"These species infused by God are called by contemplatives, deiform and deific; because of their greater likeness to the knowledge of the saints who in heaven are attached to God by himself, than to that of men who are only led to him while on earth in the ordinary way by species drawn from sensible objects."[4]

St Francis de Sales seems to make allusion to this mode of contemplation when he recommends Philothea and Baroness de Chantal not to be too desirous of the much-talked-about "deific union."

The second way in which God supernaturally enlightens the contemplative "consists, not in the creation of a new form, species or image; but only by infusion" of a very powerful extraordinary light whereby the soul knows God very perfectly.[5]

Finally, the third way is the beatific vision: the soul sees "God in his essence through the light of glory." In heaven this vision is permanent. Here below, it can only be passing and momentary. "Such were the visions of Moses and of St Paul."[6] In agreement with several writers, Richelieu believes

---

[1] Chap. xxxi, Migne, p. 1127.   [2] *ibid.*, p. 1125.
[3] The writer lets it be understood that this mode of knowledge is "special to certain souls to whom God wishes to give a degree of particular exaltation." Migne, p. 1125.
[4] Chap. xxxi, Migne, p. 1126.
[5] *ibid.*   [6] *ibid.*

that the contemplative may be raised during brief moments to intuitive vision.

These theories regarding contemplation are expounded with remarkable clearness. They disclose a practised theologian. They also give to the *Treatise on Christian Perfection* a special interest : that of reproducing mystical theories much in vogue at the beginning of the seventeenth century. But the work of Richelieu remains entirely outside the general run of the French School, which began with Bérulle.

II—PIERRE DE BÉRULLE—THE TREATISE "DES GRANDEURS DE JÉSUS"

THE chief of the French School is Pierre de Bérulle, the founder of the Oratory of France. His most famous disciples are Condren, St Vincent de Paul, Olier, founder of the seminary of St Sulpice, St John Eudes, and Blessed Grignion de Montfort. Bossuet is also a disciple of Bérulle and owes a great part of his spiritual teaching to him.

Pierre de Bérulle was born February 4, 1575, at Sérilly, in Champagne.[1] His father, Claude de Bérulle, was adviser to the Parliament of Paris. His mother, Louise Séguier, daughter of President Séguier, trained him early in piety and inspired him with a deep distaste for worldly pleasures. He made his studies in the Paris University, first of all at the colleges of Boncourt and Burgundy, where he studied literature ; afterwards at the college of Clermont, conducted by the Jesuits and rendered famous through young Francis de Sales, where he followed the much esteemed courses in philosophy and theology ; finally at the Sorbonne.

It was while he was studying philosophy, about 1593, that he grew in the sense of the sovereignty of God and of the dependence of the creature, which afterwards brought him to give so prominent a place in his spirituality to the virtue of religion. Once the young Bérulle even gave one of his fellow-scholars "a discourse so uplifted beyond that which he could have learnt from his master, in order to explain the depen-

---

[1] Bérulle's first biographer was Germain Habert, Abbot of Cérisy, *La vie du Cardinal de Bérulle* . . ., Paris, 1646. Later, Batterel and Goujet each composed a *Life* of Bérulle, which was not published. In 1817, the Oratorian Tabaraud published a *Histoire de Pierre de Bérulle* . . ., Paris. Finally, the Abbé Houssaye wrote three volumes on Bérulle, which are an authority : *M. de Bérulle et les carmelites de France*, Paris, 1872; *Le Père de Bérulle et l'Oratoire de Jésus*, Paris, 1874; *Le cardinal de Bérulle et le cardinal de Richelieu*, Paris, 1875. See also A. Perraud, *L'Oratoire de France au XVIIe et au XIXe siècle*, Paris, 1865. Above all H. Bremond, *Histoire littéraire du sentiment religieux en France*, Vol. III, *L'École française*, pp. 3 ff.

dence which creatures have upon God, as much in their being
as in their operations, and to show they have to be closely
bound to him by the disposition of their will as well as by the
disposition of their essence," that it was inferred that he
" could not have derived this teaching from any other school
than that of the Holy Spirit."[1]

Bérulle expounds these same ideas in his first work : *Brief
discours de l'abnégation intérieure,* published in 1597 with
the approbation of André Duval, one of his most famous
masters at the Sorbonne. It is upon these that he rests the
whole doctrine of abnegation :

" There are," he says, " two foundation stones of this
abnegation. The first, a very low estimate of all created
things and of oneself above all, acquired by the frequent
thought of their baseness, and by the daily experience of
one's nothingness and infirmity. . . . The second is a very
high idea of God, not by a high insight into the attributes
of the Divinity, which is not necessary and which few have;
but by the total submission of self to God in order to adore
him and give him all power over us and what is ours without
reserving any personal interest however sacred."[2]

In this little treatise, Bérulle takes pleasure in humiliating
fallen human nature. He only speaks of it to show contempt
for it and to demean it. He desires man's soul to regard
itself " as the most vile and useless creature of all, nay, as
dust, mud, and a mass of corruption : so that these things,
which, though most vile, are nevertheless useful in some
ways, wherein it is of no use except to offend God.[3] It is
difficult, in this passage and in a number of others, to fail to
see traces of that Augustinian pessimism which is to be met
with so frequently in the French School. And, as it seems
to me, there is more than this. Bérulle wishes to react
against the humanism which exalted human nature too
highly. Did this reaction begin at the Sorbonne when he was
studying there?[4] It is certain that, especially since the Reformation, the attention of theologians was greatly drawn
towards the writings of St Augustine, which had been so
much misconstrued by Luther. And we know that all the
theology of the seventeenth century was very deeply impregnated with Augustinianism.

[1] Houssaye, Vol. I, p. 103.
[2] *Œuvres complètes de Bérulle,* Migne, Paris, 1856, p. 879. Bérulle
published this little treatise on abnegation by order of his spiritual
director, the Carthusian Beaucousin. Houssaye, I, p. 142. It is a
sort of adaptation from a writing by a Milanese lady, *L'Abrégé de la
Perfection.* Cf. *Œuvres de Saint François de Sales,* IV, p. ix.
[3] *Œuvres complètes,* p. 880.
[4] This needs to be made clear. Bérulle's professors at the Sorbonne
were Asseline, who became a Carthusian, Philippe de Gamaches, and
André Duval. *Cf.* Houssaye, I, p. 122.

Bérulle was ordained priest June 5, 1599, and in the same year he became honorary chaplain to Henry IV.[1] He exerted his zeal chiefly in the direction of souls and in controversy with heretics.[2] His principal work, however, at this epoch was the introduction of St Teresa's reformed Carmelites into France. We know how he was aided in this difficult enterprise, or rather stimulated therein, by Mme Acarie.

But that which interests us mostly is what went on within Bérulle's soul, whence arose his spirituality.

At the same time that he conceived " a very high estimate of God " and " a very low estimate . . . of self," Bérulle felt himself more and more drawn towards the mystery of the Word incarnate. One Christmas night, as Germain Habert relates,[3] whilst Bérulle—he was then about seventeen years old—was assisting at Matins and Mass of the Feast, he suddenly became deeply recollected, and, being rapt in spirit, received such lights regarding the Incarnation and birth of the Son of God as are alone granted to the divinely privileged. Fr. Pacificus, a famous Capuchin, to whom he opened his mind, was struck with wonder. He was again favoured " with a similar revelation " the year after his ordination in 1660, when he made his " election " retreat with the Jesuits at Verdun. The self-humiliation of the Word incarnate was to him the most powerful motive for humbling himself in order to serve God truly :

" In thinking of the incarnation of Jesus Christ," he says, " I weighed deeply and at length in the depth of my soul this sovereign goodness of the Word eternal, who, as very God, is so exalted above all created things, and has indeed deigned to humiliate and abase himself so low as to place on his throne so vile and abject a nature, and has indeed willed to be associated and united therewith so closely that no greater or more intimate union can be found. As the Incarnation is the foundation of our salvation, I have also weighed most deeply how great ought to be the abjection of self, by which he who is resolved to labour for the salvation of his soul must begin, since the Son of God deigned to begin it in this mystery, by the humiliation and abasement of his divine and eternal person."[4]

Bérulle's favourite considerations as to the incarnate Word are on the interior states, the intimate dispositions, and the operations of the Holy Spirit in his most holy soul; and also

[1] Shortly after his ordination, in July 1599, Bérulle published, at Troyes, under the pseudonym of Léon d'Alexis, his *Traité des énergumènes* in connection with the affair of the so-called possessed woman, Marthe Brossier, which so excited Paris. Houssaye, I, pp. 147 ff.
[2] In 1609 Bérulle published in Paris *Trois discours de controverse* (on the mission of pastors, the Mass, and the Real Presence).
[3] *Vie du cardinal de Bérulle,* Book I, chap. iii, Houssaye, I, p. 198.
[4] *Œuvres complètes,* Migne, pp. 1293-1294.

on his life in us, our participation in his state. This thought, apparently, was suggested to him by meditation on the Epistles of St Paul and on the Gospel of St John. The renewal of biblical studies, and especially those of the New Testament, is due, as we know, to Erasmus and the humanists who have given us critical editions of the sacred books. After them, Luther forced Catholic exegetes to study St Paul more closely; for did not the heresiarch draw the principal points of his teaching from the Pauline epistles? Thus, he had to be answered; hence arose a great number of commentaries on the Evangelists and on St Paul. The most famous were the *Commentaries on the Gospels* by the Jesuit Maldonatus († 1583), and those of his confrère, like himself a Spaniard, Francis Tolet († 1596) on the Gospel of St John and on the Epistle to the Romans. Bérulle was not unacquainted with these works. He also studied the Greek Fathers, who throw special light on the operations of the Holy Spirit, the Spirit of Jesus, in the souls of the faithful.

Thus little by little—as far as we are able to see—did the spirituality of Bérulle become elaborated. It was completed in 1611, when the Oratory of Jesus was founded, wholly consecrated to Jesus Christ, the Sovereign Priest.[1]

Some years after this foundation Bérulle was led to give an ample, and even somewhat prolix, exposition of his spiritual teaching.

He did not confine his devotion to the Word incarnate to himself alone. He preached it to the Carmelites and strove to inspire his brethren of the Oratory with it. With this end in view, " he had composed a form of aspiration to Jesus Christ, filled with the highest conceptions of the relationship of the Word incarnate with God the Father and with us. As this book was far above the understanding of the ordinary faithful, he had only communicated it to some of the Oratorians, more advanced in the ways of perfection; then to certain Carmelites of eminent piety, but this with great discretion. In accordance with his invariable custom of never separating the Mother from her divine Son, he joined with this first aspirational prayer a second in which he rendered homage to the greatness of the Blessed Virgin and vowed himself to her service."[2]

That which was new in this devotion was this vow of servitude to Jesus and Mary.

This little book was indiscreetly communicated to the enemies of the Oratory, who caused it to be censured in 1621, both by the University of Louvain and that of Douai. Bérulle,

[1] See Houssaye, Vol. II, on the foundation of the Oratory.
[2] Houssaye, II, p. 401.

urged by his friends, answered these opponents in his masterly
work on the *Grandeurs de Jésus*,[1] divided into twelve discourses. Though it was above all a doctrinal work, it was
also polemical. From time to time Bérulle descends from the
heights to which his thought on the Word incarnate ascends
in order to inveigh against his adversaries. "These *Discourses*," he says in the dedication to the King, " [are]
without rancour or without bitterness." The reader, however, does find a little, to his great regret. He is so charmed
by the talented views of the writer on the wonderful prerogatives of the Word incarnate and on his relations with the faithful, and so edified by the pious upliftings, that he suffers in
finding himself occasionally back to the vulgarities of controversy.

Neither is this treatise easy reading. The style has
nothing in it to attract. It is long-winded and sometimes
too subtle. But "the deep knowledge of the writer . . .
the accuracy of language and his long acquaintance with
antiquity are to be admired."[2] The legitimacy of the vow
of servitude is soundly demonstrated; it is drawn from the
very analysis of the dogma.

The human nature of Jesus, stripped of his own personality, is "essentially in a state of servitude, and remains in
this state, permanent and perpetual, with regard to the
Divinity, by its own nature and condition." It belongs exclusively to the Word. This state of servitude forms all its
greatness and is the principle of all the graces with which it
is crowned. It was also the condition of our salvation.
Ought not we also to place ourselves in a state of servitude as
regards the Word incarnate? If our whole being belongs to
Jesus, must it not participate in his life and character?

"With this desire," exclaims Bérulle, "I make to thee,
O Jesus my Lord, and to thy deified humanity, a humanity
truly thine in its deification, and truly mine in its humiliation,
in its sorrows, in its sufferings : to thee and to it I make an
oblation and entire gift absolute and irrevocable, of all that
I am through thee in being, by nature and in the order of
grace. . . . I leave myself then wholly to thee, O Jesus,
and to thy sacred humanity, in the most humble and binding
condition which I know, the condition and relation of servitude; which I acknowledge to be due to thy humanity as
much on account of the greatness of the state to which it is
raised through the hypostatic union, as also on account of

---

[1] The complete title is : *Discours de l'estat et des grandeurs de Jésus
par l'union ineffable de la Divinité avec l'Humanité, et de la dépendance
et servitude qui lui est due et à sa très-sainte Mère ensuite de cet estat
admirable.* The work is prefaced by a Dedication to the King and
followed by a *Narré de ce qui s'est passé sur le sujet d'un papier de
dévotion.*

[2] Houssaye, II, 416.

the excess of voluntary abasement to which it became reduced
and humbled for my salvation and glory, in its life, its cross,
and in its death. . . . To this end and this homage I set and
place my soul, my state, and my life, both now and for ever
in a state of subjection and in relations of dependence and
servitude in regard to thee and to thy humanity thus deified
and thus humiliated together."[1]

The state of servitude of Christ's humanity is the starting-
point of the christological spirituality of Bérulle. Everything, let it be noted, becomes reduced to that principle; a
principle to throw light on which is the end the whole treatise
has in view.

The Virgin Mary was chosen to be the Mother of the Word
incarnate. Her incomparable dignity of Mother of God,
then, renders legitimate the vow of servitude made also to
her, which Bérulle expresses in these words:

" I vow and dedicate myself to Jesus Christ, my Lord and
Saviour, in the state of perpetual servitude to his most holy
Mother the Blessed Virgin Mary. In perpetual honour of
the Mother and the Son, I desire to be in a state and condition of servitude as regards her office of being the Mother of
my God, in order to honour more humbly, more holily, so
high and divine a rank; and I give myself to her as a slave
in honour of the gift which the eternal Word has made of
himself as Son, through the mystery of the Incarnation that
he deigned to bring about in her and through her."[2]

" Are there, O holy Virgin," continues Bérulle, " to be
found minds so small and so insensible to thy greatness, in
the light of our mysteries, that they can find fault with this
domination, and with this kind of servitude which looks to
her and honours her?"[3] Blessed Grignion de Montfort only
follows the Berullian teaching when he counsels total consecration, as a slave to Mary.[4]

Bérulle is not content with justifying the vow of servitude
to Jesus and Mary. He also looks at the various aspects of
the mystery of the Incarnation.

The third and fourth discourse of the treatise on the
Grandeurs de Jésus are devoted to the study of the unity of
God in this mystery. The Incarnation " is a work surpass-
ingly one " : the unity of person in Jesus Christ. It is also
the Incarnation which makes the unity of the divine plan.
" It is the centre to which are related all things in the world
of nature, of grace, and of glory." Through it God the

---

[1] *Grandeurs de Jésus*, Discourse II. *Œuvres*, pp. 181, 182 ff.
pp. 490, 1206, etc. The first Discourse is a kind of general introduction
on the Incarnation.
[2] *Œuvres complètes*, p. 527.   [3] *ibid.*, p. 529.
[4] *Cf.* A. Lhoumeau, *La vie spirituelle à l'école du B⁺ L. M. Grignion
de Montfort*, Paris-Rome, 1904, pp. 106 ff.

Father "gathers everything to himself." Bérulle would have been faithful to the logic of his idea had he affirmed, after Duns Scotus, that the Word would have become incarnate even had the fall not taken place. But he was held back by fidelity to Thomist teaching. "If," he says, "there had been no sinners on earth, there would have been no God-man in heaven or on earth."[1]

Bérulle then treats of the ineffable intercourse of God in the mystery of the Word incarnate.[2] Of all the divine communications that are realizable, there is none that is comparable to that brought about through the Incarnation. It is no longer the simple presence of God by nature or by grace. It is so intimate a union between the divinity and humanity in Christ, that the two natures have the same subsistence and that their acts can only be imputed to the single person of the Word. The acts of Christ are "divinely human and humanly divine." The Word is first of all communicated to human nature in order afterwards to communicate divine life to souls. The Incarnation is the great manifestation of the incomparable love of God for us.

Finally, in the last three discourses, Bérulle explains the three births of Jesus: his birth from all eternity in the bosom of the Father, his birth in time of the Virgin Mary, and his birth in glory on the day of his resurrection. This noteworthy part of the treatise contains the principles of devotion to the mysteries of Christ, of which we shall speak at greater length further on.

The considerations on the incarnate Word in ..e treatise on the *Grandeurs de Jésus* are constantly recurring under the pen of Bérulle, in his *Vie de Jésus,* left unfinished, in his *Elévations sur les mystères,* which were imitated and surpassed by Bossuet, as also in his *Opuscules de piété* and in his *Lettres spirituelles.*[3] Nothing could turn away his mind from meditation on the "mystery of Christ"; neither the affairs of court in which he mingled nor honours. Like St Paul he could say: "my life is Christ." He died on October 2, 1629, at the altar while celebrating "the votive Mass of the Incarnation, and before a picture of that mystery."[4]

---

[1] *Œuvres,* p. 324.　　　　　　　[2] In *Discourses* V-IX.
[3] All these works of Bérulle, with those mentioned above, were published by Fr. Bourgoing in 1644, with a noteworthy preface. Migne reproduces this edition, Paris, 1856.
[4] Houssaye, III, p. 493.

III—BERULLIAN SPIRITUALITY—ITS GENERAL CHARACTERISTICS

DEVOTION to the Word incarnate, a special regard for the virtue of religion, the Augustinian conception of grace; such are the characteristics of the spirituality of Bérulle and his school.

The founder of the Oratory in France deserved to be called " the apostle of the Word incarnate " by Pope Urban VIII. This appellation very well describes Bérulle; it is also the " substantial summing up " of his writings.[1] Fr. Bourgoing said to the priests of the Oratory in his Preface to the *Œuvres* of Bérulle :

" His way of grace and his very holy disposition, which was the origin, the base, and the foundation of all the rest which he received from God, and even of the renewal which he made in the Church, is his close connection with, and special belonging to, the person of Jesus Christ our Lord in his sacred humanity, and also to his holy Mother. Such was this belonging that all his prayers and upliftings, all his practices, and all his writings of piety, partake of it and breathe the odour of it. . . . Whichever way we turn in reading his books, we find him always in that holy and divine passion for the special love of Jesus and Mary, and in an ever ardent zeal to impress it on others. This could not be said in few words, for he was so tied to Jesus Christ, and was in such great contempt and forgetfulness of self in order to be all in all to him, that his care, his thought, his actions, and his labour had regard only for Jesus, and Jesus was his centre and his whole environment. If he spoke or wrote, it was of Jesus; if he laboured, it was for Jesus; if he undertook anything, it was through the guidance of the Spirit of Jesus."[2]

Jesus, says Bérulle, is the true sun, towards which the earth and our hearts ought to be continually moving :

"A surpassing mind of this century "—Bérulle is speaking of Copernicus—" is ready to maintain that the sun is the centre of the world and not the earth; that it is motionless and that the earth, in accordance with its circular shape, moves as regards the sun, by this contrary opinion satisfying every appearance which compels our senses to believe that the sun is in continual movement round the earth. This new opinion, little known in the science of the stars, is useful

---

[1] A. Perraud, *L'Oratoire de France au XVIIe et au XIXe siècle,* Paris, 1866, p. 71.

[2] *Œuvres complètes du Card. de Bérulle,* Migne, p. 95. There is the same testimony from Germain Habert, *La vie du Cardinal de Bérulle,* Paris, 1646, pp. 622 ff.

and ought to be followed in the science of salvation. For Jesus is the sun, motionless in his greatness, moving all things. Jesus is like unto his Father and, being seated on his right hand, is as immovable as he and gives motion to all. Jesus is the true centre of the world, and the world ought to be in continual motion towards him. Jesus is the sun of our souls whence they receive all grace, light, and influence. And the earth of our hearts should be in continual movement towards him in order to receive in all its parts and powers the favourable aspects and benign influences of this great luminary."[1]

Shall we say that Bérulle is another Copernicus, who has produced a revolution in Christian piety by causing all its manifestations to converge on the person of Christ? Herein, perhaps, we may find certain exaggerations among the historians of the Oratory:

"The whole world admits," writes Amelote in the life of Fr. de Condren, "that God was indeed thought of before the Congregation of the Oratory, but also that to it is due the revived attention of minds to Jesus Christ. I do not wish to say that this essential devotion was effaced from the Church or that there was none other than this Elias [Bérulle] who kept faithful to his Master. . . . There were Magdalens and St Johns before Fr. de Bérulle, but in truth the bulk of Christianity had grown cold in the ancient and necessary devotion to Jesus Christ."[2]

Thus, too, Fr. Bourgoing, but with more delicacy:

"This ancient and primitive devotion [the devotion to Jesus] which was in its highest fervour in the time of the apostles and of the early Christians, who thought only of Jesus and spoke only of him."[3]

Jesus was not, indeed, an abstract ideal for the earliest believers. They had a very clear sense of his presence in the Church and in the hearts of Christians. Jesus was unceasingly suggested to them as the living ideal of sanctity. Particular attention was devoted to his spiritual presence in souls. Without speaking of the Epistles of St Paul, it suffices to recall the letters of St Ignatius of Antioch, wholly overflowing with the love of Christ. Later on, the great christological controversies strongly focussed Christian thought on the person of Jesus.

"We find this devotion," continues Bourgoing, "during the course of the heresies of Arius, of Nestorius, of Eutyches, and of the Monothelites, attacking the divine person and the mysteries of the Word incarnate, which, in opposition,

[1] *Grandeurs de Jésus*, Discourse II, *Œuvres*, p. 161.
[2] *La vie du P. Charles de Condren*, Paris, 1643, Part II, chap. vi, pp. 88-89.
[3] *Préface aux Œuvres du Card. de Bérulle*, Migne, p. 98.

kindled the love of the faithful towards him and made him to be the better known."

He might have added that the mystics of the Middle Ages passionately loved Christ and, following St Bernard, directed the piety of the faithful towards him. St Gertrude, St Francis of Assisi, St Bonaventure, the author of the *Meditations on the Life of Christ,* Ludolph the Carthusian, to cite only the most famous, maintained Christian piety by meditation on the mysteries of the Saviour's life.

But—let us grant it—the Doctors of the Sorbonne in the fifteenth and sixteenth centuries had put a veil—a philosophical veil—over the divine face of Jesus, and had thus concealed him from the eyes of many. St Francis deplored it in his *Letter* to Asseline. When young Bérulle studied theology at the Sorbonne he was able to testify to the fact that metaphysical speculations made men too forgetful of Christ. In Christian gatherings preachers did not preach Jesus Christ enough. Bourgoing was right in saying:

"It must be admitted that this piety . . . had grown very cold, that the doctors made no special point of teaching Jesus Christ, nor had Christians eagerness to learn him; and that in these last days, through a special mercy of God, it is in some degree restored. We hear preachers preach Jesus Christ more often, to make him loved and adored in his sacred humanity, to give the people a better idea of the dignity of Christian grace and of the majesty of Jesus who is its author. . . . These beautiful and divine truths were suggested and upheld by the word, by the life, and by the writings of him [Bérulle] who is the subject of this discourse, and being declared by the mouths of apostolic preachers, have greatly tended to form Jesus Christ in Christian souls."[1]

Berullian devotion has its personal note. It does not resemble that of St Bernard, the Franciscans, or the Jesuits in every point. It is not addressed specially to the humanity of Jesus, but to Jesus in his entirety. Bérulle deduces his spirituality from a dogmatic analysis of the mystery of the Incarnation. He is, according to the most true expression of Urban VIII, "the apostle of the Word incarnate":

"It must then be noted," says Bourgoing, "that this servant of God and friend of the Bridegroom chiefly regarded and adored the divine person of Jesus Christ our Lord united to our nature—that is to say, himself, considered in his personality, in his divinely human being; not only as God, nor yet as man, or in his humanity taken separately, but rather as God-man, in his substantial status, which comprises his greatness and his abasement, his divine and human sonship

[1] *Œuvres,* Migne, p. 99.

in one same person and the attributes of either nature in the single hypostasis of the God-Word."[1]

All the dogmatic aspects of the Incarnation are successively considered : the person of the Word, his eternal generation from the Father, the procession of the Holy Spirit from the Father and the Son, the humiliations of the Word in his Incarnation, the manner in which he appropriates to himself human nature, the status and perfections of this nature united to the Word, the theandric compound which is Christ, the mysteries of his earthly life. From each of these dogmatic aspects Bérulle deduces moral lessons, as also their corresponding religious duties. For Christ is "the great sacrament of piety"; he is "the primitive sacrament of the Christian religion."

Piety is thus united to dogma. Metaphysical considerations are intermingled with prayers and high thoughts. Theological science is transformed into love. Bérulle is as much affective as he is speculative. He makes the philosophical veil, which was hiding Christ, transparent. "A Christ who was the object of science was not enough for him, he needed a Jesus who was the principle of life. Laying hold of all which the school teaches as to the adorable person of the Word, the union of the divine nature with the human nature in Jesus Christ, the communication of life which works between the two, 'the mystery of Christ' (of which St Paul speaks in Col. iv, 3), directs a loving attention to mysteries apparently till then considered only scientifically."[2]

The virtue of religion—its second characteristic—holds a prominent place in French spirituality. It remembers, above all, that the adoration of God is the Christian's first and principal duty. "Bérulle," says M. Bremond,[3] "created in the spiritual world of his time a kind of revolution, which may be described by the barbarous yet almost necessary word *theocentric*."

The historians of the Oratory attribute to Bérulle the merit of having "renewed" the spirit of religion :

"That which our honoured Father," writes Bourgoing, "renewed in the Church, as far as God gave him the means to do so, is the spirit of religion, the supreme homage of adoration and reverence due to God, to Jesus Christ our Lord, to his every state and all his mysteries, to his life, his actions, and his sufferings. This is the spirit which he strongly desired to maintain among us, that with which he himself was possessed and wholly enraptured, that which

[1] *Préface*, Migne, 97-98.   [2] Houssaye, II, pp. 249-250.
[3] *L'école française*, p. 23.

appeared in all his writings, all his prayers and aspirations.
For in them he speaks only of honouring, adoring, and of
doing all things to the honour of the Son of God, of his life
and of his mysteries—man's indispensable duties towards the
divine majesty and of Christians towards Jesus Christ."[1]

"It is he [Bérulle]," says again Amelote, "who has
to-day revived this buried virtue [respect towards God], and
who has aroused our century to recall this most ancient of
all our duties. . . . As it is impossible to read the treatises
of St Augustine with a tranquil mind without becoming
humble or those of St Teresa without loving prayer, so also
we cannot see those of Cardinal de Bérulle without becoming
filled with respect for God and the mysteries of his Son."[2]

Neither Bourgoing nor Amelote say that "of a tranquil
mind." They arraign devout humanism and censure those
who have "more familiarity with God than reverence
towards him":

"Many are moved to God," continues Bourgoing, "by
reason of his goodness, few through deep adoration of his
greatness and his holiness. Tender souls are more affected
by the sweetness of devotion, and in a certain freedom and
familiarity with God, than in an abasement and holy terror
before him. Our Lord is often enough looked upon as
Father, Saviour, and Spouse; rarely as our God, our
Sovereign, and Judge."[3]

On this subject how far are we away from St Francis de
Sales?

"Here [with Bérulle] we are taught to be true Christians,
to be religious with the primitive religion which we profess in
our baptism, and to be of the number of those who adore
the Father and his Son in spirit and in truth. We learn to
adore the divine greatness and perfection, the designs, the will,
the judgements of God and the mysteries of his Son; which
was less in use before and could not then be so too much."[4]

Amelote is quite as severe:

"It is certain," he says, "that in this century, in which
there appears to be so much holiness, we see in souls more
familiarity with God than reverence towards him, and there
are to be found many Christians who love God, but few who
have due respect for him. Amidst an infinite number of
good people, among whom all sorts of virtues are practised,
there is nothing more rare than the virtue of religion; each
one is readily moved to charity, there are a great number
of penitents, people are incited to perform all kinds of
holy deeds; but he who probes into minds will no doubt
admit that respect towards God is scarcely known, and that

[1] Preface to Œuvres de Bérulle, pp. 102-103.
[2] La vie du P. Charles de Condren, Part II, chap. v, pp. 80, 85.
[3] Préface, p. 103.   [4] ibid.

it is not in a profound adoration of his greatness, but only in freedom towards him, that children are brought up. . . . This licence produces in their minds a thousand excesses, it nourishes them in vain complacency, it deadens the stimulus of fear, makes us extremely dainty, chokes humility in its source which is the sense of the majesty of God."[1]

The virtue of religion, correctly understood, does not necessarily engender fear, still less "a holy terror." It is obvious that from the point of view of adoration humanism was looked on critically by the Oratorian School. Against such humanism, at the beginning of the seventeenth century, some opposition had arisen, to which the Oratory was no stranger, an opposition which Jansenism was later on to exaggerate.

But Jansenism and Bérulle are far apart. The virtue of religion which he advocates is a purer Christianity. It consists above all in adoration :

"There is nothing in him [Jesus] which does not deserve homage, honour, deep reverence and submission from all creatures in heaven, on earth, and in hell : *ut in nomine Jesu omne genu flectatur coelestium, terrestrium et infernorum* (Phil. ii, 10). It is the most essential act and exercise of religion, the first obligation of the creature towards God, the chief duty of the Christian towards Jesus Christ our Saviour."[2]

In the *Avis* on the manner of performing prayer, which precedes the famous *Meditations* of Bourgoing, we are recommended to have in view " as the aim and end of prayer, the reverence, recognition, and adoration of the sovereign majesty of God, through that which he is in himself rather than through what he is to us, and to love rather his goodness for its own sake than for the return it gives us or through what it is to us." Doubtless, we must "ask for the grace of God and virtue," but less for ourselves than because through them God is " glorified in us, and because it is his most holy will to give them us."[3]

M. Olier, who so well understood and so well expounded Berullian spirituality, makes, as we know, adoration the first point in his method of prayer :

"Christianity," he says, " consists of these three points, and the whole of this method of prayer[4] is comprised in

[1] *La vie du P. de Condren,* Part II, chap. v, pp. 80-82.
[2] Bourgoing, *Préface,* p. 86.
[3] *Méditations sur les Vérités et excellences de Jésus-Christ Notre-Seigneur,* Paris, 1631, Ve *Avis.* At the beginning of this edition are found XXIV counsels on the manner of performing prayer. These *Méditations* have often been republished, lastly in 1906, Paris, 3 vols. In his funeral Oration for Bourgoing, Bossuet said that these *Méditations* " are in the hands of everyone." They are a beautiful expression of Bérullian spirituality.
[4] The Sulpician method of prayer, as we shall see later, has two special elements : *adoration,* the source of which is plain, and *communion,* in which, through prayer and grace, we make our own the

them : to know, to regard Jesus, to become united with
Jesus, and to act in Jesus. The first leads one to reverence and
to religion ; the second to union and unity with him ; and the
third to action, not alone, but joined to the virtue of Jesus
Christ, which we have drawn to ourselves by prayer. The
first is called adoration ; the second communion ; the third
co-operation."[1]

Augustinianism is another characteristic of the French
School. Bérulle calls St Augustine " the Eagle of the
Doctors, and the great master of St Thomas the Prince
of the School."[2] He considers him to be the most humble,
the most learned, the holiest, the most prudent, the most
modest, and the most religious " doctor that this earth has
produced," and that God has yet given to his Church.[3]

He admired in him the marvellous gift of uniting with the
highest speculations, most touching affective outbursts :

" Consider this great Saint," he once said to his disciples ;
" he has, through a singular power from Jesus Christ and
by his grace, privileges which are humanly speaking in-
compatible : he is very learned and very humble, which is
rare ; he is very speculative and very affective, which is not
less rare ; and, whereas in most doctors we meet with nothing
but knowledge, in this one we find a certain spice of wisdom
which gives relish to all he says and has the unusual gift
of making the truth to pass from the mind to the heart."[4]

From this point of view Bérulle greatly resembles St
Augustine. Like him he also admired Plato and impressed
this admiration on his disciples. He grouped around him
" in the bosom of the Oratory a small circle of Platonists "
who laboured actively " to make the doctrines of the Academy

---

states of the Word Incarnate. This method was also inspired by
that of St Francis de Sales, and by that of Luis of Granada. In the
conclusion, especially, are found the thanksgiving and offering which
belong to the Granada method.

[1] *Introduction à la vie et aux vertues chrétiennes,* chap. iv. Bossuet
is inspired by Bérulle when he writes on the duty of adoration :
" Religious adoration is a recognition of the highest sovereignty in
God, and in ourselves of the most complete dependence. . . . ' Prayer '
—says St Thomas (II-II, q. 83, art. 1), and the same must be said of
adoration, of which, according to St Thomas, prayer is a part—' is
an act of the reason, for the object of adoration is to put the creature
in his own order, that is to make him subject to God.' " *Sermon sur
le culte dû à Dieu,* Lebarq, new edition, by Ch. Urbain and E.
Levesque, V, p. 108.

[2] *Œuvres de Bérulle,* Migne, p. 346.

[3] *id.,* 154.

[4] Habert, Abbot of Cérisy, *La Vie du Cardinal de Bérulle,* Book III,
chap. xi, Houssaye, III, pp. 399 ff.

prevail over those of the Lyceum.''[1] At the beginning of the seventeenth century, in spite of the efforts of the University,[2] Aristotle lost a part of his prestige in France.

But it was not only the intellectual temperament of Augustine which so charmed Bérulle. His teaching as to grace captivated him. Meditation on the Gospel of St John and on the Epistles of St Paul, rendered fruitful through the reading of St Augustine, moved Bérulle to give a new direction to the study of grace. " Setting aside the questions disputed in the School, seeking in the words of the Son of God with St Augustine as guide, a light too much neglected, he [Bérulle] saw above all in grace, a divine state, the special characteristic of which is to bind men closely to the humanity of the Saviour. This link is not only primary, in the sense that the blessing of grace is due to the merits of the incarnate Word; it is actual, because Christians live from his divinely human and humanly divine life, which is communicated to them through the Holy Spirit, thus making each of them another Jesus Christ.''[3] This conception of grace, a living bond which unites us with Christ, an overflowing into us of the divine life, is a fundamental point in the Berullian system.

Grace, the divine life within us, thereby exercises its sovereignty over us. Bérulle, whilst of course maintaining human freedom, places the efficacy of grace in high relief. In the accomplishment of good works he sees primarily the action of God. His conception of the action of God in us is clearly Augustinian and Thomist. He even showed himself "disturbed to see the arising of new systems which appeared, in order to protect human freedom, to restrict the domain of God. He compelled his confreres to uphold the teaching of St Augustine and St Thomas.''[4] Several of the Oratorians even exaggerated these tendencies and embraced Jansenism.

Berullian spirituality, in accord with the principles of St Augustine, " counts more on grace than on personal effort in order to cling to Christ." Fr. Bourgoing explains this with his customary precision :

" With regard to the attachment and binding to Jesus and Mary and to their mysteries, which are so often repeated in these works [of Bérulle], these expressions indicate a power, an authority, and a sovereignty on the part of grace and the spirit of Jesus over us which render us his, both as belonging to him by the right which he has over us, and by our submission and abandonment to his divine power.

" In order to understand this, we must know that there

---

[1] Houssaye, III, p. 381.
[2] With regard to the relations between Bérulle and Descartes, see Houssaye, III, pp. 382 ff.
[3] Houssaye, II, p. 250.　　　　[4] *ibid.*, III, p. 401.

are two kinds of operations employed in the sanctification of
the soul : the work of God in the soul and that of the soul
towards God. The first is what is called *grace,* and the
second *virtue.* . . . We call grace the work of God in us,
especially when it is sufficiently powerful to destroy the
hindrances which are opposed to it, and to draw from out the
soul the roots of that tree which God has not planted in his
creature—that is, the secret ties of self-love and of the old
Adam. We call virtue the operations of the soul thus prevented, assisted and sustained by grace and devoted through
it to God. Now, the one of these two operations which turns
us and binds us to God, to Jesus, and to the Blessed Virgin,
is the work of God and of his grace; and the creature has
no other part in it than what is given him by this same grace,
which is a voluntary adherence to this operation, followed by
desires, affections, and practices conformable to it, as also
by the rejection of all things contrary thereto. In the same
way there are two sorts of belongings and bindings to Jesus
and to his mysteries : the one which consists entirely in the
work of God, which forestalls our thoughts, our desires,
and our cares, although it requires to be followed by them
and cannot usefully subsist without our correspondence ; the
other which consists in our thoughts, desires, and devotions
in the use of grace. The writer [Bérulle] speaks chiefly of
the first.''[1]

The method of prayer of St Sulpice is based on these principles, of which the second point, *communion,* is thus explained by M. Olier :

" Why do you call the second part *communion?*—Because
in this part we give ourselves to God in order to enter into
participation in his gifts and in his perfections. This participation is called *communion,* especially by the Greek Fathers,
because God thereby gives us his common riches. The participation of the body of Jesus Christ is called sacramental
communion, because this sacrament makes common to us the
good things of Jesus Christ and communicates to us his
greatest gifts; and the participation which takes place in
prayer is called spiritual communion, because of the gifts
which God communicates to us therein by the simple intimate
operation of his Spirit. The soul which experiences some
secret operation should hold itself in repose and in silence,
in order to receive the whole extent of the gifts and of the
communications from God, without acting by itself or making
any effort which might disturb the pure and holy operations
of the Holy Spirit.''[2]

[1] *Préface,* Migne, pp. 86-87.
[2] Olier, *Catéchisme chrétien,* Part II, chap. viii. With regard to
the Sulpician method of prayer, see Letourneau, *La méthode d'oraison
mentale du séminaire de Saint-Sulpice,* Paris, 1903.

Bossuet says the same thing in connection with the prayer of simplicity :

" Then the soul, leaving the reasoning of meditation, makes use of a sweet contemplation which keeps it peaceful, attentive, and susceptible to the divine operations and impressions which the Holy Spirit imparts to it ; it does little and receives much ; its labour is sweet and nevertheless fruitful. . . .

" This prayer is prayer with God alone, and a union which contains, in an eminent degree, all the other particular dispositions, and inclines the soul to passiveness—that is to say, that God becomes the sole interior Master, and that he works therein more particularly than in the ordinary way ; whilst the less the creature labours, so much the more powerfully does God work ; and since the work of God is a repose, the soul in a certain manner becomes in this prayer like unto him, and, moreover, receives therein marvellous effects ; and as the rays of the sun make plants to grow, blossom, and fructify, so does the soul, which is attentive and calmly exposed to the rays of the divine Sun of justice, receive from it the better those divers influences which enrich it with all sorts of virtues."[1]

Tronson makes use of another image in order to express the same teaching :

" When we wish to dye cloth," he says, " and give it a colour different from what it had before—say a white cloth to be coloured scarlet—it may be done in two ways : either by applying the colour to it, which takes much time, labour, and trouble, or by putting the cloth into the dye, which is done without trouble ; for after having soaked it for some days it is taken out entirely scarlet, and scarlet of a more permanent nature than if applied. It is the same with virtues ; there is a dye enclosed within the heart of Jesus Christ, and when a soul is plunged therein through love, through adoration, and through the other duties of religion it easily takes this dye ; so that it is found, after remaining therein for some time, more filled with virtue than if it had performed many acts."[2]

Should this be called quietism ? No. It is simply a spirituality of Augustinian type, which places in relief the action of God and of Christ in our sanctification. It is op-

---

[1] *Méthode courte et facile pour faire l'oraison en foi et de simple présence de Dieu*, III, v.

[2] Tronson, *Entretiens sur l'oraison*, Discourse VII. Letourneau, *La méthode d'oraison mentale du séminaire de St Sulpice*, pp. 133-134. Louis Tronson was born in Paris, 1622, and died, Superior General of St Sulpice, in 1700. See a list of his works in the *Bibliothèque sulpicienne* of L. Bertrand, Vol. I, pp. 123-155. Migne published them in one volume, Paris. L. Bertrand also published three volumes of Tronson's *Lettres choisies*, Paris, 1904.

posed in this by that spirituality which accentuates the role
of the will in the act of virtue.[1] But neither Bérulle nor his
disciples misunderstood the necessity for the *co-operation* of
the will with divine action. The third point of the Sulpician
method of prayer, *co-operation,* consists precisely " in corresponding and co-operating faithfully with the grace received.
Good resolutions are then formed, occasions for carrying
these out during the day are foreseen." Nevertheless, whatever be the determination of our will, we must never forget
that in our good works we depend far more on the virtue of
the Holy Spirit than on our own will.[2]

Finally, it is not denied that the French School, when
speaking of fallen human nature, is inspired by Augustinian
pessimism. On this point, even more than on others, it
reacted against the occasionally somewhat exaggerated
optimism of the humanists.

[1] M. Houssaye thus differentiates the school of Berullian spirituality
from that of St Ignatius : " One is more theological, the other more
moral; the one leaves speculation in order to descend to what is
practical, the other rises from the practical to speculation ; the one
gives grace as much as is possible without prejudice to freedom, the
other relies on freedom as much as is allowable, whilst respecting divine
grace." II, p. 431. This opposition between the two spiritualities
was one of the causes of the conflict which very soon arose between the
Oratorians and the Jesuits.

[2] Olier, *Catéchisme chrétien*, Part II, chap. viii.

CHAPTER XIII

BERULLIAN DOCTRINE—THE TEACHING OF BÉRULLE
AND OF HIS DISCIPLES: CONDREN AND OLIER

THE fundamental principle of Berullian teaching, as we already know, is drawn from the total dependency of human nature, deprived of its personality, on the divine Person of the Word. Bérulle unceasingly recalls it.[1] He makes as his excuse for dwelling at such great length on this aspect of the mystery of the Incarnation that everything springs from it. The humanity of Christ cannot belong to the Word and receive from him the marvellous gifts which sanctify it except on condition that it cannot belong to itself. So, too, the Christian who desires to be united with Christ, to cling to him and live his life, must first of all renounce himself, cease to belong to himself. " If any man will come after me," Jesus said, " let him deny himself " (Matthew xvi, 24).[2] We must, then, " in this twofold way, practise the plan which our Lord himself has traced for us. To look into our soul and discard all that is not in conformity with our divine model : this is the *abnegat semetipsum*. Then, to labour to put therein all that conforms to the Spirit of Jesus Christ : this is the *sequatur me*."[3] The two parts of this plan are correlative. The more we renounce ourselves, the more we cling to Christ, and *vice versa*. Union with Christ and renunciation of self take place in us at the same time. Logical priority, however, belongs to renunciation.[4]

[1] This more especially is the subject of Discourse II, Migne, 158.

[2] " The spirit of the school of Jesus," says Bérulle (*Œuvres*, pp. 1167-1168), " and the summing up of all its teaching, is the spirit of abnegation, and it is to this that all these truths and all our practices are reduced, which also comprises all the dispositions which he requires of us. . . . It is a spirit unknown on earth before him [Jesus]. The academicians had never heard of it; philosophers, who spoke of so many things, knew it not."

[3] M. Lebas, *Supérieur général de Saint-Sulpice: Souvenirs de ses enseignements*, Paris, 1913, p. 239. M. Lebas well understood and admirably set forth Berullian teaching.

[4] " Christian life has two parts : life and death. The first is the foundation of the second. This is reiterated in the writings of St Paul . . . Death must always precede life. And this death is nothing else than the entire destruction of the whole of ourselves in order that all that is opposed to God in us being destroyed, his Spirit may become implanted there in purity and in the sanctity of his ways. It is then by death that we must enter into the Christian life " (Olier, *Introduction à la vie chrétienne*, chap. iii).

346

Let us, then, see, first of all, how Bérulle and his disciples conceived this renunciation, this abnegation. We shall after this see in what our clinging to Christ and participation in his life and mysteries consist.

I—BERULLIAN ABNEGATION

THE practice of abnegation is imposed on us, according to Bérulle, because we are *creatures, sinners,* and *members of Christ living in him by grace.*

"Abnegation," he says, "is founded on the greatness of God, and on the state of the creature drawn from nothing and tending to nothingness by his own condition and owing to sin, and also on another kind of nothingness of self through grace."[1]

Thus there are three kinds of nothingness which serve as a motive for our abnegation : the nothingness from which God draws us by creation; the nothingness in which Adam places us through sin; and the nothingness into which we must enter in order to cling to Christ. Nothingness of nature, "nothingness of grace" or sin, nothingness which Jesus operates within us in order to unite us to himself; such are the foundations of Christian abnegation.[2] Condren, the first successor of Bérulle in the direction of the Oratory, insists chiefly, as we shall see, on the nothingness of nature; M. Olier on the nothingness of grace or sin; Bérulle dwells, above all, on the nothingness brought about in us through the necessity of clinging to Christ.

A—ABNEGATION ACCORDING TO BÉRULLE

We already know Bérulle's teaching. In order to have no other being or life but in Jesus, we must annihilate all that is of ourselves and of Adam within us. The humanity of Christ was only able to be hypostatically united to the Word by being deprived of its own personality :

"As the humanity of Jesus," he says, "has no other being, life, and subsistence than in the divinity, we also must have no other life and subsistence than in his humanity and in his divinity—that is to say, than in him as God and man, the life, the salvation, and the glory of men. This state, considered well from every point of view, forces us very straitly, very strictly, and very continually to die to ourselves, to renounce ourselves."[3]

A state of death in ourselves, a state of life in Jesus, such is our condition. The less we are ourselves, the more Christ

---

[1] *Œuvres*, p. 1167.   [2] Bérulle, *Œuvres*, pp. 1165, 1170.
[3] *id.*, p. 1161.

is in us. The ideal to be sought after is the complete sub-
stitution of the Spirit of Christ for our moral ego after the
example—Bérulle does not cease to repeat it—of the humanity
of Jesus in whom the Person of the Word takes the place of
human personality :

" O admirable counsel of uncreated Wisdom," exclaims
Bérulle, " who deprives the humanity of Jesus of its human
person in order to bestow upon it the divine Person ! O
what a deprivation ! O what a denudation, which is in its
entirety both the preparation for the new life of the God-man
and the model for the new life of the spiritually just ! For,
as the eternal Son of God in his human nature is without
human personality—that is to say, is without a human ego,
substantially and personally—so also the adopted son of
God [the Christian], led by his grace, ought not to possess
one morally and spiritually.

" I honour, then, this stripping of the humanity of Jesus
of its own subsistence, and afterwards in honour of this same
stripping and, in so far as thy greatness [O Lord] and my
own condition bear it to thy honour and glory, I renounce
all power, authority, and freedom which I have to dispose of
myself, my being, and its every condition, circumstance, and
possessions ; I resign them wholly into the hands of Jesus,
his divine soul, and his humanity, anointed and consecrated
by the divinity itself ; and I resign these in honour of this
same humanity for the accomplishment of all its will and all
its power over me. I go further and desire that there be
no longer any of myself in me ; I desire to say with St Paul :
Vivo ego, jam non ego, vivit vero in me Christus (Gal. ii, 20).
And, according to the profound consideration of St Augustine,
I desire that the spirit of Jesus Christ be the spirit of my
spirit and the life of my life. And as the Son of God, by
right of subsistence, is in possession of human nature which
he has united to his person, so also I desire that by right of
special and particular power, Jesus deign to enter into possession of my mind, my state, and my life, and that I be nothing
but bare capacity and simple void in myself, filled with
emptiness and never again of myself."[1]

Hence, the opposition, so well analyzed by M. Olier,
between the spirit of ownership " which strips us of the
plenitude of the Word, of his life and operation," and the
Christian spirit. Hence also the duty of practising a negation of self by which " we no longer hold to anything."[2]

The disciples of Bérulle said again : " We ought to be
wholly changed into him [Jesus], consumed and lost in him,"

---

[1] *Œuvres*, p. 181.

[2] *Introduction à la vie chrétienne*, chap. xi, section viii. *Cf.* section
ix : " The possessor dwells in himself, the Christian leaves himself.
The possessor is filled with himself, the Christian is empty of himself."

like a consecrated host which has no longer anything but the appearance of bread. Let us inwardly be Jesus Christ and have humanity but in appearance.[1]

"Interior renunciation" is then "the best disposition to prepare us so to yield to the spirit [of Jesus] that it possess us."[2] By him we shall tend to Christian perfection which is thus defined by Bérulle:

"Jesus is all, and ought to be all in us, and we ought to be nothing, to treat ourselves as nothing, to be nothing in ourselves and have our being only in him. As we are by him and not by ourselves so also we should be for him and not for ourselves. This is what we should begin on earth that it may be finished in heaven, where Jesus Christ will be all in all. This is the perfection to which it becomes us to aspire."[3]

Our Lord said one day to St Gertrude the Great: "I desire this only, that you come to me wholly empty so that I may fill you; for it is from me that you will receive that which will make you pleasing in my sight."[4] This is the eternal plan of holiness.

This emptiness of self is not produced by efforts of the will. We must not forget that Bérulle is an Augustinian. According to him the interior renunciation needed for perfection is the result of grace which incorporates us with Christ. The important thing is not to be opposed to this grace:

"The life and form of grace," he says, "which God now gives to man is a kind of grace of annihilation and of the cross, and grace, either earthly or heavenly, is a way of grace which draws the soul out of itself by means of a kind of annihilation and transports it, fixes it, and grafts it into Jesus Christ, as, in him, our humanity is grafted into his divinity. . . . And, as in the Incarnation, there is a kind of annihilation of human nature, which is stripped of its own proper subsistence or human person in order to become one with the divine Person of the Word; so also in the grace which flows from this adorable Incarnation, as from a living source, there is a kind of annihilation in ourselves and permanent fixing in Jesus. Annihilation both of power and of subsistence, but with this difference, that the power in us which precedes the grace of Jesus Christ, being only a power which leads to our undoing, is truly set aside, and we are drawn into his own power in order to accomplish our work. But our subsistence is not taken from us in the same way; it is only annihilated

---

[1] De Condren, *Considérations sur les mystères de Jésus-Christ*, Paris, 1882, p. 196. Olier, *Traité des Saints Ordres*, Part III, chap. vii.

[2] Olier, *Introduction à la vie chrétienne*, chap. iv.

[3] *Œuvres*, p. 1179.

[4] St Gertrude, *Revelations*, Book IV, chap. iv.

as regards our use of it in morality, and in its authority and not in its existence."[1]

In fact, we always retain our personality and also the liberty to resist the action of grace.

B—Abnegation according to Condren

Condren,[2] the disciple of Bérulle and second Superior of the Oratory, specially insisted on interior annihilation, depending on the abnegation of self, which has as its motive the nothingness of the creature as much as its tendency to sin.

Condren was the most powerful interpreter of Berullian teaching. He wrote nothing himself. He said one day to M. Olier : " Ordinarily those who abstained from writing, from the love of Jesus Christ, were rewarded with the gift of illuminating souls, a gift much more useful for the Church than that of writing."[3] He possessed this gift to a marvellous degree. St Jane de Chantal said after several talks with him : " If God gave our blessed Founder [St Francis de Sales] to the Church in order to instruct men, it seems to me that he has made Father de Condren capable of instructing angels."[4]

Condren, according to Bérulle, " received the spirit of the Oratory from the cradle."[5] How well, too, did he know the way to impress it on his disciples ! Olier, Eudes, Saint-Pé, to cite only the chief of these, owed to him the best of their Berullian teaching.

The state of a victim, the condition of inward annihilation, is everything with Fr. Condren, it is also the summing-up

[1] Bérulle, *Œuvres*, p. 1166.

[2] Charles de Condren was born of a noble family at Vaubuin near Soissons, December 15, 1588. He felt himself drawn at an early age to the priesthood. He studied at the Sorbonne and, like Bérulle, had as masters Philip de Gamaches and André Duval. He was ordained priest September 17, 1614, and entered the Oratory June 17, 1617, in spite of Duval, who wished to have him as his successor in his chair at the Sorbonne. Condren was charged with the direction of several houses of the Congregation. On the death of Bérulle in 1629, he was elected Superior General of the Oratory. About 1631 M. Olier put himself under the direction of Fr. de Condren and received the invitation from him to found the seminaries. Condren died in 1641. The spiritual conferences given by Condren to his religious are noteworthy. They inspired the writings of his disciples : the *Trésor spirituel* of Fr. Quarré, the *Nouvel Adam* of Fr. Saint-Pé, the *Royaume de Jésus* of St John Eudes, the *Introduction à la vie et aux vertus chrétiennes* of M. Olier.—The Oratorian Denys Amelote wrote *La vie du P. Charles de Condren, second supérieur général de la Congrégation de l'Oratoire,* Paris, 1643, pp. 284 ff. Cf. H. Bremond. The disciples of Condren published his *Discours et Lettres*, Paris, 1643; *L'idée du sacerdoce et du sacrifice de Jésus-Christ par le P. de Condren*, Paris, 1677 (Quesnel's edition). Fr. Ingold published the *Considérations sur les mystères de Jésus-Christ*, Paris, 1882.

[3] Faillon, *Vie de M. Olier*, Paris, 1873, Vol. I, p. 151.

[4] *ibid.*, p. 139.   [5] *ibid.*, p. 138.

of all he taught. We must annihilate within us our evil inclinations; we must also annihilate ourselves in order to acknowledge our nothingness before God.

And first of all, in order to imitate and do honour to the humiliations of the Word in his Incarnation: *Exinanivit semetipsum,* Bérulle taught " that there is . . . a basis for the abnegation which is in the being of God united personally to the humanity; in which Scripture teaches us that there is an emptying of himself; a supreme emptying of the first and highest Being, which must be honoured by way of abnegation. The Son of God gave sovereign honour to his Father by his Incarnation which is the emptying of his divine Person."[1] We must enter into nothingness " with the Son of God, emptying himself in order to make reparation."

Condren, who meditated specially on the priesthood and the sacrifice of Jesus Christ, notes the exercises of this priesthood and the elements of this sacrifice in these annihilations of the Word incarnate.

Sacrifice is offered to God for several ends. It is offered for thanksgiving, for the satisfaction due to his justice, and also for securing his benefits :

But " it is primarily instituted," says Condren, " in order to give recognition to his greatness and to render homage to his divine perfections, but more particularly to three of them. It is in order to honour the sanctity of God—by which he is so great, so pure, so withdrawn in himself, so far from creatures . . . that the creature . . . is destroyed and consumed in his presence. . . . In the second place in order to do honour to his sovereign rule, not only over life and death, but over being itself. For God is the sole author of being and none but he is able to give it. . . . In the third place sacrifice is meant to recognize and do honour to the plenitude of God—that is to say, that God suffices in himself and that no creature is necessary to him. . . ."[2]

" Sacrifice, then, responds to all which God is. It regards him as the sovereign Being, to whom all being is sacrificially due. It views him in his proper and incomprehensible greatness and perfection, as being himself above every name, all light, every thought; above all adoration and all love. In offering all to God we protest that he is all; in destroying all before God we declare that he is nothing at all of all that is in the universe, and that all this is not at all God."[3]

The sacrifice of Jesus Christ, which lasted " all his life, from the first moment of the Incarnation until eternity,"[4]

[1] *Œuvres de Bérulle,* p. 1167. *Cf.* 1171.
[2] *L'idée du sacerdoce et du sacrifice de Jésus-Christ,* pp. 38-41, Paris, 1901. I shall cite this Benedictine edition. Early in it will be found just reasons for attributing the ideas in this work to Condren.
[3] *id.,* p. 52.   [4] *id.,* p. 60.

consisted in annihilating himself before God, in being perpetually a victim.

Let us not confine ourselves to honouring his victim state. United to Jesus let us sacrifice all that we have to God, let us annihilate ourselves before him, let us be victims with him :

" Then," exclaims M. Olier in this connection, " let every creature perish before my God ! And as our Lord, in sacrificing himself, claimed to annihilate all things and make of them all a sacrifice in himself, because he united everything in his person ; it is fitting that we condemn and sacrifice all things apart from him, which are so much the less holy as they are the less in him."[1]

If we sacrifice ourselves fully it is to belong wholly to God. The sacrificial victim is only truly received by God, truly accepted by him, when it is destroyed and consumed. Thus we must sacrifice all that we have, and all that we are, in order to be " nothing except in God and for God."[2] The less we are ourselves the more we shall be Christ. " The soul," declares Condren, " ought to be nothing in order that Jesus Christ in it may be all."[3] The greatest grace which God is able to give us is to suffer nothing in us but himself. The more we are empty of self the more we shall be filled with God. We ought to become new men to be modelled on Christ. That which is thrown into the mould must first be melted. We must then destroy and melt in ourselves the old Adam in order to become Christ.[4]

Looked at in this light Berullian annihilation, however obscure at first, is clearly understood.

C—Abnegation according to Jean-Jacques Olier

M. Olier[5]—the one of Bérulle's disciples who expounds Berullian teaching most clearly—teaches, like his master,

[1] Olier, *Introduction à la vie chrétienne,* chap. i.
[2] Condren, *L'idée du sacerd.*, p. 52.
[3] Condren, *Discours et Lettres,* Paris, 1643, Letter XXI, p. 381.
[4] Grignion de Montfort, *De la vraie dévotion à la très Sainte Vierge,* pp. 172 ff.
[5] Jean-Jacques Olier, founder of the seminary of St Sulpice, was born in Paris, September 20, 1608. He studied at the Sorbonne, and at the age of eighteen was appointed [commendatory] Abbot of Pébrac, in the diocese of Saint-Flour. Urged by his family to seek honours, J. J. Olier lived a somewhat worldly life. Converted by the Blessed Virgin at Loretto, in Italy, he placed himself under the direction of St Vincent de Paul, and was ordained priest May 21, 1633. He preached missions. Mother Agnès de Langeac, of the Order of St Dominic, foretold that he would found seminaries. *Cf.* Jeuné, *Une mystique dominicaine, La Vénérable Agnès de Langeac,* Paris, 1924. In 1635 M. Olier chose Fr. de Condren as his director, and became

that inward annihilation is " the best disposition " for the Holy Spirit to take possession of our soul :

" As soon as we let ourselves be reduced to nothingness unto this divine Spirit in our whole being, we find ourselves firmly disposed by him to every virtue and in a state of preparation and inclination to practise them all."[1]

The necessity for this annihilation and mortification is, above all, rendered justifiable by the Pauline teaching—constantly recalled by M. Olier—of the opposition between the spirit of the flesh and the Spirit of Jesus.

Man before the fall was in a perfect state. All his faculties, controlled by grace, were directed towards goodness and were of themselves uplifted towards God. Since the sin of Adam he is " in a strange disorder and in entire opposition to God."[2] Let us not forget that M. Olier is, like many of his contemporaries, an Augustinian, who exaggerates the ravages of original sin :

" Before being restored by baptism . . . the soul, in itself and in its outward and inward faculties, is entirely clothed with sin, and we might say, in a certain sense, that it has even lost its natural being, since, from the most pure spirit which it was, it becomes flesh through alliance with the body by becoming lost in the senses thereof and by allowing itself to be led by its evil inclinations."

Baptism, it is true, " restores " the soul :

" But the soul inwardly restored by the Spirit is encompassed by a flesh which remains corrupt and which is not sanctified by baptism, or purified from its evil inclinations. . . .[3]

---

associated with the little group of disciples who were destined to found seminaries. It was at this time that M. Olier had a great inward trial, believing himself abandoned by God. When he had overcome this he began the seminary of Vaugirard; he then became Curé of St Sulpice. He built the seminary of St Sulpice, and died in Paris, 1657, attended by St Vincent de Paul. Faillon, *Vie de M. Olier*, 4th edition, Paris, 1873, 3 vols ; Monier, *Vie de Jean-Jacques Olier*, Paris, 1914, 1st vol. only. *Œuvres complètes de M. Olier*, published by Migne, Paris, 1856; these are : *Introduction à la vie et aux vertus chrétiennes; La Journée chrétienne; Explication des cérémonies de la Grand' Messe de Paroisse; Le Catéchisme chrétien pour la vie intérieure; Traité des Saints Ordres; Lettres spirituelles, Pietas seminarii, l'Esprit d'un directeur des âmes d'après M. Olier,* edited by de Bretonvilliers. See also *Pensées choisies,* extracts from unpublished *Mémoires* of M. Olier, published by G. Letourneau, Paris, 1916. *Cf.* L. Bertrand, *Bibliothèque sulpicienne ou Histoire littéraire de la Compagnie de Saint-Sulpice,* Vol. I, Paris, 1900.

[1] *Introduction à la vie chrétienne,* chap. iv.
[2] *Journée chrétienne,* Preface; the first part of the *Catéchisme chrétien* explains the same teaching.
[3] *Journée chrétienne, ibid.* With regard to the Augustinian pessimism of M. Olier, see the explanations by J. D. Icard, *Doctrine de M. Olier expliquée par sa vie et par ses écrits,* 2nd edition, Paris, 1891, pp. 37 ff.

III.

" The Christian, in fact, possesses two lives—the life of Adam and that of our Lord; the life of the flesh and that of the Spirit. These two lives are opposed to each other; it is needful for one to be wholly annihilated in order that the other become absolutely perfect. Now, so long as we are here below, the life of the flesh is never wholly destroyed. By a special privilege, however, and in reward for heroic mortifications or for great faithfulness to the Holy Spirit, it happens to the soul to feel itself occasionally dead to this imperfect life; but this is never other than for a time and in part. Moreover, the life of Jesus Christ within us is never in this world so peaceful or wholly perfect. We must always have the sword in hand in order to overcome our enemies and those of God; it is always necessary for us to labour in order to mortify and destroy the old man."[1]

This opposition between the flesh and the Spirit is, then, the great motive of mortification :

" It is by these two exercises that we must begin the interior and divine life. We must first of all labour for the mortification of self; and then, being dead to the flesh, we must endeavour to live by the Spirit. Without this, we shall never do anything, and all other exercises will only serve to our loss. All the rest is like a salve which encloses our evil without removing it, which hides it and in no way heals it."[2]

This mortification is pushed very far by M. Olier. The Christian consists of flesh and spirit. The flesh is " all the old man in us; all man in so far as he is unregenerate, and as he is opposed to the Holy Spirit which we receive at baptism. . . .[3] We have within us either Jesus Christ or the flesh. It is necessary for us to do all through the motion of the Holy Spirit, which is charity, which disposes us to do all things for God."[4] The flesh cannot do any good thing. " During the whole of this life, it is so corrupt, spoilt, soiled, and perverted that it can never be converted to God; it cannot be subjected to him, says St Paul : *Legi enim Dei non est subjecta; nec enim potest* (Rom. viii, 7)."[5]

We must, then, " hate our flesh." Man, " in his actual state, ought to be accursed, calumniated, persecuted."[6] By himself he is nothingness and sin.

Because by himself he is nothingness he should love contempt, abjection, and forgetfulness, which are the first arm of the cross. Because he is nothing of himself but sin he

---

[1] *Olier,* unpublished texts by G. Letourneau, *Pensées choisies,* p. 48. " The Christian man, according to the teaching of St Paul, comprises two things, one is called the flesh, the other the spirit. It is thus that man is divided in Scripture." *Catéchisme chrétien,* Part I, lesson xiv.

[2] *Introduc. à la vie chrétienne,* chap. viii.

[3] *Catéchisme chrétien,* Part I, lesson v.

[4] Olier, *Mémoires;* Icard, *op. cit.,* p. 60.

[5] *Catéch. chrét.,* Part I, lesson xvii.

[6] *ibid.*

should love pain, suffering, and persecution, which are the second arm. Finally, always followed by sin he should endure poverty, which is the third part of the Christian's cross.[1] Thus it is that he should renounce "all desire of honours, pleasures, and riches—in a word, all the desires of sin which are in us and are opposed to the cross of Jesus Christ."[2]

Creatures are a perpetual cause of temptation for our fallen nature. We are not secure from them except by renouncing all the pleasure which they are able to procure for us, and by seeking our satisfaction in God alone :

"It is necessary for the soul to be in fear and distrust of self ; it must testify to this distrust by avoiding occasions and encounters in which it may satisfy the heart by love and delight in some creature. It should make its pleasure and joy depend on sacrificing to Jesus all joy and pleasure which it may have apart from himself. And when taking part in those things in which by Providence it is obliged to be occupied, such as eating, drinking, and conversation with creatures, it must be sparing in all, must discard what is superfluous, and must renounce, in the use of them, the joy and pleasure to be found therein, uniting and giving itself to Jesus as often as it feels itself tempted to enjoy something apart from him and not himself."[3]

May a Christian rightly enjoy any pleasure not thus supernatural?[4]

These exaggerations are to be found in all the representatives of the French School. All, through the reaction against that humanism which exalted the goodness of man beyond measure, accentuated Augustinian pessimism. We have already noted it in the works of Bérulle.

St Vincent de Paul also said :

"What else have we in ourselves but nothingness and sin? Let us, then, hold it as certain that in all things and everywhere we deserve to be repulsed and always despised, because of our natural opposition to the sanctity and perfections of God, to the life of Jesus Christ, and to the operations of grace ; and that which convinces us of this truth the more is our natural and continual inclination to evil and our impotence for good."[5]

"Sin has perverted all that is within us," declares St

---

[1] *Catéch. chrét.*, Part I, Lessons x-xix.

[2] *ibid.*, Lesson vi.

[3] *Journée chrétienne*, Part I. The disposal of those hours of the day not occupied with special exercises.

[4] "If there be something which is not sin within us, it is from grace, from the Holy Spirit which operates in us only through his mercy." Olier, *Mémoires*, in Icard, *op. cit.*, p. 60.

[5] *Vie de Saint Vincent de Paul*, by Abelly, Book III, chap. xxx. Icard, *op. cit.*, p. 64.

John Eudes, " in both body and soul, from head to foot. It
has filled the higher part of our soul with darkness and
malice, and has set all the passions of the lower part in
disorder."[1]

Blessed Grignion de Montfort, too, teaches that " all that
is within us is corrupted through the sin of Adam and by our
actual sins; not only the senses of the body, but also the
powers of the soul."[2]

Let us also recall Bossuet's frankly Augustinian treatise on
concupiscence.

M. Olier particularly insisted on the corruption of fallen
man. Why this insistence? " His habitual reading of the
Epistles of the Apostle [St Paul], and the trials to which it
pleased God to subject him for nearly two years at the
beginning of his sacerdotal life, greatly contributed to inspire
him with the thought of the impotence of nature to do good,
and of the corruption of fallen man. During these trials
God seemed to have withdrawn from him that natural virtue
which sustains the body; his soul was as though it were
unable to control the senses; as regards spiritual powers he
was filled with langour and in a kind of stupefaction impossible to understand. He remembered nothing, he was unable
to learn anything; if he wanted to speak, words failed him.
Another kind of equally grave sorrow was that, deprived of
all sensible supernatural gifts, distressed by every kind of
temptation, he looked upon himself as rejected of God."[3]

II—ADHERENCE TO CHRIST

THIS total mortification, without which Jesus cannot live
completely within us, is much more the effect of the Holy
Spirit than it is the result of our efforts.

" I pray God," wrote M. Olier to a nun, " to reign in you
and, as king and absolute prince, to destroy all his enemies
that might rise in you to his prejudice and your own. It is
he who should destroy you and sacrifice you in every impulse; I mean in all that belongs to yourself and is not of
him. For he should live solely in you, unceasingly keeping
down the flesh beneath his feet."[4]

Our cleaving unto Christ will be the best means of morti-

[1] *Le Mémorial de la vie ecclésiastique, Sur l'abnegation de soi-même,*
quoted by Icard, *op. cit.,* p. 66.
[2] *Lettre circulaire aux amis de la croix,* n. 6, Icard, p. 5.
[3] Icard, *op. cit.,* p. 62. See also Faillon with regard to this trial
of M. Olier, *Vie de M. Olier,* Vol. I, Book VII; Monier, *Vie de Jean-
Jacques Olier,* I, Book I, chaps. x-xi, Paris, 1914. M. Bremond,
L'école française, pp. 430 ff., reduces M. Olier's trial to simple neurosis.
[4] Olier, *Lettre XXIX,* Migne, p. 768. New edition of the *Lettres,*
Paris, 1885, Vol. I, p. 239.

fying our evil instincts. Here we come to the newest and
most attractive part of Berullian teaching.

We cling to Jesus, we unite ourselves to him by participation in his mysteries :
"In order to be a perfect Christian," says M. Olier,
"we must participate in all the mysteries of Jesus Christ,
this loving Redeemer having expressly performed them in
person so that they may be most abundant and special sources
of grace in his Church."[1]
These mysteries are events in the life of Christ. Each one
of them "possesses something particular not only in its effect
but also in its state."[2]
Let us note this word *state*. To understand it properly we
must distinguish between the outward and the inward side
of the mystery. The former is transitory ; it consists in the
deeds which Christ performed, actions which are past and
are not, in fact, repeated. The latter is permanent, and consists in "the dispositions and inward feelings which our
Lord had" in each of his mysteries.[3] These dispositions do
not change, they are permanent in Jesus, because they are
intimately bound up with the Incarnation :
"The Incarnation," says Bérulle, "is a permanent state,
and is permanent eternally. God perpetually makes a gift
of his Son to man ; this Son who is the gift of God himself
gives himself incessantly to our humanity ; the eternal Father
unceasingly begets his Son in a new nature."[4]
The intimate dispositions of Christ, then, do not change.
They form part of that permanent state which is the Incarnation. That is why the Berullian School calls the internal
sentiments which Jesus had in his divers mysteries the *states*
of the Word incarnate. They thus express the permanence
of these sentiments, which renders the mysteries of Christ
always actual and always productive of grace in our souls.
Bérulle thus explains this teaching :
"The mysteries of Jesus Christ are in some circumstances
past, and in another way they remain and are present and
perpetual. They are past as regards their performance but

[1] *Catéchisme chrétien,* Part I, lesson xx.
[2] Bérulle, *Œuvres,* p. 350. M. Olier (*ibid.*) explains : "Each mystery
has won sanctifying grace for the Church and divers states and special
graces which God distributes to souls . . . in the more ordinary way
at the time of the solemnity of the mysteries."
[3] Olier, *Introduction à la vie chrétienne,* chap. iii. Bérulle says the
same thing : "As in us there is a soul and a body and all is but one ;
so also in the mysteries of the Son of God there is the spirit performing
and suffering this mystery, the light of grace of the mystery, the
intention to establish some effect from the mystery, and the body or
action of the mystery." *Œuvres,* p. 1053. See also *Le Royaume de
Jésus,* by St John Eudes, Part III, VII, pp. 322 ff., Paris, 1924.
[4] Bérulle, *Œuvres,* p. 921.

they are present as regards their virtue, and their virtue never passes, nor will the love with which they have been accomplished ever pass. The spirit, then, the state, the virtue, the merit of the mystery is always present. The spirit of God, by whom this mystery was wrought, the interior state of the external mystery, the efficacy, and the virtue which render this mystery living and operative within us, this state and virtuous disposition, the merit by which he has gained us for his Father and merited heaven, life, and himself; even the actual taste, the living disposition, through which Jesus has brought about this mystery, is always alive, actual, and present to Jesus. So much so that if it were necessary for us, or if it were pleasing to God the Father, he would be quite ready to depart and to accomplish this work, this action, this mystery, afresh."[1]

In other words it is the same Spirit which animates Christ and the faithful, the head and the members. The spirit of God which produces in the soul of Christ these permanent dispositions " expands in all " Christians, " and causes all of them to become participants . . . in these same sentiments."[2]

" This obliges us," continues Bérulle, " to treat the things and mysteries of Jesus, not as things past and abolished, but as things present, living, and even eternal, from which also we have to gather a present and eternal fruit."

In order to make himself better understood, by way of example he sets forth the mysteries of the infancy and of the Passion of the Saviour :

" The infancy of the Son of God," he says, " is a passing state, the circumstances of this infancy are past, and he is no longer a child; but there is also something divine in this mystery which goes on in heaven and works a similar manner of grace in souls on earth, whom it pleases Jesus Christ to attach and dedicate to this humble and first state of his person. We even find that Jesus Christ has found a means of fixing a part of his Passion in his state of glory by keeping his wounds therein; for if he could keep some mark of his Passion in his glorified body, why should he not keep some of it in his soul, in the consummated state of his glory? But what he keeps of his Passion, both in body and soul, is life and glory, and he suffers in neither the one nor the other, and it is this of his mysteries which remains in him and makes a way of grace on earth, which is assigned to chosen souls to receive. And it is through this way of grace that the mysteries of Jesus Christ, his infancy, his suffering, and the others, continue and live on earth for ever."[3]

---

[1] *id.*, pp. 1052-1053.
[2] Olier, *Introduction à la vie chrétienne,* chap. iii.
[3] Bérulle, *Œuvres,* p. 1053.

To contemplate the states of Jesus and to appropriate them to oneself, such is the method of the Berullian School. "This school," writes M. Letourneau, "loves to contemplate, first of all, the marvels of the divine life in the soul of Jesus, in his intelligence, in his will—that is to say, in his heart—it exalts, it extols on every occasion this interior life of the soul of Jesus. Then it completes it by considering how this divine life flows from the head to the members of the mystical body of Jesus; how the faithful, from the time of holy baptism, reproduce in themselves the death and the life of Jesus Christ."[1]

"The life which we have on earth," says Fr. Eudes, "is only given us to be employed for the accomplishment of the great designs which Jesus has for us. This is why we ought to make use of our time, our days, and our years, to co-operate with Jesus and to labour with him in this divine work and the completion of his mysteries in us; and we should co-operate therein by good works, by prayer, and by frequently applying our minds and hearts to the contemplation, adoration, and honouring of the divers states and mysteries of Jesus in the different times of the year; and give ourselves to him for him to work in us through these same mysteries all that he desires to do therein for his pure glory."[2]

All writers of the French School teach the need for real Christians to reproduce within themselves the mysteries of Christ. In their writings they dwell on the divers mysteries and states of Jesus. Each of them, however, has his preferences, his particular attractions. Bérulle is devoted to the mysteries of the earthly and heavenly life of Jesus, Condren to those of his life of sacrifice on earth and in heaven, and Olier to those of his eucharistic life.

A—ADHERENCE TO CHRIST BY PARTICIPATION IN THE MYSTERIES OF HIS EARTHLY AND HEAVENLY LIFE—BÉRULLE AS INTERPRETED BY OLIER

To be another Christ is to appropriate his mysteries, chiefly the Incarnation, the Childhood, the Crucifixion, the Death,

---

[1] *Écoles de Spiritualité. L'école française du XVIIe siècle*, p. 9. Extract from the *Recrutement sacerdotal*, Toulouse, 1913.

[2] *La vie et le royaume de Jésus dans les âmes chrétiennes*, Part III, V, pp. 312-313, Paris, 1924. Bossuet offers this prayer to Jesus at the beginning of his *Élévations sur les mystères:* "In order to know thee well, O my God and dear Saviour, I ever desire, with thy grace, to consider thee in all thy states and all thy mysteries, and to know with thee at the same time thy Father who has given thee to us, and the Holy Spirit proceeding from you both."

the Burial, the Resurrection, and the Ascension.[1] Herein let us take M. Olier, the best writer of the French School, as our guide.

The mystery of the Incarnation " brings about in us a complete stripping and renunciation of ourselves, and in addition produces a reclothing with our Lord through total consecration to God."[2] These graces correspond to the state of annihilation of Jesus in the Incarnation, and to the state of most close union between the human nature and the divine in the single Person of the Word.

In the mystery of the Incarnation, the sacred humanity of Jesus is annihilated by the privation of his personality. The latter has no interest of its own nor does it act for itself. It seeks only the interest of the heavenly Father whom it regards in all things. " In the same way we must become annihilated as regards all our own designs and all our interests, having none but those of Christ, who is in us to live in us for his Father."[3]

The humanity of Christ, hypostatically united to the Word, is wholly consecrated to God, wholly clothed with the divinity. It lives only for God; it belongs to him in a most perfect manner. At the very moment that this humanity was annihilated by being deprived of its own personality, it acquired " the plenitude of the divinity, and an infinite capacity to receive all the operations of the Holy Spirit."[4] Thus, " when we strip ourselves of ourselves we are reclothed with Jesus Christ."[5] Christ is living within us. He fills our souls with his desires and his dispositions. The Christian is thus, if we may so express it, a little incarnation in which are produced spiritually all the mysteries of the Saviour's life.

Finally, we are consecrated to the service of God with Jesus:

" A third effect of this mystery [the Incarnation] is a grace of entire consecration to the service of God. When Jesus Christ enters the world he offers himself with all his members to his Father. . . . Thenceforth, his faithful servants, under the action of the Holy Spirit, become capable of adoring the infinite Majesty, of praising him and rendering him the duties due to him."[6]

---

[1] " Three lives [in Jesus] to which the whole life of men and of angels should be dedicated, three precious moments to which all the moments of our mortality and of our eternity should be consecrated : the moment of the Incarnation, in which Jesus begins to be Jesus and the Word begins a new and incarnate life. . . . The moment of the wayfaring and meriting life [of Christ]. . . . The moment of his heavenly and glorious life, in which Jesus is triumphant in life, in glory, and in immortality." Bérulle, *Œuvres*, p. 393.

[2] Olier, *Catéchisme chrétien,* Part I, Lesson xx.

[3] *ibid.*

[4] Olier, *Pensées choisies,* p. 41. Cf. *Catéchisme chrét.*, *ibid.*

[5] *Pensées choisies, ibid.*   [6] *ibid.*, p. 42.

Bérulle was the first to express so strongly this state of the perfect adorer which Christ acquires through the Incarnation :

" Jesus, on account of his state, is the sole adorer of the divine persons and emanations, whom the angels adore indeed in heaven through the action of their understanding and their will, but not with the kind of adoration of which we speak, which is very different : for we speak of an adoration belonging to a state and not in action ; of an adoration which does not emanate simply from the mind and is dependent on its thought, but one that is solid, permanent, and independent of powers and acts, and one that is vividly impressed in the depth of the created being and on the circumstances of its state. And thus we say that before this new birth there was nothing which, of itself and owing to its natural or personal state, adored and rendered homage to these divine objects."[1]

The humanity of Christ, annihilated and wholly consecrated to God, is a living and permanent declaration that God is all and that the creature is nothing, which is the essence of adoration.

Jesus causes the faithful to participate in his state of adoration :

" At the moment of the Incarnation," writes M. Olier, " our Lord consecrated himself entirely to the Father, himself and all his members. . . . He continues ever to live with the same dispositions that he had during his whole life ; he never interrupts them and ever offers himself, in himself and in all his members, to God in all those circumstances in which they ought to serve him, honour him, and glorify him. . . .[2] Our Lord, in order to extend his holy religion in God's direction and to increase it in our souls, comes into us and leaves himself on earth in the hands of his priests, as a sacrifice of praise, to join us with this state of sacrifice, to adapt us to his praise, to communicate to us inwardly the sentiments of his religion. He spreads himself in us, he instils himself in us, he embalms our soul and fills it with the inward dispositions of his religious spirit ; so that he makes our soul and his but one, which he animates with the same spirit of respect, love, praise, and the inward and outward sacrifice of all things to the glory of God his Father ; and thus he places our soul in fellowship with his religion, in order to make us in himself true religious of his Father."[3]

Jesus Christ " is alone the true and perfect religious of God."[4] The faithful will be united to him in order to render

---

[1] *Grandeurs de Jésus*, Discourse XI. The second birth of Jesus (*Œuvres*, p. 363). The first birth of Jesus is that of the Word in the bosom of the Father. *Cf.* pp. 933, 1058, 1059, etc.
[2] Olier, *Catéchisme chrétien*, Part I, lesson xx.
[3] Olier, *Introduction à la vie chrétienne*, chap. i.
[4] Olier, *Traité des Saints Ordres*, Part III, chap. vi.

their duties to God in the same spirit of religion. The priest, above 'll carry out this obligation. " The religion of Jesus Christ towards God is what should properly be the desire of the priest." Like his Master, he should be a " true religious of God." He ought to render to God the duties of religion due to him for all men. " He must give himself up to the spirit of our Lord in order to satisfy this duty."[1] This teaching is the foundation of M. Olier's *Traité des Saints Ordres,* and of his *Explication des cérémonies de la Grand' Messe de paroisse:*

" You should adore," counselled M. de Condren, too, " this continual love of the soul of Jesus for God and this inclina- that he had to honour him in every action, in all the suffer- ings, occurrences, and circumstances of his life; thus you should love Jesus Christ in his dispositions towards God.

" You should give yourself to him in order to enter into this same disposition and to live therein in union with him."[2]

Condren put this teaching into practice chiefly when he prepared to recite the divine Office. He then protested, says his biographer Amelote, " that it was not in his own name, as St Paul says, but in the name and in the Person of Jesus Christ and as one of his members, grafted and living in him, that he dared to converse and treat with the eternal Father, whereby he acted not as a simple creature but as the son of God in Jesus Christ, and that he was nothing in himself, but Jesus Christ alone lived within him."[3]

M. Olier, inspired with these thoughts, composed the mag- nificent prayer for the divine Office which is found in the first part of *La journée chrétienne,* from which we quote a few passages :

" My God, who takest thy delight and pleasure in our Lord Jesus Christ, who alone giveth thee, in virtue of thy Holy Spirit with which he was filled, all the honour and praise that the holy prophets and patriarchs, the apostles and their disciples, the angels in heaven and the saints on earth, have offered thee; express in our soul throughout thy whole Church, what he alone renders thee perfectly in heaven.

" Grant, O my Lord Jesus, that thy Church may spread abroad that which thou hast enclosed within thyself alone, and outwardly express that divine religion which thou hast for thy Father in the secret of thy heart, in heaven and on our altars. . . .

" Therefore, O my God, grant that all these praises and

[1] *Saints Ordres, ibid.*
[2] *Lettre* X, *Discours et lettres du R. P. Ch. de Condren,* Paris, 1643, pp. 338-339.
[3] *La vie du P. de Condren,* Paris, 1643, Part I, chap. xvii, p. 122. See also Eudes, *Royaume de Jésus (Œuvres complètes,* Vol. I, p. 470), in which will be found an excellent method for saying the Divine Office in a holy manner.

canticles, these psalms and hymns, which we are about to sing to thy honour, be only the expression of the inner spirit of Jesus Christ, and that my mouth may say to thee only what the soul of my Saviour says to thee within itself.

"Clinging, then, to thy spirit, O my Lord Jesus, who art the life of our religion, I desire to render to thy Father all the homage and all the duties due unto him, which thou alone understandest and thou alone renderest to him in thy sanctuary.

"Annihilate, my God, everything in myself, who am a miserable and shameful sinner; I adore thy Son, the true and only and perfect religious of thy name; and I unite myself to thy Holy Spirit in the purest part of my soul in order to glorify thee in him."

The first state in which we find the Son of God in the world is his childhood: and that also is the first state that we should contemplate and adore, all the more so in that it endured and included many days, many months, many years, which does not apply to his other mysteries and actions . . . a duration so much the more considerable in that this state of childhood is a state which carries with it very great abasement to so high a dignity as that of the incarnate Word, and the privation of many things due to so great a Majesty.[1]

"The abasements and privations of the state of infancy are reduced to three: dependence, indigence, and impotence; dependence unto indigence, indigence unto impotence. What impotence to be unable to help himself in his needs, or to seek help from others or to ask it in words!"[2]

We should, then, adore Jesus in his state of childhood, have true devotion to this mystery, and imitate the virtues which the Saviour practised therein: obedience, innocence, purity, and simplicity:

"The infancy of our Lord," wrote M. de Renty, the great propagator of devotion to the Child Jesus, "is a state in which we must die to all and in which the soul waits for and receives orders from God in faith, silence, and respect, in innocence, purity, and simplicity, and lives day by day in abandonment, looking in a manner neither before nor behind; but uniting with the holy Child Jesus who, dead to himself, receives every order from his Father. . . . We must . . . as it seems to me, follow these footprints of Jesus Christ our model by the grace of his infancy."[3]

---

[1] Bérulle, *Œuvres*, p. 1008.
[2] *ibid.*, p. 1014. *Cf.* p. 1448
[3] *Vie de M. de Renty,* by Fr. Jean-Baptiste de Saint-Jure, Paris, 1664, p. 286. Respecting M. de Renty, see Bremond, *L'École française*, pp. 523 ff.

We must ask our Lord, at every time, but especially at Christmas time, " to fill us with the spirit of his holy Childhood."[1] This is the spirit needed by the Christian. Did not the Saviour say : " Unless you be converted, and become as little children, you shall not enter into the kingdom of heaven " (Matt. xviii, 3)? The virtues of the state of Christian infancy are, in fact, indispensable to those who wish to belong truly to God. It is first of all the renunciation of our own spirit and the total abandonment of self to Jesus in order to let ourselves be led by him, like a child who surrenders itself in all that concerns it to those who have charge of it. Furthermore, these virtues are those which call to mind the special characteristics of the child, complete indifference, simplicity, purity, sweetness, and meekness, and finally innocence. M. Blanlo (†1657), one of M. Olier's disciples, has very clearly expounded this wholly Berullian teaching in his well-known treatise : *L'enfance chrétienne.*[2]

When it exhorts us to participate in the mysteries of the Crucifixion, the Death, the Burial, the Resurrection, and the Ascension of Jesus, the French School merely comments on St Paul.

According to the great Apostle, we are so closely united to Jesus, living the same life, that we are crucified with him, *Christo confixus sum cruci* (Gal. ii, 19); dead with him, *commortui* (2 Tim. ii, 11); buried with him, *consepulti* (Rom. vi, 4; Col. ii, 12); risen with him, *si consurrexistis cum Christo* (Col. iii, 1); and seated with him in heaven, *consedere fecit in caelestibus* (Eph. ii, 6).

" The crucifixion of our Lord," says M. Olier, " gives us, in virtue of the Holy Spirit, the grace and strength to crucify all our lusts, or all the obstacles which are opposed to the development of the supernatural life in our souls, which prevent Jesus Christ from increasing and becoming realized within us."[3]

We appropriate " the state of crucifixion " of Jesus by constant mortification of the flesh, of the old man. Thus is spiritual crucifixion produced in us :

" The conflict which we must maintain to this end," continues M. Olier, " is that which St Paul prescribed to the whole Church and to each one of the faithful when he said : *Crucify within you the old man with his concupiscences* (Gal.

---

[1] Olier, *Lettre* LIX, Migne, p. 802. M. Olier desired devotion to the childhood of Jesus to be one of the devotions of his seminary (*Pietas seminarii*, IX).

[2] The first edition appeared in 1665 ; numerous other editions followed.

[3] *Pensées choisies*, pp. 47-48. Cf. *Catéchisme chrétien*, Part I, Lesson xxi.

v, 24). Let us, then, through this mortification, sanctify our hearts and our bodies. Let us inwardly crucify our passions in testimony of our union with Jesus Christ and our participation in the grace of the cross."[1]

After the crucifixion comes the death. We participate in the death of our Lord " by communion with the grace and state of death " which he has merited for us.

M. Olier states clearly in what this state of death consists:

" It is," he says, " a state in which the heart cannot be moved in its depths; and although the world shows it its beauties, its honours, its riches, it is the same as though these were offered to a dead man who is motionless and without any desires, insensible to all that is offered him. The Christian, in this state of inward death, is inwardly undisturbed by all that the senses show him, all that the wickedness of the world arouses; outwardly he may be agitated in this life, but inwardly he is ever at peace; he remains insensible to all and esteems it as nothing, because he is dead in our Lord: *Mortui enim estis* (Col. iii, 3) . . . [and] because of the divine life which absorbs all that is mortal in [his soul]."[2]

We have also been buried in the tomb with Jesus Christ. " This burial of the body of our Lord signifies our inward entombment and includes its grace. We should, like the corpse buried beneath the stone, be entire strangers to the world and insensible to all things on earth."[3] But though in a state of burial—" that is, in the total destruction of being " —it also proclaims to us the production of a new life. For " Christ willed his life to be born again from amidst the tomb wherein death " had placed him.[4]

This new life of the Christian resembles that of the risen Jesus:

" In the same way as our risen Lord is changed, and, so to speak, no longer follows the conduct of human nature which loves life and fears death; so holy souls, through the mystery of the Resurrection, should be renewed and established in a new state of sanctity. God has taken possession of them, and has, as it were, changed them into himself. . . . This resurrection life . . . gives inclinations and impulses similar to those of the blessed. . . . But on earth, because this life goes on only in spirit, and because we have in our members dispositions and feelings wholly opposed thereto, we

[1] *Pensées choisies*, p. 50. Cf. *Pietas seminarii*, xiv-xv.
[2] *Catéchisme chrétien*, Part I, lesson xxii. Cf. *Pensées choisies*, pp. 51-52. In his *Traité des Saints Ordres*, Part I, M. Olier explains at length that the clergy, even more than the faithful, should participate in this state of the death of Christ. It is " the first foundation needed in order to aspire to the high dignity of the clerical state."
[3] M. Lebas . . ., p. 234.
[4] Cf. Olier, *Catéchisme chrétien*, Part I, Lesson xxiii.

have ever to fight against the old man, which will never be overcome until the day of judgement.''[1]

Even more perfect is the grace of the mystery of the Ascension. The state of Christ, seated at the right hand of the Father, is, in certain respects, more divine than that of Christ risen from the dead :

There appeared '' still some infirmity in our Lord Jesus Christ after his Resurrection. He had still certain marks, and seemed sometimes to strip himself of the perfect glory of his consummation in God and his total resemblance to his Father. He still rendered his humanity palpable and visible to the eyes of his apostles ; he ate with them. But on the day of his Ascension his glory no longer suffers either interruption or suspension ; the brightness of it can no longer be borne by the eyes of men : having entered into the splendour of God the Father, he remains hidden in his bosom and is not apprehended by our senses. . . . The soul which enters into this state of the divine Ascension of our Lord Jesus Christ . . . no longer declines from union or unity with God, nor descends to the lowliness of human infirmity. It is no longer yielded to passion or self-love ; it no longer admits within itself any return to the creature. . . . This state is that of perfect souls, inwardly consummated in God, into the being and life of whom they have passed in virtue of a most true and perfect union.''[2]

It might be said that these souls are already, '' by happy anticipation, in the region of eternity.''

He who would truly honour Jesus and fully live his life cannot rest content with merely keeping the mysteries which the liturgical year suggests to his devotion. Our Lord must be adored universally, '' in every one of his mysteries and in all his states.'' To this end Bérulle instituted '' the solemnity of Jesus '' :

'' The idea of this feast,'' he says, '' is to look to, love, and adore the Son of God in regard to what he is in himself, in his two natures, in his divine person, in all his greatness, in his powers and office, in his states, in his goodness, and in his operations ; but chiefly in what he is in himself and in all his known and unknown greatness, for it is our greatness and what makes us blessed.''[3]

The interior principle which animates Christ, the interior life of his soul, such is the chief aim of this feast. The

[1] Olier, *Pensées choisies*, pp. 52-53. Bérulle calls the Resurrection of Jesus his third birth, the birth of immortality (*Œuvres*, pp. 388 ff.).
[2] Olier, *Catéchisme chrétien*, Part I, Lesson xxv.
[3] Bérulle, *Œuvres*, p. 1070.

Oratorians, moreover, should daily honour the interior of
Jesus by reciting this prayer :

" Grant us the grace, we beseech thee, O Lord, unceasingly
to celebrate this ineffable and most divine life of the Word
in thy humanity and thy humanity in the Word of life."[1]

Condren paraphrased it thus :

" I adore thee, my Lord Jesus Christ, in all the holy intentions and inclinations of thy spirit during thy life on earth
and now in eternity; I renounce all my own and I desire by
the help of thy grace henceforth to live in thy intentions and
dispositions in all I must do throughout my life; I desire my
soul to be united to thine in the same love, the same desires,
the same dislikes, the same spirit and attitude towards all
things."[2]

Thus to have inclinations and dispositions like those of
Jesus is to participate in his inner life, which is defined by
M: Olier with his customary clearness :

" The interior life of Jesus Christ consists in his dispositions and inward feelings towards all things; for example, in
his reverence for God, in his love for his neighbour, in his
annihilation of self, in his horror of sin, and in his condemnation of the world and its maxims."[3]

His exterior life, " his sensible actions," his " visible practice of virtue " " arise from the depths of his divine interior."
What, then, is important to know, to venerate, and to imitate
is this divine interior. If we think, if we feel with Christ,
we shall act like him. Moreover, M. Olier desired to establish the faithful, and especially priests, in this interior life,
and to inspire them with devotion to it.[4] After his death, in
accordance with his intentions, the feast of the *Interior Life
of our Lord* was instituted, as was also that of the *Interior
Life of Mary*.[5]

We must " live in the spirit of Jesus," counselled Fr.
Eudes :

[1] Faillon, *Vie de M. Olier,* Paris, 1873, Vol. III, p. 70.
[2] Letter X, *Discours et Lettres,* pp. 337-338.
[3] *Catéchisme chrétien,* Part J, lesson i. Cf. *Introduction à la vie
chrétienne,* chaps. ii, iii.
[4] This devotion is the subject of the first article of his *Pietas
seminarii.* It is given as the summing up of all the piety of the
seminary.
[5] Fr. de Condren was the creator of this devotion to the Interior Life.
He made M. Olier recite this prayer : *Veni, Domine Jesu, et vive in
hoc servo tuo, in plenitudine virtutis tuae, in perfectione viarum
tuarum, in sanctitate Spiritus, et dominare omni adversae potestati in
Spiritu tuo, ad gloriam Patris. Amen.* M. Olier modified it as
follows : *O Jesus vivens in Maria,* in order to unite in the same devotion
the interior life of Mary and that of Jesus. See Faillon, *Vie de
M. Olier,* Vol. I, p. 168, 4th edition.

"This truth," says M. Olier in the Preface to *La journée chrétienne,* "that we should live as Jesus Christ lived on earth, according to his manner of life and feelings, has given me the idea of drawing up certain practices and suggesting divers intentions in order to do every one of our works holily."

He teaches us in this admirable "little work" to associate ourselves with the mysteries of Christ "in all the exercises of the day." For example, when we go to bed at night we should "look upon our bed in faith as the very tomb of the Son of God, in which we sleep to rise next day in a spirit of joy with the risen Christ."[1] It is thus that we realize the words of St Paul: *Christ is my life.* All our actions, even the most ordinary, such as walking, the sight of the sun or of birds and flowers, should be performed in union with Jesus.

Bossuet makes a striking application of this method to the death of a Christian in his *Réflexions sur l'agonie de Jésus-Christ,* most Berullian in thought and expression:

"Christians," he says, "have so great an interest in knowing the mysteries and in taking to themselves the sentiments and dispositions of Jesus Christ, their adorable Saviour, in all his states, that they should apply themselves thereto unceasingly; but, above all, to those great and terrible mysteries of his Passion and death, by which he completed the work of our eternal salvation by the redemption, and ended his holy life."

The devil specially attacks the dying in their last hour. But Christ, in his agony, triumphed over him, and has triumphed not only for himself, but "already in advance for Christians when they reach this state."

And, above all, the dying are associated "by a right of union, fellowship, and intercourse, which exists between the head and the living members, with the divine deeds of the soul of Jesus Christ, and with the heroic virtues which he practised in his state" of agony. Jesus endured his agony, so to speak, for Christians; he did in their place what they should do when death approaches:

"All that he then did was done in discharge of their obligations and as a supplement to what they would be unable to do at that time. He appropriated to himself the natural pain felt by the soul when struck with the sombre and fearful thought of inevitable separation: he sanctified it in a spirit of submission and penance, of sacrifice and homage to the sovereignty of his Father. He offered this agony of his children and all its consequences by a movement of love communicated to them thenceforth, if they are in a state to take part in it, and he transferred it to them under the eyes and

[1] *Journée chrétienne,* Part II.

into the bosom of his Father, to supplement their impotence, if their darkened reason rendered them incapable of actually entering into his dispositions. If they are unable to have these themselves, they have them in Jesus Christ; and to have them in him is to have them in themselves by the right of fellowship which the grace of their union with him creates between him and them."

Thus it is that Christ renews and perpetuates his sacrifice, " not only in the mystery of the divine Eucharist, but also in the death of all true believers."

When we assist souls in agony, " instead of embarrassing them . . . with a thousand confused acts of haphazard fancy, we should make them from time to time fix their eyes gently on the sight of what Jesus Christ is to them and what they are to him; impress them with an entire confidence in him and in what he has done for them; make them see him dying with them, charging himself with their interests and their obligations, in order to excite in them the desire of union and fellowship with him in all the dispositions of his agony and death."

" It is in this spirit that they should receive the Holy Viaticum " through which " the High Priest " fully hallows the death of the faithful :

" Thus the Christian being united, then, not only to the adorable body of Jesus Christ in his sacrament, but also to his heart; entering, by submission and by clinging to him, into all his designs; desiring to dispose of his being and of his life as does the great Sacrificer, becomes a priest with him in the death; and at this last moment achieves the sacrifice whereto he had been consecrated at baptism and which he ought to have carried on throughout his life."[1]

The French School looks upon everything in the Christian religion from the point of view of Jesus, and so it especially inspires devotion to the Blessed Virgin and the saints :

" To speak of Mary," says Bérulle, " is to speak of Jesus; for they are so joined together, and she is the greatest vessel of his grace and the most rare effect of his power."[2]

To consider the eminent dignity of his Mother is also " to honour Jesus," so close is the bond between Jesus and Mary. The best way of making manifest our devotion to the Blessed Virgin is to contemplate the life of Jesus in her and to strive to participate in it.

Jesus lives in Mary in a unique way from the first moment of the Incarnation until the virgin birth. During that time :

[1] See also in St John Eudes, *Le royaume de Jésus*, pp. 520 ff., a similar exercise, " For a Christian death."
[2] *Œuvres*, p. 433.

III.

" Jesus is in Mary as a son in his mother, drawing his life from hers. He is in her as her son and as her God, giving her life as he receives life from her. He is in her as in his earthly paradise; for all is holy, all is delightful in the Virgin. The shadow of sin is not and has never been there. And Jesus finds in her his joy and his repose, and out of her he found none but sinners and sin. He is in her as in a heaven, for he is living in life and glory, seeing God and rejoicing in his divine essence. He is in her as in a temple in which he praises and adores God, in which he pays his duties to the eternal Father, and pays them as much for himself as for all created being."[1]

But Jesus lives in Mary in a permanent manner, by the fulness of his Spirit with which he filled her superabundantly :

" What our Lord is to his Church," says M. Olier, " he is *par excellence* to his holy Mother. Thus he is her inward and divine plenitude; and as he sacrificed himself more particularly for her than for the whole Church, he gives her the life of God more abundantly than to the whole Church. . . .

" We must then consider Jesus Christ, our all, living in the most holy Virgin in the fulness of the life of God, as much in that life which he received from his Father as that which he obtained and merited for men through the ministry of the life of his Mother. . . .

" There is nothing more wonderful than this life of Jesus in Mary, the holy life that he pours continuously into her, the divine life with which he animates her, loving and praising and adoring God his Father in her, giving a worthy supplement to her heart wherein he abounds with pleasure. All the life of Jesus and all his love in the remainder of the Church, even in his apostles and his dear disciples, is nothing in comparison with that which he has in the heart of Mary. He dwells there in plenitude; he works there to the full extent of his divine Spirit, he is but one heart, one soul, one life with Mary."[2]

The saints should be considered and honoured as the living members of Christ :

" For it is he alone who fills all the saints with his grace and his glory; in them he is their whole life, their grace, and their virtue; he is all that is of God in them, God who in Jesus is all in all, perfecting in himself his whole creature."[3]

In the Berullian School Christ is truly " all in all." This

---

[1] Bérulle, *Œuvres*, pp. 493-494.
[2] *Journée chrétienne*, Part II, end.
[3] *ibid.*—The French School gives special honour to those saints who lived with our Lord on earth. Bérulle specially honoured St Mary Magdalen. M. Olier desired particular honour to be given to St Joseph, St John, and the Apostles in the seminary of St Sulpice (*Pietas*, x-xii). See Eudes, *Royaume de Jésus*, pp. 345-350.

it never forgets, above all, when it honours the Blessed
Virgin and the saints.

B—ADHERENCE TO CHRIST IN HIS STATE OF IMMOLATION AND AS VICTIM, ACCORDING TO CONDREN

All the leaders of the French School are apostles of the
Word incarnate; each one, however, in his own special way;
"Bérulle by a more general 'adherence,' in some way, to
the Person of the Word incarnate; Condren by a somewhat
more particularized adherence to Christ dead and risen again,
finally, M. Olier by an adherence to the most deep, the most
religious, the most persevering, and consequently the most
'really' active and efficacious annihilation of the same
Word"[1] in the Eucharist.

It is M. Olier himself who points out these different lines:
"Our Lord has made me see," he wrote to his director,
"that willing to renew the primitive spirit of the Church in
these days, he raised up two persons in order to begin this
design: Monsignor de Bérulle, to honour him in his Incarnation; Fr. de Condren, in the whole of his life, his death, and,
above all, in his resurrection; but there remains to do him
honour after his resurrection and his ascension, as he is in
the most august sacrament of the Eucharist. . . . He has
willed to bestow upon myself, as successor to Fr. de Condren,
the grace and spirit of this adorable mystery."[2]

In the preceding pages the teaching of Bérulle, defined and
developed by Condren and, above all, by Olier, has been
explained. We have now to learn the particular views of his
two most famous disciples. Let us first take those of Fr.
de Condren.

The chief object of Fr. de Condren's devotion is the
victim state of the Word incarnate and his condition of
interior annihilation and total immolation.

The victim state, according to Condren, is that which sums
up the whole life of Christ on earth and in heaven. All the
circumstances of his earthly life are the different parts of
his one sacrifice which is further continued and completed in
heaven.

"Let this," he says, "be our foundation, that his
[Christ's] whole life, from the first moment of the Incarnation right on into eternity, is the true sacrifice,[3] the redeem-
ing sacrifice.

[1] Bremond, *École française*, pp. 490-491.
[2] Faillon, *Vie de M. Olier*, II, p. 209, Paris, 1873.
[3] *Idée du sacerdoce et du sacrifice de Jésus-Christ*, p. 60, Paris, 1901.
The conception of the sacrifice may be found completely expounded by
M. Lepin, *L'idée du sacrifice dans la religion chrétienne principale-
ment, d'après le P. de Condren et M. Olier*, Paris-Lyons, 1897.

It is as priest that the Word incarnate has saved the world, and he has saved it by his sacrifice :

" The eternal design of God owing to the fall of Adam was to reconcile men to himself by means of a mediator. . . . God willed that this mediator should be priest, and that he should exercise his mediation and labour for his reconciliation of the whole human race as priest, not merely through some sacerdotal act, such as intercession and prayer, or by some other simple satisfaction offered to God; but through the noblest and most excellent of all satisfactions, the act special to the priesthood, which is oblation and sacrifice."[1]

The Word incarnate is, then, essentially a priest. Christ was appointed priest by the Incarnation itself. His life was but one single sacrifice " the different parts of which are made up of the divers mysteries."[2] The victim of this sacrifice can be none other than Christ himself, who sacrificed himself to the glory of God the Father, in expiation for the sins of men.

Condren, then, looked upon all the mysteries of the life of Christ as parts of his priesthood and sacrifice. The spirit of annihilation and immolation is that inner disposition of Jesus which he chiefly accentuates. Bérulle spoke doubtless of the priesthood of Christ; he founded the Oratory in order that the clergy should " tend towards the perfection of the priesthood." Nevertheless, in the French School, the doctor of the priesthood and sacrifice of Christ is Condren. It is, above all, by him that St Vincent de Paul, M. Olier, and Bossuet were inspired, in the beautiful pages they have left us on the priesthood.[3]

In order to explain his teaching Condren distinguishes five parts of the sacrifice :

" The first is the sanctification, or the consecration of the victim; the second, the oblation of the victim; the third, the slaying or immolation; the fourth, the burning or consuming; the fifth, the communion."[4]

In these sacrifices of the old law he thinks he finds " all the parts required to make a completed sacrifice."

But the important thing for us is to know how Condren discovers them in Christ's sacrifice :

" In the first place," he says, " the sanctification of Jesus Christ as victim takes place at the Incarnation; for in this mystery the Saviour was sanctified and consecrated by the divinity itself : *Quem Pater sanctificavit* (John x, 36)."

---

[1] *ibid.*, pp. 1-2. [2] *ibid.*, p. 87.
[3] We should read, in this connection, the beautiful work by J. Grimal, S.M., *Le Sacerdoce et le sacrifice de Notre-Seigneur Jésus-Christ*, 3rd edition, Paris, 1923. The work of Fr. Giraud, *Prêtre et Hostie* (Eng. trans., *Priest and Victim*) is well known to all.
[4] *L'idée du sacerdoce*, p. 45.

The humanity of Jesus was sanctified through the very sanctity of the Word to which it was personally united. By the Incarnation, Christ again was consecrated priest for ever :

"And that which is singular in Jesus Christ," says Condren, " is that by this mystery in which he is consecrated and sanctified to be the victim of God, he is also consecrated priest for all eternity."[1]

Christ, the most holy priest, " the victim sanctified for God," was, then, from the first moment of the Incarnation destined to offer himself in sacrifice.

This offering—which is the second part of the sacrifice—" is also made from the moment of the Incarnation " :

" Jesus Christ, seeing that the justice of God could not be satisfied by the sacrifices of animals made under the old law, and having perfect knowledge of the will of his Father, who gave him a body only in order that he might become his true victim, replacing those of old, he addressed him in these words : *But a body thou hast fitted to me: then said I, Behold, I come that I should do thy will, O God* (Heb. x, 5, 7)."[2]

This oblation " is not transitory or momentary." It constitutes the permanent state of the incarnate Word, his perpetual state of a victim, by which he unceasingly renders to God " the first duty of the creature " and " the first act of religion," which is " that of adoration and sacrifice " :

" Jesus Christ will never cease to offer himself to God his Father by a permanent and eternal oblation; with this difference, that whereas from the moment of the Incarnation and during all his life, the Son of God offered himself to his Father, as a victim to be one day slain in his honour . . . since his death and resurrection, he offers himself as a victim once slain and ever living before God in order to adore him."[3]

This victim state is actually that of Christ glorious in heaven, where he consummates his sacrifice. It was likewise that of the mortal Christ accomplishing his work of redemption on earth. The Christian who celebrates the mysteries of the life of the Saviour must then strive to make this victim state his own and to be in communion with the dispositions of immolation and annihilation which belong to it.

The destruction or immolation of the victim—the third part of the ancient sacrifices—does not always follow the oblation immediately. This is why the Son of God " waited until the thirty-third year of his age " in order to be immolated on Calvary.

But all sacrifice necessitates the destruction of the victim : "[For]," according to Fr. Condren, " sacrifice having

---

[1] *Idée du Sacerdoce*, p. 61.   [2] *ibid.*, p. 65.   [3] *ibid.*

been instituted in order to acknowledge God as the author of all being and to do honour to his sovereign dominion over all created being, it requires the consuming and entire destruction of that being."[1]

Death is one of the ways of destroying the victim. It is not the only one. Moreover, all sacrifice does not necessarily require such death. The sacrifice of the cross, however, is brought about thereby, because Christ, like the scapegoat of the old law, was " burdened with all the sins of the whole world, which were laid on him by God."[2] Hence, he had to die in order to destroy sin.

The slain victim was afterwards consumed by fire, which is " a figure of the glory of the Lord " : it was thus by being consumed " as though changed and transformed into God." It seemed " that thereby God entered into communion with the sacrifices that were offered him." Thus were made plain " the nature and true virtue of that sacrifice which is to unite us most closely to God."[3]

The consuming of Christ " was not done by fire, but by the truth typified by fire—that is to say, by the glory of God '" at the moment of the Resurrection. The humanity of Christ " was not only changed into the representation of the glory of God, but was transformed into the very glory of God, without losing anything, however, of the reality of human nature " :

" It is through the Resurrection," says Condren, " that this sacred victim was freed from all that was earthly and vile ; that it was wholly reclothed with a glory which becomes the only Son of the Father . . . that it entered into a wholly divine state, according to these powerful, but none the less most true, expressions of St Hilary (*De Trinit.*, xi, 40) : *Ne ex parte Deus fit, sed totus Deus.*[4]

Finally, " the fifth part of the sacrifice is the communion. To communicate is to participate in the victim, or to take one's part in it." In the ancient law there were three parts of the victim : one was burnt, which was " God's part whereby he communicated, as it were, in the victim."[5] The second was given to the priest, the third to the people.

God really communicated in the sacrifice of Christ. How so? By receiving in his breast the risen Saviour who, on the day of his Ascension, returned finally to the glory of the Father :

" Now this return and this new entrance of the Son of God into his Father is called communion, inasmuch as in this mystery the whole Christ is in the bosom of his eternal Father . . . he is received . . . and as though eaten by his

---

[1] *Idée du sacerdoce*, p. 40. [2] *id.*, p. 69.
[3] *id.*, p. 70. *Cf.* pp. 48 ff. [4] *id.*, p. 71.
[5] *id.*, p. 53.

Father, if we may speak thus of so spiritual and divine a matter."[1]

All the faithful, " as much in heaven as on earth," also communicate in the risen Christ, living in the glory of the Father.

" The blessed communicate for all eternity in this victim in his state of consummation and glory."[2] They communicate in this victim by being associated with his perpetual offering. For, according to Condren, there is in heaven a permanent sacrifice; the uninterrupted oblation of Jesus united with the saints :

" Jesus Christ offers himself and all the saints with him as his members to the most Holy Trinity, and the saints also offer themselves and with themselves offer Jesus Christ their head, through Jesus Christ, with Jesus Christ, and in Jesus Christ himself : and it is through this wonderful secret that Jesus Christ is in his person, and in his members at the same time, perfect victim and eternal priest according to the order of Melchisedech."[3]

The Mass is no other " than this great sacrifice " of heaven, made present on earth by the eucharistic consecration :

" This great sacrifice which Jesus Christ makes to God in heaven with his saints, in offering himself with them, is the same sacrifice which the priests offer, and the whole Church offers through them on earth, in holy Mass. For it is the same victim [host] which they offer him; since it is his body and blood really present, united to God and subsisting in the Word in this mystery. It is the same priest who offers it through his ministers, and it is on the same altar, which is the subsistence or person of the eternal Word, that it is offered. It is also in the same temple—that is to say, in the bosom of the eternal Father. This sacrifice is offered there to the same God as in heaven; and finally, not only is the victim therein the same, but therein it is in the same consummation and the same glory as in heaven. The difference is this, that though it is as really present there as in heaven, it is not so, however, in a visible manner."[4]

The faithful, then, on earth communicate in the same victim as do the elect in heaven :

" When the saints, as much on earth as in heaven, communicate in Jesus Christ, it is in Jesus Christ consecrated, offered, slain, and consummated that they communicate, and Jesus Christ bears eternally in his adorable humanity this

---

[1] *Idée du sacerdoce*, p. 74.   [2] *id.*, p. 78.   [3] *id.*, p. 79.
[4] *id.*, p. 79. *Cf.* Olier, *Traité des Saints Ordres*, Part III, chap. iii : " Is it not the same Jesus who, offering his body and Blood in heaven for us to God his Father, multiplies this divine sacrifice amongst us day by day, through his priests, in holy Mass?"

state of consecration, oblation, immolation, consummation, and glory which makes the communion eternal in heaven."[1]

Will this celebrated theory of sacrifice some day enter into the dogmatic teaching of the Mass?[2] For Fr. Condren it was, above all, the foundation of his asceticism. That which is attractive in it is the "consummation" of Christ in God. This part of the sacrifice of the Saviour contains all the others, "his consecration, his oblation, and his death."[3] This it is which Condren chiefly accentuates. He speaks of it constantly in his letters, and he deduces from it this consequence : that we should strip ourselves of ourselves and annihilate ourselves in order to be consummated in God with Christ :

"Leave yourselves to God," he writes, "in the consummation of Jesus Christ which he has effected, and to Jesus Christ in the loss of himself in God in order that God may be all in all in him; and, losing all desire of life and being for yourselves, let all your disposition be that God be in you."[4]

The consummation of Christ in God was represented more perfectly in the holocausts than in the other sacrifices. In the holocausts, in fact, the victim was burnt so that it might be wholly consumed in God :[5]

"For it is he [Christ] who offered himself to God as a whole and perfect holocaust, of which nothing was left that was not consumed in the ardent furnace of the divinity.

"Now we ought to belong . . . to God in this intention of Jesus Christ," says Fr. Condren, "so that he may consume us wholly in himself, intending to lose all that we are, but especially all that is of the old Adam."[6]

It is, in fact, by uniting ourselves with Christ, by clinging to his annihilating consummation, that we shall belong wholly to God. Sacrifice strips us only to enrich us, annihilates us only to make us greater, slays us only that we may be made to live in God. It makes us like the saints in heaven, where Jesus Christ "and the saints with him" are "in a state of consecration or appropriation to God . . . in a continual oblation both of Jesus Christ and of themselves . . . consummated in glory."[7]

[1] *Idée du sacerdoce*, pp. 80-81.
[2] *Cf.* De la Taille, S.J., *Mysterium Fidei*, Paris, 1921, pp. 176 ff.
[3] *Idée*, p. 80. See Olier, *Traité des Saints Ordres*, Part III, chap. v.
[4] *Discours et Lettres*, Letter XXI, Paris, 1643, p. 381.
[5] *Idée du sacerdoce*, p. 50 : When therefore the fire consumed the victims, God, who was figured by it, seemed to unite himself with these victims and enter into communion with their sacrifices.
[6] *Considérations sur les mystères*, p. 75. Brémond, p. 368.
[7] *Idée du sacerdoce*, p. 81.

" In this way, he [Jesus] is not only consummated in God as our head, but he is so also in his members, in whom he establishes himself in order to be consumed anew in them, being already so in his own person. It is to this that we should also tend with him; for we should freely cede to him all that we are so that he may effect in us the design which he has of there being everything instead of ourselves."[1]

As his biographer bears witness, Condren lived what he taught; his teaching ruled his every act:

" Here," says Amelote, " is the main point on which was centred one of Fr. Condren's great devotions, and therein God made it apparent from his childhood that he willed to bestow on him most singular graces. After having been vowed as a host by his parents and having had the spirit of sacrifice infused into his soul from his earliest years, having finally attained the vigour of his manhood and of his enlightenment, he became devoted to God himself and gave himself to Jesus Christ in order to be a host with him to the glory of the Father. He bound himself by this vow [of host] to the laws written by the Holy Spirit for the victims [of the Old Testament], and though unable to keep them to the letter, he had at least the intention of fulfilling them mystically."[2]

He annihilated himself so thoroughly, so thoroughly effaced himself in order to leave a place for Jesus only, that he " was only," as M. Olier testifies, " what he seemed outwardly and in appearance, being within quite another self, being really the inner spirit of Jesus Christ and his hidden life; so that it was rather Jesus Christ living in Fr. Condren than Fr. Condren living in himself. He was like the host on our altars: outwardly we see the accidents and appearances of bread, within it is Jesus Christ. It was thus with this great servant of our Lord, so singularly beloved of God."[3]

C—ADHERENCE TO CHRIST THROUGH THE MYSTERIES OF HIS EUCHARISTIC LIFE, ACCORDING TO JEAN-JACQUES OLIER

" Our Lord," says M. Olier, " desiring to draw mankind to his Father, has given himself twice to them: once, in the weakness of the flesh, through his Incarnation; the other in the power of his divine life, through the most holy Sacrament. By the first he came to establish his Church and merit his grace; by the other to renew it and perfect it."[4]

M. Olier, who desired to renew and perfect the clergy,

[1] *Consid. sur les myst.*, p. 76.
[2] *Vie de P. Ch. de Condren*, Part II, chap. xxxii, Paris, 1643, pp. 319-320.
[3] Faillon, *Vie de M. Olier*, Vol. I, pp. 149-150.
[4] *ibid.*, II, p. 207.

devoted himself to doing honour to the incarnate Word
" as he is in the august sacrament of the Eucharist."[1]

The Eucharist is the " memorial of all the mysteries of
Christ." They are there in the living state. " The inward
spirit which gives them life is present there."[2] The great
desire of the Saviour is to impart himself to us. Jesus hides
himself in the Host, he the " universal mediator of grace,"
in order " to communicate to us his own life."[3] His sacrament has no other object " than to give us as nourishment
all his mysteries and to communicate to us their life and
virtue."[4]

These Berulian principles are expressed in the *Pietas
seminarii,* the spiritual directory of the Seminary of St
Sulpice. M. Olier thought that the true formation of the
priest was produced, above all, by participation in " the state
of Jesus Christ in the most holy Sacrament." In this he
was inspired by his own experience :

" Since our Lord deigned to make me a participator in his
state of the Host in the most holy Sacrament," he wrote to
his director, " speaking truly, it is no longer I that live : it
is he himself who lives in me. Each day after Holy Communion I feel him diffused all through me, as though I felt
his presence in all my members, although in Holy Communion
he is not wedded to the body, which will only be purified in
the day of judgement. He leads me, he animates me, as
though he were my soul and my life. He performs in a
measure in my regard, what he did to [his] sacred humanity,
leading me, stopping me, opening my lips, closing them,
directing and regulating my sight—in a word, doing all for
me. Willing that I should represent him in his adorable
sacrament, he is not content thus to come into my heart to
consume it in himself, but he dwells in me in order to produce in souls the effects of divine communions and diffuses
himself thence in them as through a Host and a sacrament."[5]

By Holy Communion Jesus " comes to change our natural
dispositions into his own." The priest, thus changed into
Jesus Christ, acts effectually on souls :

[1] Faillon, *Vie de M. Olier,* II, p. 207.
[2] *Pietas seminarii,* IX : *Memoriale omnium mirabilium [mys-
teriorum] Christi, et interiora eorum nobis praesentia semper
[exhibit].* The edition by Labbe de Champgrand, Bourges, 1879,
p. 139. I cite the autograph text which differs slightly from the
ordinary one.
[3] *id.,* II : *ibique Christum delitescentem ut mediatorem omnis
gratiae . . . ut communionem propriae vitae suae amplectetur
[Seminarium],* p. 17.
[4] *id.,* IV : *Ad hoc enim Christus vivit in hoc sacramento, ut det
nobis in escam omnia mirabilia sua, vitamque eorum et virtutem
largiatur,* p. 47.
[5] Faillon, *id.,* p. 228. M. Olier wrote this for his director who had
ordered his penitent to put in writing what passed in his soul. This
explains the very personal nature of this passage.

"I feel," said M. Olier, "his virtue go out of me and be borne to them [souls] in order to communicate to them his lights and grace, as he does through the holy Eucharist."[1]

It is, then, through the Eucharist that we become truly priests.

Let us not be surprised after this at the high place that is given to devotion to the Blessed Sacrament in the *Pietas seminarii*.[2] It is the principal devotion of the seminary, the house where the clergy are formed.[3]

Adoration of the Eucharist is our first duty. And since the Eucharist contains all the mysteries of the Christian religion : mysteries such as the Holy Trinity, and mysteries which belong to time—that is to say, the Incarnation and Redemption—these are the mysteries that we should adore first of all.

"There [in the Eucharist] the seminary should, with perfect piety, adore the divine life eternally hidden in the breast of the Father and eternally poured forth in the Son and the Holy Spirit; a life which continues to be poured out in them under the eucharistic species by unceasing generation and spiration. In this same life, flowing from the Father into the humanity of Christ, and spreading most abundantly into all his mysteries so that all receive his plenitude, the seminary, after having rendered him the worship and homage due to him, should ask unceasingly to participate."[4]

The greatest desire, moreover, of Christ is to make us participate, by means of the Eucharist, in his life and the virtues of his mysteries, "chiefly in his solemn act of religion towards his Father, in his most tender charity towards his neighbour, in his deep annihilation of himself, and in his irreconcilable opposition to the world and to sin."[5]

M. Olier has developed these thoughts magnificently in the third part of his *Traité des Saints Ordres*,[6] in which he shows how priests ought to "conform to Jesus Christ, as Host, in the most holy Sacrament" : Host of praise and Host consummated in God and wholly devoted to men in an annihilating immolation. We find here, restated with regard to the Eucharist, the sacrificial teaching of Condren.

In the Eucharist, in fact, Jesus is "God's true and perfect religious" :

[1] Faillon, *id.*, p. 229.
[2] Seven articles (ii to vii) out of the twenty-three deal with this devotion. It is also referred to in articles ix, xi, xii, and xiii.
[3] *Cultu praecipuo se devovebit [seminarium] Sanctissimo Corporis et Sanguinis Christi Sacramento*, Art. ii.
[4] Art. iii, autograph text, Champgrand, p. 31.
[5] Art. iv, Champgrand, p. 47.
[6] Especially chapters iii-vii.

" God cannot be more greatly honoured than by this divine Host : for it contains within itself all religion and all worship of God. There is no sort of praise, of respect or of homage that is not enclosed in it, and ·not derived from it in the Church.

" This divine Host is the summing-up of all religion : so that he who offers it to God, offers him at the same time all the honour, all the homage, all the canticles, all the psalms, all the hymns recited throughout the Church ; and at the same time offers him all the respect, all the reverence, and all the adoration presented to him in heaven [since the eucharistic sacrifice is the very sacrifice of heaven, visibly offered here below]."[1]

What a beautiful theme for meditation, for the priest who celebrates Mass or makes his visit to the Blessed Sacrament ![2] To unite ourselves with the adoration of Christ in the Eucharist, to make it our own, in order to offer it to the Father, is not this, as M. Olier counsels in the *Pietas seminarii,* to communicate " with the religion of Jesus Christ always hidden in the Eucharist, and unceasingly seen in the sight of God, in order to intercede through perpetual worship and prayer?"[3] The Eucharist is thus " the sustenance of unceasing prayer " which enables us to offer to God, in the intimacy of our hearts, a continual sacrifice of praise.

Sacerdotal piety is not only a religious piety. It is also " a piety of charity and zeal." Christ in the Eucharist is the " centre of the Church's religion." It draws to him " all people from the extremities of the earth like lines to their centres." The most holy Sacrament is thus the principle of the Church's unity. Through it the priest also becomes a centre which draws souls in order to unite them together and to give them to God.[4]

M. Olier was particularly moved by the annihilation of Christ in the Eucharist. It recalled to his mind the inward annihilation taught by Condren. It was to him also a living interpretation of the *Agnoscite quod agitis, imitamini quod tractatis* of the *Pontificale.* It must also be said it provided him with one more occasion of expressing the wholly Augustinian contempt which we should have for ourselves :

" From this same source of the Eucharist," he says, " there emanates—let us be persuaded of it—the true annihilation of the heart which Christ chiefly proclaims in this august sacrament and there makes manifest to the whole Church, much more than in the other mysteries of his holy

---

[1] *Saints Ordres,* III, chap. vii. Cf. *Pensées choisies,* Letourneau, pp. 54 ff.
[2] M. Olier suggests this also to the faithful in *La Journée chrétienne: Exercice pour la visite au très saint Sacrement.*
[3] Art. v, Champgrand, p. 61.   [4] *Pietas seminarii,* vi.

life. For, although the Word made flesh annihilated himself by taking the form of slave, by rendering himself like
to men, and, in all outward appearance, man; nevertheless,
in the Eucharist he lies wrapped in that which is most
common in nature, in the mere accidents of bread and wine,
where he hides himself as one dead.[1] The substance of the
bread is annihilated, or rather changed into Christ. This
reminds us that, by virtue of this sacrament, we should also
annihilate ourselves and become transformed into Christ:
the Holy Spirit giving us life inwardly and the outward man
in us, which is worth nothing and only fit to be cast aside
and trodden under foot, being destroyed. Then let the pupils
of the seminary consider themselves as the most uselss and
most contemptible servants of the Church and of all the
faithful, let them place themselves in spirit at the feet of all,
like dead and putrid dogs, objects of contempt to all the
world. They should esteem themselves inferior to all and
never uplift themselves in thought, but be ever drawn to what
is humble."[2]

Let us not forget that this inward annihilation has as its
end to consummate us in God. The fire of sacrifice only
destroys the victim in order to change it in a manner into
God, to whom it is offered:

"The priest," M. Olier teaches, "ought to be so pene-
trated with divine fire and so consummated in God, in order
to reach that perfection known as priesthood, that nothing
is left of his first weakness, nothing of his unruly affections,
so that all in him may be made divine."[3]

He will, then, communicate "in horror for sin, love of
penance, and in reprobation of all evil" with the God of the
Eucharist.[4] He should offer himself with Christ to the end
that he may be slain with him, and that all depravity in his
heart and in his senses may be wholly destroyed.[5] Thus it is
that he will belong entirely to God.

[1] Bossuet expresses the same idea: "These sacred species are the
envelope in which is enclosed the body of your Saviour, and as the
winding sheet wherewith he is covered." *Meditations,* The Last
Supper, Part I, 63rd Day.
[2] *Pietas seminarii,* vii, Champgrand, pp. 95-96.
[3] *Saints Ordres,* Part III, chap. v: "It is not enough to become
dead to self and to become annihilated in order to perform a perfect
sacrifice, it is necessary for the victim to return to God."
[4] *Pietas seminarii,* viii.   [5] *Saints Ordres, ibid.*

CHAPTER XIV

THE TEACHING OF THE FRENCH SCHOOL ON
THE PRIESTHOOD

THE French School, the chief end of which was the sanctification of the clergy, studied the Christian priesthood with extraordinary love. It drew its inspiration from what St Chrysostom, St Jerome, St Gregory the Great, St Bernard, and the author of the *Imitation* had said regarding it. Faithful to its method it looked at the priesthood in its relationship to the mystery of the Incarnation. Its views are so profound and so complete that, apparently, nothing can be added to them. The mystery of the priesthood was considered under every aspect by Bérulle, Condren, Olier, St Vincent de Paul, and Bossuet. How many generations of clerics have meditated on this teaching and prepared themselves, by endeavouring to live it, to receive holy Orders worthily!

" Our priesthood," says Bourgoing, " depends on, and is a likeness of, that of Jesus Christ, and his is a model for our own."[1] The French School views the priesthood first of all from the standpoint of Christ rather than of ourselves.

" Of all the qualities and glories which the Son of God acquired in our nature through the Incarnation, the highest and most exalted is the dignity of High Priest according to the order of Melchisedech."[2]

" The unction wherewith Jesus Christ was consecrated High Priest is the divinity itself, which, from the first moment of the Incarnation, filled and sanctified his sacred humanity, as balsam or perfume impregnates the paste with which it is mixed, or fire enters into red-hot iron and penetrates it, or, finally, as the sun shines in splendid brilliance through a crystal globe which contains its rays."[3]

Just as the Incarnation endures for ever, so " Jesus Christ is anointed and consecrated priest for all eternity."

---

[1] Bourgoing, *Préface aux Œuvres de Bérulle*, Migne, p. 103.
[2] *ibid.*, 103.
[3] *ibid.* The same teaching is found in Bossuet, *Sermon sur J. C. objet de scandale*, 2nd point, Lebarq, new ed., I. p. 467. *Elévation sur les mystères*, thirteenth week, 1st and 2nd Elév. Grimal, *Le Sacerdoce et le Sacrifice de N.-S. J.-C.*, pp. 85 ff.

The function of Christ as High Priest is to glorify his Father by sacrificing himself in order to save souls :

The priesthood of Jesus " has three aspects, one towards his Father in order to glorify him, another towards himself in order to sacrifice himself, and a third towards our souls in order to sanctify them and reconcile them to God."[1]

The first reason for the institution of the priesthood, according to the French School, is the necessity of giving God the adoration which is his due :

" Can the creature who is nothing but dust and sin," asks Bourgoing, " adore his God, acknowledge him worthily, and give him the glory due to his supreme Majesty? Jesus Christ our Lord, who came into the world to make good this lack and to give supreme honour and glory in our nature to God his Father, by means of a wonderful device, instituted the Order of priests in his Church in order to place himself in their hands and to perpetuate through their ministry that adoration and infinite glory which is due to an infinite God. This it is which is performed by the sacrifice of the altar."[2]

Jesus exercised his priesthood " on himself and ever lived his life on earth in an act of active and passive sacrifice " : being both priest and victim. All his life was one sacrifice, " the last consummation " of which was made on the cross.[3] By this he merited pardon for the sins of men and the grace which he confers on them. He performed with surpassing excellence the functions of his priesthood.

The sacerdotal character of the priesthood is " the type and likeness " of the priesthood of Jesus Christ. It unites the priest closely and irrevocably to the High Priest :

" By it," teaches Bourgoing, " we priests are clothed with the very Person of Jesus Christ, we speak, we act, we consecrate, as though we were his very self ; and, in a manner, a wonderful assumption of our person takes place through the Person of Jesus Christ in order to perform this great work of the holy Eucharist, and produce his body and his blood at the altar."[4]

There is between Jesus and his priest a kind of identification. Jesus preaches by the mouth of the priest, consecrates the Eucharist through his ministry, remits sins through him. The acts of the priest are the very acts of Christ :

" Thus the priest is in the Church," declares M. Olier, " like a living Jesus Christ and a Jesus Christ head of his Church, who has not only a plenitude of grace and divine

---

[1] Bourgoing, *ibid.* *Cf.* Eudes, *Royaume de Jésus,* pp. 468 ff.
[2] Bourgoing, *ibid.* *Cf.* Olier, *Saints Ordres*, Part III, chap. vi.
[3] Bourgoing, *ibid.*, p. 107.
[4] *ibid.*, p. 106.

riches for his own perfection, but has them also for all people.''[1]

Hence, the powers of the priest are extraordinary :

"The powers and functions of the priest consist," continues M. Olier, "in producing Jesus Christ; in giving the Holy Spirit to the Church and in sanctifying the faithful; in giving even the eternal Father by giving Jesus Christ to the faithful in Communion.''[2]

This power to produce Christ in the Eucharist raises the priest so high that the writers of the French School dare compare him to the Blessed Virgin. Like her, the priest is associated with the power of the Father to produce Jesus :

"The Blessed Virgin entered into participation in the power of the eternal Father to engender the Word. And it was on that account that she was so holy and possessed a spotless womb in which to conceive and bring forth this divine Son. The priest also is called to take his share with the eternal Father in the power of engendering his Son. He produces him, in fact, day by day on our altars, as the eternal Father engendered him formerly on the day of the Resurrection. . . .

" If the sanctity of the Blessed Virgin be so great, because she brought forth Jesus Christ in his weakness, co-operating with the eternal Father in the temporal generation of his Son, how great should be the sanctity of priests, called to co-operate in the divine and glorious generation [in the Eucharist]?''[3]

The priest again has the power of giving the Holy Spirit to souls :

"The eternal Father," again says M. Olier, "not only associates himself with the priest in the power of engendering his Word and of reproducing him daily in glory [on the altar], but again in that of sending the Holy Spirit and giving him to men, so that he keeps nothing to himself that he does not communicate to the priest.''[4]

When the priest remits the sins of the faithful, administers the sacraments to them, confers grace on them, it is certainly the Holy Spirit whom he sends them. "By Holy Communion " with Jesus Christ " he also gives the eternal Father as well as the Holy Spirit.''[5]

The priesthood, then, places the one who is clothed with it in special and most intimate relationship with the divine Persons :

"The priesthood," says Bourgoing, "through its inward conditions and its outward functions, binds us to God and to men : it binds us to God by a holy association with the eternal Father, with his only Son, and with their Holy Spirit; it

---

[1] *Saints Ordres,* Part III, chap. ii.   [2] *ibid.*   [3] *ibid.*
[4] *ibid.*   [5] *ibid.*

unites us also with the Church. . . . And this association of the priest with the divine Persons is the most lofty that can be, and that which is most perfect in our association with them through Jesus Christ. . . . For we offer the Son to the Father, by virtue and through the work of the Holy Spirit; and we enter into the Person of the Son in order to sacrifice this great, unique and eternal Host of praise to the Father through the Holy Spirit.''[1]

How great, then, is the excellence of the sacerdotal dignity ! The writers of the French School declare themselves powerless to express it :

'' What in the world is as great as the ecclesiastical state?'' asks St Vincent de Paul. '' Principalities and kingdoms are not comparable to it. You know that kings cannot, like priests, change bread into the body of the Saviour nor can they remit sins.''[2]

But, also, how great should be the sanctity of the priest !

'' Who can say what dispositions are required in the ecclesiastical life, with regard to all its objects what virtues should be practised; what abstention, what uplifting, what appropriation to God do not so great a work and so holy a ministry demand of us? All inward perfection and communion with God in his highest eminence is inferior to the holiness demanded by this state.''[3]

'' The priest,'' according to M. Olier, '' is a prodigy of grace, and if the word monster could be used in a good sense, it might be said that he is a monster of sanctity.''[4]

With what zeal did the reformers of the clergy of the seventeenth century, thoroughly nurtured in these great ideas on the priesthood, labour in order to sanctify priests ! This is how St Vincent de Paul exhorted his brethren of the mission on the vigil of a retreat of ordinands :

'' Now, then, gentlemen and brethren, we are on the vigil of this great work which God has placed in our hands; to-morrow, O my God, we must receive those whom thy Providence has resolved to send us in order that we may help thee to make them better. Ah ! gentlemen, how great a saying is this : to make ecclesiastics better ! Who can comprehend the height of this work? It is the highest of all.

'' To be employed in making good priests and to co-operate therein as second efficient and instrumental cause is to perform the office of Jesus Christ who, during his mortal life,

---

[1] Bourgoing, *Préface,* p. 105.
[2] *Correspondance, discourses, documents,* ed. Coste, Vol. XI, p. 9, Paris, 1924. M. Olier wrote : '' God has given two prodigies to the Church—the priest and the Blessed Virgin.'' *Saints Ordres,* Part III, chap. vi : '' The dignity of a priest [is] of fearful extent and of inconceivable obligation.'' *Ibid.*
[3] Bourgoing, *ibid.,* p. 105.
[4] *Saints Ordres,* Part III, chap. vi.

seems to have undertaken the task of making twelve good priests his apostles, and therefore willed to dwell several years with them to instruct them and form them for this divine ministry."[1]

[1] Coste, *ibid.*, Vol. XI, pp. 8-9.

CHAPTER XV

ST VINCENT DE PAUL AND ST JOHN EUDES[1]

S T VINCENT DE PAUL,[2] like Fr. Condren, received
"the gift of enlightening souls" and not that of
writing. Like him he published nothing during his
lifetime. He had, moreover, a sort of worship for
the second Superior of the Oratory. "When he
heard of his death," M. Olier relates, "he threw himself on
his knees and struck his breast, accusing himself, with tears
in his eyes, of not having honoured this holy man as much
as he was worthy to be honoured."[3] Vincent was a disciple
of the Oratory. He had frequent relations with Fr. Bérulle,
and imbibed his teaching.

Vincent was certainly Berullian, like all the saintly persons
of his time. Nevertheless, he owes something to St Francis
de Sales.[4] He was given the direction of the Paris Visitan-

---

[1] Blessed Grignion de Montfort (1673-1716) does not belong to the
period dealt with in this volume. He, however, belongs to the French
School by his teaching. His *Traité de la vraie devotion à la Sainte
Vierge* is well known. *Cf.* A. Lhoumeau, *La Vie spirituelle à l'école
du B. Grignion de Montfort*, Paris-Rome, 1904.

[2] The principal biographies of St Vincent de Paul: *La Vie du
vénérable serviteur de Dieu, Vincent de Paul,* by Messire Louis
Abelly, Bishop of Rodez, Paris, 1664; *La Vie de Saint Vincent de
Paul,* by Pierre Collet, Priest of the Mission, Nancy, 1748; *Vie
de Saint Vincent de Paul,* by Th. Nisard, Paris, 1844; *Saint Vincent
de Paul, Sa vie, son temps, ses œuvres, son influence,* by the Abbé
Maynard, Paris, 1860, of which there were several editions; *Histoire
de Saint Vincent de Paul,* by Mgr. Bougaud, Paris, 1891; *Saint
Vincent de Paul,* by E. de Broglie, Paris, 1898, 5th edition. The
Lettres and *Conférences* of St Vincent de Paul have been published
at different dates. The edition of M. Coste, *Saint Vincent de Paul,
Correspondance, Entretiens, Documents,* Paris, 1920-1924, is now
authoritative. The spiritual teaching of St Vincent de Paul was
summed up by Abelly, by the Abbé Maynard, and by E. Motte, *Saint
Vincent de Paul et le Sacerdoce,* Paris, 1900. Only the chief characteristics of St Vincent's teaching are given above.

[3] Faillon, *Vie de M. Olier,* Vol. I, p. 139. Vincent de Paul was
born at Pouy, near Dax, in 1576. Ordained priest in 1600, he
travelled on matters of business to Marseilles and suffered imprisonment on his return. From 1610 to 1611 he was chaplain to Queen
Marguerite. He became Curé of Clichy in 1611. Shortly afterwards
he entered the family of the Gondi. He founded the Mission in 1625,
and later on the Sisters of Charity in 1633. He died September 27,
1660.

[4] He often spoke of the Bishop of Geneva with great veneration.
Coste, *Entretiens,* Vol. XI, pp. 221, 254, etc.; Vol. X, pp. 277 etc.

dines by the Bishop of Geneva himself. He assisted, no
doubt, at some of the spiritual conferences addressed by their
holy Founder to his beloved daughters. He read his books.

It would be interesting to compare the *Entretiens* of St
Vincent de Paul to the Sisters of Charity with the famous
Entretiens spirituels of St Francis de Sales to the Visitandines. Vincent first of all followed the same method. His
Conference " was not a monologue. The sisters asked questions and made observations."[1] We know that occasionally
St Francis de Sales' Conferences consisted solely of answers
to questions asked by the nuns. But these latter were in
the ordinary way educated, and quite capable of asking
questions. The Sisters of Charity at that time were of the
people, ignorant, timid, not daring to speak. Vincent had
to change his method and himself catechize[2] the sisters.
Yet might not these interrogations cover the more timid and
ignorant sisters with confusion?

" If there be any among them unable to answer," said
Vincent in order to encourage them, " I beg them not to be
troubled thereat; for those who have but little to say are
often the best, and those who understand and say things
suggested to them easily do not sometimes do so well,
although there may be some who both say and do well."[3]

There was the same resemblance in the choice of subjects.
Apart from exhortations respecting the Rules and functions
of the Sisters of Charity, Vincent insisted on simplicity,
mutual and cordial respect, gentleness, humility, and indifference.[4] Occasionally the Bishop of Geneva's actual expressions are to be found, particularly, in the Conference on the
eighth article of the Sisters' Rules, on *la pratique de ne rien
demander et de rien refuser:*

" The first reason," says St Vincent, " which should make
us observe this rule is because it is a practice which leads us
to indifference, which makes a soul who has reached it hardly
know what she does or does not wish, and be attached only
to God, wishing nothing else than what he wishes, and as he
wishes it. Oh ! the happiness of one who is in this state !"[5]

He wrote these lines, attributed to St Francis de Sales, to
Blessed Louise de Marillac about 1629 :

" I praise God for it, Mademoiselle, that you have been
thus resigned to the holy will of God, praying that both you

---

[1] Coste, *Entretiens,* Vol. IX, pp. xiii-xiv.

[2] *ibid.,* p. 94.

[3] *ibid.,* p. 95. Like St Francis de Sales, St Vincent did not ordinarily
write his Conferences.

[4] See the *Entretiens aux filles de la Charité*, Vols. IX and X. The
subjects explained in the *Entretiens* to the Missioners are similar.
Vol. XI.

[5] *Entretiens*, Vol. X, p. 273.

and I may ever have the same willingness and unwillingness with him and in him, for this is an anticipation of paradise."[1]

Like the Bishop of Geneva again he was slow to decide, fearing always to "encroach" on Providence and to act on his own initiative and not according to the designs of God:

"Oh! What treasures are hidden in holy Providence," he wrote to Louise de Marillac, "and how highly do those honour our Lord who follow his Providence and do not override it. I recently heard it said of one of the great ones of the kingdom that he had learned this truth from his own experience: he had never of himself undertaken but four things, which instead of leading to success had turned to his disadvantage."[2]

"One of the characteristic features of the life of St Vincent de Paul was his holy habit of considering our Lord in everything and everything in our Lord. Moreover, as the Church reminds us in his Office, apart from his loving Saviour, there was nothing that could captivate his heart: *Auditus dicere: Rem nullam sibi placere, praeterquam in Christo Jesu.* . . . Herein, said his first biographer [Abelly], lay all his morality and all his policy. . . . It was his principle and the foundation on which he relied solely, as on a firm and sure rock, for the erection of his spiritual building."[3]

The spirituality of St Vincent de Paul is in fact Berullian. It is also wholly practical, directed always towards action. Vincent did not stop at feelings. He looked on them, above all, as stimulants, which urge us on to the single performance of duty:

"Let us love God, my brethren," he said, "let us love God, but let this be at the expense of our arms, and in the sweat of our brows. For very often many acts of the love of God, of goodness, benevolence, and other similar interior affections and practices of a tender heart, although very good and most desirable, are, none the less, much to be suspected when we never come to the practice of effective love."[4]

Neither did St Vincent de Paul stop at theories. Not that he despised them: far from that! But he appreciated them only in so far as they were the guiding principle of sanctification for oneself and for others:

"If, each time we enlighten our understanding," he said to young ecclesiastical students, "we try also to enkindle our

---

[1] *Correspondance*, I, p. 70. In the *Lettre* XLIX to Louise de Marillac he counsels her to read "the book *On the Love of God*, by [S. F. de S.] . . . notably that part of it which deals with the will of God and indifference." *Correspondance*, I, p. 86.

[2] *ibid.*, Vol. I, pp. 68-69.

[3] E. Motte, *Saint Vincent de Paul et le sacerdoce*, p. 9.

[4] *Entretiens*, Vol. XI, p. 40.

will, let us rest assured that study will serve us as a means of going to God, and let us hold it as an undoubted maxim that in proportion as we labour for our inward perfection, we enable ourselves the more to bear fruit for our neighbour. This is why, in studying to serve souls, we must be careful to nurture our own piety as well as our knowledge, and on this account to read good and useful books and refrain from reading those which only serve to satisfy curiosity; for curiosity is the plague of the spiritual life."[1]

Though he despised pure curiosity, Vincent de Paul gave great attention to those simple theological opinions which have a practical bearing. He wrote, in 1631, to François de Coudray, Priest of the Mission at Rome :

" One eminent in teaching and piety said to me yesterday that he is of the opinion of St Thomas : that he who knows not the mystery of the Trinity and of the Incarnation, dying in this state, dies in a state of damnation; and he maintains that this teaching is the foundation of Christian doctrine. Now, that touched me so greatly and still so affects me that I fear being myself damned because I am not unceasingly occupied in the instruction of the poor. What a pity to think of it ! Who will excuse us before God for the loss of the numbers who might be saved by the little help they might have had?"[2]

We would remark that this feeling of fear is to be found much more in the writings of St Vincent de Paul than in those of the Bishop of Geneva : therein is a great difference between the two Saints.

This fear, however, does not exclude holy joy. If holy thoughts should be transformed in us by grace into vigour expended in the service of God, this transformation will be the better brought about, the greater our inward gaiety. St Vincent de Paul desires this Christian gaiety because it is a stimulant to good :

" I beg you," he counselled Louise de Marillac, " to be full of gaiety. Oh ! How much is it needed by people of goodwill !"[3]

This gaiety, he said again, is willed by God.[4] We ought

---

[1] *Entretiens, ibid.,* pp. 28-29. The spiritual teachings of Vincent de Paul on prayer and the Christian virtues are always very practical. These are the counsels he gives, which in his idea should be followed immediately. This practical note is also again found in his instructions to the Missioners on preaching. *Entretiens*, Vol. XI, pp. 257 ff. Vincent herein insists on the great principle that the preacher ought to " preach God " and not to preach himself. *Ibid.,* p. 276.

[2] *Correspondance,* Vol. I, p. 121.

[3] *ibid.,* p. 145.

[4] *ibid.,* p. 85 : " Be you gay also, Mademoiselle, I pray you, since it pleases God for you to be so." *Ibid.,* p. 109 : " Farewell, my dear daughter, keep yourself very cheerful." *Ibid.,* p. 147. " Nevertheless be very cheerful and do cheerfully what you have to do."

to honour it in the Heart of our Lord and strive to draw it
to ourselves.[1] This attraction for inward joy and holy mirth
is a point of resemblance with the Bishop of Geneva.

St Vincent de Paul warned his disciples against all exaggeration in spirituality. Fr. de Condren said of him that he
possessed " the character of prudence."[2] It was indeed one
of his dominant qualities. One is struck in reading his
Lettres and his *Entretiens* with his strong common sense and
the correctness of his appreciations. " He had," says Maynard, " in the highest degree, that common sense which
Bossuet called the master of human life; a common sense
more rare, perhaps, to the extent he had it, than what is
called genius, because it implies a combination and balance
of most numerous and opposite faculties : a perception which
grasps an idea or a matter, a comprehension which embraces
every bearing, a discernment which perceives every circumstance and foresees every consequence, a judgement which
regulates them and puts them in action and execution."[3]
One day he gave a serious " warning " to his brethren at
the seminary " on the subject—which at first seemed surprising—of excess to be avoided in the love of God." Is it
possible to love God too much?
Three or four pupils of the seminary, desirous of imitating
the saints who kept themselves unceasingly in the presence
of God and made acts of divine love all day long, were " so
taken up with making continual acts of love, day and night,
ever on the strain," that they fell ill. The intention was
good, but how reprehensible was the thing itself !
" Whatever we can do," declared St Vincent, " we shall
never love God as we ought, that is impossible; God is
infinitely lovable. Nevertheless, we must take great care
that though God commands us to love him with our whole
heart and with our whole strength, his goodness does not
will, however, that this should go so far as to injure and ruin
our health by dint of acts; no, no, God does not ask us to
kill ourselves for that."[4]
This " excess," this extravagance . . . comes, ordinarily,
from an inordinate desire for progress, from self-love and
ignorance, because it is a desire to make virtue and spiritual
things perceptible to our senses. We would " at one bound

[1] *Correspondance,* Vol. I, p. 160 : " Please be careful of your health
and honour the gaiety of our Lord's heart." *Ibid.,* p. 28. " Nevertheless keep wholly cheerful and in so doing honour the holy calm of our
Lord's soul."
[2] Faillon, *Vie de M. Olier,* Vol. I, p. 313.
[3] *Saint Vincent de Paul, sa vie, ses œuvres, son influence* (1874),
Vol. IV, pp. 294-295.
[4] Repetition of the prayer of August 4, 1655. Coste, Vol. XI, p. 17.

mount to an eminent degree of virtue . . . and draw God to us by dint of strength and machinery." Now, we should wait until God gives us the gift of prayer by which he communicates himself to us "without effort, in a perceptible way, wholly sweet, gentle, and loving." Then, "we feel ourselves without trouble in the presence of God; it becomes natural and never ceases, and this takes place with much satisfaction." This does not result from our own effort but is the fruit of our persevering prayer. Nothing is gained by "splitting our heads to make ourselves feel this virtue [of love] as if it were natural." We may lose greatly by such efforts. When health is ruined we come to feel "disgust with everything connected with devotion, disgust with goodness, disgust with the holiest things, a disgust from which we recover only with the greatest difficulty and trouble."[1] Moreover, Vincent "implores directors" of the seminary to prevent any renewal of such excesses.

The sharpness of this reprimand lets us see that St Vincent de Paul is much more inclined to asceticism than to mysticism. Doubtless he was acquainted by experience with the mystical state, although he makes few disclosures on the subject. He did not consider himself to be a mystic. This is the sense of his declaration in the account of the famous vision in which he saw the soul of St Jane Chantal rising to heaven in the form of a globe of fire. He who had this vision, he says, " is not subject to having them and never had but this one."

His extraordinary humility prevented him, moreover, from believing himself favoured by particular graces. St Vincent de Paul—as everyone knows—has, with great sincerity, said "much evil of himself," both in his *Correspondance* and in his *Entretiens*. Thus he had the right to exhort others to contempt of self; and he used this right largely. His spirituality shows very marked preference for that which represses our natural pride, which produces a sense of our baseness and nothingness.[2]

When he speaks of prayer—which he does admirably[3]— he occasionally refers to passive states, in which God acts

[1] Repetition of the prayer of August 4, 1655. Coste, Vol. XI, pp. 215-223.
[2] See *Entretiens,* Coste, Vol. XI, pp. 51-61, 323, 393, etc.
[3] See chiefly *Entretiens,* Vol. IX, pp. 26, 35, 407; Vol. X, pp. 564, 571, 582; Vol. XI, pp. 83-93, 183, 356, 401, 403, etc. "Give me a man of prayer and he will be capable of everything; he could say with the holy Apostle ' I can do all things in him that sustains and strengthens me.' " Vol. XI, p. 83. " Now then, let us all give ourselves up to this practice of prayer, since it is thereby that we arrive at every good. If we persevere in our vocation it is thanks to prayer; if we do not fall into sin, it is thanks to prayer; if we remain in

almost alone in the soul. But he does this in passing without insisting. His end is to lead his brethren to affective prayer which he so greatly loved. A beautiful treatise might be written from what he has said on this degree of prayer. He unceasingly counsels us " not to loiter with reasoning during prayer," but to " be diligent in making acts of affection."[1] It made him very happy when, during the exercise of vocal prayer, one member of his company admitted his love for this kind of prayer :

" God be praised !" he said one day, repeating these words four or five times; and this was in connection with what M. Coglée, a priest of his Congregation, had said, that in repeating his prayers he was very little hindered by reasoning in them, striving chiefly to make acts of affection. M. Vincent strongly praised this way of acting and said that it was thus that we should behave in meditation—that is, loitering but little in seeking for reasons, but rather inclining to acts of love towards God, acts of humility, of regret for our sins, and so on; for what have we to do with reasoning when we are convinced of that on which we wish to meditate? " Oh, how I wish the Congregation had this practice of at once following the lights which God bestows, rather than of leaving them in order to loiter in seeking for reasons which are useless at such a moment, because there is no need for them. . . ! I beg the priests to ask this day at holy Mass this grace for the Congregation; and the clerics and our brethren and the seminary, at holy Mass and Communion; and let their second intention at Communion be to gain this grace of God for the little Congregation."[2]

The spirituality of St Vincent de Paul is entirely " informed " by charity towards one's neighbour and zeal for the salvation of souls. This charity is our Saint's dominant virtue. All his teaching is inspired by it. It is this which speaks in his *Lettres* and in his *Entretiens*. Everything is subordinate to it; this it is which suggests all projects and brings a good result to all enterprises. It made Vincent practise almost constant heroism. It also led him to demand this

---

charity, if we are saved, all is through the grace of prayer. As God refuses nothing to prayer he also grants nothing without prayer—*Rogate Dominum messis*—not anything, not even the spreading of his Gospel and that which his glory most demands." Vol. XI, p. 407.

[1] " When we want to have a fire, we make use of a steel; we strike it, and, as soon as the sparks fire the tinder, we light a candle; and he would make himself ridiculous who, having lighted his candle, continued to strike the steel. In the same way, when the soul is sufficiently enlightened by considerations, what need is there to seek for others. . . . Do you not see that it is a loss of time and that we ought then to apply ourselves to inflaming the will and exciting its affections by the beauty of virtue and the ugliness of the contrary vice?" Vol. XI, p. 406.

[2] *Entretiens*, Vol. XI, p. 401.

heroism of his brethren. He desired them to be ready " to endure all for the salvation of souls " :

" Are we ready," he once asked them, " to endure the troubles which God will send us, and to stifle our natural impulses; to live the life of Jesus Christ and no other? Are we prepared to go to Poland, to Barbary, to India, in order to sacrifice our inclinations and our lives to him? If so, let us thank God. But if, on the contrary, there are those who fear to quit their comforts, who are so delicate that they complain if the least thing be lacking them—in a word, if some among us are still the slaves of nature, given to the pleasures of sense, like this miserable sinner who speaks to you, who, at the age of seventy [-seven], is still wholly worldly; let them deem themselves unworthy of the apostolic state to which God has called them, and let them be covered with confusion at seeing that their brethren exercise it so worthily and that they themselves are so far from their spirit and courage."[1]

Is there any spirituality which is more provocative of zeal and more fruitful in works of charity?

But God will not be truly honoured and Christ glorified, souls will not really be saved, unless the Church has good workmen :

" Oh, gentlemen," said Vincent in this connection, " what a great thing is a good priest ! What cannot a good ecclesiastic do ! What conversions can he not obtain !"

Hence the institutions founded by St Vincent for the sanctification of the clergy. Hence, also, the fiery exhortations he addressed to his brethren who were charged with training priests :

" O my Saviour !" he exclaimed one day, " how greatly should the poor missioners give themselves to thee in order to help form good ecclesiastics, since it is a work most difficult, most exalted, and most important, for the salvation of souls and for the progress of Christianity !

" If St Vincent Ferrer was incited to perfection in the hope that God would one day raise up good priests and apostolic workers in order to uplift the ecclesiastical state and to dispose men to prepare for the last judgement, for how much greater reason should we, who see the ecclesiastical state becoming renewed, incite ourselves more and more to perfection in order to co-operate in this most desirable restoration !"[2]

[1] *Entretiens*, Vol. XI, pp. 411-412.
[2] *ibid.*, pp. 7-8.

APPENDIX

ST JOHN EUDES[1] AND PUBLIC DEVOTION
TO THE SACRED HEART

THE Feast of the Heart of Jesus, celebrated for the first time in the Congregation of St John Eudes on October 20, 1672,[2] appears to be a transformation of the Berullian *Feast of Jesus* and the Sulpician *Feast of the Interior of Jesus*.[3] Cardinal Bérulle, as we know, instituted the *Feast of Jesus* for the Oratory in order to do honour, " not to some special mystery " of the life of Christ, but " to his divine person and all included in the adorable union of the God-man."[4] He

---

[1] St John Eudes was born at Ré, near Argentan, in the diocese of Séez, November 14, 1601. He made his studies at Caen with the Jesuits, and entered the Oratory, March 25, 1623. He left the Oratory in 1643 and founded the Congregation of Jesus and Mary at Caen, which was devoted to the work of seminaries and missions. In 1651 he founded the Congregation of Our Lady of Charity, known as the Good Shepherd, charged with the care of female penitents, a Congregation that was approved by the Holy See in 1666. He died at Caen in 1680. He was greatly assisted in the founding of his works by the advice of Marie de Vallées, a famous mystic born in the diocese of Coutances. *Vie du vénérable Jean Eudes . . .*, by Fr. D. Boullay, Paris, 1903-1908; *Le Bienheureux Eudes*, by Henri Joly, Paris, 1907. *Les Œuvres complètes du Bienheureux Jean Eudes* were published by Frs. Dauphin and Lebrun, with good introductions, at Vannes, 1905-1911. His best known works are *La Vie et le Royaume de Jésus*, Caen, 1637, Vol I of the *Œuvres complètes*, and the *Cœur admirable de la très sacrée Mère de Dieu*, in twelve books—the first eleven deal with the Heart of Mary and the twelfth with the Heart of Jesus. Regarding St John Eudes and the devotion to the Heart of Jesus, see Ch. Lebrun, *Le Bienheureux Eudes et le culte public du Cœur de Jésus*, Paris, 1917; Henri Bremond, *L'école française*, pp. 629 ff; Bainvel, *La dévotion au Sacré-Cœur de Jésus*, Paris, 1917, 4th edition. L. Garriguet, *Le Sacré-Cœur de Jésus. Exposé historique et dogmatique de la dévotion au Sacré-Cœur*, Paris, 1920.

[2] St John Eudes ordered this feast in a circular letter addressed to his religious, July 29, 1672. The first revelation respecting the Sacred Heart at Paray-le-Monial took place December 27, 1673. On July 20, 1685, St Margaret Mary and her novices celebrated, though quite privately, the Feast of the Sacred Heart. In 1689 the Visitandines of Dijon kept the Feast of the Sacred Heart publicly. St John Eudes was then really the first to keep the public Feast of the Sacred Heart of Jesus. From 1643 or 1644 he had instituted the Feast of the Heart of Mary.

[3] M. Bremond well explains the Bérullian origin of the devotion to the Sacred Heart, *L'École française*, pp. 629 ff.

[4] Bourgoing, Preface to the *Œuvres* of Bérulle (Migne, p. 99; Bérulle's Office is in Migne, p. 1707 and in the supplement.

wrote the Office for this himself, which was approved at Rome, February 1, 1625. The object of this feast is general : "Those who call this solemnity," says Quesnel, "the *Feast of the Glories of Jesus* do not give a sufficiently large idea of it, for it includes the humiliations as well as the glories, and is not properly the special feast either of the one or of the other, but of him who is the subject of them and their foundation."[1]

After the death of M. Olier, his disciples celebrated a similar feast : that of the *Interior Life of our Lord*. The object of this feast is general, like that of the Berullian feast. It is not, however, concerned with the Person of Jesus, but "the interior dispositions with which our Lord accompanied his mysteries and all the actions of his life, such as his religious feeling towards his Father, his charity towards his neighbour, his annihilation of himself, his horror of the world and of sin : and the fruit suggested from this feast is an abundant participation in these dispositions, according to the counsel given by St Paul to the faithful : *Have in yourselves the mind of Jesus Christ.*"[2]

St John Eudes kept the *Feast of Jesus* in a most holy way.[3] He also had a tender devotion to the *Interior Life of Jesus,* which was observed at the Oratory, although they did not celebrate its feast.[4] We are justified in thinking that devotion to the Person of Christ and to his Interior led St John Eudes to the devotion of the Sacred Heart of Jesus.

The Berullian School occasionally calls the *Heart of Jesus* the Interior of the divine Master, the whole of his dispositions, the chief of which is love.

According to M. Olier, the Interior of Jesus is his " noble Heart," the source of religion to the Church :

" The praises of the Church," he says, " and all the feelings of love which she gives her God in heaven, are none but the very feelings of Jesus Christ. They are his own praises which he sheds in our hearts in order to spread his religion further and multiply his praises by multiplying those who glorify the Majesty of God. Whence all the praises that the saints have ever rendered to God are derived *from the Heart of Jesus* and from his plenitude : *De pleni-*

---

[1] Preface to Quesnel's translation of the Office of the *Feast of Jesus . . .,* Paris, 1673.

[2] Faillon, *Vie de M. Olier,* Vol. III, p. 70. The Office of this feast was approved May 15, 1668, by Cardinal Louis de Vendôme, Legate *a latere.* About the same time the seminary of St Sulpice also celebrated the *Feast of the Interior of Mary* and the *Feast of the Priesthood of our Lord.* The Office of the latter feast was that which Fr. Eudes had drawn up for the *Feast of the Divine Priesthood,* already kept in his Congregation.

[3] *Œuvres du Bienheureux Eudes,* XI, p. 22.

[4] Faillon, *ibid.*

tudine ejus omnes accepimus, as St John says. It is of this
plenitude that we have received some share. It is this *great
Heart,* in which is comprised all that is so vastly spread
throughout the Church : *plena est omnis terra gloria ejus.*
All our temples resound only with the praises which are rendered to God *in this beautiful Heart.* All our hearts and our
temples are but the echoes which retell and repeat the har-
monious sounds rendered to God *by the Heart of Jesus.* *O
noble Heart of Jesus,* adorable source of our religion ; but
source, too, and plenitude of all our respect for God, since
all is derived by us from thee !"[1]

The Interior of Jesus, " his Heart," is also the principle
of all sanctity in the Church :

" It is with the works of sanctity which are performed in
the Church," continues M. Olier, " as it is with the praises
she renders to God. All acts of virtue practised by the whole
Church have been performed by the *Heart alone of Jesus
Christ,* so that indeed our Lord alone has performed *inwardly*
what the whole Church and the succession of every century
has practised throughout the ages. St Paul calls the Church
plenitudo Christi, in so far that what Christ practised *in his
Heart* afterwards overflowed into the Church, and it enlarged
his Heart and increased according to the same St Paul : *in
augmentum corporis facit, in aedificationem sui in caritate.*"[2]

The great happiness of the Christian should be to contemplate the interior of Jesus, his soul, his Heart—which for
M. Olier were synonyms—and to participate therein :

" This *divine interior,*" he goes on, " which it pleased the
goodness of God formerly to make known to me, is the most
beautiful and wonderful thing in the world. O my Jesus,
nothing is equal to thee in thine *inner self,* and God grant
that I may be eternally lost in adoration of thy sanctity ! *O
adorable interior ! O deified soul ! O soul* wholly in God to
my eyes, wholly changed into God, having nothing of the
weakness which exists outside thine adorable Person ! O
my Jesus, how deceived are they in seeing thee, and how
little of thee do we see, by contemplating thee from without !
Men look upon thee thus and despise thee, but faith, penetrating to *thy Heart,* makes thee to be seen otherwise. And
it is this *adorable interior* which we must unceasingly contemplate, which gives virtue to all that is external in thee,
without which thy works would not be of such value before
God. It is this immense love, this deep religion, this respect,
this devotion, and this wonderful piety which causes God to
love thee and to contemplate himself in thee. Oh ! blessed

---

[1] *Mémoires,* April 27, 1642. Icard, *Doctrine de M. Olier,* Paris,
1892, pp. 226-227. Similar expressions, *Mémoires,* August 27, 1642.
Icard, p. 242.

[2] *Mémoires,* April 27, 1642. Icard, p. 227.

be thou, *adorable Heart* of my Jesus; and be thou blessed, praised, and adored by all men for ever !"[1]

St John Eudes loved to think of the Heart of Jesus as the symbol of the interior of the divine Master, as portraying all the collective dispositions of his soul: "This Heart," he says, "represents all that is internal, but chiefly love."[2] It is, again, he says, "the admirable Heart of Jesus which is the principle . . . of all the mysteries contained in the other feasts"[3] of our Lord. The Feast of the divine Heart, according to Fr. Eudes, is able to sum up all others, just as does the Berullian *Feast of Jesus* and the Sulpician *Feast of the Interior of Jesus.*

But the Eudist conception of the Heart of Jesus is complex. It is not drawn from Bérulle alone.

St Francis de Sales, as well as the mystics of the Middle Ages, also drew St John Eudes' attention to the Heart of Jesus.

The Bishop of Geneva, after Bérulle and Condren, "is the favourite master of Fr. Eudes . . . While Bérulle and his disciples especially contemplated the greatness of the incarnate Word, St Francis de Sales stops in preference to contemplate his Heart ' so loving and so desirous of our love.' The Heart of Jesus takes a high place in the works of the holy bishop, especially in the *Treatise on the Love of God,* and it was the reading of these works that began to direct Fr. Eudes' thoughts and affections to the Heart of the divine Master. Thus, from the time of his writing *Le Royaume de Jésus,* he learnt to think of Jesus as the King of Hearts."[4]

"It seems," rightly wrote Lebrun, "that it was the thought of the wound in the Sacred Side of the Saviour

---

[1] *Mémoires,* July 8, 1642, Icard, pp. 243-244. Fr. Grou, S.J. (†1803) thus expresses this : " The Heart of Jesus is his interior; there is nothing more intimate in man than the heart. To be firmly devoted to this adorable heart is then to strive to penetrate into it by the help of meditation or prayer, in order to know the dispositions, the emotions, the objects suggested by it, the motives which make it act." *L'intérieur de Jésus et de Marie,* Paris, 1909, p. 368.

[2] *Œuvres complètes,* VIII, p. 432.

[3] *ibid.,* p. 313.

[4] Lebrun, Introduction to *La vie et le royaume de Jésus,* Paris, 1924, p. 62. It is above all in the fourth part of the *Royaume de Jésus* that St John Eudes speaks of the Heart of Jesus. He there makes allusion to the *Treatise on the Love of God,* by St Francis de Sales, above all in that passage in Book V, chap. xi : " Yes, indeed, Theotimus, divine love, seated in the Heart of the Saviour, as on his royal throne, looks through the cleft of his pierced side into all the hearts of the children of men; for this Heart, being the king of hearts, keeps his eyes day by day on hearts." St Francis de Sales in his *Lettres* often recommends private devotion to the Heart of Jesus. So also does St Vincent de Paul, Coste, *Correspondance,* Vol. I, pp. 27, 71, 114, etc.

which led mystics of the Middle Ages to the contemplation and love of the Sacred Heart."[1] St John Eudes, under the guidance of these mystics, was also led by the same way to the Heart of Jesus. No doubt it was the Benedictines of Holy Trinity of Caen who brought to his knowledge the writings of St Gertrude and St Mechtilde, in which the Heart of Jesus is so often mentioned. A particular passage, too, in the *Revelations* of St Bridget greatly impressed him. The Saint relates that "as he hung on the cross, the divine Saviour suffered pains so acute, so piercing, so violent and terrible, for love of us, that his Heart was cloven asunder and broken." This was the immediate cause of his death.[2]

The Franciscan tradition also had its influence on Fr. Eudes. St Bernardine of Siena declared, in an eloquent sermon, that the Heart of Christ is "a most ardent furnace of love to inflame and kindle the whole universe."[3] What impression must not such a thought have produced on St John Eudes, who, "from the beginning of his career," invited the faithful to contemplate not only the grandeurs of Jesus but also, and above all, "the immensity of his love for us?"[4]

Theologians have some difficulty in giving a *full* definition of the object of the devotion to the Sacred Heart. We often find among them different points of view in matters of detail. It is not surprising to find a certain lack of clearness in the thought of Fr. Eudes. We must not forget that he lacked a guide and advanced in a region as yet unexplored.

"In the God-man," he says, "we adore three hearts which are only one same heart. . . . The first heart of the God-man is his corporal heart, which is deified, as are all the other parts of his sacred body, through the hypostatic union they have with the divine Person of the eternal Word. The second is his spiritual heart. . . . The third is his divine heart . . . three hearts in this wonderful God-man which are but one heart. . . ."[5]

The word heart obviously is not always taken in its strict sense. St John Eudes gives it all the meanings he finds in Holy Writ.[6] Let us endeavour to explain what he under-

---

[1] *Le Bienheureux Jean Eudes et le culte public du Cœur de Jésus*, Paris, 1917, p. 61.

[2] Lebrun, *ibid.*, p. 62. St John Eudes recalls this statement of St Bridget in his work *Le Cœur admirable*, Book XII, chap. xiii, in his circular letter of July 29, 1672 and in the Office for the Feast of the Heart of Jesus.

[3] Book XII of the *Cœur admirable* is a commentary on this thought of St Bernardine of Siena. Lebrun, *op. cit.*, p. 67.

[4] *Royaume de Jésus*, Introduction, p. 39.

[5] *Cœur admirable*, Book I, chap. ii.

[6] Thus he finds in Holy Writ that the word "heart" signifies eight things. *Œuvres du B. Eudes*, VI, pp. 33-36.

stands by these "three hearts," which are the three elements
of the object of his devotion.

Historians of the devotion to the Sacred Heart declare that
" the heart of flesh of the God-man did not enter into the
devotion " of Fr. Eudes. This word " heart " had always in
his writings a symbolic sense. It is " the immense love of
Jesus for his Father and for men in all his mysteries and in
all his manifestations."[1] Fr. Lebrun declares that to think
thus is to be mistaken. He has no trouble in showing that
the material " corporal" heart of Christ was not outside the
perspective of St John Eudes.[2] In this the Eudist devotion
approaches that of Paray. It deviates from it, however, in
that the heart of flesh of the Saviour does not hold the same
place as in the *Revelations* made to St Margaret Mary. Fr.
Eudes, as though he feared too great an innovation, passes
rapidly over the " corporal heart."

The "spiritual heart" is, without a doubt, the principal
element in his devotion, and this element is Berullian. Here,
the heart is a symbol. It typifies the very Person of Christ
and also his interior, " the higher part of his soul, with all
the natural and supernatural perfections which are contained
in it, such as its natural faculties, the memory, the
understanding, and the will, the plenitude of grace and of
virtue with which it was crowned, and the wonderful life of
which it is the principle."[3] Although the heart typifies the
summing-up of the dispositions of Christ, it is, above all, the
symbol of love, the love of Jesus for his divine Father, for
his most holy Mother, and, above all—as St Margaret Mary
teaches—his love for us.[4]

We indeed find in the object of the Eudist devotion to
the Heart of Jesus, elements which St Margaret Mary placed
in relief later on. But they are blended with others that are
not retained. Devotion to the Heart of Jesus was to become
more simple. It was to have as object the Heart of flesh of
Christ, symbol of the immense and reparatory love that he
had for us : " This is the Heart which has so loved men "
our Lord was to declare to St Margaret Mary.

One of the elements of the Eudist devotion, which has not
been retained, at least as it was, is the " third heart," the
" divine heart."

Under this name St John Eudes signified specially the
Holy Spirit.

"The third [Heart of Jesus]," he says, " is his divine
Heart which is the Holy Spirit, with which his adorable

---

[1] *Cf.* Lebrun, *Le Bienheureux Jean Eudes et le culte public du Cœur
de Jésus,* pp. 56-57.
[2] *ibid.,* pp. 57-63.
[3] *ibid.,* p. 64. *Cf.* Brémond, pp. 648 f.
[4] *Cf.* Lebrun, *op. cit.,* 66-71.

humanity has always been more animated and vivified than
with his own soul and his own Heart."[1]

The Berullian School, when it speaks of the interior of
Jesus, does not forget to remind us that it is the Holy Spirit
who is its author and principle. It is he who created in the
soul of Christ those most perfect dispositions which we so
admire.[2] Fr. Eudes no doubt desired to recall this teaching
when he speaks of " the divine Heart " of the God-man.

But this is not the only thing signified by this expression
" divine Heart." It also means the divine love of Christ.
" In Jesus," says Fr. Lebrun, " since there are two natures,
there are also two operations and therefore two loves : a
human love which springs from the human will, which is
created and ended like all that is human, and a divine love,
identified with the divine essence, which is, like it, uncreated
and infinite. It is this uncreated love which Fr. Eudes
ordinarily signifies under the name " divine Heart of Jesus."[3]
It cannot be denied that several passages in the works of
St John Eudes authorize this interpretation. Here, again, the
Eudist devotion is at one with modern writers.[4]

St John Eudes was not only the promoter of public devotion
to the Sacred Heart, he was also its theologian. He caught
a glimpse of all the aspects of the new devotion.

[1] *Cœur admirable,* Book I, chap. ii.
[2] M. Olier, in a manner, made this teaching clear, as regards the
Interior of Mary, in an engraving produced from the designs of the
famous painter, Le Brun, representing the *Vie intérieur de la Sainte
Vierge:* " The most holy Virgin is seen in the clouds, her hands crossed
on her breast, in which the Holy Spirit, in the form of a dove, distributes all the riches of his grace. Her eyes are raised to heaven and
fixed on the monogram *Jésus Sauveur des hommes,* in order to signify
that, though the Holy Spirit was always the principle of her actions,
love for Jesus and for the salvation of souls was its end and object."
Faillon, *Vie de M. Olier,* Vol. III, p. 77. In the picture of the Sacred
Heart, designed by Sister Joly, of Dijon, for St Margaret Mary, a dove,
symbolical of the Holy Spirit, is placed above the Heart of Jesus.
Lebrun, *op. cit.,* p. 75.
[3] *Op. cit.,* pp. 76-77.
[4] According to these, the divine love of Jesus, with his human love,
is the formal object of devotion to the Sacred Heart.

INDEX

This Index reproduces the French " Table analytique " with additional references

A